JESUS
AND THE KINGDOM
OF GOD

G. R. BEASLEY-MURRAY

WILLIAM B. EERDMANS PUBLISHING COMPANY

THE PATERNOSTER PRESS

To Ruth
in gratitude
for our years of partnership
in the service of the Kingdom

Copyright © 1986 by Wm. B. Eerdmans Publishing Co.
All rights reserved
Printed in the United States of America
for
William B. Eerdmans Publishing Company
255 Jefferson Ave. S.E., Grand Rapids, Mich. 49503
and
The Paternoster Press Ltd.
3 Mount Radford Crescent, Exeter, Devon, UK EX2 4JW

Library of Congress Cataloging-in-Publication Data

Beasley-Murray, George Raymond, 1916–
Jesus and the kingdom of God.

Bibliography: p. 417
Includes indexes.
1. Kingdom of God—Biblical teaching.
2. Jesus Christ—Teachings.   I. Title.
BS2417.K5B43   1986   236   85-20739

ISBN 0-8028-3609-7

British Library Cataloguing in Publication Data

Beasley-Murray, George R

Jesus and the kingdom of God
1. Kingdom of God——Biblical teaching
I. Title
231.7'2   BS 2417.K5

ISBN 0-85364-394-6

CONTENTS

CONTENTS

CONTENTS

CONTENTS

Preface

The twentieth century has been marked from its outset, and is likely so to continue to its close, by an uncertainty as to who Jesus was. This uncertainty has been acute among New Testament scholars and has spread among theologians. The problem is to no small extent bound up with the difficulty of ascertaining what Jesus thought of himself and of his calling. Its complexity has been increased through a conviction that the traditions relating to Jesus have been radically modified by those who handed them on in the earliest Christian communities and by the evangelists themselves. R. H. Lightfoot's famous words about Jesus in the gospels express the mood of the time: "For all the inestimable value of the gospels, they yield us little more than the whisper of his voice; we trace in them but the outskirts of his ways."[1] So we find a recent writer stating, "We do not have the evidence available now to speculate realistically about Jesus' so-called messianic consciousness."[2] There is, however, one area in the testimony of the gospels to Jesus the authenticity of which is agreed on by virtually all New Testament scholars—namely, the teaching of Jesus on the kingdom of God. It pervades the entire proclamation of Jesus recorded in the gospels and appears largely to have determined the course of his ministry. While this has been commonly acknowledged, its significance for interpreting Jesus has been strangely ignored. This work is offered as a contribution toward clarifying this element in the teaching of Jesus and its implications for the question of who Jesus is.

The length of the work is a reflection of the complexity and profundity of the instruction of Jesus. The concentration of thought in few words that characterizes his sayings eludes cursory examination. Moreover, a frequent failure adequately to relate this teaching to the Old Testament and contemporary Jewish literature has made necessary the provision of a brief overview of their content. Prolonged meditation on the teaching of Jesus concerning the theme that dominated his life produces a remarkably consistent image. To provide an opportunity for such attention to Jesus is the aim of this book.

I record my grateful thanks to Dr. Larry Kreitzer, research student/lecturer of King's College, London, for kindly furnishing the indices for this work.

Part I | # The Coming of God
in the Old Testament

1 | Theophany in the Old Testament

Georges Pidoux commences his treatment of the coming of God in the Old Testament with the affirmation that "The faith of the Old Testament rests on two certainties, equally profound and indissolubly bound together. The first is that God has come in the past, and that he has intervened in favour of his people. The other . . . is the hope that God will come anew in the future."[1] Pidoux's interest centered in the latter of those certainties. More commonly the accent in theophany studies has fallen elsewhere. In the earlier Old Testament narrative writings there are many accounts that relate appearances of God or of an angelic representative to individuals or groups, and it is these that have attracted the attention of scholars in the past. Julius Morgenstern wrote two extensive articles on Old Testament theophanies.[2] The first was primarily a study of the glory of God in the Old Testament, which he defined as "the material form in which Jahwe was thought to reveal himself to mortal eyes."[3] His concern was to trace the development of concepts of God in the theophanies from crude beginnings to the lofty heights of later Old Testament teaching. In a similar strain, James Barr examined the Old Testament accounts of the divine appearances in human form, their relation to the "angel" of the Lord, the glory, the presence (*pānim*) of God, and the significance of these for understanding anthropomorphism in the Old Testament. "It is in the theophanies, where God lets himself be seen," he stated, "that there is a real attempt to grapple with the form of his appearance."[4] J. Lindblom took as his point of departure the notion of a deity's link with a holy place, originally conceived of as his dwelling but later perceived as a consecrated place he visited from heaven. It was his thesis that the Old Testament narratives of Yahweh's appearances to individuals ought to be understood as theophanies at sanctuaries.[5]

Study of theophany from these angles is of evident importance, but it is noteworthy that of these three contributions the last two make no mention of the many representations in the Old Testament of God's coming for judgment or for deliverance, and while Morgenstern recognizes them he accords them only a very subordinate place. The idea of a coming of God to communicate with individuals entails different images from the notion of a coming of God to bring judgment or to effect the deliverance of a people and bestow "salvation." C. Westermann characterized this distinction as a *coming out* of a place for action among men and a *coming to* a place to speak to them; applying these concepts to the coming of God, he named the former *epiphany* and the latter *theophany*.[6] The suggested nomenclature is doubtful, but the distinction in view is clear. Making an effort at clarification, E. Jenni postulated a threefold differentiation in the use of the verb *to come* with God as subject in the Old Testament, distinguishing (1) revelation meetings, (2) comings of God in cultic events, and (3) comings of God for judgment and salvation, which are celebrated in hymnic and prophetic passages.[7] This is a useful analysis of the material. The first group of passages includes accounts of God's coming to converse with man, whether directly or through a messenger (as in Judg. 6:11; 13:6ff.), or a dream (e.g., Gen. 20:3; Num. 22:9), or an encounter at night, as in the appearance to the child Samuel (1 Sam. 3:10). The second group embraces a whole range of experiences in connection with worship (observe the implications of Exod. 20:24), and is reflected in praise, such as that in Psalm 24, and expressions of personal religion, such as that in Psalm 27:4. The third is by far the largest group and to its examination we now turn.[8]

The simplest and possibly oldest form of a theophany for divine action in the Old Testament is in Judges 5:4–5, at the beginning of the Song of Deborah:

O Lord, at thy setting forth from Seir,
when thou camest marching out of the plains of Edom,
earth trembled; heaven quaked;
the clouds streamed down in torrents.
Mountains shook in fear before the Lord, the lord of Sinai,
before the Lord, the God of Israel.

A closely similar statement occurs in Psalm 68:7–8. With these we should compare the brief oracle that stands at the head of the book of Amos (1:2):

The Lord roars from Zion
and thunders from Jerusalem:
the shepherds' pastures are scorched
and the top of Carmel is dried up.

A comparison of these passages discloses that two ideas are expressed in them: the *coming forth of the Lord*, and the *reactions of nature at his coming*. This twofold structure is basic to the theophany of action; it is expressed in a variety of ways and is assumed even in passages in which only one of the pair is mentioned.[9] The third passage alludes to a feature characteristic of theophany descriptions that can be taken for granted in the first two: the Lord goes forth with all the accoutrements of the storm. Above all his coming is associated with clouds. This finds representation in all kinds of ways, particularly in the Psalms.

Whereas most descriptions of the theophany are brief, some are elaborate, as the magnificent poem of Habakkuk 3. The beginning of the composition takes up the traditional theme announced in the Song of Deborah and weaves variations upon it:

God comes from Teman,
the Holy One from Mount Paran;
his radiance overspreads the skies,
and his splendour fills the earth. . . .

The prophet describes the effects of the divine manifestation: the mountains are shattered; they sink and writhe; the waters rage; the sun and moon stand still; the nations tremble. The purpose of this manifestation is made known in verse 13:

Thou goest forth to save thy people,
thou comest to save thy anointed;
thou dost shatter the wicked man's house from the roof down. . . .

The Lord thus comes to judge the wicked and save the righteous.

An instructive account of a theophany occurs in Psalm 18, which tells of the response of the Lord to a man in need. When the "bonds of death" held him in their grip and the "bonds of Sheol" were tightening about him, he cried to the Lord:

He heard me from his temple,
and my cry reached his ears. . . .
Smoke rose from his nostrils,
devouring fire came out of his mouth,
glowing coals and searing heat.
He swept the skies aside as he descended,
thick darkness lay under his feet.
He rode on a cherub, he flew through the air;
he swooped on the wings of the wind.
He made darkness around him his hiding-place
and dense vapour his canopy.
Thick clouds came out of the radiance before him,
hailstones and glowing coals.
The Lord thundered from the heavens
and the voice of the Most High spoke out. . . .
He reached down from the height and took me,
he drew me out of mighty waters.

Here again we have a vivid picture of God appearing as the Lord of the storm. The clouds are both the vehicle of his coming and the means of concealing his glory (cf. Hab. 3:4). The reactions of nature at this manifestation of the Lord are described:

The earth heaved and quaked,
the foundations of the mountains shook;
they heaved, because he was angry. . . .
The channels of the sea-bed were revealed,
the foundations of earth laid bare
at the Lord's rebuke,
at the blast of the breath of his nostrils.

The Lord of heaven and earth thus comes in all his glory, shaking the world to its foundations, causing the mountains to heave and the ocean floor to be exposed—all for the aid of one sick man! This is a clear expression of the associations in a Hebrew's mind when he thought of the coming of God to aid his people: the stepping forth of the Creator evokes the trembling of the whole creation.

In passing, it may be remarked that whatever the history of the imagery used by the psalmist in his description of God's coming to him, and however it may have been understood in earlier times, for him it was a means of portraying the infinite power of the Lord who came for his help. The Psalmist was not seriously claiming that after his prayer a storm took place, followed by an earthquake and volcanic eruption that shook the mountains and raised the sea bed. His intention was to declare that when the Lord came for his deliverance he came with power and glory, and creation was subject to its master.

At this point we may raise the question of where God comes *from* as he steps forth for action in the world. Deborah's Song gives one answer: he who is known as "the Lord of Sinai" came marching from Seir, out of the plains of Edom. The like is stated in the opening of the Blessing of Moses in Deuteronomy 33:2, and also in Psalm 68:17. This would appear to reflect the original conception of the theophany in Israel. It is basic to the earliest accounts of the Sinai theophany in the book of Exodus (see for example Exod. 19:20). The latter usage is common in most prophetic portrayals of theophany. There are variations, some of which are patently explicable: Amos speaks of the Lord roaring from *Zion* and thundering from *Jerusalem* (Amos 1:2); Ezekiel sees the storm cloud wherein the Lord appears to him coming from *the north* (Ezek. 1:4); the poem in Isaiah 30 simply declares that the Lord comes "from afar" (v. 27). But fundamentally the Israelite looked for God to come for his interventions on earth from heaven.

More important than the place from which the Lord comes is the *purpose* for which he comes. The passages we have considered provide the answer: the Lord comes for the punishment of the wicked and the deliverance of his people. A survey of the references in the Old Testament to the coming of God would show that a preponderance of passages feature the former motif, which reflects the early associations of the language of theophany with battle, and of the coming of God with the "wars of the Lord." Schnutenhaus points out that the term *go forth* (*yāsā*), frequent in theophany descriptions, conjures up the picture of soldiers mobilized and going forth to action at the front.[10] The link between theophany and holy war is illustrated in Judges 4:14; the description of the coming of the Lord in Deborah's song relates to the Lord's intervention for Israel in the battle with Sisera's forces. In the prophetic literature the coming of Yahweh is frequently proclaimed as taking place for judgment of nations. On the other hand, it should not be overlooked that the earliest reference in the Old Testament to a theophany for action (in Judg. 5:4–5) was recited at the coming of the Lord for the deliverance of his people. Similarly, the prophets of Israel looked for the Lord to come for salvation, not for judgment alone. The notion of the coming of Yahweh at the end of history entails both concepts, and to this we must turn later. But at this point we might simply recall the tender message of Deutero-Isaiah, expressed in the words of comfort of chapter 40:

> Here is the Lord God coming in might
> coming to rule with his right arm.
> His recompense comes with him,
> he carries his reward before him.
> He will tend his flock like a shepherd,
> and gather them together with his arm;
> he will carry the lambs in his bosom
> and lead the ewes to water.

The picture of Yahweh coming as a shepherd strikes a new note in the theophanic music but remains in harmony with the hope of Israel. The Lord is to come in grace, bringing salvation to his people—and not to his people alone. Isaiah 64 expresses a yearning for a powerful theophany wherein the name of the Lord will be made known to his enemies and the nations tremble at his coming; chapters 60–62 anticipate that the nations themselves will share in the blessed conditions that God's coming will initiate. In reading the darker portrayals of God's coming to the world we ought not to neglect the glimpses of those who saw that the darkness of the storm cloud gives way to the light of the Lord and that the light will in the end scatter the darkness.

In connection with the recognition that God comes for salvation, it is well to observe that in certain passages of the Old Testament theophany descriptions are intertwined with reminiscences of the battle of the god of heaven with the forces of primeval chaos. This feature most clearly appears in Psalm 77:16:

> The waters saw thee, O God,
> they saw thee and writhed in anguish;
> the ocean was troubled to its depths.

In this verse and those that follow it, the reactions of nature are depicted before the description of the Lord coming with the weapons of the storm; but the concentration of attention on the writhings of the waters in anguish almost certainly reflects the defeat of the chaos powers by the superior might of the Lord. Other references to the linking of the two traditions can be found in Psalms 104:7–9 and 114:3ff.; Nahum 1:4; and Habakkuk 3:8. The interesting feature of Psalm 77 is its conjunction of the conquest of the primeval waters with the historical event of the Exodus, when by the power of the Lord Israel crossed the sea. Israel's "redemption" is described in terms of a theophany, such as that by which the chaos waters were subdued.

The same sort of thing appears to be true of the theophany described in Psalm 114. And we find the same association in contexts that have no direct reference to a theophany. In Isaiah 51:9–10 the prophet pleads for God to act again for the deliverance of his people:

> Awake, awake, put on your strength, O arm of the Lord,
> awake as you did long ago, in days gone by.

The paradigm of God's almighty power is then cited:

Was it not you
who hacked the Rahab in pieces and ran the dragon through?

That is, you, and no other, slew the dragon of the waters. Let none glorify Marduk or Baal! But the prophet has in view not primeval times, but an event in history:

Was it not you
who dried up the sea, the waters of the great abyss,
and made the ocean depths a path for the ransomed?

The Lord of the chaos waters manifested his power over the sea by bringing his people through it on dry ground. And the Lord of creation and of the Exodus will show his power for deliverance again:

So the Lord's people shall come back, set free,
and enter Zion with shouts of triumph,
crowned with everlasting joy. . . .

The theology of theophany in the light of God's mastery of creation and his redemption at the Exodus, coupled with hope for the future, is entirely at one with the theology of future deliverance enunciated by Deutero-Isaiah.

But this raises an important question: Where did this concept of theophany come from? It is commonly accepted that the notion of the Lord as conqueror of the chaos powers was taken by Israel from her neighbors. Has the same thing happened with the idea of theophany? If so, where did it come from? The answer is more complex than is sometimes supposed. Gunkel's researches made popular the view that Israel adopted the myth of the chaos battle from Babylonia, which recounted the conquest of Tiamat by Marduk.[11] Doubtless that was one source which flowed into Israel's traditions, but it cannot be overlooked that in the Ugaritic myths of Ras Shamra the same exploits are attributed to Baal, in the story of his subjugation of Prince Yam (= the sea).[12] There is a striking parallel between material in the Baal texts and the allusion to the myth in Isaiah 27:1. Baal is addressed by Mot (= death) as follows:

When thou smotest Leviathan the slippery serpent,
and madest an end of the wriggling serpent,
the tyrant with seven heads,
the heavens wilted [and] dropped slack as the belt of thy robe. . . .
I myself was consumed like blood-red
funeral meats [and] I died. (*Baal*, 1.1.1ff.)

In this text the event is spoken of as having taken place in the past, whereas the Isaiah text anticipates it happening later. It would appear that the tradition of the conquest of the monster of the sea came into Israel from both Babylonian and Canaanite sources.[13]

The notion of a deity who flies with the storm clouds and commands the powers of nature was common among Israel's neighbors. The Babylonians held

Adad to be such a god. A typical theophany hymn in honor of Adad can be cited by way of example:

> When the Lord is full of wrath, the heavens tremble before him,
> When Adad is angry, the earth quakes before him.
> The great mountains fall down before him,
> before his wrath, before his fury.
> Before his roaring, before his thundering
> the gods of heaven fly away up,
> the earth gods go down into the earth,
> the sun goes into the firmament of heaven,
> the moon disappears in the heights of heaven.[14]

In due time the functions of Adad were absorbed by Marduk, who took his weapons of lightning, fire, and winds and in his chariot issued forth to battle with Tiamat. But similar attributes are accorded to Baal in the Ugaritic literature. Like Marduk, Baal assumes the functions of Adad, and actually takes his name (*Hadad*). He is variously called Baal, the prince lord of the earth;[15] the victor Baal;[16] Baal, the most high;[17] and most characteristically "the Rider on the clouds." Jeremias points out, however, that the parallels with the Old Testament tradition of theophany extend beyond Babylonian and Canaanite religion. The idea of the theophany of the storm god is widespread in Sumerian religion; Ishkur son of Ellil also has the title "he who rides on the storm wind," and the trembling of the heavens (and of the mountains and of the gods themselves) is not infrequently mentioned in connection with the appearances of the storm gods Ellil, Ninurta, Inanna, Ishtar, and Nergal. In Egyptian texts the god Seth is the god of the storm, and in Hittite myths the storm god Teshub is the decisive and ruling god. It is Jeremias's conviction that while we are compelled to believe that Israel shared in this common theophanic tradition, we cannot be sure which nation Israel took any individual picture or expression over from, or indeed whether it was at home in many; it is natural to think of Israel's immediate neighbor, Syrian Palestine, from which the Ras Shamra texts come, as the most likely source for borrowing, but that is as far as we may go.[18]

Are we then to conclude that the concept of theophany itself was taken by Israel from the religions of its neighbors? This by no means follows. We have to distinguish between concepts and their modes of expression. As we have noted, the fundamental theophany form in the Old Testament has two parts—the coming of God and the turbulent reactions of nature. It is in the second member of the theophany—the alarm of the natural order—that we can observe the closest parallels between Israelite and non-Israelite theophany descriptions. The fundamental idea is expressed in the first member, in the description of God's coming forth for action among men. The mode of his coming and the accompaniments that mark it are of secondary importance. Jeremias has searched the traditions of the religions of Israel's neighbors in the ancient world and finds that the concept of a deity going forth to the aid of men is largely absent from them. He concludes that this vital element stems from the Sinai tradition, which embodies Israel's experience of the Exodus.[19] The setting of the earliest theophanic text in the Old Testament, the Song of Deborah (Judg.

5), suggests that the preservation of this theophany tradition in Israel took place in the triumph songs of Israel's battles.

Once the Israelite mind was seized with the conviction that Yahweh had powerfully come forth to their aid and continued to do so in times of need, it was natural that images then in use should be employed to represent and give expression to the thought. More specifically, Israel's experience of Yahweh as the all-holy God and Redeemer led her to recognize in him the almighty Creator. When her poets and prophets depicted the Lord of Hosts stepping forth to judge and redeem, it is understandable that familiar pictures drawn from the religious world about them were used to describe the majesty of the Creator in his coming and his limitless power over the creation he had made. In adopting representations of Yahweh as the Lord of the storm they naturally excluded, by that use, all other divinities from such a prerogative. In a similar way, when they proclaimed Yahweh as the subjugator of the chaos powers, they thereby claimed that he alone transforms chaos into order and brings new things into being, just as he alone is the slayer of "dragons" in all ages, past, present, and future.[20]

The decisive element in the theophany descriptions of the Old Testament, accordingly, is the concept of the coming of God; the descriptions of accompanying phenomena in the natural order are to be viewed as parabolic. The "parables" are not unimportant—they point to the irresistible might of the Lord in his coming, for the resources of creation are his, and nothing in creation can resist his will—but the supremely important matter is that God *comes* into the world, now in the present and (in the teaching of the prophets) in the future, and in his coming he reveals himself. Theophany means "God's self-manifestation in the midst of historical, worldly event."[21] The descriptions of it in the Old Testament express "the livingness, the dynamic, indeed the passion of Yahweh. *He comes to act!*"[22] When the eschatological perspective is added to the historical dimension, the concept of theophany stands for the coming of God into the world for the revelation of his glory and accomplishment of his purpose for the world he has made. The nature of that coming, the meaning of the revelation in the coming, and the understanding of the divine purpose achieved in the coming require the prophetic word for their elucidation; but it is God who comes, or there is no redemption, no revelation, and no establishment of the divine will.

2 | The Day of the Lord in the Old Testament

It is commonly acknowledged that the Day of the Lord in the Old Testament is not a date but an event. We know it best from those descriptions that represent it as the occasion of God's intervention in judgment upon the nations, bringing an end to man's rebellion and initiating the period of God's saving sovereignty (e.g., those in Joel 2 and Isa. 13–14). It forms the boundary between history and the kingdom of God. Since it includes many elements, the Day is sometimes spoken of in the plural—that is, as "those days" (Jer. 5:18)—or as "the time" that is coming.[1] The phenomena of the Day of the Lord are complex, and it is desirable to clarify the concept by considering its development and the variety of ways in which it is used.[2]

The phrase provides a good illustration of the Hebrew concept of time as content rather than duration. For the Day of the Lord is not a calendar day but an event in which the Lord acts. It has its analogies in such Old Testament expressions as "the day of battle" (1 Sam. 13:22), "the day of snow" (2 Sam. 23:20), "the day of harvest" (Prov. 25:13), or more significantly the "day of Midian" (Isa. 9:3), which was the occasion of Midian's defeat by Gideon and his men (Judg. 7:19ff.). This last instance is instructive, for in the phrase "the day of Midian," the genitive is objective; it denotes an event, a calamity that happened *to* Midian. That is in accord with a common use of *day* in Hebrew. Czerny brings together evidence from P. A. Munch and Moses Buttenweiser that indicates that when *day* in Hebrew (= *yōm*) is followed by the genitive, it frequently means "a day of bad luck" for the one named.[3] But there is no question of the Day of the Lord signifying a day of hard luck for the Lord! Clearly the genitive in this case must be subjective; it denotes a day on which the Lord *acts*, bringing disaster on the subjects of his wrath. This is an important datum, for it indicates that the Day of the Lord is an occasion (1) that involves God acting in the historical sphere, (2) that entails judgment for those for whom the day comes, and (3) that occurs at such time as is determined by the Lord (not necessarily at the end of history).

As to the nature of the disaster or judgment that the Day of the Lord brings, one cannot but notice the frequency with which descriptions of the Day are dominated by figures drawn from warfare; they depict God as a mighty Warrior who issues forth to do battle with his enemies, whom he overwhelms by his power and over whom he gains undisputed victory. Isaiah 13, an oracle against Babylon, is a typical example of prophetic representations of the Day. It develops the images of war with its accompanying terror, desolation, and death. While the prophecy is directed against Babylon, the heavens and the earth are said to be shaken in that day and disaster comes upon the whole world (see vv. 11ff.). In verses 3–5a it is said that the Lord will execute his judgment on Babylon by the agency of armies from other countries, whereas verse 5bc speaks of the Lord acting directly, "coming to lay the whole land waste." This duality of thought is typical of prophetic portrayals of the Day.

Isaiah 34 again tells of the Lord's anger against all nations, "against all the host of them: he gives them over to slaughter and destruction" (v. 2); yet the prophecy is actually against Edom. The cosmic accompaniments of Edom's judgment are even more marked than in that against Babylon:

> All the host of heaven shall crumble into nothing,
> the heavens shall be rolled up like a scroll,
> and the starry host fade away. (V. 4)

Edom's fate is portrayed as akin to the sacrifice of beasts; the land will drink deep of blood, and the soil be sated with fat (v. 7).

This last figure is developed in Zephaniah's description of the Day of the Lord, which may be viewed as the portrayal par excellence of that Day. The prophet begins by declaring that the Lord will sweep the earth clean of man and beast, birds of the air and fish of the sea. The description of the Day as one of wrath, anguish, and affliction, destruction and devastation, murk and gloom, cloud and fog reaches its climax in the picture of "a day of *trumpet and battle cry* over fortified cities and lofty battlements" (1:16). Similar descriptions of the Day of the Lord in terms of destructive warfare are recorded by Jeremiah (e.g., in chapters 4–7 and 46–51), although he does not employ the technical phrase *Day of the Lord*, and by Ezekiel (e.g., in chapters 7, 21, 25, and 30). The prophecy in Joel 2 is noteworthy in that the "great and terrible day of the Lord" (v. 11) is described as the coming of a destructive plague of locusts, and these are depicted as though they were armies advancing to battle. Von Rad has suggested that the use of military imagery is the result of traditional associations of the Day of the Lord: "Once the concept of the Day of Yahweh had been mentioned, the stereotyped images were bound to follow."[4]

It would seem reasonable to believe, accordingly, that among the Hebrews the Day of the Lord connoted above all the overthrow of the enemies of the Lord as in a day of battle. And this points to the origin of the concept: it rose to prominence in Israel's early history, when the nation entered the promised land and sought to subdue its peoples under the Lord's leadership. In the conquest of the land, it was the Lord to whom the Hebrews looked for victory; they provided armies for his use. The overthrow of Jericho took place at the instruction of the "captain of the Lord's army" (Josh. 5:13ff.); the role of the Israelites was secondary. The divine aid in the battle against the five Amorite kings was decisive, when, as the book of Jashar records, Joshua cried,

> Stand still, O Sun, in Gibeon;
> stand, Moon, in the Vale of Aijalon.

The author of the book of Joshua states that "Never before or since has there been such a day as this day on which the Lord listened to the voice of a man; for the Lord fought for Israel" (Josh. 10:14). This tradition of the holy wars of the Lord gave Israel a picture of a Lord who had power at all times to intervene in history to subdue those who set themselves against him. Scholars have long recognized that the prophets of Israel took their pictures of the salvation of the future from the nation's experience of redemption in the past: they looked for God to bring about a new Exodus (Isa. 51:9–11), to refine them in a fresh experience of the desert (Hos. 2:14), to give them a new covenant (Jer. 31:31ff.) and another David (Ezek. 34:24), and to refashion Zion in glory (Isa. 51) to become the center of the earth (Isa. 2). It is in harmony with this mode of thought that the deliverance of Israel from its destroyers should be thought of in terms of a new conquest, comparable to the subjugation of the land before the chosen people in its early years.[5]

It is comprehensible therefore that there should be a certain plasticity in the idea of the Day of the Lord and in its application. If it is the case, as is increasingly recognized, that the unique element in Israel's eschatology is its relation to history—the history that is under the sovereignty of God at all times and that is heading for a goal of his determination—then one can understand that the prophets saw *all* the future as subject to the Lord, and so could speak of impending judgments on contemporary nations in terms of the Day of the Lord in the same way they would speak of the event that will bring history to its climax. This is particularly applicable to Isaiah and Jeremiah in their prophecies, but not alone to them.[6] The author of Lamentations looked back on the destruction of Jerusalem, which for long years had formed the burden of Jeremiah's warnings, and said,

> Thou didst summon my enemies against me from every side,
> like men assembling for a festival;
> not a man escaped, not one survived
> *in the day of the Lord's anger.* (2:22)

Here the calamity that overtook Israel is spoken of as one would refer to the Day of the Lord, and it is viewed as having already taken place. There may be other examples in the Old Testament of this way of looking at catastrophes that have occurred in the past.[7] Accordingly, Von Rad laid down the following principle: *whenever and wherever great political complications were to be seen on the horizon, especially when hostile armies approached, a prophet could speak of the coming Day of Yahweh.*[8]

Whatever uncertainty may exist regarding the origin and development of thought concerning the Day of the Lord, the first clear emergence of the expression in the Old Testament—in the famous saying of Amos (5:18)—denotes the eschatological event:

> Fools who long for the Day of the Lord,
> what will the Day of the Lord mean to you?
> It will be darkness, not light.

The implication is plain: the prophet's contemporaries understood that the Day of the Lord would be a day of calamity for the earth, but they were assured that its desolations would meet other nations and that it would issue in the elect people being made lords of the world. The fault of Amos's generation lay not in looking forward to the Day but, as Vriezen puts it, in not taking it seriously enough.[9] They did not reckon with the underlying presupposition of the Day of the Lord—namely, the holiness of God, which entails judgment for *sinners*. The Day of the Lord is not upon Gentiles as such, but upon the rebellious against the Lord, whoever they may be.

This was the new and all-but-unbelievable element in the message of Amos and his prophet contemporaries: the people of the covenant are to be the objects of the destructive action of the Lord in the day of his warfare with the world. The enemies of God are none other than the people of God! This astounding message was neither lightly received by the prophets nor lightly handed on by them. We know what agonies of heart it created for Hosea and Jeremiah, and Isaiah was by no means unmoved by it.[10] Nor should it be assumed, as was frequently maintained by earlier scholars, that these prophets had rejected the belief that the Day of the Lord was related to the reign of God, as though the Day of the Lord would bring total annihilation to the world and Israel would perish in the universal ruin. The evidence of the prophets' own writings is against interpreting their message in terms of unrelieved pessimism.[11] From Israel's earliest times, the notion of a Day of the Lord included both destruction and deliverance, the former having the latter in view as its end. In the maturer reflection of the prophets these twin motifs were linked with the holiness and *hesed* of God, his wrath and his love, and they issued in a tension of judgment and salvation—for the people of God as for the rest of the nations.[12] The task of the preexilic prophets was to awaken the conscience of their people and call upon them to repent, that they might survive the impending judgments. The severity of their language and the appalling nature of their images derived from the nature of the tradition they inherited, but it also reflected their desperation to bring about the conversion of their people. When, in the early years of the sixth century B.C., judgment fell in the devastation of Israel and the deportation beyond the Euphrates, the tone of the prophets changed; emphasis shifted from the judgments of the Day to the salvation promised by the Lord. Nevertheless, it is noteworthy that the prophets of the restoration continued to emphasize the necessity for conformity to the holy demands of God for all who would dwell under his sovereignty, and they seem to have concluded that nothing short of a miracle of God by his Spirit could accomplish it.[13] According to Malachi, the Lord himself will purify and refine his people on the day of his coming: "He is like a refiner's fire, like fuller's soap; he will take his seat, refining and purifying" (3:2–3).

14

This last citation raises a point of interest and importance. It is set in a context of skepticism about the reality of divine justice in this world (see Mal. 2:17). The answer to such an attitude is an assertion of the coming of the Lord to enact judgment and make his people pure:

> Behold, I send my messenger to prepare my way before me,
> and the Lord whom you seek will suddenly *come* to his temple.

The question is then asked,

> But who can endure *the day of his coming,*
> and who can stand *when he appears?*

No answer is given, but it is said that the Lord himself will bring about the purification of his people, and take in hand the wicked:

> "Then *I will draw near to you,* for judgment."

This day of judgment upon evil men is viewed as the day of the Lord's *coming,* of his *appearing,* the day when he *draws near* for judgment. *The Day of the Lord is the day of the coming of God.*

This conjunction of thought is common in the prophets. The Day of the Lord, the coming of the Lord, and the action of the Lord are not only related concepts but are at times actually interchangeable. Von Rad observed this and noted that "There is something peculiar about the expectation of the Day of Jahweh, for wherever it occurs in prophecy the statements culminate in an allusion to Jahweh's coming in person."[14] By way of illustration, we can cite Isaiah 2:12ff., 13:4–5, and 34:2ff.; Jeremiah 51:25, 36ff.; and Ezekiel 7, 26, 28, and 30.

One cannot but notice how similar the descriptions of the Day of the Lord are to the theophany accounts, which have in view the coming of God to set right what is wrong in the earth. The simple couplet of Isaiah 35:4 sets forth the idea with admirable brevity:

> See, your God comes with vengeance,
> with dread retribution he comes to save you.[15]

It is likely that there was a consciousness among the prophets and song writers of Israel of the relatedness of the concepts of the Day of the Lord and theophany. Not only is there likeness in the content of the descriptions, but the language and the imagery used in the portrayals of the events tend to overlap, and images proper to one are freely applied to the other.[16] Could it be that they go back to the same root? Von Rad suggests that they may: "There can be no doubt that the same principle is at work both in the old stories of the theophanies in bygone wars and in the prophets' descriptions of the future day of Jahweh. The various constitutive elements and conventional stock subjects of the former reappear one after another in the prophets' predictions."[17] The same *principle,* yes; but the theophanies saw the principle enacted one stage further back than the "wars of the Lord"—namely, in the event of the Exodus, when the tribes were rescued from an alien power and the terror of the waters and were adopted as the covenant people. It is likely that in Israel's traditions the theophany concept was primary and the Day of the Lord a specialized application of it. Both concepts were readily adapted to eschatological hopes, the theophany representations being especially appropriate in respect of Israel's deliverance, and those of the Day of the Lord in describing the judgment of the nations. The chief point to be observed is that the Day of the Lord would witness a revelation of God similar to his manifestations in earlier critical times; the revelation would be in the historical sphere, as God cleansed the earth of its sinners and established his good purpose.

3 | The Kingdom of God in the Old Testament

In the Old Testament, the ultimate purpose of the future coming of the Lord and the Day of the Lord is the establishment of the kingdom of God. To what extent was this hope of the kingdom integral to Israel's thought, and how significant did it appear to the people?

If linguistic phenomena were to be our guide, we might well be led to answer "very little." The expression "kingdom of God" does not occur in the Old Testament. That could be an accident, for reference is made to the kingdom that Yahweh rules—but in nine passages only, and these in restricted areas of the Old Testament.[1] By contrast, the term *king* is applied to Yahweh forty-one times in the Old Testament.[2] Yet Eissfeldt is widely followed in contending that the absolute "hymnic" naming of Yahweh as king is first datable in Isaiah's vision (Isa. 6:5).[3] How then should it be affirmed by L. Köhler that "The one fundamental statement in the theology of the Old Testament is this: God is the ruling Lord,"[4] or by Martin Buber that "The realisation of the all embracing rulership of God is the *Proton* and *Eschaton* of Israel"?[5] The answer does not lie in repudiation of the dicta of these scholars, but in a readiness to acknowledge the limitations of linguistic studies (concepts can be expressed in a variety of ways) and in observing the emphasis of these writers on the *ruling activity* of God rather than on the abstract notion of a *kingdom*. It was Yahweh's sovereign action on which the attention of Old Testament writers focused, and it was the manifestations of his sovereign power that called forth their worship. Even when later writers did come to speak of the kingdom of God or of heaven, they did so chiefly in order to describe the rule of God.[6]

How early in its history did Israel think of God in terms of "king"? Since man's pictorial thinking about God depends on his experience of the world in general, many have held that Israel could not have thought of God as king until the nation had a king of its own, and therefore presumably not before the time of David. Eissfeldt, however, argues that the concept of God as king was known in Israel's earliest times, since the term *melek*, "king," is basic to Semitic thinking. All Semitic peoples thought of their gods as kings, he maintains; the term denotes more than merely the head of a monarchical state; it can also mean "prince" or "leader and counselor," and so it could have arisen in a period before the Semites had experienced the concept of "kingdom."[7] Buber similarly maintains that the significance of *melek* in early Israel was shaped by the nomadic existence of the tribes; in such a milieu, the *melek* was the accompanying God who guided his people through unknown areas to good pastures and afforded them protection from their enemies. From the time of the patriarchs on, God was believed in and understood in this fashion, although the events of the Exodus from Egypt, the revelation at Sinai, and the wilderness wanderings gave a new depth to this understanding and conditioned Israel's subsequent thinking about God.[8]

The importance of this insight lies in the fact that it underscores the close relationship of the concept of God as King to Israel's history and experience of God. The Exodus event and its aftermath were of critical significance for Israel's understanding. It was precisely in connection with a series of divine interventions—the deliverance of the tribes from Egypt, their experience of theophany and the covenant with Yahweh at Sinai, and their subsequent entrance into the promised land—that the revelation of the Name was given to Moses in the desert, and through Moses to the people (cf. Exod. 3:14 with 6:6–7).

The interpretation of the divine name ("I AM . . .") accordingly conveys more than the simple thought that God is the existent One; it suggests that God is and will be with his people and that he acts and will act for them. "God's name is his being," says H. D. Preuss, "but his being is his working"—and this interpretation may be held independently of one's view of the precise connotation of the Name.[9]

The implications of these ideas are considerable. The notion of the kingship of God is flexible, open to application and development as the people of Israel advanced in their organization. Chiefly it was recognized that the kingship of Yahweh relates to his sovereign acts on behalf of his people through all times. Notable instances of his exercise of sovereignty took place in times past, but of necessity no time limit can be set to that sovereignty. The statement "The Lord is King" (Ps. 93:1) is as absolute as "The Lord is God" (Ps. 100:3). The understanding of this axiom of religion, however, was decisively influenced by Israel's experience of a series of manifestations of the divine sovereignty, at the heart of which was the revelation of the divine glory at Sinai and the covenant there made between Yahweh and Israel. In light of G. E. Mendenhall's researches on the legal background of the Mosaic covenant and the understanding of the Hittite vassal treaty form current in that era, there seems little reason to resist Buber's observation that the covenant at Sinai was a royal or kingly covenant in which Israel came under the rule of Yahweh and the people were constituted as his domain (see Exod. 19:5–6).[10] The covenant fashioned the tribes into a community belonging to the Lord. In Buber's language, it was a *theo-political* act;[11] Israel came under the suzerainty of Yahweh, and so henceforth were the people of the Lord.

The significance of this event for the development of Israel's thought about the future is apparent. Israel's unique achievement of an eschatology in relation to history was conditioned by the uniqueness of the revelation it experienced, the covenant into which it entered, and the history in which it was set and to which the whole complex gave rise.[12] From the events at Sinai onward, the tribes were a group on the march under Yahweh; they were on the way to a new life in a new land, to a future that was in the hands of the Lord. In later times the Exodus was understood as being inextricably bound up with the possession of the promised land, the whole process constituting a manifestation of Yahweh's presence with and working for his people. In Deuteronomy 33:2 and 26–27, for example, the Exodus and conquest are viewed as the effects of a continuing series of theophanies for the deliverance and establishment of his people, and an indication of what may be expected from the "God of Jeshurun" at any time.

It was natural to conclude that the kingship of Yahweh relates to the future as well as to the past and present. Paradoxically, it was precisely Israel's concern to keep alive the traditions of its origins that encouraged its expectations of the future. The Israelites in the land remembered their nomad past and what Yahweh had done for them in their time of wandering. Nomad religion is in any case essentially a religion of promise.[13] The people remembered the leading of Abraham to the land of promise and how the word to Abraham was fulfilled in the mighty acts of the Exodus and bestowal of the land. The Lord who led Abraham from Ur and the fathers from Egypt to the promised land is the Lord who continues to lead the nation into the future, which is *his* future, the future of *his* providing. To the Jew settled in the land, the entire process was ever and again experienced in the festivals he celebrated. Von Rad did well to emphasize the importance of this element in Israel's life: the nation was perpetually reminded that it had been called into being through a series of divine interventions, the effect of which lasted into the present. Thus it became a fundamental element of Israel's understanding that the nation had been founded through a succession of acts of God for their salvation, forming a God-controlled continuity, a history, and that this history was moving forward to a future according to God's will. Israel's eschatology was the end product of its consciousness of God in history.[14]

If, therefore, it is right to acknowledge, with Buber, that Yahweh's covenant with Israel was *theo-political*, we may also recognize, with H.-D. Wendland, that in the Bible history is perceived to be *theo-teleological*.[15] For as surely as the basis of hope is Yahweh in his word and deed, so the content of the hope is Yahweh himself, acting in accordance with his revelation—which is the same as affirming that in the Old Testament, hope in the coming of the kingdom is hope in the coming of the Lord.

As to the nature of the kingdom that comes, the texts that describe it are well-known and scarcely need to be cited *in extenso* here. Naturally a development in the delineations of the kingdom is discernible, from those intimations we find in certain early preprophetic passages (e.g., Gen. 49:9ff.; Num. 24:3ff., 17ff.; and Deut. 33:13ff.) to the clearer utterances of the preexilic prophets about the kingdom and the Messiah (e.g., Isa. 2:1ff., 4:1ff., 9:1ff., 11:1ff., 30:15ff., and 32:1ff.; Jer. 23:5ff., 24:5ff., 30–31, 32, and 37ff.; and Ezek. 30:15ff., 32:1ff., and 40–48). Undoubtedly the greatest exponent of the future kingdom of God is Deutero-Isaiah; standing almost at the close of the exile he proclaims the impending "consolation of Israel" in a kingdom that comes through God's new creative activity (see, for example, Isa. 40:1–11, 41:17–20, 43:1–7, 44:24–28, and 48:6–13). The descriptions of the Kingdom of God in

Isaiah 25–26 are unique in their anticipation of resurrection for the kingdom, which is depicted as a feast provided by God for the nations, a time when "the veil that shrouds all the peoples" will be removed and death will be swallowed up forever (25:6ff.). The oracles concerning the kingdom in Isaiah 65–66 are characterized by their fullness of detail; they, too, are unique in stating that the Lord is to create new heavens and a new earth as the setting of the kingdom (65:17; 66:22), although their portrayal of conditions in the kingdom depicts life wholly in terms of this world. The book of Daniel represents a further stage of the understanding of the kingdom contained in Isaiah 25–26 and 65–66. Curiously, however, although Daniel gives highly dramatic representations of the coming of the kingdom (e.g., in chaps. 2 and 7), little is said about the conditions of the kingdom; the author is principally concerned to stress the certainty of its coming by Yahweh's intervention, and so to provide encouragement for the people in their sufferings.

Any summary of the prophetic teaching concerning the nature of existence in the kingdom of God would have to note the following three features:

1. *The universality of the rule of Yahweh.* The prophets stress Israel's whole-hearted allegiance to the Lord (see, for example, Isa. 26:1–15; 28:5ff.; 33:5ff., 17–22; and 44:5; Ezek. 11:17ff. and 20:33ff.; Hos. 2:16–17; and Zech. 8:1–8), but the turning of the nations to God is integral to the hope of the kingdom. Sometimes this idea of turning is combined with pictures of the submission of the nations to Israel as well as to Yahweh (e.g., in Amos 9:11ff.; Mic. 4:13 and 7:8–17; and Isa. 49:22–26 and 60:4–16), but many passages depict the inclusion of the nations in the salvation of the kingdom (e.g., Isa. 25:6–7, 45:21–22, 51:4–5, 52:10–11, and 56:3–4; Jer. 3:17; Zeph. 3:8–9; and Zech. 8:20–21 and 14:9).

2. *The righteousness of the kingdom.* This is represented in a variety of ways: sometimes in descriptions of the righteousness of the Messiah that overflows to the people (e.g., in Isa. 11:3–5 and Jer. 23:5–6), sometimes as a characteristic of the people generally (e.g., in Isa. 26:2 and 28:5–6), but most often as the action of the Lord for the cleansing and renewal of the people (e.g., in Isa. 1:25–26, 4:3–4, and 32:15–16; Jer. 31:31–32; and Ezek. 36:25–26 and 37:23–24—not forgetting Isa. 52:13–53:12!).

3. *The peace of the kingdom.* This includes the absence of war (as in Isa. 2:2–3 and 9:5–6; Mic. 5:4; and Zech. 9:9–10) but also peace in the animal kingdom (as in Isa. 11:6–7 and 35:9). Both these features are linked with the concept of the return of the paradisal age—hence the expectation of the luxuriant fruitfulness of nature (see Isa. 35 and 41:17–18; Ezek. 47; Hos. 2:21–22; Joel 4:18; and Amos 9:13). More important, this "peace" extends to the life of man in his relations with God and with others, for peace is an all-embracing synonym for salvation (see Isa. 12, 21:17–24, 33:17ff., and 41:21–22; Jer. 31:1–14; Hos. 2:14–15 and 14:4–5; and Zeph. 3:14–20).

Thus, the goal of history is reached in the revelation and universal acknowledgment of Yahweh's sovereignty, the triumph of righteousness, and the establishment of peace and salvation in the world.

What role does the Messiah play in all this? A number of the texts we have cited prominently feature the Messiah's place in the kingdom, but in others he finds no mention. And this constitutes a problem. The royal Psalms celebrate the rule of Yahweh alone: "The Lord is king, let the earth be glad" (Ps. 97:1; cf. 99:1). "Salvation is of the Lord" (Ps. 3:8) is a salient Old Testament conviction, and in Isaiah 33:22 we read,

> The Lord our judge, the Lord our law-giver,
> the Lord our king—he himself will save us.

Zechariah 14:9 makes the unequivocal statement that "The Lord shall become king over all the earth; on that day the Lord shall be one Lord and his name the one name." That appears to allow of no other sovereignty in the day of the kingdom than that of Yahweh. Yet there are passages in which a different prospect is presented. The difficulty may be illustrated by a comparison of the two texts Isaiah 40:9–10 and Zechariah 9:9–10. Both passages appear to employ the "herald's call," proclaiming the advent of a king to conquer his enemies and/or save his people (cf. the related language in Isa. 35:4, 52:7, and 62:13); in the one case, however, the king who is heralded is Yahweh, and in the other he is the Messiah. But how could this be?

One explanation is that the two concepts—the coming of Yahweh and the coming of the Messiah—are strictly alien to one another; the Messiah is a kind of "double" of Yahweh, and therefore when the coming of Yahweh is taken with seriousness he is superfluous. This view has been espoused by Gressmann and Mowinckel, and it is interesting to see how differently they are motivated in it. Gressmann holds that the Messiah was originally the divine primeval man in the midst of paradise; possibly the original myth spoke of the primeval king as a man who died and returned to heaven to dwell in the sun, from whence he now rules the world as the sun god.[16] Such a speculation is very doubtful. There is no proof that the messianic concept derived from the myth of the primal man.[17] Despite the lofty attributes sometimes attributed to the king and the Messiah in the Old Testament, neither the king nor the Messiah was viewed in Israel as "metaphysically" divine. Nor should the link between the messianic hope and the Davidic covenant be forgotten: the Messiah for whom Israel looked was to be another David, not another god. Mowinckel, however, takes a very different stance. He sees the messianic concept as rooted in the kingship in Israel—in its "ideology of kingship"—and holds that faith in the coming Messiah is thus inseparable from faith in the restoration of the state, the nation, and the monarchy. To the extent that Israel's king is a representative of God and man, a channel of divine blessing to Israel, the Messiah is also mediator of the blessings of the kingdom to come, but as soon as the essentially religious nature of the kingdom is stressed, Mowinckel contends, the Messiah becomes needless, a relic of an outworn theology, and so he largely disappears from view until a new understanding of the Messiah becomes current in apocalypticism and in Christianity.[18]

Part of the price of maintaining this position is the necessity of denying that the prophets developed an eschatology. According to Mowinckel, eschatology is present only where there is an expectation of a cataclysmic end of this world and its supersession by a new cosmos, and since the prophets were dominated by a this-worldly view of the kingdom of God, he says, they looked for a Messiah who would realize the ideals of Israel's kingship in this world. Such an outlook, he says, must be classed *preeschatological*. Moreover, he holds that the lofty ideals embodied in the Servant Songs of Deutero-Isaiah, although relating to an individual figure, should be divorced from messianic expectations, for in the prophetic circles from which the songs issued the figure of the Messiah was displaced by a *prophet* Servant of the Lord. In contrast to Gressmann, therefore, who divinizes the Messiah and makes of him a god, Mowinckel reduces him to a monarch in the theocracy of Israel's future—a great figure, to be sure, but too small to fit into the fulfillment of Israel's authentic eschatological hope. And that hardly does justice to the real expectations of the prophets.

We shall return to Mowinckel's contentions, but meanwhile a more adequate view of the Messiah—a view that harmonizes with a great deal of what Mowinckel has written about the Messiah—is that he is *the representative of Yahweh in his kingdom, in whom Yahweh is present and through whom he acts.*[19] The principle of representation is deeply embedded in the faith and institutions of Israel, applying alike to priests and prophets and kings. That these figures and institutions should find their apex in the representative capacity of the Messiah should occasion no surprise, especially when we recall the role of such leaders as Moses and David in the history and tradition of Israel. Inasmuch as the Messiah is the consecrated ("anointed") ruler through whom Yahweh rules the people and the representative of the people, the term "Mediator" is not falsely applied to him.

Generally speaking, the great messianic passages of the Old Testament proceed on the principle that the subjugation of the evil powers in the world, the submission of the nations to God, and the establishment of the new order of the saving sovereignty are the effect of the working of Yahweh, and that the task of rule in the kingdom of God is given to the Messiah. This is in harmony with what we have seen of the Day of the Lord in the Old Testament; it is Yahweh who comes in judgment upon the rebellious of mankind and who effects the deliverance and salvation of his people; the Messiah belongs to the new order. And that is the teaching of the well-known descriptions in the prophets of the Messiah and his rule (e.g., in Isa. 9:1–7 and 11:1–9; Mic. 5:1–4; Jer. 23:5–6; and Ezek. 34:22–24). Even in the prophecy concerning the prince of peace in Zechariah 9:9–10, the language and structure of which are so strikingly similar to the announcement of Yahweh's coming in Isaiah 40:9–10, the victory is the Lord's; the King-Messiah and his rule are Yahweh's gift to his people.

All this is typical of the prophetic messianic oracles, with the exception of one prophet and his followers—namely, Deutero-Isaiah. For if Cyrus is named by the prophet as the Lord's Anointed (see Isa. 45:1ff.), and therefore as a kind of Messiah, this is to indicate that the Lord is planning to use Cyrus to initiate those processes by which the deliverance and salvation of Israel are to come to pass:

> I say to Cyrus, "You shall be my shepherd
> to carry out all my purpose,
> so that Jerusalem may be rebuilt,
> and the foundations of the temple may be laid." (Isa. 44:28)

Cyrus as the Lord's anointed is the instrument of Yahweh, and his conquests are of the Lord's ordaining; but Cyrus is not raised up *after* the kingdom comes but *in order that* it may come.

This is not without parallel in the Old Testament, as the quasi-messianic psalms 2 and 110 attest, and it is wholly characteristic of the Servant Songs of Isaiah 42, 49, 50, and 52–53. Throughout the poems the dependence of the Servant on the Lord is assumed and indeed emphasized, but the role of the Servant in the time of the Lord's salvation is to be his instrument in its establishment in the earth. The first of the songs makes this clear:

> He will make justice shine on the nations. . . .
> never faltering, never breaking down,
> he will plant justice on earth,
> while coasts and islands wait for his teaching.

The second song states that the task of the servant is to bring Israel back to God—indeed, yet more:

> I will make you a light to the nations,
> To be my salvation to earth's farthest bounds.

To be "light" and "salvation" to the world are elsewhere predicates of the divine action (e.g., in Ps. 27:1).

The fourth song is difficult to interpret. There is good reason, however, for believing that it means to set forth the sufferings of him through whom mankind is purged from sin and guilt, that they may find a place in the kingdom:

> So shall he, my servant, vindicate many,
> himself bearing the penalty of their guilt.
> Therefore I will allot him the many for his portion,
> and he shall apportion the strong as spoil. (Isa. 53:11–12)

If we are meant to understand that the servant of whom such things are written is an individual (and I find it difficult to believe otherwise), we can assume that he has a unique role to play in bringing the Lord's salvation to the world. Is it really likely, as Mowinckel maintains, that such a one has *displaced* the Messiah? One cannot dismiss out of hand the idea that the prophetic circle that gave us this picture of the servant had concluded from the failure of the monarchy that there would be no Messiah in the impending kingdom of God. And yet we have to face the paradox that this is the group that reproduced the idea of a quasi-Messiah raised up by Yahweh for his people's deliverance (i.e., Cyrus) and gave expression to the belief that one must come who shall play a more vital role in the coming of the kingdom than the Messiah, as traditionally conceived, and who in that kingdom shall have power. Is this not better understood as a *reinterpretation* of the messianic hope, rather than a *substitute* for it?

Whatever be the truth of this matter, one thing is indisputable: in the Old Testament prophetic teaching *the Messiah is uniquely related to God and man, and as the representative of Yahweh he is the instrument of his rule.* Strictly speaking one is not affirming in that statement more than the members of an Israelite court would have affirmed of the reigning monarch in Jerusalem. But how much more is one affirming if one goes on to state that in the prophets the Messiah is *Son of David par excellence*? Mowinckel would have no hesitation in answering that "The Messiah is the future eschatological realisation of the ideal of kingship."[20] The answer is impeccable, but in light of all the evidence we have examined, including that of Isaiah 40–55, should we not be more specific? If we further ponder such statements as that in Zechariah 9:9 ("Behold, your king comes to you") in relation to Isaiah 40:9 ("Behold your God . . . comes with might"), there seems some justification for the view of H. H. Wolff that *the Messiah is the form of the appearance of Yahweh the Lord.*[21] We have seen what emphasis is laid in the theophanic traditions of the Old Testament on the coming of Yahweh for the deliverance of his people. Similarly, the Day of the Lord is none other than the coming of Yahweh to set right the injustices of the earth. And it is equally plain that the hope of the kingdom of God is understood in the Old Testament as the coming of Yahweh to establish his sovereignty of salvation. Nor is this a late development in the thought of Judaism. It is astonishing that so acute a student of eschatology as Mowinckel should overlook the significance of the fact that the coming of Yahweh was a primary datum in Israel's faith and that it was bound to affect the development of Israelite expectations of the future profoundly, from earliest times to the emergence of a full-fledged eschatology. It is false to Israel's religion first to characterize the prophetic hope of a kingdom of God ruled by the Messiah as preeschatological nationalism projected into the future rather than the "religious" hope of the coming of Yahweh for his eschatological kingdom, and then to affirm that the coming of Yahweh made the Messiah superfluous. *There could never have been a stage in Israel's history when the kingdom of God was looked for apart from the coming of Yahweh.* On the contrary, as Eichrodt has affirmed and many others would be prepared to support, *"the religious core of the whole salvation-hope . . . is to be found in the coming of Yahweh to set up his dominion over the world."*[22] The hope of the kingdom was not founded on an inherited messianic hope; rather, the messianic hope was integrated into Israel's hope in Yahweh, as truly as the covenant with David was subsequently related to the Sinaitic covenant. It is understandable, however, that the expectation of the coming of the Messiah would have strengthened and sharpened the hope of the kingdom in the minds of the populace.[23]

The changes in the place accorded the Messiah in descriptions of the kingdom of God in the Old Testament are certainly perplexing, although the fragmentary nature of the collections of prophetic oracles accounts for not a little of this. Mowinckel himself acknowledged that the Davidic Messiah is so natural an element in prophetic expectations of the future that he is often not mentioned but tacitly assumed.[24] We ought not therefore to check through the books of the Old Testament to see where the Messiah finds no mention and then declare that the authors of these works did not look for the Messiah in the coming kingdom. Positively, we may affirm that for those circles in which the coming of the Messiah was an attested element in the expectation of the coming of the kingdom of God, the name "Immanuel"—*God with us*—is not a misleading representation of the Messiah. In these passages what Wolff called "God's will to appear" in the earthly realm is anticipated as an abiding reality in the

Messiah: "As in the pillar of fire, as in the Angel, as in the prophetic word, so Yahweh appears in the Messiah; not in such a fashion that he is restricted thereby, but rather he himself, and none other than he, appears to men, as one who has fellowship with them and deals with them, and that in a manner in which he cannot normally be with them if they are not to perish from the sight of his full presence."[25]

Here is an expectation of the future firmly rooted in the Old Testament revelation and in Israel's history and experience of God, which corresponds to the hope of God's people in all ages; the prospect of "seeing God" and dwelling in his presence has always been viewed by his people as the ultimate blessing of the final order of existence. We should take care not to overlook one characteristic element in this expectation in particular, however: when Yahweh comes to bring his kingdom, it is to this world that he comes and in this world that he establishes his reign. The hope of Israel is not for a home in heaven but for the revelation of the glory of God in this world, when "the earth shall be full of the knowledge of the glory of the Lord as the waters fill the sea" (Hab. 2:14). As God's claim on man encompasses the totality of his life, so God's salvation for man encompasses the totality of human existence, including our historical existence. The claim and the promise alike find their fulfillment in the Messiah. In him man has his sufficient representative before God, and in him God's presence is signified and the rule of the world is actualized. In the person of the Messiah God's purpose in history finds its embodiment.

A time was to come when men should learn that the kingdom that comes embraces this world and the cosmos and the ages of ages, that in that kingdom the individual has a meaningful place in the corporate totality of redeemed mankind, and that at the center of all stands the throne of God and the Lamb. Such a vision is beyond the horizon of the Old Testament, but it stands in the line of its development. At this juncture it is sufficient for us to observe the harmony of the hope of God's rule and of God's anointed in it, and to know that both are the result of the coming of the Lord for the salvation of the world.

4 | **The Coming of God in Daniel 7**

The vision of the Son of Man in Daniel 7 has long engaged the attention of scholars, not only by virtue of its intrinsic interest but because of its significance for the understanding of the gospels.

The chapter falls into two parts, consisting of the vision (vv. 1–14) and the interpretation (vv. 15–28). The vision itself is made up of two sections, that of the four beasts (vv. 1–8) and that of the divine judgment (vv. 9–14).

The vision of the beasts is dominated by the tradition of the chaos monster of ancient myth.[1] But this is given a complex form in that not one beast but four are presented. The adaptation of the myth and its application to world powers was already established in the prophetic tradition; in Daniel it is combined with the concepts of a series of world ages and four empires of world history (see chap. 2). This fusion of ideas has been further extended so as to include the climactic appearance of wickedness in a development of the fourth beast, the "little horn" of verse 8, which appears to represent Antiochus Epiphanes; he is presented as manifesting the characteristics of the chaos monster beyond his predecessors. The application of this "cartoon" to the contemporary oppressive political power serves both to show its antigod ("chaotic") nature and its sure fate: as the chaos monster was conquered by a champion of heaven, so also the tyrant faces an annihilating judgment from the ruler of the universe.

The second section of the vision has a tone different from that of the first and opens up a new prospect. Verses 9–10 and 13–14 are in poetic style, or at least in exalted prose. Because they are clearly distinct from the context, they are frequently held to be originally independent of the vision of the beasts.[2] Some have considered them to be a later interpolation into the chapter,[3] but this suggestion does not commend itself; whatever may be thought of the origin of the two visions, they form an integral part of the chapter, so it is better to view verses 1–14 as a vision in two acts,[4] or as consisting of two phases of a single tableau.[5] Admittedly the stanzas of verses 9–10 and 13–14 are brief and may not have been connected originally within a single paragraph; they give the impression of being excerpts from a larger context, rather than a self-contained composition.

The likeness of the man-like figure who comes with the clouds of heaven to the deity known as the rider of the clouds (e.g., Baal in the Ugaritic literature) and of the one "Ancient in Years" to El in the court of the gods (whose gray hairs and gray beard are frequently mentioned in the same texts) make it plausible that the original setting of the vision of the heavenly court in verses 9–10 and 13–14, like that of the beasts in verses 2–8, fell at some point within the myth of the subjugation of the chaos monster. The varied forms of the myth that have come down to us differ widely, but some of them have important features in common with Daniel 7. The Ugaritic Baal cycle, for example, describes the scene in the court of El, at which a demand is made by the god of the sea, Yām, that Baal be delivered to him. El is ready to do this, but Baal goes out and fights Yām, overcomes him, and proclaims his kingship. Instead of returning to El's court, however, Baal goes to his home in the north and sends a message to El requesting permission to build a palace, without which he cannot effectively exercise his rule; the request is granted.

In some respects, the Akkadian Creation Epic has closer affinities with Daniel's vision, in that the assembly of the gods is convened to determine what shall be done in face of the threat of Tiamat to attack them. Marduk, the storm god, is asked to be their champion, and he assents, providing that the gods agree to make him supreme among them. An assembly is called for this purpose and Marduk's demand is met, whereupon Marduk battles with Tiamat, kills her, and makes heaven and earth out of her body. In gratitude the gods build him a palace (Babylon!) and proclaim his fifty glorious names, the last of which is "Lord of the Lands."

In the Hittite myth the Song of Ullikumis we again read of an assembly of the gods called in face of danger from the powerful sea god and of the deliverance wrought by the storm god, though the outcome is lost to us through bad preservation of the tablet.

In all of these myths, the pattern of *threat* from the sea monster, *assembly* of the gods, *deliverance* by the storm god, and his consequent exercise of *sovereignty* is clear.[6] Similarly, in the first stanza of Daniel 7:9–10 we read of the assembly of the court of the "Ancient in Years." The assembly has been called to consider the misdeeds of an offender and to pass judgment on him (the books were opened). By setting the poetic stanzas in their present context (vv. 2–8) the apocalyptist has linked the judgment scene with the myth of the rising of the monster from the sea against the powers of heaven, thereby identifying the offender with the monster. Furthermore, the two court scenes (vv. 9–10 and 13–14) are separated by an account of the monster's destruction (vv. 11–12). Whoever arranged the material in this fashion did so because he was recapitulating the patterns of a source as he found it and because the story contained within itself the elements of this well-known complex of ideas, recognizable by those for whom he wrote.[7]

In the myth of the conquest of the dragon, it is the cloud-rider who does battle with the beast and overcomes it. El is a peaceful god who presides over the court of the gods and pronounces decisions within the court.[8] It is possible, therefore, that in the original vision the man-like figure is given dominion because *he* overcame the monster. Such an understanding of the source can be accommodated to the vision exactly as it stands in chapter 7. The Ancient in Years convenes the court and determines the judgment to be executed on the monster: it is to be slain. The carrying out of the sentence, assumed in verse 13, is stated in the intercalated verse 11; since the sovereignty that belonged to the monster is handed over to the cloud-rider, it is natural to deduce that the latter is the one who kills the monster and receives the dominion as his reward.[9]

It is of course also possible that the apocalyptist modified his sources in light of the use to which the chaos myth had long been put in Israel's traditions. In the Old Testament generally, Yahweh is the conqueror of the sea monster, just as he is described as the rider on the storm clouds. The writer of the vision may have intended his readers to interpret the destruction of the beast as the work of Yahweh. In that case, the kingdom is given to the man-like one not as a reward but through the sovereign *hesed* of God. Nevertheless, the former interpretation commends itself, not least because in this passage the cloud-rider is, after all, the man-like figure, not the Ancient in Years, and in a context describing the monster's raging, his going forth on storm clouds is most likely to have been for combat.

It is important to observe that in the Old Testament passages in which the chaos myth is applied to Yahweh's reduction of tyrannical historical powers (e.g., Isa. 27:1 and 51:9–10, and Ezek. 32), Yahweh *comes to earth* to execute judgment and to deliver his people. The same would appear to be the case in Daniel 7. We observe that in verses 9–10 the description of the throne of the Ancient in Years is reminiscent of Ezekiel's vision of the chariot throne. In Ezekiel the chariot is the vehicle of a theophany to the prophet in an alien land. In Daniel the materials did not allow such a description; only a hint of the movement of the deity is given (i.e., in the vision rather than in the interpretation). But inasmuch as the author of Daniel wished to relate the court scene to the oppression of the nation by a tyrant *on earth*, it is likely that he intended it to be understood of an intervention of God *on earth*. Although he could have viewed the court scene as taking place in heaven and the judgment as being carried out on earth, it would accord with the nature of his materials and the picture he was conveying to assume that he had in view the theophany pattern. The convening of the court for the judgment of the monster-tyrant is thus conceived of as a theophany, not to a locale in the heavens but, in accordance with the nature of theophanies throughout the Old Testament, to the earth scene where the monster is doing his evil works.

Two features encourage this interpretation of the writer's intention. First, the immediately succeeding stanza describes the one like a man "coming with the clouds of heaven." Many exegetes of recent times, it is true, maintain that since the man-like one approaches the Ancient in Years on clouds, he is depicted as *ascending* from earth to heaven. But such a deduction results from overlooking the origin of the picture. In the source, the man-like figure is a divine being who rides on clouds to engage in his works, above all when he goes out to battle. How did the Jewish editor of the primitive text wish it to be understood? Surely in the same manner as all representations of God coming on the storm clouds of heaven—namely, to earth. Here I would cite K. H. Müller's view of the matter:

Nowhere in the Old Testament, Jewish or Talmudic literature do "clouds" ever play a role so long as the concern is to give expression to the communication and the movement of heavenly beings among each other in the transcendent sphere, withdrawn from the eyes of men. It is only when one of them steps forth from his hiddenness that epiphany clouds and cloud vehicles are brought into the picture.[10]

Hence, in a Jewish adaptation of the myth under review it would be natural for a theophany of God to the earth to be depicted as being followed by a like theophany of his agent.

Second, we should not overlook the indications given in the interpretation of the vision about how the court scene was understood. In verses 21–22 it is stated that the oppression of the tyrant continued *"until the ancient in Years came.* Then judgment was given in favor of the saints." Even if this interpretation was not added by the one who originally narrated the vision, it at least indicates how an early redactor interpreted the scene in verses 9–10 and how the writer who gave us the book of Daniel understood it. The author/redactor interpreted the session of the divine court as the equivalent of a theophany to the earth, accompanied by the theophany of the man-like rider on the clouds.[11]

We should now turn to an examination of the interpretation of the vision recounted in the second half of chapter 7. A summary interpretation is given in verses 17–18: verse 17 explains the vision of the four beasts, and verse 18 explains the vision of the judgment scene. The man-like figure is not mentioned by name, but in verse 14 the gift of sovereignty is made to him, and in verse 18 it is given to the "saints of the Most High." Similarly, in verse 27 it is stated that "the kingdom and the dominion . . . shall be given to the people of the saints of the Most High." It has therefore been commonly assumed that the author of Daniel 7 interpreted the "one like a son of man" as a symbol for the faithful people of God. Since there is no mention of the Messiah in the book, it is thought that the apocalyptist and his circle had rejected belief in the Messiah, perhaps because earlier hopes had been discredited.

While accepting the view that the man-like one represents the faithful in Israel, some believe that this does not exclude the possibility that he also stands for the representative of the people, whether or not the name *Messiah* be accorded him. In chapter 7, as elsewhere in Daniel, a fluidity in the concepts of king and kingdom is apparent. In verse 17 the four beasts are said to represent four kings, though they are clearly kingdoms. The description of the first kingdom in verse 4 is dominated by the experience of one king, Nebuchadnezzar (cf. chap. 4), just as the description of the fourth beast in verses 7–8 and 19–22 has in view the nature of its last king. Similarly, in Daniel 2:37 Nebuchadnezzar, not his kingdom, is declared to be the head of gold, and 8:21 reflects a like phenomenon. Indeed, in Daniel 7 interest is concentrated not on the Seleucid Empire but on the tyrant Antiochus Epiphanes; hence, the slaughter of the beast in verse 11 is replaced by references to the conquest of the antigod ruler, and the replacement of his sovereignty by that given to the man-like figure.

In recent years a fresh application of this interpretation has emerged. Ever since M. Noth's investigation of this theme, it has become increasingly common to view verse 27 as part of a final redaction to interpret the vision, and its understanding of the *saints* is discounted for the earlier interpretations.[12] It has been urged that the term *saints* ("holy ones") normally denotes supernatural beings—always so in Canaanite literature and frequently so in the Old Testament (e.g., in Ps. 89:5–7; Zech. 14:5; and Deut. 33:2) and in Daniel outside chapter 7 (e.g., in 4:13 and 8:13); in the Qumran literature it is the title par excellence given to angels.[13] It is suggested, therefore, that verse 18 signifies that the kingdom is given to the angelic hosts. The world is ruled by the powers of heaven instead of the evil powers. When the vision was edited so as to apply it to the time of Antiochus Epiphanes, the same concept was still in view in the references to the saints of the Most High added in verses 22a and 25a. But when in the light of the intensified war of Antiochus against the Jews verses 21, 22b, and 25b were penned, the picture was changed; here the saints are under the heel of the tyrant. Accordingly, the term in these instances was applied to the Jewish people, as also in verse 27.[14]

This dissection of the chapter has not gone without challenge, but in the course of discussion a mediating view has been proposed in relation to the "holy ones." It is suggested that in chapter 7 they may be understood *both* as the holy people on earth *and* the angelic holy ones in heaven.[15] Or the "holy ones" may be angels, but "the people *of* the saints of the Most High" denote *the people on earth who are destined to belong to the holy ones in heaven.*[16] Such an idea comports with the views of the Qumran community as they are expressed, for example, in the War of the Sons of Light against the Sons of Darkness (12:6ff.):

> Thou, O god, [art terrible] in the glory of thy majesty, and the *congregation of the holy ones are amongst us* for eternal alliance . . . for the Lord is holy, and *the King of Glory is with us, a people of saints.*[17]

According to this latter interpretation it is possible to see in the man-like one an angel representative of the saints of the Most High and of the people destined to belong to them, just as in the later chapters of Daniel (especially chap. 10) we read of angel representatives of the nations. It has often been remarked that Gabriel in Daniel 8:15 is described as "one with the semblance of a man" (cf. 9:21), and that Michael in 9:21 is spoken of as "your prince"—that is, as Israel's leader—whereas in 12:1 Michael is described as "your great captain who stands guard over your fellow countrymen." Accordingly, it is conceivable that *the man-like figure is Michael, leader of the hosts of heaven and representative of the saints on earth.*[18] This view has been supported by J. J. Collins on the basis of an elaborate parallelism between the vision of Daniel 7 and the visions of chapters 8–12, especially of chapters 10–12. In this last vision the struggles of the nations on earth are seen as concomitants of conflicts among their angelic patrons in heaven:

> The earthly battles are only one dimension of what is happening in a two-story universe. Corresponding to the kings on earth and their conflicts are the patron angels of the peoples and the battles waged betweeen them.[19]

The hope of Israel's rescue from Antiochus therefore rests upon the intervention of Michael. His victory in heaven will result in their deliverance on earth and the resurrection from the dead, when the wise will "shine like the stars" and so become one with the angelic host in heavens. Accordingly, Michael is the representative of the people of the saints of the Most High in Daniel 7 also, the "one like a son of man" to whom rule is given in heaven and on earth.

How are we to decide between these conflicting views? We can but examine the evidence freshly in hope of finding clues to guide us.

First, regarding the alleged development in the interpretation of the vision in verses 15–27, whatever the sources of the vision in verses 1–14, it is unlikely that the sole interpretative comments on it by the author are confined to verses 17–18. The material used is so complex and the message it was desired to convey so important that the seer would not have been satisfied with so brief a comment. It is likely that verses 17–18 were set down as an immediate key to the vision and that the writer elaborated the interpretation in the light of his contemporaries' situation. In addition, the chapter is more unified than some represent it to be. Both Collins and M. Casey, to take examples from representatives of different viewpoints, agree that chapter 7 does not require a hypothesis of interpolation by a later editor and that distinctions should not be drawn between the "saints" in verses 21–22 and in the rest of the chapter. Collins, however, views the "holy ones" as angels; Casey views them as faithful members of God's people.

Second, it is not true that outside chapter 7 of Daniel the term *saints* always means "angels." In Daniel 8:24 the equivalent in Hebrew of the Aramaic expression for "people of the saints" is used of Israel in a sense that *excludes* the holy ones of heaven. That should be set alongside the fact that in Daniel 7:21, 22, 25, and 27, the term *saints* can be interpreted in an identical manner.

It is true that Collins contests this last point. He believes that the statements in 7:21–25 reflect not merely the concept of battles in a two-story world on earth and in heaven but that they reflect a *mixture* of these: the tyrant of *earth* does battle against the powers of *heaven*. Accordingly, we read that "As I still watched, that horn was waging war with the saints and overcoming them until the Ancient in Years came. Then judgment was given in favor of the saints of the Most High" (vv. 21–22). Again, "another king shall arise . . . and he shall wear down the saints of the Most High" (vv. 24–25). Now I grant that it is within the realm of possibility, in light of Daniel 8:10–12 and 11:36, that these passages could mean that Antiochus Epiphanes fought against heaven and overcame the angelic forces until the Ancient in Years came and ended the conflict; it is *possible*, but *improbable*. The mythological language of the vision of 8:10–12 is not intended to convey the notion that Antiochus trod angels underfoot. A similar idea is in view in the parallel 11:36: Antiochus exalts himself above every god, and utters blasphemies against the God of gods. But this is "fighting" of a different order from that spoken of in 10:20–11:1 and of the wars of the kings in 11:2–45. When Daniel 7:21–25 speaks of the "horn" waging war against the saints and overcoming them till Yahweh's deliverance, of the king "wearing down" the saints and trying to alter the law, and of the saints being delivered into his power "for a time and times and half a time" (i.e., the period of great distress of the people of God), it seems evident beyond reasonable doubt that the reference is to the persecution of Antiochus and that the "saints of the Most High" denote the saints of earth, not of heaven.

This presumption is confirmed by the expression in verse 27, "*the people* of the saints of the Most High." The most natural understanding of that phrase is that it identifies the people with the saints of the Most High; there is no hint within the vision or its interpretation that the expression signifies the association of the faithful of Israel with the hosts of heaven in the kingdom of God.

Third, the relation of Daniel 7 to the rest of the book calls for some consideration. Collins dissociates it from the early chapters and links it closely with chapters 8–12; there is ground, however, for linking it no less with chapters 2–6, which are written in Aramaic (as is chapter 7), not in Hebrew (as are chapters 8–12). Now, we are not anxious to pit one section of Daniel against another, but it is evident that chapter 7 has obvious connections with chapter 2, especially in that they both employ the four-kingdoms division of history. Daniel 2:44 states that "In the period of those kings the God of heaven will establish a kingdom which shall never be destroyed; *that kingdom shall never pass to another people*; it shall shatter and make an end of all these kingdoms." The italicized portion of the statement puts in a negative form the positive affirmations made in 7:18, 22, and 37—namely, that the kingdom is given to the saints of the Most High, and that "they shall retain it for ever and ever." We would need a strong reason to drive a wedge between the eschatology of chapter 2 and that of chapter 7, ascribing to the latter an understanding of the nature of the kingdom of God not glimpsed in the earlier one.

Fourth, we should express the relation between Daniel and the Qumran writings with care. Certainly we find in the latter a unique consciousness of fellowship between the elect on earth and the hosts of heaven. Not that the term *holy ones* cannot denote the elect of earth; according to H. W. Kuhn it has that meaning not only in 1QM 10:10, where it is generally recognized, but also in 1QM 3:5; 6:6; 16:1, and possibly in 12:8 (assuming Yadin's interpretation).[20] That apart, there is no doubt that the Covenanters believed (1) that they formed one company with the angels in this time, (2) that the angels would be with them in the final battle of this age, and (3) that they would form one fellowship with them in the kingdom of God. This consciousness of unity with the angels in their inheritance is frequently expressed in the Qumran literature. But *where is there in Daniel 7 (or anywhere else in the book) a comparable statement that the heirs of the kingdom of God are the angels above and the saints below and that they form one community in the kingdom?* The idea is so striking and it would have been such an inspiration to the people of God in their persecutions for the faith that it would surely have been expressed with plainness by the seer had he held it.

Fifth, if the identification of the saints in chapter 7 with angels is deemed improbable, the identification of the one like a man with Gabriel or Michael is no more plausible. The difficulty is not merely that neither Gabriel nor Michael is mentioned in chapter 7. Their role in chapters 10–12 is to contend with hostile spiritual powers on behalf of Yahweh and Israel, and yet not a hint is given that either of them is to be enthroned in the age to come—whereas the man-like one is given dominion over all nations in the kingdom of God. Why is there no mention of this in Daniel 12:2–13, after the statement of Michael's support of Israel in the time of trouble? If the views of the Qumran apocalyptists are to be invoked, we may recall that while Michael and the angels are ascribed a lofty place in the coming age, the rule and the priesthood are committed to the royal and the priestly Messiahs (or, according to at least some of the Covenanters, to a Messiah who performs the functions of priest and king). Michael may be a mediator, but he is not the Messiah.

So we return to the question of the identity of the man-like one in the vision of Daniel 7. We have postulated that the original figure was the storm god common to many Semitic religions and that he appears in the vision because he plays the traditional role of conqueror of the sea monster. But of course neither the seer nor any prophet before or apocalyptist after him had the remotest intention of setting forth a pagan deity as representative or savior of Israel. In the Old Testament it is the Lord who rides on the storm, slays "monsters," and delivers his people. In our vision, the monster is a caricature of Antiochus Epiphanes, raging against the Lord of creation. Who, then, is the rider on the clouds? The interpretation in Daniel 7:15–27 mentions only the saints of the Most High. We might then ask whether the man-like one is a *corporate symbol* for a nation or a *representative* of the nation. The former is possible; indeed, many would say that is the only justifiable interpretation, since the explanation that follows the vision mentions the saints of God alone as recipients of the kingdom. Nevertheless, the notion of a representative of the saints may be closer to the intent of the vision:

1. It does not cancel out the former, but includes it. Contrary to the commonly held opinion, it was unusual for later Jews to have an expectation of the kingdom of God without a representative of the people and of the kingdom.

2. The use of the symbol of the cloud rider in the vision favors a personal rather than a corporate interpretation of the figure. The Ancient of Years in the vision clearly denotes an individual rather than an abstraction such as heaven or a corporate notion such as "dwellers in heaven." The monster stands for a king who reigns over an earthly dominion. Moreover, elsewhere in the Old Testament the rider on the clouds is Yahweh, not a symbol for a group. It is to be expected, then, that in this vision the cloud rider should denote the representative of the rule of God and (in light of the interpretation) the representative of the people to whom the rule is given.

3. In the prophetic tradition, the Messiah holds just such a position as representative of Yahweh in his final sovereignty and representative of the people privileged to be included in the rule. This concept is sometimes referred to without use of the term *Messiah*, as we see in the Servant Songs of Deutero-Isaiah, in which the concepts of servant leader and servant people flow together.

4. It is the view of not a few that the vision in verses 13–14 represents an eschatological form of the ancient Semitic ritual for the proclamation of a king[21] or of the enthronement festival of Yahweh himself.[22] If we are right in believing that the seer has utilized the chaos myth, this hypothesis would need no modification, since the relation between the conquest of chaos and exaltation to rule was integral to the myth, and it would strengthen a "messianic" rather than a purely corporate interpretation of the chapter.

The obvious objection to these observations is the fact that neither the Messiah nor a quasi-messianic figure appears in the interpretation of the vision in chapter 7. If the apocalyptist did anticipate that such a figure would represent the people, he seems to have taken him for granted; his concern was to depict the consolation of the saints of God in the kingdom that lay ahead of them. This may indeed be the case. The author's overriding purpose was to encourage the suffering saints by emphasizing the hope of their deliverance and vindication in the kingdom of God. The central vision of verses 9–10 and 13–14 suffices to show what must happen to bring this about: God's judgment of the tyrant and the coming of his kingdom. It appears that a reference to the Ancient of Years slipped into the interpretation of the vision (v. 22) only as an afterthought—so incidental a matter that most of the commentators have failed to notice that it is there! It is therefore not so surprising that the man-like one receives no mention in the interpretation. The meaning of the vision with respect to the divine intervention was clear enough, and the seer concentrated on its relation to God's oppressed people.

A parallel to Daniel 7 rarely brought into the discussion is worthy of examination—namely, the vision of the overthrow of the dragon in Revelation 12. Here a different version of the ancient myth is reflected, but the primitive pattern is maintained. The chaos monster appears as the seven-headed dragon of the deep who wages war with the inhabitants of heaven. His intention to devour the child of the heavenly woman is frustrated when the child is rapt to heaven and the dragon is cast down to earth, where he persecutes the offspring of the woman. The story is briefly told. No word is given of the part played by the child in the overthrow of the monster, but every reader knew that the child was destined to slay the dragon, and that that is why the dragon sought to kill him. This story was not freshly minted by the Christian apocalyptist. It appears to have been taken up first by a *Jewish* apocalyptist, who saw in it a mode of presenting Old Testament messianic prophecy. He declares that the male child is "destined to rule all nations with an iron rod" (v. 5), and so identifies him with the king-messiah of Psalm 2; and the mother becomes the messianic people (vv. 13–17). But the Jewish apocalyptist gives a twist to the story: it is not the "child" who conquers the dragon, but Michael and his angels, who hurl the dragon out of heaven (vv. 7–9). A song is then sung celebrating "the victory for our God, the hour of his sovereignty and power, when his Christ comes to his rightful rule" (v. 10). This means that the dragon is overthrown by *Michael*, that the victory belongs to *God*, and that the rule is given to the *Messiah*. A further modification in the tradition is made by the *Christian* seer: in verse 11 it is stated that "the brethren" have conquered the dragon "by the sacrifice of the Lamb and by the testimony which they uttered"—that is, the dragon was conquered by the Christ-Redeemer after all; his exaltation to heaven resulted from his sacrificial death, and so he received the rule in the divine kingdom and his followers share his victory.

The interesting feature of this vision lies in its use of the dragon myth. The author has taken his material straight from the ancient myth, making it a vehicle of messianic prophecy. In the Jewish adaptation, Michael is introduced in the setting of the conflict with the powers of evil, although for the Christian seer his role is of secondary importance. In both Jewish and Christian traditions, Michael takes his place alongside the Messiah, but the rule is given to the Messiah, not to the angel.

The significance of the parallel can be variously assessed. I would suggest that it is important because it illustrates how an apocalyptist could utilize a form of the chaos myth to set forth the hope of the messianic kingdom for the consolation of God's people. Alike in Daniel 7 and Revelation 12, the figure of a god is made to do service for the representative of the people of God. In Daniel he is "like a man"; in Revelation he is a "man-child" whose growth to full stature is not allowed by reason of the exigencies of this version of the myth. In both accounts the (quasi-) messianic figure has a prominent role in the vision, but in both he disappears thereafter. Unfortunately, we cannot be certain of the extent of the Jewish redaction in Revelation 12; if, as is plausible, the whole of the song in verses 10–12 comes from the Christian apocalyptist, the Messiah of the preliminary vision disappears entirely in the Jewish interpretation handed on to us. If verse 10 comes from the Jewish apocalyptist, reference to the Messiah is limited to a single phrase in the song—"the authority of his Christ." Whether or not verse 10 originated with the Jewish apocalyptist, the purport of the vision is to show that the hope of the pagans is fulfilled in the messianic kingdom of biblical prophecy. Accordingly, it was simple for the Christian apocalyptist to make a few additions to show its true fulfillment in the crucified and risen Redeemer.[23]

If we cannot claim too much for the parallels in the visions, their existence should at least illustrate the necessity of caution in pressing the silences of Daniel 7 relating to the Messiah and the kingdom.

We may summarize the discussion of the vision and its interpretation in Daniel 7 as follows:

1. As in the prophetic tradition before it, the vision accords a prime place to the coming of Yahweh to subdue evil and to deliver his people. The differences in the images employed should not detract from our recognizing the importance of that motif in the chapter.

2. The coming on the clouds of one like a man should be interpreted in terms of theophany, as should the coming on the clouds of the Ancient in Years. This accords with the form of the myth adapted in the chapter and the use to which it is put in the vision.

3. The gift of the kingdom made to the one like a man is meant to provide consolation to the people of God. There is insufficient evidence to interpret the vision as including angelic powers in the rule of the new age.

4. The messianic interpretation of the one like a man is not demonstrable, but it is plausible and even probable. The man-like one represents the saints in the kingdom, as the interpretation emphasizes, but inasmuch as the sovereignty over the world is that of God exercised through the "man," he is also the representative of God. This dual role of the "man" accords with the messianic traditions of the Old Testament.

Part II

The Coming of God in the Writings of Early Judaism

5 | Theophany in Apocalyptic Literature

In considering the ideas set forth in works belonging to the apocalyptic literature and the writings of the Qumran Sect, which form a specialized group within the larger whole, it is essential to recognize the complexity and variety of thought expressed within them. It is legitimate, obviously, to speak of the "apocalyptic movement," just as it is right and necessary to speak of the prophetic movement in Israel, but the latter embraces a wide range of emphases within the preexilic, exilic, and postexilic times, to say nothing of the developments in the later additions to the prophetic literature that shade into apocalyptic proper. Similarly, the literature we classify as apocalyptic is extraordinarily varied; we might compare it to a river fed by many streams from the hills that issues into a lake that itself has outlets flowing in various directions. Accordingly, we should resist the temptation to lay down axioms of apocalyptic thought as though they were believed *ubique et ab omnibus*.

The origins of this literature underscore the necessity for this caution. That apocalyptic writers drew on the writings of the canonical prophets can hardly be denied. In this sense it is legitimate to view apocalyptic as the "child" of prophecy. But there was another parent, to say nothing of a considerable number of relatives. J. C. C. Collins has drawn attention to the link that existed between the Jewish apocalyptic movement and similar phenomena that existed in the contemporary world of the Middle East:

> Throughout the Near East from Egypt to Persia, Hellenistic rule was met by national resistance. Messianism, as the desire for the restoration of native monarchy, was by no means a peculiarity of the Jews but was a feature of the entire Near East in the Hellenistic period. The ways in which the national aspirations of each state were expressed also had much in common throughout the area.[1]

Collins adduces as one illustration of this situation the widespread use of the scheme of the four kingdoms. The division of history into four world kingdoms followed by some form of divine intervention was adopted and adapted by Persians, Jews, Romans, those from whom the Romans took it, and whoever wrote the oracle embedded in the Fourth Book of Sibylline Oracles; significantly, in every case the scheme is hostile to the Greeks, who always form the fourth kingdom.[2] Thus, in addition to the factor of religious oppression, of which we are all familiar, there was a political influence present in the formation of apocalyptic, through the loss of national independence. The revival of ancient myths and of interest in native traditions was part of the general resistance to Greek rule in the literature of other countries in addition to Israel.[3] All of this is to say that Israel took part in an international movement of thought in producing its apocalyptic literature; its contacts were horizontal and vertical as its representatives responded with other nations to a current situation and with them drew on a cultural inheritance from the remote past.

We must, therefore, recognize the developing nature of apocalyptic thought. That entails more than a simple differentiation between earlier and later stages of literature. For example, if it is true, as is generally acknowledged, that dualism is the basic feature of apocalyptic, it is misleading to cite its expression in 4 Ezra and 2 Baruch as normative for apocalyptic generally. The roots of *temporal* dualism lie in the prophetic movement. Wherever the Day of the Lord and the Coming of God were viewed eschatologically, there the essentials of the contrast between this age and the coming age were present. This concept became increasingly emphasized in the prophetic writings, above all in those of Deutero-Isaiah, in which stress is constantly laid on the sovereign intervention of God to bring about the salvation of the kingdom in the immediate future (see, for example, Isa. 40:9ff., 42:13ff., 43:16ff., 51:4ff., and 54:1ff.). Undoubtedly the apocalyptists sharpened the contrast and added the dimension of a *special* dualism to the temporal—the contrast of the world above and the world below to that of the present age and the coming age. Yet despite the spatial dualism of Daniel, the concept of the kingdom in that book stands closer to the view of the kingdom of God presented in Deutero-Isaiah than that found in 4 Ezra. Moreover, the abandonment of the present age to the powers of evil in apocalyptic thought should not be exaggerated. It would be wrong to charge the two canonical apocalypses with harboring such an attitude. Daniel, for example, records that Nebuchadnezzar is told that he will be humbled "until you have learnt that the Most High is sovereign over the kingdom of men and gives it to whom he will" (Dan. 4:25), and the Seer of Revelation teaches that even the Antichrist and his minions are under the hand of God as they blaspheme his Name and wage war on his people (Rev. 13:5ff.). Daniel's view is echoed more than once in the Psalms of Solomon (e.g., 2:33ff., 8:25ff.), while in 1 Enoch 84 the rule of God over creation is extolled in a manner scarcely surpassed in the Old Testament psalms or prophets. This is not the whole story of the apocalyptists' attitude of the relation of God to the world, of course, but these comments should serve to remind us that we are not dealing with a unified literature in apocalyptic. We need to bear this steadfastly in mind as we look at its treatment of the subjects of concern to us, as we should in any endeavor we might make to relate contemporary Jewish eschatological thought to the teaching of Jesus.

We turn then to the theme of *the coming of God in apocalyptic writings*. This is not a subject in which investigators in this field have commonly shown interest. Nevertheless it may be worth mentioning that one early explorer into apocalyptic found it possible to write that "We find the natural germ of apocalyptic in the anthropomorphic idea of the national divinity in pre-Jahwism; the ancient theophanies are little apocalypses."⁴ A more recent author, Klaus Koch, expounded the same idea with greater fullness. Concerning the apocalyptic writers he affirmed, "Apocalypse means not only the revealing of details (revelation as the communication of doctrine) but the disclosure of possible participation in the final and unique, all encompassing coming of God among men. An apocalypse is therefore designed to be 'the revelation of the divine revelation,' as this takes place in the individual acts of a coherent historical pattern."⁵

In truth there are frequent allusions to the coming of God in apocalyptic literature, though many of these are not to be classed as theophanic compositions in the old prophetic style. We find, for example, various references in the Testaments of the Twelve Patriarchs to God's coming, most clearly of all in the Testament of Levi:

> They said to me: Levi, thy seed shall be divided into three offices, for a sign of the glory of the Lord who is to come. (8:11)⁶

There is also the extraordinary statement in 2 Enoch 32:1, wherein the Lord recounts his words to Adam consequent on his sin:

> I said to him: Earth thou art, and into the earth whence I took thee thou shalt go, and I will not ruin thee, but send thee whence I took thee. Then I can again take thee at my second coming.

The "second" coming denotes God's appearing in judgment and salvation at the end, in contrast to his "first" coming to the earth to bless his creatures (as in 2 Enoch 58:1—"the Lord came down on to earth for Adam's sake, and visited all his creatures which he had created himself").

Apart from such casual references to the coming of God there are longer descriptions of the event, written after the style of the biblical theophanic poems. The best-known example is the opening oracle of Enoch:

> The Holy Great One will come forth from his dwelling,
> And the eternal God will tread upon the earth, [even] on Mount Sinai,
> [And appear from his camp]
> And appear in the strength of his might from the heaven of heavens.

This announces the theme of the apocalypse as a whole. The traditional features of convulsions of earth and the fear of mankind before the presence of the Lord are mentioned, together with a new feature characteristic of this book—namely, the terror of the "Watchers," the fallen angels; the coming of God issues in judgment and deliverance in the Kingdom. The poem concludes with two further stanzas, which are cited in the letter of Jude in the New Testament:

> And behold! He cometh with ten thousands of his holy ones
> To execute judgment upon all,
> And to destroy all the ungodly. . . . (Vv. 14–15)

Another passage in similar style is found in the Assumption of Moses, wherein the traditional accompaniments of theophany and of the Day of the

Lord appear yet more fully than in the Enoch citation. God's kingdom, it is said, will appear throughout all his creation, and Satan will be no more:

> For the Heavenly One will arise from his royal throne,
> And he will go forth from his holy habitation
> With indignation and wrath on account of his sons. . . .

Here the coming of God is motivated "on account of his sons"—that is, by reason of the sufferings they endured at the hands of their oppressors. The writer tells how at his coming forth from heaven all nature goes into confusion—earth, mountains, sea and rivers, the sun, moon, and stars—and judgment falls upon the Gentiles, especially because of their idolatry, but the chosen people are made glad and are exalted "to the heaven of the stars."[7]

Perhaps the most overwhelming representation of the coming of God in all this literature is that which occurs in the third Thanksgiving Hymn of the Qumran community. The speaker thanks God for freeing him from "the pit" and setting him "on the crest of the world." He then contemplates his insignificance and his weakness. What strength does he possess that will enable him to survive when the hour of God's judgment strikes,

> when the final doom of his rage
> falls on all worthless things . . .
>   when with his mighty roar
> God thunders forth,
> and his holy welkin trembles
> through dread of his glory,
> and the hosts of heaven give forth their voice,
> and the world's foundations rock and reel;
>   when warfare waged by the soldiers of heaven
> sweeps through the world
> and turns not back until final doom
> —warfare the like of which
> has never been?[8]

The "final doom of his rage" bursts upon the world "when with his mighty roar God thunders forth": that is the old language of the theophany of God in the storm, but in this passage the element of fire, formerly associated with the lightning, becomes a raging river that consumes even the granite of the mountains.

N. Messel has drawn attention to this tendency of the apocryphal, pseudepigraphic, and Qumran writings to stress the destructive effects of the divine intervention in the world at the last day rather than the coming of the Lord as an event, and Jeremias has confirmed it.[9] It may be linked with the Jewish experience of oppression, which is one of the factors prompting the creation of this literature, and thus to a consequent emphasis on the wickedness of man and the evil of the times. Nevertheless, the hope of the apocalyptists and of the circles for which they wrote was undoubtedly directed to the coming of God to abolish evil and to establish righteousness in the world.

6 | The Day of the Lord in Apocalyptic Literature

In the writings we are examining, the coming of God is the advent of *the Judge*. As the writer of 2 Baruch 48:39 expressed it, "The Judge shall come and will not tarry." The significance of this element in the apocalyptic literature was apparent even to its earliest investigators. The dictum of H. T. Andrews is often cited: "Apocalyptic arose out of prophecy by developing and universalising the conception of the Day of the Lord."[1] F. C. Burkitt more simply affirmed that "The doctrine of the apocalypses is the doctrine of the Last Judgment."[2] Burkitt had in view the general expectation of Judgment at the end of history to which the apocalytists bear witness. His lack of differentiation between a judgment that forms a term to the historic process and an assize for all generations of history is in no small measure a reflection of the lack of clarity within the apocalyptic writings themselves. Nevertheless there is justification in D. S. Russell's description of the apocalyptic day of judgment as "a specialisation of the prophetic Day of the Lord."[3] Features of the prophetic descriptions of the Day of the Lord are elaborated in these writings, and various attempts are made to systematize them.

It will be recalled that Old Testament descriptions of the Day of the Lord frequently include convulsions in nature such as are proper to theophany descriptions, but that they especially stress confusion in the heavenly bodies. All these features find mention in the apocalypses, but it is evident that they are sometimes linked with the wickedness of earth's inhabitants rather than viewed as the recoil of creation before the Creator. An example of this appears in 1 Enoch 80:2ff.:

> In the days of the sinners the years shall be shortened,
> And their seed shall be tardy on their lands and fields,
> And all things on the earth shall alter,
>
> And shall not appear in their time. . . .
>
> And the moon shall alter her order,
> And not appear at her time. . . .

And many chiefs of the stars shall transgress their order.
And these shall alter their orbits and tasks,
And not appear at the seasons prescribed to them.

And the whole order of the stars shall be concealed from the sinners,
And the thoughts of those on the earth shall err concerning them. . . .
Yea, they shall err and take them to be gods.

And evil shall be multiplied upon them,
And punishment shall come upon them
So as to destroy all.

There is a related description in 2 Esdras 5:1ff. that includes freakish manifestations of all sorts of horrors among the cosmic phenomena of the last day. Such
things happen because righteousness is not to be found on the earth (v. 11). The
like applies to the lengthy description of the portents at the end in Jubilees
23:13ff.

Prophetic portrayals of the Day of the Lord give much space to the warfare
that will take place at that time. In such descriptions the invading armies, which
are often represented as merciless in their slaughter of people, are viewed as the
scourge of the Lord, the agents of his judgment. This too is recognized by the
apocalyptists, but they tend to lay emphasis on bloodshed as the expression of
men's wickedness at the end of the age. The two elements are brought together
in the oracle of 1 Enoch 100:1ff.:

In those days in one place the fathers together with their sons shall be smitten

And brothers one with another shall fall in death
Till the streams flow with their blood. . . .

And the horse shall walk up to the breast in the blood of sinners,
And the chariot shall be submerged to its height.

A unique turn is given by the Qumran community to the expectation of
wars in the end time, for they believed that God had appointed as his scourge
not heathen armies but themselves; through them judgment and destruction
would be executed on the heathen and on the apostates of their own people
alike. The concept is succinctly stated in the Commentary on Habakkuk, verse
3:

By the hand of his elect God will execute judgment upon all heathen nations; and
when these are chastised all the wicked among his own people will also be
punished.

The nature of the war is described in The War of the Sons of Light with the Sons
of Darkness, wherein it is made clear that the course of the war is wholly in the
hands of God and wholly determined by him. It is to last for forty years,
punctuated with sabbath years (every seventh), when no fighting will take
place. The entire congregation is to take part in the first week of warfare, which
will be directed to Israel's ancient neighboring foes (the Edomites, the Moabites,
etc.) with a view to clearing the holy land, and then to the "Kittim" in Assyria
and Egypt—presumably the Romans. The remaining years of battle, which will
be fought by divisions of the community in turn, will be against the kings of the

north and for the subjugation of the nations comprising the sons of Shem, Ham, and Japheth. The issue of the war is not in doubt. Though in the earliest phase the "sons of Belial" are permitted to be victorious at times, "the great hand of God shall subdue Belial and all angels of his dominion, and for all men of his lot there shall be eternal annihilation" (1QM 1:14–15). At the end God and his angels join the Sons of Light to gain the final victory (19:1ff.), and the issue is the glory of God and the salvation of Israel:

> The kingdom shall be the Lord's
> and Israel for eternal sovereignty.

Mention was earlier made of attempts to systematize constituent elements in the Day of the Lord. A good example of this can be found in 2 Baruch 25–27, in which the tribulations of the last time are divided into twelve parts, each being characterized by one or more woes. But no apocalypse sets forth the end time judgments in so elaborate and systematic a fashion as the book of Revelation in the New Testament. John the Seer organizes the judgments into three series of seven, using the symbolism of breaking seven seals of the scroll of God's covenant to give the kingdom, sounding seven trumpets announcing judgment and the kingdom, and pouring out seven cups of wrath on the earth (Rev. 6–11, 15–16). It is significant that each group concludes in the same manner—namely, with the occurrence of thunder, loud noises, lightning flashes, and earthquake (Rev. 8:5, 11:19, 16:18ff.), which represent a residuum of nature's response to the coming of God associated with theophanies in the old prophetic tradition. For John the Seer the Day of the Lord is the Day of God and the Lamb (Rev. 6:16–17), and it leads to "the kingdom of our Lord and of his Christ" (Rev. 11:15).

7 | The Kingdom of God in Apocalyptic Literature

Burkitt recognized that it was necessary to provide a complement to his statement that the doctrine of the apocalypses is the doctrine of the Last Judgment, for when God arises in judgment he will bring in his everlasting kingdom: "*The Kingdom of God—that is the central idea.* It is the New Age, the new state of things that will come about when the great agony has ended by God's victorious intervention on behalf of his saints, when he comes, or sends his representative to come, to set the world aright."[1] It is interesting that Burkitt should have been so general in his utterances about the Last Judgment and the Kingdom of God. This may have been intentional, but there is considerable sensitivity about this issue. For the nature of "last" judgment is related to the nature of the kingdom that is expected. Unfortunately the kaleidoscopic nature of the apocalyptic writings makes it difficult for us to be sure about the basic convictions of some of the authors concerned—visual images do not lend themselves to systematic treatment of doctrine—but it is clear that the apocalyptists were not without convictions concerning the kingdom, and it is also clear that they did not all think alike.

The simplest interpretation of the issue of the last times involves viewing it as being ushered in by *the coming of God and the Day of the Lord*, which will entail *the overthrow of evil powers and the establishment of the kingdom of God in this world.* This was essentially the prophetic view, and in such an expectation the accent is always on the Day of the Lord rather than on a so-called "Last Judgment." This may well be the thought of the author of Daniel. Although the judgment scene in Daniel 7:9–10 is described in transcendental terms, it nevertheless relates to the judgment of an earthly tyrant and his empire; it is a transposition of the prophetic Day of the Lord into the key of an assize by the heavenly powers, but the kingdom to which it leads is upon this earth. At the close of the book there is a fleeting reference to a resurrection of "many who sleep in the dust of the earth" (12:2). If some rise to everlasting life and some to everlasting shame, that assumes a judgment that distinguishes between them, but no further light is shed on the event. This illustrates the fragmentary nature of apocalyptic representations of the end. There is no indication that the kingdom of the one like a son of man in Daniel is a temporary kingdom; on the contrary, it is stressed that "his dominion is an everlasting dominion, which shall not pass away, and his kingdom one that shall not be destroyed" (Dan. 7:14; cf. vv. 18, 27).

This view of judgment and the kingdom of God is apparently shared by the authors of 1 Enoch 6–36, and 83–90, both of whom wrote their works early in the apocalyptic movement. The view can also be found in the third book of the Sibylline Oracles and the Psalms of Solomon, and possibly in the Testaments of the Twelve Patriarchs as well.

With the precedent already set in a late Old Testament passage (Isa. 65–66), it was inevitable that an increased emphasis on the transcendent features of the future kingdom would lead to an expectation that *the coming of God will issue in a judgment of all generations of mankind, and a kingdom of God in a transformed creation.* Such appears to be the expectation in the Similitudes of Enoch (chaps. 37–71 of 1 Enoch). Daniel's judgment scene had obviously been pondered by the author of the Similitudes, and he reproduces it in terms that go beyond what the author of Daniel had in mind. The Son of Man, so titled (i.e., rather than "one like a son of man"), is associated with the "Head of Days" in the judgment, and is appointed to carry it out. The theme of his judgment of the kings and the mighty is frequent in this work, and it clearly includes punishment after death:

> He will deliver them to the angels for punishment,
> To execute vengeance on them because they have oppressed his children and his elect,
> And they shall be a spectacle for the righteous and for his elect. . . . (62:11–12)

The universe is to be renewed as a worthy setting of the kingdom:

> I will transform the heaven and make it an eternal blessing and light:
> And I will transform the earth and make it a blessing:
>
> And I will cause mine elect ones to dwell upon it:
> But the sinners and evil-doers shall not set foot thereon. (45:4–5)

A contrast between the judgment of the unrighteous and the felicity of the righteous in the kingdom constitutes a pronounced theme in the Similitudes (see, for example, 1 Enoch 38–39; 41:1–2; 46–48; 50–51; 53; and 58).

The contrast between a kingdom of God within this world and a kingdom of God within a transformed creation was bound at some time to lead to an attempt to combine both expectations. This we find in the hope of *the coming of God and the Day of the Lord that leads to a messianic kingdom within this world, at the end of which the judgment takes place and the kingdom of God is set in a new creation.* Such is the fundamental expectation in 1 Enoch 91–104, with its so-called Apocalypse of Weeks, and more notably in 2 Esdras and 2 Baruch. There is however a difference of accent in the exposition of this view. In 2 Esdras the messianic kingdom is of limited duration and is speedily dismissed:

> My Son the Messiah shall be revealed, together with those who are with him, and shall rejoice the survivors four hundred years. And it shall be, after these years, that my Son the Messiah shall die, and all in whom there is human breath. Then shall the

world be turned into the primaeval silence seven days, like as at the first beginning, so that no man is left. (7:28ff.)

A lengthy account of the Last Judgment follows, when the resurrection of the dead is to take place, the Most High will appear on his throne of judgment, the furnace of Gehenna and the paradise of delight will be revealed, and God will pronounce his decisions over the resurrected nations. For this writer the messianic kingdom belongs not simply to *this world* but to *this age*, and it is sharply distinguished from the kingdom which is the goal of creation.

In 2 Baruch the messianic kingdom is accorded a greater significance than it is in 2 Esdras, although both works belong to the same period. A summary of the teaching of Daniel 7 is provided in the vision and interpretation of 2 Baruch 36–40: four kingdoms are to arise in the world, the last of which will be "harsh and evil far beyond those which were before it," but it will be replaced by "the principate of my Messiah." The armies of the fourth kingdom will be destroyed and the Messiah will convict and put to death their leader in addition to protecting the rest of God's people.

> And his principate will stand for ever, until the world of corruption is at an end, and until the times aforesaid are fulfilled. (40:3)

It is in harmony with this picture of the messianic kingdom that the description of its felicity in chapters 73–74 concludes with the following statement:

> For this time will mark the end of corruption
> and the beginning of incorruption.
> This is why the predictions will be fulfilled in it.
> Also it is held far from the evil and it is wholly near for those who will not die.
> (2 Bar. 74:2–3)[2]

The "predictions" that will be fulfilled in the kingdom of the Messiah are presumably those of the Old Testament prophets. For this reason the time of the Messiah's revealing is described as "the consummation" (69:5), "when the time of the age has ripened" (70:2). Yet some representations of the future kingdom in 2 Baruch speak as though the present age is followed immediately by a new world. This uncertainty of reference is illustrated in 2 Baruch 30:1–2:

> When the time of the advent of the Messiah is fulfilled, *he shall return in glory.*

What can the writer mean by the statement that the Messiah will "return in glory?" Some interpreters assume that it relates to the coming of the Messiah to the earth for the initiating of the messianic kingdom.[3] The difficulty in this apparently simple interpretation is that 2 Baruch 30:1 follows a description of the messianic kingdom that is introduced in 29:3 with the following declaration:

> And it shall come to pass when all is accomplished that was to come to pass in those parts, that the Messiah shall then begin to be revealed.

For this reason some commentators believe that the reference to the Messiah's returning in glory denotes his return to heaven, from whence he came, after which the resurrection for the eternal kingdom in the new world takes place.[4] Ulrich Müller objects that such an expectation is without example in Judaism and concludes that the offending clause must be a Christian interpolation describing the parousia of the Messiah Jesus.[5] It is nevertheless difficult to see why a Christian interpolator would place the statement in so unsuitable a position when he could so easily have inserted it in 29:3, which is followed by a description of the marvels of the messianic kingdom very much in the spirit of Papias. The statement should be left. It can be said to have a precedent in 1 Corinthians 15:28, and it implies that the messianic dominion will yield to the dominion of God, after which there will follow the general resurrection and a truly "last judgment" (30:2–5).

The understanding of the kingdom and the judgment in the Qumran community is not easy to determine, and there are differences of opinion about it. On the one hand, the prominence of the "Messiahs from Aaron and Israel" in the kingdom led J. Pryke to speak of their rule as a "messianic interregnum."[6] On the other hand, the description of the coming of God in the third Thanksgiving Hymn (3:28–36) might lead one to look for the kingdom in a renovated world. One has the impression that the outlook of the community was closer to that of the book of Daniel than of later apocalypses, though with the spread of years covered by the scrolls it is but to be expected that variations in thought would occur among its members. The Manual of Discipline (4:7ff.) provides a clear expression of belief about the kingdom in this literature. The "visitation" of those who walk in the ways of truth is said to be "healing and great peace in a long life, multiplication in progeny together with all everlasting blessings, endless joy in everlasting life, and a crown of glory together with resplendent attire in eternal light." Conversely those who walk in the spirit of deceit will know "many afflictions by all the angels of punishment, eternal perdition by the fury of God's vengeful wrath, everlasting terror and endless shame, together with disgrace of annihilation in the fire of murky hell." While the doctrine of resurrection is not incontrovertibly evidenced in the scrolls, this passage among others presupposes what Kurt Schubert calls "at least a rudimentary belief in a resurrection of the dead"[7] together with a judgment that has final consequences.

There appears to be an element in the expectation of the kingdom of God that appears in the writings of the Qumran community that makes it different from the apocalyptic literature produced by other Jewish sources. Although the members of the Qumran community lived in an ardent anticipation of the coming of the kingdom, as H. W. Kuhn has stressed, they also believed that they were already participating in the eschatological salvation, that they already belonged to the heavenly Jerusalem (1QH 6:24ff.) and enjoyed the hidden paradise later to be revealed (1QH 8:5ff.).[8] Confining himself to the Book of Hymns (or Psalms of Thanksgiving), Kuhn observed that the salvation in which the community rejoiced included the follow elements: (1) rescue from death and introduction into eternal life, along with cleansing from sins and the concept of new creation; (2) entry into the inheritance of God's people and the "lot of the angels"; (3) the gift of the Holy Spirit of the last days; and (4) the possession of knowledge which is the experience of salvation.

The first two elements are reflected in 1QH 3:19ff.:

> I praise thee, O Lord,
> for thou hast redeemed my soul from the pit;
> and from the Sheol of Abaddon
> thou didst draw me up to an eternal height,
> so that I may walk about in uprightness unsearchable,
> and know that there is hope for him
> whom thou didst fashion from the dust unto eternal foundation. . . .

The third can be illustrated from 1QH 16:8ff.:

> I know that no man beside thee can be just.
> I therefore entreat thee, through the Spirit
> which thou didst put in me
> to bring unto fulfilment thy lovingkindness
> thou hast shown unto thy servant . . .
> to cleanse me with thy holy spirit
> and draw me near to thee in thy good pleasure,
> according to thy great lovingkindness. . . .

The fourth element can clearly be seen in 1QH 11:7–14, but also in the following passage from the Manual of Discipline:

> By his righteousness my sin is wiped out. For from the fountain of his knowledge he has released his light. My eye has beheld his wonders, and the light of my heart has beheld the secret of what happens and is happening for ever.
> From the fountain of his righteousness, his justice, a light has come into my heart from his wondrous mysteries. My eye has beheld what is happening for ever, wisdom which is hidden from man, knowledge and prudent discretion [which is hidden] from mankind, a fountain of righteousness and a well of strength as well as a spring of glory [which is hidden] from the assembly of humanity. (11:2ff.)

The emphasis in these passages and those that speak of entrance into the "lot" of the angels suggests a guarantee of participation in the new world because it has already begun to be realized in the community. Kuhn observes that here the apocalyptic and priestly self-understanding of the group flow together. The application of the temple concept to the congregation meant that they felt God's saving presence in the community. The community was the place in which the believer stood in the divine sphere of life, and in its fellowship there was no separation between earth and heaven, between the present and the eschatological time of salvation. "Hence," states Kuhn, "it can be said that the righteous is set in heaven (III.20), stands in fellowship with the angels before God, and the eschatological blessings of salvation have already been assigned for his possession (XI.5ff.). Thus he already has risen from the dead (XI.12), and is newly created (III.21; XI.13–14; XV.15ff.)."[9]

According to Kuhn this view of the Qumran community has been aided by the peculiar juxtaposition of past, present, and future in Hebrew thought. In the sphere of the cult past events can be re-presented, and such re-presentation is especially likely to happen in the proclamation. In a like manner, present and future can flow together. Moreover, the spheres of death and life (the upper world of God) are also viewed as present in this world as active forces (note how the righteous is set in heaven in 1 QH 3:20). This does not exclude the prospect of resurrection and new creation; an exclusive either/or of present and future is not applicable here.[10]

If this interpretation is established—and it would appear to be well-founded—it will have implications relating to the eschatological proclamation of Jesus and of the early church. It would enable us to see that the juxtaposition of present and future notions of the eschatological kingdom is not so foreign to Jewish eschatology as was once thought.

8 | The Messiah in Apocalyptic Literature

The question of the role of the Messiah in the kingdom of God in apocalyptic thought is as complex as the apocalyptists' ideas on the kingdom of God itself. This is not without reason, since one's understanding of the kingdom of God is bound to affect one's view of the Messiah in the kingdom. An anticipation of a purely earthly kingdom of Israelite domination over the nations invites the idea of a purely earthly Messiah-king of the order of David, such as we find in the Psalms of Solomon (chaps. 17–18). The concept of a kingdom of God within a new creation would call for a Messiah with attributes beyond those of man in this world, which is what most scholars find in the Son of Man in the Similitudes of Enoch (whether they hold him to be the Messiah or not). A view that combines a temporary kingdom set in this world with a kingdom that will follow in the new creation complicates to no small degree the messianic concept, which accounts for the fact that the ways in which it is described in 4 Ezra and 2 Baruch are by no means identical.

Is the Messiah a necessary element in the expectation of the kingdom of God, however? Some writers apparently did not believe so, for the Messiah finds no mention in a number of apocalyptic writings, notably Jubilees, 1 Enoch 1–36 and 91–104, Assumption of Moses, 1 Baruch, 2 Enoch, and various books of the Apocrypha (1 and 2 Maccabees, Tobit, Wisdom, Judith, and Ben Sira). It is not unreasonable, therefore, to suppose that the Messiah plays a very minor role in apocalyptic literature.

Ulrich Müller goes beyond this opinion. Excluding the Similitudes of Enoch, in which he finds a Son of Man who is a superhuman figure appointed to be judge and regent in the kingdom of God but who is not identified with the Messiah, he maintains that the expectation of an earthly Messiah-king had no place at all in apocalyptic thought before 4 Ezra and 2 Baruch. The Psalms of Solomon are exceptional but explicable, he maintains, in that they represent the Pharisaic reaction to the Hasmonean kingship. In their rejection of the Hasmonean usurpation of kingship, the Pharisees looked to God to raise up a king of David's line in the future, says Müller, but the apocalyptic movement itself rejected the messianic expectation. He holds that the reasons for this are clear: on the one hand, the change of fortune for Israel was expected to come from

God alone, since he alone directed the plan of the world in hand, the Messiah being but an earthly king; on the other hand, the apocalyptists no longer looked for a restoration of the (idealized) time of David but looked instead for God to create something new of cosmic proportions and to transform the entire world. Accordingly, Müller affirms that "We have to hold firmly that apart from the late writings 4 Ezra and 2 Baruch the Messiah has no real function in the apocalypses of Judaism."[1]

This judgment is by no means uncommon. It is related to the conviction that we should not look for eschatology in the prophets of the Old Testament since it does not emerge until the work of apocalyptists who awaited a transcendental kingdom of God. According to such a view, eschatology must have been confined to very restricted circles in Judaism prior to the Christian era, and oddly enough the Judaism that finally adopted the transcendental kingdom as the real object of hope was nonapocalyptic! Such considerations apart, Müller's position is puzzling, for it entails the belief that the entire literature associated with the Qumran community and its related groups is of no consequence for Jewish messianic interpretation. This is a serious implication, for the Qumran literature covers virtually the whole period during which Jewish apocalyptic literature was produced. If any community in history could be viewed as apocalyptic, surely it was this one!

A single statement from the Manual of Discipline epitomizes the messianic expectation of the congregation of Qumran. It is laid down that the men of the community are to be judged in accordance with the first regulations delivered to the community "*until the coming of a prophet and the Messiahs from Aaron and Israel*" (1QH 9:10–11). Set in the context of the community's writings, this statement expresses a belief in the coming of *three* eschatological figures in the end time: a prophet, a Messiah from "Aaron" (i.e., a priest Messiah), and a Messiah from "Israel" (i.e., a king Messiah). These figures correspond to three passages from the Old Testament of significance to the Covenanters that are brought together in their writings: Deuteronomy 18:18–19, with its promise of a prophet who will be sent as Moses was; Numbers 24:15ff., containing a prediction of a "star" out of Jacob and a "scepter" out of Israel; and Deuteronomy 33:8ff., granting to Levi the Urim and Thummim by which knowledge of the divine will can be ascertained.[2] It will be noted that the Messiah of Aaron is mentioned before the Messiah of Israel. This accords with the conviction that the Anointed Priest is superior to the Anointed King, which is indicated by the prescribed order of seating in a community feast, a description of which in 1QS 2:11ff. appears to be the anticipated Messianic Feast, since it envisages the event of God "begetting" the Messiah to be with them:

> The High Priest of the Congregation of Israel shall enter, and all the fathers, the sons of Aaron, the priests. . . . And they shall be seated before him, each man according to his position. And after them shall sit the Messiah of Israel; and there shall be seated before him the heads of the thousands of Israel, each according to his position. . . .

Doubt has been raised about this interpretation of "the Messiahs from Aaron and Israel," on the grounds that there are passages in the Covenanters' writings that refer to the Messiah in the singular (as in the last citation). In particular, the Zadokite document has the following statement:

> These shall escape during the period of visitation, but the rest shall be handed over to the sword *when the Messiah comes from Aaron and Israel.* (9:10)

The relation between these two modes of messianic reference is difficult to assess. A number of scholars hold that the reference to the Messiah in the singular in the passage just cited is the result of a correction by a later scribe who did not know what to make of a statement about "Messiahs" in the plural.[3] And of course there are not a few who maintain, on the contrary, that the plural reference is the offender and should be corrected to the singular.[4] The inclination of scholars now is to let both texts stand and refrain from any incautious attempts to reconcile them. Apart from the fact that the group that produced the Zadokite document may not have been settled in Qumran—they referred to themselves as sojourning "in the land of Damascus" (8:6)—it has been affirmed that "Palaeographical analysis indicates that the two messiahs' doctrine was central to the community at least until the invasion of Pompey (63 B.C.E.) and that the messiah of the line of David became more prominent, especially in the first century of the Christian era."[5]

In this connection it is noteworthy that the twofold messianic concept is found in the Testaments of the Twelve Patriarchs, which appears to have been one of the works emanating from the Covenanters, composed in various stages and extensively interpolated by Christian hands.[6] In this work we find various passages which tell of a Messiah who will spring from Levi (see especially Test. Reuben 6:5–12 and Test. Levi 18:2–14), while others speak of a Messiah who will arise from Judah (e.g., Judah 17:5–6, 22:2–3, 24:1ff.). Some passages bring the two together; the Testament of Simeon 7:1–2 does so in a typical fashion:

> And now, my children, obey Levi and Judah, and be not lifted up against these two tribes, for from them shall arise unto you the salvation of God. For the Lord shall raise up from Levi as it were a High-priest, and from Judah as it were a King.

This idea of the salvation of the Lord arising both from Levi and from Judah appears frequently in the Testaments (e.g., in Levi 2:11, Dan 5:4, Naphtali 8:2–3 [cf. 5:2ff.], and Gad 8:1). It makes difficult the supposition that a whole set of references to one of the two Messiahs is the result of corrective editorial activity.[7] The Testament of Judah 21:1ff. is of particular significance in that it expresses the rationale that inspired the idea of Levi's superiority over Judah:

> And now my children I command you to love Levi, that ye may abide, and exalt not yourselves against him, lest ye be utterly destroyed. For to me the Lord gave the kingdom and to him the priesthood, and he set the kingdom beneath the priesthood. To me he gave the things upon the earth; to him the things in the heavens. As the heaven is higher than the earth, so is the priesthood of God higher than the earthly kingdom.

The outlook reflected in this passage is in harmony with, and perhaps largely due to, the description of a restored Israel and its worship in Ezekiel 40–48, wherein the weight of emphasis lies on the new Temple and its ordinances, and the "Prince" has little of the glory elsewhere accorded to the Messiah in the Old Testament.

On the other hand, we should note that, in harmony with the belief of the Covenanters that the Lord had appointed them to be executors of his judgments among the nations, the two Messiahs have a role to perform in bringing about the deliverance that will issue in the kingdom. The royal Messiah appears to include among his functions that of commander of the troops in the final war.[8] Curiously, a comparable warlike function is attributed to the priestly Messiah in the Testament of Joseph 19:8ff., a vision in which the flock of God is delivered from attacks of beasts by a lamb in company with a lion, though the deliverance is actually wrought by the lamb. In the messianic hymn of the Testament of Levi 18:2ff., the Levitic Messiah is accorded not merely an exalted position in the kingdom but a position from which he mediates its blessings:

> Then shall the Lord raise up a new priest.
> And to him all the words of the Lord shall be revealed;
> And he shall execute a righteous judgment upon the earth for a multitude of days.
>
> And his star shall arise in heaven as of a king.
> Lighting up the light of knowledge as the sun the days,
> And he shall be magnified in the world. . . .
>
> And in his priesthood shall sin come to an end,
> And the lawless shall cease to do evil . . .
> And he shall open the gates of paradise,
> And shall remove the threatening sword against Adam,
> And he shall give the saints to eat from the tree of life,
> And the spirit of holiness shall be on them.
> And Belial shall be bound by him,
> And he shall give power to his children to tread upon the evil spirits. . . .

This representation of the Messiah is hardly surpassed in any of the Old Testament prophetic descriptions. It has been suspected of being a Christian psalm, and yet every line of it is in harmony with Jewish apocalyptic expectation of the messianic kingdom, and of Qumran views in particular. Of particular significance are verses 6–7 of this passage:

> The heavens shall be opened
> And from the temple of glory shall come upon him sanctification,
> With the Father's voice as from Abraham to Isaac.
> And the glory of the Most High shall be uttered over him,
> And the spirit of understanding and sanctification shall rest upon him [in the water].

The bracketed closing phrase is clearly a Christian interpolation, but does anything beyond that phrase come from a Christian hand? There is no need to assign more. The opening of heaven from which the voice of God proceeds appears frequently in apocalypses,and the whole passage combines motifs from Psalm 2, Genesis 22, and Isaiah 11:2. The astonishing feature of the passage is not the glory and the voice from heaven, but the characterization of the Speaker: "*with the Father's voice* as from Abraham to Isaac." The implication is clear: the Messiah is Son of God.

Here we touch on a very debatable issue. Hitherto it has been considered by scholars as axiomatic that no Jewish writings prior to the Christian era represent the Messiah as Son of God. Such a concept, it has been believed, was incompatible with Jewish notions of divine transcendence. Over against the Christian proclamation of the Christ as the Son of God, the Rabbis laid it down that "God says I have no son."[9] In light of the writings that are becoming available to us from Qumran, it is becoming increasingly clear that this judgment requires revision. In their opposition to the Christians, the Rabbis appear to have overreacted to traditions that stemmed from pre-Christian Judaism. We have already referred to the regulations for seating at the Feast in 1QS 2:11ff. These relate to a session of the Council of the Community: "*in the event of God begetting the Messiah to be with them. . . .*" It is generally recognized that this language reflects Psalm 2:7, which speaks of the king at his coronation as "begotten"— that is, as set in the relation of adopted son of God.

In the scripture collection 4QFlor 1:6-7 a summary of 2 Samuel 7:11–14 is given in which verses 11b and 14a are explicitly cited. After the latter verse ("I will be to him a father, and he will be to me a son") the following comment is made:

> This is the Shoot of David, who will stand up with the interpreter of the Law. . .
>
> This is the Shoot of David which is fallen who shall stand to save Israel.[10]

Here is an identification of the "son" of Nathan's prophecy with the Messiah who will arise in the last days.

Again there is a Daniel apocryphon from Cave 4 that, while not in the best state of preservation, nevertheless includes lines of vital importance clearly written. J. A. Fitzmyer reproduces it as follows:

> [But your son] shall be great upon the earth, [O King! All (men) shall] make [peace], and all shall serve [him. He shall be called the son of] the [G]reat [God], and by his name shall he be named. (Col. 2) He shall be hailed (as) the Son of God, and they shall call him Son of the Most High. As comets (flash) to the sight, so shall be their kingdom. (For some) year[s] they shall rule upon the earth, and shall trample upon people, city upon ci[t]y, (*vacat*) until there arises the people of God, and everyone rests from the sword.[11]

Unfortunately we are not in a position to state who it is that this paragraph refers to. It is written in apocalyptic style, and relates to some human being described in the last third of the first century B.C. Fitzmyer points out that these titles "Son of God" and "Son of the Most High" are not applied to one called a Messiah or Anointed One: "If my apocalyptic interpretation proves to be right, then they would be applied to the son of some enthroned king, possibly an heir to the throne of David."[12]

We are therefore still not in a position to say with incontrovertible assurance that the Messiah was called "Son of God" in specified circles of pre-

Christian Judaism, but the evidence is pointing in that direction. W. Grundmann, in a searching essay devoted to the question of whether the Messiah was viewed as Son of God in the Judaism contemporary with the Qumran Community, was at pains to point out that whereas the writings of Qumran hint that the Messiah was so regarded, all the texts we possess refrain from using the title. His comment on the psalm of the Testament of Levi 18 is typical: "Behind Testament of Levi 18 there stands a tradition which truly spoke of God's son, which nevertheless avoids making the statement."[13] The like is said of 1QS 2:11–12 and 4Q Flor 1:6–7. But Grundmann wrote without knowledge of the Daniel apocryphon. The latter still leaves us in uncertainty concerning its subject, but at least it provides what Grundmann failed to find: clear use of the title *Son of God* in a non-Hellenistic context applied to an individual with a significant function among mankind.

The accumulating evidence is leading scholars to the conviction that the Qumran sectaries did in fact view the Messiah as Son of God. Indeed, the evidence is encouraging fresh explorations of contemporary Jewish literature that suggest that Jews of this period were ready to extend the concept of Son of God beyond the Davidic King of the Scriptures.[14] After reviewing the evidence, H. Braun affirmed that in the Qumran literature the Messiah is regarded as Son of God, and with van der Woude he goes on to state that this understanding of the Messiah is not unique to Qumran, but is simply Jewish.[15]

There are two brief references to the Messiah in the third book of the Sibylline Oracles that need not detain us.[16] But we might note that 1 Enoch 90:37ff. brings the Apocalypse of Weeks to a conclusion with a typical apocalyptic employment of animal symbolism:

> I saw that a white bull was born, with large horns, and all the beasts of the field and all the birds of the air feared him and made petition to him all the time. And I saw till all their generations were transformed, and they all became white bulls.

Müller would excise the reference as a secondary addition to an apocalypse that could not use the figure of a Messiah,[17] but Hengel views it as a fitting climax to the vision:

> The Messiah is born, and finally all the beasts—not only the sheep of Israel—are changed back into their perfect primal form of the patriarchal period: they become white bulls, like the pious fathers from Adam to Isaac (90:19–42). Thus at the end of history is restored again what Ben Sira called the incomparable 'splendour' of Adam, and the Essenes the glory of Adam. The apocalypse ends, taking up the universal prophecies of salvation from O.T. prophecy . . . with a portrait of salvation for all mankind which breaks the bounds of all national limitations.[18]

The Psalms of Solomon present no new development of thought about the Messiah, simply recalling readers to the ancient hope in the Messiah who is Son of David. The prayer in the seventeenth psalm (vv. 23–24) that God may send the Messiah expresses *in nuce* the outlook of the Psalmist:

> Behold, O Lord, and raise up unto them their king, the son of David,
> At the time in the which thou seest, O God, that he may reign over Israel thy servant.

And gird him with strength, that he may shatter unrighteous rulers,
And that he may purge Jerusalem from nations that trample her down to
destruction.

The Messiah thus has the task of delivering Israel and "shattering" their
oppressors.

A wholly different picture of the one whom God is to send is provided in
the Similitudes of Enoch (1 Enoch 37–71).* It is improbable that the origin of
its visions of the Son of Man go back to a source independent of Daniel 7. On the
contrary, it is more likely that the author of the book of Daniel alone was
responsible for redacting the ancient myth in which the one like a son of man
came into the court of the Ancient of Days to receive dominion, and that the
author of the Similitudes made the Danielic vision the starting point for his
portrayals of the Son of Man. That would appear to be the simplest explanation
of chapter 46, the foundational vision of the Son of Man in the Similitudes; it
reads very much like an adaptation of Daniel 7, and the subsequent references to
"*this*" or "*that* Son of Man" depend on the explanation given in 46:3.[19]

The functions of the Son of Man in the Similitudes are fundamentally those
of the Messiah in the writings of the apocalyptic era—namely, judgment of the
Gentile rulers and exercise of sovereignty in the kingdom of God—only they are
set in a different key: the Son of Man is appointed to hold a forensic judgment of
"the kings and the mighty" (46:4ff., 48:8ff., and chaps. 62–63), and he is to
reign over the righteous after resurrection from the dead takes place (45:3,
48:4ff., 49:1ff., 51:1ff., and 62:13ff.).[20] But who is the Son of Man? The second
parable begins in chapter 45, in which the "Elect One" is depicted on the throne
of his glory as judge of sinners and ruler in the kingdom. It is natural to view the
vision in chapter 46 of the Head of Days and "that Son of Man" who went with
him as revealing the identity of the Elect One described in chapter 45. Such is
the conclusion of Morna Hooker and U. B. Müller; but whereas Hooker holds
that the Son of Man is the Elect One par excellence among the elect people of
God,[21] Müller suggests that the Elect One is the figure depicted in Isaiah 42:1,
just as "He [who] shall be the light of the Gentiles" in 1 Enoch 48:4 is the same
figure depicted in Isaiah 42:6 (the same ideas are set in juxtaposition in the
second Servant Song of Deutero-Isaiah, Isa. 49:6–7).[22] This latter suggestion is
attractive and may be right. It would suit the conviction common in the British
tradition of scholarship that the concepts of Son of Man and Servant of the Lord
hover between corporate and individual interpretations, the transition being
natural to the Semitic mind.[23] On the other hand, without contesting this
conviction, we would do well to note that the presence of a corporate concept of
the Son of Man in the Similitudes is unlikely in view of the highly personalized
representations given of him there.

More difficult is the question whether or not the Son of Man in the Similitudes is conceived of as a heavenly figure, the highest of the angels. Certainly the

---

*The question of the date of this section of the Enoch writings is so complex that a
discussion of it at this point would only serve to distract our attention from matters more
immediately at hand, and so we will defer a consideration of this question to a brief
excursus following this chapter, on pp. 63–68.

descriptions of him in the judgment scenes are exalted, and language used of him suggests his preexistence with God:

> The kings and the mighty and all who possess the earth shall bless and glorify
> and extol him who rules over all, who was hidden,
> For from the beginning the Son of Man was hidden,
> And the Most High preserved him in the presence of his might,
> And revealed him to the elect. (1 Enoch 62:2–3)

From this and related passages in the Similitudes it has been concluded that the Son of Man is a preexistent heavenly being hidden in the presence of God till his manifestation at the end of the times.[24] There is one factor that complicates this picture of the Son of Man, however—namely, the fact that he is identified with Enoch in the closing parable of the Similitudes. To Enoch it is said, "Thou art the Son of Man born unto righteousness" (71:14ff.). Those who view the Son of Man as a superhuman being generally view this passage as having been interpolated or redacted to yield the present text. This is a questionable procedure for dealing with a text that happens to be inimicable to a particular interpretation. It would seem that two chief possibilities lie open before us. Conceivably the picture of the one like a man in Daniel 7 inspired the conception of a messianic figure of transcendental nature who would act as both judge and ruler in the kingdom of God, and the writer of the Similitudes concluded that Enoch either was (at his translation) or was yet to be installed into that position of honor by God.[25] The other possibility is that the Danielic vision was linked by the author of the Similitudes with the picture of Enoch in Genesis 5:24 and that features of that Enoch may have given substance to the Son of Man figure. Maurice Casey sees support for this in 1 Enoch 70. In verse 1 of that chapter, the manuscript U, supported by V and W, reads "The name of that Son of Man was raised aloft while he was still alive to the Lord of Spirits." The text goes on to describe how he was "raised aloft on the chariots of the spirit" (i.e., translated to heaven) and set between the winds of the north and west; there he saw "the first fathers and the righteous *who from the beginning dwell in that place*" (v. 4): the language about the "preexistence" of the Son of Man could well be explained by that passage. Enoch is then represented as one who was born, lived his life on earth, saw visions of himself as the eschatological judge, was translated to heaven, and is to be revealed in that capacity as deliverer of his people and executor of the divine retribution on their oppressors.[26] Both of these interpretations comport well with the ambiguous evidence of the Similitudes of Enoch, and the choice between the two is fairly even. It would appear that we would do well to keep an open mind on the issue.

Whatever our judgment on this matter, it seems clear that the author of the Similitudes linked the figure of the Son of Man with that of the Messiah, since according to his presentation, the functions of the Messiah are to be carried out by the Enoch–Son of Man. In two places he is explicitly referred to as God's "Anointed" (1 Enoch 48:10 and 52:4), and there is insufficient ground for excising those references from the text. They comport with the view that the figure of the Son of Man represents an interpretation of the Servant of the Lord of Deutero-Isaiah. In that case, we find in the Similitudes three Old Testament figures with messianic representative functions (Messiah, Servant of the Lord, and Son of Man) brought into alignment, and Enoch declared to be destined to fulfill the roles of all three. It is hardly surprising that in due time readers of the Similitudes were so fascinated by the figure set before them that they ignored his relation to the humbler Enoch.

To what extent did later readers find inspiration in the Similitudes for developing their interpretations of the expected Messiah? If members of the Qumran sect were aware of the existence of the book, it would not seem that they found any such inspiration in it. There are, however, indications that the picture of the Son of Man in the Similitudes exerted an influence within certain apocalyptic circles toward the end of the first century A.D., most notably among those that produced 4 Ezra and 2 Baruch. In both these books the Messiah is presented as judging and destroying the Gentiles and delivering and protecting his people.[27] The delineation of the Messiah in 4 Ezra has contrary elements. According to 7:29, the Messiah will die with "all in whom there is human breath" at the conclusion of the temporary kingdom. This concept, though, is inharmonious with the vision in chapter 13 of the Man who flies with the clouds of heaven, cuts out for himself a great mountain, and destroys hostile armies with the flaming fire of his breath. It is evident that this Messiah has taken on features of the Son of Man. Interestingly, however, both the term *Man* (rather than Son of Man) and the reference to the mountain that is cut out by the Man recall Daniel 2 and 7 rather than the Similitudes of Enoch. The divine mode of travel (with clouds) and the theophany weapons are also more clearly reminiscent of Daniel than of the Similitudes. It looks as though Daniel's vision has influenced the author of the vision of the Man from the Sea in much the same way that it influenced the author of the Similitudes,[28] although the later seer had the precedent of the earlier interpretation to aid him.

A similar procedure is apparent in 2 Baruch. The vision of the cloud with black and white waters in chapter 53 presents a picture of a threatening cloud that is destroyed by lightning. The vision does not entirely correspond to the interpretation that follows it. The threatening cloud is a storm cloud like that to which Gog is likened in Ezekiel 38:9ff., and the lightning represents the Messiah in his swift appearance to attack and destroy the enemies of God's people. Like the vision of the Man from the Sea and its interpretation in 4 Ezra, the vision of the Cloud and the Lightning and its interpretation in 2 Baruch presents a combination of motifs drawn from the traditional figure of the Messiah and of the Son of Man who comes from heaven.[29] But the fusion of the two traditions is more thorough in 2 Baruch than in 4 Ezra; as we have seen, 2 Baruch states that the messianic time is "the consummation of that which is corruptible and the beginning of that which is not corruptible" (74:2) and that when the time of the advent of the Messiah is fulfilled "he shall return in glory" (30:1). In short, there is a cleavage between the messianic thought of 2 Baruch and 4 Ezra, perhaps because the former treats the Son of Man conception with greater seriousness than does the latter.

Finally we may note that in the fifth book of the Sibyllines there is another echo of the Son of Man concept:

There came from the firmament of heaven a blessed man, bearing the scepter in the hand, which God gave him. And he won fair dominion over all . . . and destroyed every city from its foundation with sheets of fire, and burnt up the families of the men who before wrought evil, and the city which God loved he made more radiant than the stars and the sun and the moon. (51:4ff.)

The description of the coming of the "blessed man" and the nature of the kingdom he inaugurates again reveals the influence of the Son of Man tradition.

If we were to attempt any conclusions from this review of the messianic conceptions in Jewish apocalyptic literature, we should comment at once on their variety. The groups that gave us the literature associated with Qumran, the Psalms of Solomon, the Similitudes of Enoch, 4 Ezra, and 2 Baruch exhibit a wide diversity of thought relating to the messianic idea—although it is doubtful that the variations in the concept in any instance are intended to imply a repudiation of the figure of the Messiah himself.

Further, the evidence we have reviewed cannot be said to indicate that the messianic hope was of secondary importance in the apocalyptic movement. On the contrary, a significant role is frequently ascribed to the Messiah (or his equivalent[s]) in descriptions of the end of the age and the kingdom of God. For the apocalyptists, as for the Jewish people generally, the initiative for salvation and judgment is believed to reside with God. But the Jewish religion has always been acquainted with the idea of mediators, and the Messiah can be viewed as the Mediator par excellence. That he is not mentioned at all in some apocalyptic works is in some cases attributable to the fact that they are presenting unrelated subject matter (as in certain works of the Apocrypha) and in other cases to the fact that he is simply being assumed.[30] We should endeavor to pay more attention to what is said positively of the Messiah rather than draw uncertain deductions from the silence of authors.[31]

Finally, while it is true that the conception of the Kingdom is related to the conception of the Messiah, the evidence does not encourage a simplistic correlation of the two. In part this is because of a lack of clarity in the apocalyptists' ideas on the kingdom of God; notions proper to an earthly kingdom of God, for example, find themselves in juxtaposition with those more appropriate to a transcendent kingdom. The anticipations of the kingdom in the Qumran writings are so variable as to give the impression that at times the kingdom is viewed as purely earthly and at times as set in a transformed world. The relation of the kingdom to the resurrection is also unclear; the resurrection is at times set in the earthly kingdom and at others in the new world. The messianic figures are by no means closely correlated with the nature of the kingdom. The Messiah in the temporal kingdom of 4 Ezra is purely human, but this is not the case in 2 Baruch, and the concept in the book of Revelation is different again. In addition, if our interpretation of the Son of Man in the Similitudes of Enoch is correct, the notion of a purely transcendent kingdom of God is not necessarily accompanied by a concept of a wholly transcendent Mediator.

It may well be that the nature of the kingdom is not so determinative for the understanding of the Messiah as is a writer's concept of the mediatorial function of the Messiah in the kingdom. We might recall that in some Old Testament descriptions of the Messiah he is viewed as the form of Yahweh's presence in the kingdom. Indications of a similar concept of the Messiah can be found in some of the works we have considered, and these should be set alongside others in which the Messiah is of less significance. We will have to take this variety into account when considering the New Testament conception of the role of the Messiah in the kingdom of God.

The Date of the
Similitudes of Enoch

The majority of scholars in the present century have accepted a pre-Christian date for the Similitudes, doubtless to no small degree influenced by R. H. Charles, whose arguments and conclusions were followed virtually without modification by G. Beer in Germany.[1] Charles's position rested largely on a single assumption: that the "kings and the mighty," whose judgment by the Son of Man features prominently in the Similitudes, represent the later Maccabaean princes and their Sadducean supporters.[2] The "kings and the mighty" are characterized in this book by their denial of the Lord of Spirits; this "denial" is thought to indicate an apostasy on the part of Jews rather than a rejection of true religion by Gentiles. The Sadducean elements are indicated by their refusal of the messianic hope (46:5), the heavenly world (45:1), and the coming judgment (60:6). The Similitudes reflect persecution of the righteous by oppressive rulers, which according to Charles points to the era of Alexander Jannaeus, whose rule commenced about 103 B.C. As it is believed that no hint of the Roman presence in Palestine is to be found in the book, a date prior to 64 B.C. is postulated. But since Alexandra, who succeeded Jannaeus, reversed earlier policies and favored rather than oppressed the Pharisees, Charles pushes that date back prior to 79 B.C. (the date he assigns to the beginning of Alexandra's reign). Accordingly, he sets the Similitudes in the period of 94 to 79 B.C.

The widespread acceptance of this conclusion is a critical curiosity in view of the improbability of its basic assumption. For there is no likelihood that the kings and the mighty are viewed by the author of the Similitudes as *Jews*. Let the reader consult afresh 1 Enoch 41:2, 45:2, 46:7, 48:10, and 63:7, in which reference is made to those who deny the Lord of Spirits. Foremost among these are the kings and the mighty, of whom it is written,

All their deeds manifest unrighteousness,
And their power rests upon their riches,
And their faith is in the gods which they have made with their hands,
And they deny the name of the Lord of Spirits. (46:7)

A similar understanding of the kings and the mighty is reflected in the vain confession they make in the judgment before God:

We have now learned that we should glorify
And bless the Lord of kings and him who is king over all kings . . .
For we have not believed before him
Nor glorified the name of the Lord of Spirits . . .
But our hope was in the sceptre of our kingdom,
And in our glory. (63:47)

It is unnatural to interpret these and related passages in the Similitudes as descriptive of Jewish rulers and Sadducees. The writer has in view oppressors of the Jews who do not acknowledge the God of Israel. Admittedly this would not unconditionally exclude tyrannous and cruel rulers in Israel from being numbered with them, but the language is formulated with respect to heathen powers from which the Jewish nation suffered again and again.

For this reason J. B. Frey dissented from Charles's view and argued that the Similitudes have to be related to the period of persecution by Antiochus Epiphanes, when there was heathen oppression against Jewish religion and no lack of renegades among the Jews.[3] He dates the Similitudes shortly after the death of Antiochus.[4] This would satisfy the language used of the oppressors of the faith in Israel, but it raises difficulties relating to historical allusions of another kind in the book.

There are two passages in the Similitudes that earlier writers tended either to ignore or to play down but that Jonas C. Greenfield refers to as "two historical references which no sort of sophistry can suppress."[5] These are 1 Enoch 56:5–7 and 67:7–13. The former reads as follows:

> And in those days the angels shall return,
> And hurl themselves to the east upon the Parthians and Medes:
>
> They shall stir up the kings, so that a spirit of unrest shall come upon them,
> And they shall rouse them from their thrones . . .
> And they shall go up and tread under foot the land of his elect ones,
> [And the land of his elect ones shall be before them a threshing-floor and a highway,
> But the city of my righteous shall be a hindrance to their horses.

Charles's suggestion that in this passage the Parthians and Medes are expected to play the role assigned to Gog is plausible, for language used of Gog in Ezekiel 38 is reproduced in it. To account for how the Parthians and Medes came to be viewed in this way, one would have to assume that events transpired that had forced the Jewish apocalyptist to recognize the immense power of the Parthian empire. Such events clearly did occur: the Roman armies under Crassus suffered an overwhelming defeat at the hands of the Parthians in 53 B.C., and—more startling to the Jews—the Parthians invaded Syria in 40 B.C., advancing to Jerusalem, installing Antigonus as king and high priest there, and lifting a garrison in the city. Some scholars have objected to relating these events to 1 Enoch 56:5–7 on the grounds that far from viewing them with horror, the Jews widely welcomed them.[6] That is a misleading estimate of the situation if the accounts of Josephus are correct, however; one gathers from his descriptions that it was a time of great confusion and strife, increased by the harshness of Hyrcanus and Herod, but also by the treachery of the Parthians themselves.[7] The importance of the episode lies in the fact that it provides an example of the ability of the Parthian forces to strike in Israel's territory despite the presence of the Roman power. These events of the middle of the first century B.C. were not necessarily recent from the author's point of view, but they clearly remained a vivid memory in Jewish minds and were a warning object lesson for the apocalyptist.

The second passage that according to Greenfield reflects a historical circumstance is 1 Enoch 67:7–13, which gives an obscure description of a valley through which streams of fire proceed that serve both to heat the waters therein and to punish fallen angels and the wicked of mankind. The writer states,

> Those waters shall in those days serve for the kings and the mighty and the exalted, and those who dwell on the earth, for the healing of the body, for the punishment of the spirit. . . .

He further predicts that "in those days"—namely, the days of judgment—the water will become cool, but

> because these waters of judgment minister to the healing of the body of the kings and the lust of their body, therefore they will not believe that those waters will change and become a fire which burns for ever.

It is not unreasonable to see here a reference to Herod's endeavor to recover from the tormenting condition of his body, described in fulsome detail by Josephus. On the advice of his physicians, the King

> went beyond the river Jordan, and bathed himself in warm baths that were at Callirrhoe, which besides their other general virtues were also fit to drink; which water runs into the lake called Asphaltitis.[8]

Herod's efforts were in vain, and he died not long afterwards. It can be assumed, in the light of the knowledge of this event by Josephus many years later, that the king's resort to the healing waters became widely known.

These two passages are the clearest reflections of time to be found within the Similitudes. It is noteworthy that both reflect happenings with the lifetime of Herod the Great, the one in the early days of his rule and the other at the close of his life. It is to be observed that the passages in question do not link the events reflected with expectations of the immediate future. The Parthian power is recognized as capable of striking powerfully within Palestine, and the waters to which kings and the mighty can go for healing will one day become a means of their punishment. Accordingly,the period following Herod's death, but not necessarily *immediately* after it, is indicated as a possible time for the composition of the Similitudes.

If the period reflected is not necessarily *shortly* after Herod's death, how long after it should the Similitudes be set? It has long been a notion attractive to some that they should be placed in the era marked by the rise of the Christian Church—sufficiently long after its beginning for the proclamation of Jesus as the Son of Man to become widely known. Three variations of this view have found support: (1) that the Similitudes were produced as a rival Jewish messianic interpretation in response to the Christian teaching of Jesus as the Son of Man,[9] (2) that the Similitudes are a Jewish writing but that descriptions of the Son of Man were interpolated into it by a Christian author,[10] or (3) that the Similitudes are a Christian composition that was incorporated into the earlier collection of writings ascribed to Enoch.[11]

A current revival of these views has been stimulated by the fact that to date no fragments of the Similitudes have come to light among the Qumran manuscripts, whereas fragments of all the remaining sections of 1 Enoch have been discovered. This has led Matthew Black to consider it likely that the Similitudes have been inserted into the book of Enoch, either by a Christian or a Jewish Christian author, but in any event through the inspiration of the gospels, in a manner comparable to the Christian interpolations into the Greek version of the Testaments of the Twelve Patriarchs.[12]

J. C. Hindley argues for a Jewish origin of the Similitudes but is encouraged to believe that the background for 1 Enoch 56:5–7 is best seen in events of the years A.D. 115–117, when a victorious Parthian army invaded Syria, possibly taking Antioch for a while, and when revolts of Jews broke out simultaneously in Cyprus, Egypt, and Cyrene and an earthquake accompanied by a flood occurred in Antioch (see 1 Enoch 53:7).[13]

J. T. Milik has argued at length for the Christian composition of the Similitudes, calling attention not only to their absence from the Qumran literature but also to the silence of early Christian writers on them between the first and fourth centuries. According to this view the Similitudes belong to the literary genre of the Sibylline literature, the Christian production of which flourished in the second to the fourth centuries. These assumptions encourage Milik to find the background of 1 Enoch 56:5–7 not in the Parthian invasion of 40 B.C., nor even in that of the early second century A.D., but in the victorious campaigns of Sapor I in the latter half of the third century A.D.[14]

What are we to say of these views? Responding to the claim that the Similitudes come from a Christian author, Frey long ago said a sufficient word: "No specifically Christian doctrine is met in its pages."[15] The figure of the Son of Man exalted by God in the new age is not "specifically Christian"; indeed, linguistic evidence strongly indicates that Daniel 7 is the source of the figure that appears in the Similitudes. It would be unthinkable for a Christian exponent of the Son of Man–Messiah to exclude all reference to the role of the Son of Man as redeemer of the world through his suffering and his resurrection. Moreover, the identification of the Son of Man with Enoch in the final vision of the Similitudes (71:14–17) raises an insuperable difficulty for a Christian origin of these prophecies. Supporters of the Christian view of the work are compelled either to modify the text to avoid the identification with Enoch, or to separate the final vision from the rest of the Similitudes and attribute it to a different writer; neither of these alternatives commends itself to scholars as probable.

Certain factors point to the first century of the Christian era for the composition of the Similitudes. First, if there is any plausibility in finding an echo of Herod's resort to the healing waters of Callirrhoe in 1 Enoch 67:7–13, then the Parthian intervention in Israel in Herod's early rule is more likely than one remote in time from that event; that is, in both instances the two events should belong to the same era. Second, whereas the concept of the Son of Man as a messianic figure is not found anywhere in the Jewish apocalyptic literature of the first century B.C. or in the Qumran literature,[16] it does appear to have influenced the view of the Messiah in 2 Baruch, and it is reflected also in the vision of the Man from the Sea in 4 Ezra 2.[17] These two works belong to the end of the first century A.D. and reflect messianic views that were gaining currency among Jews of that time. Since it was an era in which relations between Judaism and Christianity were not only strained but almost severed, it is more likely that these interpretations of the nature and role of the Messiah were prompted by a Jewish work than by Christian proclamation. Third, the representation of the "kings and the mighty" in the Similitudes suits well the Jewish view of their Roman rulers.

This last point needs some elaboration in light of the fact that it has been dismissed by some notable scholars. Jewish apocalyptic writers in the latter half of the first century B.C. and in the first century A.D. had little reason to regard their Roman overlords any differently than their predecessors had. The lofty estimate of the Romans held by some Jews in the time of Judas Maccabaeus (reflected in 1 Macc. 8:1–16) was naive and untypical of the Jewish populace during the period we have in view. Pompey's capture of Jerusalem was attended by no little slaughter, and his sacrilegious entry into the holy of holies caused a shock wave throughout Jewry, standing as a sign of what could be expected of the Romans. The plunder of the Temple by Crassus a few years later confirmed the worst fears of the Jews. A contemporary apocalyptist's view of Roman forces in Palestine is found in the Psalms of Solomon, in which Pompey is referred to as "the sinner" (2:1), "the dragon" (2:29), and "the insolent one" (2:30).

A similar attitude of implacable opposition and hatred toward the Roman rulers is manifest in the Qumran scroll that describes the final eschatological conflict, "The War of the Sons of Light against the Sons of Darkness." In this work the duty of the Sons of Light is set forth as the annihilation of the Sons of Darkness, prominent among whom are the so-called "Kittim," who now must quite certainly be recognized as the Romans.[19] Yadin states that in this war scroll "The persecution by the Kittim is the main theme, and they are the main enemies."[20] The armies of Rome are viewed as the "troops of Belial," evil in nature and under the rule of the evil one. Their fate is described with all clarity in the eighteenth column of the scroll:

> When the great hand of God shall be raised up against Belial and against all the army of his dominion for eternal discomfiture . . the Kittim shall be smashed without remnant and survivor, and there shall be an upraising of the hand of the God of Israel against the whole multitude of Belial.

This war scroll belongs to the latter part of the first century B.C. The attitude to the Romans revealed both in it and in the Psalms of Solomon was shared by many Jews in the century that followed. W. R. Farmer emphasizes that Palestine in this time was "an occupied country."[21] There was more than enough cause for apocalyptically minded Jews to view their Roman rulers as one with the oppressors of earlier times and so to characterize them all as "kings and the mighty," opponents of true religion and oppressors of God's people, the heathen whom God is to judge by the hand of his appointed Representative.[22]

We are directed therefore to the first half or middle of the first century A.D. as the most likely time for the composition of the Similitudes of Enoch. The latter alternative would ease the problem of the absence of this work from the Qumran collection: its circulation would have been comparatively late for it to have been included in that collection.[23] Whether other factors operated to make the Covenanters reject the work is difficult to say. A date in the early years of the Christian era certainly helps to account for differences between it and the rest of 1 Enoch on the one hand and between it and the Qumran writings on the other.[24]

We are brought then to the startling realization that the evidence points to the Similitudes as having been written at the same time as or during the generation after the ministry of Jesus. Does this suggest that the idea of the Son of Man as messianic representative was in the air, as it were, at that time? Its absence from the Qumran writings should caution against undue haste here. It would appear rather that in the tradition of the teaching of Jesus and in the Similitudes we have the precipitate of two parallel movements of thought leading back to one source—namely, the vision of Daniel. New Testament scholars convinced of the origin of the Similitudes in the second or first centuries B.C. have persistently rejected this as improbable; now, however, with the revised estimate of the date of the Similitudes, and with our knowledge of the intense interest in the book of Daniel among the Qumran group, this judgment will have to be reconsidered. Whether the evangelists or the tradition before them was influenced by the Similitudes is a question that has to be judged in the light of the use of the Son of Man concept in the Jesus tradition, especially in relation to his teaching on the kingdom of God and his role in its coming. Meanwhile, the way is open for a fresh assessment of the place and the significance of the Son of Man in the eschatological teaching of Jesus.[25]

Part III

The Coming of God in the Teachings of Jesus

9 | Sayings of Jesus on the Coming of the Kingdom of God in the Present

1. THE PROCLAMATION OF THE KINGDOM OF GOD
Mark 1:15

This passage, set by Mark as the climax to his prologue to the ministry of Jesus,[1] is intended to supply a summary of the gospel preached by Jesus, of which the teaching of Jesus in the body of the gospel can be viewed as exposition.

As with the prologue as a whole, most scholars assume that verses 14–15 are Mark's own composition. On this basis different estimates of their pertinence to the teaching of Jesus have been drawn. W. Kelber, for example, believes that the passage "provides the hermeneutical key not primarily to the ministry of Jesus, but first and foremost to Markan theology. . . . Mark put on the lips of Jesus the program and leading motif of his own theology."[2] This is contested by a majority of exegetes, who maintain that if the formulation is ultimately Mark's, the content must have derived from earlier tradition. R. Pesch goes so far as to argue that the formulation itself and its place in the prologue come from the Markan *source*.[3] Some of the terms employed reflect Christian usage, but a distinction must be drawn between different ways in which identical terms can be used. The phrase in verse 14, for example, "the good news of God," which describes the message of Jesus in verse 15, appears to have originated with Hellenistic Judaism in its teaching of monotheism to the Gentile world, which would have been adopted and adapted by Christian missionaries in their own proclamation.[4] Naturally its content in the Christian mission would have been determined not by Hellenistic Judaism but by Christian belief in the redemption wrought by God in and through Jesus Christ, the crucified and risen One who is to come again. In the passage before us "the good news of God" characterizes *the preaching of Jesus concerning the kingdom of God*; there is no need to postulate an identity of meaning between that message and the church's proclamation of Easter, whether in Mark's mind or in that of any other writer on whom Mark depended. "Unity" is not the same as "identity," as the relation between the Christian and the Jewish use of "good news" should show.

Lohmeyer long ago suggested that the content of verses 14–15 may have been supplied from an early Christian catechesis;[5] that suggestion has been developed by W. Trilling, who contends that it is the catechetical tradition that formed the *Sitz-im-Leben* for verses 14–15.[6] In the formulation of the catechesis the proclamation of Jesus concerning the kingdom of God is assumed to have provided the chief elements. Recognition of the positive relation between the details of the Markan summary and records of the preaching and teaching of Jesus in Mark and in the other gospels has led to a consensus of late about the essential authenticity of the *content* of Mark's summary.[7]

The summary divides itself naturally into four elements: (1) the time is fulfilled, (2) the kingdom of God has "drawn near," (3) repent, and (4) believe in the good news.

Critical attention has centered on the second point ever since C. H. Dodd challenged the hitherto unquestioned interpretation of *engiken he basileia tou theou*. His statement of the issue is well known, but we would do well to recall it again in view of its importance to our discussion:

> In the LXX *engizein* is sometimes used (chiefly in past tenses) to translate the Hebrew verb *nāga* and the Aramaic verb *metā*, both of which mean "to reach," "to arrive." The same two verbs are also translated by the verb *phthanein*, which is used in Mt. 12.28, Lk. 11.20. It would appear therefore that no difference of meaning is intended between *ephthasen eph' humas he basileia tou theou*, and *engiken he basileia tou theou*. Both imply the "arrival" of the Kingdom. With an eye on the presumed Aramaic original, we should translate both: "The Kingdom of God has come."[8]

The debate set in motion by those few lines has continued to the present day. Soon after the appearance of *The Parables of the Kingdom*, J. Y. Campbell contested the correctness of Dodd's use of the LXX. He observes that in the LXX when *engizein* is used in the perfect it translates not *metā* but *qārab*, which means "come near," "approach." Similarly, of the 158 times *engizein* is used in the LXX, in the majority of occasions (110 times) it translates *qārab* or *nāga*, both meaning "to come near." Campbell concluded, "The LXX affords no good evidence that *engiken* ever means 'has come.'"[9] K. W. Clark followed this up by examining *engizein* in noneschatological passages in the New Testament, and concluded that in these *engizein* signifies nearness, not arrival; consequently, there was no reason to assume that it means anything different in eschatological passages.[10]

Dodd countered Campbell's arguments with a fuller review of the evidence. He pointed out that whereas Campbell took *engiken* at its face value and tried to make *ephthasen* of Matthew 12:28 conform, he himself took *ephthasen* at its face value and tried to make *engiken* conform: "I believe his task is the harder," commented Dodd.[11] Essentially Dodd concentrated on the meaning of the Hebrew verbs *nāga* and *metā*, citing the judgment of Brown, Driver, and Briggs for the meanings for both of *reach, attain, come to*, and *arrive*, pointing out that *engizein* and *phthanein* do occur among the verbs used in the LXX to translate these words. He emphasized that in the LXX, as in Hellenistic Greek in general, *phthanein* has the meaning "arrive," and that this should be accepted unless it is impossible in any given passage. On examining the occasions on which *engizein* translates *nāga* or *metā*, he maintained that in six of the eight occurrences the proper meaning of the Hebrew verbs is preserved, and the other two show how the idea of approach may pass into that of arrival.[12]

From this point on the contest resembles a long-drawn-out tennis match, which it would be fruitless to describe here. In a review of the linguistic arguments on Mark 1:15 and related texts, R. F. Berkey has pointed out the ambiguity that surrounds the meaning of the Semitic and Greek terms involved, an ambiguity that inheres in the thought they have to express: "Imminent nearness and actual arrival do frequently overlap; thus it is extremely difficult to speak of the one without also speaking of the other, and practical distinctions break down." In view of the varied ways in which the terms are used in the Bible, and the significance of Jesus in his word and action for the kingdom of God, Berkey is led to state that "I am convinced that neither phrase (Mark's *engiken he basileia* and Q's *ephthasen eph' humas* . . .) suggests nearness at the expense of arrival, or arrival at the expense of nearness."[13]

Scholars are increasingly coming to feel that some such judgment has to be made about the sayings we are considering, and especially about Mark 1:15. The linguistic arguments do not appear adequately to account for the utterances in which the disputed terms occur. As Kelber has put it, the basic deficiency in these arguments "lies in their failure to come to grips with the semantic significance of *words in their contextual settings*."[14] Now this applies particularly to Mark 1:15, in that the statement begins not with *engiken* but with *peplerotai ho kairos*, which appears to mean that the measure of time assigned by God for the fulfillment of the promise of the kingdom has been "filled up," and so come to its end. If it has reached its limit, there is no further waiting. On this Trilling is emphatic: the "time" has become *really* full, not only "almost" or "nearly":

> One must read the prophets to grasp the immense dynamic of the expectation, the unbroken and ever newly awakened faith in an "absolute future" of God. Only then does one know what this statement says in which the faith of early Christianity has become shaped. *The unsurpassable future of God has begun.*[15]

This underscores the inadequacy of the notion voiced by some scholars that Mark 1:15 means that the time of waiting is over and the kingdom is to come in the near future. *If the time before the kingdom is finished, the time of the kingdom has begun.* This is confirmed by the observation that the two clauses of Mark 1:15 are set in synthetic parallelism. It is this conviction that has led to a sweeping change of view regarding the meaning of Mark 1:15. A. M. Ambrozic speaks for many when he says,

> Grammatically and stylistically the two statements are alike; verbs in the perfect tense precede their respective subjects, and the completed action is thus emphasized. The first clause enunciates clearly that the divinely decreed time of waiting has come to an end. The decisive manifestation of the saving God, promised in the prophecies quoted in verses 2–3, must therefore be taking place. The second member of the parallel can be seen as interpreting the first; it states the same truth. The only difference between the members: the first looks backward, while the second looks to the present and future; the first announces the end of the old era, the second proclaims the beginning of the new.[16]

A question of first importance arises at this point. Mark wished to indicate that with Jesus the waiting time came to an end and the kingdom of God broke into history, but did Jesus himself think that? Here the exegetes are divided. Trilling is uncertain.[17] Reploh is quite clear: the church of Mark's day understood that the old time had ended and the era of the kingdom of God had begun with Jesus, but Jesus himself understood that the old time ended with his proclamation and the new was *impending*.[18] This position is difficult to justify. We have already observed the force of the parallelism between *peplerotai* and *engiken*. It will now be valuable to consider the relation between Mark 1:15 and such statements as those contained in Matthew 11:5–6 and 12:28 (to say nothing of the parables of the kingdom), which imply that the new time has begun with Jesus. It is curious how frequently one hears that Jesus sometimes spoke of the kingdom as future and sometimes as present, and that Mark 1:15 represents the former emphasis. But Mark 1:15 does not denote *one* strain of teaching about the kingdom among others. It is a summary of the message that Jesus brought to his nation and that is unfolded in the gospel. That Jesus included in his proclamation the message of the coming revelation of the divine kingdom is not to be denied, but that is comprehended within Mark 1:15. For the kingdom that is the subject of his proclamation is the kingdom of the future. Jesus did not proclaim, like the deluded enthusiasts of Thessalonica, that the *end* of history had arrived. The general thrust of his teaching on the kingdom of God, as we shall see, implies that in his word and work there is an *initiation* of the sovereign action of God that brings salvation and is to end in a transformed universe. It is precisely this thrust of the proclamation—the decisive beginning of the promised coming of God to bring the saving sovereignty—that makes *engiken* so suitable a term to employ in this summary of his message of the kingdom.

It will be noted that we are using the terms *kingdom* and *sovereignty* interchangeably. That should require no justification today. It was a cardinal element in Schlatter's interpretation of Jesus that the kingdom of God has to be viewed as a *dynamic activity of God*, operative in, with, and through him.[19] G. Gloege followed Schlatter and also found the unity of present and future eschatology in Jesus' teaching in this dynamic concept of the rule of God; he saw the same "living-organic unity of working" expressed in Mark 1:15 and summarized the passage as declaring that "the new aeon has in its present-future identity of operation already broken in."[20] This understanding of the thought of Jesus is being freshly taken up by other scholars as well, who are applying it to the interpretation of Mark 1:15 in particular. Pesch cites it in this context,[21] as does Becker at greater length. In the estimate of Becker, "God's sovereignty as the sovereignty which comes is now coming to pass."[22]

That leads to a further observation, which is commonplace enough but not always related to this discussion: the sovereignty of God proclaimed by and manifested in Jesus is unrecognized by the world and apparent only to eyes of faith. That was true during the ministry of Jesus despite his parables, allusions, and open declarations (see Mark 4:11 and Matt. 11:25 and 12:28). Yet the sovereign action of God must by its very nature finally disclose itself in the consummate glory of the Creator-Redeemer. This imperceptibility of the divine sovereignty moving toward ultimate disclosure is by no means expressed in

Mark 1:15, but it is fittingly enclosed by it. Its presence in Jesus moves to its manifestation in the hour of God's appointing, when that which is operative in the present becomes known to all in the unveiled glory of God.[23]

The call to "repent" in the light of the completion of the time and the presence of the kingdom is rooted in the prophetic call to "turn" to God. There is no need to reject this element of the proclamation on the grounds that it may have been imported into the preaching of Jesus from that of John, as though John preached repentance and Jesus preached the kingdom of God.[24] Admittedly the accent in Jesus is different from that of his Jewish contemporaries, who thought of repentance as the necessary precondition for the bestowal of the divine sovereignty. Jesus on the contrary bases the call for repentance on the prior fact of the dawning of the new time: "The movement of 'turning' corresponds for Jesus to the movement of God which takes place first (Lk. 15:11–32); the demand for turning is subordinate to the proclamation of salvation (not in the first instance the threat of judgment), the decisive motive for him is the experience of the incomprehensible goodness of God."[25]

What of the final element of the summary, "Believe the good news"? In the judgment of many, this must be attributed to Mark, since the "good news" is indelibly associated with the redemptive acts of Jesus Christ—supremely, his death and resurrection. But this is a questionable position to maintain. We must not forget the determinative passages about the good news of the kingdom in Isaiah 40:9, 52:7, and 61:1ff. The representation here made, that Jesus called on men to believe the good news that the time was complete and the kingdom of God was operative among them, ought not to be confused with the later proclamation concerning Jesus as the crucified and risen Christ of the new age. Of course Mark will have assumed the unity between the good news of the kingdom preached by Jesus and the good news of redemption preached by the apostles and missionaries of the church. As Schnackenburg points out, Mark reports that Jesus both proclaims the inbreaking kingdom and declares that it is necessary that the Son of Man should suffer (9:31–32, etc.); hence, "the good news of Jesus develops into the good news of the cross and resurrection."[26] But that Jesus preached the good news of deliverance to Zion, proclaiming "Your God is King" (Isa. 52:7), is evident in the summary of Mark 1:14–15 and the remainder of the gospels. Accordingly, with Pesch we may recognize that "Announcement of the fulfilled time, nearness of the sovereignty of God, and demand for repentance and for faith in the good news of God's sovereignty can be considered as an important document of the proclamation of Jesus."[27]

2. THE KINGDOM OF GOD AND DEMONIC POWERS
Matthew 12:28, Luke 11:20

This statement is one of the few logia in the gospel traditions relating to the kingdom of God that is universally acknowledged to be authentic.[28] Its clarity is such as apparently to make its meaning unambiguously plain: "If it is by the finger of God that I cast out demons, then the kingdom of God has come upon you" (RSV)—that is, the exorcisms of Jesus show that the eschatological rule of God is present among men in and through Jesus. This understanding of the

75

saying nevertheless has been rejected by certain scholars through the present century, and not a little ambivalence and confusion can be found in discussions concerning it. So crucial is the significance of the saying that it will be necessary for us to examine it with care.

Albert Schweitzer did not discuss the meaning of Matthew 12:28, but simply took it for granted that the logion implied the coming of the kingdom of God *in the imminent future*.[29] Martin Werner, following in his footsteps, maintained the same viewpoint, but in doing so put forward an interpretation that is frequently echoed in current writings: "It is not the kingdom which is present in the deed, but *a sign that it will shortly break in*."[30] This position has been consistently maintained by E. Grässer[31] and by H. Conzelmann in all his writings,[32] and was elaborated by R. H. Fuller.[33] Admittedly Fuller goes beyond most who share this view in that he agrees with Dodd in understanding *ephthasen he basileia* to mean "the kingdom of God has arrived upon you," but he assumes that this mode of speech reflects the prophetic device of speaking of a future event as though it were already present.[34]

Some leading New Testament scholars observe ambivalence in Matthew 12:28. Bultmann, for example, deduces from the saying that Jesus "sees God's reign already breaking in, in the fact that by the divine power that fills him he is already beginning to drive out the demons." Nevertheless, he adds, "All that does not mean that God's reign is already there, but it does mean that it is dawning."[35] It is unclear what is meant by the statement "God's reign is already breaking in" if the reign is not "already there." Nor can we be sure what the phrase "is dawning" signifies; some writers use that expression to indicate that the kingdom is in the process of coming. Conzelmann similarly affirms that the kingdom of God is not yet here, but that "it already casts its light in that *it becomes operative in Jesus*" that "the kingdom is future, pressing near and *now active in Jesus' deeds and preaching*."[36] If the kingdom of God means the sovereignty of God powerfully active for the salvation of men in fulfillment of the ancient promise, how is it "operative in Jesus" and "active in Jesus' deeds and preaching" but not "present"? Grässer likewise supports the idea that Jesus' sayings about the kingdom place it exclusively in the future, insisting that the logion speaks of the presence of the *signs* of the kingdom and not of the kingdom itself; and yet he cites with approval Norman Perrin's affirmation that this question becomes academic "as soon as we recognize that the claim of the saying is that certain events in the ministry of Jesus are nothing less than an experience of the kingdom of God."[37] I confess perplexity at these admissions of the present *operation* of the divine sovereignty in Jesus alongside an insistence that that sovereignty was not *present* in him, both deductions being allegedly derived from Matthew 12:28.

One cannot avoid the conclusion that the exegetes in question are embarrassed by the saying and have to find ways of muting its testimony. Bultmann did not deal with its meaning in his earlier works, but he found that he had to do so when reviewing Kümmel's *Verheissung und Erfüllung*.[38] In face of Kümmel's protest against scholars forcing all the sayings of Jesus on the kingdom into a single channel (that of the future kingdom), Bultmann answered that they have to be contained within the circle of possibilities that are given in the concept of the sovereignty of God. With regard to Matthew 12:28 he said,

> The understanding demanded by the author would be the kind of correction of a concept held by Jesus in common with his hearers that could be accepted only if it was expressly (polemically) stated in the words of Jesus, as e.g. the correction of the concept of the Day of Yahweh in Amos 5:18–20. Of that however there is no question in Matthew 12:28; here rather the meaning of the concept "rule of God" is presupposed as common to Jesus and his hearers, and the word affirms, "The event for which you hope and on which you speculate now breaks in! Now the situation is serious!"[39]

We might make two observations at this point. First, when Bultmann wrote this statement he had had no opportunity to examine the Dead Sea Scrolls and was in no position to learn that they attest to the consciousness of a community that believed that the salvific realities of the eschatological kingdom of God already existed among them; in these writings there is precedent for the (admittedly more striking) proclamation of Jesus concerning the presence of the sovereignty of God in his words and deeds.[40] Second, the saying is not solitary; the parables of Jesus are related to it in a manner that Bultmann did not choose to acknowledge but that is basic to the contemporary understanding of the parables. The apparently plain meaning of a saying of Jesus must not be rejected on the basis of our uncertain knowledge of the thought of his contemporaries.

A further example of this same tendency to reject the seemingly clear import of Matthew 12:28 is Conzelmann's attitude toward it. He maintained that the distinction between present signs of the kingdom and the presence of the kingdom must be "firmly held in face of the famous *ara ephthasen eph' humas he basileia tou theou*; especially we would emphasize that the pressing of details (choice of word, time) of a logion handed on only in translation is methodologically doubtful."[41] The same notion is alluded to in his work on New Testament theology: "The word *phthanein* means 'to arrive.' But we do not know the Hebrew equivalent. This word, too, might point *to the present sign* of the coming kingdom."[42] Now why should Conzelmann be so uncertain about the adequacy of the translation of a saying from its Semitic original that he is unable to accept that *ephthasen* is a trustworthy equivalent of the term Jesus used? He does not treat the sayings of Jesus in that manner generally. There is no question of "pressing details" in Matthew 12:28, but simply of willingness to accept its plain meaning. The sole difficulty in the way of admitting the straightforward thrust of this saying is that of reconciling it with an uncompromisingly futurist interpretation of Jesus' teaching about the kingdom of God—an attitude that gets one into trouble with a great deal of other material in the synoptic traditions. In fact this attitude would seem to suggest that if a particular view of the eschatology of Jesus makes it impossible to accept the plain meaning of the Greek text of Matthew 12:28, so much the worse for the Greek text of Matthew 12:28!

Are we justified, however, in speaking so confidently of the meaning of the

Greek text of this statement? Let us look at the evidence, as attested by the linguists, grammarians, and exegetes.

Liddell and Scott define the meaning of *phthano* as "to come or do first or before others." Further significations are classified as (1) "be beforehand with," "overtake," "outstrip" (see 1 Thess. 4:15); (2) "come first" or "act first," or, with prepositions, "come first" or "arrive first" (1 Chron. 28:9; Matt. 12:28, cf. 1 Thess. 2:16); *phthano eis* = "arrive at," "attain to" (Rom. 9:21; Phil. 3:16); absolutely of time = "arrive," "extend," "reach"; and (3) "be beforehand" (no New Testament citation provided). Later lexicons tend to simplify these definitions. Moulton and Milligan illustrate extensively the original meaning of "anticipate," "precede," which appears in 1 Thessalonians 4:15, but then state, "Apart from 1 Thess. 4:15, the verb in the N.T. has lost its sense of priority, and means simply 'come, arrive,' as in Mt. 12:28; 1 Thess. 2:16; Rom. 9:11; 2 Cor. 10:14. . . ."[43] Three paragraphs of illustrations from the papyri illuminate this use of the term. Bauer, after giving the primary meaning "come before," "come earlier," "be beforehand," which appears in 1 Thessalonians 4:15, is content to define its common use in the New Testament as "arrive"; for this meaning Matthew 12:28 is listed with the rest of the New Testament passages. Blass and Debrunner similarly state, "The meaning is 'to arrive, come,' as in late Greek . . . and modern Greek; 'to precede' only in 1 Thess. 4:15 . . . The form and usage are comparable in the LXX."[44] G. Fitzer, in his article on *phthano* in the Kittel *TDNT* provides a more extensive review of the use and meaning of the term than can be found in the lexicons. He points out that even in profane Greek, in addition to its basic meaning of "come first," "do first," "be first," it acquires the sense "to reach," "reach to." In the LXX, used absolutely, it no longer means "come first" but "to come" in the sense of "to arrive," "to get there," "to attain to." In the New Testament other than 1 Thessalonians 4:15, it is used with a prepositional phrase and always means "to arrive at," "to reach," "to come or attain to." This last meaning is intended in Matthew 12:28; in this case Fitzer considers it immaterial whether one reads the passage as "the kingdom of God has reached you," or "come to you." He adds, "At any rate, apart from the *ara*, with its emphasis on the conclusion, the contribution that *phthano* makes semasiologically and with the aorist form to the shaping of the saying is perfectly clear."[45]

So much for the linguists.[46] What of the exegetes? Here it is worthy of mention that *all* the contributors to *TDNT* who have had occasion to allude to the meaning of Matthew 12:28 have without exception expounded it as demonstrating the presence of the kingdom of God in the ministry of Jesus. Typical of their statements on Matthew 12:28 is that of G. Schrenk:

> The triumphs against demons are regarded by the Synoptists as decisive indications of the new situation, which consists in the coming into effect of the divine rule.[47]

Or of W. Foerster:

> Jesus is conscious that he now breaks the power of the devil and his angels because he is the One in whom the dominion of God is present on behalf of humanity.[48]

Commenting on Matthew 12:28, E. Schweizer states that

> The distinctive of the saying lies in the fact that the presence of the Spirit (of exorcism) is interpreted as the presence of the *basileia*.[49]

With these writers the majority of New Testament scholars have long been in agreement. E. Percy, for example, long ago pointed out the inadequacy of viewing instances of the "banning of the demons" as signs that proclaim the nearness of the coming kingdom: "They are a piece of the kingdom itself; where Satan is driven back, the rule of God begins."[50] Similarly, T. W. Manson was impressed with a comparison of the exorcism referred to in Matthew 12:28 and exorcisms in the Gentile world. He cited Arbesmann's description of the elaborate preparations that had to be made to enable men to be in contact with the deity; Porphyry had stated that "When they [the evil demons] have departed, the parousia of the god may take place." On that Manson commented that "This is in sharp contrast with our text, where the exit of the evil spirits is the result of the Divine presence, not the preparation for it. This is the difference between the Gospel and other religions."[51]

There is no point in continuing to list the opinions of scholars on the meaning of Matthew 12:28. Clearly the major issue in the saying is its implications for the coming of the kingdom of God in relation to the ministry of Jesus. The division that has developed concerning its meaning may have been unduly sharpened by those who drew the battle lines. Schweitzer's attitude toward the complexity of eschatological thought is revealed in his dictum "Progress always consists in taking one or other of two alternatives, in abandoning the attempt to combine them."[52] Anyone who approaches the eschatological teaching of Jesus from that viewpoint renders himself incapable of rightly interpreting it. On the other hand, C. H. Dodd's contribution to grasping the significance of Matthew 12:28 has been diminished by his undue emphasis on realized eschatology, by his insistence that if the kingdom came with the ministry of Jesus there can be no room for talk of a future coming of the kingdom; that view, too, is untenable in the light of Jesus' teaching, and it has predisposed some scholars to deny what most have viewed as the transparent meaning of Matthew 12:28.

Admittedly there is a disposition on the part of most scholars to effect the kind of compromise that Schweitzer despised but that this saying in its relation to the rest of Jesus' teaching seems to demand. Those who insist that the logion indicates the presence of the kingdom of God in the deeds of Jesus nevertheless recognize that it is the *arrival* of that kingdom being spoken of here, not its *consummation*. Those who stress the pure futurity of the kingdom nevertheless endeavor to give some kind of recognition to the operation of the kingdom of God in the ministry of Jesus.

Among those who stress the futurity of the kingdom, E. Jüngel has striven more than most to do justice to Matthew 12:28. When considering how the *future* kingdom can be affirmed as *present* he writes, "Manifestly the near future of the sovereignty of God so projects into the present that the power of the divine sovereignty is already, indeed precisely now effective."[53] Admirable as his intention is here, however, it seems to me that he can construe "the near future of the sovereignty of God" as the fundamental thought of Jesus only by juggling some words. Is it the *power* of the divine sovereignty that is at work in Jesus, or *the divine sovereignty at work in power?* If the sovereignty of God is God royally working to save and to judge, there is no doubt that it is the latter concept that is expressed in Matthew 12:28. But it is precisely this that Jüngel and his colleagues are anxious to avoid saying.

As he proceeds, Jüngel moves even closer to an admission of what he does not wish to say: "We have to understand 'futurist' not in the sense of delay as distance [*Ausstand als Abstand*], but in the sense of a future standing in the present; the future of the divine sovereignty projects into the present as the finger of God."[54] If the divine sovereignty "projects into the present" as the powerfully operative finger or hand of God, it *moves into the present.* Indeed, Jüngel states that the future "stands" in the present. In that case, the future has become presence-with-future. That is what the text actually implies of the kingdom: the emancipating power of God at work in Christ shows that the divine sovereignty that is destined to bring deliverance in the future is operative for that purpose in the present. Thereby the futurity of the kingdom is in no way diminished, let alone eliminated. The kingdom promised for the world is the divine sovereignty that delivers and transforms humanity in the entirety of its relations, extending to cosmic transfiguration. Manifestly that had not come to pass when Jesus addressed his hearers: the future alone could bring that. Nevertheless, a decisive entry of the liberating kingdom had occurred in the advent of Jesus. The reality of that event and its significance are not lessened on the ground that the completion of God's sovereign will for man's redemption had not yet been achieved. The rule of God in and through its representative had *begun*, powerfully and effectually.

3. SIGNS OF THE PRESENCE OF THE KINGDOM OF GOD
Matthew 11:5–6, Luke 7:22–23

The sayings in which this paragraph culminates, Matthew 11:5–6 and Luke 7:22–23, are reproduced by the two evangelists without any verbal divergence. They are so characteristic of what we know of Jesus that their authenticity is virtually unchallenged in contemporary scholarship.[55] Less agreement exists as to the context in which they are set. Scholars have variously argued that the inquiry of John the Baptist to which the sayings provide an answer originated (1) in the tendency in the primitive church to make John a witness to Jesus, (2) in the belief that John's urgent exposition of the kingdom of God excluded the possibility of his looking for a Messiah, or (3) in the notion that if John had thought that Jesus was the Messiah, he would surely have directed his disciples to him.[56] These objections by no means cohere with one another, and none is plausible enough to counter the evidence of the gospels. John's inquiry can hardly be construed as testimony to Jesus: he *questions* whether Jesus can be the "coming one," and no early Christian community would have fashioned "testimony" in that manner. John's eschatological preaching was undoubtedly urgent, but it did include an expectation of the coming of one "mightier" than he—and he would scarcely have referred to almighty God coming to judge mankind in such terms! The loose terminology used to describe him—"the Coming One"—is most likely an authentic echo of John's speech.[57] The relation between John's movement and that of Jesus during John's lifetime has been needlessly complicated by an overemphasis on the fact that the two groups later parted irrevocably. It is clear that the movement of Jesus was rooted in that of John. The records relate Jesus' conviction that John was sent "from heaven"; it is not likely that they were falsified to suggest that John thought the like of Jesus.

Whatever motive John may have had in formulating his message to Jesus, the comprehensibility of his question is clear. John had proclaimed God's impending retribution, the coming of one who would baptize not with water but with the Spirit of God and with fire, who would cleanse God's threshing floor, gather wheat into the barn, and burn chaff with an inextinguishable fire. Directing his message to the king as well as the people, he was imprisoned for his testimony. And what was Jesus doing? Puzzling things, from John's viewpoint: preaching, healing, and driving out demons. And what is his message of the kingdom? Beatitudes, parables of the gracious rule of God, prospects of feasting in the kingdom of God. Where was the thunder of judgment? Where was the rebuke of the wicked? Why this use of power over demons but not over evil men? Why did Jesus consort with them in their feasting? Why did he allow the prophet of God's righteous wrath against sin to rot in Herod's jail without a word of protest? Could this possibly be the Messiah?

Jesus' answer is in complete accord with what we know of his preaching concerning the kingdom of God: it is indirect and yet couched in terms of the sovereign acts of God that were being performed through him. Jesus refers John to the reports he had heard of his ministry—which were set in a tonality that had escaped John. Like a famous predecessor to whom he was compared, John had thought of theophany only in terms of earthquake, wind, and fire; now he is asked to contemplate a different kind of theophany, a "sound of gentle stillness." Scriptures from the Old Testament are cited that set Jesus' deeds in a context other than that which John had contemplated—the context of God's coming for the salvation of his people. The items Jesus recounts are reminiscent of Isaiah 35:5–6 and 61:1, but the links to similar passages should be observed—especially the links to Isaiah 29:17–19 and 42:6–7, and possibly to an echo of resurrection from Isaiah 26:19.[58] Bultmann is mistaken in thinking that Jesus was not referring to his own works but was taking the colors of Deutero-Isaiah and using them to "paint a picture of the final blessedness which Jesus believes is now beginning."[59] Bultmann found it possible to say this because he dissociated the saying of Jesus from the question of John the Baptist. But in their context, the words of Jesus are luminously clear: the deeds that perplex John are signs that God's awaited sovereignty is in action in the world. And the most important deed for John to ponder and understand is the last of the six: "the poor have the good news preached to them." The announcement of the kingdom, according to Isaiah 61:1–2, is a proclamation of jubilee—good news of liberation for the people of God, good news of grace, forgiveness, renewal of life. It is this proclamation that gives meaning to the acts of grace and power performed by Jesus. By it men are enabled to know the time and to seize the opportunity it presents to experience the salvation brought to man.[60] This was the key to John's failure to comprehend the actions of Jesus. He had rightly marked the lightning and thunder of the last times in the books of the prophets, but the nature of the kingdom also portrayed therein had not made the same impression upon him. He failed to recognize the kingdom when it rose above his horizon, just as he failed to recognize the one who brought it.

About one issue we must be clear: the deeds that culminate in the word of Jesus must be understood in terms of the Old Testament presumptions of a salvation *begun*. Those who have failed to see the like in Matthew 12:28 have also denied it regarding this passage, and they adduce similar arguments to support their view here. R. H. Fuller, for example, maintains that the events of Isaiah 35:5–6 characterize the journey through the wilderness but that the decisive act that culminates in the messianic salvation is the return to Zion mentioned in Isaiah 35:10. Similarly, he contends that the miraculous healings of Jesus, described by pictures drawn from Isaiah 35:5–6, are signs that the messianic age is dawning rather than that it has dawned: the messianic salvation itself is yet to come.[61]

This contention of Fuller and others like him rests on a misunderstanding of Isaiah 35. The prophet's description does not *culminate* in the coming of God but *begins* with it. The composition follows on the prophecy of the terrible theophany in chapter 34, which describes the desolation of Edom accompanied by the "crumbling of the host of heaven into nothing" (Isa. 34:4). By contrast, the coming of God for the salvation of his people is declared in chapter 35; they are to see how the creation which reacts in terror before the almighty Judge blossoms in beauty at the revelation of his glory: "These shall see the glory of the Lord, the splendour of our God" (v. 2), as they traverse the wilderness and thirsty land, transfigured in fruitfulness and splendor like Lebanon and Carmel and Sharon.[62] With this hope the prophet strengthens the feeble arms and steadies the tottering knees of his contemporaries:

> See, your God comes with vengeance,
> with dread retribution he comes to save you.
> *Then* shall blind men's eyes be opened,
> and the ears of the deaf unstopped.
> *Then* shall the lame man leap like a deer,
> and the tongue of the dumb shout aloud. . . .

As the Lord's "ransomed" and "redeemed," they are to walk the Way of Holiness, the scene of God's splendor, and enter Zion "crowned with everlasting gladness," for the reign of God which spells salvation has come. The essential element in this picture is not the decree of Cyrus permitting the return of exiles but the coming of God that brings redemption. When Jesus alludes to this passage, he is likewise suggesting that the saving sovereignty is present in the events of his ministry. E. Schweizer affirms with respect to this passage that "The eschaton announced by the prophets is not about to dawn; in the actions of Jesus it *has* dawned."[63] Naturally the nature of the pictures employed suggests that the presence of the time of salvation in Jesus' ministry anticipates the revelation of its fullness in the future, when the glory of God will manifest itself not simply in the humble deeds of grace performed by Jesus but in the trans-figured humanity of the new world. This, however, does not diminish the fact that in this utterance of Jesus eschatology has been "Christologized," and para-doxically "historicized," to use Schürmann's language.[64] In the word and deed of Jesus the awaited redemptive sovereignty of God has entered history.

Following on the declaration of Matthew 11:5, the beatitude of verse 6 is startling in its unexpectedness:

"Happy is the man who does not find me a stumbling block."

Its appropriateness in a message to John is apparent: when one is looking for and proclaiming the coming of a representative of God to judge the world, accompanied by all the accoutrements of theophany (the Spirit's power, the flame of fire, convulsions of heaven and earth, and the destruction of the wicked), to be directed to Jesus in his ministry as the manifestation of God in his kingdom is shattering. To recognize in such a man and such deeds as he was doing the eschatological kingdom of promise demanded an enormous adjust-ment of thought and a fresh assessment of the scriptures. Nor was this true only of John the Baptist; the Pharisees, Zealots, and many others among the Jews had been nourished by an unqualified apocalypticism. The passage under consid-eration may be viewed as a summary of the appeal made by all the parables of Jesus for men to see in his ministry the sovereignty of God at work.

But why are those for whom Jesus is not a *skandalon* "blessed"? Is it because they have gained a better understanding of the Bible? No, something of greater import than that is at stake here. Those for whom the words and deeds of Jesus constitute cause of stumbling, stumble into *ruin*. They fail to recognize in his word and deeds the call of God, and so the sovereignty that he announced and invited men to participate in is lost to them. On the other hand, those who do not stumble because of the word and deed of Jesus recognize in his message and action God at work for the salvation of men; in faith and obedience they submit themselves to that sovereignty and experience its gracious power. The beatitude thus implies that in his word and deed Jesus is the revelation of God's kingdom operative in the present and that to come under that sovereignty for salvation one must recognize his authority and submit to his way.[65] It sets forth the same claim of Jesus in relation to the kingdom of God that we note in Matthew 10:32–33 and Luke 12:8–9, but with a difference that must not be overlooked. Jüngel, overlooking the difference, declares with respect to Matthew 11:5–6 that "The present of Jesus as eschatological time of salvation is now so thematic that the person of Jesus himself becomes eschatological criterion for the future of the divine sovereignty."[66] The statement is impeccably correct, but it ought to be linked with Matthew 10:32–33 rather than Matthew 11:5–6. For on what basis is the import of Jesus as "eschatological criterion of the divine sovereignty" limited to the *future* of that sovereignty? Does he not have the same significance for the *present* sovereignty of God? Assuredly so, and that was the issue for all to whom the word of Jesus was directed. God in his gracious, sovereign power as Redeemer is encountered in the word and work of Jesus, and through him that sovereignty is experienced in the present, even as it is to be inherited through him in the future.

4. BLESSED EYES AND EARS
Matthew 13:16–17, Luke 10:23–24

The context of this saying is not known. Both evangelists were influenced in their positioning of it by the contrast it implicitly establishes between the disciples, who are given to know and understand the revelation through Jesus, and the multitude, which does not comprehend it. Matthew accordingly conjoins the saying with logia that tell of the revelation to the disciples of the secrets of the kingdom conveyed through parables, contrasting their privilege with the situation of those who hear without understanding (Matt. 13:10–15). In Luke the saying follows the thanksgiving of Jesus for the revelation to the "simple" (*nepioi*) of the signs of the kingdom in his ministry and of the Father through the

The essential content of the saying is recognizably the same in Matthew and in Luke, although there are divergences of minor import. Luke's "Blessed are the eyes *which* see" suits the form of beatitude better than Matthew's "Blessed are the eyes *because* they see."[67] Matthew contrasts the disciples with "many prophets and righteous men," whereas Luke contrasts them with "many prophets and kings." Later scholars tend to assume the originality of Luke on the grounds that the term *righteous* is characteristic of Matthew, and he may be assumed to have introduced it at times on his own authority.[68] Twice in passages from his own source Matthew conjoins *prophets* and *the righteous* (10:41; 23:29), but with Luke he shares one passage that links a prophet with a ruler in relation to the last day (cf. Matt. 12:41–42 and Luke 11:31–32). It is not a matter on which to dogmatize, but we might note in the first place that this could well be another instance of variant renderings of an Aramaic version of the saying,[69] and in the second place that while prophets were obviously intent on seeing the kingdom of God, one would not associate Israel's kings generally with such longing, whereas the righteous may be assumed to have yearned for the establishment of righteousness in the kingdom. Assuming that Matthew's inclusion of "ears that hear" as well as "eyes that see" is right, we may tentatively construct the original of the saying as follows:

> Blessed are the eyes which see what you see,
>   and the ears which hear what you hear.
> Amen I say to you, that many prophets and righteous men
>   desired to see what you see and did not see them,
>   and to hear what you hear and did not hear them.

We can most readily grasp the meaning of the saying by comparing it with two comparable beatitudes from the Psalms of Solomon. The first concludes a description of the messianic reign of David's Son.

> Blessed be they that shall be in those days,
> In that they shall see the good fortune of Israel which God shall bring to pass in the gathering together of the tribes. (17:50)

The second is set in the final psalm of the book:

Blessed shall they be that shall be in those days,
In that they shall see the goodness of the Lord which he shall perform for the
generation that is to come. (18:7)

These beatitudes concern members of the future generation who are to witness
God's mighty acts in the establishment of the kingdom and who will experience
Israel's good fortune under the reign of the Messiah. Blessed *will* they be in *those*
days! The beatitude of Jesus relates to the disciples about him, for to them it has
been given to "see with their eyes" and "hear with their ears"—manifestly the
fulfillment of the visions of the prophets in the salvation (the "righteousness") of
the divine sovereignty. The commonsense comment of T. W. Manson on this
passage is difficult to resist: "The point of the saying is that what for all former
generations lay still in the future is now a present reality. What was for the best
men of the past only an object of faith and hope is now a matter of experience."[70]
Fuller's contention that the disciples witness only the signs of the *coming*
kingdom, and thus "not its arrival, but its dawning,"[71] is an unjustifiable weakening of the import of the saying. The prophets and the righteous longed to
experience not simply the signs of the kingdom to come but the reign of God
itself. That the visions of the prophets were to receive more complete realization
in a fuller manifestation of the kingdom of God would not have been disputed,
but the language of Jesus demands an acknowledgment of the actual arrival of
that reign, not merely its *impending* arrival. Closer to the heart of this saying is
Lohmeyer's comment that "To the question, 'How long is the night?' the answer
is now given: 'The night is past, the day has broken. It is wedding day' (Mk.
2:14f.)."[72]

5. THE SERMON AT NAZARETH
Luke 4:16–30

In view of Mark's very different account of the visit of Jesus to Nazareth,
diverging from Luke's both in content and in time, the origin and value of Luke's
narrative have long been matters of debate.

Most commonly it is assumed that Luke's report is an expansion of Mark's
either by Luke's own free composition[73] or with the aid of other sources.[74]
Contrary to this view, many are convinced that *Luke's narrative was formed on
the basis of an account parallel to Mark 6:1–6 but independent of it.* Schürmann's
investigation of the problem led him to this latter conclusion; he contends that
the expansion took place at an early, pre-Lukan stage, and he assigns the whole
to the Q source.[75] The argument for the independence of the Lukan tradition
and for a pre-Lukan formation of the narrative is persuasive, but the assignment
of the tradition to the Q source, and the corollary assumption that Matthew
knew of Q but chose not to use it, is less plausible. The strongest evidence for
such a view is not the linguistic data but the striking congruence of the narrative
with other Q material.[76] On the other hand, Luke's special source is not without
related teaching,[77] which suggests a common interest and agreement with Q in
this area. Most scholars who reject dependence of the Lukan material on Mark
assign it to the Lukan special source.[78]

Bound up with this issue is the problem of whether the narrative reproduces in some degree a continuous report of what took place at Nazareth or whether it has been compiled from a series of independent passages, some of which may have had no connection with the Nazareth visit. From Spitta on, attempts have been made to analyze the material on the basis of the latter assumption. Spitta himself held that Luke enlarged a report of the sermon of Jesus presented in verses 16–21 and 24 by adding verses 22–23 and 25–27.[79] In their attempts to analyze the passage, most of his successors have agreed that verses 16–21 form an integral whole. Uncertainty prevails (1) about whether Luke's *kai elegon* in the midst of verse 22 indicates that the question "Is not this Joseph's son?" was independent of verse 22a, (2) about whether verses 23 and 24 were transmitted separately, and (3) about the relationship between verses 23 and 24 and the preceding narrative.[80] In view of the introduction to verse 25 ("But of a truth I say to you") and the difficulty of relating 25–27 to the early ministry of Jesus, it is common to regard these verses as an independent unit that was brought by the compiler into this context.

Decisions on these issues are difficult to arrive at, and it would entail a lengthy detour for us to attempt to settle the problems. For our purposes this is not of first importance, since our interest lies in verses 16–21, and with the rest of the narrative as it sheds light on that passage.

The passage of scripture Jesus is said to have read in the synagogue breathes the spirit of the Servant Songs of Deutero-Isaiah (it begins with an echo of the first of the Songs, Isa. 42:1). The prophet's message is concentrated in the good news of "liberty to the captives, release to those in prison."[81] This is less likely to refer to return from exile than to full emancipation for those who have known the bitterness of captivity but not the "glorious liberty of the sons of God" depicted in the visions of Deutero-Isaiah. Accordingly, the prophet's successor employs the figure of the release proclaimed at the opening of the year of Jubilee on the day of atonement (see Lev. 25:8ff.). Like a herald he announces

A year of the favor of Yahweh,
A day of the recompense of our God.

The parallelism appears to be synonymous: God's kindness creates a release from burdens of the present for salvation in the kingdom and a recompense that restores wholeness to his afflicted servants.[82]

But if this was indeed the meaning intended by the prophet, that was not how it was interpreted by Jews of later times. The language of emancipation in the great jubilee was recognized, but it was understood to signify release for God's faithful ones and divine vengeance on the nations. We can get some indication of the way in which at least some contemporaries of Jesus read this passage by studying the Qumran Melchizedek fragment (11QMelch).[83] In this document citations are made from passages relating to the year of Jubilee (Lev. 25:13; Deut. 15:2); these are linked with Isaiah 52:7 and Psalms 82:1–2 and 7:8–9, and all are interpreted in the light of Isaiah 61:1–2. After referring to Leviticus 25:13 and Deuteronomy 15:2, the text continues as follows:

Its interpretation, at the end of the days, concerns those in exile. . . . Melchizedek . . . will bring them back to them and he will proclaim liberty for them to set them free and to make atonement for their sins. . . . This word in the last year of jubilee . . . that is . . . the tenth year of jubilee . . . for that is the time of the acceptable year of Melchizedek. . . .

The heavenly one standeth in the congregation of God, among the heavenly ones he judgeth, and concerning him he says: Above them return thou on high; God shall judge the nations . . . and Melchizedek will avenge with the vengeance of the judgments of God . . . from the hand of Belial and from the hand of all the spirits of his lot. . . . That is the day of a slaughter and that which He says concerning the end of days by means of Isaiah the prophet who says: How beautiful upon the mountains are the feet of him that bringeth good tidings. . . . And he that bringeth good tidings, that is the anointed by the Spirit.[84]

Three points emerge from the citations of this fragment. First, the impending jubilee being proclaimed is the last one in history. Described as the "last year of jubilee," it is also said to be "the *tenth* year of jubilee"—that is, the conclusion of Daniel's seventy weeks of years determined before the consummation (see Dan. 9:24ff.): seventy times seven years equals 490 years, which represents ten jubilees of seven weeks of years. The Qumran group, like other Jewish apocalyptists, had no difficulty in relating Daniel's seventy "weeks" to their own day. Accordingly, they understood Isaiah 61:1–2 as a proclamation of the advent of the kingdom of God in terms of the final jubilee.

The second point made in the fragment is the fact that the day of release for the chosen of God is also the day of vengeance, the day of the judgments of God. Belial and his evil spirits are singled out in accord with the apocalyptic tradition and the exposition of Psalm 82 current in the community; but the judgments extend to evil men as well.

The third point is that Melchizedek is identified with the one who will proclaim the day of release, who is described as the prophet of Isaiah 52:7 who brings good tidings and "the anointed by the Spirit" of Isaiah 61:1. Further, as the anointed bearer of good tidings, he appears also to be the instrument who puts into effect the release of the elect and the judgment on wicked spirits and men. The "acceptable year of the Lord" becomes "the acceptable year of Melchizedek," and since "the vengeance of the judgments of God" are carried out by Melchizedek, in effect they become "the vengeance of the judgments of Melchizedek." As the "heavenly being" (= God!) described in Psalm 82 as judging among "the heavenly ones on high," Melchizedek is represented as a supramundane Messiah executing the will of God for salvation and judgment.

These three elements of interpretation—the eschatological understanding of the jubilee proclaimed in Isaiah 61:1ff., the duality of grace for the elect and vengeance on the rest, and the identification of the proclaimer of the jubilee with the agent of God authorized to put it into effect—are of unusual significance for understanding Luke's narrative of Jesus in Nazareth. To these should be added two other principles of interpreting the Old Testament current in Qumran: first, that the object of prophesy is presumed to be the end, and the present time is presumed to be that end; and second, that words of salvation are directed to the community, but words of judgment are directed to those outside the community.[85] While the Qumran community had its own application of these principles, there can be no doubt that they were widely shared by contemporary groups in Israel during the period of Jesus' ministry. But how do they relate to the proclamation of Jesus himself?

Jesus was handed the book of Isaiah, and he read from Isaiah 61. The text is reproduced from the LXX by Luke, as is natural, but two modifications call for our attention. The clause "to heal the broken in heart" is omitted in our earliest manuscripts, although it does appear in some not unimportant manuscripts. Whether the omission was accidental on Luke's part or deliberate it is not easy to say,[86] but it has the effect of throwing the weight of the citation on the good news of *release*. This emphasis is further underscored by the second peculiarity of Luke's text: the fifth line, "to set at liberty those who are oppressed," comes not from Isaiah 61:1–2 but from Isaiah 58:6. It is frequently suggested that this betrays the influence of Hellenistic Christianity on the ground that the link has been made possible through the common term *aphesis*, "release," which occurs in the LXX of both passages, whereas the Hebrew terms it translates are different. The issue is not so obvious. It is not as though Isaiah 58:6 is an insignificant saying that could be trailed in simply by a catchword. It occurs in a polemic against those who fast in the name of the God of Israel but act in a manner contrary to his will:

> Is not this what I require of you as a fast:
> to loose the fetters of injustice,
> to untie the knots of the yoke,
> to snap every yoke
> *and set free those who have been crushed?*

The italicized clause is the one conjoined in Luke 4:18 with Isaiah 61:1. It is closely allied in thought with the characterization of the release that God is to grant: that which he gives, he demands of men! There need be no Greek catchword in the saying for us to see its relation with Isaiah 61:1. The term *aphesis* is, in fact, constantly used in the LXX (e.g., throughout Lev. 25) to denote the release made at the jubilee; hence, it is comprehensible that it should be employed in Isaiah 58:6. Naturally Jesus would not have switched from Isaiah 61 to Isaiah 58 and back again in his reading of scripture, but if he conjoined the two in his exposition, that would suffice to have stamped the recollection of his use of the passage in the tradition. We should note, however, that the introduction of the clause from Isaiah 58:6 strengthens even more the stress on the proclamation of release, and this emphasis reaches its climax in the concluding line of Jesus' sermon text: "*to proclaim the acceptable year of the Lord.*" Just as the message of Jesus to John (Matt. 11:5 // Luke 7:22) reaches its culmination in the citation from Isaiah 61:1, "the poor have the good news preached to them," so here the proclamation of the good news to the poor finds its apex in the announcement of the acceptable year of the Lord.

We may assume that the hearers of Jesus would have understood the passage as relating to the great day of release for their people, the final Jubilee of history. When Jesus proceeded to affirm, "Today this scripture has been fulfilled in your hearing," they would have understood him to be announcing that the Jubilee had arrived, that the acceptable year of the Lord had begun. And that is what Jesus wished them to understand. This is no prophecy of an *impending* emancipation from heaven. What the scripture speaks of has attained its fulfillment in its pronouncement by Jesus. The statement is not simply a scripture quotation, therefore; it is a declaration that the time has arrived. As G. B. Caird expressed it, "He has not merely read the scripture; as King's messenger he has turned it into a royal proclamation of majesty and release."[87] Moreover, the Spirit of the Lord has anointed him to make known this good news and to put it into effect. Jesus had been sent with the word of release, which is a word of power; he had been sent to "set free those who had been crushed." The *proclamation* of release is accompanied by *acts* of release, as elsewhere in the preaching of Jesus.

Thus we can see why Luke preferred this narrative to Mark's summary of the preaching of Jesus in Mark 1:15. Although the fundamental meaning of the two passages is the same, Luke was able to emphasize the element of fulfillment contained in Mark 1:15 and to make plain without ambiguity the presence of the divine sovereignty in the proclamation and deeds of Jesus. Only instead of using the symbol of "sovereignty of God," Luke set forth the reality under the symbol of the jubilee release that brings salvation.[88]

Luke's portrayal of the reaction of the people of Nazareth is ambiguous, and it has been variously interpreted. If Mark's account were set aside, it would be possible to read verse 22 as signifying that Jesus' sermon received unqualified approval from those who heard it. Indeed, the NEB rendering of the passage could encourage that interpretation: "There was a general stir of admiration; they were surprised that words of such grace should fall from his lips. 'Is not this Joseph's son?' they asked."[89] Not even this question about Jesus' identity necessarily implies criticism; it could simply express astonishment that a son of Nazareth could speak so wonderfully.[90] Most scholars assume that Luke means for us to see a change of attitude in the people, however: first they express admiration, then offense that such claims should proceed from one of their own. It is also possible to read the whole statement as conveying hostility: the people of Nazareth attest with astonishment the "powerful words" of Jesus but reject them because he is the son of Joseph.[91]

If it is the case that Jesus' message was received with unqualified approval, then his statements in verses 23–24 would appear to be unmotivated—unless, indeed, we are to understand that he would attack his hearers without provocation, as surely we are not. Those who hold that the report indicates both admiration and hostility in their response suggest that the admixture may be the result of Luke's having conjoined two different reports of the event, one expressive of admiration and one of criticism. Most exegetes have been reluctant to accept the third possible reading of this passage—namely, that Jesus' message met with unequivocal unbelief—but it is nevertheless most likely that this is how Luke intended us to understand the narrative.

What then is the cause of the rejection of Jesus by his fellow townsmen? The implication of the concluding question in verse 22 is that Jesus' origin constituted the offense: a man of Nazareth was arrogating to himself the authority to proclaim the inauguration of the jubilee release of the kingdom of God. The proverb cited in verse 24 agrees with such an interpretation. Should we read verse 23 as a subsidiary complaint of the people of Nazareth then? According to Schürmann, the fact that Jesus had worked wonders in Capernaum but not in Nazareth made the Nazarenes indignant at having been denied a share in the good things they heard he had brought, and thus unreceptive to his message.[92] In isolation the statement could be read in that way, but in context it seems to have more in common with the advice of Jesus' brothers recorded in John 7:3–4: "You should leave this district and go into Judaea, so that your disciples there may see the great things that you are doing," on which the evangelist commented, "For even his brothers had no faith in him." The same appears to hold good of Luke 4:23: it is an utterance of unbelief. In this sense it is linked closely in content with verse 24; Luke's rendering of the proverb indicates that "No prophet in his native place has, in the estimate of his people, *God's* approval."[93] The authority and the message of Jesus were alike rejected. The demand by the citizens of Nazareth that he perform works in Nazareth is akin to the demands of Pharisees and others for signs, which Jesus consistently denied (cf. Luke 11:29 // Mark 8:11; Luke 23:8–9, 35ff. // Mark 15:29ff.).

We should investigate verses 25–27 using the same assumptions. Taken by itself, this passage can be understood to suggest that as Elijah was sent in time of famine to a heathen widow rather than to one of his nation, and as Elisha was led to heal a leprous heathen soldier but none within Israel, so Jesus was sent not for Israel's salvation but for the salvation of the Gentiles.[94] But such a reading leads to the conclusion not that Jesus went beyond Israel because he was rejected at Nazareth but rather that he was rejected at Nazareth because he went to others[95]—and this view of the "sending" of Jesus fits the records of the ministry of Jesus as little as it fits the narratives of Elijah and Elisha. Elijah was sent to Israel in a time of apostasy, and began his ministry with a message of judgment, thereby anticipating the messianic judgments of the eschaton, since the famine lasted *three and a half years*![96] Jesus, too, was sent to Israel, but with an offer of the salvation of the eschaton. In going to his people at Nazareth in the course of that "sending," he experienced rejection; accordingly, he gave warning that his nation risked suffering what their fathers suffered in the times of Elijah and Elisha: they might lose God's blessings, which in this case were the ultimate gifts of the final jubilee, and then witness them being allotted to others.

Such a pronouncement would have been cause for more than mere disagreement; it would have constituted an unforgivable offense so far as the inhabitants of Nazareth were concerned. They held it to be axiomatic that the *Mebasser* (the Announcer) of the good news would introduce both the liberation of Israel and judgment upon the Gentiles, and yet Jesus stated that the very opposite would occur: Israel was facing judgment and exclusion by the Announcer, and the Gentiles were being offered the emancipation of the kingdom. The rage of the Nazarenes at *this* preaching would have been duplicated in every synagogue in Israel where it was heard. The fact that the indignation eventually came to be shared by the teachers and leaders of Israel to the point that they acted to silence the *Mebasser*, and the fact that Israel then proceeded to reject the good news, which then led to its being proclaimed to the Gentiles, could account for Luke's decision to place the episode at Nazareth at the beginning of his story of the ministry of Jesus.

Whether Jesus actually declared the content of verses 25–27 to the people of *Nazareth* is disputed. But despite uncertainty on this point, the fact remains that the passage is extraordinarily apt in its present setting. It underscores a characteristic common to Jesus and the Old Testament prophets that distinguishes them from the Qumran community and their fellow apocalyptists: Jesus and the prophets directed words of judgment to the people of God as well as to the nations, whereas the Qumran teachers exempted their own community from all words of judgment. The sentiment underlying verses 25–27 thus marks Jesus off from every contemporary Jewish preacher in his native land other than John the Baptist. Coupled with the suggestion that he has been sent to initiate by proclamation and action the emancipation of the last jubilee, this emphasis serves to underscore the uniqueness of his vocation in relation to the kingdom and the people of God.

6. THE VIOLENT KINGDOM
Matthew 11:12, Luke 16:16

Among the sayings of Jesus concerning the kingdom of God, this one is generally considered to be one of the most obscure and difficult to interpret.[97] In view of the marked difference between its contexts in Matthew and in Luke, it is likely to have been handed on in the Q tradition as an independent saying. Its form differs in the two gospels, in part through the redactional activity of the two evangelists, but perhaps more decisively through differences of rendering of an Aramaic logion in the versions of Q available to the evangelists. The substance of Luke's first clause ("Until John it was the Law and the Prophets") appears *after* Matthew's version of the saying, in verse 13 ("All the prophets and the law foretold things to come"), and in its place we have the phrase, "From the days of John the Baptist until now." It is likely that Matthew refashioned the saying in order to link the reference to John the Baptist in this verse to the reference in verse 14. On the other hand, the second and third clauses are more obscure in Matthew than they are in Luke, and we gain the impression that the language in the latter has been clarified along one line of interpretation (a not illegitimate one, as we shall see). Thus it is generally believed that we can approximate to the original form of the saying by combining the first clause of Luke's version with the second and third clauses of Matthew's.[98] This produces something along the following lines:

ho nomos kai hoi prophetai mechri (ton hemeron) Ioannou,
apo tote (heos arti) he basileia tou theou biazetai,
kai biastai harpazousin auten.[99]

Translation and interpretation of this saying are difficult because the verbs in the second and third clauses can have both favorable and unfavorable meanings, and *biazetai* can be either middle or passive in voice.[100] Bauer informs us that the term *biazomai* is chiefly used as a deponent middle verb with the idea of applying force, and a long line of exegetes, enthusiastically represented by Otto, has interpreted the term in that fashion here: "the kingdom of God exercises force."[101] With Luke 16:16 in mind, most of those who interpret the second clause in this manner interpret the third clause as an expression of intense eagerness and determination to possess the salvation of the divine sovereignty: "violent men press their way into it by force." Other scholars, however, are impressed with the negative associations of *harpazousin* and *biastai* and contend that the second and third clauses should be understood as standing in synonymous parallelism; thus, they render the passage as follows: "the kingdom of God is being violently attacked, and violent men are ravaging it." Interpreted in this fashion, the saying can be understood to apply to various kinds of opponents of the kingdom, including such would-be advocates as the Zealots. Nevertheless, *harpazousin* is most commonly understood to denote action that "robs" men of the kingdom (cf. Phil. 2:6 and Matt. 23:13). Those who adopt this view generally assume that Luke's incorporation of the saying is in accordance with his basic concern for the gospel mission in the world. Deciding among these various interpretations is no easy matter; even so sober an exegete as Grundmann feels compelled (in his commentaries on Matthew and Luke) simply to state the options and declare his inability to make a decision among them.[102]

Inasmuch as the difficulty of interpreting this saying is largely attributable to the ambiguity of Greek terms, various scholars, including A. Dalman, M. Black, and D. Daube, have investigated the Semitic background to see if clarification can be found there.[103] To the best of my knowledge, A. Resch was the first to mention a theory, later put forward by Black, that may serve to explain the difference between the versions of this saying in Matthew and Luke.[104] It involves the Hebrew term *pāraṣ* (= Aramaic *peraṣ*), which has a variety of meanings in both earlier and later literature. Its root meaning is "to break through," and it is variously used in the Old Testament to connote all of the following actions: breaking through a wall, Yahweh's breaking out in violent action (especially in judgment on men), the violent action of men, breaking over the limits (and hence "to increase," "to spread"—including to spread or make known news), and also a milder application of force, the pressure of persuasion upon people.[105] The fundamental meaning of "breaking through" and "tearing down" continues to appear in later Talmudic Hebrew and in Aramaic[106] and is conveyed by a variety of verbs in the LXX, including *biazesthai* and *parabiazesthai*, but most frequently by *diakoptein*, meaning "to cut through" or "to break through" (especially to break through the lines of the enemy), together with varied applications of destructive force.

It would be much easier to understand the saying if we could assume that the basis of the second and third clauses was an Aramaic statement along the following lines:

malkutha dishemaya peraṣath,
uporeṣin peraṣu bah.

Such a construction might underlie the renderings in both Matthew 11:12 and Luke 16:16. It might naturally be translated into English as "The kingdom of heaven is powerfully breaking out (into the world), and violent men are strongly attacking it." This would suit perfectly Matthew's version of the saying (providing that *biazetai* is understood as a middle rather than a passive verb): "The kingdom of heaven is exercising force (in the world) and violent men are ravaging it." Such a reading accords with the common use of the Greek term.

We would do well in this regard to note the use of the Hebrew term in Exodus 19:24, 2 Samuel 5:20 and 6:8, and Psalm 60:1 (Heb. v. 3), in which the focus is on the violent action of God in judgment. In light of these passages, Black wondered whether Jesus had in mind God's breaking into the world in deeds of judgment, with which Matthew 12:28 could be linked.[107] This might be the case, although 2 Samuel 5:20 also intimates the powerful intervention of God on behalf of his people. We should also take note of Micah 2:13, in which the prophet's pronouncement of judgment upon his people is followed by the promise that God will intervene to deliver and restore them. In the spirit of Isaiah 40:10–11, the Lord is pictured as gathering together the remnant of Israel as a flock:

> I will herd them like sheep in a fold,
> like a grazing flock which stampedes at the sight of a man.
> So their leader *breaks out* before them,
> and they all *break through* the gate and escape,
> and their king goes before them,
> and the Lord leads the way.

Daube cites an anonymous Midrash that states that this is a description of the way God will reveal his kingdom.[108] It illustrates how the term *pāraṣ* can have the connotation of breaking out for redemption as well as for judgment, and that in an eschatological context.

As to the "attacking" of the violent men, it is noteworthy that in John 10:12 *harpazousin* connotes the "ravaging" of sheep by wild beasts, which corresponds to a usage of the term that occurs frequently in the LXX: the figure of a beast mauling a man is sometimes used of God's actions against sinful men (e.g., in Hosea 5:14 and 6:1) but still more often in reference to the actions of men against others (e.g., in Micah 3:2 and 5:8; Nahum 2:12; Ezekiel 19:3, 16; and Job 16:9). The term is also suitably used to express the hostile actions of men against the reign of God as manifest in its representatives. The same term (*harpasai*) appears in Matthew 12:29, and a strengthened form of it (*diarpasai*) appears in Mark 3:27, although in these New Testament passages it is God's representative who attacks Satan's kingdom and plunders his goods.

If *peraṣath* stood in the original saying, Luke's *euangelizetai* is explained. In 1 Samuel 3:1 and 2 Chronicles 31:5 the term *pāraṣ* signifies the making known of information ("no vision was made known," "As soon as the command spread abroad . . ."). It is quite conceivable that one who knew the Old Testament association of the word would interpret *malkutha dishemaya peraṣath* as "the kingdom of heaven is made known." It is more likely that the version of the saying in Luke 16:16 was passed on to Luke by one who interpreted the Aramaic form in this fashion than that Luke himself changed the word in order to make the saying conform to his outlook on mission. We cannot be so confident that

Luke interpreted the following *pas biazetai . . .* as "everyone forces his way into it," although *biazetai* can have that meaning. There is an interesting parallel in 2 Maccabees 14:41: *ton de plethon . . . ten aulaian thuran biazomenon,* "the multitude was forcing the outer door."

To this point we have concentrated on the second and third clauses of the saying. Now we should turn to the first clause, which involves the period to which the kingdom's appearance and its opposition belong. Luke's version is usually preferred: "Until John it was the law and the prophets, since then . . . the kingdom of God." The term "until" *(mechri)* has an inclusive sense: "up to and including" John. John the Baptist is viewed as concluding the period denoted by the law and the prophets; the era of the kingdom of God is to follow. The period of preparation for the kingdom came prior to Jesus; with the coming of Jesus the period of the proclamation and presence of the kingdom had arrived.

Matthew 11:13 appears to be similar: "All the prophets and the law prophesied until John." But his opening clause in verse 12 has a different emphasis: "From the days of John the Baptist until now the kingdom of heaven exercises force." That opening phrase manifestly includes the time of John's ministry; the NEB renders it "Ever since the coming of John the Baptist. . . ." Matthew has already had to make a certain redistribution of his terms by transferring the opening line of the saying to its end. It is quite possible that the first line in his source read "The law and the prophets were until the days of John the Baptist."

How then did the next line begin? Clearly, it began with the preposition *apo,* as it does in Luke; but it must have been extended somehow. There would appear to be no more natural phrase than *apo tote,* "from then," "from that time." But where would Matthew have gotten his *heos arti* from? Did he frame it, or was it in his source? We should note at this point that *heos arti* occurs nowhere else in the synoptic gospels and that Luke's *apo tote* occurs nowhere else in Luke's writings. This strongly suggests that a tradition common to both of the sayings transmitted both of the phrases. Dalman, then, would appear to have been justified in believing that the Aramaic tradition underlying the logion was *min haka ulehala*—that is, *apo tote heos arti.*[109] But such a reading implies that John the Baptist's ministry occurred during the time of the speaker. This would seem to substantiate the case of those exegetes who, for various reasons, see in our logion not *two* periods (either placing the law, prophets, and John in one period and Jesus and the kingdom in another, or placing the law and prophets in one period and John, Jesus, and the kingdom in the other), but rather *three* periods: (1) the period of law and prophets, climaxing in John's ministry; (2) the period of John's ministry, serving as the introduction of the eschatological period (cf. Matt. 11:10 and 14); and (3) the period of Jesus, in whom the kingdom operates among men in power.[110] John the Baptist forms the bridgehead between the old order and the new, not in such a fashion as to belong to *neither,* but in such a fashion as to belong to *both.* This accords with the teaching of Jesus, which on the one hand links the two of them together and on the other hand recognizes differences between them (e.g., see the immediately succeeding passage, Matt. 11:16–19, which contains elements of both connection and differentiation). It accords with the kerygmatic tradition (see Acts 10:37), and the gospels that make the proclamation of the saving event in Jesus Christ begin with the ministry of John the Baptist. Nor is this merely a convenient date; the ministry and the movement of Jesus took their rise from the ministry and the movement of John. Jesus did not come from outside and take advantage of the effect of John's preaching on the populace; rather, he identified himself with John and proceeded outward from within his movement. When Jesus challenged the Jewish leaders to recognize that John's ministry was authorized "from heaven" (Mark 9:30), he suggested the same sort of thing that this passage is suggesting—namely, that the kingdom of God was breaking into history in John's ministry and that Jesus exploited the breach and brought through it the powers of the kingdom of heaven in abundance. Of course John was by no means as significant in relation to the kingdom as was Jesus; but even so, though he was a prophet, John was also "more than a prophet," and had a unique service to perform in relation to that kingdom.

It is doubtless in immediate reference to the fate of John the Baptist that Jesus added the closing line of this saying: "violent men are ravaging it" ("it" being the kingdom lately introduced among men). The new Jezebel was more successful with the new Elijah than her predecessor had been with the former prophet: John had been silenced in prison, and his fate was clear. Jesus also experienced powerful opposition from Jewish authorities, and in the events that had overtaken the Baptist he was given a reminder of the characteristic response to God's messengers in the world. The kingdom of God in the person(s) of its representatives was being "ravaged" by its opponents.

The unexpected nature of this element of the saying should not be overlooked. In apocalyptic writings, persecution and hostility are the lot of the people of God in this age. Suffering at the hands of oppressors and tyrants in the period of tribulation that precedes the kingdom is also to be expected. The Qumran community could calmly predict defeats as well as victories for God's people in the final war, despite the presence of the armies of heaven with them in the time of battle. But to think of the kingdom of God suffering powerful opposition once it had come among men was an extraordinary notion. There was certainly no question of Jesus contemplating the defeat of the kingdom of God, but it is evident that he took the opposition to God's saving action in the world seriously. The most natural interpretation of his language suggests that he was giving warning that the powerful opposition would be directed toward God in the persons of his representatives rather than simply toward men to hinder them from gaining the kingdom.

Herein lies the prime significance of this saying. On the one hand, it affirms the presence of the kingdom of God in the period following the appearance of John the Baptist. We should not allow the fact that certain elements of the saying are somewhat obscure to divert us from perceiving its general thrust, which clearly implies that the kingdom of God was powerfully operative among men in the labors of Jesus and that it was making a beginning in the work of John. On the other hand, the presence of the kingdom during this period was distinguished by resistance to the rule of God by evil men (and evil powers?). Obviously this stage in the ongoing presence of the kingdom will eventually be superseded by a stage in which the divine sovereignty will be established beyond the possibility of any sort of resistance. But that prospect lies beyond the horizon of this saying.

Having noted that the resistance of the violent attackers subdues the one who begins the eschatological time, one is prompted to wonder what will happen when their violence is directed to the sole representative and bearer of the divine sovereignty. Will the power of God's sovereignty be manifested in their destruction, or will it permit its representative to suffer in the same way and achieve a victory in a manner as yet undisclosed? This, too, lies beyond the horizon of the saying. The issue *is* raised, however, and tacitly answered in terms of the relation between John's fate and the destiny of Jesus in Mark 9:11–13 (// Matt. 17:10–13). In the logion we have been considering, the suffering of the representative of the kingdom of God is simply treated as a mark of the presence of the kingdom in this time.

7. THE LEAST IN THE KINGDOM
Matthew 11:11, Luke 7:28

If we interpret Matthew 11:12 // Luke 16:16 as affirming that the kingdom of God breaks into this world through the ministries of John the Baptist and Jesus, what are we to make of the saying in Matthew 11:11 // Luke 7:28? T. W. Manson's interpretation is simple and direct: "John is the greatest man that ever lived—outside the kingdom of God."[111] Jüngel agrees with Manson on this point, and proceeds to argue that such a statement is irreconcilable with the idea that John could have initiated the eschatological period; he therefore contends that we must interpret Matthew 11:12 and Luke 16:16 as excluding John from the period of the kingdom.[112] But the results of careful exegesis that point to the link between John and Jesus in the new age cannot be so easily discarded.

From time to time the notion is revived that the reference to "the least" in the kingdom of heaven in this passage (*mikroteros,* literally, "the less") is in fact a reference to Jesus, who is less than John in the estimate of men but is destined to be revealed at the end as greater than the greatest.[113] Most scholars reject this as an artificial interpretation, however. Schnackenburg, Michaelis, and Grundmann (after an apparent change of mind) follow Schlatter in contending that Matthew 11:11 has nothing to do with the question of John's place in the kingdom of God but rather that it serves to make the point that greatness in the kingdom of God is accorded differently than greatness among men in this age—it is a matter of grace rather than of human achievements—and that every disciple can and should acquire such greatness.[114] But I find this interpretation to be quite as unlikely. Is it not possible simply to recognize that the man who formed the watershed of the ages, who bridged the gap between the period of promise and the period of fulfillment, and who by his proclamation opened a way for the kingdom of God was an initiator who did not truly belong to the age he helped to usher in? Inasmuch as the evangelists did include the sayings that characterize John as the "angel" who goes before the Lord and as the Elijah who was to prepare his way (see Matt. 11:10ff., Luke 7:27, and Mark 9:13), they must have viewed him in this manner, and if these sayings are dominical, they must indicate that this was Jesus' understanding also. It may well be that the fact that John stood on the threshold instead of within and alongside the bearer of the kingdom is to no small degree attributable to the fact that he had to suffer the attacks of the violent opponents of the kingdom; the ministry in Galilee began after his imprisonment. E. Schweizer appears to be suggesting as much in the following:

> The contradiction can probably be resolved by assuming that God's kingdom refers to an event that announces itself in the opposition to John, his imprisonment and execution; it becomes present for whoever has ears to hear and eyes to see in the ministry of Jesus, his preaching, actions and death; and it will be visible to all and fulfilled in the glory to come (cf. 13:1–50). For Jesus, as for Matthew, both are important: the activity of the kingdom of God commences with the Baptist, but only Jesus himself makes it present for those who have ears to hear.[115]

8. THE INCALCULABLE KINGDOM
Luke 17:20–21

This passage is a clear example of an "apophthegm," or pronouncement story; the narrative setting is limited to a mere introductory clause.[116] Most scholars assume that it circulated in the tradition as an isolated unit.[117] It is likewise the critical consensus that Luke found the saying in his own source rather than in Q (since it is not in Matthew's gospel) and that he himself conjoined it with the Q discourse on the end of the age (vv. 22–37). There are some scholars, however, who maintain that the evangelist found the whole passage, verses 20–37, already combined in Q, and that Matthew, while knowing of the existence of verses 20–21, decided to omit them.[118]

Bultmann calls an identification of the questioners with Pharisees into doubt by noting that the opponents of Jesus are frequently described as Pharisees without due cause.[119] Schnackenburg likewise calls this identification into doubt by suggesting that the introduction was not integral to the statement of Jesus in the earliest tradition.[120] This issue is not a matter of fundamental importance, however; the current tendency is to consider the identification plausible while recognizing its uncertainty. As A. Rustow has rightly observed, the saying in verses 20b–21 fits no group more suitably than Pharisees.[121]

Difficulties in interpreting the passage arise out of ambiguity in its key terms, notably the *parateresis* of verse 20 and *entos* in verse 21.

In Greek literature the simple meaning of *parateresis* as "watching" is extended to the kind of observing undertaken by scientists and physicians, the "observation" of signs and symptoms that precedes deduction, and the observation of the heavenly bodies in astronomy and astrology; it is also used to denote the observance or keeping of rules and commandments.[122] The combination of the preposition *meta* with *parateresis* yields a tolerably clear meaning; in this instance it signifies the manner or accompanying circumstance of the observation. Bauer interprets the assertion that the kingdom does not come *meta paratereseos* to mean "so that its approach can be observed."[123] But in what sense is that to be taken?

E. Percy has insisted on taking the statement of verse 20b at face value, contending that the phrase "The kingdom of God does not come in such a manner that it can be observed" relates to those who are awaiting it, that men are not able to observe or be aware of the coming of the kingdom for the reason stated in verse 21b—namely, that it is a purely inward phenomenon: "the kingdom of God is in your inmost being" (*in eurem Inneren*).[124] The difficulty with this simplistic interpretation is that it ignores a great deal else that Jesus says about the kingdom in both its present and future manifestations. Questions about the meaning of *entos* aside, it seems clear that the signs of the presence of the kingdom were such that John the Baptist should have been able to recognize it (Matt. 11:5), and the opponents of Jesus should have been aware of it (Matt. 12:28). The parable of the fig tree (Mark 13:28–29) is also pertinent here, regardless of whether it relates to the present or future kingdom.

What applies to the popular view expressed by Percy also applies to the more sophisticated exposition of Norman Perrin. Along with others, he has been impressed with the use of this saying of Jesus in the Gospel of Thomas, where it appears (or is alluded to) no fewer than three times:

> Jesus said: If those who lead you say to you: "See, the Kingdom is in heaven," then the birds of heaven will precede you. If they say to you: "It is in the sea," then the fish will precede you. But the Kingdom is within you and it is without you. If you (will) know yourselves, then you will be known and you will know that you are the sons of the Living Father. (Log. 3)

> His disciples said to Him: When will the Kingdom come? Jesus said: It will not come by expectation; they will not say: "See, here," or: "See, there." But the Kingdom of the Father is spread upon the earth and men do not see it. (Log. 113)

> His disciples said to Him: When will the repose of the dead come about and when will the new world come? He said to them: What you expect has come, but you know it not. (Log. 51)[125]

The interesting feature of logion 113 is its rendering of *meta paratereseos* by the phrase "by expectation" (Coptic *gosht ebol*), which again appears in logion 51 as "what you expect." Quispel suggests that Thomas is independent of Luke in this instance, since both *meta paratereseos* and *gosht ebol* can be seen as renderings of the Aramaic verb *ḥur*.[126] Perrin concurs with Quispel on this point,[127] accepting it as a confirmation of his earlier conviction that Jesus rejects all apocalyptic speculation (and with it the apocalyptic conception of history), that contrary to current apocalyptic ideas Jesus affirms that the kingdom of God is a matter of human experience (it is *entos humon*): "It is to be found wherever God is active decisively within the experience of an individual and men have faith to recognize this for what it is."[128]

Despite the attractiveness of this view, it rests on dubious assumptions. The independence of the Gospel of Thomas from the canonical gospels is sharply contested, both generally and with respect to the logia we are discussing.[129] W. Schrage rejects the notion that *gosht ebol* is an alternative rendering of a common Aramaic *ḥur* that lies behind *meta paratereseos*. He points out that the Coptic term in the Sahidic New Testament is the equivalent of *apokaradokia* in Romans 8:19 and Philippians 1:20, and it appears again linked with the kingdom of God in Mark 15:43 (*prosdechomenos ten basileian tou theou*, "await-ing the kingdom of God"). *The author of the Gospel of Thomas is opposed to the expectation of the kingdom of God itself.* His transformation of the biblical con-cept of the kingdom of God into a vehicle for Gnostic thought is apparent in logia 3 and 51: the invisible presence of the kingdom is conceived of as "parti-cles, drops or sparks of the divine world of light. . . . The eschatological kingdom of God is thus here also spiritualized."[130] Having seen how the baby can be tossed out with the bath water in this way—tossed into the Gnostic sea—we stand forewarned about attempts to read too much meaning into the phrase *ou meta paratereseos*.

A third attempt at solving the problem of the troublesome phrase focuses on the use of *parateresis* to mean observation of the heavens. A. Strobel con-tends that the verb is being used to denote a very specific variety of this sort of observation in Luke 17:20–21.[131] He notes that the Jews regularly observed the heavens to determine the dates of new moons, and above all that of the passover. They viewed the passover night as "a night of watching": "It was a night of watching by the Lord to bring them out of the land of Egypt, so this same night is a night of watching kept to the Lord by all the people of Israel throughout their generations" (Exod. 12:42). Why a night of watching? In due course the answer was given: "In it you were redeemed, and in it you will be redeemed" (Mekh. Exod. 12:42, 20a). That is to say, the memorial of redemption from Egypt became united with the eschatological expectation of the kingdom of God: the kingdom would come on the night of the Passover! Significantly, Aquila ren-dered the phrase *lel shimmurim* as *nux paratereseos*, "a night of observation." Strobel maintains that Luke 17:20b is a specific denial of the contemporary Jewish "observation" of the passover night as the occasion on which the king-dom of God would come and thus that the formulation must be Luke's, since Luke knew that Jesus was opposed to such apocalyptic reckoning, and he would have been inclined to frame the saying in accordance with the teaching of Jesus relating to the presence of the kingdom.[132] Ingenious as this interpretation is, such a delimitation of the phrase *ou meta paratereseos* would scarcely be war-rantable unless it were set in a context that made the application evident, and we have no indication that this is the case. Doubtless it is a striking example of apocalyptic speculation with which the teaching of Jesus cannot be reconciled. A. Rustow (who views the saying as dominical) wishes to acknowledge this; noting that the question addressed to Jesus can relate both to a year and to a time within the sacral year, he suggests that *ou meta paratereseos* is intended to exclude *every kind of reckoning of the time, including that based on the Passover Haggada.*[133]

Can we say more with confidence about Luke 17:20? I believe that we can, and we can take as starting point Riesenfeld's definition of *parateresis* as "the rational-empirical observation and fixing of signs and symptoms."[134] In es-chatological contexts it is possible to contemplate "signs and symptoms" from two different viewpoints. The one proceeds from a belief that God works ac-cording to a fixed timetable in history,[135] that he has communicated its details to certain elect seers, and that a comparison of such revelations with events in world history will indicate where one is in the plan of the ages.[136] All such speculations take it as axiomatic that the end of time is near, and the nearer the end appears to be, the more confidently the prophecies are formulated and proclaimed.[137] In contrast to this there is the conviction that the "times and seasons" are in God's hands (see Acts 1:7) but that he has given intimations as to the nature of the times that conclude this age in order that his people might maintain faith and obedience and so gain the final salvation. It is to such "signs" that the parable of the fig tree relates (Mark 3:28–29)—a parable that is suitably followed by exhortations to watchfulness (Mark 13:33ff.). But these passages do not give any sort of specific answer to the question posed in Luke 17:20a, and certainly no sort of calendar date.

It is not unreasonable to appeal to this distinction in considering the meaning of *ou meta paratereseos* in Luke 17:20. Resorting to apocalyptic time-tables is alien to the mind of Jesus, as Luke 17:20b makes clear. But that statement should not be construed in such a manner as to overrule his teaching, elsewhere attested, that for those with eyes to see there are "signs" that point to God at work in judgment and salvation for the achieving of his purpose in the world.[138]

The negative assertion that the coming of the kingdom of God is not observed is balanced by the affirmation that "the kingdom of God is *entos humon*." This second chief clause is preceded by another negative assertion, however: "Neither will they say, 'Look, here! or, there!'" The *parateresis*-clause speaks of speculation as to *times* of the kingdom's appearance, but this other negative assertion speaks of the *place* where it will appear. Riesenfeld notes that in apocalyptic thought temporal and local aspects are closely related and concludes that the two negative statements can be regarded as virtually synonymous.[139] He is correct in this, although we ought not to overlook the fact that Mark has a statement similar to that in Luke 17:21a in his eschatological discourse in Mark 13:21: "And then if anyone says to you, 'Look, here is the Christ! Look, there!' do not believe it." Matthew cites not only this form of the saying in his version of the discourse (Matt. 24:23) but also the Q form (Matt. 24:26), which Luke reproduces in Luke 17:23. All these yield a positive clause: "If anyone *says* to you . . ." (Mark 13:21; Matt. 24:23), "If they *say* to you . . ." (Matt. 24:26), "They *will say* . . ." (Luke 17:23). How then are we to account for the negative form in Luke 17:21a, "They will *not* say . . ."? The context may supply the answer. If verse 21b is in fact referring to the presence of the kingdom, then Luke's "They will not say . . ." would really mean "They cannot rightly say," for the awaited kingdom has already come, in contrast to verse 23, in which the future revelation of the kingdom and/or Messiah is in view. It is also possible that Luke found verse 21a as a floating item of tradition, and introduced it into the saying in verses 20b and 21b partly because he considered it to be fitting in this context and partly because he thought it provided a suitable link between the logion and the discourse of verses 22 and following. The passage from 20b to 21b is smooth, and it does make a striking utterance. That the two clauses originally formed a unified saying is a possibility we should seriously consider.

As to the meaning of *entos humon*, Noack's review of the interpretation of Luke 17:20–21 shows that all of the various understandings of *entos* that have been suggested in modern exegesis had already been propounded in earlier works.[140]

The lexicon of Liddell and Scott, even in its revised edition of 1940, recognizes only one meaning for *entos*, that being "within."[141] Such has been the common interpretation in the church, and it is reflected in most of the early versions,[142] in the Gospel of Thomas,[143] and in the Oxyrhyncus papyrus 654.[144] While the latter two documents reflect a Gnostic understanding of the text, that is not the case with the interpretation adopted by Athanasius, which was already attested in his time and which was maintained through the centuries. He set Luke 17:21 in parallelism with Deuteronomy 30:14:

> Moses taught saying, "The word of faith is within your heart [*entos tes kardias sou*]." Whence also the Savior . . . said, "The kingdom of God is within you [*entos humon*]."[145]

Johann Arndt strengthened this link between "the word of faith in the heart" (which is how Paul renders the passage from Deuteronomy in Rom. 10:7ff.) and Luke 17:21 by combining it with another Pauline dictum, "The kingdom of God is not eating and drinking, but righteousness, peace, and joy, inspired by the Holy Spirit" (Rom. 14:17).[146] This has been the standard interpretation since Arndt first proposed it at the beginning of the seventeenth century. In seeking to establish the interpretation on form and redactional critical grounds, R. Sneed has maintained that Romans 14:17 is an expanded paraphrase of Luke 17:20–21. "The correspondence between Romans 14:17 and Luke 17:20–21," he says, "suggests that during the oral period there circulated a saying whose point was that Jesus has said that the Reign of God is not realized by Mosaic observances, but by the reception of the Holy Spirit."[147]

The difficulty about this view is that in the Bible generally, and in the teaching of Jesus particularly, the kingdom of God is not represented as the immanence of God in the soul (as Harnack suggests)[148] or as a principle at work invisibly in the heart of the individual (as Wellhausen suggests),[149] and in Luke 17:20–21 there is nothing to indicate a promise of indwelling by the Holy Spirit (as Sneed suggests). Typically the rule of God is referred to in terms of God's sovereign activity in the world, manifested in deeds of judgment and deliverance, and in terms of man's coming under that rule or entering its sphere of saving grace. The Pauline word about the kingdom of God as "righteousness, peace, and joy, inspired by the Holy Spirit" is no exception; it should be understood in light of the prophetic teaching on *God's* establishment of righteousness, peace, and joy in the world.[150] No interpretation of a saying of Jesus on the kingdom of God can be right that diminishes its strictly eschatological content.

In contrast to the tradition that translates *entos* as "within," the Old Syriac translates it as "among" (*bainathkon* = "among you"), and some of the early Fathers were attracted to this interpretation. The majority of modern scholars also favor this meaning here, having the weighty support of Bauer (who reiterates his support for this reading in the fifth edition of his lexicon). Strobel maintains that Luke generally holds the biblical usage to be of greater account than the classical usage. With others before him, he views the rendering of

Exodus 17:7 as almost paradigmatic. "Is the Lord among us or not?" (Heb. *beqirbenu*) is reproduced in the LXX by *ei estin Kurios en hemin e ou*, in Aquila by *entos hemon*, and in Symmachus by *en meso hemon*. Strobel contends that this evidence gives a clear indication of how we ought to understand Luke 17:21b.[151]

While the majority agree that this understanding of *entos* suits Luke 17:21–22 well, the question remains whether we should understand the term in the context of the appearance of the kingdom of God in the future,[152] or of the presence of the kingdom in Jesus among his audience.[153] Bultmann's brief statement of the former view is representative: "The meaning is: when the kingdom comes, no one will ask and search for it any more, but it will be there on a sudden in the midst of the foolish ones who will still want to calculate its arrival."[154] Virtually all of those who have interpreted the saying in this fashion have had to include that phrase "on a sudden" or its equivalent. It is hard not to agree with those who protest that this is not a legitimate procedure. As Otto has forcefully stated,

> It is a peculiar method of interpretation, which interpolates rather than explains. The word put in parenthesis ["suddenly"] would then be the real point of the discourse, and on it alone everything would depend. Christ would then have forgotten to express the real point of his discourse. What he really wanted to say he would not have said, and what he actually said he would not have wanted to say.[155]

If the idea of suddenness is removed, the future application of the saying is rendered very tame—"The kingdom of God does not come with observation . . . when it comes it will be among you"—a statement that Rustow regards as "thoroughly trivial and no more than a naked tautology."[156] However, there is the added difficulty that Luke employs *entos* nowhere else in his writings, consistently expressing the idea of "among" with the term *mesos*;[157] we might well wonder why he would have chosen to use *entos* in this passage if "among" was the meaning he wished to convey. In the end, then, while it is possible to understand *entos* as "among," it must be considered a doubtful interpretation.

In fact the passage has been accorded a less dubious interpretation from early times. Cyril of Alexandria maintained that Jesus' answer to the Pharisees in Luke 17:20 implies that we should earnestly seek to attain the kingdom, for it is *entos humon*—that is, "it is in the scope of your choices, and it lies *in your power* to receive it."[158] This interpretation was revived by C. H. Roberts on the basis of evidence from papyri ranging from the end of the first century to the end of the third century A.D.,[159] although the cogency of this evidence has been disputed. Subsequently A. Rustow has adduced a wider range of citations from Greek literature to illustrate just such a meaning for *entos* and has thereby made it clear that it is possible in Luke 17:21b.[160] I believe that this is the most plausible interpretation of the term here, for it suits the context of the saying, its meaning is consonant with other teachings of Jesus on the kingdom (unlike *entos* = "within"), and there is no objection from the side of the linguists (unlike *entos* = "among"). According to this interpretation, Jesus is simply telling the questioners not to concern themselves with trying to determine when (or where—recall v. 21a) the kingdom of God is to appear, but rather to be aware that the kingdom is *within their reach*—which is to say that it lies in their power to enter it and secure its blessings. The unexpressed corollary of the saying would then be, as in Mark 1:15, "Repent, and believe the good news."[161]

Our discussion suggests that the last clause of Luke 17:20–21 constitutes the climax of the saying. The kingdom of God has entered the present in and through Jesus, and the possibility of experiencing its saving power lies within the range of all who hear the good news. There is insufficient warrant for viewing either of the main clauses, verse 20b or 21b, as deriving from Luke rather than from Jesus, whatever the interpretation of verses 20a and 21a. The passage is closely related to other sayings of Jesus concerning the presence of the kingdom of God in and through his ministry. It does not deny the expectation of the revelation of the presence of that kingdom any more than do the other utterances of Jesus. Otto may well have been right in saying of the passage that "It was meant to shatter the dogmatism of a finished eschatology and burst its too narrow limits."[162] He who reckons only with future hope must come to terms with God's royal working in the present if that hope of the future is to be realized.

9. THE SECRET OF THE KINGDOM
Mark 4:11–12

It is now commonly agreed that this saying, which has been inordinately debated through the years, is not a Markan construction, but was taken by Mark from a previously existing tradition and inserted into the context of the parable of the Sower.[163] It is a plausible conjecture that verse 10 originally related to a request of the disciples for an explanation about the parable of the Sower and that Mark adapted a question about "the parable" in the singular to parables as such, in order to lead into the statement of Jesus in verses 11–12, which speaks of "parables" in the plural.[164] If we assume that verses 11–12 were an originally independent unit, we will do well to distinguish between the intent of the saying as Mark records it and the intent behind the saying in the tradition from which he adopted it. This becomes apparent as soon as we ask to whom the saying relates: "To *you* is given . . . to *those outside*. . . ." In Mark's setting, the "you" means "those about him with the Twelve" (v. 10), a unique designation that is not used anywhere else by Mark. Kelber suggests that it arises through a conjoining of the phrase in Mark 3:34, "those sitting about him," whom Jesus acknowledges to be his true kinsfolk, with "the Twelve," thus connoting the immediate group of disciples plus a larger group of Jesus' followers. Kelber goes on to suggest that "those outside" must have been family of Jesus, who stood "outside" the house in which Jesus was teaching (Mark 3:22ff.).[165] But such an interpretation seems most implausible: why look to the remoter context of chapter 3 (viz., 3:33) rather than the immediate context of chapter 4?[166] Certainly the original logion could not have been envisaged in so restricted a manner as Kelber suggests. In Jewish writings generally "those outside" are those outside *Israel*, or unbelieving Jews.[167] The contrast in verse 11 is most naturally construed as a contrast between the circle of Jesus' disciples on the one hand and the "multitude," the general population of Israel, on the other.

It is the disciples of Jesus, then, who are given "the secret of the kingdom of

God."[168] What is this revelation that is communicated to the followers of Jesus? With a unanimity rare in discussions on dominical sayings, New Testament scholars agree that it is the inbreaking of the kingdom of God in the word and deed of Jesus.[169] The term *musterion* is well suited to convey this revelation. While its use in the world of Hellenistic religion is not unrelated to its use in the New Testament,[170] the background for its appearance in Mark 4:11 is clearly the context of Jewish apocalyptic, in which it denotes the purpose of God in the history of the world, which will be realized in his universal rule revealed in the last times. One needs only to read the second chapter of Daniel to become aware of the importance of this concept; in the description of Nebuchadnezzar's dream and its interpretation, the term *rāz* (= *musterion*) occurs no fewer than seven times.[171] Its most characteristic meaning appears in Daniel's statement to the king:

> "The secret about which your majesty inquires no wise man, exorcist, magician, or diviner can disclose to you. But there is in heaven a god who reveals secrets, and he has told King Nebuchadnezzar what is to be at the end of this age." (Dan. 2:27–28)

This consciousness that the elect of God are the recipients of the secrets of God is marked in the literature of the Qumran community, in the hymns of which the Teacher of Righteousness has the function of revealing the secrets of God to the elect in the face of opposition from "prophets of falsehood" and mockery of many.

> As for them, they are hypocrites;
> the schemes are of Belial which they conceive,
> and they seek Thee with a double heart
> and are not firm in Thy truth. . . .
> Through me Thou hast illumined the face of many
> and caused them to grow until they are numberless;
> for Thou hast given me to know Thy marvellous mysteries
> and hast manifested Thy power unto me in Thy marvellous council
> and hast done wonders to many because of Thy glory
> and to make known Thy mighty works to all the living.[172]

As in Daniel, the content of the "mysteries" is the rule of God which he is to establish in the end of the times.[173]

The writer of the Similitudes of Enoch is an heir to this tradition. In a manner comparable to that of the Teacher of Righteousness, the Son of Man in the Similitudes has the role of making known the "hidden things" of the last times. He is, of course, a more exalted figure, and he himself belongs to the mysteries of the end:

> I asked the angel who went with me and showed me all the hidden things, concerning the Son of Man, who he was, and whence he was, (and) why he went with the Head of Days. And he answered and said to me:
>
> This is the Son of Man who hath righteousness,
> With whom dwelleth all the righteousness,

> And who revealeth all the treasures of that which is hidden,
> Because the Lord of Spirits hath chosen him.[174]

In light of this background, and in view of the teaching of Jesus on the kingdom of God in his parables and his nonparabolic sayings on the kingdom, it is more than a pious guess that in Mark 4:11 the secret of the kingdom given to the disciples relates to the realization in and through Jesus of God's purpose in the establishment of his saving rule. Its description as a "secret" belongs to the tradition. The fact that it continues to be a secret in spite of Jesus' proclamation is tied to the nature of the kingdom he brings. In contrast to the expectation of a reign established in might and splendor by the Son of David or inaugurated in the blood, power, and glory of the apocalyptic Warrior-Lamb, it is a rule of liberating grace, welcomed by the poor in spirit but rejected by the populace at large and their leaders, a kingdom of humble beginnings that faith alone can perceive to be the true fulfillment of the promise and thus destined to be the glorious embodiment of God's will for judgment and salvation. The secret of the kingdom therefore contains as an essential element the secret of the representative and agent of the kingdom: the lowly proclaimer of the kingdom is God's chosen one, through whom his will to salvation is effected on earth.[175]

In contrast to the privileged who are given the secret of the kingdom, those outside receive all things en *parabolais*. The contrasting parallelism of the two clauses in verse 11 suggests that *musterion* and *parabole* must correspond in meaning. As *musterion* means "secret," so *parabole* means "enigma" or "riddle," in accord with the Semitic *māshāl* tradition. The use of the term *ginetai*, "becomes," has occasioned some difficulty. "It is a strange expression to describe teaching," Vincent Taylor has noted.[176] The difficulty is alleviated when it is recognized that its subject *ta panta* is not the teaching in the parables, nor even "preaching in general,"[177] but the whole ministry of Jesus, his teaching as well as his action. *All* that Jesus says and does in relation to the kingdom of God is an enigma to those whose eyes have not been opened to the significance of his mission. Hence it does not matter greatly how we render the term *ginetai* so long as we recognize that it links the whole ministry of Jesus with the "riddle" of his secret.[178]

It is quite understandable that Mark applied this saying to the parables of Jesus themselves, since they frequently deal with the supreme topic of Jesus' instruction, the kingdom of God. Moreover, there is an enigmatic quality about a number of them. Admittedly many moderns have denied this, insisting that they are in fact simple. "The parables," says Schniewind, "are clear as the sunshine; children and simple people understand them immediately."[179] Ironically, that statement follows Schniewind's exposition of the parable of the Sower, which he summarizes with the dictum, "The normal result of the word of God is failure." Scarcely a scholar would agree with him today! He missed the point of Mark's basic parable of the Kingdom! This illustrates a feature of the Semitic *māshāl* that differentiates it from the Greek *parabole*: its message frequently is not immediately apparent. Moreover, Mark would have been aware that the parable plays a unique role as a form of conveying prophetic oracles (e.g., the "parables" of Balaam in Num. 23–24 and those of Ezekiel in Ezek. 16,

17, 19, 23, and 24; another example would be the Parables of Enoch in 1 Enoch 37–71, although Mark may well have been unfamiliar with these).

How would Mark have understood the second part of the saying—"that they may look and look, but see nothing, and hear and hear, but understand nothing, lest they turn (to God) and be forgiven"? The passage has often been interpreted as bitter irony, on the assumption that the words in Isaiah 6:9–10 reflect the prophet's experience of seeing his message rejected, the language of purpose being used to express result. More recent studies question this interpretation, however. In light of the fact that the scriptures conjoin divine predestination and human responsibility, the words would appear to express the judgment of God on the nation that rejects his call. The obduracy of the people was foreseen as a part of the sending of the prophet, a part of the bringing to pass of the "strange work" of God in Israel, a "destruction decreed by the Lord God of Hosts for the whole land" (Isa. 28:21–22). The prophet's word is considerably disturbing; indeed, if it were the only note he sounded, we might well be appalled by it. But we know that there are other elements in his message. The prophet through whom ears are deafened, eyes blinded, and wits dulled is the prophet of the remnant, a proclaimer of final redemption, and a herald of the Messiah. As von Rad has reminded us, "We must learn to read the saying about the hardening of the heart with reference to the saving history."[180]

Whoever preserved this citation in the tradition of Jesus' words must have recognized that the situation of the nation in Isaiah's day was strangely repeated in the day of Jesus and that judgment on the impenitent nation was unavoidably bound up with his ministry. Mark would not have hesitated to interpret the *hina* and the *mepote* as expressive of purpose—"in order that . . . lest. . . ." The guilt of the people matched the predestination of God; the rejection of the message of Jesus matched the concealment of the mystery of the kingdom; the judgment on blindness entailed the divine rejection of the nation as nation. Nevertheless, just as in Isaiah's day the hardening of the nation had been qualified by the creation of an obedient remnant, so in Jesus' day the blindness of the people was qualified by the calling of a remnant of believing disciples. And as hope of a deliverance and a messiah was made known by the prophet, so the message of Jesus included the proclamation of a redemption now inaugurated. He promised a day in which the hidden would be unveiled (see Mark 4:22) and the rule of God would be universally manifested (see Mark 4:26ff., 30ff.). *Thus, the veiling is clearly temporary.*[181]

Mark will have viewed the saying in this fashion, but what of Jesus? Since Jülicher set forth his views on the matter many scholars have been inclined to dissociate the saying from Jesus and set it to the account either of early church tradition or of the evangelist himself.[182] There has been a critical reaction to this view of late. Holding that verses 11–12 constitute an independent saying in the tradition that originally referred not to the parable but to the enigmatic character of the mission of Jesus to Israel, some recent scholars have argued that there is no good reason to suppose that they ought not to be attributed to Jesus. The idea that the secret of the kingdom is given to disciples but hidden from others is paralleled elsewhere in the gospel traditions, notably in Matthew 11:25–26 // Luke 10:21:

"I thank thee, Father, Lord of heaven and earth, for hiding these things from the learned and wise, and revealing them to the simple. Yes, Father, such was thy choice."[183]

Thus, more and more scholars are coming to accept the saying in Mark 4:11–12 as authentic, although many hold that by setting it in this context Mark obscured its original significance.[184] It is most plausibly conjectured that Jesus made the statement at the end of his Galilean ministry, when it had become apparent that the majority of the people had rejected his proclamation.[185] Despite the tragedy implied in the conclusion of the saying, we will misunderstand its intention if we view it as a gloomy utterance. It is, after all, directed to the disciples, and the emphasis falls on the first and positive statement: the secret of the kingdom is theirs, given to them by the Lord of history, whose lordship continues to encompass Israel even in its unbelief. It is fundamentally a word of encouragement to the followers of Jesus, who may rejoice in their association with him through whom the kingdom comes. Those who reject the word of the kingdom are powerless to prevent its coming; they turn the word of grace into a word of judgment, but they remain under the sovereignty of the Lord of the kingdom.[186]

10 | Parables of Jesus on the Coming of the Kingdom of God in the Present

1. THE STRONG MAN BOUND
Mark 3:27, Matthew 11:29, Luke 11:22

This similitude is bracketed by Mark as one of the two so-called "parables" with which Jesus answered the charge that he had power to perform exorcisms because he was in league with "the prince of the demons" (v. 23). The picture is simple: no one can walk into a strong man's house and carry off his property unless he is able first to overpower the strong man and render him helpless; then he can take what he will of his goods.[1]

The elements of the picture are reminiscent of several Old Testament passages, notably Isaiah 49:24–25 (cf. also Isa. 53:12 and 59:15–20):

> Can the prey be taken from the mighty,
>   or the captives of a tyrant be rescued?
> Surely, thus says the Lord:
>   "Even the captives of the mighty shall be taken,
>   and the prey of the tyrant be rescued,
> for I will contend with those who contend with you,
>   and I will save your children."

The context is that of Yahweh's restoration of his people from exile in the time of redemption and judgment. In consequence of this promised deliverance and judgment,

> "All flesh shall know that I am the Lord, your Saviour,
>   and your Redeemer, the Mighty One of Jacob."

Recognition of this Old Testament background led Rudolf Otto to believe that the Stronger One in the parable represents God. He has suggested that the comparison reflects the ancient Aryan-Iranian idea of the warfare between the God of heaven and his evil foe, a tradition strongly maintained in Jewish apocalyptic and reproduced in detail in Revelation 12. Thus, Otto contends that in the simile of Mark 3:27, God is the Stronger One who takes the spoil from the Strong through the exorcist Jesus.[2]

Theologically this interpretation is impeccable. Jesus made no claim to act independently of God. Indeed, the point of the controversy between Jesus and his opponents in connection with his exorcisms was the identification of his inspiration—whether it was from the devil or God. Nevertheless, Otto's view assumes a rather inflexible apocalyptic; Jesus' parable clearly moves on a plane different from that of transcendental apocalypticism. It leads us to contemplate not a cosmic struggle in heaven between the forces of God and the devil, but rather the work of an individual powerful enough to challenge a strong man in his own home and take from him his ill-gotten possessions. If the associations of the imagery indicate that it is *God's* work being done in the overthrow of the Strong One, then the focus of attention must be on the *agent* who is doing it. Moreover, while it is true that the parable has no formal connection to its context, it is commonly accepted that the evangelists have preserved the general context in which it should be understood—namely, that of the accusation that Jesus was an instrument of the devil. The thrust of the simile is directed to that indictment: Jesus is the *adversary* of Satan, not his associate, and his exorcisms manifest not an agreement but a rescue operation. In fact, the exorcisms signify the defeat of the devil. The Strong Man is helpless to prevent them, for he has been floored and tied up, and must perforce watch his goods go! The one who tied him up is the one who directs the removal of the furniture. That can be none other than Jesus, in whom a power superior to that of the devil is operative.

A further point calls for consideration. Most exegetes have been content to deduce from the parable the obvious lesson that the exorcisms of Jesus signify a defeat for the devil. Yet in all the versions of the parable that have come down to us, the plundering of the Strong Man's house takes place only *after* he had been defeated:

> No one can break into a strong man's house and make off with his goods unless he has *first* tied the strong man up; *then* he can ransack the house. (Mark 3:27, NEB; the Gospel of Thomas reads virtually the same.)

This suggests that the liberating actions of Jesus are grounded upon a defeat of Satan that has already been accomplished and that has made it impossible for Satan to prevent Jesus from freeing his prey. We need not push the allegory beyond any reasonable limits to see that it is conveying the idea that Jesus is an adversary who has bested his opponent and is exploiting his victory.

If this interpretation is correct, one might naturally ask when it was that Jesus secured Satan's defeat. Luke 10:18 has been cited in this connection, but it does not help us materially, inasmuch as it does not tell us when Satan's fall from power took place; there is no indication of whether it happened in connection with the mission of the Seventy, or through an event in the ministry of Jesus as a whole, or even whether we should understand the statement as a prophetic anticipation of the outcome of the ministry. On the other hand, the synoptic gospels do contain an account of an encounter between Jesus and the devil in which Jesus was the victor—namely, the temptation narrative. Jülicher cautions us against associating the account of the temptation of Jesus with the parable of the Strong Man on the grounds that in the narrative Jesus is attacked but successfully defends himself, whereas in the parable Jesus is the attacker who seizes the devil's possessions; accordingly, Jülicher maintains that "neither the Pharisees nor the evangelists, still less Jesus himself, will have read out of the temptation story a binding of Satan."[3] But is this a correct way of looking at the matter? Mark, at least, would almost certainly have denied it. In the prologue to his gospel he recounts the proclamation of John the Baptist concerning the coming of "one who is stronger" than he, who will baptize in the mighty Spirit of God (Mark 1:7–8); the collocation of one who is "stronger" with the possession of the Spirit is significant in view of the fact that Mark links the two features in the parable and its context. Mark also states that Jesus was "driven" by the Spirit into the wilderness (1:12–13). Traditionally the wilderness is the home of evil spirits, and so the suggestion is implicitly made that Jesus was driven off to meet the devil. For what purpose? To be destroyed by him? To undergo an endurance test? Surely not. He on whom the Spirit descended at his baptism and who was led by the Spirit into the wilderness is represented as sent to contest the field with him who holds it, that by the defeat of the devil the way to the new world might be opened. That would have been the vantage point from which Mark would have understood the parable of the Strong Man, and in this he may well have been right.[4]

We should acknowledge at the beginning that all these speculations concerning the intention of the parable are uncertain. Fortunately, a more important element of the parable is not so uncertain: the concept of the overthrow of the evil powers as the precursor of the kingdom of God, and even as the concomitant of its coming, occupies a firm place in apocalyptic Judaism.[5] The Qumran Community had its own peculiar modification of the expectation, and it is also prominent in the book of Revelation. Since the early Christian centuries, the picture of the binding of Satan related in Revelation 20:1–3 has been linked with the Markan parable of the Strong Man; in that passage the "binding" connotes the subjugation of the devil at the parousia of Christ, and is the immediate precursor of the kingdom of Christ. Of yet greater pertinence is the description of the ejection of Satan from heaven related in Revelation 12, to which Otto attaches so much importance. The vision in its present form bears the marks of a prior redaction by a Jew, who saw in the myth of the child-redeemer a picture comparable to the messianic hope of the Old Testament; in harmony with the outlook of the Jews of his time, he represented the overthrow of the devil and his angels as the work of Michael, the protector of Israel. The Christian apocalyptist reasserted the importance of the Redeemer: by his insertion of the song in verses 10–11 he affirmed that the victory over Satan was attributable not to Michael and his angels but to Christ in his death, whose sacrifice nullified the accusations of the Accuser and enabled the confessors of the Crucified to share his victory. The final triumph, to be witnessed at the close of history, has therefore been decisively anticipated in the midst of history. That faith is at the heart of apostolic Christianity. The parable of Jesus, however, asserts that the victory over Satan took place in the ministry of Jesus—indeed, apparently at its *commencement*. This was a distinctive note in the proclamation of Jesus, although it was overshadowed in the earliest church by the overwhelming significance of his death and resurrection. As Grundmann has pointed out, this constitutes strong evidence that the parable is in fact authentic.[6] The ministry of Jesus itself is characterized by triumph over Satan. The conquest began at the outset of the ministry, and it was manifested in his continuing works. That was why his life was a constant challenge to men to make a decision about their relation to the kingdom of God; in his deeds, his word, and his fellowship there was power for emancipation, for life in freedom under the saving sovereignty of God.

The simile of Jesus is very short, but it opens wide horizons. It embodies in a nutshell the teaching conveyed in the nonparabolic sayings of Jesus.

2. THE TREASURE AND THE PEARL
Matthew 13:44–46

It is probable that these two parables were originally separate in the gospel tradition, as they are in the Gospel of Thomas, and as certain differences of language and form between them would suggest.[7] Nevertheless, they have the same basic message. Matthew was guided by right instinct in bringing them together if they were not already joined in his source.

Yet a third parable appears in the Gospel of Thomas which is often thought to have a similar intent:

> The Man is like a wise fisherman who cast his net into the sea, he drew it up from the sea full of small fish; among them he found a large (and) good fish, that wise fisherman, he threw all the small fish down into the sea, he chose the large fish without regret. (Log. 8)[8]

Some exegetes view this as an independent parable, embodying the same message as the parables of the Treasure and the Pearl, though adapted by Thomas for a Gnostic application.[9] It is more likely to be an alternative version of the parable of the Dragnet,[10] however, and we shall leave it out of our consideration of the parables of the Treasure and the Pearl.

What then is the lesson conveyed by these two parables? It would seem, as H.-D. Wendland has put it, to be "the incomparable worth of the kingdom, which surpasses all earthly things, for which everything must be offered up."[11] The treasure is valuable beyond anything the laborer could dare to imagine that he would possess. The pearl is such that no merchant could ever hope to lay hands on it.[12] Because this is so, the last clause of Wendland's statement, "for which everything must be offered up," is not the happiest way of expressing the mood of the parable. The word *must* is correct in relation to the procedures involved in the stories but not in relation to the spirit of the occasions that are described. The point is that the worth of what has come to the finders is so great that they are happy to pay whatever price is necessary to get it. As Jüngel has put it, "The joy on the part of the finder corresponds to the superior worth of the treasure; as joy in the greater over the less, it *self-evidently* (not sacrificially!) makes renunciation, if that which is of greater worth can be gained."[13] In a similar vein, E. Linnemann points out that the finders are presented with the chance of a lifetime to acquire something of enormous value; if it demands all that they possess to scrape together the required sum, they are still fortunate to have the chance of securing what is there. "We can in fact best formulate the point of comparison as *risking all in view of a unique opportunity*."[14]

The implication of the parables then is clear: Let every hearer be sure to get the treasure! Let every hearer be sure to secure the pearl!

The object of value in these parables is the kingdom of God. But is it a treasure one hopes to receive in the future, or is it offered as gift in the present? Awareness of the kingdom as an eschatological reality in the teaching of Jesus has led a number of scholars to assume that in these parables he is indicating that the kingdom will be possessed solely in the future, that he is establishing the same sort of emphasis present, for example, in the beatitudes. J. D. Crossan has strongly opposed this interpretation as entailing a grave misunderstanding of the teaching of Jesus. He contends that these two parables (along with the parable of the Fish) provide the key to all the parables of Jesus. He argues that as a whole the parables set forth the kingdom's "temporality" and that the modes in which they do this are present in both parables we have under review. He suggests that this temporality of the kingdom can be seen in its *advent* as gift of God, in its *reversal* of the recipient's world, and in the fact that it empowers recipients to *action*. If we apply these categories to the parable of the Treasure, we see (1) that the future projected by the laborer is overturned by the *advent* of the treasure, which opens for the man a new world, causing him to (2) *reverse his past* and sell all he possesses, by which measure he is able to secure the treasure and thus (3) open up new possibilities for *action* that he did not have before. In light of this, Crossan states his conviction that

> the basic attack of Jesus is on an idolatry of time, and that this is the centre whence issued forth what Yeats called that 'Galilean turbulence' which set Jesus against all the major religious options of his contemporaries. . . . The one who plans, projects, and programs a future, even and especially if one covers the denial of finitude by calling it God's future disclosed or disclosable to oneself, is in idolatry against the sovereign freedom of God's advent to create one's time and establish one's historicity. . . . It is the view of time as man's future that Jesus opposed in the name of time as God's present, not as eternity beyond us but as advent within us.[15]

If Crossan is suggesting that Jesus opposed the sort of apocalyptic interpretation of the kingdom that would restrict it to the future, then the language he uses to describe Jesus' assertions concerning God's saving action in the present is quite in order. The vivid miniatures portrayed in the two parables depict the joy of laying hold on something in the here and now, an experience of God's gracious giving that transforms life. Moreover, this interpretation agrees with the message of the sayings of Jesus relating to the incursion of the divine sovereignty into the time of his present. If, then, this is what Crossan intends to say when he speaks of the "idolatry of time," we can rightly stand with him. But if he is suggesting that because Jesus emphasized the present as God's present he was not interested in the future as *God's* future, it is difficult to follow him. The last thing that can be attributed to Jewish apocalyptists is a view of time as *man's* future, for in their view God alone can deliver man from the forces of evil, in the face of which man is impotent. The good news of Jesus is the declaration that the time of God's expected action has come into the present. The glory and the grace set beyond the horizon of history is also operative in all its transforming powers now—*God's* glory, *God's* grace, *God's* transforming power. But it is important to observe that it is not just *any* present that Jesus is speaking of in his parables. It is the present of his activity, characterized by the overthrow of the Strong Man and the dawn of a new day. It is the kingdom promised for the future that has come into the present in and through his word and work. His parables are intended to convey to his contemporaries the challenge to acknowledge that what has come with him into the present is nothing less than the kingdom of the great and glorious future. Accordingly, it is fundamental to our understanding of what Jesus is saying that we realize that the God who comes in the present, who enables men to reverse their lives, and who empowers them for new action is the God of the future also, and hence that his kingdom belongs to the *present-and-future*.

We come closer to the mind of Jesus if we speak of the kingdom of God as represented in the parables before us not with abstract terms such as "temporality," but rather with such terms as *salvation*, with all its richness of associations in the prophets and the developing tradition of the people of God. Otto has made this point admirably:

> The thing of which the parables were meant to treat is the kingdom neither as a constraining power, nor as claim to sovereignty, nor as realm of power, nor even as concrete supramundane condition, but as the blessing of salvation, the blessing pure and simple, and purely and simply a blessing.[16]

3. THE LOST SHEEP, THE LOST COIN, AND THE TWO LOST SONS
Luke 15:4–32

The first two of this trilogy of parables are frequently viewed as twin parables. Certainly they are similar in intention, but, as with the parables of the Treasure and Pearl, it seems most likely that the evangelist is responsible for their being placed together. Matthew set the parable of the Lost Sheep in a different context (Matt. 18:12ff.), in which it applies to a situation within the church. The parables of the Lost Coin and the Prodigal Son are peculiar to Luke.

Is Luke's *situational* context right? There is ground for believing that it is. The three parables continue the banquet motif of chapter 14.[17] They are well suited to provide an insight into the reason Jesus associated with "sinners" and held table fellowship with them. What in the eyes of scrupulous observers of the law (as interpreted by Jews of that time) was construed as reprobate behavior on the part of Jesus is set forth as characteristic of the nature and action of the sovereign God. The people who are despised by the righteous matter to God, and they mattered to Jesus—which is but another way of saying that God values them, as a small farmer values a lost sheep because he cannot afford to lose even one, and as a poor woman values a lost coin, and as a father values the sons who wander off from him (whether in lands afar off or in a heart afar off).

We need not concern ourselves with the details of the parables of the Lost

Sheep and Lost Coin; they are adequately dealt with elsewhere.[18] The farmer and the housewife are depicted as seeking till they find that which was lost. The point of both parables is epigrammatically stated by Linneman: "Finding creates boundless joy."[19] In the address of Jesus to his hearers, that principle signifies "It creates joy in the heart of God, and it should create joy in yours too." We should bear in mind that Jesus is not merely excerpting an item from an accepted list of the attributes of God; he is relating to the concrete situation in which he and his hearers are involved. In the labors of Jesus among those estranged from God—in his preached word and in his association with them—the Lord God himself is seeking and finding and rejoicing. The saving sovereignty of God is at work where men least expected it.

Crossan holds that the parable of the Prodigal Son depicts in sharpest focus the double elements of a situational reversal: both parts of the parable end with virtually identical words (vv. 24 and 32), but they finish by showing the prodigal inside the house feasting and the elder son outside the house pouting.[20] This underscores the unspoken appeal of the parable—that other elder sons should heed the lesson and come inside the Father's house lest they miss the banquet. Nevertheless, there is more to the parable than this. Overarching all the exquisite touches of the story, a supreme reality can be discerned—namely, that the Lord of the kingdom is love as well as power and justice. If God's kingdom signifies his sovereign action, so too his quickness to forgive the wayward of humanity and to restore them to the fellowship with him that they have forfeited signifies the sovereign love of God. The "righteous" who are scandalized by such procedures are not condemned; rather, they are called on to recognize the fact that God is a merciful and compassionate Father and that they too need his mercy since they stand in danger of losing that which is foremost in their aspirations—the joy of fellowship with God and his family in the festivities of the kingdom.

Two points warrant emphasis here. First, we should note that the parable of the Prodigal Son is indeed a parable of the kingdom, as in their varied ways all the parables of Jesus are. If the church had grasped this insight early on, it might have avoided the one-sided view of eschatology that it has clung to through the centuries. Traditionally it has associated the coming of the kingdom of God above all with judgment, and with connotations of condemnation at that. Yet here in the parable of the Prodigal Son Jesus presents the sovereignty of God in terms of a love that delights in restoring the wayward to the fellowship of love. Nor should we regard this emphasis as somehow aberrant, a departure from what is norm everywhere else. That the salvation provided in the kingdom of God is depicted in terms of the lost being found, the dead being brought back to life again, and the Father's house being filled with the sound of joyous banquet is wholly in accord with the message and conduct of Jesus.

The second point we should note is that the parables in Luke 15 serve both to portray the attitude of God toward those beyond the pale of religion and respectable society, and also to reveal the rationale of the way of Jesus, which appeared unseemly to many of his contemporaries. It follows that the action of Jesus reveals the character of God. And it does more than just reveal that character. In the words of Jeremias,

Jesus thus claims that in his actions the love of God to the repentant sinner is made effectual. Thus the parable [of the Prodigal Son], without making any kind of christological statement, reveals itself as a veiled assertion of authority: Jesus makes the claim for himself that he is acting in God's stead, that he is God's representative.[21]

These parables indicate yet again an aspect of the sovereign activity of God in the word and deed of Jesus. As the parable of the Strong Man shows God's sovereignty as the power that can deliver men from evil to life in the freedom of God, so the parable of the Prodigal Son shows God's sovereignty as the power of love that can draw men from their lost condition into the fellowship of the Father's house.

4. THE UNMERCIFUL SERVANT
Matthew 18:23–25

The parables of the Treasure and Pearl tell of the exultant joy of discovering the kingdom of God. The parable of the Prodigal Son portrays the divine sovereignty as illimitable love. The parable of the Unmerciful Servant reveals the grace extended to us under the divine sovereignty, but instead of "a song of jubilation which celebrates the new peace with God," it turns out to be a parable of judgment carrying a dire warning.[22] It speaks of the mystery of sin, which is never so heinous as when a man is shown the redeeming love of the kingdom of God and then proceeds to grind it into the mire.

Everything in the parable is set on an astronomical scale. It is the nearest thing to a tale from the Arabian nights in the teaching of Jesus; it could have come from Scheherazade herself, had she been a disciple! Surely those exegetes who want to cut down the figures (e.g., from ten thousand talents to ten) have locked their imaginations in their filing cabinets.

The first "impossible" thing in the story is the extent of the administrator's debt. We take it that the man was responsible for the finances of a large area in a foreign land. Even so, the sum of ten thousand talents would have been beyond a Palestinian peasant's comprehension. It should never be translated into modern currency equivalents (any more than the twelve thousand stadia of the City of God should be rendered into kilometers or miles), but it may help us to grasp the amount involved if we understand that it represents a hundred million dinars (i.e., the wages for a hundred million working days) or that in 4 B.C. the whole of Galilee and Peraea paid only two hundred talents in taxes. Jeremias is on target in pointing out that this sum combines the highest figure available to the ancients with the greatest currency unit known in the world of Jesus.[23] To all intents and purposes the debt was illimitable.

The second "impossible" feature of the story is the reaction of the king to the plea of his administrator for mercy. The king had arrested the man and ordered his wife and children to be sold as slaves to provide some compensation for the debt. The man pleaded that he be given some time so that he might repay *all* that he owed. This was a useless plea; he could never have raised the sum required. Perhaps we are to infer that precisely because the king recognized the total inability of the man to meet his debt, his munificence was all the more extraordinary: he released the man from arrest, removed the threat hanging over his family, and remitted the debt. Here was royal bounty indeed! Infinite indebtedness was met with matching compassion.

The third "impossible" element in the story is the hardness of the freed debtor after he has received the incredible generosity of the king. He walks out of the king's audience chamber and meets a subordinate who owes him a hundred dinars—a mere five-hundred-thousandth part of the debt from which he had just been released. He takes the man by the throat and demands instant repayment of the debt. The unfortunate official makes the same plea to his colleague that the latter had made to the king: he asks for time to repay. Unlike the senior official, the subordinate could have made good on his promise to repay—it was, after all, only a hundred dinars. His plea is nevertheless denied; he is handed over to the torturers till the debt be paid. That action is as incomprehensible as the generosity of the king. Not surprisingly, wrath that had been averted came upon the unforgiving man to the uttermost.

The primary application of the parable is transparent. Linneman points out that the *tertium comparationis* of the parable is in verse 33: "Should you not have had mercy on your fellow servant as I had mercy on you?" Via agrees, but suggests that verse 33 really needs verses 32 and 34 to secure its force. One is inclined to agree with that, especially when reading the passage in the NEB:

> "You scoundrel!" he said to him; "I remitted the whole of your debt when you appealed to me; were you not bound to show your fellow-servant the same pity as I showed you?" And so angry was the master that he condemned the man to torture until he should pay the debt in full.

Via summarizes the passage as follows: "To receive (18:32) without giving (18:33) is self-destructive (18:34)."[24] That is not simply a law of existence; it belongs to the way of the kingdom of God.

Perhaps this affirmation calls for further comment. It holds good, I believe, not merely on account of the introductory words of the parable (18:23), but because of the place of the parable itself in the teaching of Jesus as a whole. The parable is not intended to convey a timeless truth about God's rule but rather a timely truth about the "now" of God's redeeming action. In commenting on this parable, Ernst Fuchs emphasized its pertinence to the present as a unique time: "The one question is what possibilities exist for our dealing with the present, when the present carries eschatological obligations." In characterizing the nature of this eschatological present he made two assertations: "The present . . . is the advance working of God's coming," and "The present must correspond to the inexorableness of God's judgement."[25] We can validly consider these two statements to be complementary insights into the teaching of Jesus generally and into the parable of the Unmerciful Servant in particular. We spend our present existence between these two poles of the eschatological situation, and by them it is determined. In the final analysis both are equally important, but it cannot be denied that for Jesus the essential characteristic of the present time (i.e., *his* present) is the abounding grace of the divine sovereignty. In the parable of the Unmerciful Servant he presents it in terms of emancipation from the bondage of guilt. For the man who opens his life to that grace and allows it to be the determining factor of his living, it is a fount of a new life. The purpose of the parable was to challenge the hearers of Jesus to allow the divine sovereignty to be the determining factor of their lives.

5. THE LABORERS IN THE VINEYARD
Matthew 20:1-16

To simplify identification, I use the traditional name of this parable, although the name suggested by Jeremias—"The Good Employer"—more accurately suggests the focus of the story: it is the owner of the vineyard who dominates the scene from first to last, and it is his action to which the kingdom of heaven is likened. Of course the laborers also figure prominently in the story; their role is underscored by the repetition of the proverbial saying both before and after the parable: "Many who are first will be last, and the last first" (Matt. 19:30) and "Thus will the last be first, and the first last" (Matt. 20:16). The first use of the statement is taken from Mark, whom Matthew follows in concluding the account of the Rich Young Ruler with these words.

It is generally supposed that Matthew inserted the repetition of the saying at the conclusion of the parable in order to emphasize what he understood to be its point. While it is in fact likely that Matthew made the insertion, it may well be unfair to attribute a wooden interpretation of the parable to him on the basis of 20:16. It may be, as Bonnard has suggested, that he wished to emphasize the fact that, in contrast to the Rich Ruler and all he represents, "The last to be called are *the first to taste the sovereign goodness of the master.*"[26] Such a conjecture is not wholly unworthy; Matthew may have had it in mind to establish a link between this parable and another he was shortly to relate, about two sons asked to work in their father's vineyard, the "first" of which said that he would work but then failed to do so, and the second of which (the "last"?) said that he would not work but then went on to do so. According to Matthew's account, Jesus then said, "I tell you this: tax-gatherers and prostitutes are entering the kingdom of God ahead of you" (Matt. 21:31). Nothing could be closer to the parable of the Good Employer than this, indicating that Matthew knew full well that the "last" are the publicans and sinners and the "first" the Pharisaic objectors to Jesus and his ministry.

The natural inclination of anyone coming into contact with the story for the first time is to be perplexed at the conduct of the employer. It is an extraordinary practice to pay men working all day long in the burning heat of a Palestinian summer the same wage as those who worked for an hour in the cool of the early evening. Our sense of justice evokes sympathy with the men who were indignant against their employer. But that attitude changes if we bear in mind two elements of the parable's background—the social and the religious.

Regarding the social context, we should recognize that the parable was set in conditions of dire unemployment, which was a real factor in the Palestine of Jesus' day, with consequent proverty and hunger, both for workers and for their families. As Jeremias observes, "It is because of his pity for their poverty that the owner allows them to be paid a full day's wages. In this case the parable does not depict an arbitrary action, but the behavior of a large-hearted man who is compassionate and full of sympathy for the poor."[27]

The second element is the religious context of the parable. Jesus had achieved notoriety for associating with the "last," people whom the "first" considered to be the dregs of society—not merely socially but religiously as well. The publicans and sinners were despised for living in disregard of the law of God and the traditions of the Fathers. To claim that the kingdom of God could belong to such seemed to some outrageous! These people had no part in it, they insisted, and the man who preached otherwise was teaching contrary to the holy law of God. But the parable expounds another view—namely, that God is compassionate as well as holy.

Many exegetes of this passage have noted that the teaching of the parable and the situation that called it forth must be understood together, but none has grasped it more acutely than Fuchs. He stresses the point that the parable is not intended to exemplify the kindness of God in a general way but rather that it is meant to reveal a distinctive action of God, to make us think in terms of an *act* of God's kindness. This action, or "conduct," of God is related to the conduct of Jesus with respect to publicans and sinners. In particular, we are meant to note the fact that he celebrated a meal with them: even if it is not suggested that this was a messianic meal, it is nevertheless plain enough that it served to celebrate God's *basileia*. Jesus viewed this act—and indeed his entire conduct toward these people—as a specific expression of God's kindness. Accordingly, Fuchs says of this feature of Jesus' ministry that

> He appeared not simply as the preacher of some possible kindness of God, of which all stood equally in need. Instead Jesus clung to this kindness, as to an event known to him; and he did not shrink from demonstrating the correspondence between this event and his own conduct towards those under judgment. Jesus acted in a very real way as God's representative, and said himself, "Blessed is he who takes no offense at me" (Mt. 11:6). A declaration of this kind relates not to Jesus' personal qualities, not to a dogmatic assessment of his person, but to his conduct and to his proclamation. Coming from Jesus, the parable then declares: *"This is how things stand with regard to God's kindness—I know it and am showing it to you—it is like a great lord who once. . . ."*[28]

It is certainly true that the parable does not yield a dogmatic assessment of the "person" of Jesus, but as Linneman observes, in dependence on Fuchs, "There lies an enormous claim, if Jesus answers an attack on his behavior with a parable which speaks of *God's* action!"[29] As we have seen, that claim has continually emerged in our consideration of the parables of Jesus.

Before we conclude our consideration of this parable, we should take up a final question. The implications of the parable for those described as the "last" and their relation to the kingdom of God are clear: they are the ones to whom God shows his compassionate love, the ones who are granted a place in his kingdom. But what of the more problematic implications concerning the "first" to the kingdom? Should we assume, as some have, that since in the parable they receive the same wages as the others, all must inherit the kingdom, the first as well as the last? Such an interpretation presses the details of the parable to extremes; surely it yields results that do not comport well with the teaching Jesus elsewhere addressed to Pharisees who opposed him. Via lays emphasis on another element in the parable—namely, the word of the employer to the spokesman of the grumbling workmen: "Take your pay and go home!" Admittedly the men would have had to go home in any case, but in Via's view the order makes their departure a dismissal. He sees in this a significant point, coming as it does at the conclusion of the parable: "It does not teach that while some need grace, others do not, but rather suggests why some do not receive it. Because of their impenetrable legalistic understanding of existence, grounded in the effort to effect their own security, they exclude themselves from the source of grace."[30] This view seems in accord with the intention of the parable; indeed, it not only vindicates the conduct of Jesus but points to the call for conversion that is implicit in this parable, as it is in so many of the related parables of Jesus. The parable of the Laborers in the Vineyard, like the life of him whom it mirrors, does more than reveal the nature of God: it enables those who receive its message to enter the kingdom of God. It is a grave responsibility to hear a parable of Jesus!

6. THE GREAT FEAST
Matthew 22:1–14, Luke 14:16–24

The parable of the Great Feast has come down to us in two sharply distinct traditions. It is unmistakably one parable, but it is doubtful that a single tradition was modified by the evangelists to produce the two variants we now have.

Luke's version is simpler than Matthew's, and it is closer to the version in the Gospel of Thomas (log. 64) than it is to Matthew's. In Luke and in Thomas, the host of the feast is described simply as "a man," no reference is made to the ill treatment of the servants bringing the invitations or to the destruction of the city of the murderers, and the excuses the people give for not attending are recognizably related (although they are elaborated in the Gospel of Thomas). The description of the occasion as a celebration for the marriage of a king's son rather than as a private individual's party can best be explained as the result of Matthew's having conflated the original version of this parable with that of the man without a wedding garment attending the marriage feast for a king's son. It is an essential part of the situation depicted in Matthew 22:11ff. that the celebration is a *wedding* feast, and yet the silence of the man when questioned as to his dress and the wrath of the king at the insult rendered do not comport with the idea of guests being herded in from the streets. Rather than postulating an unusually inept bit of free composition by Matthew, it is more plausible to assume that he found a short parable about a feast arranged by a king for his son and conjoined it with the parable of a feast arranged by a man for his friends, incorporating the introduction to the second parable into that of the first. Thus, he would have replaced the statement with which Luke begins his parable ("A certain man was giving a big dinner party . . .") with a description drawn from the second parable ("There was a king who prepared a feast for his son's wedding . . ."). Naturally, the second parable would have been truncated by such a treatment, but the essential point of the main parable would not have been affected; if anything, the enormity of the rejection of the invitations to the feast is greatly increased by the fact that the host is depicted as a monarch.[31]

It is likely that once Matthew had represented the host as a king, he was then led to add the other features that distinguish his version of the parable from Luke's—namely, the attacks by the invited on the servants (note the plural; Luke speaks of only one servant) and the wrath of the king, which led to the sacking of the city (Matt. 22:6–7). These elements in the tale appear to have been traditional, and are not simply reflections of the fall of Jerusalem. Their present form recollects elements in the parable of the Wicked Husbandmen, which is recorded in the previous paragraph. In that parable, too, groups of servants are sent, badly treated, and even murdered; in that parable, too, the wrath of the landowner issues in bringing "those bad men to a bad end" (21:41); and in that parable, too, the landowner's son is prominently featured (more so than in the parable of the feast). Why has Matthew done this? Surely because he perceived the connection of basic ideas in the two parables—specifically, the sending of representatives by a man of position, the rejection of the call issued, and the grave consequences suffered by those who rejected the call, both parables having in view the arrival of the eschatological hour.

It may be assumed that the basic image in this parable—the great feast provided by one with resources to give it and to invite many to it—reflects the long-standing symbol of the kingdom of God as a feast. Recent investigators into the parables have strangely rejected this notion. Nevertheless, in view of the familiarity and popularity of this symbol among the Jews, one has to ask whether Jesus could have told this story without being aware of the effect the image would have had on his hearers. There are some images that inevitably evoke associations through long use. Among the Jews, the Exodus would inevitably evoke associations with the promised land, harvest would bring to mind the idea of end of the age, the desert would suggest the demonic, light would signify salvation—and the image of a feast would naturally suggest the kingdom of God. In saying this I do not mean to advocate a simplistic approach to interpretation of these images, nor am I suggesting that any passage that happens to include one of the images should automatically be treated as an allegory; I simply mean to suggest that such images were commonly used as signals to alert listeners about the direction a story was likely to take, and that being the case we would do well to explore such possibilities ourselves. Just as it was natural for Jesus to employ the harvest image in various ways to embody his message of the kingdom, so it would have been natural for him to use the picture of the feast, which would have connoted the idea of good things and life from the dead to all those familiar with Isaiah 25:6ff.

If this parable is in fact about the kingdom, then two significant elements immediately fasten in the mind. The first is the proclamation *everything is now ready*: the beasts are slain, the preparations are complete, the tables are spread, the guests have only to come in and eat. The second is that although those originally invited have spurned the invitations, others have joyfully accepted them; the newly invited guests are streaming into the house and taking their places at the tables, and the house is getting full. The picture does not suggest that God in his merciful providence will arrange a great feast for mankind *some day*. On the contrary, the parable indicates that *the feast is spread*. The Jewish hope is characteristically expressed in the exclamation of a guest sitting at table with Jesus, reported in Luke 14:15: "Happy the man who shall sit at the feast in the kingdom of God!" Whether or not Jesus spoke the parable in that setting, there is no doubt that it was directed precisely to that kind of man making that kind of utterance. Such men have to take in the fact to which they have thus far been blind: the banquet is already ordered, the invitations have been sent out, and they have not accepted theirs! The situation is not unlike that reported in Luke 17:20–21, in which Pharisees question Jesus about when the kingdom of God should come and he replies, "The kingdom does not come with observation . . . for in fact *the kingdom of God is within your reach*." Ironically, according to Luke, Jesus was sitting at table with Pharisees when the pious exclamation about the feast of the kingdom was made, and one gathers that the atmosphere was charged. How different when Jesus is at table with the tax-gatherers and other outcasts! In such a setting the participants experience grace and salvation—they rejoice! That is the sort of table fellowship that celebrates in the here and now the feast of life extended to all mankind. This the Pharisees cannot comprehend, and therein lies their danger. As Linneman has aptly put it,

> The Pharisees do not believe that the kingdom of God is beginning *now*, and see no connection between this event and Jesus' table fellowship with the lost. But Jesus places the situation in the light of a parable in which some people are not prepared to respect the fact that *the meal has already begun*, and have to put up with the consequences. Anyone who is not willing to be summoned to the first course does not get to taste the meal proper.[32]

The situation of present grace and imminent threat is portrayed with added force in the episode of the Wedding Garment. The guests are depicted as occupying the dining hall ("The hall was packed with guests," Matt. 22:10). The king came in to see the company at table and noticed a man who did not have a wedding garment. This, we now realize, does not denote a special garment made for a notable event, but simply a clean garment, one that had been washed for the occasion. The question addressed to the offender is mild enough: "Friend, how do you come to be here without your wedding clothes?" Had he possessed no other garment, or had he been brought in from the street without having received an opportunity to change, he could have said so. It is assumed that the man could have been properly attired and should have been so but that he had chosen to attend the feast otherwise. In so doing he had insulted the king, the occasion, and his fellow guests. When asked for an explanation, he had none to give, and accordingly he was forthwith ejected.

We hear yet again in this parable the echo of the proclamation of Jesus "*Repent*, for the kingdom of God is upon you." This man had neither repented nor sought grace where it could be found. Alike the teaching and the conduct of Jesus indicate that to the repentant, garments of salvation for the day of redemption are available, and they are for wearing *today*, for *now* is the day of salvation.

There is in this parable a curious ambivalence relating to present and future salvation, however. The banquet is ready, the guests have arrived, the hall is packed, and the feast is in progress. The arrival of the king constitutes the climax of the joy of the occasion. But for one, at least, it is the hour of judgment; since it entails an exclusion which is final, it is the *last* hour. How can this be so? The parable appears to be one of those utterances of Jesus wherein distinctions of time seem out of place, when men are confronted with the ultimate issues of grace and judgment, and a decision is demanded of them. Setting out from this parable, Sallie TeSelle wrote of the parables of Jesus that "It is not primarily knowing about the kingdom that appears to be crucial in the parables, but rather deciding when confronted by it." In such circumstances, however, people are apt to find themselves in the position of "identifying with one of the two guest lists"![33]

As with other parables of Jesus, there is good news and bad news here. For those who allow it to be good news it means joy *now*, in anticipation of a coming consummation, for in the fellowship of Jesus one is given a proleptic experience of the feast of the kingdom of God, which is present grace with eternal blessings. The righteous whose hope is based on God's promise to those who merit it perceive this as a threat to their existence—to their present way of life and to their expectation of the future. In that situation nothing in all the world is so hard as to accept a gracious invitation. But the decision regarding that invitation determines whether one is inside the hall or outside it, whether one "lives" or "dies."[34]

7. THE MUSTARD SEED AND THE LEAVEN
Mark 4:30–32, Matthew 13:31–32, Luke 13:18–19

These two short parables are frequently regarded as twins. They appear to have been united at least as early as the Q tradition, for they are linked in both Matthew and Luke, even though they are placed in different contexts. On the other hand, they could hardly have formed a pair in the source available to Mark, for he provides only the parable of the Mustard Seed and appears not to have known of the parable of the Leaven. The Gospel of Thomas includes both parables, but places them in separate contexts. Moreover, while Matthew and Luke coincide closely in their rendering of the parable of the Leaven, Matthew has conflated the Markan and Q wordings of the Mustard Seed parable, and in so doing has modified both. Luke gives what appears to be a fresh introduction to the parable of the Leaven (13:20), which suggests that at some stage in the tradition before him the parable was isolated. Evidently the two parables were brought together because of their similarity.

It is commonly acknowledged that whereas Mark's wording of the Mustard Seed parable is superior to that of Q (= Luke), the form of the parable in Luke is likely to be more original than Mark's, for in Luke it reads like a little narrative, like the parable of the Leaven and Jesus' parables generally. Minor verbal differences in the traditions of the parables need not detain us, for the general picture in both of them is clear. There has, however, been some difference of opinion concerning the significance of the Old Testament allusion (hardly a citation) that concludes the Mustard Seed parable. Mark tells how the seed germinates and grows taller than any other plant, so that "the birds of the heaven settle beneath its shade." Virtually all exegetes have assumed that the passage alludes to the tradition in Ezekiel (17:23 and 31:6) and Daniel (4:10–12) of a great tree, beneath which the beasts find shelter and in the branches of which birds lodge. The imagery in these passages denotes a kingdom embracing many nations. Crossan has protested against linking the parable with this prophetic and apocalyptic tradition. He observes that the Old Testament passages relate to a *tree*, not a *bush*, and that they always contain the parallelism of resting beasts and nesting birds; in his view, there is only one passage in the Old Testament that could rightly be considered to be reflected in the Mustard Seed parable—Psalm 104:12:

> The birds of the air nest on their banks,
> and sing among the leaves.

Here is a picture of nesting birds without mention of a tree, and without the parallelism of beasts in the shade and birds in the branches. Significantly, there is nothing apocalyptic about it; it is merely an expression of God's care for nature. The parable of the Mustard Seed, suggests Crossan, is similarly free of apocalyptic images; like the parable of the Sower, it simply has in view "the gift-like nature, the graciousness and the surprise of the ordinary."[37]

Although this is scarcely an issue of outstanding importance, we may note that Crossan's argument is not very convincing. Psalm 104:12 has much less in common with the imagery of the parable than the Ezekiel and Daniel passages mentioned. The former is a segment of a psalm of praise for creation and the providence that sustains it. The passages in Ezekiel and Daniel, on the other hand, have in view a sovereign power in the world, as does the Mustard Seed parable, which relates to the sovereign power of God! Each of these three descriptions makes references to the *growth* of the plant or tree; moreover, Ezekiel 17:22ff. depicts the planting of a *small shoot* that grows to become a great tree, and has in view Israel's restoration under the divine sovereignty. The affinity between these ideas and those of the parable of the Mustard Seed is obvious; to presume that it is less pertinent than Psalm 104:12 is indeed curious.

As to the content of the two parables, their emphasis is commonly presumed to lie in the *contrast* they present between the beginning and the end of God's sovereign action: the mustard seed is inconspicuous among seeds, but it becomes conspicuous for its height among plants—"a midget of a seed among seeds, but a veritable tree among herbs."[36] Similarly, a little leaven mixed with dough makes the whole a bubbling mass, so great is its power.[37] Most scholars agree that the stress in the parables falls on the beginning and the end of the operation of the kingdom and that the *process* that lies between is ignored. We can appreciate this emphasis, particularly in contrast to views on the "parables of growth" that emphasize the long process required for the growth of the kingdom, from its beginnings in the ministry of Jesus to its distant end in the grand finale of history. But N. A. Dahl has issued a caveat that reminds us of another element in the picture that we ought not to forget. Recognizing the legitimacy of the concern that we should view the parables through the eyes of first-century Palestinians rather than the eyes of twentieth-century man, Dahl calls attention to the fact that "the growth of the seed and the regularity of life have been known to peasants as long as the earth has been cultivated. . . . To Jews and Christians organic growth was but the other side of what was essentially the creative work of God who alone gives growth."[38]

Dahl's point is well taken. It means that along with the contrast between the beginning and the end of the sovereign action of God we have to recognize the continuity between them, and therefore their unity. "We have to do with a single event," Polag has remarked in this connection, "with the destiny of a single object."[39] The single event, the single object, is the coming of the kingdom in its totality, beginning and end and whatever may lie between. When this thought is related to the ministry of Jesus among men in Galilee and Judea it becomes a paradoxical, not to say incredible, idea for many a Jew to accept. It was all but impossible for Jews nurtured in the expectation of the kingdom of God manifest in a revelation of the almighty King of creation working in and through his powerful representative, the Messiah, to identify those expectations with what Jesus was doing among his untutored disciples and the crowd of followers drawn from the "people of the land," whom they considered cursed for not knowing the law (see John 7:49). With this in mind, some scholars have speculated that Jesus may have deliberately chosen the images of yeast (which the cult held to be unclean) and the tree with the birds (which could be understood to represent a kingdom under the judgment of God) as iconoclastic symbols of the kingdom of God. Surely by Pharisaic standards his followers were worldly and unclean![40] That Jesus had such an intent is by no means impossible; in the case of the parable of the Mustard Seed, it would depend on which Old Testament passage(s) Jesus may have had in mind. In any case, we should note that this interpretation involves viewing the situation from the point of view of the blindness of men who do not perceive what is taking place in their midst. Since the parables reckon with the unity of the beginning and the end of the divine sovereignty, we can assume that Jesus was calling on his listeners to consider the nature of this beginning in the light of the end they already knew about. Long ago Lutgert pointed out that our two parables do not simply speak of the contrast between beginning and end but of the contrast between *cause* and *effect*. The *cause* of what is happening is God active in and through Jesus; the *effect* is the powerful initiation of the divine sovereignty.[41] What has begun is the mighty work of God that will end in the transformation of creation.[42]

Approaching the parable from this vantage point, Otto goes on the offensive. The way to dispel any doubts about whether Jesus was the Coming One that might have stemmed from the agony of a John the Baptist or the scorn of the Pharisees was to open the eyes of the doubters to what was happening in the ministry of Jesus:

> In the present case Christ puts something before man's eyes which is already in action around himself and his hearers as a miraculous process which they ought to perceive and rightly understand as being such. . . .

It is the kingdom of God as an eschatological sphere of salvation, which breaks in, makes a small unpretentious beginning, miraculously swells, and increases, as a divine "field of energy" it extends and expands ever farther.[43]

If this is in fact the intent of the parables, then they too are presenting us with a picture of the kingdom as existing in the present. The parables set forth not as dogma but as a self-evident fact the presence among men of the long-awaited kingdom of God in the work of Jesus. They suggest that the ministry of Jesus is nothing other than the sovereign working of almighty God to embrace the world and bring salvation to it. Jesus may have delivered these parables to dispel the unbelief of critics and bolster the wavering faith of his disciples, but we should note that the stories also serve to challenge them to enter the sphere of salvation that has arrived in him and to experience the power of the saving sovereignty that has made its decisive beginning in his work.

Finally, we should observe once more that the parables reflect upon the speaker himself. If the divine sovereignty is present in his action, and if the way to experience it is through listening to and exercising faith in his word, then we are confronted with the demand to recognize his unique role in that sovereignty. As Ambrozic has put it, "There is no other kingdom than the one which Jesus is bringing. There are no other authoritative words about it besides the ones which Jesus is speaking. There is no other way into it apart from the one Jesus is pursuing."[44]

8. THE SEED GROWING SECRETLY
Mark 4:26–29

Despite the brevity of this parable, there has been a considerable difference of opinion as to where the accent in it falls. There are three basic elements in the parable: first, the farmer and his action (v. 26, he sows; v. 27, he sleeps and rises; v. 29, he reaps); second, the seed and its fate (v. 26, it is sown; v. 27, it germinates and incomprehensibly grows; v. 28, it reaches maturation for harvest); and third, the earth and its power to fructify (v. 26, it receives the seed; v. 28, it produces *automate*). The point of view that places emphasis on the first element is as old as the Gospel of Thomas, in which the parable is drastically reduced to read as follows:

> Let there be among you a man of understanding; when the fruit ripened, he came quickly with his sickle in his hand, he reaped it.[45]

Indications of where others feel the stress of the parable falls can be found in the moves of scholars to designate the parable with what they feel to be more appropriate names. B. T. D. Smith and J. Jeremias, for example, have referred to it as "The Parable of the Patient Husbandman," and K. Weiss has called it "The Parable of the Confident Sower." The traditional title lays stress on the second element: "The Seed Growing Secretly" calls attention to the power of the seed to grow once it has been sown. This feature has not received the principal stress in most recent expositions of the parable.[46] Instead, modern treatments have tended to emphasize the third element, the action of the earth described as *automate* in relation to the seed committed to it, since it is this that leads to the harvest in which the parable culminates. This view has been supported by R. Stuhlmann, who contends that the term *automatos* means not "of itself" but "without visible cause," "incomprehensibly," or even "effected by God." It is this last nuance that he argues is especially appropriate in Mark 4:28.[47] He goes on to suggest that the *tertium comparationis* of the parable refers to the certainty and the incomprehensibility of the coming of the harvest after the seed has been sown.[48] This interpretation accords well with the common view of the parable—namely, that it sets forth the coming of the reign of God as a process attributable solely to the miraculous working of God. Those who adopt this view generally link the second and third elements in the parable, stressing that the *seed-in-the-earth* is the heart of the matter, and holding that the man who sows and reaps is a purely incidental figure.

While we might appreciate the intent of such an interpretation, it remains the case that apart from the farmer's action there could be no talk of sowing or reaping. He may not be of *primary* importance in the parable, but without him there is no parable at all! In light of the parable's structure, it is not unreasonable to suggest that we should take account of all three elements in it and so should acknowledge the contribution of all three to the total situation to which the kingdom of God is likened. It is not without significance that all three elements find mention both in the beginning of the parable and in its close. All three have an indispensable place in the total picture.

Let us freely recognize that the parable moves to an unmistakable climax in the harvest. The use of language found in Joel 3:13—"Put in the sickle, for the harvest is ripe"—strengthens what in any case is evident: it is the harvest of the kingdom of God with its accompanying judgment that is depicted. Both the certainty of the event and the stress on the fact that the coming of the kingdom is the result of the miraculous working of God are in harmony with the teaching of Jesus generally, and also with Jewish apocalyptic teaching generally. What distinguishes the parable from related apocalyptic literature is the suggestion that *a sowing has taken place with which the almighty working of God is conjoined and which must therefore inexorably issue in the final harvest of the judgment and kingdom of God.* If we recognize that, all the emphases of the parable will fall into place.

It requires no allegorical treatment of the parable to recognize the ministry of Jesus in word and deed in the initiation of the process that leads to the God-given harvest. The parables of the Mustard Seed and Leaven contrast the inconspicuous nature of the initiation of God's rule in the ministry of Jesus with the great end to which it leads. This parable gives assurance that what has begun with Jesus is sure to reach its destined end in the final kingdom of God because that future lies in the hands of God. But not the future only: it is important for the hearers of Jesus to grasp that God's sovereign action is even now operative with Jesus, and that it will continue to be so unremittingly until it issues in the final kingdom of glory. Thus we can see that this parable brings together and fuses into a single teaching the complementary motifs (1) that the work of Jesus is authorized and enabled by God, (2) that the ministry of Jesus and the final acts of judgment and salvation to come are expressions of God's sovereign action, and (3) that the miraculous working of God in both the present and the future constitutes a unified whole.[49]

This point deserves special attention, for among recent writers on the parables there has come about a remarkable convergence of views in relation to it. This is best illustrated in Kümmel's review of contemporary trends in parable interpretation, in which he adduces this parable as a test case for the soundness of the new approach. He affirms the necessity of taking into account the *whole* picture presented in the parable, contending that when this is done the parable conveys its full message for those who heard it in Jesus' day as well as for those who hear it today:

> The hearer of Jesus . . . is called on both to await with assurance the coming of the sovereignty of God as the completion of the divine action in the world, and to see this certainty grounded in the fact that it has already been "sown"; and that can only mean concretely that the future sovereignty of God has already begun to work with Jesus. But from this viewpoint it also becomes plain that the parable cannot be understood according to its original intention, nor be made known to the hearer of today, unless this link between the prophetic announcement of the divine sovereignty through Jesus and the eschatological estimate of his present is grasped. The parable sets the hearer in the saving action of God which belongs to the end time, which has begun with Jesus and awaits its completion; only if this message of his is taken seriously can it communicate to the man of today, even as to the first hearers of Jesus, the good news of the final salvation of God, declare to him this salvation, promise it to him and encourage him to advance towards it because it has already begun.[50]

It remains for us to ask what circumstances called forth this parable. Arguments that the parable is meant to counter an impatience for Jesus to engage in the kind of action the Zealots urged or to create messianic demonstrations are dubious, since confidence rather than caution is the keynote of the parable. In general, exegetes have been so eager to dismiss the significance of the period of growth between sowing and harvest that they have tended to overlook the concept of the "measure" allotted by God to the period prior to his gift of the kingdom.[51] But in the context of this parable that idea is significant: the sowing has been appointed by God, the harvest has been appointed by God, and the time between is subject to his will. It would be quite in keeping with the intent behind the parables we have already studied if the primary purpose of this parable were less the voicing of opposition to certain hearers of Jesus than it were the encouragement of anyone willing to receive it. We might quite properly assume that the parable's call for faith in the almighty power of God to fulfill his redemptive purpose is complemented by a call for faith that recognizes in the ministry of Jesus the initiation of the divine intention to establish judgment and redemption. If this is in fact a right reading of the situation, it would be hard to improve on Lohmeyer's summary of the purpose of this parable—that it presents its recipients with an "appeal to see as he saw who first saw and spoke this story of the kingdom of God."[52]

9. THE SOWER
Mark 4:1–9, Matthew 13:1–9, Luke 8:4–8

The position assigned to this parable in the synoptic gospels, along with the fact that it is accompanied by an interpretation, indicates the importance that the evangelists attached to it and its message. Ironically, contemporary discussions of the parable reflect great confusion as to its meaning. Linnemann goes into some detail discussing the narrative elements within it but concludes that its meaning is lost and irrecoverable.[53] Scholars have championed no fewer than four different features as the heart of the parable: the Sower, the Soils, the Seed, and the Harvest.

In his introduction to the interpretation of the parable Matthew explicitly refers to it as "the parable of *the Sower*" (Matt. 13:18). If, as is likely, he views the Sower as a reflection of Jesus, he would consider him to be more important than the land or the process of gathering the harvest. Michaelis follows this lead: "The figure of the Sower," he says, "has so to be set before the eyes of the hearers that they see in him a man who has failure upon failure, but whose work yet also finds success."[54] On the other hand, many exegetes have referred to the parable as "The Parable of the Four Soils" (in the German tradition "The Parable of the Fourfold Field"). The emphasis implicit in this designation is clearly in harmony with the interpretation supplied by the evangelists, and the scholars who have employed it have tended to treat the parable as an allegory. In some cases, an emphasis on the element of disaster in the parable has been a by-product of this treatment. For example, Guardini has suggested that the parable depicts "the unspeakable tragedy of almighty truth and creative love doomed, for the most part, to sterility,"[55] and Schniewind has deduced from it that "The normal result of God's word is failure."[56] The validity of such interpretations is doubtful, as we shall see. Meanwhile, we should note that the parable places less stress on the poor qualities of the soils than on the hindrances (birds, weeds, scorching sun) that prevent the seed from bearing fruit.

Should we then recognize the chief element in the parable to be the *seed*? J. D. Kingsbury contends we should do so on the grounds that the force of the parable lies not in the simple notion that the harvest symbolizes the Day of the Lord but in the picture of Mark 4:8a (Matt. 13:8a): "Others fell on good ground and kept bearing fruit." Says Kingsbury, "The Sower is a parable of the Kingdom because it lays stress on the word of proclamation, the vehicle by which God brings his kingdom to men even now."[57]

Neither the importance of the seed in the parable nor its implicit relation to "the word of the Kingdom" (Matt. 13:19) should be denied. Still less, however, should we deny the importance of the *harvest* in the total picture of the parable. An analysis of the form of the parable indicates that it does not present us with a fourfold description of the fate of the seed but rather (in Mark and Matthew) with "a formal balance and contrast between three situations of waste and failure and three situations of gain and success."[58] Mark emphasizes this by his describing each of the first three sowings of seed in the singular and the last in the plural: "some seed (*ho men*) fell beside the path . . . some seed (*allo*) fell on the rocky ground . . . and some seed (*allo*) among the thorns . . . and *other seeds* (*alla*) fell into the good earth." With this in mind, we might note that there is some merit in Dahl's contention that "The general sense of the parable is not that the fate of the seed depends on the nature of the soil, but the fact that the sower can get an extremely rich harvest even though most of the seed has been lost."[59]

Summing up this part of the discussion, one cannot resist the conclusion that here, if anywhere in the parables of Jesus, the belief is justified that a parable may be accorded more than one point—or at least that in the exhibition of one important message there may be subsidiary features of real significance. We have, in fact, a peculiarly complex picture set before us in the parable. Assuming that the evangelists are right in representing this as a parable about the kingdom of God, it is best viewed not simply as a portrayal of the coming of God's kingdom in the world in spite of unfavorable circumstances but as a depiction of *the mission of the kingdom of God*—its operation in the world in word proclaimed and word enacted, opposed in a variety of ways, but coming in spite of all with fullness of blessing.[60]

Some may question the legitimacy of using the phrase "the mission of the kingdom of God" to describe the thrust of this parable, but to do so serves the purpose of calling attention to a characteristic of the instruction of Jesus that we have consistently noted in the course of our study thus far: throughout his teaching, he depicts the coming of the kingdom of God not solely in terms of the majesty of the theophany, the Day of the Lord, and the Last Judgment (although he by no means denies any of these elements) but he pointedly likens the kingdom of God to the open arms of the Father, to the strong arms of a seeking shepherd, to the boundless mercy of a forgiving creditor, to the generosity of an employer who takes on eleventh-hour laborers, to a treasure at hand for the finding. These are representations of a divine sovereignty engaged in action among needy humanity in the present time, with blessedness in store for the future. To put it another way, the blessedness God has in store for men he brings to them in the here and now. How does he do that? Through the bearer of the kingdom, as he goes in God's name to the people who have received the promise of the kingdom. *The mission of the one who proclaims the kingdom and bears its grace is none other than the mission of God acting in sovereign graciousness toward men.*

The contribution of the parable in illuminating the situation encountered in the mission of the kingdom is its depiction of the naturalness—one might say the *expectedness*—of obstacles and opposition of many kinds. What if there is resistance to the word of proclamation (note the charge of blasphemy against Jesus for declaring forgiveness, Mark 2:7) and revulsion at the deeds of the kingdom (Jesus being accused of being the agent of Beelzeboul, Mark 5:7), rejection in the unbelief of those who see and hear (Mark 6:22ff.), and a forsaking of the bearer of the kingdom by those who once welcomed his ministry (John 6:66)? This is the situation in which the kingdom of God has to operate—a fallen world which needs the saving sovereignty of God. It belongs to the context of the divine mission, as truly as thorns and thistles and birds and paths and scorching heat are part and parcel of a farmer's work in producing a harvest. Jesus understood this, accepted it, and explained it to his hearers in this parable.

But if realism requires recognition of thorns and thistles and obdurate hearts and unyielding opposition, we should also note that the fact that the world is made and sustained by God and that the word of promise partakes of his omnipotence dictates that these harsh realities will never amount to more than the *context* in which the work of grace operates. Guardini's words about "the unspeakable tragedy of almighty truth and creative love doomed . . . to sterility" are true to life, but how did he bring himself to include the phrase "for the most part" without any qualification? This is not true to the whole parable, any more than it is to the total message of Jesus about the kingdom of God. The figure of the harvest calls to mind the end to which the sovereignty of God is working, an end elsewhere represented as the harvest of the Seed growing secretly, the full growth of the mustard plant, the leavening of the whole mass of dough, the joyous feast of God for the whole world. Not infrequently 2 Esdras 8:41–42 is compared with the parable of the Sower to note the use of the same symbols by a near contemporary of Jesus. But let us recall that it is Jesus speaking, not the author of 2 Esdras! How differently the two employ their symbols!

> Just as the husbandman sows much seed upon the ground and plants a multitude of plants, and yet not all which were sown shall be saved in due season, nor shall all that were planted take root, so also they that are sown in the world shall not all be saved.

The pessimism of this simile reflects an outlook on God and the world as different from that in the parables of Jesus as the arctic wastes are from Galilee. There's realism in Jesus, but it is the realism that lives in the assurance of God's power to fulfill his *good* word.

Since related parables of Jesus teach not only the advent of the kingdom in power at the end but its incursion into the life of man in the present, it is likely that we are intended to understand the parable of the Sower in the same way. The mission of the sovereign God constitutes more than just a promise of untold blessing in the future; it also serves to convey untold blessing in the present. To a degree the images in the parable of sowing and reaping do not suit the reality they illuminate. The sowing itself is a representation of the approach of the saving sovereignty to man. Moreover, the image of a thirtyfold, as compared with a hundredfold, harvest does not comport with the reality of resurrection to life in a new world in the fellowship of God, although it is comprehensible in relation to the sovereignty of God operative in the ministry of Jesus, in which we can assume that there will inevitably be differences in the ways people respond to the experience of God's sovereign graciousness. The parable provides us with a representation of the effectiveness of the sovereignty of God in the mission of Jesus, making a decisive beginning despite all opposition and anticipating the final glory to which God is guiding the present.[61]

The context in which Mark places the parable of the Sower may well provide a clue as to what occasioned Jesus to tell it. The gospel narrative preceding the parable includes reports of the following: a series of incidents in which Jesus comes into conflict with Jewish opponents (2:1–3:6); a subsequent departure from the synagogue to minister in public, chiefly beside the lake (3:7); accusations of scribes from Jerusalem that Jesus worked by the power of the devil; the separation of Jesus from his family (3:20ff.); and the appointment of the Twelve to be associates with Jesus in his ministry (3:14ff.). There then follows the scene of Jesus preaching from a boat to crowds assembled on the lakeside, and of his declaring to them the parable of the Sower (4:1ff.). This narrative reflects a topical arrangement of the evangelist's material rather than the chronological succession of events as they occurred; nevertheless, the mounting opposition to Jesus, along with the continuing hearing that he received among the people, would provide a fitting context for the message of the parable, which suggests that he was neither deterred by the opposition nor deceived by the acclamation. Jesus uses the parable to speak to his audience about their own situation: if any are dismayed by a growing opposition to Jesus that he does not attempt to dispel, let them take into account the realities of God's work among men, which may be resisted for the time being, but which is nevertheless powerfully working towards its appointed end, and which can be experienced by all who are ready to respond to God's gracious approach. The parable accordingly provides encouragement to the dismayed, and a call to faith to the uncommitted.

Note on the Interpretation of the Parable
of the Sower in Mark 4:14–20

We have explored the parable of the Sower without making any reference to the interpretation of the parable given in Mark 4:14–20. Questions of the authenticity of the passage raised by such scholars as J. Jeremias (see *The Parables of Jesus*, trans. S. H. Hooke, rev. ed. [London, 1963], pp. 77–79) are formidable. Jeremias has argued that the eschatological point of the parable is lost in the interpretation: "The emphasis has been transformed from the eschatological to the psychological aspect of the parable." C. E. B. Cranfield disputes Jeremias's view, however, suggesting that "The harvest of v. 20 is eschatological not psychological, and the implication of vv. 14–20 as a whole is that the seriousness of the question how the Word is received derives from the fact that it is the Word of the kingdom of God that has come near to men in Jesus, and that their final destiny depends on their reception of it" (*The Gospel according to St. Mark*, Cambridge Greek Testament [Cambridge, 1963], p. 161). Both A. M. Ambrozic (*The Hidden Kingdom: A Redaction-Critical Study of the References to the Kingdom of God in Mark's Gospel*, Catholic Biblical Quarterly—Monograph Series, 2 [Washington, 1972], pp. 100–101) and W. L. Lane (*The Gospel of Mark*, New International Commentary on the New Testament [Grand Rapids, 1974], pp. 162–63) concur with Cranfield's interpretation. Those scholars who recognize that the parable is not solely concerned with the harvest, that it also takes account of the difficulties encountered by the mission of the kingdom, find that the basic idea of the interpretation comports with the range of the parable's meanings. Schnackenburg has suggested that the interpretation shows "a freedom of applied instruction which is conscious of its original meaning and presupposes it" (*God's Rule and Kingdom* [London, 1963], p. 152). That judgment does justice to the observable data.

---

10. THE TARES AND THE WHEAT
Matthew 13:24–30

It is evident that in following and expanding Mark's chapter of parables, Matthew chose to omit the parable of the Seed Growing Secretly and substitute the parable of the Tares and the Wheat. In view of certain formal similarities between the two parables, it was perhaps inevitable that someone should raise the question of whether Matthew rewrote Mark's parable and transformed it into what we now have in the parable of the Tares.[62] As it turns out, however, few scholars have been persuaded that this happened; most contend that the Tares has a distinctive plot and a message of its own, different from that of the Sower or of the Seed Growing Secretly.[63] More recently some scholars have urged that the original parable was shorter than its present length and that Matthew expanded it to include ideas of concern to him, but the arguments they have thus far advanced for such an occurrence are hardly compelling in their plausibility; moreover, their arguments tend to cancel one another out.[64] The version in the Gospel of Thomas is certainly shorter, but further study indicates that Thomas has reproduced a pruned version rather than that Matthew has elaborated a version similar to that in Thomas. One has the feeling that Thomas either wished to give only the gist of the parable or that he simply failed to discern its message (note that he omits the all-important words, "Let both grow together").[65]

The situation described in the parable was by no means an everyday occurrence, but examples of this kind of deed have been noted in various parts of the world in ancient and modern times.[66] In Palestine it was not uncommon for darnel seeds, or bearded wheat, which are grown for feeding poultry, to be accidentally mingled with ordinary wheat used for sowing. When this occurred, the darnel was commonly rooted out along with other weeds in the field. The deduction of the farmer that an enemy had been at work in his field indicates that an unusually large amount of the darnel was observable. This explains why he would not allow his servants to attempt to root out the darnel: by this time the roots would have mingled with those of the wheat, and removing them would have endangered the harvest. Hence the decision to let both grow to the harvest, when the wheat alone could be gathered into sheaves and the darnel bound into bundles for later use as fuel.[67]

Bultmann considered the story to be "a pure parable" rather than an allegory, as Jülicher and others have maintained.[68] But what is the message of the parable? The instinct of exegetes to focus on the command "Let both grow together till the harvest" (v. 30) is surely right, since this command establishes the point that the present is not the time for separating the "good" from the "bad": that is for God to do in the revelation of the final kingdom and judgment. But what kind of separation is it that the parable is suggesting we ought not to attempt, and what sort of people are involved? It has been popularly assumed that the good seed represents true Christians and that the darnel represents spurious believers within the Christian communities; the parable is said to teach that we should avoid trying to separate *true and false members of the church*. Employing this understanding of the parable, Augustine made effective use of it in his controversy with the Donatists, and the view he established has lasted into the present era. It is noteworthy, however, that the Donatists protested that Augustine had misused the parable, since Jesus said that the field was the *world*. They argued that the parable did not speak to the dispute between Augustine and themselves, because the issue at hand was not whether ungodly men should be tolerated in *the world* but whether they should be tolerated in *the church*. Trench responded to this objection with some warmth himself: "It must be evident to every one not warped by a previous dogmatic interest that the parable is, as the Lord announced, concerning 'the kingdom of heaven,' or the Church."[69]

Trench's statement gives us an indication of how theology has changed over the centuries. The ecclesiastical application of the parable to no small degree reflects the experience of the church as a "corpus mixtum," encouraged beyond all horizons of the New Testament communities by the Constantinian settlement, the state churches of Europe, and a noneschatological understanding of the kingdom of God. The combination of these factors has led to a misunderstanding of even the interpretation of the parable supplied by Matthew in verses 36–43. For there can be no doubt that when Matthew stated that the field was the world he was referring to the whole of mankind, over which the Son of Man was exalted as Lord; for Matthew, the kingdom of the Son of Man (v. 41) was as truly an eschatological phenomenon as the kingdom of the Father (v. 43).[70] As with other parables of the kingdom, we must understand the parable of the Tares within the context of the ministry of Jesus if we are to understand it at all.

In this parable, as in all the parables of growth, the picture of sowing reflects the initiation of the saving sovereignty of God in the word and deed of Jesus. But whereas certain of the other parables suggest that the divine intervention is more modest than was awaited, the negative factors are here given more prominence. Along with the powers of the kingdom of God among men there is a contrary force, and it is apparently formidable enough to threaten the promise of the future.

It is difficult to know how much emphasis we should put on individual features in a parable of this kind, but the prominent element in this parable—the "enemy action," as it were—is deeply significant for Jesus' ministry. Jesus himself spoke of the kingdom of God as being under violent attack (Matt. 11:12) and on many occasions referred to his ministry in terms of conflict with evil powers. By the finger of God he cast out demons (Matt. 12:28), and by the same Spirit he was stronger than the Strong One who held men captive (Mark 3:27). His successes led to allegations that he was an agent of the devil, and these accusations became part of the contrary forces directed against him. Not without reason Jesus could characterize these events as a countermovement to the divine sovereignty operative in his ministry.

But why did he permit it to continue? If he was stronger than the "Strong Man," why did he not declare war against the agencies of wickedness? This matter falls in a different category than that of the scandal Jesus created by consorting with the religiously unclean; rather, it reflects the scandal he caused for John the Baptist, who was troubled by the question of why Jesus would allow Herod to carry on in his evil ways without rebuke if he were indeed the Coming

One. It also reflects the scandal Jesus constituted to the Zealots, who wondered why he should hesitate to exercise his power to destroy the Roman tyranny and deliver the righteous if he were indeed empowered by the sovereignty of God. The associates of the Qumran Community would have been similarly scandalized, questioning why Jesus had no program for ridding the earth of the sons of darkness in preparation for the holy kingdom of God if indeed he had authority from God to do so.

It is in the context of concerns such as these that the picture in the parable of the Tares comes alive. Its purpose is to point to the fact that along with the new thing that has come into the world with Jesus—namely, the incursion of the divine sovereignty—evil is also at work among men, an enemy opposing the work of God. To this problem the command "Let both grow together till the harvest" presents a solution different from that offered by any of Jesus' contemporaries, a solution based on a different understanding of the time in which they stood. God had been graciously pleased to make the redeeming power of his sovereignty in and through Jesus operative in the present. The task of Jesus in this time was not to mediate the judgment of God on men but to be the agent of the redemptive powers of the kingdom. Having faith in God's sovereignty, he knew he could leave the future to God—hence his appeals for the reverse of separation from sinners: he called for showing the divine compassion to them, thereby offering them the opportunity to repent and experience the divine sovereignty. The occasion on which Jesus and his disciples were making their way to Jerusalem and Samaritan villagers refused them hospitality because they were Jews provides a perfect example of the attitude which the parable seeks to contradict: when the representatives of the kingdom of God are confronted by hostility, their task is not to respond with hostility in kind but to manifest the divine sovereignty in a patience consonant with that of the King, who has ever been long-suffering towards his erring creatures (Matt. 5:45).

The command "Let both grow together till the harvest," then, signifies a rejection of the impatience of the righteous and a call for the patience of God. The parable in which the call is set, like the other parables of growth, takes its point of departure from the reality of the saving sovereignty of God among men in the present. But more than the others, this parable emphasizes the fact that the function of the divine sovereignty in this time is to *save* men, not to judge them. God's sovereignty certainly manifests itself in judgment as well, but judgment will be revealed in God's time; till then it is the responsibility of the faithful to share the attitude of the Lord of the kingdom toward the impenitent and in the spirit of divine grace show them the power of redeeming love. The parable also reminds those who have hitherto been unresponsive to the word of the kingdom that it remains possible for them to open their lives to grace now, that the harvest God will someday reap can mean life for them rather than the loss of it.

Note on the Interpretation of the Parable
of the Tares and the Wheat, Matthew 13:36–43

As with the interpretation of the parable of the Sower in Mark 4:13–20, there is considerable evidence to indicate the evangelist's hand in the composition of the interpretation of the parable of the Tares and the Wheat. Jeremias's demonstration that the interpretation exhibits "a simply unique collection of the linguistic characteristics of the evangelist Matthew" (see *The Parables of Jesus*, pp. 82ff.) is all but irresistible. The same cannot be said, however, of his comments on the leading concepts employed in the interpretation, and above all his insistence that the kingdom of the Son of Man is a designation of the church.

It may not be out of place to observe a couple of points here. First, the interpretation is harmonious with the parable itself. As Michaelis has suggested, "The parable formally demands such an interpretation of its individual features" (*Die Gleichnisse Jesu*, Die urchristliche Botschaft, 23te Abteilung [Hamburg, 1956], p. 50). Second, we might note that the scope of the interpretation is limited. Schniewind suggests that it ought not be called an "interpretation," since it only serves to explain the self-evident (*Das Evangelium nach Matthäus*, Das Neue Testament Deutsch [Göttingen, 1956], p. 171). Perhaps it would be better to say that it excerpts certain features from the parable for the sake of clarity and assumes the rest. Apparently the evangelist believed that once he had identified the leading elements in the parable its intention would be plain.

It has been suggested that behind Matthew's interpretation there lies a tradition that preserves elements of the instruction of Jesus. Among those holding this view are Schlatter (*Der Evangelist Matthäus* [Stuttgart, 1948], pp. 445–46), Schniewind (*Das Evangelium nach Matthäus*, pp. 171–72), Michaelis (*Die Gleichnisse Jesu*, pp. 50–51), Bonnard (*L'Évangile selon Saint Matthieu*, Commentaire du Nouveau Testament [Neuchatel, 1963], p. 204), and Hill (*The Gospel of Matthew*, New Century Bible Commentary [Grand Rapids, 1972], p. 235).

---

11. THE DRAGNET
Matthew 13:47–50

This parable has obvious similarities with the parable of the Tares and Wheat, and equally obvious differences from it. The likenesses are accentuated by the interpretation in verses 49–50, which in its entirety reflects the interpretation of the Tares.[71] But the differences must not be overlooked. One such difference involves the idea of separation. In the parable of the Tares and Wheat the alien elements are introduced after the preliminary sowing, whereas in the parable of the Dragnet the different kinds are gathered at the same time. Further, in the parable of the Tares and Wheat a distinction between the present and the future is implicit in the command to wait before making a separation ("Let both grow together until . . ."), whereas in the parable of the Dragnet the catch is followed almost at once by the separation of the different kinds of fish.

The relationship between these two parables has evoked different reactions from exegetes. Otto has argued that the parable of the Dragnet must originally have consisted of verse 47 only: "The kingdom of heaven is like a net which was thrown into the sea and gathered fish of every kind." He goes on to suggest that the picture has nothing to do with categorizing men as good and bad, but simply represents them as different—"of every kind," like the animals in Genesis 1:25:

> Jesus does not speak of the good and bad and of their fate in the last judgment, but of a present miracle of the divine power, which, already breaking in, already working, succeeds in bringing together men of every kind who otherwise would never have met—a marvel to behold, a sign for seeing eyes.[72]

Appealing as this interpretation may be, it is based on an arbitrary judgment. Otto appears to have overlooked the fact that in a Jewish setting, fishing of this kind cannot be undertaken without separating the clean fish from the unclean (cf. Lev. 11:10), and fish deemed fit to eat from those regarded as inedible.[73] Jesus' audience would naturally have assumed that a catch of fish would have to be followed by a sorting of fish.

On the other hand, Jeremias has gone to the other extreme in arguing that the main point of the parable is the element of separation. He paraphrases the opening clause of the parable as follows:

> It is the case with the coming of the kingdom of God—to wit, as with the sorting out of the fish.[74]

In fact, however, the parable is formulated as a single sentence, and its intention is surely to affirm that the kingdom of heaven is like the action set forth in the *whole* statement:

> The kingdom of heaven is like a net which was thrown into the sea and gathered fish of every kind; when it was full, men drew it ashore and sat down and sorted the good into vessels but threw away the bad. (RSV)

It is the entire action of throwing out the net, gathering fish of every kind, drawing in the net, and sorting the fish on the shore that Jesus is setting before his audience as a picture of the kingdom of heaven.

It is likely that it was precisely this inextricable connection between large-scale fishing and the sorting of the catch that made the image attractive to Jesus. Whoever goes fishing in this way knows that the catch will be mixed and that it will have to be sorted later. In Jüngel's words,

> To the gathering function [of the net] corresponds the separating function [of the fishers]. Without the gathering the catch of fish is not possible, without the separating it would remain meaningless. The separation presupposes the gathering; the gathering proceeds to the separation.[75]

Putting such stress on this conjunction of functions may appear to be laboring the obvious, but it is the key to the parable that the kingdom of heaven is likened to both together—that is to say, *the spreading of the net and the gathering of the fish are, along with the separation that follows them, integral to the eschatological event.* That insight is not trite; it is of supreme significance. For the reality symbolized by the catch of fish is God's sovereign action: his kingdom is at work among men, as truly as his judgment will manifest it.

Seine nets necessarily gather fish *of every kind.* Can it be that Jesus is addressing the parable to the disciples, as part of a directive for going out on mission to Israel—as "fishers of men," as it were? Many scholars have suggested that this is the case.[76] Others protest vigorously against it. Lohmeyer stresses the fact that it is God's kingdom, God's sovereignty, God's might that is being portrayed here—"let men call it what they will, the word or will or finger of God."[77] The reminder is salutary, although the question then becomes how God is exercising his sovereign power. In light of the other parables of Jesus, one answer alone is possible: God is gathering men of every kind through the ministry of the word and deed of Jesus. If indeed any reference to the disciples was intended in this parable, it must be only by virtue of the fact that they are associated with the ministry of their master.

Granting this to be so, what could have prompted Jesus to picture God's sovereign operation in this way? In all probability he did so because he knew that this aspect of his ministry would not only be unfamiliar to his listeners but would actually be offensive to many of them. The phrase "of every kind" holds the key to the offense. It was not so much the problem that Jesus' ministry led him to associate with every kind of person—to eat with tax collectors and "sinners," for instance—but that it was his intent to reject all barriers of any kind in communicating the good news of the kingdom of God to the nation. As God's "Evangelist," he "showed to all the divine grace in its universal greatness and brought the divine forgiveness to all."[79] This is so familiar a feature of the ministry of Jesus that we are in danger of overlooking how greatly he differed from what we know of his contemporaries in this respect. John the Baptist in the wilderness, waiting for the penitent to come to him; the Essenes in Qumran, watching and waiting for the call to march to the Day of the Lord; the Pharisees keeping their skirts clear of the defiled; the Sadducees maintaining the cultus in the temple and trying to maintain good relations with the Romans; the Zealots raising the flag of God against his foes—all of these had visions of the kingdom of God far different from that in the parable of the Dragnet.

In the setting in which Jesus delivered this parable, the image of the dragnet was peculiarly apt. Everybody recognized that a fisherman had to take all kinds of fish in his net. Everyone knew that the fish that were caught had to be separated once the boat reached shore. That was simply part of the business of fishing. And that is how it is with the kingdom of God.

From what we have said thus far, it should be evident that the parable of the Dragnet has an important feature in common with the parable of the Tares and the Wheat—namely, that it has nothing to do with the problem of the mixed church and the separation of true and false members. Rather, it represents God's gracious approach to the common people through Jesus. "The kingdom of heaven is like . . ." is the theme. The modern counterpart would not be the mixed church but the church taking the good news of redemption to Skid Row, to the casinos of Las Vegas and Monte Carlo, to clubs where homosexuals and transvestites gather, to taverns and dance halls and discotheques where long-haired youths stamp to loud music, and to those thousand and one places where men and women gather for leisure and pleasure but where many Christians would not want to be caught dead, let alone alive. So far as many are concerned, the fishing boats have been transformed into arks, and the nets have been left on the shore to rot; it is understandable that such would come to believe that the parable was intended to address the church about the church. But in Jesus' day there were still *fishing* boats!

One cannot help but wonder whether among those who listened to the parable from the lips of Jesus there were any who had been gathered by the net but had not yet taken to themselves the word of the kingdom he preached. For such the parable would have given not a hint of the delights of the kingdom of God, but it would have provided a powerful motive for listening further and responding fully to the word of proclamation: the separation that God himself had ordained and would effect lay ahead. The challenge to decision presented by the parable is luminously clear.[79]

12. THE BRIDEGROOM AND HIS FRIENDS; OLD CLOTHES; NEW WINE
Mark 2:18–22

These three parabolic sayings are bound together by the common theme of the new situation created by the ministry of Jesus and its relation to the old. Their origin and composition are still debated. Verse 19a is widely considered to be a dominical saying. Bultmann has suggested that it was an unattached logion that was worked up into an apothegm—verses 18–19a—in order to defend the church's conduct of not fasting at a time when it was attempting to distinguish itself from the Baptist sect. Bultmann goes on to suggest that verses 19b–20 were subsequently added to this apothegm, reflecting the changed attitude of the *later* church to fasting, and that the evangelist then appended the two parabolic sayings of verses 21–22 to the combined passage.[80] Bultmann's argument concerning verses 18–19a has not been generally accepted, but agreement is widespread that verses 19b–20 reflect the church's practice of fasting; many scholars contend that this point is substantiated by the fact that in verse 19a the language concerning the bridegroom is parabolic, whereas in verse 19b it appears to be allegorical, and in verse 20 this representation has been conjoined with what a few hold to be a prediction of the passion.[81]

Despite the impressive support for this view, there remains reason to question it. Jesus was known to approve fasting under certain conditions (see Matt. 6:16ff.). Was the earliest church more radical than Jesus in this matter? And would its teachers have later presumed to transform a saying that in the tradition was believed to affirm one mode of conduct (namely, repudiation of fasting) in order to promote the opposite (namely, observance of fasting)?[82] It would be interesting to know if the early church ever did ban fasting or need a reason to justify fasting; the argument that it did impose such a ban for a time and then reverse the decision is based on very insubstantial evidence.[83] Moreover, the presumed difference between the subject of verse 19a and verse 19b is not immediately obvious. Wellhausen saw no difference between the two halves of the verse at all, and he also noted that he failed to find adequate grounds for separating verse 19 from verse 20.[84] Vincent Taylor has argued that verse 19 is in fact a single unit, citing the basic unity of thought and the structural parallelism of the text.[85] Two recent discussions of the parable have strongly asserted a similar position.[86] A. Kee maintains that there is nothing in verses 19b–20 that is not present or implied in verse 19a; he notes in particular that the clause "while the bridegroom is with them" (verse 19a) assumes that he will be taken away (verse 20). However, on the basis of this assumption, Kee has joined others in contending that the entire passage must be a later interpolation. The argument goes something like this: Matthew 6:16ff. tells us that Jesus enjoined fasting in the right spirit; since we know that he encouraged fasting in secret to God, we might expect that he would have responded to the question recorded in verse 18 by saying something like "How do you know that we don't fast?"—and since he did not respond in this fashion, we can assume that the text that does appear was inserted later.[87] But surely this assessment depends on a misreading of the intention not only of Mark 2:18–22 but probably of Matthew 6:16ff. as well. The three parables in this passage were not delivered in order to formulate a church rule on fasting but rather to describe the new situation that had come about through the ministry of Jesus.

If verses 19–20 are in fact a unified whole, the question of the authenticity of verse 19a is obviously important for our understanding of verses 19b–20. Since there are no typically Markan links connecting verse 18 with verse 19 or connecting verses 18–20 with verses 21–22, we can provisionally assume that Mark found the whole paragraph in the controversy series of 2:1–3:6 and left it relatively untouched.[88] Verse 18 provides a plausible setting for verse 19a and may well have provided the original context for the saying of Jesus. In any case, it is difficult to believe that verse 19a was delivered or transmitted as a statement complete in itself, for it is clearly meant to follow something.[89] If the emphasis in verses 19–20 is in fact on the joy of Jesus' presence with his disciples, as opposed to the severity of the regimen of fasting pursued by the disciples of John the Baptist, then we can at least say that verses 19b–20 provide a not inappropriate conclusion to verse 19a. It may well be the case that this question simply cannot be resolved. At least it is not of prime importance; the chief significance of verses 18–22 is the light the passage throws on Jesus' estimate of the present time.

According to Mark's narrative, disciples of John and the Pharisees[90] were engaged in a fast, and some people asked Jesus why his disciples (and, by implication, Jesus himself) were not. We can assume that the occasion was not one of the legally prescribed fasts, such as that enjoined for the Day of Atonement (Lev. 16–29, 23:27), which Jesus and his disciples would have observed. Nevertheless, the way in which the question is framed gives the impression that the questioner considered their decision not to fast to be a failing. The Jewish sects of the first century had developed an interest in fasting that Muddiman describes as "very nearly obsessive."[91] To go beyond what was prescribed in the law was held to be mark of piety, and to neglect such practices was held to be a sign of doubtful devotion. We know that the Pharisees customarily fasted twice weekly (cf. Luke 18:2). How frequently John's disciples fasted we do not know, but it is evident that they followed in the steps of their master, of whom Jesus said, "John came, neither eating nor drinking" (Matt. 11:18). While the Pharisees and John's disciples must have had different motives in fasting, they would have shared the conviction that fasting was closely bound to repentance— although the Pharisees would have undertaken their fasting as a means of expiating sins or perhaps to acquire merit, whereas John's disciples would have stressed the relation of fasting to the imminent end of the age and engaged in their fasts as an "eschatological demonstration" of repentance in prospect of the impending day of judgment.[92]

The reply of Jesus recorded in verse 19 gives a striking indication of the difference between the emphasis of his proclamation and that of John, between the kinds of life the two led, and between the movements they created:

"Can you expect the bridegroom's friends to fast while the bridegroom is with them? As long as they have the bridegroom with them, there can be no fasting."

The situation of Jesus with his disciples is comparable to that of a bridegroom with his "friends"—that is, the guests whom he has invited to the wedding.[93] In such a setting, fasting has no place. "On the contrary," says Billerbeck, "the chief duty of the friends and wedding guests of the bridegroom consisted in their contributing to their utmost to the delight of the bridal pair during the wedding celebration. For this reason they were even freed from certain religious duties of the more serious sort."[94]

The general implication of the saying is clear, but we should look more closely into the details of the point being made. Jeremias has suggested that the phrase "while the bridegroom is with them" is a paraphrase for "during the wedding festival," so that the thrust of the saying is "Can one weep at a wedding?" The answer, of course, is No. "Similarly," says Jeremias, "it would be nonsensical for the disciples of Jesus to fast when they have the joy of the coming age of salvation, and they already possess the gifts of salvation."[95] While this interpretation harmonizes with the intention of the saying, reflecting as it does the arrival of the new age and the feast of the kingdom as a wedding celebration, it does have its weak points. In substituting "wedding" for "bridegroom," Jeremias appears to have been motivated by a desire to avoid at all cost the equation "the bridegroom = Jesus." In support of his understanding, Jeremias points out that the Messiah is not identified with a bridegroom anywhere else in Jewish literature; when associated imagery is used in that literature—namely, the idea of betrothal in this age and "marriage" in the age to come[96]—the role of bridegroom is filled exclusively by Yahweh, and the role of bride is filled exclusively by his people Israel. But, this explanation aside, Jeremias's interpretation has the effect of turning a statement about *relationships* in the unique situation of the present into an impersonal statement about the nature of the *time*.

The focus of the saying is not on the gifts of salvation that are inherited in the kingdom (cf. Matt. 11:5) but on the privilege of the disciples to enjoy fellowship with their master at his festive table. Moreover, this emphasis is clearly important within the context of the saying, which was prompted by a veiled criticism of the disciples (and obliquely of Jesus himself) for feasting when they might better have been fasting. Jesus' answer does not suggest that the time had come for men to be merry in general; rather, it points to a specific situation: *the bridegroom is present, and it is only appropriate that his companions should celebrate.* Thus, the underlying point of the parable is not so much that the time has called forth the bridegroom as it is that the bridegroom's presence determines the time and what takes place in it.[97] Admittedly, such an understanding of the saying assumes that Jesus was making an implicit claim to be the Bridegroom of the eschatological kingdom, but does that really constitute a problem? Is it not quite in keeping with the seriousness with which he viewed his vocation as representative of the divine sovereignty in this time, itself unparalleled within Judaism, that he should go beyond any representation of the Messiah that had appeared previously in Jewish literature? Goppelt summarizes the parable by saying that "Fasting . . . is suitable for one who awaits God's rule, not for the one who brings it."[98]

Returning to the idea that in this parable Jesus is making an *implicit* claim to be the Bridegroom of the people of the kingdom, we might note Roloff's suggestion that in this passage Jesus is not employing picture language that reflects an obvious state of affairs but rather is employing enigmatic language.[99] For us, who ponder the saying in the context of the teaching of Jesus, its intent is plain, but it would not have been so evident to the original hearers. On the contrary, it is a good example of the function of a parable to "tease" the mind, as Dodd put it, to evoke reflection on the significance of what was said.

If verse 19a is enigmatic, verses 19b–20 are even more so. Verse 19b adds little to the preceding clause beyond strengthening the main idea through repetition: "The bridegroom's friends cannot fast so long as the bridegroom is with them." The phrase "so long as" anticipates the eventual departure of the bridegroom, and it is this that constitutes the subject of verse 20:

> Days will come when the bridegroom will be taken from them, and then they will fast on that day.

What exactly is meant by this statement?

Some exegetes have maintained that the language relating to the "removal" of the bridegroom denotes no more than that he must leave his friends, that it stands in contrast to the emphasis laid on his presence with them, and that it is not meant to suggest that the departure may be forcible or through death.[100] But if this is indeed the intent of the verse, then it is most unusual that the term *aparthe* was chosen to convey it, for the verb in the passive connotes removal through the agency of another (or others).

Muddiman has noted the close association of thought between the parable of the Bridegroom and Joel 2:16, which in context reads as follows:

> Blow the trumpet in Zion,
> proclaim a solemn fast, appoint a day of abstinence . . .
> *bid the bridegroom leave his chamber*
> *and the bride her bower.*
> Let the priests, the ministers of the Lord,
> stand weeping between the porch and the altar
> and say, "Spare thy people, O Lord . . ."

Muddiman suggests that the statement about the bridegroom in this passage provided the inspiration for the parable of the Bridegroom, and that the passive verb *aparthe* in Mark 2:20 has replaced a verb in the active voice (*apairo* in the active can be intransitive, in which case it means "depart"). Support for this interpretation can be found both in Logion 104 of the Gospel of Thomas, which reads "When the bridegroom *comes out* of the bridal chamber, then let them fast and let them pray," and in the reading in the Venetian Diatessaron, discovered by Quispel: "The bridegroom will not be with them, but will *go away*."[101] If such was the intent of the original statement, the passive *aparthe* may have been introduced under the influence of Isaiah 53:8.[102] If such were the case, the saying in its original form could be viewed as an assertion of the authority of

Jesus in relation to fasting, comparable to his authority regarding the sabbath and the forgiveness of sins. Certainly the link between the Markan passage and that in Joel is striking, but it is questionable whether it is so clear that we can safely use it as a key to determining the meaning of the parable with regard to the time when fasting will be appropriate. The main thrust of the Markan saying is not so much to emphasize the fasting that lies ahead as to stress the joy of the present, when Jesus is able to hold table fellowship with his friends. Verse 20 simply serves to fill out the picture and underscore the positive element in verse 19.[103]

It would appear therefore that it is most natural to interpret verse 20 as denoting an anticipated removal of Jesus, and to assume that the approximation of the language to Isaiah 53:8 ("his life is taken from the earth," *airetai apo tes ges he zoe autou*) indicates that he will be removed through his death. The fasting would then relate to the grief of the period that would follow.[104]

But precisely what is that period? The later church assumed that it was the interval between the departure of Jesus from the world and his parousia, and so saw in the saying a call for Christians to fast. But the parable is more closely akin to John 16:16–22, which speaks of a short period of desolation among the disciples that will be followed by a joyous reunion with the Lord and a resumption of fellowship with him:

> "Are you discussing what I said: 'A little while, and you will not see me, and again a little while, and you will see me'? *In very truth I tell you, you will weep and mourn, but the world will be glad. But though you will be plunged in grief, your grief will be turned to joy.* A woman in labour is in pain because her time has come; but when the child is born she forgets the anguish in her joy that a man has been born into the world. So it is with you; *for the moment you are sad at heart; but I shall see you again, and then you will be joyful, and no one shall rob you of your joy.*"

This is followed by a promise that the resumed fellowship will lead to the disciples' participation in the powers of the divine sovereignty; it will initiate a new experience of effective prayer to the Father (see vv. 23–24).

The Johannine pericope suggests an interpretation of Mark 2:19b–20 that is entirely harmonious with the other Markan references to the passion of Jesus. At least it illustrates how the joy of the presence of Jesus with his disciples can give place to a period of fasting without its overshadowing the joy of the present, since the latter period itself gives way to further and fuller experience of the divine sovereignty in Jesus.

The two parables that follow the parable of the Bridegroom—the parables of the Old Coat and the New Wine—expose the power of the new situation that has come into being with Jesus. A. Kee sees in the two parables not a contrast between the old order and the new order manifest in Jesus, but rather an emphasis on the value of the old order: the old coat is worth mending, and the old wineskins must be preserved. Kee maintains that the parables warn of the danger of loss in the face of the imminent coming of the kingdom and cry to the hearers of Jesus, "Stop, or you may lose everything!"[105] But this misses the point of the parables, which are both meant to point to the power of the new age that has come with Jesus—a power that is in some respects destructive of the old order. The new wine is too powerful for the old wineskins and will burst them; the new cloth could render the old coat useless. Admittedly, one must be careful not to allegorize the comparisons employed by Jesus beyond reasonable limits, but Muddiman is not unjustified in pointing to the similarity of opposites in the two parables, that of shrinkage and expansion: both spell danger to the old![106] These two little parables are deeply significant in the extent to which they convey Jesus' warning that the power of the new age cannot be accommodated to all the forms of the old. They indicate that Jesus' mission to fulfill the law and the prophets (Matt. 5:17) could not be accomplished through the forms of the old order, nor would it leave them intact; such a mission called for new modes of expression—such as, indeed, those that Jesus exemplified in his ministry.[107]

| # The Relation of Jesus to the Kingdom of God in the Present

Having surveyed some of the dominical sayings and parables concerning the kingdom in the ministry of Jesus, we would now do well to assess their implications for the relation of Jesus to that kingdom. Of course, we can do this only in a provisional way; no such assessment would be thorough that failed to take into account his statements concerning the future of the kingdom. On the other hand, these statements about the future of the kingdom present certain problems peculiar to themselves, problems that can be resolved only through a consideration of the relation of Jesus to the present kingdom. There is no simple escape from this vicious circle; for want of a better alternative, we will simply proceed to investigate the relation of Jesus to the kingdom of God come in the "present" (i.e., the "present" of his ministry) on the basis of the material we considered in Chapter 10.

We have seen that certain sayings depict the kingdom of God as operative in powerful *acts* of Jesus that bring liberation from evil forces (Matt. 12:28) and healing to men's bodies (Matt. 11:5). Other sayings, such as the sermon in Nazareth (Luke 4:18–21) and the summary of Jesus' preaching in Mark 1:15, imply that the kingdom becomes effective in the *word* of Jesus. In some passages (e.g., Matt. 11:5 and 13:6–7), the deeds and word of Jesus are linked as complementary indications of the presence of the kingdom. Luke 17:20–21 and Mark 4:11–12 suggest that the *totality* of the action and speech of Jesus signifies the presence of the kingdom. The parables reflect the relation of the present kingdom to Jesus in a variety of ways: the parable of the Strong Man Bound presents the kingdom in the action of Jesus, the parable of the Great Feast presents the kingdom in the proclamation of Jesus, the parable of the Bridegroom and his Friends gives a picture of the kingdom in the table fellowship of Jesus, and the parables of growth assume the kingdom to have been initiated in the ministry of Jesus generally. Our task is to define the role of Jesus in relation to the kingdom of God so as to do justice to all this varied evidence.

Otto solved the problem by assuming that in the parable of the Strong Man Bound, the figure described as the Stronger than the Strong is God, whose victory over Satan in heaven (see Rev. 12:9) was witnessed by Jesus in a vision—"I saw Satan fall from heaven like lightning" (Luke 10:18). Otto proceeded to deduce that Jesus was borne on the tidal wave of that victory in his proclamation and action, and thus that the saying "clearly presupposed that Christ did not himself bring the kingdom of God, but that his own appearance was actually only a result of the fact that the kingdom had already come, that the powers of this kingdom were working in him and through him, but in such a way that he himself was part and parcel of this in-breaking entity of the kingdom, which was superior even to him." Thus Otto formulated his famous dictum: "It is not Jesus who brings the kingdom. . . . On the contrary, the kingdom brings him with it."[1]

Clearly, however, the exposition of the parable on which Otto bases his thesis is implausible—and thus the opposition posed in the epigram is equally doubtful. Let us freely recognize that the last thing anyone would assert of Jesus is that he acted or spoke in conscious independence of God. If we bear in mind the fact that Jesus understood the kingdom of God to consist primarily in God's acting in salvation and judgment, then it will be quite apparent that he was indeed "borne along" by God's sovereign action in his ministry. It is axiomatic that Jesus does not lead God but rather that God sends, guides, empowers, and sustains him. Nevertheless, as the gospel records witness, Jesus exploited to the full the authority committed to him. It was precisely his *exousia* that first impressed his contemporaries. If it astonished them to hear him use the formula "It was said to them of old time . . . but I say to you" with respect to the law of God, it was no less astonishing to hear him declare "Today this scripture has been fulfilled in your hearing" with respect to the promise of the kingdom (Luke 4:21). Such a declaration would scarcely have been countenanced had it not been matched by equally impressive and telling deeds. The relation of Jesus to the kingdom of God is such that no single formula can do justice to it. We will do well to adopt a fuller vocabulary to represent its nature. In this respect, precision of language is less important than the fullness of significance that Jesus' words imply.

The parable of the Strong Man in Mark 3:27 depicts Jesus as the *Champion*, or *Contender for the kingdom of God*, who by virtue of his conquest of Satan rescues those held under the Evil One's thraldom. Luke 10:18 may conceivably extend this rescue function to the disciples associated with him in his mission.

We can assume that the role of *Initiator of the kingdom* of the last days belongs to Jesus in association with John the Baptist in the saying Matthew 11:12. John serves as a bridge between the period of law and the prophets and the period of the kingdom, but the kingdom is operative in Jesus in a fuller sense than it is in John. The parables of growth point in a similar direction, implying as they do that a decisive beginning of the divine sovereignty has taken place in the word and work of Jesus.

In the exorcism saying, Matthew 12:28, we see Jesus as the *Instrument of the kingdom*; it is by the "finger of God"—the powerful working of the Spirit of God—that Jesus performs the liberating acts of the divine sovereignty.

In Luke 17:20–21 it is not unfitting to see Jesus as the *Representative of the kingdom of God*. Had the interlocutors of Jesus recognized the nature of his ministry, they would not have needed to ask when the kingdom of God was to come.

In various passages Jesus is depicted as the *Mediator of the kingdom* and its blessings. This is notably the case in the parable of the Bridegroom and his Friends (Mark 2:18–19), since it is the presence of the Bridegroom that gives the character of wedding festival to the present and mediates to others the fellowship of the royal feast. It is little more than a matter of preference whether we use the term Mediator or *Bearer of the Kingdom of God* to signify Jesus as he is referred to in Matthew 11:5, with mention of his healing and transfiguring powers.

Again, we need take but a short step to speak of him as *Revealer of the Kingdom* in such passages as Matthew 13:16–17, for example. Certainly that concept is present in Matthew 11:25–26 // Luke 10:21–22 and the related passage of Mark 4:11–12. In the parables of the Lost Sheep, the Lost Coin, and the Prodigal Son, Jesus makes reference to the fact that he associates with the lost souls of society in order to grant them the opportunity to experience the saving sovereignty of heaven; in the course of defending himself against the criticism he received for doing so, he depicts the ways of *God*—and yet the very contours of these parables reflect the ways of *Jesus*. Along these lines, Fuchs has observed that "We are confronted by a very daring line of conduct on the part of Jesus: he dares to affirm the will of God as though he himself stood in God's place."[2] Jesus' self-defense thus constitutes a revelation of God in his sovereignty. This being the case, we find in the conclusion of Jesus' message to John the Baptist the ultimate word on his relation to the kingdom of God: "Happy is the man who does not find me a stumbling block" (Matt. 11:6). To recognize in Jesus the Revelation of the kingdom is to find the way into the kingdom, while to stumble over the truth of his person is to stumble into ruin.

What name, then, shall we give to him whose role in the operation of the divine sovereignty is so crucial? In his teaching on the kingdom of God, Jesus portrays himself as Champion of the kingdom, Initiator of the kingdom, Instrument of the kingdom, Representative of the kingdom, Mediator of the kingdom, Bearer of the kingdom, Revealer of the kingdom. These names have been coined on his behalf—Jesus claimed none of them for himself—and yet they are demanded by his words. What then of the ancient and honorable title of Messiah? Jesus did not claim this title either in any of the passages we have considered. Nevertheless, if it is the case that the sayings of Jesus lead us to postulate his functions relative to the kingdom represented by those terms, do not those sayings and functions indicate that he *assumed* for himself the function of Messiah? This is a point of no small controversy. The voice of critical scholarship either trails off into silence or becomes strident over it.[3] In the end, however, we are compelled to say Yes for the simplest of reasons.

In Jewish literature generally, the relation of the Messiah to the divine sovereignty is ambiguous. The Old Testament presents the Messiah not as the agent through whom the kingdom comes, but rather as the agent of the kingdom after God has established it. In some apocalyptic writings the Messiah has a role in the coming of the kingdom, but the function that Jesus assigns to himself in relation to the kingdom goes well beyond anything said of the Messiah in the Old Testament or in the apocalyptic and rabbinic teaching of his day. Since we would do well to have a term to denote the manifold function of Jesus with respect to the kingdom of God, and since the title *Messiah* is the acknowledged umbrella term to denote the representative of the kingdom, it is difficult to avoid appropriating it for Jesus. It might be argued that the term is insufficient to convey *all* that he is in relation to the kingdom of God, but if that is so, then certainly nothing *less* than that will do to describe him.

11 | Sayings of Jesus on the Coming of the Kingdom of God in the Future

1. THE DISCIPLES' PRAYER
Matthew 6:9–13, Luke 11:2–4

Of the two forms of the prayer taught by Jesus to his disciples, the Matthaean is the longer, and far better known through its use in the churches. Since it is unlikely that anyone would have further abbreviated the very short prayer taught by Jesus, and since liturgical texts tend to be expanded through use, it is generally agreed that Luke's version is original in its *extent*, whereas a comparison of the two texts suggests that Matthew's is more original in its *wording*.[1] Many scholars contend that the shorter version of the prayer in Luke was expanded to the form in Matthew through the addition of elements of prayer used by Jesus.[2] We can be almost certain that the existence of the two versions is not attributable to editing by the evangelists, however; both forms of the prayer easily revert into Aramaic, in which language they exhibit both rhythm and rhyme—a highly unusual feature, which Jesus' prayer shares with the daily prayer of the Jews, the Tefillah.[3] This would indicate that Matthew and Luke have preserved for us versions of the prayer that were being used in different Christian communities of their day. In keeping with his conviction that the sermon in Matthew 5–7 represents an early pre- or post-baptismal catechism for Jewish Christians and that the version in Luke 6 represents such a catechism for Gentile Christians,[4] Jeremias argues that the versions of the prayer in Matthew and Luke belong to Jewish Christian and Gentile Christian catechisms on prayer, respectively (even though the prayer appearing in Luke is not included in the great sermon).[5] Our consideration of the prayer will of course be conditioned by our interest in the light it sheds on Jesus' teaching about the kingdom of God.

As background to our study of the prayer, we should note its significant relationship to the Kaddish, the ancient Aramaic doxology that was used to end Jewish synagogue services, which reads as follows:

> Magnified and sanctified be his great name
>   in the world which he has created according to his will.

> May he establish his kingdom
> in your lifetime and in your days and in the lifetime of all the house of Israel,
> even speedily and at a near time.

That a doxology concluding worship should be formulated in such terms shows how deeply the hope of the kingdom of God was rooted in the religious aspirations of the Jews of Jesus' time.

More pertinent for a comparison of Jewish prayer with the pattern prayer of Jesus than the Kaddish, however, is the so-called Tefillah or Amidah, commonly known as the Eighteen Benedictions. This prayer was recited three times daily by pious Jews, in conscious imitation of the sacrifices offered daily in the temple at Jerusalem. In contrast to P. Billerbeck, who thought it precarious to compare the Disciples' Prayer with the Eighteen Benedictions, on the grounds of the uncertain date and use of the latter,[6] K. G. Kuhn maintains that the comparison is quite in order, since the Tefillah in its Palestinian recension (shorn perhaps of its doxologies, which were added later) would have been in use in the first half of the common era and may well go back to pre-Christian times. Kuhn emphasizes the fact that both prayers have the distinctive feature of rhyme throughout, both are divided into two sections (one section relating to the present age and the other to the future age), both are individual in intent and yet can be used in public prayers (the Tefillah was the constitutive prayer for the three daily synagogue services), and both are expressions of the faith and hope of the communities that used them, the differences of content between them arising from the different theological emphases of the Synagogue and of Jesus.[7] This last point will engage us when we examine the presuppositions of the prayer of Jesus about the kingdom of God.

In addition to the difference in content there is another major difference between the daily prayer of the Jew and that taught by Jesus: the former is very lengthy, while that of Jesus is very brief (in Aramaic extraordinarily so!). The Eighteen Benedictions consist of a core of twelve benedictions preceded by three introductory benedictions and followed by three blessings. So long did it take to recite them that some questioned whether it was necessary to go through the whole prayer three times a day. R. Akiba and R. Joshua were prepared to say that if a man was not fluent he could recite "an Abbreviated Eighteen":

> Give us discernment, O Lord, to know thy ways,
> and circumcise our heart to fear thee,
> and forgive us so that we may be redeemed,
> and keep us far from our sufferings,
> and fatten us in the pastures of thy land,
> and gather our dispersions from the four corners of the earth,
> and let them who err from thy prescriptions be punished,
> and lift up thy hand against the wicked,
> and let the righteous rejoice in the building of thy city
> and the establishment of the temple
> and in the exalting of the horn of David, thy servant,
> and the preparation of a light for the son of Jesse, thy Messiah;
> blessed art thou, O Lord, who hearkenest to prayer.

In the abbreviation, as in the full prayer, the first half relates to concerns of this life and the latter half to the kingdom of the Messiah. Both the content and the relative order of the two groups of prayers form an instructive contrast to the petitions in the prayer of Jesus, although they relate to the same fundamental concerns of this life and of the kingdom of God.

In the prayer of Jesus, concern for the kingdom of God is given precedence. In the version in Luke, the request concerning the kingdom is set in two petitions; in Matthew there are three. In both forms of the prayer, however, concern for the kingdom takes priority over concern for personal needs. It is in fact likely that we are meant to understand these petitions regarding personal needs specifically within the context of the coming of the kingdom of God; the same may well be true of the prefatory address, "Father."

That Jesus taught his disciples to address God as *Abba* is clear from Luke's version. Matthew's "Our Father" is a rendering of *Abba* for community use, making it a joint utterance of the children in the family of God. The novelty of this mode of prayer seems clear. Despite sundry protests to the contrary, the researches of Jeremias seem to have established that Jesus' use of *Abba* in prayer to God is unique.[8] Even if some exceptions may be unearthed to qualify Jeremias's assertion that "There is *no analogy at all* in the whole literature of Jewish prayer for God being addressed as *Abba*,"[9] it remains the case that Jesus stands alone in his undeviating use of this mode of address in his prayers to God (the only exception is the cry of desolation on the cross, which cites Ps. 22:1); it is one with the awareness of his relation to God that is reflected in his teaching, one with his awareness of his vocation with respect to the reign of God.

In pondering the significance of the fact that he taught his disciples to address God in this fashion, we should bear in mind the significance of the context in which Jesus gave them the prayer—namely, the coming of that kingdom of which he was the representative and instrument in the present. As mediator of the kingdom he was the means of bringing men under the saving sovereignty of God *now*, of permitting them to experience its blessings *now*. Supreme among those blessings was the permission to know God in his forgiving grace. Matthew 5:9 makes it clear that in the kingdom of God, Jesus' followers will indeed be known as sons of God; we are likewise told that God will confess these sons to be such in the judgment. It is wholly in accord with the role of Jesus in the coming of the kingdom that he enabled his disciples to enter into a relation with God comparable to his own through their reception of the word of the kingdom and that he encouraged them to anticipate its completion in the advent of the kingdom at the end.

Some exegetes have suggested that the prayer for the coming of the kingdom of God was originally presented by Jesus in a single brief petition: "Your kingdom come." Those who read the passage in this way then hold that the clause "your name be hallowed" is a little doxology added by Jesus; Jews customarily added such doxologies when making mention of God (e.g., "The Holy One of Israel, *blessed be he*, said . . ."). Following the Lukan version, the opening section of the prayer would then read as follows:

> Father—hallowed be your name—
> Your kingdom come.[10]

While it is not impossible that the words were originally expressed in this fashion, neither is it very likely. On the one hand, although it is true that like his contemporaries, Jesus frequently used periphrases to avoid the name of God,[11] he was not in the habit of uttering a doxology with every mention of God's name, and not at all with the appellation *Abba*. On the other hand, the example of the Kaddish suggests that the clause could be a prayer for the sanctification of the name of God *through the revelation of his sovereign rule*. Luke's opening twofold petition and Matthew's threefold petition clearly present a parallel structure that features the kingdom of God as the subject of desire in each case:

> Your name be hallowed,
> Your kingdom come,
> Your will be done,
>   As in heaven, so on earth.

The primary intent of this section of the prayer, then, is to present a plea that God put forth his almighty power so that his name might be hallowed, his kingdom come, and his will be done among humanity.[12]

Recognizing the parallelism in the passage also helps to shed light on the meaning of each individual petition and the contribution each makes to the total picture of the kingdom for which prayer is being made. In this context the prayer for the sanctification of the divine name denotes a plea for God to act in such a manner that his name be acknowledged in all the world as "holy and terrible" (Ps. 111:9 RSV). It is more than a prayer for mankind to confess that truth of God; it implies a desire for the sovereign God to unveil his glory in the judgment and salvation that initiate his kingdom in order that men may see who he is and give him the glory due to his name. As A. Polag has put it, "The revelation of the glory of God before the world is sought, which has for its consequence the recognition of God's holiness through men."[13] The prayer presupposes that this condition does not exist in the present. While God's name is held in awe by some, it is ignored and even contemned by others. The prayer echoes the concern for the honor of the name of God evinced in some of the Old Testament prophetic writings. Ezekiel especially elaborates this theme as he speaks of the disgrace brought to the name of God by his people, and the action of God to vindicate it:

> It is not for your sake, you Israelites, that I am acting, but for the sake of my holy name, which you have profaned among the peoples where you have gone. I will hallow my great name, which has been profaned among those nations. When they see that I reveal my holiness through you, the nations will know that I am the Lord, says the Lord God. I will take you out of the nations and gather you from every land and bring you to your own soil. I will sprinkle clean water over you, and you shall be cleansed. . . . I will give you a new heart and put a new spirit within you. (Ezek. 36:22ff.)

In this passage the hallowing of the name of God is an act of God that reveals his glory in rescuing his people from their distresses and in transforming them into a people holy in character as well as in name; God is thereby seen as the Holy One who creates salvation and establishes righteousness in the earth.

The stress given to the petition for the sanctification of the name of God within the prayer for the kingdom of God reminds us that Jesus understood prayer for the kingdom to be primarily prayer for the greater glory of God. While it is a part of the nature of God that his glory is manifest in the blessing of man, the recognition of the primacy of God and the call for adoration and obedience is characteristic of the emphasis of Jesus in all his teaching, and is itself an inheritance from the prophets who were before him.

The second petition of the prayer, "Your kingdom come," presents a similar request for God to act in his power and love to bring about judgment and salvation in his creation, although it is more comprehensive than the first one. All the Old Testament prophetic pictures of deliverance through another Exodus and salvation in the kingdom of God come to expression in this brief petition. It entails the revelation of God's glory (Isa. 40:1–11), the universal acknowledgment of his kingship (Isa. 26:1–15), the universal sway of his righteousness (Isa. 4, 11, 32, etc.), universal peace in his creation (Isa. 2), and above all, in the latest reaches of Old Testament hope, the conquest of death and the wiping away of tears from all eyes (Isa. 25:8). Brief as it is, no more comprehensive prayer than this can be prayed. The Seer of Revelation endeavors to illustrate what it will mean in his closing vision of the City of God that descends from heaven to earth (Rev. 21:9–22:5). Jesus himself gives few such pictures in his instruction on the kingdom, although he does adduce the image of the messianic feast at which people from all the world will "sit down" with Abraham, Isaac, and Jacob in the kingdom of God (Matt. 8:11–12), at which people will gather with rejoicing in the banquet hall of God (Matt. 22:1) and eat and drink with him in a new way (Mark 14:25). Needless to say, this prayer can be answered positively only by an act of God. Deliverance from all evil, including the ultimate enemy of man, and resurrection for life in God's kingdom can come about solely through God's intervention and recreative activity. In the final analysis, "Your kingdom come" is a prayer for God himself to come and achieve his end in creating a world.

In light of the significance of the second petition, the third petition appearing in Matthew's gospel, "Your will be done," is very pertinent, and ought to be interpreted in the same way. Obviously it expresses the idea that men should turn from their wickedness and act in accordance with God's will as it has been made known to them. Nevertheless, it is not primarily a prayer that the disobedient be converted and obey God's laws; rather, it is a plea that God will act in such a way as to realize his "good pleasure"—namely, the purpose he intended for the world when he created it, to which end he is bringing about a redemption. In the context of a world actually wandering from God, it is his saving will that lies at the center of this petition. This restatement of the prayer for the coming of the kingdom in terms of the fulfillment of God's will is in complete accord with Christ's preoccupation with the Father's will in his own life, as the prayer in Gethsemane reminds us (Mark 14:35).[14]

The addition of the phrase "as in heaven, so on earth" is best viewed as relating to the entire threefold petition for the sanctification of the name of God, the coming of the kingdom of God, and the fulfillment of the will of God. The Father who graciously relates himself to us as we respond in faith and obedience to his approach is the Lord of the universe. *In heaven* his name is hallowed, his rule acknowledged, and his will performed without end; here the prayer is made that the name of God will be sanctified, the sovereignty of God will be established, and the good pleasure of God will be fulfilled *on earth* as well. So fundamental is this to the ministry of Jesus in relation to the kingdom that it is surprising that some exegetes have been uneasy about this element in the prayer of Jesus. Schlatter is not one these, however; he boldly affirms that "Precisely because Jesus longs for the kingdom of heaven his love belongs to the earth, for the sovereignty of heaven comes to pass as God reveals to men his almighty grace."[15] Certainly the concern for both heaven and earth is in harmony with his teaching on the kingdom of God generally. Apart from the remarkable juxtaposition of the first and third beatitudes (Matt. 5:3 and 5), the basic notion of the coming of the sovereignty of God is a movement from heaven to earth, from God to man. In the context of this prayer, Jesus is seeking an act of God to produce a "movement" that will be a part of the greater "movement" God has already initiated in Jesus. Heaven has already invaded the earth in the mission of Jesus; here he is praying for a completion of what God has begun in him, for a securing of his purpose to unite heaven and earth. As H. Traub has expressed it,

> Not only does the Matthaean formula comprehend heaven and earth, it also implies a new interrelation of heaven and earth effected by God's saving action. . . . The formula *hos en . . . kai epi* expresses the new participation of heaven in earth which in the saving work of Jesus Christ has replaced the division of heaven and earth.[16]

What then is the relation between the prayer for the ultimate revelation of the kingdom of God and the ministry of the kingdom taking place in the labors of Jesus? We can assume that it consists primarily in God's bringing the saving sovereignty he has initiated in Jesus to a victorious conclusion at the end of the age. These two points are clear: it is *this* kingdom that is to be brought to completion, and it is to be brought to completion *at the end of the age.* It may very well be the case that Jesus had no other application than this in mind when he gave the prayer to his disciples. In view of his overall instruction on the kingdom of God, however, and in light of the fact that the prayer was given as an example of the sort of issues for which prayer should be made, it is not out of the question to suppose that this petition might constitute an appeal for God's blessing on the sovereignty initiated through Jesus' ministry—a request that his name might be revealed to men in saving action through his word and acknowledged by them in faith and adoration, that his sovereignty might be experienced by those who perceived in Christ's deed and word the kingdom of God drawing near to them, and that his good purpose be accomplished among men who submit to his sovereign pleasure. If we distinguish between the immediate intention of the prayer and its wider implications, we need not set ourselves so quickly to building fences around it, as though to forbid unwonted straying by those inclined to ponder the meaning of the prayer for their lives.

Whereas the eschatological spirit of the first half of the prayer is generally recognized, the petitions of the second half, relating to the personal needs of those who pray, are divorced from the prayers for the kingdom by many scholars. Their treatment of these petitions proceeds as though the latter were delivered separately from the rest of the prayer. They assume, and understandably so, that the petitions for bread for the day, for forgiveness of sins, and for grace to resist temptation have to do with the needs of people at all times and in all places. And yet we must steadfastly bear in mind that the prayer was not delivered to everybody everywhere; it was given to those who had responded to the word of the kingdom through its Bearer and who were thereby privileged with him to address God as *Abba*. It is such who petitioned God to complete that work of grace that made its beginning in the world during their lifetime. Inevitably, the lives of those who enter into this situation are radically affected, including their attitude to bread, the forgiveness of sins, and the testings of life (see, for example, Matt. 6:25–33 and Luke 12:22–31). On the other hand, some exegetes press beyond this, and maintain that the petitions of the second half of the prayer are so bound up with those of the first half that they should be viewed as aspects of the coming of the kingdom which constitutes the focus of the whole prayer.

Jeremias is the most eloquent exponent of the idea that the petitions of the second half of the prayer are essentially connected with the eschatological emphasis of the first half. Taking his cue from Jerome's report that in the Aramaic Gospel of the Nazaraeans the term *epiousios* in the petition for bread was rendered "tomorrow" (*mahar*), he understood the petition to mean "Give us today our bread for tomorrow." Then, noting that in Jewish parlance "tomorrow" can mean the future—that is, God's tomorrow—he concludes that the prayer is actually requesting that God give us today the *bread of the time of salvation*: "Jesus grants to them, as the children of God, the privilege of stretching forth their hands to grasp the glory of the consummation, to fetch it down, 'to believe it down,' to pray it down—right into their poor lives, even now, even here, today."[17] He similarly assumes that the request for forgiveness is made with an eye to the day of judgment that approaches with the kingdom of God, in which only God can forgive. Happily the disciples of Jesus, by their association with him and reception of his word, know that they belong already to the age of forgiveness and salvation; accordingly they may pray: "Grant us this one great gift of the Messiah's time already in this day and in this place." Finally, Jeremias holds that the petition regarding temptation is likewise made with the final great testing in mind, the time when Satan will be rampant and apostasy will be a fearful possibility; that being the case, he contends that the petition actually means "O Lord, preserve us from falling away, from apostasy!"[18]

Despite the attractiveness of this view, and the fact that it is advocated by an impressive array of scholars, I cannot bring myself to believe that this is what the second group of petitions really means. In particular, the interpretation of the prayer for bread for the coming day as a request for the present bestowal of the powers and blessings of the age to come seems unnatural. In his detailed account of the possible meanings of *epiousios*, Foerster concludes that the term is not intended to convey an indication of time at all, but rather an indication of *measure*—that is, it defines the amount of bread for which we pray: "Bread for the coming day" is simply "the bread which we need."[19] It is true that the prayer for forgiveness might justifiably be related to the final judgment—the idea of judgment is surely as much a part of the revelation of the kingdom of God as any other aspect of life, all of which have to to be lived in its light (see Matt. 6:1–4, 5–6, 16–17)—but it should also be remembered that Jesus makes a point of stressing the fact that we must forgive others here and now if we would be forgiven by God (see Matt. 5:25–26, 6:14–15, 18:21–35; Mark 11:25). The petition for deliverance from the power of temptation is analogous to the warning of Jesus in Gethsemane (Mark 14:38 par.), and that is hardly to be referred to the final tribulation.

We can see, then, that there is substantial reason to believe that the second group of petitions should be understood *in light of* the situation presumed in the first group but not as an *extension* of them. The disciples of Jesus, standing under the saving sovereignty of God brought in and through Jesus, pray for the ultimate revelation of that sovereignty in all its glory. In that setting, under the kingdom of grace and anticipating the kingdom of glory, they make petitions that befit such a situation: for bread that is needed (but no more); for forgiveness, in order that the divine fellowship might remain unbroken; and for the upholding hand of God in the hour of temptation, since the flesh is weak, the opponent strong, and the hour is momentous. This is not "the *apocalyptissimum* of apocalyptic" as Schulz has suggested. Rather, it is a consequence of the recognition that to be associated with the Bearer of God's kingdom is to be caught up in the advent of God's new world, and hence to experience its salvation in the present (though not as it will be experienced in the future); it is to be implicated in the battle with evil, and so in need of grace to prevent a fall; and *therefore* it is to anticipate with deepest yearning, yet with confidence, the revelation of the glory of God and the kingdom of God and the accomplishment of his good pleasure.

Thus we can see that while the prayer of Jesus may not be from first to last a set of eschatological petitions, it is dominated from first to last by the reality of the kingdom of God. The prayer is a perfect embodiment of the maxim of Jesus, which in the Q tradition forms the conclusion of his call to cease from anxiety over the everyday needs of life:

Seek his kingdom,
and the rest will be yours as well. (Luke 12:31 //Matthew 6:33)

Since the coming of the kingdom is the supreme concern of existence, Jesus calls on men to make it theirs also. They are not merely to *believe* in its coming, but to *seek* it—to set their hearts on gaining it, and to set their hearts on serving it. This will liberate them from anxiety, since God extends his sovereign care to all who seek his kingdom.

It is particularly instructive to compare the prayer of Jesus with the daily prayer of the Jews, the Tefillah, which, unlike the Kaddish, combines prayers for the coming of the kingdom of God with prayers for the needs of the people. We have already noted that the prayers for life precede the prayers for the kingdom of God in the Tefillah. We should also note, however, that the prayers for life are themselves preceded by three benedictions that celebrate the greatness of God in history and in creation, so that God is worshipped before any petition is made. Nevertheless, the order of the petitions in Jesus' prayer undoubtedly reflects a different set of priorities on his part: the kingdom *first* is his watchword.[20]

The nature of the petitions for both the kingdom and human needs in the Tefillah and Jesus' prayer suggests a difference not merely of emphasis but also of the concept of the kingdom of God between the thought of Israel's spiritual leaders and that of Jesus. In the Tefillah the sanctification of the Name is mentioned in the third Benediction immediately preceding the petitions, and it is viewed as a timeless reality:

> Holy art thou,
> and thy Name is to be feared,
> and there is no God beside thee.

In contrast, Jesus prayed for the sanctity of the Name in terms of the revelation of the glory of God in the establishment of his kingdom so that it might be acknowledged by men.

In the Benedictions, prayer for the kingdom is made in terms of a restoration of Israel's former glories as a nation, somewhat in the spirit of the Psalms of Solomon:

> Blow the great horn for our liberation,
> and lift a banner to gather our exiles. . . .
> Restore our judges as at the first,
> and our counsellors as at the beginning;
> and reign thou over us, thou alone. . . .
> Be merciful, O Lord our God, in thy great mercy,
> towards Israel thy people,
> and towards thy temple and thy habitation,
> and towards the kingdom of the house of David, thy righteous one.

This strikes a note absent not only from Jesus' prayer but from his teaching on the kingdom of God as a whole; it presents the concept of the Son of David who rules in the kingdom, whereas Jesus presents the concept of the Son of Man who brings redemption for the kingdom. It is not liberation from Gentile political powers or the restoration of Israel's ancient polity that concerns Jesus, but rather emancipation from spiritual powers that bring ruin to men.

The difference between the Eighteen Benedictions and Jesus' prayer in the matter of the petition for the provision of food is also significant. The former reads as follows:

> Bless for us, O Lord, our God, this year for our welfare,
> with every kind of the produce thereof,
> and bring near speedily the year of the end of our redemption;
> and give dew and rain upon the face of the earth
> and satisfy the world from the treasuries of thy goodness,
> and do thou give a blessing upon the work of our hands.

This is a wholly comprehensible and suitable prayer for men in an agricultural community. It links with prayer for temporal needs a petition for liberation from the oppression that constantly destroys the toil of honest and peace-loving people and desolates the land. The focus of the prayer is a request for God's mercy on the land in the year lying ahead, that the plowing and sowing and reaping might not be in vain, but rather be prospered by the blessing of dew and rain and whatever else God may be pleased to give from the treasuries of his goodness.

In the "Abbreviated Eighteen" the petition for bread reads "Fatten us in the pastures of thy land." Expressed in terms akin to those in the prayer of Jesus, it can be summarized as follows: "Give us our bread in the coming *year*." Jesus bade his disciples ask "Give us our bread for the coming *day*." Why the difference in the period of time? The Bible reader might naturally recall that the manna was given to the fathers in the desert day by day, enough for a single day. The historian might observe that the Palestinian peasant was paid each day for his labor, and being thus accustomed to think in terms of provision for one day's food for his toil, it would have been natural for him to offer a prayer consonant with that kind of existence. Both observations are pertinent, but we should not overlook the fact that the Tefillah was prayed by the landowners as well as by the peasants! The basic difference between the prayers reflects a difference between the concepts of hope and calling that underpin them. Jesus taught that life under the reign of God is life under his divine grace and authority, which involves fresh experiences of grace as well as demands for service both today and tomorrow, while always holding before us the prospect of an indeterminable revelation of final glory. Jesus took it for granted that those who pray for the kingdom of God to come will want it to come, will look for it to come, and will be ready for it to come. He assumed that when his disciples prayed, they would do so with the attitude to which he referred in his parables of "watching" for the divine sovereignty. This is the posture of faith that so petitions *Abba*.

It is entirely in keeping with this intent that Jesus does not bid his disciples to pray, as the Abbreviated Eighteen has it, "Keep us far from our sufferings," but rather, "Let us not succumb to temptation." The battle for the kingdom has been triumphantly joined through the Bearer of the kingdom in his encounter with the great opponent; the follower who knows the present redemptive power of the divine sovereignty does not pray to escape trial but to obtain grace to conquer it till the conclusion of the emancipation.

The difference between the disciple of Jesus who prayed for the kingdom and the Jew who paused in the midst of his daily tasks to worship God and seek his blessing was a matter of their respective concepts of the kingdom of God. It was not a matter of how much enthusiasm they experienced in their hope of the coming of the kingdom or even a matter of how near they considered the end to be. Rather, it was a matter of conviction concerning Jesus—namely, that he was the one God had appointed to be Bearer of the kingdom—and this in turn went back to Jesus' own awareness that the sovereignty of God, promised of old through the prophets, was at work in the world in his work and word. Having been consecrated by the Father to fulfill his appointed task, he was aware that every day was momentous, that every work done for God brought nearer the climax of service for the kingdom that God was seeking. Liberation, emancipation, and redemption were on the way! The time of salvation had begun; Jesus was now moving toward the consummation of the work.

We should look for the ultimate source of Jesus' prayer, then, in the summary of his proclamation that appears in Mark 1:15. This is the essential message of his ministry, and he shaped it into a prayer for his disciples. Those who look to him as the Mediator of the kingdom of God will continue to pray it.

2. THE BEATITUDES
Matthew 5:3–12, Luke 6:20–23

We are so used to viewing the beatitudes of Jesus as the introduction to the Sermon on the Mount that it requires an effort to recognize that the beatitudes are as much a compilation as the Sermon itself. Four of the beatitudes are in Q (those in Luke), and of these the last one is different from the first three in form and content, and was almost certainly delivered by Jesus later in his ministry than were the others. Moreover, there are other beatitudes attributed to Jesus than the nine reproduced in the Matthaean collection—namely, those in Matthew 11:6 // Luke 7:23; Matthew 13:16 // Luke 10:23; Luke 11:28; and Acts 20:35. We may also note Matthew 24:46 // Luke 12:43; Luke 12:37–38; and John 20:29. Most of these are eschatologically related, but we would not readily place any of them with the nine in the Sermon. The peculiar nature of the nine beatitudes as declaratory blessings and revelation concerning the kingdom of God and its heirs makes them unusually suitable for heading the catechetical summary of life under the sovereignty of God that constitutes the Sermon on the Mount.

What of the woes that accompany the beatitudes in Luke 6:24–26? These are so closely linked with the four beatitudes in Q that one gets the impression that they were originally delivered with them. Certainly they balance the beatitudes remarkably, and by their contrasts they serve to clarify the meaning of the beatitudes. J. Dupont has suggested that since the correspondence between the woes and the beatitudes appearing in Luke is so close, Luke must have composed the latter with a view to elucidating the significance of the former.[21] While we cannot rule out the possibility that this is the case, we might note that the Lukan content of the beatitudes is almost certainly the more original of the two forms, and it is not impossible that each was complemented by a woe in the same context as the beatitude. It is instructive to note further that there is a collection of Jesus' woes recorded in Matthew 23 that is unrelated to those in Luke 6:24ff., and that contrasting beatitudes and woes were not unknown in Judaism.[22]

If we ask whether any of the beatitudes were uttered together, we enter a realm of conjecture. It is evident that the first two in Luke are related through their connection with Isaiah 61:1ff. The "poor" of the first beatitude are the "poor" to whom the good news of the Jubilee is made known (Isa. 61:1), and the "mourners" are those whom the *mebasser* of the prophecy is sent to comfort (Isa. 61:2). As we noted earlier, a line from Isaiah 58:6 is inserted into the citation of Isaiah 61:1 recorded in Luke 4:18; the sentence immediately following (Isa.

58:7) continues the description of the Lord's requirements as "sharing your food with *the hungry*." It is not impossible therefore that the first three beatitudes (of Luke) were delivered at the same time, since the poor, the mourners, and the hungry may be viewed as collectively constituting the needy of humanity whom God wills to save.[23]

The relation between the beatitudes in Matthew 5:3 and 5:5 is as intriguing as the relation between those in verses 3, 4, and 6. There is a significant textual tradition that conjoins the two together as follows:

> Blessed are the poor in spirit,
>   for theirs is the kingdom of heaven.
> Blessed are the meek,
>   for they shall inherit the earth.

While the textual authorities for the usual order are superior to those that recommend the conjunction of verses 3 and 5, many scholars believe that the established order is largely attributable to the influence of Isaiah 61:1ff. on the text. In his edition of the Greek text, Tischendorf adopted the order as given above, as does the Jerusalem Bible and its French predecessor, the Bible de Jérusalem. M. Black has suggested that in the Aramaic tradition they formed a single stanza.[24] Not a few scholars maintain that in the original the order of the verses in Matthew was 3, 5, 4, although those who agree on this point still hold a variety of views regarding the origin of the beatitudes.[25] It is tempting to assume that essentially they belong together, but there is a difficulty with such an assumption: the term for "poor" in the Hebrew text of Isaiah 61:1 is *anawim* (*ptochoi* in the LXX and gospels); the term for "meek" in Psalm 37:11 is also *anawim* (*praeis* in the LXX and gospels)—and thus the two beatitudes actually refer to the same subject! The "poor" are the meek! Not surprisingly, some scholars have concluded that Matthew 5:5 is a variant of Matthew 5:3, couched in the form of a citation of Psalm 37:11. There is, of course, a simpler possibility: if the beatitudes were spoken by Jesus on various occasions, there is no reason why he should not have uttered *both* beatitudes. While the first accords with his frequent citation of Isaiah 61:1, the formulation of inheritance in the kingdom in terms of Psalm 37:11 more clearly conveys the thought of Isaiah 58, and constitutes a vivid alternate expression of the promise of the first beatitude (and of the rest!).

There is a somewhat similar relation between Matthew 5:10 and the Q beatitude Matthew 5:11–12 // Luke 4:22–23. The content of verse 10 is essentially the same as that of verses 11–12, but it rounds off the chain of beatitudes by pronouncing the same blessing as that in the first of the group of eight in verse 3. It could have been formulated as an abbreviation of verses 11–12 in the style of the other beatitudes.[26] It could equally well have been uttered by Jesus as an expression of a principle illustrated through the generations of God's people and finding fresh application in his day. In the longer beatitude the situation has been sharpened through the scandal of attachment to Jesus; on the whole, it seems to me less likely that Matthew would have formulated an abbreviation of the statement that involved replacing the specific *heneken emou* ("for my sake") with the vaguer *heneken dikaiousunes* ("for the sake of righteousness") than that Jesus himself would have formulated the briefer statement and later made a more specific declaration in light of the situation that had developed in his ministry.

The question of whether the beatitudes were originally delivered in the second person, as in Luke, or in the third person, as in Matthew, has been debated at length. It does not appear as if the question will ever be finally resolved, although an increasing number of scholars believe that Matthew is right in this feature, and with good reason. The general form of beatitudes uses the third person in the Hebrew Old Testament, in the Jewish noncanonical writings, and in Greek and Latin literature, although enough exceptions can be found in all these groups to preclude the formulation of a rigid rule concerning the form of beatitudes.[27] Among the beatitudes of Jesus we are considering here, the last one is set in the second person plural in both Matthew and Luke. Curiously, all of the thirteen beatitudes in the New Testament outside the group in the Sermon are set in the third person except for 1 Peter 3:14, which echoes the last beatitude!

The question of whether Luke received the first three beatitudes in the third person and conformed them to the form of the fourth or whether Matthew found them in the second person and changed them to the normal style of beatitudes (apart from the last one, which resisted such change) is essentially moot. Dupont brought three considerations to bear on the problem which are of importance. First, we note that in the first three beatitudes Luke *begins* with the third person and then *changes* to the second; on this Dupont comments that "We have run through many hundreds of macarisms, and we do not remember having met one constructed in this manner."[28] (The normal pattern for a beatitude in the second person would be conveyed by *asherekem* [in Aramaic, *tubekon*]—"Blessed are *you* poor . . ." and so forth.) Thus, Luke is not presenting three beatitudes in the second person but rather three beatitudes begun in the third person and continued in the second, followed by a fourth wholly in the second person. Second, Dupont notes that Luke stands alone among the synoptic writers in using the term *humetera*, "*yours* (is the kingdom of God)"; in his view, this form of the beatitude clearly reflects Luke's unique mode of editing. Third, Dupont cites Cadbury's observation that Luke has a predilection for transmitting sayings of Jesus in direct language, whereas Matthew and Mark tend to present them in a more general fashion.[29] In light of all this evidence, it does seem likely that Luke adopted the same process in recording the first three beatitudes, thereby keeping all four in the same form.[30]

The last preliminary question relating to the beatitudes concerns the number that we can with confidence attribute to Jesus. In his first work on the beatitudes, Dupont maintained that the four in Q could be viewed as original, and that the other five in Matthew were of Matthew's creation. He held that the Matthew began by adding explanatory phrases to the authentic beatitudes in verses 3 and 6, proceeded to add verse 5 as an explanatory doublet of verse 3 in the same spirit, then added verse 10 as an anticipatory doublet to verses 10–11, and finally composed the beatitudes in verses 7, 8, and 9 to indicate the ethical qualities that the poor, afflicted, and hungry who inherit the kingdom of God should have.[31] The only qualification Dupont later added to this hypothesis was the suggestion that the final beatitude was adapted to the situation of Christians in the church, although he continued to hold that the core of the beatitude reflects the thought of Jesus.[32]

Dupont's "genetic" theory of the development of the beatitudes assumes that Matthew worked as an evangelist rather than as a journalist, as a teacher of the mind of Christ rather than as a reporter. Nevertheless the leap from recognizing that Matthew made interpretative *insertions* into authentic beatitudes of Jesus to contending that Matthew *created* a number of beatitudes is not well founded. The beatitudes are rightly viewed as expositions of Jesus' proclamation of the kingdom, summarized for us in Mark 1:15. But if we reduce the authentic beatitudes to those in Luke 6:20–21 (plus the later 22–23 stripped down), then we should note that they contain no equivalent of the keynote of Mark's summary: "Repent." This would in no way cast doubt on their dominical origin, but it should serve to remind us that it would be wrong to treat these three beatitudes as so exclusively an expression of Jesus' proclamation of the kingdom of God that any utterances suggesting an ethical interest must be secondary. The ethical emphases in the beatitudes of Matthew 5:7–9 can be found in other instruction of Jesus recorded elsewhere. The beatitude pronounced on the merciful in verse 7 invites comparison with Luke 6:36: "Be merciful even as your Father is merciful"; the comparison is particularly significant because mercy is uniformly recognized as a supreme quality of God, and it is but natural to affirm that those who are merciful will themselves receive mercy in the great day of testing. The same is true of the beatitude in verse 9: God is the source of peace and the supreme peacemaker, and those who promote reconciliation among his children thereby demonstrate their likeness to God as his children. The beatitude of verse 8 expresses the fundamental principle by which Jesus lived, the principle that infuriated his adversaries—namely, that authentic purity or holiness is not an external condition maintained through observance of cultic laws of clean and unclean, but is rather of the *man*, made manifest in words and deeds, as the controversy described in Mark 7:1–23 indicates. Apart from verses 11–12, the content of verse 10 is also illustrated elsewhere in the teaching of Jesus (e.g., in Matt. 10:16–25, 28, and 34–35; and 23:34ff.). While the beatitude in verse 10 could certainly have been introduced as a succinct expression of the longer verses 11–12, the fact that Jesus expressed the idea contained in it with some frequency suggests that he might well have uttered it in the form of a short beatitude in the style of the earlier ones in Matthew's series as well.

In considering the meaning of the individual beatitudes, we are confronted with the problem of the redactional activity of Matthew and Luke. Most scholars agree that the briefer Lucan version of the first three Q beatitudes is the original form, as was the case with the Lord's Prayer. The relation of these beatitudes to the consolatory prophecies of Deutero- and Trito-Isaiah, particularly of Isaiah 61 and 58, suggests that as the prophecies in Isaiah were addressed to one people, so the beatitudes of Jesus on the poor, the hungering, and the sorrowful were addressed to a single group of people. Luke appears to have had in mind the needy in society without qualification; Matthew characterizes them as needy in a spiritual sense. With characteristic thoroughness, Dupont has investigated the religious and historical background of the concepts involved and demonstrated that Luke's presentation is in harmony with the whole sweep of Israelite religion and history and the religious inheritance of Israel's Semitic neighbors: it is the glory of God (and of the king as his representative) to care for the poor, and the God of Israel is intent on doing precisely that, in history and in the new age.[33] One wonders whether this would have been less apparent to Matthew, who had been trained in the Jewish religion, than it would have been to Luke. The idea is typically expressed in the oracles of Isaiah 61, in which these beatitudes are rooted. The prophet proclaims the year of the Lord's release of all in bondage, a year of Jubilee that will fulfill the promise of the kingdom. It is important, however, to note whom the prophecies are addressed to—namely, *the Lord's poor, broken-hearted, grief-stricken people*, for whom he has planned his "day of recompense." It is prophesied that when the Lord's purpose is accomplished, these people will be perceived to be "oaks of righteousness, the planting of the Lord," "the priests of the Lord . . . the ministers of our God," "a people whom the Lord has blessed." In addressing these people in his beatitudes, Jesus was not making declarations to the world's proletariat in the spirit of Karl Marx; he was proclaiming the good news of the kingdom of God to men and women gathered about him to hear the word of God—the poor, broken people for whom none cared except God, who had prepared his kingdom for them.

This interpretation is most clearly shown to be appropriate in the case of the beatitude in verse 5. There is an obvious connection between this beatitude and Psalm 37:11, one of five verses in that chapter that speak of the "poor" inheriting the land (see also Ps. 37:9, 22, 29, and 34). The "poor" (*anawim*) are described in the psalm as those who trust in the Lord and commit their way to him, in contrast to the self-sufficient men of the world. Matthew would have been aware of this background of the term "poor" in the Old Testament, which would account for his making the addition in question to the first beatitude: he knew that his Jewish readers would assume it, but he would have wanted his non-Jewish readers to understand the term as well. To what extent such a consideration would have occurred to the Gentile Luke it is impossible to know. Several scholars have suggested that he "secularized" the beatitudes beyond the intention of Jesus. On the other hand, while Matthew's additions in verse 10 ("persecuted *for righteousness' sake*"), and possibly in verse 8 ("pure *in heart*"), were made in the same spirit and may be viewed as justifiable, it is clear that his ethical emphasis has considerably modified the content of verse 6: the addition of "thirst" to "hunger" is a common enough feature of Old Testament language, but the addition of the words "for righteousness" as the object of the hunger and thirst has the effect of making the beatitude refer exclusively to religious yearning, which was not the intention of the original utterance.

We should also take note of Luke's insertions giving indications of time. In the second and third beatitudes (Luke 6:21), he has inserted the term "now" ("Happy are those who hunger *now* . . . who weep *now* . . ."), thereby underscoring the contrast between present distress and future hope. His addition of the phrase "in that day" in 6:23 has a similar effect. Far from being a reference to the last day, wherein the persecuted will be acknowledged and rewarded,[34] the phrase is meant to focus on the present, to emphasize in paradoxical terms the privilege of suffering for the sake of one's association with the representative of the kingdom of God, the Son of Man: "on *that* day, when men express their hate . . . , rejoice, and leap in dance!"

The extent to which Luke has redacted the beatitude in 6:23 is uncertain. A common version of the first part of the beatitude would require the omission of the word "persecute" that appears in Matthew and the phrase "hate you and exclude you" that appears in Luke. Just as "persecute" is a favorite term of Matthew, so Luke frequently employs the term "hate." If he means the unusual term *aphorisosin* ("exclude") to be understood generally rather than in its specialized sense denoting excommunication from the synagogue, then his intent might have been to convey a simple representation of opposition to the disciples of Jesus. We will discuss the relation of Matthew's *heneken emou* ("for my sake") and Luke's *heneka tou huiou tou anthropou* ("for the Son of Man's sake") later; at this point we may just observe that it was not Luke's custom to insert into his text references to the Son of Man that were not in his source. The fact that the phrase appears here suggests that it was indeed original with Jesus in this context.[35]

The second part of each beatitude presents the prospect of new circumstances that will offer "happiness" to the "poor." These promises are summed up in the first and eighth beatitudes in the phrase "theirs is the kingdom of heaven." The remaining beatitudes give commentary on and content to the statement— importantly so, inasmuch as Jesus did not give the sort of apocalyptic descriptions of the kingdom of God we find in Revelation 20–22; these brief depictions of the blessedness of the heirs of the kingdom indicate at least some of the elements of what Jesus wished to convey when he referred to the kingdom of heaven or kingdom of God.

First we must determine what is meant by the statement "theirs *is* the kingdom of heaven." Is it given to them in the here and now, or is it pledged to them for the future, as their "inheritance"? The rest of the beatitudes describe a *future* reward for the "blessed" (e.g., "they shall be comforted . . . they shall inherit the earth . . . they shall be satisfied . . . they shall obtain mercy . . . they shall see God . . . they shall be called sons of God . . . your reward is great in heaven"). Some exegetes nevertheless urge that since elsewhere in Jesus' teaching he makes reference to both a present and a future form of the kingdom of God, the same should apply to the blessedness pronounced in the beatitudes; accordingly, in the beatitudes Jesus is teaching that the kingdom and its blessings are already given to the "poor" in this time, although they will not be given completely until the end of the times.[36] This is logical enough reasoning, and it may be a legitimate deduction from the teaching of Jesus as a whole, but the fact remains that there is not a hint of that thought within the beatitudes themselves. If we are concerned to understand their *intention*, we must acknowledge that it is the prospect of future glory that they set forth. The observation of a pagan made to Rabbi Meir serves to illustrate where the accent falls in the beatitudes of Jesus: "Ours is this age, yours is the age to come."[37] The same emphasis is implicit in Jesus' saying concerning the children—namely, "of such is the kingdom of heaven" (Matt. 19:14 par.)—which is to say that the kingdom is theirs when it appears.[38]

If we want to relate the teaching of Jesus on the in-breaking of the kingdom in his ministry generally with that in the beatitudes specifically, the key point to be stressed is this: they both declare that when the kingdom which has broken into the world with its representative comes in its fullness at the end, it is the "poor" to whom it will be given. Such an emphasis by no means entails any negation of present grace; it simply serves to provide an assurance that the consummation of God's salvation comes for them. No greater gift could be given by God to man than this. To those who have nothing, *everything* is given. As Luke recognized, that signifies a complete reversal of human conditions and values in the kingdom of God.

We have seen that at a very early date the beatitudes circulated with the third (Matt. 5:5) set in conjunction with the first (Matt. 5:3). Whatever the truth is about the *earliest* state of the textual tradition,[39] it is worthwhile to consider them together, if only to be reminded that the kingdom of heaven is fundamentally the kingdom of earth. While the majority of Christendom has been in the habit of thinking of "heaven" as the place for which the children of God are destined, Jesus makes the startling statement that the poor ("meek" = *anawim*) are to possess the *earth*. This accords with the prophetic and apocalyptic traditions almost in their entirety. We have already noted that Jesus does not give apocalyptic descriptions of the kingdom such as that contained in the book of Revelation, but we can assume that he would have shared the fundamental notion of the kingdom of God that the Seer represents through his picture of the city of God descending from heaven to earth: the kingdom of God *comes* from heaven to earth, and earth will be fitted to be the scene of such rule. Strangely, the concept of a "new creation" does not appear in the eschatological instruction of Jesus.[40] As Schniewind suggests, it is enough that he offers hope for the earth and hope for a new world through the promise of his resurrection.[41]

In the same way that the beatitude on the poor in Matthew 5:5 cites Psalm 37:11, the beatitude on the "grief-stricken" in Matthew 5:4 takes up the prophecy of Isaiah 61:2, which states that the task of the *mebasser* is "to comfort all who mourn" (LXX = *parakalesai pantas tous penthountas*). Matthew reproduces the terms, but with the verb in the passive, since it is God who is to console his people. The context of the phrase in Isaiah 61:1ff. indicates that the reference is not simply to mourners for the dead; the description of those addressed as "poor," "brokenhearted," and "captives" opens the term up to include the wretchedness of the people as a whole. Luke's term for the mourners, *hoi klaiontes* ("those who weep"), is therefore close to the intent of *penthountes* in Isaiah 61:1–2: the poor are full of grief for all that has overtaken them.[42] Grundmann draws attention to the broad application of the beatitude in his comment that "Whatever in human distress calls forth the grief of men, the grief-stricken is consoled with the assurance that God takes to his heart the mourner."[43]

Among the Jews, "Comforter" was one of the names given to the Messiah, and "consolation" known to be one of his gifts.[44] The phrase "the consolation of Israel" used in Luke 2:25 is an inclusive description of the kingdom of God; Schlatter has suggested that for Jews it signified nothing less than resurrection.[45] The "consolation" to be accorded to the mourners, then, is the gift of the kingdom of God with all its blessings. In rendering the beatitude "you shall laugh," it may have been Luke's intent to narrow its focus to one aspect of the salvation. It is often thought that this version is reminiscent of Psalm 126:1ff., in which the laughter constitutes an expression of delirious joy at the deliverance effected by the Lord, when even the nations marked the notable acts of the Lord for Israel. This nuance may well be implicit in Luke's wording of the beatitude: God's sorrowing poor will have their tears turned to happy laughter through the intervention of the Lord.[46] This is a feature of prophecy, old and new (cf. Isa. 25:8 and Rev. 21:4).

The beatitude promising happiness for the poor and the sorrowful is followed by a similar beatitude regarding the "hungry and thirsty."[47] We have already observed that the Lukan version keeps the beatitude within the orbit of the consolatory prophecies of Isaiah 58 and 61; the Matthaean addition to the beatitude provides an interpretative amplification in the same spirit as the additions in verses 3 and 10.[48] On the basis of the shorter reading, the promise given to the hungry and thirsty is highly pertinent: "they shall be satisfied" relates to the satiety that the Lord will ensure with the feast of the kingdom. The paradigmatic Isaiah 25:6 describes the lavish provision that will be made in that day, although the prophet's language is intended to conjure up less a picture of full bellies than one of unimaginable delight through the gracious deed of God: in that day the Lord will cause all earth to know him; he will vanquish death and banish sadness. The feast for the world is thus a picture of boundless happiness in the presence of God. How appropriate, then, is such a beatitude on the lips of him who ministered as the Mediator of the kingdom of God to the poor and outcasts! Matthew's interpretation of the hope has a largely similar content. If he had in mind hungering and thirsting to see God's righteousness established in the earth,[49] then his image of the feast of the kingdom would be much the same as that of Deutero- and Trito-Isaiah, for whom righteousness and salvation are virtually synonymous (see Isa. 45:22–25, 46:12ff., 61:10–11, and 62:1–3). If it was his intent to suggest that the acquisition of personal righteousness is the key without which none shall enter the kingdom (cf. Matt. 5:20 and 6:33), then he would have been thinking of the happiness of the feast in terms of the joy of the presence of God as it is expressed by the psalmist in Psalm 17:15:

> As for me, I shall behold thy face in righteousness;
> when I awake, I shall be satisfied with beholding thy form.[50]

Such beatitudes are sheer gospel. They exemplify the generosity of the God of grace, as do the three beatitudes that follow in Matthew 5:7–9. There is no suggestion in them of a *quid pro quo* in the last judgment, as though the merciful, the pure, and the peacemakers could lay claim to any approbation of the Almighty or pride of place in the kingdom of God on the basis of merit. Nevertheless there is a difference of accent in these beatitudes; the focus is not on the helplessness of those whom God makes heirs of his kingdom but on those qualities of God's poor, sorrowful, and hungry that call forth his approval in the last day. One is reminded of the prophetic word of Isaiah 66:2:

> This is the man to whom I will look,
>> he that is humble [*ani*] and contrite in spirit,
>> and trembles at my word.

In reproducing these sayings, we do not doubt that Matthew is assuming that it is necessary for the people of the new covenant to aspire to these qualities if they want to be accepted in the last day, but we do him an injustice if we interpret them as reflecting a legalistic intention. These beatitudes embody the spirit of the Sermon on the Mount and are in harmony with teaching of Jesus given elsewhere on entry into the kingdom of God (see Matt. 5:20 and 7:13–27; Mark 10:13–27 and 12:28–34).

The happiness of the merciful is mentioned first. The term Matthew uses (*eleemon*) is used in the Greek Old Testament to render the Hebrew *hannun* ("gracious"), which is applied by the Old Testament writers exclusively to God, with one exception—Psalm 112:3, which expounds a beatitude on the man who fears the Lord and who like him is gracious, compassionate, and generous. The spirit of that psalm is reproduced in many a rabbinic saying. In the Sayings of the Fathers, mercy is said to be the sign of the true Jew; he who is merciful to men belongs to the seed of Abraham, and he who does not show mercy does not belong to Abraham's descendants.[51] In the Sermon, Jesus calls on men to be merciful as God is merciful (Luke 6:36). The beatitude in verse 7 quite simply states that the merciful are happy, since they will receive mercy when they appear before God. This "mercy" represents not merely acquittal at the bar of God but the gracious verdict that gives entrance into the kingdom. Such is the import of Matthew 25:31–46: those who show pity in action for the relief of the needy are welcomed into the kingdom prepared for such, while those who show no mercy to the needy are excluded from it.[52]

The happiness of the "pure in heart" could originally have been attributed simply to the "pure"; Matthew may have added the words "in heart" in order to clarify its meaning, as he added the words "in spirit" to the first beatitude. Most scholars agree, however, that the longer phrase should stand. Burney has suggested that it is essential to the meter and the assonance of his Aramaic rendering.[53] It is widely believed that the beatitude reflects the psalmist's answer to the question, "Who shall ascend the hill of the Lord? And who shall stand in his holy place?"—namely,

> He who has clean hands and a pure heart. . . . (Ps. 24:3)

Not only does the precise phrase occur here (LXX *katharos te kardia* = *bar lebab*), but the eschatological blessing within the beatitude is anticipated in the psalm:

> He will receive blessing from the Lord,
> and vindication from the God of his salvation.

It is noteworthy that while the psalm has a cultic setting, the concept of purity it presents is similar to that of the prophetic outlook—an inner cleanness that is expressed in right action, in sincerity toward God and man. Such a notion of purity is closely related to the holiness rooted in God's adoption of a people and in their dedication to him. Those who are by such a reckoning "pure" exhibit a Godlike holiness and a desire to experience the holy fellowship of the kingdom of God.[54]

In any case, we are told that the authentically pure will "see God." None of the beatitudes makes it clearer than this that the end in view is the ultimate happiness that God can bestow on man—the vision of God in the perfected glory of his kingdom. This is not the language of "inaugurated eschatology," or whatever term be used to denote life under the saving sovereignty of God in the present; it is a reference to the final end, the goal of man's creation. Schniewind postulates that the emphasis in this beatitude is on the critical moment of the revelation of God in his glory and his acceptance of man, the *Einmaligkeit* ("solitary action") of the judgment, rather than on the eternal enjoyment of the presence of God in his kingdom; the beatitude is thus related to passages such as Matthew 25:41ff. and is in keeping with the Old Testament view that God hides his face from the wicked and shows it to the righteous as he rescues them (see especially Ps. 80, with its refrain "Restore us, O God, let thy face shine, that we may be saved").[55]

There is merit in Schniewind's interpretation of this beatitude; certainly it comports well with the outlook of the two beatitudes that flank it, both of which have to do with the action of God in the judgment. If the cultic background of Psalm 24 is assumed in the saying, it points to the culmination of the whole process of worship in the temple, since the phrase "to see the face of God" is commonly used in reference to attendance at the temple feasts and its worship (see Exod. 23:14–19; Isa. 1:11–12); this would agree with the expressions used in Revelation 22:3–4. We should also note that similar language is used in reference to appearing before a king in his court (see, for example, Gen. 43:3–4; cf. 2 Sam. 14:24ff.) and even of being in the service of a king (see 2 Kings 25:19). In the eschatological perspective, both elements of Israelite background could contribute to the complex of ideas associated with the gracious act of God in the last day: he takes the part of his own in their deliverance and welcomes them into his fellowship, which comprises both the priestly and the royal service of the children of the King of Kings.[56]

The beatitude pronounced upon the peacemakers is a promise of the same sort of happiness as that promised to the merciful—a happiness that consists in participation in the nature and works of God. Peace is God's great gift to the world; it is the most comprehensive word used to denote the salvation of his kingdom. The Rabbis frequently sang the praises of peace. They professed that God's name was peace (Judg. 6:24) and that the first word the Messiah would speak when he appeared would be "Peace," in accordance with Isaiah 52:7.[57] They often cited the exhortation in Psalm 34:14 to "Seek peace, and pursue it," and they viewed Aaron as the chief exemplar of the virtue, calling on their fellows to seek it as he did.[58] As Foerster has observed, "One might almost say that the role which peacemaking assumes among the Rabbis comes nearest to the NT concept of love, and takes the place in later Judaism which the requirement of love occupies in the NT."[59] Accordingly, it is wholly in accord with the traditions of his people that Jesus affirmed the happiness of the peacemakers.

Strangely enough, Billerbeck could find no saying in rabbinic literature to the effect that the peacemakers will be called "God's children."[60] That it should come from Jesus is entirely natural, in view of his teaching and experience of God as Father. Having initiated his disciples into an intimate relationship with God, as evidenced by his teaching them to call on him as *Abba*, he states that when God grants them mercy and allows them to see his face at the time of the judgment, he will also declare before all creation that they are his children. The language of the beatitude may well be reflecting that in Hosea 2:1, which notes that the day would come when the name given to the faithless people, *Lo-ammi* ("Not my people"), would be removed in favor of another:

> It shall no longer be said, "They are not my people," they shall be called *Sons of the Living God.*

Doubtless we are meant to understand that when God declares that the peace-makers are his sons at the judgment, he will thereby be welcoming them into the fellowship of his family in its perfected environment within the kingdom. In this respect, this beatitude is closely related to the one that precedes it.

The happiness of the "persecuted" is affirmed in two forms, a shorter form in verse 10 and a longer form in the Q sayings of verses 11–12. It is likely that the phrase in verse 10, "for the sake of righteousness," was added later, as was the reference to righteousness in verse 6, but the issue is disputed.[61] While Matthew appears to have been responsible for the addition of verse 6, it is uncertain that he is similarly responsible in verse 10: there is a clear echo of the beatitude in its present form in 1 Peter 3:14, which suggests a tradition earlier than the evangelist's work. Polycarp reproduces a macarism that combines the first and last beatitudes: "Happy are the poor and the persecuted for the sake of righteousness, for theirs is the kingdom of God" (*Phil.* 2:3). The combination serves as a reminder that we should understand the persecuted to comprise the poor, the sorrowful, and the hungry who are oppressed by the godless precisely because they are the people of God. From the time of Daniel on, the sentiment of verse 10 would have been cherished by devout Jews who looked for the consola-tion of Israel.[62] In this sense, Jesus could well have uttered the beatitude without modification as an expression and endorsement of the faith and hope of his people.

The form given to the beatitude in verses 11–12 is more specific in its description of the nature of the persecutions experienced. It is pointed out that the cause of the disciples' sufferings is their attachment to the persecuted representative of the kingdom of God. The common features of Matthew and Luke characterize the opposition as a revilement and defamation of the disciples for the sake of Jesus or of the Son of Man. The defamation is described in Matthew as "uttering every kind of calumny" (NEB, literally, "speaking every evil thing in a lying manner"). Luke's version is uncertain; the term *aphorizo* could reflect judicial language of excommunication from the synagogue (Schür-mann contends that the "casting out" of the name reflects the uttering of a curse on one so rejected).[63] It is possible, however, that the language is intended in a more general manner, denoting exclusion through social ostracism; since Luke does not suggest that Jewish authorities were invoking procedures of excommunication against Christians anywhere else, this interpretation is perhaps preferable, but the matter remains open.[64] In any case, the exclusion that takes place is effected because of the disciples' connection with Jesus. Luke's mention of the Son of Man should be compared with his preservation of the phrase in the crucial Q saying Luke 12:8–9, which is absent in Matthew's version (Matt. 10:32); Luke is almost certainly right in including the reference in 12:8–9, and the same is likely to be true here. The application of the term to Jesus in his capacity as representative of the kingdom of God is apt; those who have received his word and declared their loyalty to him suffer through their association with him.

In the day when the slander and defamation take place, the disciples are to "exult" (as Matthew has it) or "leap in a dance" (as Luke has it). M. Black points out that the Hebrew and Aramaic term *dus* covers both meanings; Matthew opted for one interpretation, and Luke opted for the other.[65] Why is such extraordinary counsel offered to persecuted disciples? Two answers are given: first, "You have a rich reward in heaven"; and second, "Your forebears treated the prophets in the same way." The first answer serves to align this beatitude with those that precede it. In saying that they will receive their reward "in heaven," Jesus was not intending to lay stress on a distinction between heaven and earth; rather, the emphasis is on "with God, who dwells in heaven"—which is to say, in the "kingdom of heaven," wherein the sorrowful will be consoled, the hungry will be satiated, the pure will see God, and so on.[66] The second reason Jesus gives for the disciples to be joyful is their association with the prophets. Matthew's slight alteration ("who were before you") implies that the disciples are persecuted not simply *as* the earlier prophets were, but as the *successors* of the prophets: in enduring persecution they are numbered with them! In both Matthew and Luke it is tacitly assumed that the opposition faced by the disciples of the Son of Man is matched by an opposition that the Son of Man himself must suffer; in fact, of course, it is the opposition he faced that embroiled his followers in a like fate. This passage, then, constitutes a foreboding of the rejection and suffering of the Son of Man described in Mark 8:31, which entails suffering on the part of his disciples also (see Mark 8:34).[67]

In conclusion, we see in the beatitudes of Jesus the proclamation of the good news of the kingdom of God to the poor. That the proclamation conveys inspiration for the people of God to continue in the path of faith and hope is self-evident. Nevertheless the primary emphasis in them is on the grace that is given to God's people in being numbered among the heirs of the kingdom of God. Matthew's concern to draw attention to the ethical appeal of the beatitudes does not subvert the element of grace that shines from the first to the last beatitude.

While the proclamation is strictly in harmony with the eschatological hope of the covenant people of God, it gains power and authority through the one who declares it. Only in the last beatitude is there any reference to the proclaimer, but that is crucial: he is the Son of Man to whom the kingdom is given and through whom it comes. Those who heard the earlier beatitudes could not have known this, but many among them must have been conscious of the unprecedented authority with which the message was spoken (see Matt. 7:29). Some at least traversed the path from the reception of the first beatitudes to the reception of the last and thus have come to believe that the salvation of which the beatitudes speak had been initiated in the redemptive action of the Mediator of the kingdom of heaven. The reader of the gospel standing on the farther side of the cross and resurrection shares that assurance. We, too, may direct our gaze to the point where they looked who first heard the beatitudes—to the unveiling of the grace that is to be brought in the revelation of the glory of the kingdom. So looking, we may share the happiness of those to whom the kingdom of heaven belongs.

3. THE FEAST OF THE KINGDOM OF GOD
Matthew 8:11–12, Luke 13:28–29

The first decision to be made concerning this saying relates to its form: is Matthew's version the more original, or Luke's, or do we have to attempt a reconstruction from both? The point is not really crucial for meaning: although the order and content of the two versions are clearly different, the sense of the passage is not dramatically affected by the variations. The wording of Matthew's statement of the nations coming to the feast of the kingdom of God (8:11) is actually very close to that given in Luke 13:29. It is in the second saying that the differences most sharply appear (cf. Matt. 8:12, Luke 13:28). But again, although the difference is interesting, it is does not entail any decisive alteration of the intent of the logion.

The order of clauses in Luke 13:28–29 is the reverse of that in Matthew 8:11–12. Trilling maintains that Luke reproduced two independent sayings (the first a threat and the second a promise) and that Matthew molded the two into a single logion, citing as evidence the fact that Luke's statement is simpler and that Matthew's version includes elements that are characteristic of his writing.[68] Yet more decisive, in I. Howard Marshall's view, is the awkward Aramaism with which Luke 13:28 concludes—*humas de ekballomenous hexo.* Following Black's demonstration that this phrase constitutes an Aramaic circumstantial participle that should be translated "while you are cast out,"[69] Marshall has concluded that Luke's version of the saying must be more primitive than Matthew's version.[70] On the other hand, it would appear that the context in which Luke has set the passage has influenced both its order and the wording of 13:28. In 13:24 a warning is given that one must strive to enter through the narrow door into the kingdom of God, for many who seek to do so will be unsuccessful. This warning is followed by a related parabolic fragment telling of the master of the house who will shut the door on people claiming admission: "You may stand outside and knock, and say 'Sir, let us in!' but he will only answer 'I do not know where you come from.'" It would appear that Luke switched the order of clauses in verses 28–29 so that these preceding verses might be followed with the words "*There* shall be the weeping and gnashing of teeth"; furthermore, this redaction would also account for the addition of the words "when you see" to the phrase "when you see Abraham and Isaac . . . in the kingdom of God." Thus, we should assume Matthew's order to be the more primitive of the two versions. The antithetic parallelism of his clauses tells in his favor, and the fact that the ideas they present are so closely connected would seem to weaken Trilling's argument that they were originally two independent sentences that have been brought together here.[71] Nevertheless, the details of the two clauses as they are presented by the two evangelists will have to be settled on their individual merits.

Matthew's "many" may or may not be original (Luke presumes a simple "they," v. 29); it could reflect the well-known use of the term to represent the multitude from Gentile nations at the end time when the kingdom comes.[72] Matthew's briefer statement of the directions from which the Gentiles come to share in the feast—"from east and west"—suffices to indicate a universal movement; Luke probably filled it out along the lines of such scriptures as Isaiah 43:5–6 and Psalm 107:3.

In the next clause, the phrase "the sons of the kingdom" is more problematic. Luke's *hotan opsesthe* is most likely the result of the evangelist's effort to link the saying with 13:25–27. The Matthaean version more closely resembles standard Jewish phraseology (note such similar constructions as "sons of the bridechamber" in Matt. 9:15 // Mark 2:19, and "sons of Gehenna" in Matt. 23:15).[73] According to Billerbeck, "sons of the kingdom" simply means citizens of the kingdom, just as "sons of the city" denotes a city's inhabitants.[74]

The "outer darkness" of Matthew 8:12 is rendered the "outside" in Luke 13:29. Again, the longer version reflects established Jewish modes of speech and thought, especially with regard to the contrast between the light in which the feast of the kingdom takes place and the darkness into which those who are not allowed to attend are cast (see especially Matt. 22:11–13).[75] Nevertheless, the simpler version in Luke could be original. Interestingly, the phrase that is so characteristic of Matthew—"there shall be the weeping and gnashing of teeth" (Matt. 8:12)—also occurs in Luke 13:28, suggesting that it was likely present in the common source Q. It could be that Matthew first found the phrase in this passage, relished it, and subsequently employed it in related sayings of Jesus (e.g., in Matt. 13:42, 50; 22:13; 24:51; and 25:30).

In seeking to determine the meaning of the logion about the feast of the kingdom, it is important to note that there does not appear to be any single Old Testament passage that served as its inspiration. There are, of course, many passages in the Old Testament that speak of the nations making their way to Zion at the end of the age to pay homage to Yahweh and to Israel (e.g., Isa. 2:1ff.), but in none of these is mention made of the nations sharing in the feast of the kingdom of God. On the other hand, Isaiah 25:6ff., which provides the classic description of the feast for the nations given by God, makes no mention of the peoples streaming from all parts of the world to Zion, and naturally there is no hint of Israel being excluded from that feast. Accordingly, we have in this saying an independent formulation—and a rather drastic modification—of an idea for which the Old Testament prophets prepared. The relation of this thought to the prophetic predecessors and apocalyptic contemporaries of Jesus bears closer examination.

Jeremias gives a classic exposition of Matthew 8:11ff. He sees in it an expression of a very important concept in Old Testament prophecy—namely, that of the eschatological pilgrimage of the nations to the mountain of God— which he believes to have been among a complex of biblical ideas then current among the Jews, of which Jesus would have known as well. Jeremias maintains that an examination of the writings of the prophets enables us to piece together this complex of ideas that Jesus and his contemporaries had concerning the end time as it related to the nations. They anticipated that first *the epiphany of God* would take place, including in its scope all nations (see, for example, Zech. 2:13 and Isa. 40:5, 51:4, and 52:10). The epiphany would then issue in *the call of God* to the world to turn to him (see, for example, Isa. 25:20ff. and 55:5; and Ps. 96:3) and to come to Zion and offer worship in its temple (see Isa. 66:19–20). Then *the Gentiles would make their journey to the mountain of the Lord*, bringing gifts and the dispersed of Israel with them (see Isa. 2:2; 45:14, 23–24; and 56:7; and Zech. 3:9). Finally, they would participate in *the banquet of the Lord* (see Isa. 25:6ff.). Thus, says Jeremias, "the goal of the pilgrimage is the scene of God's revelation of himself, Zion, the Mountain of God. . . . The Gentiles will not be evangelized where they dwell, but will be summoned to the holy Mount by the divine epiphany."[76]

This representation of the "pilgrimage of the nations" has been criticized by Dieter Zeller as an artificial reconstruction; he finds it nowhere attested in this fashion, and argues that it constitutes a basic misunderstanding of the function of the "pilgrimage" in the Old Testament.[77] He contends that the origin of the concept is the celebration of the kingship of Yahweh, who manifests his rule over the nations in coming to the help of his people, and that the nations turn to God not primarily as an expression of a change in heart toward the true God but in response to the revelation of Yahweh's glory in his conquest of Israel's enemies. Zeller goes on to suggest that the nations have a double function in the delineation of the end-time events: their utter defeat as religious and political enemies serves both to remove a threat to Israel and to demonstrate the glory of Yahweh's name. The prophetic redaction combines these two elements in the epiphany of judgment and the offering of worship by the nations (see Zech. 3:8ff. and Isa. 66:5–24). There is a similar combination of the two elements in the apocalyptic literature, although in these writings the pilgrimage of the nations to Zion is deemphasized, and the conversion of the Gentiles is hardly ever mentioned at all; it is assumed that the new age will have no real place for them.[78] The chief point that Zeller seeks to make is that the idea of the stream of nations paying homage to Zion does not have an independent significance anywhere in the Old Testament or its apocalyptic successors. The basic concept itself does not include an answer to the question of how the nations come to salvation, he suggests; rather, it belongs to the revelation of Yahweh as the God of his people. The worldwide reaction to God in the context of this idea is presented more as a factor in the relationship between Israel and God as its Lord and King than as an objective comment on the destiny of the nations in their own right.

It may be that Zeller has minimized the significance of some Old Testament passages (e.g., Isa. 2, Mic. 4, and still more the Servant Songs of Deutero-Isaiah), but it should also be remembered that the Jews of Jesus' time did not separate out and exalt these passages above the more "nationalist" prophecies of the end in the works of the prophets, as tends to be the case in our own day; on the contrary, the literature reveals that the reverse took place, that the turning of the nations to the Lord was viewed as a prophecy of their subjection to Israel in the kingdom of God. There is, however, not the slightest trace of this latter tendency in the teaching of Jesus; in fact, the logion of the feast of the nations presents the opposite idea.

A. Polag argues that it is not necessary to relate the idea of the pilgrimage of the nations to Matthew 8:11–12, and in this he is probably right.[79] Perhaps we should recognize the simple fact that the tradition of the messianic feast, so movingly expressed in Isaiah 25:6ff., was accepted by Jesus as a fitting symbol of the kingdom of God. None of the accompaniments of the "pilgrimage of the nations" is alluded to in our passage. Most notably, there is no mention of the defeat of the Gentiles or their subjection to Israel in the kingdom of God; rather, the nations are described as coming from all quarters of the world to participate in the feast of God with Israel's founding fathers, whereas Jesus tells the Jews that they will be excluded from the feast. The Gentiles will not be forced to serve the Jews, but will in fact be given the privileges that the Jews considered their exclusive heritage while the Jews are expelled from the kingdom. The thrust of the saying, therefore, is a devastating declaration of judgment on Israel.

The shock of this saying is difficult for us to imagine. It was axiomatic for the Jews of Jesus' time that the kingdom of God belonged to them. It was an exercise of charity on their part to contemplate the possibility of Gentiles being admitted to the kingdom promised to them, but to think of the Gentiles *replacing* them in the kingdom of God was incomprehensible. Some recent scholars contend that it would have been too drastic an idea even for Jesus. Zeller, for example, suggests that an outright denial of the Jewish nation in these terms could never have issued from the lips of Jesus; consequently, he follows Käsemann in holding that this saying was an "eschatological judgment of holy law" of a sort that was current in the early church, and that it must have been uttered by a Christian prophet in face of the Jewish rejection of the *Christian mission*.[80]

There is something seriously wrong here. Apart from the fact that we have no evidence that Jewish Christians pronounced such a judgment on their own nation, this saying is far from standing alone in the tradition of the words of Jesus. Luke 13:28c, whether original or not, points to the real meaning of the saying: the phrase "while *you* are cast out" is directed to *Jews listening to Jesus who reject the message of the kingdom of God proclaimed by him*; it in no way implies that the whole nation was guilty of the same rejection.

We find similar utterances attributed to Jesus on many occasions. For example, he likened his generation to quarrelsome children at their games after they had given unreasonable excuses for rejecting the message of both John and Jesus (see Matt. 11:16–18 // Luke 7:31–35). He condemned Chorazin, Bethsaida, and Capernaum for giving a response to the revelation of God in his ministry that was less enthusiastic than Tyre, Sidon, or Sodom would have given had they been offered a like opportunity (see Matt.11:21–24 // Luke 10:13–15). He referred to the condemnation that the Ninevites and the Queen of Sheba will utter at the judgment, since they gave heed to the word of God that was delivered to them by Jonah and Solomon, whereas Jesus' generation would not listen to God's ultimate messenger and was blind to the divine sovereignty at work in him (see Matt. 12:41–42 // Luke 11:31–32). And he announced that his generation, in which the rebellion against God's messengers had come to a climax, would suffer the climax of God's judgments (see Matt. 23:34–36 // Luke 11:49–51).

Jesus' pronouncements of judgment upon Israel reach a crescendo in the logion in Matthew 23:34–36 // Luke 11:49–51, but the severity of the judgment in the logion of the Feast of the Kingdom is no less evident. It finds its closest parallel in a parable as authentic as any words attributed to Jesus—namely, that of the feast to which the invited guests did not go (Matt. 22:1–10 // Luke 14:15–24). Luke's conclusion to that parable, "I tell you that *not one of those who were invited shall taste my banquet*" (Luke 13:24), can be interpreted as a substantiation of the position Trilling and Zeller have adopted concerning Matthew 8:11–12. But in fact such an interpretation would be incorrect, for the parable goes on to speak of fresh invitations being sent to the common people, who gladly accepted them—and Luke understood these new guests to include both Jews and Gentiles! He goes on to speak of the festive hall being so packed with guests that there was no room for those originally invited.

Is it not clear that in these passages Jesus is condemning his generation of Jews for rejecting the word of God presented through him, and most especially condemning their spiritual leaders and those following them? These declarations of judgment in no way excluded either the "little flock" (see Luke 12:32) or those who heard and gratefully received the message of the beatitudes from participation in the kingdom of God. In this regard, S. Schulz has rightly pointed out that

> Not all Israel of the present generation falls to the eschatological judgment on the basis of the prophetic utterance, but in the context of Q it is the unbelieving and impenitent Israel represented by the Pharisees, not the Israel of publicans and sinners, which joyfully received God's second invitation. . . . Those called by Jesus, including the publicans and sinners, alone represent the chosen Israel in the end time.[81]

What lessons, then, are we to draw from this statement? First, its primary purpose is a negative one: pronouncing judgment on Jews who reject the word of the kingdom brought by Jesus. Inasmuch as all prophetic declarations of judgment are given with a view to encouraging the hearers to repent and change their ways, we may view this logion as a warning rather than as the pronouncement of a verdict and a sentence. This is especially clear in Luke's version, with its direct mode of address; the call "Strive to enter" of 13:24 sets the tone for the parable that follows and for the saying concerning the feast of the kingdom. Jesus was explaining to those who listened that they need not have the door of the kingdom shut against them, that they need not be excluded from the feast.

The positive implications of the logion are no less important. Jesus anticipates that multitudes of the nations will share with "Abraham, Isaac, and Jacob" in the feast of the kingdom of God.[82] The patriarchs are not named as the heroes of Israel, but rather as Israel's representatives: they stand for the nation that was called into being through them.[83] The absence of any hint that the Gentiles will be considered inferior as they share in the feast with Israel, coupled with the fact that the unworthy of Israel will be excluded, suggests that the Gentiles and Jews will be admitted to the feast as equal beneficiaries of God's gracious gener-osity—or in other words, that the guests at the feast form the community of salvation, the one people of God drawn from all nations.[84]

Finally, we may note that the symbol of the feast of the kingdom of God can be given either a higher or a lower interpretation. It became a standing convic-tion among the Rabbis that Leviathan, the sea monster, and Behemoth, the land monster, were being reserved as food for the elect in the feast of the kingdom of God—one even finds the expression "the Leviathan meal" for that feast.[85] The paradigmatic passage of Isaiah 25:6ff. presents a richer meaning, however. As Jeremias has pointed out, this passage is part of a body of symbolism appearing throughout the Bible in which eating and drinking serve as a means of mediat-ing the vision of God; hence, "when the festal meal on the Mountain of God is celebrated, the veil that covers the eyes of the Gentiles will be forever rent asunder, and they will behold God with unveiled face."[86] The issue of whether the reference to resurrection in Isaiah 25:7–8 is original to the text is irrelevant for our purpose: it stands written there that the Lord God will wipe away the tears from every face and "swallow up death forever." Similarly, in Matthew 8:11–12 the presence of Abraham, Isaac, and Jacob at the feast indicates that the resurrection of the dead has taken place. The feast is not an occasion of gorman-dizing (not even on Leviathan and Behemoth); instead, it is meant to represent the gladness that comes when God is known, the joy of fellowship and the life eternal that God bestows in the revelation of his saving sovereignty.

4. SAYINGS ON THE ENTRY INTO THE KINGDOM OF GOD

The sayings of Jesus that speak of entering into the kingdom of God have a special place in the body of his teaching about the kingdom.[87] Matthew has the largest number of such sayings (viz., 5:20, 7:21, 21:13, and 23:13 // Luke 11:52), together with parabolic references to the same idea (in 7:13–14 [cf. Luke 13:24–25], 25:10, 25:21 and 23, and 25:30). Mark has three logia on this theme of no little importance (viz., 9:43, 45, and 47 // Matt. 18:8–9; 10:15 // Matt. 18:3 // Luke 18:17; and 10:23 // Matthew 19:23 // Luke 18:17). We shall examine these passages, though not in this order, then consider two related sayings (in Matt. 16:19 and Luke 12:32), and finally attempt to reach some conclusions on the basis of the review.

a. Mark 9:43–48 // Matthew 8:8–9
This group of sayings in Mark almost certainly came together in the tradition prior to Mark; they were linked with verse 42 through the catchword *skan-dalizein*, "offend" or "entice."[88] Through startling hyperbolic language they convey a call for drastic action in order to attain the goal of life. The contempo-rary belief among Jews that the hand, eye, and foot are the most important members of the body in which the sinful impulse resides goes back to the old Semitic attribution of psychological functions to parts of the body.[89] It is doubtful that Jesus would have pressed this association, since he stressed the heart as the source of sinful action.[90] Amputation served as an alternative to execution as punishment for certain crimes among the Jews and others in the

ancient world, but self-mutilation was held to be an abominable practice; the demand therefore is clearly not for literal amputation or the like, but for "radical decision against one's ego to avoid perishing in the hell of fire."[91] Mark would doubtless have seen in this saying a demand that those who hear it should apply to themselves the principle that the Lord himself accepted as he made his way to Golgotha, a law of the kingdom that embraces both Master and disciples (see Mark 8:34ff.).

For our purpose it is important to observe that the "radical decision" to sacrifice something of supreme worth is made in order to enter into *life* (vv. 43, 45), and that this is defined in verse 47 as entering into *the kingdom of God*. In each case the possibility of attaining this goal is contrasted with the possibility of "going off" or being "thrown into" *Gehenna*.[92] The parallelism of "life" and kingdom of God is instructive. The life is equated with the individual's participation in the kingdom of God, which is fundamentally a corporate concept, the divine sovereignty over man and the world; individual participation in the kingdom of God is accomplished through resurrection.[93] The passage makes it quite clear that it was Jesus' understanding that entrance into the kingdom of God in the present entails participation in the kingdom that will arrive in its fullness after the judgment, since the alternative to entering the kingdom is going into Gehenna.[94]

b. Parabolic Sayings
It is fitting at this point to recall the references to entering the kingdom of God in the three parables of Matthew 25: the wise maidens go with the bridegroom into his house for the marriage celebrations (v. 10); the faithful servants are invited by their master to "enter the joy of your master" (vv. 21, 23), which may signify an invitation to "come into the feast to celebrate";[95] and the sheep on the Shepherd-King's right hand are welcomed to "come . . . inherit the kingdom prepared for you from the foundation of the world" (v. 34). Each of these representations is accompanied by a corresponding description of rejection (v. 12), or ejection into outer darkness (v. 32) or Gehenna (v. 46). There is a similar representation in the parable of the Great Feast (Matt. 22:9 // Luke 14:23); the fact that those who were originally invited missed the feast because they would not come is clear from the parable, but the point is underscored in the additional parable of the man not wearing a wedding garment (Matt. 22:11–13). Jesus presents a comparable idea with the figure of entering through the door of a building (palace, or temple?) or gate of a city (see Matt. 7:13–14 // Luke 13:23–24, which Luke extends in 13:25ff.).

c. Matthew 7:21
Judgment is described in this logion in terms of exclusion from the kingdom of God: "Not everyone who calls me 'Lord, Lord' will enter the kingdom of heaven." The saying is evidently a reformulation of the Q logion, alternatively rendered in Luke 6:46, and expressed in terms of an entrance saying.[96] It is significant as an indication of the evangelist's understanding of the entrance sayings generally.

d. Mark 10:23 // Matthew 19:23 // Luke 18:24

The shattering utterances concerning entry into the kingdom in Mark 9:43–48 are matched by the equally forceful sayings in Mark 10:23ff. The context shows equations similar to those in the former passage. The man who kneels before Jesus wants to know what he must do in order to "inherit eternal life." The language reflects two images: first, the inheritance of the promised land of Canaan, a symbol of entry into the kingdom of God promised to the Fathers (second exodus typology); and second, admission into the kingdom of God as admission into "eternal life," so called because one receives the new life through resurrection and the new age is eternal. The first image is essentially corporate, and the second is essentially individual, although the concept of inheritance itself became individualized in Judaism.[97] The response of the questioner to Jesus' statement that he should keep the commandments reflects his confident belief that he has kept the whole law, which was not an unusual conviction among pious Jews.[98] Jesus then reveals to him the one thing he lacks: *treasure in heaven*, another synonym for life in the kingdom of God, since "heaven" here means God ("in heaven" = "with God").[99] When the man declines the invitation to meet the conditions for gaining that treasure—namely, giving up his treasure on earth and following Jesus—Jesus makes the unexpected statement, "How hard it will be for the wealthy to enter the kingdom of God!" and then yet more strongly states that "It is easier for a camel to pass through the eye of a needle than for a rich man to enter the kingdom of God." The surprise of those who heard these statements would have been the greater in light of the fact that they would have assumed that possession of land within the promised land was a guaranteed part of their inheritance in the kingdom of God, a survival of the concept of the land as an eternal inheritance, wherein God's glorious reign would be revealed.[100]

Lodged between the two sayings on wealth and the kingdom of God is a yet more disturbing saying:"Children, how hard it is to enter the kingdom of God!" (v. 24). There is no limit set on the application in this logion; it is in fact a statement of universal application. The astonished disciples ask, "Then who can be saved?"—the words "be saved" indicating a fourth synonym for the eschatological redemption.[101] To that question the answer of Jesus is positively alarming: "For men it is impossible." The fact that Mark places verse 28 at this point gives the impression that the consoling assurance "But not for God; everything is possible for God" is scarcely heard; naturally God can do all things, but for whom will he do this? There follows the encouraging assurance of verses 29–30, which defines a contrast between the reluctant rich man and the disciples who have left all things to accompany Jesus in his service. Those disciples who walk with Jesus, forsaking all things to become wandering heralds of the kingdom of God, can look forward to the recompense of the age to come with blessings a hundredfold beyond all sacrifices, to be followed by *life eternal in the coming age*.[102]

It is clear that the interests and concerns of the church were in Mark's mind as he penned this narrative. The relation of discipleship to possessions would have been a matter of even greater importance to the primitive community than it would have been to succeeding generations, since following Jesus was a costly venture. Not a few wandered in the service of their Lord as the Twelve did, and many paid the utmost price for their discipleship; beyond this, all confessors of the Christ needed encouragement. For our purposes it is important to note that the subject of the narrative is the attainment of *life eternal* in *the kingdom of God*, which is final *salvation* in *the age to come*. Significantly the most disturbing saying of the passage, verse 24, is couched in the present tense—"How hard it is to enter the kingdom of God!" Yet it is apparent that the entrance in view is in the future rather than the present. Nevertheless, there is a present experience of the kingdom of God for those who follow in the way of Jesus: a fellowship of heirs of the divine sovereignty, an anticipation of the blessed fellowship with God and man in the life eternal of the kingdom of God.

e. Mark 10:15 // Matthew 18:3 // Luke 18:17

The majority of exegetes hold that Mark 10:15 is an independent saying that was placed in the context of the pronouncement story appearing in 10:13, 14, and 16 because of its similarity to verse 14.[103] The entrance into the kingdom of God mentioned in verse 15 is spoken of in the future tense. There would not appear to be any reason for suspecting that the saying is referring to anything other than participation in the future kingdom, but the condition for entry into the future kingdom is unexpected: one must "accept the kingdom of God like a child" in order to enter it. What is meant by "accepting" or "receiving" the kingdom of God? Some scholars have interpreted the phrase as signifying the acceptance of *the message* of the kingdom of God: whoever would enter the kingdom of God when it comes in the future must receive the good news of the kingdom of God brought by Jesus with the simplicity of faith manifested by a child.[104] Ambrozic contends that the saying is rooted in the wisdom tradition and that in the pre-Markan tradition it must therefore have included a reference to the "word" or "secrets" (*musteria*) of the kingdom of God ("Whoever does not receive the *secrets* of the kingdom of God shall not enter"); in that light he holds that the saying points to the necessity of receiving the gospel of the kingdom of God as a "child"—that is, as a pupil who receives instruction in the divine wisdom.[105]

I confess that it is not easy to see why Mark would have wished to eliminate either the term "word" or "secret" from the saying had he known it in that form, particularly since he was so fond of the terms "word," "gospel," and "secret." It is simpler to take the text as it stands and assume that Jesus is speaking of the necessity of receiving the kingdom of God as a child receives it. If *basileia* is the saving rule of God, why should it be thought strange to "accept" that rule, in the sense of submitting oneself to the Lord, who exercises his sovereignty in *bestowing* salvation? Or, in other words, why should it be thought strange to acknowledge the presence of the saving sovereignty of Jesus and so receive the salvation that the sovereign Lord bestows in such fashion as is possible in the present life? Schnackenburg makes a point of the fact that there is no other passage in which the present reign of God is regarded as a saving grace for individuals.[106] But I do not understand this objection. Surely granting forgiveness of sins and healing through Jesus to someone in need of both amounts to bestowing the saving grace of the sovereignty of God (by the Son of Man!) to an individual (see Mark 2:10–11). And the same thing would apply to the gifts of healing described in Matthew 11:5, which are viewed as evidences of the saving sovereignty among people; to the deliverance of individuals from Satan's power, such as that recorded in Mark 3:27 and Matthew 12:28; and to the fellowship with Christ that publicans and sinners were granted, which adumbrated the fellowship to be enjoyed in the feast of the kingdom of God (see Mark 2:19). Thus, while fully recognizing the emphasis Jesus placed on entrance into the kingdom of God as the goal of hope, we should also recognize the elements of his proclamation that conjoin with hope for the future the dynamic operation of the saving sovereignty in the present. As Pesch points out, this dual emphasis is also apparent in Jesus' exhortations to seek the kingdom of God (see Matt. 6:33) and in his intimations of the joy of finding it, as in the parables of the Treasure and the Pearl (see Matt. 13:44–45). The picture, but not the reality, changes when Jesus speaks of receiving the kingdom of God as a child: *only those who receive it in that manner now can be assured of entering it when it comes in its fullness.*[107]

f. Matthew 5:20

It is not inappropriate to pass from Mark 10:14–15 to the consideration of this saying. While it is customary to emphasize the function of Matthew 5:20 as providing a heading for the antitheses of 5:21–28,[108] there is little doubt that the saying is also closely bound with verses 17–19. Schürmann has called attention to the kinship between Matthew 5:17–20 and Luke 16:14–18; in particular, he sees a close link between Matthew 5:20 and Luke 16:15 (+ 16?), and comes to the conclusion that "Matthew in his way in 5:20 repeats Luke 16:15 (16), *whereby the same sentence structure as Matthew 18:3 is utilized (ean me . . . ou me eiselthete eis ten basileian* = 'unless you . . . you will not enter into the kingdom')."[109] I believe this link between both the structure and the thought of the two passages provides an important clue to the meaning of Matthew 5:20. It is a mistake to interpret the *perisseuein* (the "surpassing" of Pharisaic righteousness) in terms of a quantitatively larger fulfillment of the law's demands than that which the scribes and Pharisees achieve.[110] Windisch was at least on the right track when he commented that "The righteousness which opens the kingdom is here won through repentance, which the Baptist proclaimed (21.32)."[111] He would have been even more on target had he referred to the proclamation of Jesus as well as that of John, for Jesus demanded repentance not only in the light of the coming of the kingdom of God in the future but also in the face of the new thing that God was doing in the present— repentance that entailed a radical commitment "in the fulness of surrender to God's will."[112] It was this kind of repentance and faith to which Jesus pointed when speaking about receiving the kingdom of God as a child, for it is only when the kingdom is approached in this fashion that the required obedience— of a sort the scribes and Pharisees did not know (Matt. 23:3)—becomes possible. To respond wholeheartedly to the message of Jesus is to know that "eschatological superabundance" which issues in a righteousness acceptable to God and entrance into the kingdom of God in the last day.

g. Matthew 21:31, 23:13 // Luke 11:52

These two entrance sayings have two features in common: both address the failure of the Jewish leaders to respond to God's call to the kingdom through Jesus, and both present an ambiguity relating to the time of entry into the kingdom of God. The saying in Matthew 21:31 is peculiar to that evangelist; the one in Matthew 23:13 // Luke 11:52 is a Q logion.

Matthew 21:31 forms the climax of the parable of the Two Sons. One son initially refuses his father's request to work in the vineyard but later repents and goes, and the other initially declares that he will go into the vineyard but then fails to do so. After gaining from his hearers the admission that it was the former son who did the father's will,[113] Jesus makes the application: "I tell you this: tax-gatherers and prostitutes are entering the kingdom of God ahead of you." So the NEB renders the statement, from which we are presumably to deduce that the sinners of Israel are making their way into the kingdom of God in the present, while the Jewish leaders remain outside. This understanding of the saying suits those elements in the teaching of Jesus indicating that the powers of the kingdom of God are operative among men through him, and especially those elements regarding the fellowship of the kingdom of God that publicans and sinners enjoyed through his ministry to them. These factors are enough to recommend the interpretation to a number of scholars,[114] but it poses some difficulties as well; notably, it does not comport well with the entrance sayings we have reviewed thus far. For this reason Jeremias paraphrases the saying as follows: "Verily, I say unto you, publicans and harlots shall (at the Last Judgment) enter the kingdom of God rather than you."[115] He maintains that *proagousin* renders an Aramaic participle, which is timeless, and has to be rendered according to context; if this is the case, the other entrance sayings demand the future meaning. Jeremias further contends that the *pro* in the verb *proagousin* has an exclusive rather than a temporal force. This interpretation is logical enough, and it is accepted by a majority of exegetes.

The Q logion is more difficult to interpret with confidence. Behind the difference in the renderings of Matthew and Luke, we can see that a common image is being employed—namely, that of the key which unlocks the door to (the knowledge of God and) the kingdom of God. The logion assumes that the scribes and Pharisees possess the key but are misusing it, so that they neither "enter" nor permit others who "are entering" (conative?) to do so. Some scholars contend that the reference is to the kingdom of God of the last time, and so they place it with the other entrance sayings we have been considering.[116] More recent scholarship is increasingly assuming that the saying relates to the kingdom of God in the present time.[117] Perhaps we come closer to the heart of the saying if we recognize that its weight falls less on the *time of entrance into the kingdom* than on the *opposition of the scribes and Pharisees to the kingdom*, expressed in their shutting the door in the face of men (as the version of the saying in Matthew suggests) or their removal of the key of knowledge (as the version in Luke suggests) to prevent those who would enter from doing so.

The fact that Matthew placed 23:2–3a at the head of this chapter would seem to suggest that he equated the opposition referred to in the saying with the resistance of the Scribes and Pharisees to the ministry of Jesus. Elsewhere the evangelist notes their hostile opposition to his teaching (Matt. 9:2ff.) and his mode of life (9:10ff.) as well as their attribution of his powers of healing and exorcism to the work of the devil (12:22ff.), thereby slandering the Holy Spirit who was operative in him (12:31–32). A similar opposition may also be reflected in the logion of Matthew 11:12 and the parable of the Tares and the Wheat (13:24ff.). This interpretation is consonant with the acknowledgment in Matthew 23:13 that the scribes possess the keys of the kingdom, but suggests that *they misuse the keys in their opposition to the herald and representative of the kingdom of God*. It was their belief that Jesus came not to fulfill but to destroy the law and the prophets (cf. Matt. 5:17), and so as the exponents of the word of God, they sought to prevent the people from paying attention to him. A. Polag concurs with this interpretation:

> The polemic against the Pharisees and teachers of the law is not concerned with the rightness of the exposition of the law, not even with the observance of the law in itself. Neither does the moral failure stand in the foreground of the criticism. It is concerned with their inability to grasp a new action of God which corresponds with the work of God through the prophets. This incapacity doubtless is rooted in a failure to orientate themselves to God, in their self-righteousness and the rejection of repentance bound up with it. The teachers therefore are not in the position to recognize the effective operation of the kingdom in Jesus. This state of affairs becomes an object of criticism because the teachers exercise a fateful influence: through their teaching they hold back from men the knowledge of God's action and so hinder their participation in the *basileia*.[118]

Such an interpretation can afford to leave open the question of whether it is the present or future kingdom into which men are said to enter. In this saying, as in several of the entry logia we have considered, the assumption is apparent that the kingdom of God is operative in Jesus, and its powers accessible to those who are confronted by him. This saying differs from the others in that it seems to speak more clearly of entrance into the present sphere of operation of the kingdom, although it is not out of keeping with the other entrance sayings, as Jeremias demonstrates. One factor influences my own decision in the matter: the saying of Jesus in Matthew 11:1 appears to speak of people being *in* the kingdom in the present time: "Never has there appeared on earth a mother's son greater than John the Baptist, and yet *the least in the kingdom of heaven is greater than he*." Windisch, who is convinced that the entrance sayings relate exclusively to the future, is forced to understand this saying as indicating that Jesus ranked John the Baptist with the rabbis, the Pharisees, the rich, the cowards, and the half-hearted among those who are *excluded* from the kingdom of God, just as he understands Matthew 11:6 to be implying that John took offense at Jesus and is one of those who will certainly be rejected because of unbelief (see Mark 6:3 par.).[119] I find this interpretation incredible, but it is instructive to see where one is led if one insists that Jesus *never* countenanced entrance into the kingdom of God prior to the judgment. On the other hand, while it might be possible to cite Matthew 23:13 along with Matthew 11:11 as an example of Jesus' indication that one can enter into the kingdom in the present time, this interpretation remains admittedly uncertain.

5. THE KEYS OF THE KINGDOM
Matthew 16:19

In his discussion of Matthew 16:18–19 Trilling begins by affirming two "assured and generally recognized results" of earlier debates on this passage: its great age, and the secondary position of the text in relation to its context.[120] This judgment is especially true of verse 19, which incontestably has a Semitic character and may have a connection with Peter's confession.[121] Trilling indeed is uncertain whether verse 19 has any connection with verse 18, other than through the person of Peter, who is the binding link of the two logia.[122] Whatever the truth of the matter is (we shall return to that question shortly), it is clear that we can proceed to interpret verse 19 on its own merits.

Although the metaphorical use of "keys" is widely attested in the ancient world, not least among the Jews, the phrase "the keys of the kingdom of heaven" does not seem to appear anywhere outside of Christian literature.[123] We have already seen that Matthew 23:13 speaks of locking and opening the door of the kingdom of heaven, and that it is natural to link that saying with Matthew 16:19. Grundmann suggests that in the latter passage it is presumed that the power of the keys is transferred from the scribes to Peter, making him the authorized teacher of the people of God and thereby fulfilling Isaiah 22:15–25, in which Shebna is rejected and Eliakim installed.[124] Admirable as the suggestion is, it is unlikely that it captures the original intent of the saying; surely if Jesus gives the key to Peter, the overriding implication must be that Jesus himself possesses the authority it denotes, and that it is this authority which he imparts to Peter. It so happens that Isaiah 22:22 was never interpreted messianically among the Jews,[125] but its language is peculiarly suitable here, for the key given to Eliakim was of "the house of David"—literally the palace in Jerusalem—and possession of the key implied authority within the palace.

The use of the symbol in Revelation 3:7 is very instructive. It is stated that the risen Lord has "the key of David"; when he opens the door none can shut it, and when he shuts none can open it. The Philadelphian congregation is assured therefore that it is their Lord who has authority to admit people to the kingdom of God and to exclude them from it. In the face of denials by the Jews that they have any part in the kingdom of God, the Lord says, "I have set before you an opened door, which none can shut" (v. 8). Since the Christ who authorizes entrance into the kingdom has opened it for them, their place in the kingdom is secure.[126] In Revelation 1:8 the symbol of the keys is basically similar: the Christ, as the Living One who died and is alive forevermore, has "the keys of death and Hades"; through his death and resurrection he has conquered the forces of death, and so has power to open the gates of death that those who are shut within may enter the eternal kingdom of God, sharing with him in the resurrection from the dead. So also in Matthew 16:19, the presentation of the keys of the kingdom of heaven to Peter indicates that he is being given the authority to open the door of the kingdom that people may enter it.

The second and third clauses of Matthew 16:19 explain the authority entailed in the possession of the keys of the kingdom of heaven:

> Whatever you bind on earth shall be bound in heaven, and whatever you loose on earth shall be loosed in heaven.

The verbs "shall be bound" and "shall be loosed" are examples of the "divine passive," an indirect mode of referring to God's action that in this case is reduplicated by the use of the phrase "in heaven," which of course denotes "with God." It is well known that the language of "binding and loosing" is used in Rabbinic literature for scribal determinations concerning actions that are "forbidden" or "allowed" on the basis of authoritative interpretation of the Torah, although it can be used also for imposing or relieving the "ban" on offenders in relation to the synagogue. The suggestion that the metaphor is being used this way in Matthew 16:19 is increasingly challenged, however. Most modern scholarship concurs with Schlatter's judgment that "This mode of speech plainly shows that originally *the formula 'loose and bind' describes the activity of the judge.* Consequently the formula is *also* used for the loosing from the ban."[127] The language thus relates to the judge's declaration of the guilt or innocence of individuals brought before him. In Matthew 16:19 it would denote Peter's authority to declare people forgiven or condemned according to their response to the proclamation of the message of the kingdom, and thus his authority to announce their eligibility to enter the kingdom.

It may be observed that in Matthew 18:18 the extension of the authority to bind and loose to the wider group, whether to the apostles as a whole or to the local congregation, is interpreted as authority to exclude individuals from the congregation (disciplining erring members) and to admit individuals to it (presumably to readmit disciplined members after they have repented). The statement of John 20:23 is also closely related:

> Whoever's sins you forgive they stand forgiven them;
> whoever's sins you hold back, they remain held back.

Jesus spoke these words in the context of sending the apostles out to pursue his mission with the aid of the Holy Spirit. In effect he authorized the apostles as his representatives to declare to the people the message of God's promise of salvation, fulfilled in the crucified and risen Christ and received on the basis of repentance and faith. In the context of the primitive church the message and the response would have been linked with baptism, and so with admission to the community of salvation, the heirs of the kingdom of God.[128]

We must now take up a closer investigation of the connection between Matthew 16:19 and verse 18. It is not possible to determine whether the two sayings were formulated together, but it is safe to say that, contrary to Trilling's contention, they have more in common than just the person of Peter: first, both sayings speak of actions that will be accomplished in the future, and second, both sayings employ the image of a structure.

With regard to the matter of time in the sayings, we can note that when he says "I will build my church," Jesus is not suggesting that he is about to accomplish the task in the *immediate* future, in the face of growing opposition and threats on his life. But neither is he referring to a time so far into the future as some point beyond the revelation of the kingdom of God at the end (i.e., after the parousia). Rather, he is speaking of the period following his death: if he was to be the builder of the church, it is axiomatic that he would have had to do so in the period between his resurrection and the parousia. The same applies to the statement, "I will give you the keys of the kingdom of heaven. . . ." Admittedly it is possible to understand Jesus to be speaking of the immediate present in this logion,[129] but surely the period in which Peter would actually use the keys was yet to come—the period in which he exercised his authority with freedom and boldness.

The recognition of this time aspect in the two sayings has understandably led to speculation about whether verses 18–19 are post-resurrection sayings, antedated into the earthly ministry of Jesus. The evidence for such a suppposition is more substantial in this case than it is with most attempts to identify post-resurrection sayings in the gospel traditions. The closely related saying in John 20:23 is set in a post-resurrection context, and so it would appear likely that one or the other of the evangelical traditions has suffered a transfer; the question is which logion has been moved. Those scholars who attribute these logia to the post-resurrection church typically do so because they assume that Jesus did not anticipate an untimely death and hence that he would not have anticipated his resurrection, but there is evidence to suggest that both this assumption and this conclusion are unwarranted.

When we later consider the sayings of Jesus concerning his rejection and death (Mark 8:31, etc.), we will note that they are rooted in various traditions of his people—including, significantly, the tradition of the persecuted righteous man who is vindicated by God. In the period of Israel's history during which it produced its apocalyptic literature, it was assumed that this vindication would take place through exaltation in the heavenly world. If, then, we are to acknowledge the vocation of Jesus to be the representative and mediator of the kingdom of God, we cannot suppose that it would have been his assumption that this vocation was to extend no further than his death at the hands of his people: the kingdom of God is resurrection to life! The tradition that Jesus linked his death with the making of God's new covenant with his people is strong, despite and even through the failure of the people to recognize him as God's Messiah and to recognize God's call to the kingdom in his message. This was to bring judgment on Jerusalem, its people and place of worship (Mark 13:2, Matt. 23:34–36, Luke 19:41–44), but not only that: in three days, they said, he would raise another in its place (Mark 14:58 // John 2:19)! Clearly Jesus had no intention of erecting a temple of stone to replace the old one, and there is no evidence to suggest that he thought God would do so. It is most likely that he was looking forward to a replacement of Herod's temple with a temple in the Spirit as the locus of worship. The postulate that he was suggesting this would happen in the era opened by his resurrection is at least as plausible as the postulate that he was suggesting it would happen in the era opened by his parousia. And there is no doubt that *this* saying was spoken before Easter!

All of this leads us to the second feature linking verses 18 and 19: the sayings in both employ the image of a structure. The saying in verse 18 indicates that the people who are gathered by the proclamation of the good news of the kingdom of God will be built on the "Rock" (= Cepha). The "building" referred to is a house for God—hence, a *temple*.[130] This links the saying not only to the statement Jesus makes at his trial, but also to a fundamental concept of the Qumran community that finds clear expression in 1QS 8:1–10:

> In the council of the community [there shall be] twelve men and three priests, perfect in everything revealed in the whole law, in order to do truth, righteousness, justice, love of mercy, and a humble walking each with his neighbor. . . . When these things happen in Israel, the council of the community will be established in truth as an eternal planting, a sanctuary for Israel and a foundation of the holy of holies for Aaron, truthful witnesses for judgment and chosen by grace, to atone for the land and bring retribution to the wicked. This is the tested wall, the precious cornerstone, whose foundations shall not tremble nor yield from their place. It is a dwelling of the holy of holies for Aaron, in all knowledge of the covenant of justice, to offer a pleasing odor [to God]. It is a house of perfection and truth in Israel, to establish the covenant according to eternal laws. They are acceptable to atone for the land and to pass judgment on the wicked, so that there is no more unrighteousness.

The similarity between the concepts in this passage and those in Matthew 16:18–19 is striking. In the former, twelve men and three priests constitute the *foundation* of the community, which is described as an eternal planting, a sanctuary, a foundation of the holy of holies, the tested wall, the precious cornerstone, a house of perfection and truth in Israel. The council will be truthful witnesses for judgment and they will pass judgment on the wicked so that there might be no more unrighteousness. This is not to suggest that Matthew 16:18 is in any way dependent on the Qumran passage; it does show, however, that the ideas in the former passage were abroad in Judaism during the time of Jesus and the earliest church and that it would not have needed the precedent of the Easter experience to have formulated them. Taking into account the evidence we have reviewed, it would seem that there is not sufficient reason to assume a post-resurrection origin for Matthew 16:18–19.[131]

We will do well to examine the relation between the structure described in verse 18 (symbolizing the church) and the implied structure to which Peter is given the key in verse 19 (symbolizing the kingdom of heaven). The former is thought of as a temple. The latter could be envisaged as a palace (along the lines of Isa. 22:22), or a temple, or even a city (the gates of which can be opened by the key). Windisch points to three precedents in the Old Testament for the sayings concerning entrance to the kingdom of God: references to entrance into the holy land (e.g., Deut. 4:1), references to entrance into the holy city (e.g., Isa. 26:2), and references to entrance into the holy temple (Isa. 56:1–8; cf. Pss. 15 and 24). He contends that each of these "types" is represented in the entrance sayings of Jesus: Mark 10:23ff. speaks of the inheritance of the kingdom of God (the kingdom as the promised land), Matthew 7:13–14 // Luke 13:23 presents an implicit reference to the gate of a city (the narrow road leads to the gate), and Matthew 16:19 could be pointing to either a city or a house, but the possible link with Isaiah 22:22 and the juxtaposition of verse 18 suggest that the image of a house is the more likely.[132]

If Jesus is to build on Peter a "house" of God—that is, a community—and he gives Peter the key to the house of God's kingdom, the implication is plain that the community constitutes the people of the kingdom. Or again, inasmuch as verse 18 indicates that Peter is to be the means by which the community of the Messiah will be realized, and verse 19 indicates that he is to lead people into the kingdom of God, the implication is clear that the community of the Messiah can be equated with the community of the kingdom of God. Can we go further? The conditions for entering the messianic community are the same as the conditions for entering the kingdom of God: reception of the message of the kingdom brought by Jesus and repentance as he demanded. This is underscored in the paraphrase of the saying in Matthew 16:19 that appears in John 20:23, in which binding and loosing are interpreted in terms of guilt and forgiveness, possibly linked with baptism, the door of the church. In light of all this, it is tempting to ask, as Windisch did, whether the term *basileia* in Matthew 16:19 might not mean "the community under the rule of God" rather than "the rule of God" itself.[133] Such an interpretation is not impossible, and it would link the saying with those aspects of anticipation of the kingdom in the present that we have noted in several of the entrance sayings. On the other hand, it would be the only instance in the teaching of Jesus concerning the kingdom of heaven in which the kingdom denoted the community under the saving sovereignty of God. Under the circumstances, perhaps we should leave the question open, assuming in the meanwhile that the saying conforms to the regular meaning of *basileia* in the teaching of Jesus. That being the case, we can assume that Matthew 16:18–19 indicates that the community of the Messiah comes into being through the proclamation of Peter, that those who enter the community thereby enter into the kingdom of salvation, and that those who reject the community are bound in their guilt and excluded from the kingdom of salvation.[134]

6. THE LITTLE FLOCK
Luke 12:32

It is generally acknowledged that the saying in Luke 12:32 is an isolated logion from Luke's own special tradition, and that he placed it here because of the associated themes and the key terms "kingdom" and "your Father" in the immediately preceding context (Luke 12:30–31).[135] The saying differs from the entrance sayings we have considered in its formal aspects, but in content it clearly belongs with them, since the "little flock" is being promised the (future) kingdom.

Regarding the matter of the saying's form, Wilhelm Pesch has pointed out that its threefold structure is common in Old Testament sayings, comprising (1) a demand, "Fear not," (2) the mention of a name or an address to the persons in view, and (3) a statement explaining why there is no call to be afraid. Examples of the formula can be found in Ruth 3:11, Genesis 50:19–21, and 1 Samuel 23:17. The promise is usually made to indicate that a situation that appears to be fearsome is in fact harmless, and that there is indeed hope for a safe future. Significantly, the formula is frequently found in exilic and postexilic prophets, bound up with statements concerning the holy remnant in Israel (see, for example, Isa. 41:8–10, 13–14; 43:1–7; and 44:1–3; see also Jer. 23:3–4 and Mic. 2:12–13, which are related to the theme of Luke 12:32 even though they do not share the threefold structure). The connotations of the use of the form in the Old Testament seem to apply to the saying in Luke as well.[136]

The saying takes up the image of Israel as the flock of God and Yahweh as their Shepherd, a symbol often used in the Psalms (e.g., Psalm 23), and developed in the prophets as a symbol of the nation (e.g., Hos. 4:14; Mic. 7:14; Jer. 23:1–4; Ezek. 34). When Jesus uses the image, he is frequently referring to the entire people of Israel (see Matt. 10:6; 15:24; 18:12–13 // Luke 15:4ff.; Mark 6:34; and Luke 19:10). When he speaks of "the little flock" in Luke 12:32, however, he is referring to a group within the whole. Since Jesus states that the kingdom of God is appointed for them, we must assume that he is indicating that they have fulfilled the entrance requirements for the kingdom of God that he laid down in the entrance sayings. Accordingly, we can understand the little flock to be the equivalent of the faithful remnant in Israel, related to the shepherd whom God has sent to act on his behalf for the flock. Such a deduction is strongly supported by Mark 14:27, in which Jesus is identified as God's appointed shepherd and his followers are identified with the flock of God mentioned in Zechariah 13:7. The Markan saying pointedly distinguishes between the flock of Jesus and the nation, which will be the instrument through which God will "smite" the shepherd.[137]

There has been a certain reluctance among New Testament scholars to countenance the idea that Jesus formed or had in view a remnant within Israel that would receive the kingdom and be its instrument of action to the nation (and perhaps to the nations outside Israel). It has been argued that Jesus addressed his message to the whole nation, in hopes of winning the people as a whole. Indeed, his words and actions are clearly different from those of the sectarian groups in Israel, for they manifested an exclusiveness in their membership and in their relations with the people: Jesus broke through all the barriers erected by the rigorists and invited all and sundry to the feast of the kingdom of God.[138] The points made by these scholars are justified. Jesus did attack spiritual pride and elitism wherever he met it, and his whole mode of life was a rebuke to those who separated themselves from the ordinary people in the name of the Lord. Nevertheless, these perversions of the remnant doctrine were as far from the prophets as they were from Jesus. Isaiah was no sectarian! His remnant teaching was the outcome of his eschatological message: judgment lay ahead of the rebellious nation, but God in his mercy would see that a remnant would be spared—but a remnant, and no more! (see especially Isa. 1:9 and 10:20–23).

Regarding this matter of Israel's relation to the judgment of God and the kingdom of God, it would seem that Jesus had more in common with Israel's prophets than with their apocalyptic successors. His call to repentance was addressed to all the people; the prospect of participation in the kingdom of God was opened up for all who would listen to God. Failure to respond to the message of God's kingdom would mean forfeiture of the inheritance of the kingdom, irrespective of claims to religious status on which some might rely. There are clear indications in the proclamation of Jesus that he recognized that his message from God would suffer the same sort of rejection the prophets had received before him, and he warned the people of the consequences of that rejection (see Luke 13:33; Matt. 8:11–12, 11:20–26, 12:41–42, 23:29–38, and 25:31–36; Mark 12:1–12 and 13:2; and Luke 19:41–44 and 23:27–31). The saying in Luke 12:32 stands in marked contrast to the warnings addressed to the people, however: it sets the "little flock" apart from them as a remnant to whom the Father has chosen to give the kingdom.

In view of the entrance sayings on the one hand and the related citation in Mark 14:27 on the other, we may assume that the little flock comprised those who received the good news of the kingdom of God brought by Jesus and recognized in him God's messenger of the kingdom—the *mebasser* of Isaiah 61:1. The Father's selection of the group thus coincides with their acceptance of the Father's word, and Jesus sees in them "the first appearance of the eschatological flock of God coming into realization."[139] As a *little* flock they are acknowledged to be vulnerable to attack. Indeed, they are warned that hardships and persecutions are the lot of those who respond to God's word and share with Jesus in the service of the kingdom of God (see, for example, Matt. 5:11–12 and 10:16ff., 24–25, and 28; and Mark 8:34ff.). But they are also assured that the future belongs to the flock of God, according to the promise made long ago (e.g., Mic. 7:14–15, Jer. 23:3–4, Ezek. 34:22ff., and especially Dan. 7:27), and that the Father has been pleased to include them among the heirs of the kingdom: "Your Father has chosen to give *you* the kingdom."

On the basis of this evidence, then, we can view Luke 12:32 as a contrast saying, similar to the beatitudes and the contrast parables. The little flock is comparable to the little ones to whom God has revealed the secret of the kingdom—the poor, the hungry, the thirsty, the persecuted, the captives, and the crushed, to whom the kingdom belongs. As the mustard seed issues in a great plant, and the leaven affects the mass of dough, so "from the little flock there comes the glorified community in the kingdom of the Father."[140]

Thus, while it does not resemble the other entrance sayings of the kingdom of God in its formal characteristics, Luke 12:32 is nonetheless one with them in content. It makes reference to the kingdom that will be revealed at the end and provides a substantial consolation to the members of the little flock, assuring them that the Father who promises to welcome them at the end of the road will not forsake them on the way.

7. THE KINGDOM COMING IN POWER
Mark 9:1, Matthew 16:28, Luke 9:27

This saying concludes a short series of logia that Mark has placed after Jesus' first prediction of his passion and Peter's protest on hearing it (8:34–38). The introductory phrase in 9:1 (*kai elegen autois*) suggests that the saying was originally isolated, and that it was Mark who set it in its present context, doubtless because it fits well with the immediately preceding parousia saying in 8:38.[141] The saying also fits well with the material that immediately follows, however. The fact that Mark placed the Transfiguration narrative after 9:1 suggests that he saw a connection between the saying and that event. Indeed, there are many apparent connections: (1) the statement that "some" of those standing with Jesus are to see the kingdom is consonant with his taking Peter,

James, and John with him on the mountain; (2) the term "seeing" corresponds to the nature of the event as a "vision" (it is so described in Matt. 17:9); and (3) the Transfiguration is replete with eschatological associations, including the glorification of Jesus at the parousia, the appearance of the eschatological figures Moses and Elijah (see Rev. 11:3ff.), the appearance of the cloud that envelops both the representatives of the living people of God and the representatives of the glorified dead (see 1 Thess. 4:15–17), and the declaration by the Father that Jesus is his Son. Such an understanding of the Transfiguration appears to be reflected in 2 Peter 1:16–19, which represents the Transfiguration as the divine confirmation of the "prophetic word"—which is to say, the hope of the kingdom of God that will come in power at the parousia of the Lord Jesus Christ.

The belief that the prophecy of Mark 9:1 was fulfilled in the Transfiguration was the most popular interpretation in the succeeding centuries.[142] Chrysostom, for example, said that in the Transfiguration the disciples glimpsed the glory with which Jesus would come.[143] Basil of Seleucia spoke of the Transfiguration as "an image of the parousia,"[144] and John of Damascus viewed it as "a parable of his coming parousia from heaven."[145] The same tradition was maintained among the Western Fathers, through the Reformation and to modern times. Today, however, the scholar who supports this view regarding the *intent* of the saying is the exception rather than the rule.[146] Since the saying was isolated in the tradition, Mark must have been the one to set it in its present position, juxtaposed to the description of the Transfiguration; thus, the textual link between 9:1 and that event reflects Mark's interpretation of the saying. More important, it hardly seems realistic to suppose that Jesus would state that some of those standing there with him would not *taste death* before they would see the arrival of the kingdom of God if he were referring to an event that was to take place *six days* later. Despite the arguments of some scholars to the contrary, the natural implication of the language is that while certain individuals will survive to see the kingdom, others will die before the event, and that suggests a lapse of years rather than days prior to the fulfillment of the prediction.[147]

If it is the case that the lapse referred to in Mark 9:1 is in fact a matter of years rather than days, then it would clearly seem to rule out the possibility that the coming of the kingdom is being equated with the glory of Jesus in his resurrection. Calvin contends that the arrival of the kingdom mentioned here signifies "the revelation of the heavenly glory which Christ began with the resurrection and then more fully offered when he sent the Holy Spirit and worked marvellous deeds of power."[148] Luther, Melanchthon, and Karl Barth provide similar interpretations.[149] C. H. Dodd has given a modern dress to this interpretation, providing an analysis of the language in Mark 9:1. He notes that an accusative and participle in the sense of an accusative and infinitive after verbs of saying and thinking is a standard construction in Greek, and further that the perfect participle indicates an action already complete from the standpoint of the subject of the main verb; thus, he argues, one should translate the statement "*Some . . . will not taste death until they have seen that the kingdom of God has come with power*"—that is, the bystanders will eventually come to see that the kingdom of God had already been among them for some time prior to their recognition of the fact. Dodd also notes that the phrase "with power" occurs in the early Christological formulae (it is cited by Paul in Romans 1:4 in connection with the Resurrection), and he contends that the phrase in Mark 9:1 conceivably reflects this formula and its relation to the resurrection of Jesus. Thus Dodd holds that in Mark 9:1 Jesus is indicating that a time will come when the disciples will realize that the kingdom of God came with power in his resurrection.[150]

Dodd's interpretation has been sharply criticized.[151] Not everything that is grammatically possible will necessarily yield a plausible meaning. It seems obvious to most interpreters that Mark 9:1 speaks of a limited group of people who at some time in the future will experience the coming of the kingdom of God. The phrase "with power" relates to the mode in which that kingdom will come—similar to the way in which the parousia is expected to occur, "with power and great glory" (Mark 13:26). This is how Matthew interpreted the logion (see Matt. 16:28). The evidence that Mark also understood it this way lies in the fact that he set it in conjunction with 8:38 and followed it with the Transfiguration narrative, viewing the latter as a vision of the advent of the kingdom at the end.

A fresh direction in the interpretation of Mark 9:1 was taken by Gregory the Great, who dealt with the point that *some* will not taste death before the kingdom of God comes. On the basis of Matthew 13:41, he equated the kingdom with the church and proceeded to suggest that the saying is actually indicating that *some* disciples would live to see the church of God built up in strength in the world, that just as the promised land was given to Israel as an indication of its inheritance in the heavenly country, so the kingdom of God on earth would be given to the disciples as an assurance of the kingdom to come in heaven.[152] This interpretation played an important role in the Middle Ages. Favored by many Lutheran scholars in subsequent years, it has been taken up by many Roman Catholic scholars in the present century.[153] Vincent Taylor also adopted it, though with caution, suggesting that the saying refers to "a powerful manifestation of the rule of God in the Church."[154]

In view of the references in the gospels to a calamity encroaching upon the Jews, it was inevitable that Mark 9:1 came to be interpreted as a reference to the Jewish war of A.D. 66–70. Many advocates of this view freely acknowledge the eschatological aspect of the distress of the Jews and the destruction of their city. J. J. Wettstein, for example, has written concerning Matthew 16:28 that "I understand this of the coming of Christ at the destruction of Jerusalem, which gave a certain picture of the last judgment of which the previous verse speaks."[155] C. F. Keil has gone further, maintaining that the judgment on Jerusalem marked "the inbreaking of the royal coming of Christ" for the judgment of the world, "the prelude of the last days."[156] Exegetes have expressed this basic conviction in a variety of ways throughout the past century or so.[157] Nevertheless, it is one thing to acknowledge that the tribulation of Israel and the destruction of Jerusalem are set in an eschatological context (as in the eschatological discourse of Mark 13) so that the ruin of the city and its temple are placed in juxtaposition with the parousia of Christ and the coming of the kingdom of God; it is another thing to *identify* the judgment on the Jews and their city and temple with the coming of the kingdom of God. In the eschatological discourse, the tribulation of Israel and destruction of the temple are numbered among the signs that precede the parousia (see Mark 13:14–20), and Mark clearly differentiates them (note especially the parable of the Fig Tree, vv. 28–29). If they are not identified in Mark 13 and its parallels, we can be sure that the evangelists had no intention of making the identification in their renderings of Mark 9:1 and its parallels.

The view that in Mark 9:1 Jesus is anticipating the arrival of the end-time kingdom in the near future was first asserted by H. S. Reimarus, and was taken up by D. Strauss and E. Renan.[158] In view of the quarters from which the interpretation came and the implications these writers drew from it, the view was resisted at first, but beginning with W. Weiffenbach,[159] it has gradually become established as critical orthodoxy, even in the conservative critical community.[160] In contrast to the allegation that such an expectation of the end discredited Jesus as a teacher, it was (and is) maintained that the statement simply indicates that Jesus shared the anticipations of the end characteristic of the prophets of the Bible: intensity of hope and pastoral concern for the people led to a "foreshortened perspective" on the history that issues in the kingdom of God.[161]

It is probably safe to say that the majority of contemporary scholars of the teaching of Jesus are not greatly concerned with the question of whether Jesus was mistaken regarding the time of the end; nevertheless, the debate on the authenticity of Mark 9:1 continues to increase rather than diminish. Reimarus regarded the saying—along with every other saying concerning the parousia in the gospels—as a creation of the early disciples. Today Eta Linnemann rejects the saying on the ground that "there is not a single saying of Jesus which expressly speaks of the nearness of the kingdom of God, the genuineness of which is not at least contested."[162] Ironically, something of the same conclusion is reached by scholars who begin from the opposite premise. Many who take it as axiomatic that Jesus consistently assumed that the kingdom of God was close at hand in his teaching find in this saying an awareness on his part that the end is *not* at hand—since many will die before the kingdom comes—and so they attribute it to the church, which had to come to terms with the delay of the expected parousia. This point of view was affirmed as long ago as 1965 by O. Pfleiderer in his work on primitive Christianity and has also been maintained by Bultmann and various other scholars.[163]

Discussions of Mark 9:1 have inevitably called into question its relation to Mark 13:30: "Amen I say to you, this generation will not pass away before all these things take place." Mark 9:1 expresses a similar expectation, but with a difference: whereas Mark 13:30 speaks of the contemporary *generation* witnessing "all these things," Mark 9:1 appears to put a limitation on who will live to see it: "There are *some* standing here who will not taste death before they see the kingdom of God come with power." This distinctive meaning of Mark 9:1 has been affirmed by scholars of various viewpoints. Bornkamm, for example, has compared Mark 9:1 with 13:30 and Matt. 10:23 and observed that "Mark 9:1 says more precisely: even if many will die, some will experience it. Here we no longer have to do with a proclamation that the last things will break in upon this 'generation,' but with the assertion: some will still be alive at the parousia."[164] In a similar vein, Kümmel states that "It is clear that Jesus says of a limited number of persons only [*tines*] that they live to see the coming of the kingdom of God. . . . This not only confirms again the expectation of a future kingdom of God in Jesus' thinking, but also establishes the fact that this futurity is thought of as restricted. Yet the absence of an unrestricted promise to all Jesus' contemporaries to experience the kingdom of God implies that it cannot be expected within a very short period."[165] And Michaelis affirms yet more emphatically that "Although a more precise reckoning is forbidden, it must nevertheless be said that in the saying at Mark 9:1 the point of time of the last day lies at a considerable distance, insofar as it is apparent that several decades are reckoned with."[166]

I confess that I once saw no difficulty in this position. Mark 13:30 speaks of "all these things" happening in the contemporary generation, and Mark 13:32 states, "Of that day or hour no man knows"; the segments of the picture seem to fit into place perfectly: all that Jesus spoke of will take place in his generation, manifestly at the end rather than the beginning, but nobody knows precisely when they will happen. It did not occur to me that I was interpreting Mark 13:30 in the light of Mark 9:1 rather than in its own light. Nor did I appreciate that perhaps Mark 13:30 ought to be read in the light of Mark 13:32, rather than the other way round, particularly if in the latter saying "that day" and "that hour" are to be viewed as synonymous expressions for the *last* day. In reality, Mark 13:30 is more closely related to the Q saying in Matthew 23:34–36 // Luke 11:49–51, in which the emphasis falls on the doom that threatens the whole contemporary generation:

> this generation will have to answer for the blood of all the prophets shed since the foundation of the world; from the blood of Abel to the blood of Zechariah who perished between the altar and the sanctuary. I tell you, *this generation will have to answer for it all.*

In this passage there is no question about "some" surviving to the end: the whole generation will experience the Day of the Lord upon the nation. In all probability that is the prime significance of "all these things" in Mark 13:30. It is not an astrologer's forecast of the time when a notable event of the future will take place, but a declaration that judgment from God is to come upon the contemporaries of Jesus.

Keeping in mind the difference in perspective between Mark 13:30 and 9:1, we might further consider the question of how Mark 9:1 relates to the overall teaching of Jesus on the end. In general the emphasis of this teaching is that the time of the end cannot be known, and thus one should be ready for it at *all* times. This is in fact the point of Mark 13:32 and the parabolic sayings that follow in verses 33–37; it is also the emphasis in Luke 17:20–21, the so-called Q apocalypse that follows in verses 22–37, and such sayings as the parables of the Burglar (Matt. 24:43–44) and the Watching Servant (Matt. 24:45–51). A. Vögtle draws attention to this problem in his discussion of Jesus' knowledge of the time of the end. He urges that Mark 9:1 moves the coming of the kingdom of

God into the second half of the present generation and adds, "That seems to me to press urgently the objection . . . *whether it is credible that Jesus weakened the actuality and urgency of his demand for repentance and preparedness through a retarding statement of time of the kind that is recorded.*"[167] Vögtle holds that Mark 9:1 breaks the sharp point of Jesus' appeal for conversion, for people to awake out of their lethargy and with all their hearts to turn to God. In this Vögtle is surely right. For Mark and his contemporaries at the time of the composition of his gospel the saying would have had the urgency of the whole of Jesus' eschatological utterances, since they were living in the time to which the saying had relevance, but that same factor presents an argument against attributing the saying to Jesus' day, for it could not have possessed that significance for the people he addressed forty years earlier.

How then are we to account for Mark 9:1? In opposition to the common modern view that it is a consolatory prophecy uttered by a Christian prophet in the name of the Lord, Vögtle has suggested that it originated as a modification of the saying with which it is so often compared—Mark 13:30. The structure of the two sentences is strikingly similar: both begin with the introductory "Amen I say to you," and both make a strong assertion regarding people in relation to the eschatological deeds of God: "some will not [*ou me*] taste death until they see the kingdom of God" and "this generation will not [*ou me*] pass away until all these things take place." It is possible that the progress from Mark 13:30 to 9:1 was aided by an identification of "all these things" in 13:30 with the kingdom of God, thus leading to the variant "This generation will not pass away until the kingdom of God comes." From that it would have been a short step to speak in terms of individuals surviving until the arrival of the kingdom of God, instead of "this generation" continuing.[168] Schürmann contends that it is unnecessary to postulate such a step between Mark 13:30 and the redaction that produced 9:1;[169] but we should note that Luke has made precisely such a change in Mark's version of the parable of the Fig Tree immediately preceding verse 30. Mark's version reads "When you see these things happening, know that [it] is near, at the doors"; Luke's version reads "When you see these things happening, *know that the kingdom of God is near*" (Luke 21:31). It is instructive to observe that Matthew has taken the process of interpretation suggested for Mark 9:1 a step further; instead of making the kingdom of God the sole object of concern, he makes the parousia of the Son of Man the center of hope: "There are some of those standing here who will not taste death until they see the Son of Man coming in his kingdom" (Matt. 16:28). We can thus trace an ascending series of versions of the one saying: Mark 13:30, Mark 9:1, and Matthew 16:28.

Vögtle has by no means been alone in postulating that Mark 9:1 was formed through a modification of Mark 13:30.[170] But there has also been scholarly support for the opposite thesis—namely, that Mark 9:1 was the basis for Mark 13:30—from M. Horstmann and R. Pesch.[171] The latter, in his commentary on Mark, describes 13:30 as "an ad hoc formation for the pre-Markan apocalypse, which will have been inspired through Amen-sayings like Mk 9.1, Mt 10.23, 23.36."[172] In this he echoes J. Lambrecht, who has suggested that the *thought* of Mark 13:30 is essentially the same as that of Matthew 23:36, the *structure* is basically the same as that of Mark 9:1, and the *wording* is related to that of Mark

13:29 (viz., the *tauta genomena* of v. 29 is taken up in the *tauta panta genetai* of v. 30).[173]

How are we to determine whether Mark 9:1 or Mark 13:30 has the priority? According to Horstmann and Pesch the independence of 9:1 from its context and the dependence of 13:30 on its context decide the matter. But is that a proper assessment of the situation? It is generally recognized that the *tauta panta genetai* of 13:30 is related to the *tauta ginomena* of verse 29 as well as to verses 1–4. But verses 28 and 29 together constitute an independent unit, and so the original reference of the *tauta* is uncertain. If the parable of the Fig Tree in verses 28–29 is pre-Markan and circulated independently of its present context, there would seem to be no good reason to accord verse 30 a different treatment. In passing we might note that modern scholars constantly cite Mark 13:30, apart from its context, as an example of the eschatological expectations of the primitive church; why should the members of the early communities not have done the same?

We have already noted that Mark 13:30 is closely related to Matthew 23:36 // Luke 11:51. It is altogether more plausible to look to the latter passage than to Mark 9:1 for the origin of Mark 13:30. The Q saying is clearly in keeping with the overall message of Jesus to his generation, unlike Mark 9:1, which does not express the urgency of his message. Putting it another way, we might say that Mark 13:30 is pertinent to Jesus' day, whereas Mark 9:1 is pertinent to Mark's day and to the church for which he wrote. Admittedly, such a conclusion is a matter of speculation on the basis of probabilities rather than indisputable evidence, but it would appear reasonable to hold that Mark 13:30 is prior to Mark 9:1 and that it provided its inspiration.[174]

12 | Parables of Jesus on the Coming of the Kingdom of God in the Future

We have already considered a number of the parables of Jesus that relate to the kingdom of God. Our primary interest was to investigate the extent to which they confirmed the teaching of the nonparabolic sayings of Jesus that indicate that God's saving sovereignty was present in his ministry. We saw that the "secret of the kingdom of God" (Mark 4:11) was the clue to the parables with regard to the wider teaching and activity of Jesus. Having examined many cardinal sayings of Jesus that speak of the future of the kingdom of God, we should now examine the parables of Jesus that appear to have that future in view.

1. THE PARABLES OF GROWTH

It is significant that the parables in which the presence of the kingdom of God in the ministry of Jesus is particularly plain—the so-called parables of growth—make the prospect of the future climax of that kingdom equally evident. It is the consideration of this aspect of these parables to which we will turn first.

a. The Mustard Seed and the Leaven
Mark 4:30–32 // Matthew 13:31–32 // Luke 13:18–19; Matthew 13:33 // Luke 13:20–21

As all acknowledge, we here have "contrast parables" par excellence. They clearly express the contrast between the inauspicious beginning of God's saving sovereignty in Jesus and its end in universal dominion. On the one hand, they speak of the planting of a tiny mustard seed and the placing of yeast in dough; on the other hand, we are shown a plant greater than all shrubs and a mass of dough penetrated by the leaven. The contrast is heightened by the use to which the metaphors are put. A mustard plant is not a tree, although it may resemble one.[1] But the extension of the picture with the words "it forms branches so large that the birds of the air can nest beneath its shade" has the effect of turning the picture into a well-known cartoon: the mustard plant has become the tree of apocalyptic prophecy, which exemplifies the universality of a reign embracing all peoples. Curiously enough, in the best-known appearances of this image in the Old Testament (in Ezek. 31 and Dan. 4), it is used to represent the dominion of pagan rulers over the nations, which in each case was brought to an abrupt end by the judgment of God. It is not inconceivable that Jesus may have linked these examples with his use of leaven as an image of rapid growth, for when it was used symbolically it usually bore connotations of evil, as Jews were reminded at every passover. Such associations of the two symbols have the effect of emphasizing the beginning and the end of the divine sovereignty in the parables as sheer miracle: its beginning is so small, so dubious, so questionable in the eyes of men that it seems impossible to identify it with the marvelous event depicted in the prophets; yet God is in that beginning, making the first momentous moves toward the fulfillment of his purpose for the world, which will be the revelation of his dominion in power and glory, beneath which all mankind may securely and forever rest.[2]

There is, of course, a third passage in the Old Testament to which the Mustard Seed parable may be related—namely, the allegory of the cedar tree in Ezekiel 17:22ff. The oracle is less spectacular than the other two we have mentioned, but the similarities with the gospel parable are closer. It presents the picture of a small cedar twig planted with a view to its becoming a great tree, representing Israel in the kingdom of God—but the action is wholly set in the future.

The relation of present and future in the two parables can be viewed from two vantage points. We can look at the present situation from the standpoint of the future, which reflects on the present: the mighty sovereignty of God that is to be revealed in power and glory in the future is operative among men in the humble ministry of Jesus. Or we can view the present by faith as the beginning of the saving sovereignty of God that will surely issue in a triumphant vindication in the judgment and universal rule of God. In both cases the unity of the beginning and the end of God's sovereign intervention is axiomatic; it is a single saving, judging rule that is at work in Jesus and that will be powerfully revealed at the end of the age.[3] Both vantage points are of moment, alike to those who fail to perceive the significance of the ministry of Jesus and to those who count themselves as his followers. The former are called on to recognize the signs of the future in the present and to place themselves under the saving sovereignty in repentant faith in order that they might enter it when it is revealed in glory. The latter are encouraged to stand firm and to look for the completion of that to which they have committed themselves in faith and which they serve in hope.[4]

b. The Seed Growing Secretly
Mark 4:26–29

If this parable is to be viewed as a contrast parable, as most regard it,[5] the contrast clearly does not lie in the difference between an insignificant beginning and a great ending, as with the parables of the Mustard Seed and Leaven; rather, it is between the inactivity of a farmer after sowing seed and the incomprehensible but effective operation of the creative process that produces a harvest out of the seed sown.

The hearer or reader of the parable is undoubtedly expected to pay attention to what is said of the farmer's action after he has sown the seed: he does nothing! Or, more accurately, he "sleeps and rises," and so does not concern himself at all with what is happening to the seed. The reason for this behavior is also significant: the earth produces growth "of itself." How it does that the farmer does not know, but that too is of no concern to him! As P. R. Jones wryly remarks, "The farmer is planter and harvester, but not grower!"[6] Growth is part of the mystery and miracle of creation. If the mystery is beyond knowing, the miracle can yet be trusted, and the farmer can afford to go about his business until harvest comes: then is the time for decisive action.

These elements within the parable are acknowledged by all to be of central importance. A harvest is not man-made; it is the effect of God's operation in creation. So also the earnestly awaited kingdom of God cannot be brought about by the labors of man, but solely by the intervention of the almighty and sovereign God. In the estimate of most exegetes, this is the chief lesson of the parable.[7] It is recognized that there were people within the orbit of Jesus' ministry who needed to listen to that truth. Notably, the Zealots believed that God would give his kingdom as his people cooperated in destroying the nation's enemies, which they held *ipso facto* to be the enemies of God.[8] The Pharisees held that man was able to influence the coming of the kingdom of God through the power of repentance: if Israel would repent for but a day, the kingdom of God would come.[9] So far as the populace was concerned, there is little doubt that the fact that Jesus had no revolutionary program of action to introduce the kingdom of God was a stumbling block in the way of their accepting his message (see John 6:14–15, 66). This element in the parable therefore served as a necessary corrective to the poor understanding of the kingdom of God among the hearers of Jesus.

If the kingdom of God is the gift of the miracle-working God, like a harvest after sowing, the question inevitably provoked by the parable is when the sowing is supposed to take place. The answer is not given, but there is an indication that the sowing is assumed to have taken place. In the context of the ministry of Jesus, that can mean only that the miracle of God's sovereign action has been set in motion through Jesus' proclamation of the kingdom and the acts of divine saving sovereignty wrought through him. Because that work has begun, there is neither need nor place for man to attempt to take over from God; the issue of what has been started through Jesus is in the hands of God and may be as confidently expected as the harvest after sowing. As N. A. Dahl has expressed it,

> The evens of the final era have already begun to happen, the forces of the kingdom are at work; when the time is ripe, at the end of the world, God will certainly intervene without delay, cause the judgment to come and establish his kingdom in glory. To urge that Jesus, if he were the coming one, should unfold a messianic activity would be as foolish as to press the husbandman to be active in order to make the grain grow or to reap it before the time of harvest.[10]

Accordingly, while the parable is concerned with the future coming of the kingdom of God, its emphasis lies first in the identification of the coming kingdom with what is taking place in the ministry of Jesus and second in the assurance that what has been initiated in and through him needs no supplementation from men; it is in the hands of the Lord of creation, who will as certainly bring it to victory as he gives harvest after sowing.[11]

The exposition of the kingdom of God in this parable, even more clearly than that in the parables of the Mustard Seed and Leaven, is no mere defense of the mode of ministry adopted by Jesus; it is a call to recognize the nature of the present situation and to come to terms with it. The sovereign intervention of God for which Israel has been waiting has made a beginning. Its miracle-working grace is operative among them, and its future glory is on the way. The implication is unmistakable: "Recognize the nature of the time, turn to the God who has graciously drawn near, and so be ready for the glory that is coming in order that you may inherit it!"

c. The Sower
Mark 4:1–9, Matthew 13:1–9, Luke 8:4–8

Unlike the parables of the Mustard Seed, the Leaven, and the Seed Growing Secretly, no formula occurs at the beginning of the parable of the Sower to indicate that its theme is the kingdom of God. The similarity of its imagery to that of the parables of the Seed Growing Secretly, the Mustard Seed, and the Wheat and the Tares, however, favors the assumption that it has a similar theme. Mark's placement of the saying on the secret of the kingdom of God as the burden of the ministry of Jesus, and so of his parables, at the conclusion of the parable of the Sower is not misleading. The parable relates the ministry of Jesus to *the coming of the kingdom of God.*

Again we have a parable of contrasts, but differently accented than those we have just considered. This time the contrast is between the frustrations encountered in the service of the kingdom of God (the *mission* of the kingdom!) and the conclusion of the process in the abundant wealth of the kingdom revealed in its fullness (the "harvest"). As we noted earlier, the "frustrations" relate to elements of opposition to the work of the kingdom of God in the world, and this is why they figure so largely in the parable—beyond their deserving, one is inclined to say. They mirror the factors that militated against Jesus in his service of the kingdom and hindered people in responding to the message of the kingdom. Despite the seriousness of these contrary elements, the hearer and reader ought not to be misled by the amount of attention they are given any more than the Sower in the parable was deterred from his work of sowing because of them. Birds and weeds and rocks and scorching sun have to be reckoned with in the business of sowing, but (to adapt a saying in another area) greater are the processes of creation that are with the Sower than the forces against him. This needs to be emphasized, because the descriptions of contrary factors have frequently led interpreters to offer pessimistic reflections on the parable.[12] Yet the parable was surely not intended to convey such notions. It is not, for instance, stated that the field was divided into four equal parts—one fourth path, one fourth weeds, one fourth rock, and one fourth good earth. It is obstacles that are being described, not quantities of land. Fundamentally, *two* kinds of results of sowing are set before us—unfruitful and fruitful—with three examples of each being depicted. That the results of the fruitful sowing take less space to describe does not lessen their importance.[13] The conclusion of the parable forms an authentic climax: despite all the difficulties, the end of the sowing is abundant reaping. Similarly, we are to understand, the outcome of the service of the kingdom of God undertaken by Jesus is the sure and certain triumph of the kingdom that invaded the world through him.[14]

Of the adequacy of this interpretation there is no question among most exegetes. The sowing, as in the parables of the Seed Growing Secretly and the Mustard Seed, symbolizes the intervention of the saving sovereignty of God in the ministry of Jesus. The parable of the Sower shares with related parables a certain fitness to do this, associating as it does the harvest with the judgment and deliverance of God in the end of the age (cf. Joel 3:12–14). Nevertheless, as is the case with all parables and metaphors, there are limitations on how the images can be applied. The images of the sowing of seed and the growth of a plant are severely limited when it comes to representing the epoch-making entry of the divine sovereignty into the world in the ministry of Jesus, as is evident when we recall such sayings as those in Matthew 11:5, 12 and Luke 4:18ff. and 11:20. To balance the parable's emphasis on the birds and weeds and scorching sun that prevent or halt growth to harvest, we might have looked for some representation of the powerful results of the divine sovereignty at work in Jesus—that is to say, *present* fruitfulness. But the images in the parable cannot express that; they can only depict a constancy of growth with a view to the harvest of history. The sole justification of his ministry that Jesus had in view in this parable was the ultimate one: the vindication of the final glory. Yet this issue is all-important, for again we have a parable that goes beyond the assurance of the sure coming of God in the future: *what is coming is the divine sovereignty that has made its entrance into the world in the ministry of Jesus*, and not all the obstacles set in its path can prevent that great day from bursting upon the world.

The recognition of the bond between the labors producing a harvest on the one hand and the ministry that leads to the universal sovereignty of God on the other is perhaps more challenging in this parable than in the others we have reviewed, for the call to pay heed to the parable implicitly includes the demand to examine one's own response to the work of God in and through Jesus: "He who has ears to hear, *let him hear!*" It requires no undue allegorizing to perceive in the parable an appeal to the hearers and readers to renounce the hindrances to God's sovereignty at work in their midst, to open their lives to it, and to identify themselves with its representative in anticipation of the consummation of the gracious work of God now abroad in the earth.

d. The Wheat and the Tares
Matthew 13:24–30

First of all we should note that this parable deals with a situation in the ministry of Jesus. It does not have in view the problem of the mixed church of later years, nor is it concerned with the creation of a pure messianic community, such as that striven for by the Qumran Covenanters. The problem exposed within the parable is indicated in the dictum "An enemy has done this." The reference is to a movement contrary to the operation of the divine sovereignty in Jesus, a Satanic counterthrust of the kind referred to in Matthew 11–12: "The kingdom of God is powerfully breaking into the world, *and violent men are powerfully attacking it.*"[15]

What then is the answer to this display of hostility? The reply that John the Baptist would give could be stated in terms of the parable as follows: "Hasten the reaping, burn the weeds, and gather the wheat!" The preaching of John reported in Matthew 3:7–12 indicates that he looked for the Messiah to make this his *first* task on arriving, and it was precisely to prepare for that that John launched his baptismal movement. It is striking that the last words of the parable are closely akin to the concluding statement of Matthew's record of John's teaching: "At harvest time I will tell the reapers, Gather the darnel first, and tie them up in bundles in order to burn them, but gather the wheat into my barn" (v. 30, cf. Matt. 3:12). It is possible that Jesus deliberately chose to echo John's preaching in this parable, but whereas John places the shovel in the Messiah's hand to be used speedily, the parable indicates that the hour for the bundling and the burning has not yet arrived; the harvest belongs to an undisclosed future.

It is clear then, as Dahl has pointed out, that in the parable "the essential contrast is that which exists between the time when grain and weeds grow together and the time of harvest, when weeds and wheat are separated from each other, the weeds to be burned, the wheat to be gathered into the barn. When the harvest comes, and not before, the time for separation has come."[16] We should take note of the fact that it is not a contrast between the time *before* the kingdom and the time *of* the kingdom. In this parable, as in the related seed parables, the sowing denotes the initiation of the divine sovereignty that has taken place through Jesus. The distinctive feature of this parable is the contrast between the mode of operation of the divine sovereignty in the present and its expression in the future, denoted by the "harvest": in the present of Jesus' ministry, the sovereignty of God is operative among men without making any move to put down the hostility and opposition that confronts it, whereas in the future denouement it will be revealed in a decisive judgment.

In view of general opinion to the contrary, we should note that there is no suggestion in the parable that the divine sovereignty withholds judgment before harvest because humanity is unable to discern rightly between the good and the evil; on the contrary, even slaves on the land could tell the difference between ordinary wheat and bearded wheat! *They* drew the attention of their master to the presence of the spurious wheat! The danger posed to the harvest by a premature separation is an essential part of the picture; the reality in view is the inability of man to execute the judgment of God, which corresponds to the inability of man to bring about the resurrection of the dead and the final kingdom. The positive implication of the refusal to anticipate the judgment is that the sovereignty of God in Jesus in the present time has a different function—the function of its power to redeem, to bring its grace to bear upon human life in a multitude of ways. Thus, the relation between the present and future expressions of the kingdom of God presented in this parable is different from that presented in the parables of contrast. In the latter, the unity of the present and future operations of God's rule is clearly discernible; in the parable of the Wheat and the Tares it is the diversity of the two modes in which God exercises his sovereignty that is being highlighted. The present rule of God is in no way diminished, let alone denied, by the recognition that evil powers are opposed to it. As Schnackenburg has pointed out, "This co-existence of the forces of salvation and destruction should not confuse us as to the reality and power of God's rule in the present. The end will show who belongs to it."[17] If the parable implies that the divine sovereignty is manifested in the ministry of Jesus in grace, it also implies that the opposition to that work is subject to the same divine sovereignty. There is no fear that the present kingdom will fall before the powers of evil. On the contrary, the divine sovereignty to be revealed in the judgment at the end is the same sovereignty that is exercised in redemptive grace in Jesus. He therefore will continue to exercise that power with the same redeeming grace till the hour determined by the Father arrives.

e. The Dragnet
Matthew 13:47–50

The parable of the Dragnet is so similar to that of the Wheat and Tares that they are frequently viewed as twin parables with an identical meaning.[18] In fact, however, although the fundamental assumptions of the two parables are the same, there is a difference in purpose between them. In contrast to the parable of the Wheat and Tares, the parable of the Dragnet is not structured to indicate a distance between the initiation of the kingdom of God and the judgment; the picture it presents demands that the two be drawn together, for part of the business of catching fish is precisely sorting the good from the bad, the edible from the inedible. Inevitably this has led some interpreters to view the sorting as the main point of the parable.[19] But as we noted earlier, this parable is likening the kingdom of heaven to the *whole* process of catching fish, not merely the separation. The casting of the net, the gathering of fish of every kind, the drawing in of the net, the sorting of the fish, the retention of the good and rejection of the bad—all this represents the sovereignty of God in action. That means that we are not directed solely to an eschatological future but to an eschatological present also.[20] If we wish to envisage a counterpart in life to catching fish of every sort, we might recall the picture Mark gives in the opening chapter of his gospel of a whole town gathered at the close of the sabbath about the house in which Jesus was staying, and of Jesus ministering by word and deed to the needy multitude; or we might recall Jesus preaching to the crowds by the lake (Mark 4), or feasting with many "bad characters" in the house of Levi the tax gatherer (Mark 2:15, NEB), or the Johannine representation of Jesus conversing with an immoral woman by Jacob's well and then staying in a Samaritan village, communicating to them the good news (John 4). For Jesus, "gathering" people meant more than simply assembling a crowd; it meant drawing them *to God* and gathering them under the saving sovereignty.

It is likely, therefore, that Jesus told this parable in order to respond to the objections that were being elicited by his ministry to the multitudes. The spiritual leaders of Israel contemptuously viewed people of this sort as accursed through their ignorance of the law (John 7:49) and wondered how Jesus could represent his association with them as a manifestation of the kingdom of God. The answer that Jesus gives them in this parable is that the kingdom of God is mercy as well as righteousness, redemption as well as judgment; in this present time it has pleased God to reveal his sovereignty in saving grace, and the judgment will reveal its reality.

It would be difficult to bind more closely the two aspects of the kingdom of God, present and future, grace and judgment, than they are in this parable. And we should not fail to note that grace is not banished from the judgment, for beyond the separation lies the salvation of the kingdom of God for all who have not denied that grace.

2. THE UNJUST STEWARD
Luke 16:1–8

This story of a clever rascal who by the exercise of his wits turns a calamity into an occasion for feathering his nest has caused no little perplexity among both scholars and laymen, since the man's conduct is praised rather than condemned and in some way is cited as an example to be followed. The difficulty is compounded through uncertainty as to the limits of the parable. There is an increasing consensus that the introduction to verse 9 ("And I say to you . . .") marks a fresh beginning and that Luke has added a series of sayings that serve as lessons drawn from the parable.[21] He himself will then have viewed the parable to consist of verses 1–8. It is nevertheless plausible that verse 8b ("The worldly are more astute than the other-worldly in dealing with their own kind") is also an independent saying, conjoined to the earlier unit—verses 1–8a—prior to Luke, for it is not part of the story but an observation on the kind of men to whom the steward belongs, and it forms a point of attachment to which Luke added his further sayings.

The moot question is who the *kurios* of verse 8a might be: "The *master* applauded the dishonest steward for acting so astutely." If the *kurios* is Jesus, he is represented as adding his own (favorable) verdict on the actions of the character portrayed in the parable, and in that case the parable concludes at verse 7. The arguments for this interpretation are strong: (1) elsewhere in Luke, when *kurios* in an absolute sense does not refer to God, it relates to Jesus; (2) there is a close parallel to this passage in the parable of the Unjust Judge (also a man of *adikia*!) in Luke 18:6; and (3) the *kurios* commends the man for disposing of still more of his master's resources, a difficult point if the *kurios* is the steward's master. On the other hand, there are substantial reasons to view the *kurios* as the master of the steward: (1) the term *kurios* is used three times in the parable to denote the master of the steward (vv. 3, 5), and it is natural to assume that the fourth occurrence of the term in the same context should have the same reference; (2) it would be unusual for a statement such as that in verse 8a to be handed down in the tradition, for the statement is not a word of Jesus, but a *report* about a saying of Jesus relating to an element in the parable;[22] (3) it has been argued that a parable commencing with a judgment of the master relating to his steward's conduct of affairs would most fitly end with the judgment of the master relating to the steward's further conduct, for thereby an excellent balance is obtained;[23] and (4) there are grounds for affirming that the master could have responded to the actions of his steward in the manner indicated in verse 8a.

J. D. M. Derrett has supported the assertion that the master might indeed have responded to the actions of his steward in the manner indicated in verse 8b with an ingenious explanation of the situation depicted in the parable.[24] He contends that the steward is represented as having made loans to a number of creditors *and charged the usual interest on them.* The lending of money on interest, however, was contrary to the Mosaic law (see Exod. 22:25, Lev. 25:36, Deut. 23:19–20). The Pharisees had propounded a way of evading this prohibition in their business transactions by maintaining that if anybody actually possessed a portion of that which he desired to borrow, it would not be wrong for the lender to make profit on the loan. Since even the poorest man had in his possession some wheat and oil by which to live, loans were translated in terms of these commodities, and the interest was reckoned accordingly. The parable, says Derrett, tells how the steward called his master's debtors and instructed them to rewrite their promissory notes, *deducting the interest on their loans.* He thereby conformed to the intention of the law, which he had formerly evaded by charging interest on the loans. Naturally the creditors were delighted, and the steward made friends for life. But what of the master? He had lost yet more money. On the other hand, everybody would have assumed that the steward had acted according to instructions, that the master had benevolently decided to conform to the law of God and permit his representative to dismiss the usury that had formerly been charged. Thus, Derrett suggests that the steward had calculated that his master would be gratified to bask in an unaccustomed reputation for generosity and piety, and would not repudiate what had been done in his name—and the employer, taking in the calculation, would appreciate the astuteness of his rascal of a steward! If the situation was indeed as Derrett has described, it may be presumed that Jesus' audience sufficiently understood it to get the point.

D. O. Via has made the additional observation that Jesus makes use of the literary form of picaresque comedy in the parable. The latter characteristically deals with the adventures of a successful rogue, whose exploits are narrated in such a way as to elicit the approbation of readers (or onlookers in the case of a drama). Admittedly it entails a kind of "moral holiday," for it demands a suspension of the moral judgments of those who read or watch, but it appeals to the mischievous side of people and can be highly entertaining, particularly when the laugh is at the expense of the authorities (Robin Hood is such a character). It is in harmony with this type of story that the steward can be represented as winning the approval of the employer he tricked, although when judged by normally accepted standards his morals are questionable. Looking at the parable from this standpoint, Via says, "It is this element of success, which belongs to the picaresque mode, that suggests that Luke 16:8a was an original part of the parable."[25]

Assuming then that we may approach the parable from this angle, what is the message Jesus intended to convey by it? Of this there can be little doubt. We are presented with the picture of a man under threat of doom who takes resolute action to avoid it. Time was short, but he effectively used it to transform a dreaded future into one that could be anticipated with relief. The parable will have been spoken by Jesus in the context of warnings to his hearers to recognize the judgment ahead of them, and to take steps whereby doom may be avoided and entrance into the kingdom gained in its stead. This is no new note in the proclamation of Jesus. It conforms to the summary of his preaching given in Mark 1:15, with an added note of urgency. In the ministry of Jesus the salvation of God was operative as a marvelous reality, but many in Israel were blind to it, and they were incurring the judgment of heaven. As the salvation of God hastened to its revelation, so also the reckoning for those who rejected the word of the kingdom was hastening. Jesus therefore issues a call for decisive action in the present to avoid the prospect of rejection by God in the judgment and replace it with the prospect of joyous entry into the kingdom of redemption.

3. THE JUDGE AND THE WIDOW
Luke 18:1–8

It has been the fate of this little parable to have suffered total dismemberment at the hands of its exegetes. It is generally agreed that the opening sentence was added by Luke to form not only an introduction to the parable but also an interpretation of it.[26] Most expositors contend that Luke has thereby given a partial interpretation that fails to do justice to the main thrust of the parable. Jülicher thought otherwise. He believed that the original parable consisted only of verses 2–5, to which Luke's introduction is suitable. The parallelism between 18:1–5 and Luke 11:5–8 (the parable of the Friend in Need) seemed to Jülicher to be so close that he was persuaded that the two parables were originally conjoined, like the parables of the Man Building a Tower and the King Going out to Battle in Luke 14:28–32. They have an identical lesson, admirably expressed by Luke in 18:1, and on this Jülicher commented, "If one idea is assured for Jesus it is that represented in this parable."[27] By contrast, he suggests that 18:6–8 has a different intention—not to emphasize the necessity of the believer's continuance in prayer but the assurance of God's speedy answer to his people's prayers. Moreover, Jülicher contends that the attitude expressed in this passage is characteristic of the primitive Jewish church, and that the thought and language of the passage are very close to those of Ecclesiasticus 35:14–20— that, in fact, 18:6–8 may be an early interpretation of the parable based on the passage from Ecclesiasticus.[28] Many scholars agree with this essential thesis, although some prefer to refine it (1) by attributing the phrase "But the Lord said" in 18:6a to Luke, (2) by assuming that the rest of verses 6–7 forms an early exposition of the parable found by Luke in his source, and (3) by supposing that verse 8a ("I tell you he will vindicate them soon enough") is of Luke's composition but that he took verse 8b ("But when the Son of Man comes . . .") from elsewhere and placed it in its present position to bind the parable to the discourse on the parousia in the preceding chapter (Luke 17:22–37).[29]

The phenomenon of different parabolic elements fused to form a new whole is not unknown in the gospels (cf. Matt. 22:1–10 with 11–14 conjoined; and Luke 19:11–27 with vv. 14 and 27 inserted from another tradition). When it is affirmed that the thought of verses 6–8a is not congruous with the teaching of Jesus (as Jülicher argues), however, or that Jesus *could not* have uttered verse 8b, we are dealing with a highly selective attitude to what is dominical in the gospel traditions. Luke 18:6–8 is closely related to the Q apocalypse that immediately precedes the parable. The concept of the justice of God is fundamental to the Bible, not least to Jesus himself, particularly in its eschatological aspects. We recall that the Sermon on the Mount begins with beatitudes of the kingdom and ends with a parable of judgment; there is an emphasis on judgment both positive and negative in Luke 12–13; and there is an element of vindication implied in sayings such as those in Luke 12:32, Mark 14:25 with Luke 22:28–30, and the parousia passages in the gospels.

The motivation to separate verses 6–7 from verses 2–5 is bound up with the idea that the shortened parable forms a twin with that of the Friend at Midnight (Luke 11:5–8) and that verses 6–7 are not compatible with verses 2–5. The former of these views, despite its popularity, is doubtful, as G. Delling has shown.[30] The question of the compatibility of verses 6–8a with 2–5 will depend on our interpretation of both sections. Suffice it to say at present that there is reason for believing that the concepts embodied in verses 2–5 are continued in verses 6ff. and that the whole parable forms a unity, possibly reflecting and applying a notion also found in a single passage, well-known in the day of Jesus (Ecclus. 35:14). Similarly, it is true that verse 8b may have been an isolated saying that Luke brought to this point because of its fitness to the context, but if this is the case, we can only say that it suits the parable so well that Luke was fortunate to have come across it, and he was possessed of unusual insight to place it here. As it stands, however, there are adequate grounds for believing that the saying was uttered in connection with the immediately preceding sentences.

Despite differences of judgment regarding the composition of the parable, widespread agreement exists about its meaning as it now stands in Luke's gospel. The disagreement generally centers on the issue of the extent to which the second part would qualify the first. The widow, frequently conjoined with the orphan, is a traditional figure for helplessness in the world. Similarly the treatment of the widow by a judge is an equally traditional measure of the impartiality of his justice.[31] In the parable we are confronted with a judge who fails completely in the light of this standard. He is represented as a man who thought little of the judgment of God that he would one day have to face, or of the opinion of his fellows. A widow, convinced that she was being wronged by someone, besought the judge time and again to "take up her case,"[32] but without success. At length, however, the judge stirred himself to action for no other reason than the desire to get rid of the complaining woman. The lesson is drawn: if so *unrighteous* a judge could be persuaded to aid a person in need, we may be assured that the *righteous* God will certainly take up the case of his chosen ones who cry to him day and night and will right the wrongs they suffer. This he will bring about "speedily," through the agency of the Son of Man. For that day the elect must hold themselves ready.

Thus some hold that the clue to the parable is the phrase "how much more," typical of Jewish comparison, which is read into the beginning of verse 7 ("and will not God vindicate his chosen . . . ?"). On this basis, a unity can be sought between the two parts of the parable in that assurance of vindication is offered when God's people *continually* cry to him, the faith that the Son of Man seeks is the root of such believing prayer, and the lesson Luke points out in verse 1 can be applied not only to prayer generally, but to the specific need of God's people to *pray constantly for the coming redemption.*[33]

A different approach to the parable has been set forth by Derrett, who holds that the key to understanding the parable lies in recognizing that in the Middle East it was common for two jurisdictions to exist side by side in a single land. In the Palestine of Jesus' day there were two sorts of legal jurisdiction concurrently in force—namely, the courts run by the Jews in accordance with the Torah, and a second judiciary superimposed upon them as a kind of "police" or "administrative" system. The widow goes straight to the administrative judge, since he had authority to make decisions according to his own will, and she was too poor to hire a lawyer.

Why did the judge give way to the woman? The answer is stated in his own words: "This widow is too great a nuisance. I will see her righted, in case by her continually coming *she finally blackens my face.*" Such is Derrett's translation of *hupopiazein,* which literally means to hit one beneath the eye, and so to give one a black eye. The term was used in a variety of ways, but the figure of blackening the face was and is known all over Asia for disgracing a person. It reflects the phenomenon of a sallow skin turning ash-gray when disgrace is realized. To the Orientals this was a matter of great moment; they would do anything to avoid being publicly disgraced. This judge may assume the posture of fearing neither God nor man, but not even he can afford to lose his prestige. His soliloquy assumes the possibility that if he finally turns away this woman, his name and his status will suffer—whether through her slander or the deduction of others—and so at last he yields to her pleas.

Although there is obviously a gulf between this picture of an unscrupulous judge and the biblical revelation of a holy God, there is one factor that bridges the gulf: *God also has a reputation and a name to maintain.* This is a common theme in the Old Testament, illustrated in the law, the psalms, and the prophets (see, for example, Exod. 32:12; Deut. 9:28; Ps. 74:22, 79:9, and 143:11; Jer. 16:20–21; and especially Ezek. 36:21ff., 38:23, 39:7, and other passages). Accordingly, says Derrett, the key to the parable lies not in a "how much more" element, which is not expressed at all, but in the recognition of the feature the judge and the Lord possess in common—the name that must be preserved. It is in accordance with a concern for his name that the Lord will act for the vindication of his people.[34] This understanding of the parable puts the first part not only in harmony with the second part but actually makes it integral to the meaning of the second part: it makes the parable one, not two.

There is a further issue, essential to an accurate understanding of the parable, that also prepares for its final thrust—namely, the meaning of the enigmatic phrase in verse 7: *kai makrothumei ep' autois* (NEB, "while he listens patiently to them"). Every commentator has wrestled with this problem. Ott devotes many pages to a review of the interpretations the phrase has received. He rejects the idea that the phrase continues the question in the first part of the sentence, as the NEB reading suggests, on the ground that the aorist subjunctive of the verb in the main clause should then be continued in the last clause of the sentence instead of being replaced by a present indicative. The AV makes the verb concessive in meaning: "though he bear long with them," and many exegetes follow this clue in varied ways. This too is doubtful, however, for nowhere is a solitary *kai* evidenced as a concessive particle, and such a notion would ordinarily require a participle to express it.[35]

Having dismissed the alternatives, Ott suggests that the contention, urged especially by Riesenfeld, that Luke 18:7 reflects Ecclesiasticus 35:18 has much to commend it. The parallels between the two passages are remarkable, as will be seen from the Greek version of the first two lines of Ecclesiasticus 35:18:

> *kai ho kurios ou me bradune*
> *oude me makrothumesei ep' autois.*

That is,

> And the Lord will not be slow,
>   neither will he be patient with them.

Riesenfeld, however, holds that since the two verbs in this passage occur in parallelism, they should be viewed as identical in meaning; he suggests that they both express the single idea "be tardy," "keep one waiting," and that, he urges, is the intent of Luke 18:7.[36] In response, Ott quite rightly points out that synonymous parallelism does not automatically entail identical meaning of verbs employed in the parallel lines;[37] while he concedes that *bradunein* does imply tardiness, he points out that *markrothumein* conveys the idea of holding back wrath that it may not come into action (cf. 2 Pet. 3:9). Ecclesiasticus 35:18 says that the Lord will not be tardy or show grace to the wicked; Luke 18:7, on the other hand, states that what the Lord will not do for the wicked he will do for the elect: he will not close his ears to their cry but will graciously listen to them.

While this is all very pertinent, there is a further element in the relation of Ecclesiasticus 35:18 and Luke 18:7–8 that deserves notice. The Hebrew text of Ecclesiasticus 35 underlying the Greek text from which our translations are made has some important marginal readings, and in verse 18 the variant is striking. Oesterley and Box, in their commentary on Ecclesiasticus, read the passage as follows:

> Yea the Lord will not tarry,
>   *And the Mighty One will not refrain himself,*
> Till he smite the loins of the merciless
> And requite vengeance to the arrogant.[38]

The marginal reading, however, makes the second line a question, presuming a negative response:

> *The Mighty One will not refrain himself, will he?*

Luke 18:7 appears to turn the question demanding a negative response into an open question, but since it follows a question demanding a positive response, the implication would seem to be that it calls for the same positive response that the first question calls for:

> *God will vindicate his chosen ones . . . won't he?*
> *And he will be gracious to them, won't he?*

Now what has Jesus to do with Ecclesiasticus? Commonly it has been assumed that an adaptation of a statement in Ecclesiasticus must betray the hand of a redactor, but Derrett points out that this book was beloved of the Qumran community. It is not inconceivable that Jesus might, in characteristic fashion, use a cardinal passage from the community's favorite textbook, a work in which they found encouragement for their anticipated role of avengers of the Lord, in order to correct an attitude that was typical of them and that also appealed to the populace. The men of Qumran looked for the Mighty One to lead them in battle and to "smite the loins of the merciless and requite vengeance to the arrogant." Jesus implies that that was not the task of the people of God; they needed not the sword for the achievement of redemption but rather the gracious hearing of prayer for a victory beyond their power to secure and mercy for participation in it.[39]

The bearing of this discussion on the understanding of Luke 18:8b is apparent. The Mighty One may be counted on to hear the prayers of his people, and he will grant them vindication "shortly." But how will this be accomplished? The Old Testament prophets would have answered, "Through the divine intervention of the day of the Lord." In the Q apocalypse, however, the day of the Lord has become the day of the Son of Man (see Luke 17:22, 24, 26, 30), and the judgment of the Lord on a generation comparable to that of Noah and that of Lot is to be carried out through the Son of Man. In that context, the question of Luke 18:8b asks whether the Son of Man at his coming will find faith of the kind that pays heed to the word of God and seeks his kingdom before all else in the world. Such a faith stands in contrast to the attitude of the generations of Noah and Lot, which were too absorbed in the affairs of this world to pay heed to the call of God, and it also stands in contrast to the attitude of contemporaries of Jesus, who heard the call of God through him. Quite specifically, it is faith directed to the God who is in process of fulfilling his promises to the fathers and establishing his saving sovereignty in and through Jesus. It is faith of this order that prompts the earnest cry to God for the final revelation of divine sovereignty, a faith that continues to believe, despite having to wait, that the answer to the ultimate prayer is sure.

This link between the faith the Son of Man will seek and the sovereignty of God operative in and through him raises the question of whom Jesus was addressing in this parable. It is generally assumed that he was directing it to his disciples, since they are the last audience to be named by Luke (17:22). If this is the case, the disciples received from the parable not only encouragement but a reminder of the necessity for being prepared for the day when their prayers would be answered in the kingdom's unveiling. The teaching of Jesus, like that of the prophets of both Testaments, assumes that there will be a people of God— the "elect"—to inherit the kingdom for which the world was made. Luke 18:8

must not be interpreted so as to imply that Jesus had doubts about that. But like the prophets, Jesus does not cease to warn against "ease in Zion." He never equates faith's assurance with presumption in relation to the judgment. The Son of Man seeks a living faith, strong enough to endure afflictions and overcome natural impatience for vindication, a faith that expresses itself in obedient service to the end.

We know that some of the parables of Jesus were addressed not to his followers but to other members of his nation, including some who were highly critical of him. The parable of the Widow and Judge could have been spoken to Jews who were not followers of Jesus, or to a mixed company of disciples and noncommitted Jews who were interested enough in the message of Jesus to listen to him.[40] Most Jews who came to hear Jesus had their hopes set on the deliverance of their people in the Day of the Lord. They would have listened with approval to the parable, seeing in the situation of the widow a reflection of their own and finding in the concluding assurance of verses 6–8a a heartening message. The final question of verse 8b would have disturbed them, however. Are not the "elect," who cry night and day to God for vindication, the covenant people, as the scriptures teach? And yet some at least in contemporary Judaism were aware that the "elect" were not coextensive with the nation. The word of Jesus gives a fresh slant on the elect: they are those in whom the Son of Man at the revelation of the kingdom finds "faith." According to Delling, Jesus directs the gaze of the Jewish community to "the danger of not being able to stand before the coming of the Son of Man," and in verse 8b he asks, "Will the Son of Man encounter faith in the Judaism which at the present time widely rejects him, the faith which recognizes the Son of Man in the lowly and humble man in his earthly work, who is the Servant of the Lord?"[41]

The question finds a peculiarly urgent application to Jews of our Lord's day if he had in mind those who sympathized with the outlook of the Qumran sectaries. The men of Qumran were preparing to be the army of the Lord, whom God would use as instruments of his annihilation of the wicked—Romans, Gentiles, and apostate Jews alike—and to usher in, under the messiahs of Aaron and Israel, the promised kingdom. Certainly they prayed for the vindication of God's elect, for their entire existence was oriented to the events in which it would be accomplished. And they studied among their sacred writings the book that told how the Lord, the Judge, listens to the widow whose tears run down her cheeks as she accuses the man who caused them. We have seen how they read in their copy of the passage:

> Yea, the Lord will not tarry,
>   And the Mighty One will not refrain himself, will he?
> Till he smite the loins of the merciless
>   And requite vengeance to the arrogant. (Ecclus. 35:18)

The difference between this citation and Luke 18:6ff. warrants attention. First, we should note that in the Ecclesiasticus passage the people from whom God will not "hold back" are the objects of his destructive judgment, whereas in Luke 18:7 it is his own people from whom God will not hold back as he listens to their cries. Second, the "Mighty One" in the citation is Yahweh, whose instruments of judgment the Qumran members expected to be, whereas in Luke 18:6ff. the Mighty One is the Son of Man. Third, and most significant of all, the question at the end of the parable implies that the Son of Man asks no one to be an instrument of his judgment but rather warns every man to look for judgment on himself and to come to terms with the true Messiah.

It is one of the tragedies of history that the group of Jews who in many ways stood closer to Jesus than any other group known to us promulgated a messianism that directly contributed, through the Zealot movement, to the destruction of their nation. Holding on to the hope of a messianic Priest and messianic King, they were blind to the concept of a messianic *Servant*. Their Messiah-Priest, like their Messiah-King, was a warrior, and the community of priests prepared themselves to be an army of priestly warriors. Jesus recalls them to a different understanding of the way of divine vindication. Vengeance does not belong to man, for judgment is in the hand of God, and his only appointed instrument of justice is the Son of Man. Israel must turn from thoughts of bringing in the kingdom with the sword, for the Lord will do it through his Mighty One. And every man of Israel must recognize that he, too, as well as the men of Kittim and the rest of the Gentiles, must stand before the Son of Man at his coming, and give answer concerning his relation to the God revealed in *this* Christ.

4. THE BURGLAR
Matthew 24:43–44 // Luke 12:39–40

The wording of this Q parable diverges little in the versions of Matthew and Luke, but in some minor respects Matthew appears to be more primitive than Luke.[42] The introductory sentence in Matthew 24:42, "Keep awake then; for you do not know on what day your Lord is to come," does not belong to the parable, but is an independent saying that Matthew has placed here, apparently to serve as an announcement of the theme of the parables that follow.[43]

The reference of the parable of the Burglar has been disputed. C. H. Dodd contends that it has in view the crisis that was developing in the ministry of Jesus. He maintains that in Jesus' teaching the predictions of the coming of the Son of Man or of "that day" run parallel to his predictions of historical disasters, and that the coming of the Son of Man in its aspect of judgment was to be realized in the catastrophe that Jesus saw looming ahead for himself, for his disciples, and for his nation.[44] Jeremias essentially followed in Dodd's path, viewing the parable as relating to the day of the Lord, with its accompanying terrors for the godless, including unbelieving Israel. He judged the application of the parable to the parousia in the gospels to be secondary, since the parable portrays disaster, whereas the parousia is elsewhere represented as a day of joy for the disciples. Moreover, he notes that the Christological application in the second half of the parable is absent from the version in the Gospel of Thomas.[45]

Dodd's interpretation scarcely does justice to the eschatological language of Jesus, however. It goes without saying that Israel's response to the ministry of Jesus was determinative for its destiny, as he made clear in both parable and plain speech; but Jesus never suggests that his death will temporally initiate the final tribulation, issuing in an instantaneous parousia. And, indeed, Jeremias rightly dissociates himself from such a view. But he then proceeds to draw a distinction between the day of the Lord and the parousia in the teaching of Jesus on the ground that the former signifies disaster and the latter joy, and in this he is incorrect. The Q apocalypse clearly represents the day of the Lord as identical with the day of the Son of Man and with the parousia of the Son of Man; for this event the disciples will yearn (Luke 17:22), but for the generation as careless as those of Noah and Lot it will bring doom (Luke 17:26ff.), creating a separation among people entailing a "taking" of the prepared to be with the Lord in the messianic banquet and a "leaving" of the unprepared to the doom of divine rejection (Luke 17:34–35).

The understanding that the parousia is identical to the day of the Lord was preserved in the primitive church, taught by the tradition of Jesus' words. In 1 Corinthians 1:7, for example, "the revelation [*apokalupsis*] of our Lord Jesus Christ" is paralleled in the next sentence with "the day of our Lord Jesus," and both are anticipated to be an occasion of joy for the Corinthian believers.[46] When therefore Paul writes in 1 Thessalonians 5:2 that "the day of the Lord" comes as a thief in the night, he clearly views it as identical with the parousia, as the immediately preceding paragraph with its description of the coming of the Lord shows (1 Thess. 4:15–18). E. Lövestam comments that "In the oldest phase of the primitive Church that it is possible to reach, the 'thief' simile is thus in fact used about the parousia. What compelling objection then exists for the parable of the thief being originally a parousia parable?"[47] The majority of recent critics agree that there is none.[48] Certainly we ought not to allow the "non-Christological" version of the parable in the Gospel of Thomas (log. 21 and 103) to serve as evidence in the matter. Characterizing this rendering of the parable as "an unambiguously Gnostic interpretation," Schrage states, "That Thomas does not allow the exhortation to watchfulness regarding the parousia is only to be expected in face of the Gnostic eschatology, or rather the de-eschatologizing."[49] Thomas in fact transforms the thief into the kosmos ("You, however, watch out for the world"). We cannot appeal to this source against the evangelists and the primitive church in a matter so alien to its Gnostic outlook.

Once we acknowledge that the parable of the Burglar relates to the parousia of the Son of Man, its meaning is not difficult to determine: it sets forth the unexpectedness and unpredictability of the parousia. Hence, the parable calls for "readiness" (*ginesthe hetoimoi*) on the part of all. Since the event is likened to the coming of a thief, it is commonly assumed that the parousia is being viewed in terms of its aspect of judgment, bringing loss and ruin for many. The observation of Schulz on this point is noteworthy:

> For the Q community the parousia is not in the first place the great day of Jubilee (in contrast to other kerygmatic representations of primitive Christianity, e.g. the ardently yearning *Maranatha* in the pre-Pauline Lord's Supper liturgy, 1 Cor. 16:20ff.); the apocalyptic "day" of the Kyrios is not, as in the pre-Pauline community tradition (= 1 Thess. 5:2, 4, cf. also Rev. 3:3; 2 Pet. 3:10) to meet only the unrepentant Christians and unbelievers as a day of doom. The apocalyptic arrival of the Son of Man is for the Q community something feared, uncomfortably surprising

and a threatening fear which cannot be avoided, because the Son of Man at his coming will demand the fruits of the radical obedience to the law.[50]

Is not this contrast between Q and the other primitive communities drawn too sharply? We have already seen that the representations of the parousia in the Q apocalypse (Luke 17:22–23) have positive aspects for those prepared for the end as well as ruin for the unprepared; we should recall also the foundational saying in Luke 12:8–9 // Matthew 10:32–33 and the parable of the Great Feast (Luke 14:16–24 // Matt. 22:1–10). The parable of the Burglar calls attention primarily to the unpredictability of the parousia rather than to the idea that it brings loss to people. If the parousia be viewed in terms of judgment in a positive sense, it will connote vindication and salvation on the one hand and condemnation and loss on the other. The likening of the parousia of the Son of Man to the incalculable visitation of a thief does not of itself imply that the parousia is a disastrous event; rather, it is an appeal to ensure that it may be a day not of loss but of entry into the infinite gain of the kingdom of God, as Strobel points out: "The concern [in the parable] in the first instance is seen to be not a prophecy of judgment, but an exhortation and a call to lay hold of salvation."[51]

It remains to ask whether *Jesus* could have spoken the parable. Bultmann wavers on this issue,[52] but some recent scholars have refused to attribute it to Jesus on the grounds that its Christological slant reflects the church's experience of the delay of the parousia.[53] Any who acknowledge that Jesus viewed himself as the representative and mediator of the kingdom of God in the future as well as in the present will not be affronted by the so-called "Christological slant" of the parable. We have yet to examine the implications of this position in the teaching of Jesus on his own destiny. As to the issue of the delay of the parousia, we might well ask why the conviction that the time of the parousia is *unknowable* should be considered irreconcilable with the expectation that it is *near*; what reason is there to suppose that the mystery of the time is a sign of the delay of the parousia? Strobel, who cannot be said to be unaware of the problem of the delay of the end, is surely right in his assertion about the belief in the unknowability of the time of the parousia: "It is the principle handed down from of old that the time of the end is determined alone in the decree of God."[54] The parable gives no indication that that end will be delayed, but it does affirm that the time of its coming is unknowable, and by its appeal for preparedness assumes the real possibility of its imminence. In this it is one with the eschatological outlook of Jesus generally. On this issue Patsch wrote,

> It belongs to Jesus' preaching of the sovereignty of God that he proclaims it as something near, and that this nearness compels to conversion; but it is characteristic that this nearness is not chronologically fixed. Jesus speaks not of the when but of the suddenness of the inbreaking. This suddenness is inevitable; it cannot be calculated, e.g. through apocalyptic interpreting of signs. But the fact of the nearness has to be recognized in all its incalculability. The announcement of Jesus is temporal, but it is not temporally confined, for it gains its point from the emphasis on the inescapable ignorance of the time of the end, and therewith the necessary surprise, which no watching can penetrate.[55]

In conclusion, we can see that the use in early Christian literature of the figure of the thief in relation to the day of the Lord or the parousia (cf. especially 1 Thess. 5:2ff., also 2 Pet. 3:4ff.; Rev. 3:3), together with the fact that this picture appears to be foreign to the eschatological imagery of late Jewish literature,[56] points to the circulation of the parable of the Burglar among the words of Jesus in earliest times.[57] Its congruence with other attested teaching of Jesus supports the presumption of its authenticity.

5. THE WISE AND FOOLISH MAIDENS
Matthew 25:1–13

For the innocent, this well-known parable of Jesus is straightforward and contains a simple message. For the scholars, it is a battleground of contending interpretations.

The kingdom of heaven is likened to a story about ten girls and a wedding. They may have been servants, either of the bride's or the bridegroom's home.[58] They were charged to meet the bridegroom as he came to meet his bride for the marriage ceremony.[59] For this they required lamps with oil and wick, which were probably carried on poles.[60] The girls would have lit the lamps when they first received the command to meet the bridegroom, and in the period of waiting the oil burned low—hence the cry of the foolish girls, "Our lamps *are going out*" (v. 8). The relative wisdom of the girls is displayed by their having taken or failed to take a jug of oil with which to refuel the lamps, for a bridegroom frequently arrived late for the wedding. True to form, the bridegroom was delayed, and the girls fell asleep. When the cry was sounded at midnight, "Look, the bridegroom! Come out to meet him!" all the girls woke up, but the lamps of the foolish were now flickering low. Their request for oil from their friends was denied on the ground that no lamps would remain alight if the oil were shared. While they were at the shops buying oil, the bridegroom came, the wedding party entered the house for the festivities, and the door was shut. When the foolish girls arrived late and asked to be admitted to the wedding, they were turned down. "I do not know you" echoes a common formula that was used to deny individuals access to their superiors; it means, "I do not want anything to do with you."[61] The lesson drawn is "Be on the alert; for you do not know the day or the hour" (v. 13).

Of the problems raised by the parable, the first is perhaps the simplest—namely, the question of whether it should be classed as a parousia parable or whether it has in view the crisis developing in the ministry of Jesus that is leading to the eschatological tribulation. As with the parable of the Burglar, Dodd and Jeremias apply the latter interpretation to this parable.[62] They recognize that the evangelist presents the parable as relating to the parousia, but they contend that Jesus himself must have had in mind the eschatological crisis. In general, however, exegetes hold that this parable is making reference even more clearly than the parable of the Burglar to an event in the future that has to do with a *person* rather than a progression of conditions from the ministry of Jesus to a crisis of disaster. Reviewing the interpretation of this and related parables Kümmel comments,

No explanation is given why in all these parables the "coming" of *the master, the bridegroom, the thief* is constantly mentioned. On the contrary it follows also from all these exhortations to be on the alert and to be prepared that Jesus describes the coming of the Son of Man, and therewith the entry of the kingdom of God, as possibly very imminent, and in any case pressingly near, although its actual date was completely unknown.[63]

Virtually all critics concur with this conclusion (although some differ concerning the matter of the time).

A more difficult issue to resolve is whether the parable of the Maidens is to be viewed as a true parable, or whether it is an allegory concerning the parousia. Bultmann held the latter view, stating, "This is a Church formulation, completely overgrown by allegory, and having a strongly emphasized reference to the Person of Jesus."[64] Bornkamm agrees and specifies a number of items that seem to him explicable only in terms of the parousia expectation of the church: (1) the procedures in the parable do not accord with Jewish wedding customs, (2) the girls are featured rather than the bride because they represent those who are *invited* to the wedding, (3) the delay of the bridegroom and the fact that he comes in the night reflect Christian ideas of the parousia, (4) the "meeting" (*hupantesis*) is a technical term for escorting a notable person to a city on the occasion of his parousia, (5) and the cry announcing the groom's arrival recalls the eschatological cry (of angels or prophets) at the end of the world. Bornkamm therefore pronounces the parable to be "a document of the post-Easter expectations."[65]

Jeremias responded to this exposition in a twofold way. On the one hand he agreed that the evangelist would certainly have viewed the parable as an allegory: its details call for such treatment, and Matthew underscored them first by prefacing the parable with the word *tote* ("then"), thereby setting the parable in the context of the parousia described in the preceding chaper, and second by adding verse 13, with its reference to the *day* and *hour* of the parousia. Nevertheless, Jeremias holds that the original parable was not an allegory but rather that Jesus formulated a wedding scene wholly in accord with the customs of Jews in the first century in order to drive home a message relating to the eschatological crisis. Thus Jeremias holds that the bridegroom does not depict the Messiah, for such a representation was foreign to Judaism, and Jesus' hearers could not have made such an identification. Rather, he maintains that Jesus used the story to give to the crowd a warning cry to awake them from sleep, and *the evangelist* (or his tradition) made of it an allegory of Christ and the church.[66] Eta Linnemann goes further than Jeremias in denying that the points of contact between the parable and the reality of Christian faith made the parable an allegory, stating that "The narrator has used them only to secure the connection of the parable with the situation."[67]

There is sufficient cause here to give us pause before we conclude that the parable is an outright allegory. We do not feel compelled to view Jesus as the burglar in the parable of the Burglar, nor a capitalist in the parable of the Talents (Matt. 25:14ff.), nor a vulture on account of what he says in Luke 17:37. Why then should we feel compelled to identify him with the bridegroom in the parable of the Ten Maidens, as though it gives a description of his wedding night? We can freely acknowledge that the situation of the parable is congruent with the eschatological hope of the Old Testament, of Judaism, and of Jesus himself; the image of the feast of the kingdom of God might be readily adapted to the most cheerful of feasts, that of the wedding; and the picture of Yahweh taking Israel as his bride is not difficult to extend to the relationship between the Messiah and the people of God.[68] Of this there is a hint alread in Mark 2:19. Jeremias recognized that his nonallegory "at most . . . conceals a messianic utterance of Jesus which only his disciples could understand."[69] Perhaps that exactly describes the intention of the parable: it is a story with an application that can be grasped by all but that reflects a relationship with the speaker that only his own recognize.[70] But that does not make the parable an allegory.

A third issue is the motif of delay in the parable. To what extent is it a dominant feature in the story? Are we to view it as simply a part of the scenery, or is it the controlling factor, the key that makes the parable what it is and determines the message it is meant to convey? Bornkamm has affirmed the latter view; the assumption that the parable fails to mirror Jewish wedding customs confirmed his suspicions that the parable had been redacted to bring it into line with the church's later expectations concerning the parousia.[71] It must nevertheless be stated that it has been shown that every major point Bornkamm cites as being out of harmony with Jewish wedding procedures (and every point that he therefore argues must have been determined by the hope of a delayed parousia) is in fact within the range of actual wedding customs. L. Bauer has written an account of a typical Palestinian wedding in which (1) the bridegroom is brought instead of going to fetch the bride, (2) the groom enters the bride's home instead of their going to his, (3) the groom delays his arrival, and (4) the wedding takes place at a late hour:

> After having amused oneself with dancing and other entertainments, one starts the wedding-feast at nightfall. By torchlight, songs, and exultation the bride, attended by women, is later led from their parents' house to her new home where she is entertained by her companions. Suddenly—usually around or after midnight—it is announced that the bridegroom comes. The women then leave the bride alone and go with torches to meet the bridegroom who approaches at the head of his friends. After the bridegroom has entered the house, the nearest relations wish him and the bride luck and the newlyweds are left to themselves.[72]

Jeremias states that the reception of the bridegroom with lights and the long wait for his arrival continue to be characteristic in modern Arab weddings. The frequent delay of the bridegroom is usually due to prolonged argument concerning presents due to the bride's relatives.[73]

The lesson of the parable, then, is plain: the people of God must be prepared for the Lord in his coming.[74] The sleep of the girls is part of the picture; it is of no account so long as they are prepared and equipped to meet the bridegroom. For this reason we may reserve judgment as to the relation of Matthew 25:13 to the parable. At first sight it seems indubitable that Matthew has added the saying, whether or not from Mark 13:35, for the parable teaches the necessity of being *prepared*, not of remaining *awake*.[75] On the other hand, Bauer defines *gregorein* as "to be on the alert," "be watchful," "be *vigilant*," and Oepke prefers this last definition in its figurative use relating to the parousia.[76] That meaning easily passes over to "be prepared" in relation to the parousia, and it is reasonably certain that that is how Matthew intended it to be understood.[77] Such is Lövestam's conclusion:

> The concluding *gregorein* in verse 13 expresses thus—corresponding to the significance of the word in other passages—the fitting eschatologically determined posture of the faithful (in Christ) in this world. It means in the time of "night" to stand with burning lamps prepared to receive the coming "bridegroom," to be "awake" in the life of salvation (in Christ), and, concentrated on and awaiting the return of the Son of Man, to live in preparedness for this.[78]

6. THE TALENTS AND THE POUNDS
Matthew 25:14–30 // Luke 19:11–27

There can be little doubt that in these two parables we have two versions of a single parable, the traditions of which diverged prior to Matthew's and Luke's redactions. The essentials of the story are discernible from the common material. A man commits sums of money to his servants and goes abroad. After returning home, he summons the servants and investigates what each has done with his money. Two of them report a profit, and are rewarded. The third makes a speech in which he says that his master is a ruthless man in business, that he (the servant) was afraid of risking the money by trading, and that he will now hand it back to him intact. The master severely rebukes his servant for his indolence, and he hands that servant's money to the one who had gained the most. The lesson is added: "The man who has will be given more; the man who has not will forfeit even what he has."

In comparing the differences between the two versions we are at once struck by the additions Luke has placed at the beginning and the end of his version of the parable. When detached from the common material, the outline of another parable can be discerned, a parable J. A. T. Robinson called "The Parable of the Prince Royal":

> A man of noble birth went on a long journey abroad, to be appointed king and then return. His fellow citizens hated him, and they sent a delegation on his heels to say, "We do not want this man as our king." However, back he came as king. . . . [The parable relates how certain loyal subjects were rewarded with the governorship of cities, vv. 17, 19.] "As for those enemies of mine who did not want me for their king, bring them here and slaughter them in my presence."[79]

That the nobleman gives money to *ten* servants instead of *three*, as in Matthew, could be an indication of his higher status, but Luke's later description reflects the original number three (v. 16 tells of the report of the "first" servant, v. 18 of the "second," v. 20 of "the other one"). In Luke each servant is given a "mina," which was worth a hundred denarii, whereas in Matthew there is a gradation of assignments according to ability, and the sums are vastly larger—five talents, three, and one. If in Luke the ability of the servants is being tested, in Matthew the merchant entrusts great resources of capital with a view to serious trading.

What did the original parable say about this matter? It is difficult to be confident about it. The sequel in Luke's account contains some curious incongruities: for a servant to be made a governor over ten *cities* in recompense for earning ten *mina* is a startling reward, and for such a man to be additionally rewarded by being handed *one* mina is just as remarkable! These features are, of course, due to the conjunction of the two parables, and so may not determine what the original parable may have said. Despite the popularity of following Luke's account of the bestowal of the single mina, the originality of Matthew's representation appears to be more plausible. If, as we shall see later, the deposit made with the servants is a figure of the gift of the kingdom of God, the committing to men of a mina is an unsuitable figure for the reality and is not in accord with related parables and figures of Jesus for the same thing.[80]

As to the description of the activities of the servants in Matthew 25:16–18, Crossan maintains that its dramatic value in the unfolding of the narrative argues for its originality:

> The contrast between the first two servants and the third one is immediately established, and questions are immediately posed for the hearer's mind. . . . The result of having 25:16–18 present is to draw the hearer immediately into the world of the parable, so that already one is taking sides, pondering, wondering, and questioning.[81]

Did the third servant *bury* his talent as Matthew states (v. 18), or did he put it in a *soudarion*, a kerchief, as Luke says (v. 20)? If he acted as a responsible Jew, he would have buried it; R. Samuel said, "There is only one sure place for preserving money—in the earth!"[82] But we do hear of Jews putting money in a neckerchief about their necks, which was manifestly a less safe procedure; Michaelis suggests that Luke may be right in this point: it indicates that the servant was not only indolent but culpably careless.[83] This could apply only to Luke's "mina," however; a talent would be too great to carry about the neck.

What are we to say of the divergent conclusions of the parable? Luke's verse 27 must have belonged to the "Prince Royal" parable, not to that of the Pounds. Matthew's verse 30 may also be an addition to the original parable, a conjecture supported by the fact that it reflects language favored by the evangelist.[84] Matthew and Luke combine in reporting an identical saying in Matthew 25:29 // Luke 19:26. It is found also in Mark 4:25 // Matthew 13:12 // Luke 8:18, and is obviously a *Wanderwort*. Presumably it was added here at an early stage in the common tradition, and so it is likely that the parable in its earliest stage came to a close with Matthew's verse 28 (= Luke's v. 24).[85]

Scholars have proposed a variety of answers to the question of whom the parable was directed to. Their proposals fall into two basic categories: the Jewish people who are unresponsive to Jesus, and those who hear his word with a measure of acceptance and faith. The former interpretation has captured the allegiance of most modern exegetes. Dibelius views the parable as "an accusation against the Jewish people, who do not know how to use the precious heritage entrusted to them by God."[86] Dodd contends that it is directed to the Pharisee, who seeks personal security in the meticulous observance of the law: "Simple folk, publicans and sinners, Gentiles, have no benefit from the Pharisaic observance of the Law, and God has no interest on his capital."[87] Yet more commonly, the Scribes have been considered as the target of the parable, in view of their responsibility to instruct the people in the scriptures.[88] One must nevertheless ask whether the Scribes and Pharisees can justly be related to the third servant in the parable. He is viewed as lazy and wicked, with a jaundiced view of his master. The Scribes and Pharisees are criticized for many things in the New Testament but never for those faults; rather, they are accused of a misplaced zeal, often directed against the Bearer of the kingdom of God and his message. The Parable of the Talents appears to have been directed to those who professed to be *recipients* and not opponents of the message of Jesus.

This becomes clearer when we ask what reality lies behind the figure of entrusting wealth to the servants. The major issue in the proclamation of Jesus is not the nature of revelation in the scriptures but the fulfillment of law and prophets in the kingdom of God that has drawn near and become available to men. The entrusted wealth, accordingly, is likely to be a symbol of the saving sovereignty of God: offered as a gift, it becomes a powerful agency in the lives of those who receive it. The figure is comparable to those of the parables of the Treasure in the Field (Matt. 13:44) and the Pearl of Great Price (Matt. 13:45–46), but it goes beyond them in implying that to receive the gift is to accept a trust that demands a discharge in the service of God.[89]

This sheds light on the purpose of the parable. It cannot be categorized as just a crisis parable, meant to warn Israel of the coming day of reckoning, for it has positive as well as negative implications. The proclamation of the kingdom of God brings with it gifts and power that challenge God's people to become what they were meant to be—the salt of the earth and the light of the world (Matt. 5:13ff.). If this is true for the hearers of Jesus generally, how much more must it be true for followers of Jesus, to whom the secret of the kingdom of God has been given (Mark 4:11; Matt. 13:16–17)! They have been called into the kingdom in order to serve. This suggests that the third man in the parable symbolizes any person who is drawn by the proclamation of Jesus but refuses to accept the obligations of the saving sovereignty of God.

A final question must be raised concerning the parable: Has it anything to do with the parousia in its intention, or is its apparent connection with that event attributable solely to the redaction of tradition and/or of the evangelists? Without doubt the evangelists understood the parable to signify the departure of Christ from this world and his return at the parousia. This is particularly clear in Luke's version: the introductory statement in Luke 19:11 asserts that the parable was told because "they [the disciples?] thought that the reign of God might dawn at any moment." The parable shows that the Lord is to leave his servants and appoint them to complete a task in the world, after which he will return as King and reward his faithful servants and destroy his enemies. Matthew achieves the same purpose by attaching this parable to the parable of the Ten Maidens with the conjunction "for" in the opening sentence: disciples must be alert and prepared for the Lord at his coming (Matt. 25:13), *for* their situation is like that of the servants in our parable. At the other end of the parable, the closing sentence goes beyond depriving the guilty servant of his talent: the man is thrust into the outer darkness—that is, outside the kingdom of God—and hence we are to assume that the sentence is that of the Lord at the judgment. It is also possible that the call to the faithful servants to "enter the joy" of their master (Matt. 25:21, 23) may refer to going into the Master's joyful feast—that is, the Feast of the kingdom of God.[90]

We should acknowledge these elements of allegorical interpretation, but we should also note that some exegetes have so stressed them that they have failed to discern significant implications of the parable in its basic form. Both the *absence* of the master and his *return* to demand the rendering of accounts are essential to the picture of the parable. The period between the departure and return is the time when the servants carry out their master's bidding and demonstrate their worth or unworthiness.[91] If therefore the separation of the master from his servants is important for the creation of a significant present, and his return for a reckoning of accounts, there is a salient deduction to be drawn: "The picture of the parable is not possible at all apart from a certain parousia expectation."[92] Polag points out that if the reckoning alone were the point of the parable, the feature of the master's going away would have been unnecessary, as in the parables of the Unforgiving Servant (Matt. 18:23–35) and the Unrighteous Steward (Luke 16:1–9).[93] Thus we can assume that the parable of the Talents and the Pounds has an essential concern with the parousia, even apart from its redaction in the tradition and through the evangelists.

This has a bearing on Luke's introduction to the parable: "They thought that the reign of God might dawn at any moment" (Luke 19:11). Quite specifically, it is the disciples and the crowd referred to in Luke 19:7ff. who are represented as harboring such thoughts. What this means to Luke regarding the church of his own time is not immediately clear. Does it suggest that his contemporaries had similar expectations? If so, Luke was remarkably perceptive in placing the parable where he did, inasmuch as it assumes that the time for the departure of the Master is at hand—the time when the service of the Master's servants in the kingdom of God assumes urgency. Many exegetes reject such an interpretation, however; they dismiss as impossible an expectation of the parousia that maintains a balance between delay and near expectation. But other scholars have recognized that such an expectation was in fact characteristic of the Q community that handed on the early form of the parable.[94] Due consideration of Luke's eschatology, noting especially the complementary stance of Luke 21:20–24 and 21:29–31, 34–36, suggests that the evangelist held a similar expectation. If we read the parable in the light of the total eschatological instruction of Jesus, it appears that such an expectation was characteristic of Jesus also.

13 | The Son of Man and the Kingdom of God

1. JESUS AND THE SON OF MAN
Luke 12:8–9, Matthew 10:32

The question of the role of Jesus in the future of the kingdom of God is bound up to no small degree with the interpretation of the Son of Man sayings in the synoptic gospels. The sayings in question can be conveniently divided into three groups: (1) those that relate to the work of the Son of Man in the present (notably Mark 2:10, 28; Matt. 8:20 and 11:19; and Luke 19:10); (2) those that speak of his suffering, death, and resurrection (note especially the predictions of the passion in Mark 8:31; 9:31; and 10:32ff.; see also Mark 9:12; 10:45; and 14:21, 41); and (3) those that speak of his parousia at the end of the age (above all, Mark 8:38, 13:26, and 14:62; Matt. 10:23 and 24:44; and Luke 17:24ff.). This division of the sayings is convenient, but it should be observed that the groups are nonetheless related; we can view the second group as a subcategory of the first, and the third has to do with the destiny of him who suffers rejection and death at the hands of men (note that Mark 14:62 belongs to the passion narrative not just in terms of its content).

Exegetes have long questioned whether one or another of these three groups authentically reflects the mind of Jesus. The term "son of man" is a Semitism for man, properly speaking an individual of the species. There is at least one saying in the first group that reflects a misunderstanding of the term: Luke 12:10 reads, "Anyone who speaks a word against *the Son of Man* will receive forgiveness; but for him who blasphemes the Holy Spirit there will be no forgiveness"; in Mark 3:28–29 the saying runs, "All sins and blasphemies will be forgiven *the sons of men*, but whoever blasphemes against the Holy Spirit has never forgiveness." The original saying clearly speaks of "blasphemy" (i.e., slander) against *bar nasha*—that is, man as such—but in the Q source it was understood that the reference was to the Son of Man, the Christ; and yet such a reading results in a highly improbable contrast between blasphemy against the Son of Man and blasphemy against the Holy Spirit who inspires the Son of Man.[1] Bultmann believed that similar misunderstandings have occurred in *all* the sayings relating to the ministry of the Son of Man in the first group: they all relate to man, or to Jesus as a son of man, in the idiom in which "son of man" means "I," he says. He views the second group of sayings as inauthentic, as containing *vaticinia ex eventu*. It is only the third group that he considers authentic, but in these he holds that the Son of Man is distinguished from Jesus, that the Son of Man at his coming is expected to ratify the work of Jesus.[2]

The two major studies of the Son of Man in recent times, those of A. J. B. Higgins and H. E. Tödt, can be viewed as detailed expositions of Bultmann's position.[3] By contrast, E. Schweizer has endeavored to reverse this common critical interpretation by seeking to establish the authenticity of the first group of sayings and the inauthenticity of the last group.[4] His position finds support in the linguistic arguments of G. Vermes, on the basis of which Vermes includes the first and second groups among the authentic tradition but rejects the last, chiefly on the assumption that the parousia doctrine did not arise till after the death of Jesus.[5] A more radical approach to the problem, associated especially with E. Käsemann, and worked out in detail by P. Vielhauer, eliminates the Son of Man tradition entirely from the authentic teaching of Jesus.[6] Vielhauer takes his stand on the conviction that the concepts of the Son of Man and the kingdom of God belong to different strands of tradition; in the literature in which the Son of Man plays an active role (e.g., the Similitudes of Enoch), the kingdom of God is not central, he says, whereas in literature in which the kingdom of God is dominant (e.g., rabbinic literature), the individual Son of Man is absent. He goes on to say that Jesus' teaching on the kingdom of God indicates that he stands in the main line of Jewish thought, which has no room for a Messiah or Son of Man in the kingdom of the age to come, and he suggests that this is why no Son of Man saying in the gospels mentions the kingdom of God. Hence, he concludes that it may be said "with a probability bordering on certainty" that "none of the sayings of the coming Son of Man derives from the historical Jesus."[7]

Clearly the scholarly confusion on this subject is considerable. One is constrained to ask whether any factors may have been neglected in this matter that might shed fresh light on the problems. I think there may be some. Continuing scholarly research is beginning to turn up some points of significant agreement, and at least some of the mist that obscures the view seems to be diminishing.

The first point of agreement is a negative one, but it has considerable importance nonetheless. It is now generally conceded that the Similitudes of Enoch should no longer be made a starting point for investigating the Son of Man sayings in the gospels, since there is no cogent evidence for dating them prior to the ministry of Jesus.[8] Granted the notion of the Son of Man toiling in the world for the redemption of mankind is remote from the thought of the Similitudes—as remote as the Son of Man is from the world in those writings— but that scarcely constitutes a reason to strike out such representations from the gospels. It is true that in Daniel, the one like a son of man comes from heaven, in contrast to the beasts that come from the abyss, but the symbolism of that vision is not to be interpreted by means of the Similitudes of Enoch. In Daniel 7 the seer has adapted a long-established and familiar myth of the Orient to express the Jewish faith in the establishment of the kingdom of God in this world by the agency of his representative. The Jewish reader is not expected to interpret the one like a son of man as a godlike being, any more than, say, the Christian reader of Revelation 12 has to understand the woman clothed with the sun as a goddess. Daniel 7 is a visionary picture, and it would have been understood to be such by the seer's contemporaries. We know, for example, that the book of Daniel was read avidly by the members of the Qumran community, yet the Messiahs of the Qumran literature belong essentially to earth rather than to heaven, and they have tasks to perform on earth as they initiate the transition from this age to the age to come. Why should it be assumed that Jesus could not have entertained similar thoughts? Certainly the Son of Man and the kingdom of God come simultaneously in Daniel 7; the question should be asked what the corollary of that would be for one who believed that the kingdom of God was coming in his God-appointed and God-inspired ministry.

That question leads directly to the second feature of the teaching of Jesus that has a bearing on the Son of Man sayings—namely, the significance of the word and work of Jesus for the coming of the kingdom of God. Vielhauer's radical separation of the Son of Man from the kingdom of God is based on the view that belief in the kingdom of God was irreconcilable with the expectation of a Messiah or Son of Man, since the sovereignty of God denotes *God* acting in judgment and salvation. We have already considered this in connection with the Old Testament and noncanonical Jewish literature and found that the contention simply is not true. For one thing, it fails to take into account the entire movement of Jewish belief in representation and mediation in the relationships of God and man. Moreover, the first and paradigmatic appearance of the Son of Man in Jewish apocalyptic literature is set precisely in the context of the appearance of the kingdom of God among men (see Dan. 7:13–14). If there is any truth in the contention that the one like a son of man in that vision is not only the representative of the divine rule but the agent by which it is operative in the world—and I hold that there is reason to believe so—then the precedent has enormous import regarding Jesus. In his teaching on the presence of the kingdom of God we have found that he consistently speaks in terms of his being the representative and mediator of the kingdom of God in this time. It is harmonious with this fundamental principle that he should view himself as the Son of Man through whom God gives the kingdom. We will have to investigate further to determine whether his sayings actually demand such an interpretation, but for the moment I am simply concerned that we be delivered from a critical straightjacket that would prevent us from recognizing such a possibility.

Third, the linguistic evidence concerning the Son of Man demands fresh consideration in relation to the Son of Man sayings in the gospels. The long history of investigation of the linguistic evidence, going back to A. Meyer and H. Lietzmann, has been brought to a decisive issue by Vermes in his essay on the use of *bar nash / bar nasha* in Jewish Aramaic.[9] In face of protestations to the contrary, Vermes maintains that in Galilean Aramaic, *bar nasha* ("son of man") could be used in a manner similar, though not wholly identical, to the way *hahu gabra* ("that man") was used, and so it could serve as a circumlocution for "one" in such phrases as "one says," or even as a synonym for "I."[10] The significant feature of *hahu gabra*, says Vermes, is that a speaker typically uses it when he wishes to avoid undue or immodest emphasis on himself, or when he is prompted by fear or dislike of asserting openly something disagreeable in relation to himself, or when he is uttering a curse or a protestation. Vermes goes on to cite various instances from later Aramaic in which *bar nasha* occurs in a *double entente*, in which it is not immediately apparent whether the speaker is referring to man in general or to himself, and reflection is needed to find the answer. The matter is of sufficient interest to warrant quoting one such example. Rabbi Simeon ben Yohai is said to have hidden in a cave for thirteen years during the reign of Hadrian. In Y. Sheb. 38d it is stated that

> At the end of those thirteen years he said, I will go forth to see what is happening in the world. He then went forth and sat at the entrance to the cave. There he saw a hunter trying to catch birds by spreading his net. He heard a heavenly voice saying, *Dimissio* ("release"), and the bird escaped. He then said, Not even a bird perishes without the will of Heaven. How much less *bar nasha*.

The same story is recounted in Gen. Rabba 79:6, but with a modified conclusion:

> Not even a bird is caught without the will of Heaven. How much less the soul of *bar nasha. So he went forth and found that affairs had quietened down.*

The last sentence shows that *bar nasha* is meant to refer to the speaker, not to man in general (Vermes cites a variant in an Oxford codex in which "the soul of man" is replaced by "my soul").[11]

Jeremias disagrees with Vermes on the matter of relating *bar nasha* to *hahu habra*, on the grounds that the latter has a restricted denotation ("I and no other"), whereas *bar (e)nasha* maintains its generic significance ("the [or a] man," and therefore also "I" or "the [or a] man like myself").[12] In reply, Vermes questions whether *hahu gabra* does in fact have so restricted a meaning, and insists that *bar nasha* can clearly include reference to oneself, as the examples of *double entente* in rabbinic authors show.[13] J. A. Bowker has recently examined Vermes's examples and appears to prefer Jeremias's explanation of how *bar nasha* can refer to the speaker who uses the phrase (i.e., from the point of view of its generic significance), although he does agree that Vermes has succeeded in demonstrating this usage in Jewish tradition:

> At present the case does seem to be established that the phrase could carry with it a generic reference, and that a speaker could include himself within the reference. That argument is an important gain, and is a direct consequence of Vermes' work.[14]

The layman in linguistics may perhaps feel that the *manner* in which *bar nasha* gained its personal reference to a speaker is of secondary importance in comparison with the *fact* that it was so used. And the student of the teaching of Jesus cannot but be interested to learn that modesty was a motive for using the expression in this way and that it could be so employed with self-conscious ambiguity.[15] Vermes recognized the applicability of this ambiguity to the sayings in the gospels that relate to the *present* action of the Son of Man. But why stop there? Is it not evident that the ambiguity could obtain equally in affirmations concerning the future activity of the Son of Man? There is, in fact, only one saying relating to the coming of the Son of Man in which there is no ambiguity concerning his identity—namely, Mark 14:62. The context of this passage is unique, however, and the clarity of the statement is exceptional. It is conceivable that the ambiguity attaching to the phrase "son of man" and the variety of the ways in which it could be applied are precisely what recommended it to Jesus for use in his teaching on the kingdom of God and his relation to it, both in the present and in the future.

There are, of course, passages other than Daniel 7:13–14 in the Old Testament and in other Jewish writings in which the phrase "son of man" occurs, with important implications for the gospel sayings. There is, for instance, the familiar use of the phrase in Psalm 8:4, in a context of wonder that the God of creation should set store in so frail a creature as him and bestow on him so lofty a calling in the world. Bowker has called attention to the comparable statement in Psalm 144:3–4, which has a significant modification:

O Lord, what is man that thou dost regard him,
    or the son of man that thou dost think of him?
Man is like a breath,
    his days are like a passing shadow.

Here "son of man" has the sense of *man subject to death*, in contrast to God and his angels.

Bowker points out that the Targum translations of Psalms and Job emphasize this understanding of the phrase. In Job 25:6, for example, as in Psalm 8:4, the Targum has *bar nash* in both clauses ("the son of man . . . a maggot, the son of man . . . a worm!"), and in Psalm 144:4 "son of man" is substituted for "man" ("*bar nash* is like a breath"). Bowker proceeds to list a considerable number of comparable passages to illustrate further this understanding in the Targums.[16] The appearance of the phrase in the Targums on the early chapters of Genesis led Bowker to conjecture that the association of the son of man with subjection to death was attributable to his being the son of Adam, who was subjected to the penalty of death. He does not press the point, however, nor does he argue that the Targums on Psalms and Job served as an influence on the New Testament writings, although he does suggest that it is pertinent to the gospel traditions relating to the Son of Man that the two chief ideas related to the use of "son of man" in the Old Testament are his subjection to death (Psalms and Job) and his prospect of vindication (Dan. 7).

We will examine, in connection with the gospel sayings relating to the suffering and vindication of the Son of Man, other representations in the Old Testament and Judaism of figures who suffer injustice and rejection and find vindication at the hand of God (the righteous sufferer, the rejected prophet, the suffering servant, the martyr for God's cause), but at this juncture it will suffice to note the existence of various strands of Old Testament and late Jewish piety and hope that find a meeting point in the gospel traditions about the ministry and destiny of the Son of Man. An adequate exposition of these delineations must take all these into account and avoid the temptation of taking a shortcut by confining ourselves to one or two late Jewish apocalypses.

III. THE COMING OF GOD IN THE TEACHINGS OF JESUS

We can perhaps best illustrate the principles laid down in this brief introduction to the Son of Man sayings in the gospels by referring to one of them that has in recent times come to be viewed as possibly holding the key to the interpretation of the rest—namely, Luke 12:8–9. It has an immediate parallel in Matthew 10:32–33, and a more remote one in Mark 8:38 and its parallels. Kümmel commences a notable article on this Q passage with a quotation from G. Haufe: "All in all the insight impresses itself on the observer . . . that the clarification of the Son of Man problems depends to a considerable extent on the understanding of the double saying Lk. 12.8f. . . . The question as to the interpretation of Lk. 12.8f is the crucial issue of the Son of Man problem."[17] We shall accordingly make this saying the point of departure for reviewing the Son of Man sayings and let it serve as a test case for the ideas we have reviewed thus far.

First a word about the form of the saying. It is a statement in double parallelism describing the confession of Jesus that leads to the Son of Man's confession of the confessor before God, and the denial of Jesus that leads to the Son of Man's denial of the denier. Mark 8:38 reproduces only the negative element of denial; we can assume that the double form is original and that Mark's version abbreviates it.

According to O. Michel, the saying contains a "pronounced Aramaism" in *homologein en* ("confess") and the "Palestinian Semitic colouring" in its use of *emprosthen* ("before," "in the presence of").[18] It is doubtful that we should put much emphasis on the difference between "deny" in Q and "be ashamed of" in Mark on the assumption that the latter reflects the terminology of the church in mission;[19] the essential issue in the logion is the decision for or against Jesus as the representative of the divine sovereignty.

The major critical question to be settled is whether we have a Son of Man saying here. Critics have said that we do not, for two reasons. On the one hand, while Luke has the Son of Man as subject in the second clause ("the Son of Man will acknowledge"), Matthew reads, "*I* will acknowledge." Jeremias has investigated a similar phenomenon in other Son of Man sayings and concluded that where one gospel tradition has a saying with the Son of Man as subject and a parallel version has a simple "I" as subject, the reference to the Son of Man should be judged as secondary—and he contends that this rule applies in this case.[20] It has also been observed that in the negative parallel clause of Luke 12:9 the passive ("will be denied") appears with no mention of the Son of Man; this has led to the suggestion that the passive originally stood in *both* parallel clauses, in harmony with Jesus' habit of referring reverentially to the action of God by means of the passive voice. On that basis, N. Perrin has proposed that the saying should be read as follows:

Everyone who acknowledges me before men
  will be acknowledged before the angels (of God);
but whoever denies me before men
  will be denied before the angels (of God).[21]

By one means or another, therefore, these scholars eliminate the references to the Son of Man from the original logion.

These arguments have on the whole been resisted by the scholarly community, however. Most of the parallel versions of the Son of Man sayings adduced by Jeremias turn out to be related in content rather than alternative forms of identical sayings. There are a number of passages related to the saying in Mark 8:31, for example: the phrase "the Son of Man must suffer many things" is related to Luke 22:15 and Mark 10:38; the phrase "and be rejected" is related to Mark 12:10; the phrase "and be killed" is related to Matthew 23:34, 37 and Luke 13:33; and the phrase "and after three days rise" is related to Luke 12:32 and Matthew 27:63. This scarcely constitutes evidence that Mark 8:31 is a passion prediction that once circulated without the Son of Man as subject. F. H. Borsch has examined the Son of Man sayings that have alternative versions without the expression, and he came to a conclusion opposite that of Jeremias: "The various tools of source, form and redactional criticism tend to point, sometimes rather conclusively, to the priority of the Son of Man designation in traditions where there are probably parallels without the Son of man."[22]

We might also make two observations about the contention that both parallel clauses of the Q saying in Luke 12:8–9 // Matthew 10:12 originally had a verb in the passive without the Son of Man as subject. First, not only Matthew but Mark also, representing an independent tradition, has the verb in the active, and in Mark's case the subject is the Son of Man. This suggests that if the parallelism were originally more precise than at present, the Son of Man would have been subject in *both* clauses in the Q version. Second, Luke's passive verb in 12:9 is almost certainly attributable to an accommodation to the sentence that follows in verse 10, which appears as a Son of Man saying with passive verbs in both clauses:

> Everyone who speaks a word against the Son of Man will be forgiven; but he who blasphemes against the Holy Spirit will not be forgiven.

I have already suggested that this is a clear example of "son of man" being used in a generic sense, applying to man generally, but taken by the hearers of the tradition as referring to the Son of Man, Jesus. The content of the saying is theologically difficult if we attempt to view it as relating to *the* Son of Man, in which case it says that those who speak against the Son of Man in his mission will be forgiven, but those who speak against the Holy Spirit who inspires the Son of Man in his mission will not be forgiven. But it is even more difficult to reconcile the saying with verse 9, which tells us that those who deny Jesus will be denied by the Son of Man at the judgment. Luke feels compelled to retain the saying in verse 10, but he softens the apparent difference of viewpoint by omitting the reference to the Son of Man in verse 9 and putting the verb in the passive *as in verse 10*. That being the case, we ought not to cite the form of verse 9 as evidence in any speculation concerning the original form of verse 8, and in particular we ought not to use it as evidence counting against the presence of the Son of Man in verse 8.[23]

For the majority of exegetes, the question of whether the original Q logion of Luke 12:8 // Matthew 10:12 featured the Son of Man in the manner of Luke's version is settled by the apparent distinction between Jesus and the Son of Man that is introduced into the saying in the Lukan version. Such a differentiation appears in only two other texts in the synoptic gospels—namely, Matthew 19:28 and Mark 14:62—but it is more striking in Luke 12:8 than in either of the other two:

> Everyone who acknowledges *me* before men,
>> *the Son of Man* will acknowledge before the angels of God.

If the Matthaean version were the original, why should anyone create this unexpected contrast in the second clause? Or why should an originally passive verb have been changed by a redactor to produce the contrast? If the statement were a creation of a Christian prophet, how would it have come to be formulated in this manner in the post-Easter era? It would have been easier either to set the Son of Man in all four lines or to omit all reference to him. A. J. B. Higgins therefore rightly affirms that "In analogy to the principle of the *lectio difficilior* in textual criticism we should conclude that the Lucan version of the saying is to be preferred."[24] Not surprisingly, Kümmel suggests that in view of the presence of Son of Man in Luke's positive clause and in the negative clause of Mark 8:38, the saying originally transmitted in the Q tradition must have run as follows:

> He who confesses me before men
>> the Son of Man will confess before the angels of God.
> He who denies me before men
>> the Son of Man will deny before the angels of God.[25]

The primary point of the saying is that the outcome of confession or denial of Jesus before men is a confession or denial by the Son of Man before God. Herein is an advance on the scene in Daniel 7:9–10, 13–14, in that the Son of Man not only receives the kingdom but plays a decisive role in determining who shall enter it. The emphasis falls on the decisive importance of heeding the word of Jesus as the representative of the kingdom of God in this time. Its significance is well expressed by Tödt, commenting on Mark 8:38:

> He by no means appears as the lowly one, the sufferer, but demands with supreme authority that allegiance which detaches the disciple from this generation. In demanding this, Jesus utters an unsurpassable claim. No prophet in Israel ever claimed that men should confess him.[26]

Jesus demands such allegiance because he is the bearer of the divine sovereignty and therefore exercises the authority of the God who appointed him. To confess him is to acknowledge that one follows him in his company. And Luke 12:8 implies that to be confessed by the Son of Man is to be admitted to a like relation to *him*: those who confess Jesus enter the fellowship of the Son of Man in the perfected kingdom of God. The burning question then arises: Who is this Son of Man? Having cited Tödt on the authority of Jesus assumed in this saying, let us consider his answer to the question:

> In Jesus' preaching the coming of the kingdom of God and the coming of the Son of Man appear to have been announced in a parallel manner. In view of this parallel we can realize that Jesus could indeed promise to those who by following him prepare themselves to respond to the coming of the kingdom, that they will be attached to

> the future lord of the kingdom, to the Son of Man. In giving these promises Jesus appears to have pointed away from himself and spoken of the Son of Man as someone different from himself.[27]

The statement is impeccably correct, even its last sentence: Jesus *appears* to have pointed to someone other than himself as the Son of Man. The question at hand is whether he intended his hearers to understand that the Son of Man would be someone other than himself. The answer must be a clear No.

At this point we should recall the foundational element in the teaching of Jesus relating to the kingdom of God that affirms its presence in the world in and through his word and work: he was able to call for allegiance to himself only by virtue of his authority as the representative and mediator of the kingdom of God among men. It is self-evident that the kingdom of God, God's rule in judgment and salvation, is one. The kingdom that comes in Jesus is *the kingdom of God promised for the end of the times*. That is the theme of his parables of the kingdom. However difficult it may have been for some of his contemporaries to believe, Jesus was proclaiming that the promised saving sovereignty of God was operative even as he spoke. He was thereby proclaiming himself to be the representative and mediator of the kingdom of God. Observe: "of the kingdom of God"—not of a present kingdom of God as distinct from a future kingdom of God. That which is at work in the present in Jesus is the future kingdom of God. It is the saving sovereignty of which the *revelation* is coming in the not-distant future.

How then are we to define the role of the Son of Man in the kingdom of God? If we were to attempt a definition in terms of Daniel 7, we could hardly do better than to employ language I have already used of Jesus and the kingdom: the one like a son of man is set forth as the representative and mediator of the kingdom of God to a world hitherto dominated by the bestial kingdoms. That he is also viewed in the interpretation of the vision as the representative of the people who possess the kingdom does not diminish the reality of his representing the sovereignty of him who bestows the kingdom. Clearly Luke 12:8–9 recalls the language of Daniel 7:9–10, 13–14: the Son of Man confesses his confessors in the scene of bestowal of the kingdom. Accordingly, Luke 12:8–9 signifies: *He who confesses before men the representative and mediator of the kingdom of God, Jesus, will be confessed by the representative and mediator of the kingdom of God, the Son of Man.* That can signify only that Jesus and the Son of Man are one.[28]

There can be no doubt that the chief reason for confusion in recognizing the import of Luke 12:8–9 has been a failure to reckon seriously with the teaching of Jesus concerning his role in the coming of the kingdom of God. We can easily see how those who reject the idea that Jesus was saying that the kingdom was present in his words and works might be prone to a failure of this sort. Bultmann was prepared to go so far as to affirm that Jesus was *the Bearer of the Word*, who could therefore assure men of the forgiveness of God,[29] but he maintains that Jesus *awaited* the coming of the Son of Man to ratify his mission. Käsemann, as others of Bultmann's students, went further than his master: he recognizes that in the word of Jesus the kingdom of God was coming to his hearers, "setting men in its presence, and facing them with the decision between obedience and disobedience."[30] Nevertheless, Käsemann argues that Luke 12:8–9 is not a word of Jesus but rather one of his "Sentences of Holy Law," attributable to the prophets in the church.[31] The difficulty of the saying in his view is that it suggests that confession of Jesus will be the standard of judgment at the last day. But is this really a problem? Is it unreasonable to suppose that the one in whose word and work the kingdom of God comes to men, the one who by that word and work creates about himself a redeemed and redeeming fellowship who are called to inherit the kingdom and to serve as its instruments in the world, should set as the standard for entry into the kingdom of God men's response to him in his proclamation of the word of the kingdom and embodiment of its action in his ministry? Jesus did not undertake his work or proclaim his word on his own authority but on the authority of him who sent him as representative of the saving sovereignty. It is this authority that underpins the sovereign commands to follow him expressed in such passages as Matthew 10:34–38, Mark 8:34, and Luke 9:57–62, as well as the imperious words about the importance of hearing his teaching expressed in such passages as Matthew 7:24ff. and Luke 8:31–32, and the importance of heeding his works expressed in such passages as Matthew 11:20–24.

The word of the kingdom come in Jesus is bound up with his role in the kingdom, and so the recognition of his function in the kingdom is bound up with confession of allegiance to him. Luke 12:8–9 is the projection into the future of the kingdom of those axioms of Jesus' teaching relating to its bursting into the present in his word and work. This is in fact so clear that I am constrained to believe that Käsemann's inclusion of Luke 12:8–9 in his category of "sentences of holy law" and his consequent attribution of the passage to anonymous early prophets throws his whole thesis about the "sentences" into question. There are, of course, other formidable grounds on which this theory can be questioned,[32] but so far as Luke 12:8–9 is concerned we may content ourselves first with observing the fundamental unity of the passage with the teaching of Jesus on his role in the kingdom of God, and second with noting Kümmel's comment that the attitude to Jesus and the reaction of the coming Son of Man in Luke 12:8–9 finds no parallel in the "sentences" collected by Käsemann.[33]

In conclusion we would do well to recall what we previously noted about the ambiguity of the phrase "son of man." We know that speakers did use it as a circumlocution in referring to themselves, and such a usage could account for the change from first person to third person in Luke 12:8–9. But it is equally evident that the phrase "son of man" *can* be used in this fashion to refer to another individual. In Luke 12:8–9, the references to confession and denial by the "son of man" before the angels direct the hearers to recognize the allusion to the one like a son of man who comes to exercise the promised divine sovereignty without clearly indicating the identity of that son of man. A hearer may well ask whether it is intended as a reference to Jesus or to the "one who is to come," the Messiah of the future. Disciples of Jesus will almost certainly perceive who is meant and receive the message of the saying; others may divine the implication and be offended by it; still others may be in the dark as to who the "son of man" is and yet perceive the claim being made about the importance of a decision about the word of Jesus. It could be argued that this saying provides good evidence for I. H. Marshall's contention that the expression "Son of Man" was a perfect vehicle for Jesus' proclamation of the message of the kingdom of God; it is a humble term with associations of divine glory that preserves "the secrecy of self-revelation from those who had blinded their eyes and closed their ears to it."[34] It corresponds with the obscurity of Jesus as representative of the divine sovereignty (despite his unparalleled authority in the exercise of its powers) and with the hiddenness of the kingdom that is to give way to manifest splendor at the revelation of the Son of Man. How many times did people ask as they heard Jesus refer to the present service and future exaltation of the Son of Man, "Who is this Son of Man?" (John 12:34)?

2. THE SON OF MAN IN MINISTRY

a. The Authority of the Son of Man
Mark 2:10

As with the other sayings that we have considered concerning the Son of Man active on earth (Matt. 8:10, 11:19; Luke 19:10), exegetes are divided on the meaning of the saying in Mark 2:10. They variously view the phrase "Son of Man" in this saying as a circumlocution for "I," an interpolation for "I," the equivalent of "man" in a generic sense, or a title of authority.

Formerly there was no little support for the suggestion that Son of Man was the equivalent of man in a generic sense here, on the grounds (1) that most of the eschatological Son of Man sayings fall in the latter part of the ministry of Jesus (after Peter's confession), and this appears too early to be classed among those; (2) that Matthew relates that the crowd looking on praised God, "who had given such power to *men*" (Matt. 9:8); and (3) that the objection of the Pharisees to Jesus' declaring forgiveness of sins was answered by the cure of the paralytic—a miracle that constituted proof not "that he was divine, but that the claim to forgive sin was within human competence."[35] Of late, however, there has been widespread recognition that this last contention is improbable, for the idea that forgiveness of sins lies within human competence is "alien to the mind of Judaism and of early Christianity."[36] Accordingly, even as early as Wellhausen we find it suggested that "Son of Man" in this case is used in a concessive manner, to mean "although I am a man"; Klostermann interprets it as "a man (as I)"; and Colpe defines it as "man in me, Jesus."[37] Indeed, Colpe goes further in acknowledging that the indignation of the Scribes did not take into account "*the messianic actualizing of the remission of sins* as this is effected by Jesus."[38] That is as close as one can come to acknowledging that Son of Man is a title of authority in this passage without actually stating as much, for it is precisely in the exercise of authority to forgive sins that the term Son of Man is employed. Schürmann, as others before him, calls attention to the significance of the phrase "on earth":

> The contrast here is not between God with his power of forgiveness in heaven and man "on earth," but between God in heaven and the "Son of Man" on earth. There is

not only forgiveness of sins in heaven—thus through God—but also "on earth"—even because the "Son of Man" is there now.[39]

Accordingly, Schürmann suggests, Son of Man appears to be used in Mark 2:10 as a term of dignity, expressing the authority of Jesus in his ministry, and in particular his authority to forgive sins.[40]

What is the connection between forgiveness of sins and the function of the Son of Man? There is no precedent in the Old Testament or in Judaism of the Son of Man exercising the prerogative of forgiveness, and that is a pressing problem for those scholars who regard the Son of Man as a messianic concept in pre-Christian Jewish apocalyptic. For Tödt the problem is even more complicated, since in his view all Son of Man sayings relating to the earthly Jesus must be church creations, but he addresses it as follows:

> The ascription to Jesus of the power of forgiving sins is not inspired by attributes of the transcendent Son of Man. Rather is the reverse process recognizable: by calling Jesus in his unique authority Son of Man, and conceiving of Jesus' authority as including the forgiveness of sins, the community can formulate the saying that the Son of Man has the *exousia* to forgive sins on earth.[41]

This is an example of the improbabilities into which scholars are led when they start off with the Jewish apocalyptic notion of the Son of Man and fail to take into account the implications of Jesus' teaching on his relation to the kingdom of God in his ministry. Naturally there is no contact between the purely transcendent Son of Man in heaven, as depicted in the Similitudes of Enoch, and the Son of Man on earth forgiving the sins of men. But why imagine that it was *the church* that had to bridge the gap between the Son of Man and forgiveness on earth? Jesus called on men to repent in view of the approach of the kingdom of God, and, using a variety of images, he assured them of God's readiness to forgive them. It was as representative of the kingdom of God and mediator of its redemptive powers that he delivered them from the thraldom of evil and brought them under the reign of God, to enjoy the blessedness of the fellowship that is to be known in its fullness in the feast of the kingdom. In that context he spoke of himself as the Son of Man who came eating and drinking, rejoicing with repentant sinners in the fellowship of the kingdom, and as the Son of Man who came to seek and to save the lost. Why then should he not speak of himself as the Son of Man with authority on earth to forgive sins? For the Son of Man is the representative and mediator of the kingdom of God, and it was in his consciousness of being that representative and mediator that Jesus proclaimed the kingdom and mediated its blessings to men. Mark 2:10 is an application of Jesus' theology of the kingdom to one important need of man and one aspect of the kingdom of God, and it is in harmony with all the rest he taught.[42]

b. The Son of Man and the Sabbath
Mark 2:28

Scholarly interpretation of the saying in Mark 2:28 pursues lines similar to those used for other sayings on the life and action of the Son of Man, and especially of

Mark 2:10, since that saying also appears in the context of an early confrontation between Jesus and his Jewish opponents. The discussion is complicated by the relation of Mark 2:28 to 2:27. A virtual unanimity of opinion has developed that verses 27–28 were not originally part of the narrative recorded by Mark in 2:23–26 but that the evangelist attached the two sayings to the preceding episode in view of their common theme.[43] The parallelism of the sayings in verses 27–28 makes the frequently suggested identification of the Son of Man with "man" more plausible here than in any of the related passages we have considered:

> The sabbath was made for the sake of man . . . therefore the Son of Man is sovereign even over the sabbath.

It is not unnatural to assume that the "son of man" who is sovereign over the sabbath is the "man" for whose sake it was made.[44] This proposed identity, of course, can operate in another way: there is no a priori reason why the "man" of the first clause should not be the same as the "Son of Man" of the second clause, so that the saying may be read,

> The sabbath was made for the Son of Man, not the Son of Man for the sabbath; therefore the Son of Man is sovereign even over the sabbath.

Such was T. W. Manson's later interpretation of the passage, although he viewed the Son of Man as Israel represented in the community of disciples about Jesus and held that they violated sabbath observance in the service of the kingdom.[45] Like so much of Manson's writing on the Son of Man sayings, it is an attractive but unlikely interpretation, since the idea of the Son of Man as a corporate entity does not suit the Son of Man sayings generally.

As with other "present" Son of Man sayings, most interpreters view the Son of Man in Mark 2:28 as an individual—namely, Jesus. But they manifest a marked reluctance to ascribe the logion to Jesus. They typically contend that it is a Christian comment, either on verse 27 or on the sabbath issue as illustrated in the preceding narrative.[46] Such cautious scholars as C. E. B. Cranfield and W. L. Lane include themselves among those who regard the saying in this way, holding that it is an explanatory comment of the evangelist, similar to the observation introduced at the conclusion of the revolutionary statement of Mark 7:15.[47] Others take a less charitable view of the logion. There is a tendency to look on verse 28 as evidence of the church's hesitation to accept without reservation the bold statement of verse 27. H. Braun traces this attitude, especially in Matthew's version of Mark 2:23–28; on the one hand, he observes, other sayings are introduced by Matthew (the profanation of the sabbath by the priests in the temple, the presence of one greater than the temple, and the citation of Hos. 6:6), and on the other hand he omits the offensive verse 27. He suggests that Mark 2:28 is the final step in this process of weakening the impact of verse 27: Jesus as Son of Man—he and he alone—has authority over the use of the sabbath, because he is Messiah and Lord.[48] Käsemann presents a similar argument:

> The community was prepared to ascribe to its Master what it had not the courage to claim for itself. This qualifying insertion shows that it shrank from exercising the

freedom given in Jesus and preferred to take refuge in a Christianized form of Judaism.[49]

Now the heavens do not stand or fall according to whether Mark 2:28 is a saying of Jesus or not, nor according to the precise determination of its references, but one receives the impression of needless ebullience in the discussion of this saying. Braun and Käsemann have a point to make about verse 27 that is worthy of our consideration. Every commentator on the passage quotes the statement of Rabbi Simeon ben Menasja in the Mekilta—"The sabbath is delivered over for your sake, but you are not delivered over to the sabbath"—and note that this is an indication of Jewish sentiment akin to the thought of Jesus. With respect to Jesus' declaration about man and the sabbath, Israel Abrahams has said that "The Pharisees would have done, nay, did do, the same."[50] But apart from the limited scope of Rabbi Simeon's dictum,[51] it is misleading to give the impression that the sentiment expressed in Mark 2:28 was in any way representative of the Judaism of Jesus' day. Braun on the contrary refers to it as "a lonely bird on the roof." He asks, with evident feeling,

> And now shall this sabbath which, according to Jewish faith, God in heaven with all the angels ritually observe with exactitude, in order then to lay it on the chosen people of Israel as a religious observance; shall this institution which orders in the same way the realm of heaven and the realm of earth be *not* the most exalted service to the Godhead, but rather for the service of *men*?! Is it really so that it is not the setting aside of work, but the working of what is right which will perform the true service of God?! On the contrary, the antithesis of Jewish thinking can hardly be more incisively urged: the sabbath and its observance is not a religious end in itself; man is the end of the sabbath.[52]

It is quite comprehensible that the earliest followers of Jesus, before Easter as well as after, would have been as astounded by the teaching of Jesus on the sabbath as the Pharisees were. It is therefore equally comprehensible that Jesus himself should have added a statement to this saying that both strengthened and qualified his astonishing assertion.

Here I would make two observations. First, the *hoste* of verse 28, frequently rendered "therefore," need not be taken to imply the introduction of a strict deduction from its antecedent statement; it can also serve as a term of transition.[53] This is not unimportant, for it is often insisted that verse 28 must be viewed as a logical consequence of the principle of verse 27. Second, the ambiguity of *ho huios tou anthropou* (= *bar-nasha*) is nowhere more evident and instructive than in this sentence, for it is susceptible to a profound significance either way it is read. In this regard, we might note a minor difference between English and German traditions of translating Mark 2:28. Most English translators of modern times understand *kai tou sabbatou* as meaning "*even* over the sabbath," whereas the Germans prefer "*also* over the sabbath," a rendering that is perhaps the more natural. It is a question, though, what in addition to the sabbath the Son of Man is supposed to be sovereign over. The answer certainly does not lie in verse 27, and it is not self-evident in light of verse 28. There must be an allusion to some other dictum or teaching relating to the sovereignty of the Son of Man, sufficiently well-known to provide the clue to what is in mind.

Pesch contends that such a dictum holds the key to Mark 2:28: he suggests that an allusion is being made to the earliest scripture in which the sabbath is mentioned—namely, the creation narrative of Genesis 1:1–2:3. The description of the first sabbath follows the command (Gen. 1:28) that man should rule over the creatures that God made in the previous days of creation; the thought is assumed to be that as man is sovereign over the creatures of God's making in the six-day week of creation, so man is sovereign *also* over the seventh day, since it was made for his sake.[54] On this basis, Pesch opts for the view that Son of Man in Mark 2:28 must originally have meant man generically. One must admit that when the saying is viewed in the light of Genesis 1 (and Psalm 8, which celebrates man's God-given rule), the constantly voiced opinion that to view man as sovereign over the sabbath is an absurd and impossible notion is itself seen to be false; man responsible for rule under God is no more free to abuse the sabbath than he is to abuse the creation over which he has been set.

But while this is an attractive interpretation of Mark 2:28, it is not the only way of relating *kai tou sabbatou* to the creation narrative. A generation ago I heard C. H. Dodd, in a lecture on Christology, draw attention to the possibility of understanding Mark 2:28 in relation to man's appointment to bear rule over the earth. He was particularly interested in the way Psalm 8 expounds man's sovereignty over God's creatures and in the use of the psalm in Hebrews chapter 2. The psalmist marvels at the way God is mindful of *man* and cares for *the son of man*, giving him *dominion* over all the works of his hands—the collocation of the three terms is notable. The psalmist further details one by one the "works" over which man has been given dominion; it is in this light that Dodd understood Jesus' words concerning dominion "*also* over the sabbath," for as Son of Man, Jesus viewed himself as the representative man to whom rule is given. The author to the Hebrews uses the psalm in much the same spirit: he cites the psalm concerning God's regard for man, his care for the son of man, and his being crowned with glory and honor, concluding with the statement that God has put everything in subjection to him. The writer points out, however, that not everything is in subjection to man in the present time; nevertheless, we see Jesus, made lower than the angels as all men, but now crowned with the glory and honor of sovereignty by reason of his suffering death, which he endured for every man. The argument suggests that the author knew well enough that the psalm relates to man but believed that Jesus brought man's destiny for sovereignty to fulfillment in himself for the sake of man. That, as I recall, is how Dodd reasoned. And surely Mark 2:27–28 can be understood in a closely comparable manner: the sabbath was made for *man*, the crown of God's creation, and sovereignty over the sabbath, which belongs to man, is exercised now by *the Son of Man*, since he is representative and mediator of the divine rule, and so the one through whom man may experience it. The translation from *man in relation to creation* in verse 27 to the *bar-nasha in relation to the divine rule* in verse 28 is the more natural in view of the sabbath serving among the Jews as a type and anticipation of the kingdom of God.[55]

The importance of this mode of understanding the saying is twofold: it indicates that the destiny of man to rule being referred to in the creation narrative is realized in Jesus, the Son of Man, who mediates the redemptive rule of God; and it announces the sovereignty of the Son of Man in such a way that each hearer is able to understand according to his capacity. Shock and no little puzzlement would ensue whatever the interpretation of the saying, but the reserve of the Son of Man was maintained.

c. The Son of Man Who Feasts
Matthew 11:19, Luke 7:34

The authenticity of this saying is rarely disputed. On the one hand, the contrast between Jesus and John the Baptist is set forth more starkly here than anywhere else, and is hardly to be set to the account of church reflection.[56] On the other hand, the point of contrast is bound up with the element in the ministry of Jesus that gave most offense to his religious contemporaries: his table fellowship with "publicans and sinners." For Jesus the latter was significant both as an expression of the redemptive fellowship that the divine sovereignty made possible and as an anticipation of the coming feast of the kingdom; for his Pharisaic opponents it was the clearest expression of Jesus' rejection of the law as interpreted in the authoritative tradition. As Jeremias points out, "The offence after Easter was Jesus' accursed death on the cross, his table-fellowship with sinners was the pre-Easter scandal."[57]

While the authenticity of Matthew 11:19 is generally agreed on, though, there is less agreement about the significance of "Son of Man" in the saying. There is a tendency to view the expression as indefinite here, signifying "a man": "John came, neither eating nor drinking . . . a man came eating and drinking."[58] Others hold that "son of man" is being used as a periphrasis for "I" here.[59] And yet others hold that the title has replaced an original "I" as the subject of the statement.[60] In favor of the first alternative, Jeremias adduces the possibility of a wordplay in the original statement: "*bar ᵉnasha* (a man) came eating and drinking, and they say, Look, *bar ᵉnasha* (a man), a glutton and a drunkard."[61] Borsch draws a different deduction from the wordplay, suggesting that the statement was intended to convey the meaning "The Son of Man (*bar ᵉnasha*) came eating and drinking, and they say, Look a man (*bar ᵉnasha*) who is a glutton and a drunkard."[62]

Are we not confronted here with a clear example of conscious ambiguity in a Son of Man utterance of Jesus? The relation of the expression to Jesus is clear, and wordplay seems likely. Yet if we take into account the context (i.e., the parable of the Children in the Market Place, and possibly the statements of Jesus about John the Baptist and his message to John that immediately precede it in the Q source), an allusion to the eschatological Son of Man is possible. Clearly the comparison between Jesus and John involves more than the mere contrast of two lifestyles; it sets forth two complementary missions in relation to the kingdom of God, directed to the men of "this generation" (Matt. 11:16). The ministries of John and Jesus were vastly different, yet in the fulfillment of their respective roles relating to the kingdom of God and in their distinctive modes of proclaiming the kingdom, the initiation of the divine sovereignty among that generation was taking place (Matt. 11:12), and it was the condemnation of the men of that generation that they were too blind to perceive it. Thus, when Jesus contrasted John's ministry and his own, it would have been fitting for him to use the expression "Son of Man" with allusion to its function in relation to the kingdom of God, not least in view of the significance for the kingdom of his eating with the outcasts of society.[63]

We should note that this saying embodies the notion of rejection of the Son of Man in his ministry on behalf of the kingdom of God by the men of his generation. The description of Jesus as "a glutton and a winebibber" appears to be a recitation of the declaration that Israelite parents were commanded to make when they delivered a disobedient son to the elders of their city: "This our son is stubborn and rebellious . . . he is *a glutton and a drunkard*" (Deut. 21:20).[64] A son so condemned was to be stoned to death. In all likelihood, Jesus was here citing an allegation of his Pharisaic opponents, who thereby implied that such was his nature and such should be his fate. The connection between the sayings of the Son of Man in his earthly ministry and those relating to the destiny of the Son of Man to suffer and to die is particularly evident in Matthew 11:19, but it is expressed in other sayings as well, and we can assume that it is in general a part of the concept of the Son of Man who ministers among Israel on behalf of the kingdom of God.

d. The Son of Man Who Is Homeless
Matthew 8:20, Luke 9:58

This saying is said by Matthew to have been addressed to a scribe who desired to follow Jesus. This is noteworthy, in view of the strong polemic against Pharisees and scribes in Matthew's gospel; judging from the language of verse 21 ("*Another* of the disciples said . . ."), Matthew intends us to understand that the scribe became a disciple of Jesus.[65]

The exegetes' approach to this saying is not dissimilar to their approach to the saying in Matthew 11:19. Once again a number hold that the Son of Man should be understood as "man" in the generic sense. Bultmann has given it a well-known twist, postulating that the the saying is based on a proverb reflecting a pessimistic view of the homelessness of man on earth in comparison with animals, and suggesting that it entered the gospel traditions in the Hellenistic churches.[66] Few have followed him in this supposition; the generalization is patently false, and the saying is clearly best viewed as anchored in a specific situation in the life of Jesus.[67] Colpe, followed by Jeremias, understands Son of Man to mean "a man such as I" in this saying.[68] Otto maintains that Son of Man replaced an original "I."[69]

Most exegetes regard Matthew 8:20 as a genuine utterance of Jesus. Its primary emphasis is not on the situation of Jesus as such, but on what it means to follow him: a would-be disciple of his must be prepared to share the homelessness that is his lot. But why does Jesus refer to himself as Son of Man in this saying? Why does he not use a direct statement: "I have no place to lay my head"? Tödt sees the answer in the context: "Jesus is acting as the one who, with full authority, summons men to follow him. The name Son of Man is thus used to designate his sovereignty, his supreme authority."[70] While it may be true that the Son of Man sayings generally carry the implication of authority, it is better to view the accent in this passage as falling not on the authority of him who so speaks but on his mission in relation to the kingdom of God. There was no need for Jesus to have "nowhere to lay his head." There were many who would gladly have given him a permanent lodging, and in any case he had had no need in the first place to leave his home in Nazareth. His situation is illustrated in Mark's account of the early ministry in Capernaum: when Jesus went away in a lonely spot to pray, Peter and his companions searched him out and said to him, "All men are looking for you"; his reply was, "Let us move on to the next towns; I have to proclaim my message there also. *That is what I came out to do*" (Mark 1:35ff.). It was as proclaimer of the kingdom of God that Jesus was perpetually on the move, bringing to people the good news of the kingdom and the powers of the kingdom for the transformation of their lives; hence it was as the representative of the divine sovereignty seeking men that he spoke of himself as "Son of Man" in this logion.

But more: along with the itinerant ministry of Jesus in the service of the kingdom, the pathos in the phrase "nowhere to lay his head" may well allude to the opposition Jesus experienced in the course of his ministry.[71] Some exegetes, indeed, stress this aspect heavily. Bonnard believes that in Matthew's context the saying applies to "the dramatic itinerary of the Messiah, suffering right up to the cross," and Colpe remarks that "Jesus is not homeless because he has no house and no friends to see to his support but because . . . he goes to Jerusalem to his death."[72] Such comments go beyond what the text warrants.

Nevertheless, it is of no small significance that the two most characteristic sayings relating to the ministry of the Son of Man on earth apparently allude to the opposition and rejection that the Son of Man experiences in his service of the kingdom of God.

e. The Son of Man Who Seeks and Saves
Luke 19:10

Like all sayings related to the action of the Son of Man in present time, this one poses problems for those who hold that only the eschatological Son of Man sayings are authentic. Nevertheless, the objections brought against it can hardly be said to be substantial. Short as it is, the saying has elements that link it with some of the most characteristic features of Jesus' life and teaching.

Various scholars have hazarded the view that verse 10 is an addition by Luke to the story of Zacchaeus, and indeed that Luke formulated it.[73] Schmid has made the much less controversial proposal that Luke received the logion in the tradition without context and decided to set it here,[74] although clearly we cannot attribute the placement of all isolated logia in the gospels to the evangelists. Colpe was confident that Luke 19:10 is pre-Lukan, since Luke never uses "Son of Man" on his own, and the term *elthen* ("came"), used in connection with the mission of the Son of Man, is already found in pre-Lukan tradition, as Matthew 11:10 // Luke 7:34 shows.[75] Jeremias consistently maintains that Luke 19:10 is a secondary reshaping of Matthew 15:24 ("I was sent only to the lost sheep of the house of Israel").[76] Clearly the Lukan saying is harmonious with the Matthaean, especially in its present context, for Zacchaeus, like other publicans, is esteemed to be among the "lost sheep of the house of Israel," whom Jesus would seek and find.[77] Nevertheless, the differences of motive in the two sayings are so transparent as to make it difficult to view the one as a variant of the other.

The most notable feature of Luke 19:10 is its relationship to some of the elements of the ministry of Jesus that made it unique. One thinks of the concern for sinners and the outcasts of society expressed in the saying, a concern that is also reflected in Mark 2:17. Jesus' "seeking" such in order to "save" them recalls the parables of Luke 15. Lagrange speaks of the Zacchaeus narrative and of the saying with which it concludes as a *mise en action* of the parables of chapter 15.[78] The motif that lies behind the parable of the Lost Sheep is alluded to in Luke 19:10; in the discourse of Ezekiel on the faithless shepherds, Yahweh declares that he himself will undertake what they have failed to do:

I will *search for the lost*, recover the straggler, bandage the hurt, strengthen the sick. . . . (Ezek. 34:16)

The opening phrase in Hebrew—*eth-haobedeth abaqqesh*—is rendered in the LXX *to apololos zeteso*, "I will seek that which is lost" (cf. Luke's *zetesai kai sosai to apololos*). The implication is clear: Jesus is sent to carry out this work on behalf of God. In the present context it is given as the reason for his association with tax-gatherers and all like them. In the wider context of the mission of Jesus, the saying indicates why he should express his vocation in terms of the mission of the Son of Man: Yahweh's seeking and recovering his sheep is the prelude to the kingdom of God; hence, it is as Son of Man that Jesus engages in this divine task of seeking and saving the lost. Salvation is essentially an eschatological work, with the kingdom of God in view. Accordingly, "to save is the calling and purpose of the Son of Man."[79]

One further observation. Luke 19:10 is set in the context of the grumblings of onlookers that Jesus had gone to be the guest of a sinful man (v. 7). If the saying was originally independent, it is still most likely that it was evoked by the hostility Jesus met through his associating with the "unclean." The saying therefore seems to presuppose a motive similar to that displayed in Matthew 8:20 and 11:19. It is another instance of a Son of Man saying that has in view the opposition and rejection Jesus' earthly ministry received.

3. THE SON OF MAN IN SUFFERING

a. The Markan Predictions of the Passion
Mark 8:31, 9:31, and 10:32ff.

The three so-called predictions of the passion in Mark, despite their differences, are bound by a common content: in all of them *the Son of Man* is the subject of the prediction, and it is said of him that he is to be *killed*, and to be *raised—after three days*. The phrase "after three days" is surprising, for in the parallels of Matthew and Luke it is modified to the well-known "on the third day," which is the language of the primitive kerygma (see 1 Cor. 15:3–4). It is now generally agreed that the two phrases have the same meaning,[80] but Mark's adherence to the alternative expression is striking; it suggests that it was in his source and that he made no attempt to conform it to current Christian speech. It provides a hint that Mark dealt with his sources relating to the passion of Jesus with great care.[81]

In considering the three predictions, the question arises whether they are three independent predictions, viewed in the tradition as having been uttered on different occasions, or three forms of one of Jesus' statements. Jeremias favors the latter alternative.[82] If such is indeed the case, it becomes the exegete's task to determine which of the three is closest to the earliest tradition. It is generally agreed that 10:32ff. represents a developed form of the teaching, expanded in light of the events of the passion.[83] As to the remaining two, opinions are fairly evenly divided between the priority of 8:31 and 9:31, with perhaps a preponderance in favor of the latter.[84] We will take a look at the arguments regarding this matter, but at the outset we might just note that the nature of the instruction and the circumstances in which it was given suggest that the two passages may well contain independent traditions of instruction given on more than one occasion.[85]

We should turn first to the special elements in Mark 8:31: "The Son of Man must suffer much and be rejected" (*dei polla pathein kai apodokimasthenai*). The phrase reproduced in Greek appears in Luke 17:25, and the two verbs occur in Mark 9:12. It is likely that "suffer" and "be rejected" were intended to be understood in a general sense, and together express the humiliation and pain of the Son of Man. How early might such an association be? Hahn contends that the term *paschein* ("suffer") is a Greek word for which there is no real equivalent in Semitic languages, and so the saying could have arisen in this form only in Hellenistic Christianity.[86] That is by no means a necessary conclusion, however. We have yet to consider other elements of the saying, but on this point we might note the observation of Ruppert that *paschein* and *thlibesthai* ("suffer" and "be distressed"), with their connected nouns *pathemata* and *thlipseis* ("sufferings" and "distresses") are used interchangeably in the New Testament (see, for example, 2 Cor. 1:4–7 and 2 Thess. 1:4–7). Ruppert also notes that the expression *polla pathein* corresponds to the clearest statement in the Old Testament about the suffering of the righteous man, Psalm 34:19: "Many are the afflictions (*thlipseis*) of the righteous, but out of them all he will rescue them." It is Ruppert's conviction that Jesus could have had the Hebrew or Aramaic source of the saying in mind as he uttered this saying (in Aramaic!).[87] The reference to "rejection" reflects Psalm 118:22, which is also cited at the conclusion of the parable of the Wicked Husbandmen (Mark 12:10); the spirit of the psalmist's word ("The stone which the builders rejected has become the head of the corner") is not unfitting in a passion prediction that concludes with an anticipation of vindication by God.[88]

The term *dei* ("must") has evoked much discussion. Since it occurs in the LXX of Daniel 2:28[89] it has been thought to express the suffering of the Son of Man as an *apocalyptic* necessity.[90] In a less dogmatic sense, Grundmann holds that it sets forth faith in God's eternal plans and so is an *eschatological* necessity.[91] More commonly still, *dei* is regarded as the equivalent of the common New

Testament term *gegraptai* (cf. Mark 9:12, *pos gegraptai*), and so is held to denote a *scriptural* necessity that an event will come to pass. It is by no means certain that Mark would have distinguished among these nuances.[92]

Nor is it clear to me that the second chapter of Daniel has anything to do with the saying apart from providing an illustration of how *dei* can be used in Greek translation of a Semitic original. First, it should be observed that the Greek translators of the Old Testament have rendered *a simple future* by *dei* elsewhere (in Lev. 5:17, where it expresses the will of God made known, and in Isa. 30:29, where it expresses a future of prophecy). Second, the translators are not consistent in this usage in Daniel; the sentence following Daniel 2:28 has the same phrase, and it is rendered in the LXX in the same way, but in verse 45 the phrase is rendered in the LXX by the simple future *ta esomena*, whereas Symmachus gives *ha dei genesthai*. Third, the evangelists and/or their sources did not feel compelled to keep to *dei*. The second passion prediction, Mark 9:31, represents the suffering of the Son of Man with the verb *paradidotai* ("is handed over"), which Jeremias believes renders an Aramaic participle having a future meaning—"will be handed over."[93] The parallels in Matthew and Luke both read *mellei paradidosthai*; and Luke in 24:7 has *dei paradothenai*! Moreover, examples of the same kind of interchange can be found in different contexts. Mark 13:10 says of the gospel *dei keruchthenai*, whereas Matthew 24:14 reads *keruchthesetai*, a simple future with little difference of meaning. Mark 13:7 has the strong statement with respect to wars and the like, *dei genesthai*, whereas in verse 4 the eschatological-apocalyptic *hotan melle tauta sunteleisthai panta* is hardly weaker ("when all these things will come to pass" expresses an apocalyptic certainty of expectation).[94]

All this points to a tendency among those who translate Aramaic into Greek to render a simple future tense with *dei* (and *mellei*) where the context has to do with eschatological and/or apocalyptic realities and thus with the conviction that what is said belongs to the purpose of God and therefore must surely come to pass.[95] The importance of this will be immediately apparent: it suggests that the argument that the occurrence of *dei* in Mark 8:31 betrays the origin of the saying in Hellenistic Christianity since it reflects the Greek rather than Hebrew-Aramaic Old Testament is baseless. On the contrary, the evidence suggests that it comes from a community that understands how to render sacred truth in a Semitic language into Greek—that is to say, a bilingual community. In view of the likelihood that the passion predictions of Mark are intimately linked with the passion story reproduced by Mark, we might suppose that such a bilingual community could be sought in Palestinian Christianity. Pesch asks which church is more probable a candidate than the Jerusalem community, which first made known the passion story, and which from its earliest times was in touch with Greek-speaking Jews.[96] After all, the subject of *dei polla pathein* is the Son of Man, concerning whose destiny eschatological confidence, not to say assurance, is comprehensible.

The corresponding opening clause in Mark 9:31 claims our attention next: the Son of Man *paradidotai eis cheiras anthropon*, "is handed over to the hands of men." Jeremias is surely right in his conviction that an Aramaic play on words is reflected in this saying: *bar ᶜnasha* is handed over to *bᵉne enasha*—"the Son of

Man is handed over to sons of men," or, more simply, "the Man is handed over to men."[97] His further contention that *paradidotai* is a divine passive and that the mashal character of the saying points to its going back to Jesus is also plausible. While we may not concur that Mark 9:31 is the origin of the rest of the passion predictions, there is certainly no warrant for viewing it as an adaption of Mark 8:31;[98] it has good claim to being an independent tradition of the teaching of Jesus.

A major question regarding this saying is the significance of the passive mood of *paradidotai*: is it a "divine passive" *simpliciter*, so that it should be translated, "*God* will (soon) hand over the Man to men"?[99] That interpretation is in harmony with Paul's use of the term in Romans 8:32 ("He who did not spare his own Son, but gave him up [*paredoken*] for us all"), as also the kerygmatic formula in Romans 4:25 ("Jesus our Lord was handed over for our trespasses [*paredothe*]"). Yet we find different nuances in the use of the verb in other passion predictions in Mark. This is clearest in Mark 14:21: "The Son of Man goes the way appointed for him in the scriptures, but alas for that man by whom the Son of Man is being handed over (*paradidotai*)"; here the one who "hands over" is Judas, and most translators render *paradidotai* as "is betrayed." The same holds true for Mark 14:41. In the third passion prediction it is the Jews who hand over Jesus to the Romans (Mark 10:33). Now while this could indicate a later development of the understanding of *paradidotai* in the circles that were responsible for handing on the tradition,[100] it would appear to imply that from the beginning the saying was intended to embody *both* the decree of God *and* the human instrumentality through which the action was carried out; that would be entirely consistent with the idea that the "handing over" of Jesus to the will of sinful men falls within the eschatological purpose of God. Hoffmann is right in pointing out that in theological contexts it is possible to stress the divine element of the passive as though it were absolute, as in Paul, but that the perspective changes in a context that relates to the historic events of the passion, as in Mark, where both dimensions are consciously in view.[101] If such is indeed the case, then Mark 9:31 is not so distant from Mark 8:31 as is sometimes maintained; even in the latter "the Son of Man must suffer much" has in view the divine purpose as well as the human agency that inflicts suffering and rejects the representative of the divine sovereignty.

But there remains the question of the *origin* of these conceptions. We might ask in particular how such statements can be made concerning *the Son of Man*. It is possible to approach the issue by assuming that the external factors of the course of Jesus' ministry led him to reckon with the possibility—not to say probability—of an early and violent death. This view has been set forth succinctly by Jeremias, and at length and impressively by Schürmann, and it hardly needs to be reproduced at length here.[102] Yet surely the nature of Jesus' vocation from God as he interpreted it from the scriptures and through his communion with God would have been a more fundamental factor in his anticipation of the end toward which he was moving. On this much has been written and will yet be written, but there are signs of an increasing convergence of thought on this matter. There would seem to be four relevant strands of thought indicated by scripture, closely related but sufficiently distinct to warrant our distinguishing among them. The Son of Man can be said to suffer (1) as *the Righteous Man*, who is opposed by the unrighteous as he walks in the way appointed him by God; (2) as *the Prophet of the End*, the Bearer of the word of the kingdom, whose message is rejected like that of earlier prophets; (3) as *the Servant of the Lord*, whose sufferings bring to a climax his ministry of mediation of the kingdom of God; and (4) as *the Martyr* for the truth of God, whose obedience to God culminates in a sacrifice for the guilty. Of these four, the first is of greatest moment for the predictions of the passion, but the other three categories are also involved.[103]

The idea of the Righteous Man who suffers at the hands of unrighteous men is deeply rooted in the Old Testament and finds frequent expression in the Psalms. The pattern is seen in the experience of the king whose life is threatened, who prays to God for deliverance and is answered by divine intervention, and whose righteousness is demonstrated by God's deliverance (Psalm 18). The pious in Israel who find themselves in distress, often through false accusations that can lead to death, make similar prayer for deliverance, and, on finding it, typically offer thanksgiving to God with a promise or vow (see Psalms 7, 26, 56, 57, 59). Isaiah 53 can be viewed as combining the theme of the rejected prophet with that of the suffering righteous man: it is formally related to the Psalms of the afflicted righteous, it is set in the frame of a song of thanksgiving for deliverance (see Isa. 52:13–15 and 53:11–12), and in 53:11 the subject of the poem is actually called "the righteous one, my servant."[104]

It is in the book of Wisdom, chapters 2–5, however, that the theme of the suffering righteous man comes to its fullest development. Within these chapters there are two sections that are separated from each other but that correspond to one another as parts of a diptych—namely, 2:12–20 and 5:1–7. Ruppert contends that the two passages come from a Palestinian source, to be dated from the latter part of the first third of the first century B.C. He further suggests that behind this mysterious "righteous man" who was brought to a violent end and who is viewed as an actualization of the Servant of the Lord there is hidden a martyr who was faithful to the law and belonged either to the Pharisees or to their predecessors the Hasidim.[105] Certainly the lineaments of the Servant of the Lord can be discerned in the description within the diptych; they led M. Jack Suggs to characterize Wisdom 2:10–5:23 as "a homily based on the fourth Servant Song."[106] It begins with a declaration of the godless:

Let us lie in wait for the righteous man,
because he is inconvenient to us and opposes our actions. . . .
He professes to have knowledge of God,
and calls himself a servant of the Lord.
He became to us a reproof of our thoughts;
the very sight of him is a burden to us. . . .
He calls the last end of the righteous happy,
and boasts that God is his father.
Let us see if his words are true,
and let us test what will happen at the end of his life;
for if the righteous man is God's son, he will help him,

and will deliver him from the hand of his adversaries. . . .
Let us condemn him to a shameful death,
for, according to what he says, he will be protected.

Chapter 5 takes us to the judgment scene, in which the oppressors utter a different sentiment:

Then the righteous man will stand with great confidence
in the presence of those who have afflicted him,
and those who make light of his labors.
Then they will speak to one another in repentance,
and in anguish of spirit they will groan, and say,
"This is the man whom we once held in derision
and made a byword of reproach"—we fools!
We thought that his life was madness
and that his end was without honor.
Why has he been numbered among the sons of God?
And why is his lot among the saints?

The simple pattern of Psalm 34:20 has come a long way! And yet it is the same basic pattern, but extended on a broader canvas through the understanding of life, resurrection, judgment, and kingdom brought about through the apocalyptic movement. The diptych embodies the two aspects of the suffering of the righteous and his vindication in the judgment with a resurrection to glory. More specifically, the elements of suffering, rejection, putting to death, and being raised to life are all mentioned in the text. The relation of the whole to the traditional motif of the righteous sufferer who is delivered by the Lord is plain.

What of the gospel texts with which we are concerned? Of one thing we can be certain without fear of contradiction: the model of the righteous sufferer was available to those who framed the pre-Markan passion narrative. It is possible to relate virtually every element of the narrative to various psalms of the righteous sufferer, as J. Gnilka has demonstrated.[107] What applies to the passion narrative also applies to the passion predictions, which may well have been earlier linked with the story of the sufferings of Jesus.[108] These are distinguished in that they not only reflect biblical expressions of suffering and vindication but, as with the passion narrative as a whole, they each embody the *pattern* associated with the righteous man and his fate: he suffers at the hands of the unrighteous but is vindicated through the deliverance of God who lifts him high.

Less obviously, from the point of view of form and language, the theme of *the rejected prophet*, which held a prominent place in Old Testament thought and in the people's comprehension of it, may be another strand in the passion predictions. For the Deuteronomist editor of Israel's history, the story of the northern kingdom was one of constant warnings to kings and people of Yahweh's judgments or disobedience—and of fulfillment of the warnings—while his representation of Judah's history has been summed up as "an almost unbroken series of breaches of the revealed will of God."[109] Actual persecutions of prophets in Israel are not numerous in the Old Testament records. It is true that there are explicit indications that Elijah, Michaiah, and Jeremiah were persecuted by their contemporaries (see 1 Kings 19 and 22:27 and Jer. 11, 20, 26, and 37) and that Urijah the son of Shemaiah and Zechariah the son of Jehoiada were put to death by command of the reigning monarchs (see Jer. 26:20ff.; and 2 Chron. 24:21), but subsequent tradition held that such persecution was considerably more extensive and maintained that Isaiah, Jeremiah, Ezekiel, Amos, and Micah were all put to death.[110] In the time of Jesus, "Martyrdom was considered an integral part of the prophetic office."[111] Jeremias speaks of that era as the time of the great "tomb renaissance," when people built in all parts of Palestine memorials to the prophets and other martyrs as expiations for their murder.[112]

Jesus himself referred more than once to the prophets' experience of rejection and persecution. He told his disciples to rejoice when they were persecuted, "for in the same way they persecuted the prophets before you" (Matt. 5:12 // Luke 6:23). He condemned the builders of the tombs of the prophets and righteous as "sons of the murderers of the prophets"—that is to say, men of similar disposition to them (Matt. 23:31 // Luke 11:48). He cited "the Wisdom of God" that told of the killing of prophets and righteous men from Abel to Zechariah, and the judgment that would be demanded of "this generation" for its culminating wickedness (Matt. 23:34ff. // Luke 11:49–50). He lamented over Jerusalem as "the city that murders the prophets and stones the messengers sent to her" (Matt. 23:37 // Luke 13:34–35). In response to a reported desire of Herod to kill him, Jesus stated that he must continue on his way, since "It is unthinkable for a prophet to meet his death anywhere but in Jerusalem" (Luke 13:33).

These passages form a crescendo of utterances indicating not only that Jerusalem and its people reject and kill prophets but that Jesus was to add to the number of those so treated and was aware of the fact. The statements that refer to the fate of the prophets and to the fate of Jesus to suffer like them are themselves reminiscent of the passion predictions, including as they do the motifs of rejection, persecutions, and execution. Moreover, Jesus associates prophets with righteous men (see Matt. 13:17); his predictions that he will suffer like the righteous man implicitly include the idea that he will suffer as the prophet of God's last word to man. Insofar as the prophets perish in carrying out their ministry, they share the fate of the martyrs—as well as the martyrs' vindication in the kingdom of God.[113]

Clearly the suffering of *the Servant of the Lord* in Deutero-Isaiah is related to both types of suffering we have been considering. The Servant is a supreme example of the "righteous man" who endures suffering at the hands of the unrighteous. What is said of him anticipates the idea of the passion predictions. As the "Righteous One" (Isa. 53:1) he is *rejected* by his contemporaries (52:14, 53:3–4), *suffers* at their hands (50:6, 52:14, 53:7–8), is *put to death* unjustly (53:7–9), but is to be *vindicated and exalted* (52:13–15, 53:10–12).[114] The term *paradidonai* is not used, but the concept represented by it is central to the fourth Servant Song; the entire Song is marked by the dual motif of the Servant afflicted by both men and God: in the first place, "He was despised and rejected by men . . . he was oppressed and he was afflicted . . . without protection and justice he was taken away"; and in the second place, "It was the will of the Lord to bruise him, he has put him to grief." Nowhere in the Songs is it stated that their subject is a prophet, and yet he appears to stand in the succession of

243

prophetic figures of the past, like Moses, and he is represented as exercising a prophetic ministry.[115] His tongue is made by Yahweh as a sharp sword (Isa. 49:2), and he has a mission to restore Israel and bring light to the nations (49:5–6). He is the recipient of continuous revelation to speak the word that is needed (50:4), and it is as such a one that he is rejected and cruelly treated (50:6) but expects to be vindicated by God in face of his adversaries (50:7–8). We seem therefore to have in the Servant Songs a coalescence of the two figures of the suffering righteous man and the rejected prophet.

So closely does the exposition of the Suffering Servant in the fourth Song correspond to the representations of suffering and death in the Markan passion predictions (at least those that contain the *paradidonai* theme—Mark 9:31 and 14:41) that Jeremias believes that Isaiah 53 might be their source—first, because the term *paradidonai* appears in the LXX of Isaiah 53:12 (twice) and its equivalent is in the Targum of Isaiah 53:5,[116] and second, because the divine passive *paradidotai* needs a justification such as only scripture can give: "The only answer to the question how it could be possible that Jesus attributed such unlimited atoning power to his death must be that he died as the servant of God, whose suffering and death is described in Isaiah 53."[117] One appreciates the force of the argument, but the influence of the more widespread motif in Judaism of the Righteous Sufferer must not be diminished. Moreover, the *paradidonai* passages have even closer parallels in Job (9:22–23 and 16:11) than in the Servant Songs, as Pesch has pointed out.[118] The Servant Songs should be viewed as one important contributing factor to the thought of the passion predictions, along with other streams of related tradition.

The fourth element in the background of the passion predictions is the significance attached to the death of the martyrs in Judaism. When Antiochus Epiphanes attempted to destroy the religion of the Jews, he precipitated an effect he could not have foreseen: the exaltation of martyrdom in Israel. The humble "poor" preferred to suffer barbaric tortures unto death than to renounce the faith of their fathers. From this time on it could be said, "The Jewish religion is a religion of martyrdom."[119] The martyr's fate and the apocalyptic faith reacted upon and stimulated one another; God's intervention on behalf of his people was eagerly anticipated, and with it the individual's participation in the coming kingdom through personal resurrection.[120]

With these developments came another of profound significance: the sufferings of the martyr came to be understood in the light of the sufferings of the Martyr of the fourth Servant Song: they were seen as having atoning power. This conviction gathered momentum through Jewish contemplation of the martyrdom of Eleazar the priest and the Widow and her seven sons, as the second and fourth books of the Maccabees show. The story is related in 2 Maccabees 6–7, where the last of the seven sons is said to have told the king that

> I, like my brothers, surrender my body of life for the laws of our fathers.... With me and my brothers may the Almighty's anger, which has justly fallen on all our race, be ended! (7:37–38)

In 4 Maccabees that concept is elaborated. Eleazar is made to say at his end,

> Be merciful unto thy people, and let our punishment be a satisfaction in their behalf. Make my blood their purification, and take my soul to ransom their souls. (6:28–29)

Summarizing his story of the martyrs, the author affirms that

> Through them the enemy had no more power over our people, and the tyrant suffered punishment; and our country was purified, they having, as it were, become a ransom for our nation's sin; and through the blood of these righteous men and the propitiation of their death, the divine Providence delivered Israel that before was evil entreated. (17:20ff.)

While these two works, which treat the story of the Maccabaean period and in particular that of the martyrs, issue from Hellenistic Judaism, both reflect the ancestral faith.[121] Palestinian Judaism provides examples of similar views of the efficacy of the martyr's death for atonement and for bringing near the kingdom of God.[122]

The importance of this last development for the passion predictions in Mark should not be overemphasized, however; it does not provide the key to them. The significance of the martyr's sufferings was *part* of the Jewish inheritance in which Jesus and his followers shared. Not least the emphasis on vindication through resurrection, associated with the martyr's death, was integral to the hope of salvation in the kingdom of God that the apocalyptic movement had quickened. Suffering and death in the cause of God had as its counterpart resurrection unto and exaltation in the kingdom of God.[123] In this respect the martyr's suffering and destiny formed part of the background in the light of which the passion predictions of Mark have to be set.

This leads to a consideration of the second major element in the passion predictions that I have merely alluded to thus far. Each of the three main passages we are reviewing concludes with an anticipation of the resurrection after three days. Because this element of the tradition is echoed in the Christian kerygyma (1 Cor. 15:3–4), there has been a readiness on the part even of those scholars who view the tradition of a prediction of the *passion* as authentic to view the reference to the resurrection as late. One of the points I have been trying to stress, however, is the striking correspondence of the basic structure of the predictions with that of the traditions in Judaism relating to sufferers in God's cause. That correspondence has an obvious relevance at this juncture.

Fundamental to the pattern of the righteous man who suffers is his vindication after oppression; after the rise of the apocalyptic movement, that was taken to mean resurrection for the kingdom of God and vindication in the judgment. The poem of the Suffering Servant in Isaiah 52:13–53:12 embodies the same fundamental idea, and it led, as we saw in the diptych of Wisdom 2 and 5, to an enrichment of thought about the righteous sufferer and God's raising him to life and honor. Reflection on the experience of the martyrs had the same result, for the martyr is exalted to the right hand of God. Insofar as the perception developed that prophets were typically rejected by their generations, it was anticipated that they too would share in the vindication of the righteous and the

Servant and the martyrs. On first principles, therefore, it is improbable that Jesus would have anticipated a violent death at the hands of his people without at the same time anticipating a resurrection by the God who vindicates the suffering righteous, the suffering servant, the martyr, and the rejected prophet. Thus, the "three days" tradition that is conjoined to the resurrection predictions need not be dependent on the Christian kerygma for its origin at all; to the contrary, it would seem more likely that it would have originated in the same context that the kerygma itself reflects.

The resurrection on the third day "according to the scriptures" (1 Cor. 15:4) almost certainly implies a reference to Hosea 6:3 ("after two days he will revive us, on the third day he will restore us, that in his presence we may live"). But Hosea 6:3 is but part of a body of literature in Judaism in which note is taken of God's acts on the third day. In the Midrash on Genesis 42:17 there is a famous comment, "The Holy One, blessed be He, never leaves the righteous in distress more than three days." The principle is lengthily illustrated in the comment on Genesis 22:4 ("On the third day Abraham lifted up his eyes and saw the place afar off"):

> "On the third day" etc. It is written, *After two days He will revive us, on the third day He will raise us up, that we may live in his presence* (Hos. 6.2). E.g. on the third day of the tribal ancestors; *And Joseph said unto them the third day: This do, and live* (Gen. 42.18); on the third day of revelation: *And it came to pass on the third day, when it was morning* (Exod. 19.16); on the third day of the spies: *And hide yourselves there three days* (Jos. 2.16); on the third day of Jonah: *And Jonah was in the belly of the fish three days and three nights* (Jon. 2.1); on the third day of those returning from the Exile: *And we abode there three days* (Ezra 8.32); on the third day of resurrection: *After two days He will revive us, on the third day He will raise us up*; on the third day of Esther: *Now it came to pass on the third day, that Esther put on her royal apparel* (Est. 5.1)— i.e. she put on the royal apparel of her ancestor. For whose sake? The Rabbis say: For the sake of the third day, when revelation took place. R. Levi maintained: In the merit of what Abraham did on the third day, as it says, *On the third day* etc. "And saw the place afar off." What did he see? He saw a cloud enveloping the mountain, and said: "It appears that that is the place where the Holy One, blessed be He, told me to sacrifice my son."[124]

The first passage cited after Hosea 6:2 gives the clue to the idea enshrined in the third-day principle: the "tribal ancestors" *suffered for a short time*—three days only—and their suffering was ended on the third day with *liberation and a promise of life*. Virtually all the examples mentioned in the extract, other than the third day of "revelation" (i.e., that of the theophany at Sinai with the gift of the covenant to Israel), relate to deliverances of various kinds. They culminate in Abraham's vision of the place of sacrifice, which was also a place of deliverance (and which in tradition was the site of the future temple). This too was of great importance in the context, for the sacrifice of Isaac came to be viewed as supremely significant for the value of all sacrifice in Israel.[125] From all this, Lehmann concludes that the "third day" was not simply a general expression for a short time, but a determination of time stamped with special significance:

The third day brings the turning to something new and better. God's mercy and righteousness create a new "time" of salvation, of life, of victory; the third day brings a difficult circumstance from decision, through God's saving action, to a final solution which is creative of history.[126]

To look at the passion predictions in the light of this evidence is to view them in a fresh way. It does not prove that any single expression of an anticipated resurrection in the sayings is authentic, but it does show that in them we may see expressions of an assurance on the part of Jesus that after suffering he would be raised by God for his further service and glory.

I speak of "further service and glory" deliberately in view of the fact that the subject of the predictions is designated the Son of Man. The fitness of the title in these contexts can be seen in their eschatological nature: the destiny of their subject is resurrection to exaltation in the kingdom of God and participation in the judgment—and precisely this is the destiny of the Son of Man. The term is also appropriate here because it is a comprehensive designation for those who serve God through their sufferings; as Son of Man he is the righteous man par excellence, the prophet of the end time who brings to fulfillment the prophecies of the end, the embodiment of the Servant of the Lord who becomes "light" for the nations, the supreme martyr for the cause of God's kingdom. The Son of Man gathers up all these types into one figure to carry through their service at the end of the times as the central point of the eschatological process whereby the kingdom of God might come and men might participate in the kingdom.

Here we see the answer to the question persistently raised by students of the gospels: "How can the Son of Man of Daniel's vision be viewed in the first century as a humble and humiliated man, the subject of prophecies of rejection, suffering, and death?" The question is not unrelated to that of John the Baptist in prison, and the answer is not dissimilar to that given him by Jesus: Daniel 7 is not the only passage in the Old Testament that speaks of the Messiah and his service for the kingdom of God. The Son of Man of Daniel 7:13 must be understood in light of the righteous sufferer of the Psalms, the rejected prophets of the Bible and subsequent times, the Servant of the Isaianic songs, and the martyrs who have offered their lives for God's glory and their people's deliverance. In this way we see the unity that holds together the sayings regarding the Son of Man in his humble ministry, in his suffering to the death followed by resurrection, and in his parousia at the end: *the binding link is the service for the kingdom of God that the Son of Man is commissioned to achieve.* In humble service of man, in suffering unto death, in rising unto life, and in parousia in glory, he is the mediator of the kingdom of God, the representative of God and the representative of man.

b. Fire and Baptism
Luke 12:49–50

We have here a pair of sayings set in a context of Q material attached to verses 51–53. Their position is due in part to the eschatological nature of verse 49 and the surrounding context, and perhaps also to the catchword *balein* (v. 49), which appears in Matthew's parallel to Luke's verse 51 (Matt. 10:32); it may be that it was in Luke's source originally and that he changed it to the more suitable *dounai*.[127]

The language used in the saying poses few problems. Verse 49 gives indications of a Semitic background: *pur balein* is reckoned by Jeremias as a Semitism meaning "kindle fire" rather than "throw fire."[128] In verse 49b, *ti thelo . . .* is unusual Greek, but it appears to render an Aramaic mode of speech: *ti* = *mah*, which can be an interrogative particle, as in Mark 2:7, but can also perform the function of an exclamation, as the NEB translators recognized in translating the clause "How I wish it were already kindled!"[129] Verse 50a contains the expression *baptisma baptisthenai*. In discussing its syntax, Delling points out that the substantive represents an accusative of inner object to the verb. Such a construction is known in Hebrew and Aramaic as well as in Greek, but according to R. Helbing it was no longer frequently used in the Hellenistic period; accordingly, it is possible that the verse originated in a Palestinian area.[130] Verse 50b, by contrast, is in normal Greek; unlike the *ti thelo* of verse 49, the exclamatory *pos* is in keeping with Hellenistic usage. The use of *echein* with the infinitive and the term *sunechomai* are both characteristic of Luke's style, suggesting that he is likely the author of this clause.[131]

This last observation raises the question of the relation of verse 50 to verse 49. The attempts to minimize the parallelism between the two sayings and to ascribe verse 50 to Luke's literary activity are not well founded.[132] The figures of fire and flood were from early times interpreted as modes of depicting the judgment of God and the infliction of suffering. The first sentence is unique in implying that the speaker both initiates judgment *and* suffers judgment; hence, the image employed is closely related to that in the second sentence. It is more probable that Luke found the two sayings conjoined in the tradition than that he took the idea of Jesus undergoing an "immersion" of suffering expressed in Mark 10:38–39 and with it constructed the extraordinary statement of verse 49 in elaborate parallelism with verse 50. The suggestion that someone else rewrote the sentiment of Mark 10:38 to produce "*I came to be baptized with a baptism, and how I wish that it were already achieved!*"[133] and that Luke constructed from that sentence the double saying of verses 49–50 is no more plausible. The supposedly contrived saying is one of the most arresting statements in the gospels, conveying a representation of judgment without parallel in the Old Testament, late Judaism, or the synoptic tradition. To suggest that the evangelist constructed it out of another saying and then ingeniously formed it into a double set of clauses in elaborate parallelism is to strain our credulity.

The one term in verse 50 that we can with certainty set to Luke's account is *sunechomai*. His preference for the term is illustrated in Luke 4:38, where he replaced Mark's *katecheito puressousa* ("was ill with a fever") with *sunechomene pureto megalo* ("suffering from a high fever")—one of the passages often adduced as evidence of his medical knowledge. His rewriting of Mark 8:45 is likewise significant in relation to 12:49–50; he replaces *ton ochlon thlibonta se* ("the crowd is pressing upon you") in Mark 5:31 with *hoi ochloi sunechousin se kai apothlibousin*, which simply strengthens the emphasis of Mark's statement: "the crowds *are hemming you in* and pressing upon you." This meaning of *sunechomai* is close to that in Luke 12:49, making even more plausible the conjecture that Luke replaced a similar term in his source with this favorite of his. In any case, the occurrence of *sunechomai* in Luke 12:50 scarcely constitutes evidence that Luke himself was responsible for the *idea* embodied in the clause.

Verse 49 has been subjected to an extraordinary variety of interpretations through the years, particularly with regard to the significance of the "fire on earth." British Christians recall a favorite hymn written by Charles Wesley in which he uses the metaphor of the fire of *charity*, known from the Fathers on:

> O Thou who camest from above
>   The pure, celestial fire to impart,
> Kindle a flame of sacred love
>   On the mean altar of my heart.

Zahn thought rather in terms of the risen Lord's rekindling the *faith* of the disciples.[134] Plummer postulates a reference to the fire of *holiness*.[135] Others, attempting to do justice to the context, maintain that the reference is to the fire of the *division* or discord caused by the ministry of Jesus.[136] Taking a broader view of the context—namely, John's preaching (Luke 3:11) and the Pentecost narrative (Acts 2:1–3)—still others suggest that it is the fire of *the Spirit* that is being referred to,[137] or, more explicitly, "the eschatological outpouring of the Spirit who will mediate the 'judging' message of the kingdom."[138]

None of these suggestions, however, captures the primary intent of the sayings before us. A glance at a concordance will show that in all parts of the Old Testament, fire is used as an image of the wrath of God falling in judgment upon mankind. This use of fire as a symbol of divine judgment continues into late Jewish literature, as may be seen in the Qumran writings and the apocalyptic literature, and it is maintained in the New Testament.[139] It is evident in the preaching of John the Baptist (see Matt. 3:11–12 // Luke 3:16–17). In the teaching of Jesus, fire relates chiefly to the final judgment (see, for example, Mark 9:43–49 and Matt. 5:22), but it appears in the Lukan apocalypse in relation to the day of the Son of Man (Luke 17:28–30). Related descriptions of the parousia occur in other New Testament writings, such as 2 Thessalonians 1:8, 2 Peter 3:7, and Revelation 8:5 and 20:9 (and see also 1 Cor. 3:13; Heb. 12:26–29; and 1 Pet. 4:12–17). The term "baptism" in Luke 12:50 is self-evidently used in a referred sense and denotes an immersion in or plunging beneath destructive waters. The figure appears frequently in the Psalms (e.g., Pss. 18:4, 32:6, 42:8, 69:1–2 and 13–15, 88:6–7, and 124:1–5), a particularly interesting example being Psalm 69:2, the first line of which Symmachus renders *ebaptisthen eis aperantous kataduseis*; other examples of the same verb occurring in like contexts can be found in non-Septuagintal versions.[140] We should note that this baptism in the destructive waters is sometimes a punishment exacted by the wrath of God, whether upon an individual (Ps. 88:6–7) or upon nations (Ps. 9:15–17). This idea was indelibly impressed on the Jewish mind by the record of the great flood; the day of the Son of Man is accordingly compared to the flood that carried away Noah's generation (Luke 17:26–27 // Matt. 24:37–39).

Significantly, there are passages in the Old Testament in which the figures of fire and flood are combined to express calamity. In Psalm 66:12 and Isaiah 43:2, the experiences of adversity do not entail the idea of divine wrath, but in Isaiah 30:27–28 the symbols relate specifically to Yahweh's coming in judgment, and Ezekiel 38:22 combines storm and fire in representing judgment upon Gog. The connection between the flood as a judgment on evil men and the eschatological fire of the Day of the Lord eventually became a fixed association among the Jews.[141] This had the effect of leading to interpretations suggesting that Noah's flood involved both fire and water[142] and of viewing the coming judgment in terms of flood and fire;[143] even the eschatological fire itself was often described as an outpouring or flood of fire.[144]

There is some disagreement as to how pertinent this information is to Luke 12:49–50, but at least it serves to demonstrate that fire and flood were symbolically conjoined in the Old Testament and thus that the connection already existed for Jesus, even apart from John the Baptist's proclamation of the kingdom and the Messiah. The link between fire and flood is also significant in Luke 17:26ff., and so the fact that they are conjoined in Luke 12:49–50 should occasion no surprise. But the urgent question is what they have to say about the destiny of Jesus in this passage.

First, we should recognize that the complementary nature of the statements in verses 49 and 50 indicates that it is the task of Jesus both to initiate judgment (to "kindle fire") and to suffer judgment (to endure a "baptism"). The initiating and enduring of judgment is signified not alone in the successive statements of verses 49a and 50a but also in those of verses 49b and 50b—a point underscored by Vögtle, who, however, has failed to perceive the connections. In fact, Vögtle holds that the statements in verses 49 and 50 are contradictory and distasteful, and that they ought by no means to be attributed to Jesus. He maintains that verse 49 portrays Jesus as playing an active role without being immersed in the fire, whereas verse 50 portrays Jesus as undergoing the ordeal; in other words, he contends that in verse 49 Jesus yearns for the judgment, whereas in verse 50 he shrinks from the ordeal. The idea that a destructive judgment should fall upon Jesus as well as others is in Vögtle's estimate a strange one. And he wonders how such a judgment might be understood to precede the end-time judgment. If the death of Jesus is viewed as an effective atonement, how could there be room for a judgment afterward, he wonders, since judgment would presumably be canceled? And is it conceivable that Jesus should represent his mission as that of bringing judgment on his people or that he should long for it to come upon them?[145]

Questions such as these are surprising from so acute a thinker as Vögtle, for apart from the question of the authenticity of verses 49–50, the content of the passage is consistent. Verse 49 does not suggest that the purpose of Jesus' mission is to bring destruction upon Israel or that he yearned to see the nation's ruin; the parallelism between 49b and 50b indicates that Jesus is himself to be as implicated in the fire as he is in the flood of water: in both clauses the suffering is destined for him. Moreover, the parallelism of "kindled" in verse 49b and "accomplished" in verse 50b suggests that he is thinking of the anticipated suffering in terms of *achievement*; he desires not simply that the agony be over and done with but that its end be accomplished in the redemption of mankind in the kingdom that lies beyond the judgment. The idea expressed in verse 49 (viz., that Jesus is destined to bring judgment and to suffer judgment) is certainly extraordinary, but it is so in a positive rather than a pejorative sense. The only parallel in Israel's history that could be held to reflect a consciousness comparable to this would be the last Servant Song of Deutero-Isaiah (Isa. 52:13–53:12), but it is much less sharp a picture. The Maccabaean martyrs were viewed as turning away wrath from Israel by their death, but the idea that the Messiah should rescue his people from the judgment by suffering it himself dawned on no one.

It might be argued that by speaking in this way we are leaping too far ahead in the deductions drawn from the text. Does the passage really imply that Jesus is to suffer *death* by reason of the fire and the baptism? Légasse replies with a firm No on the grounds that the images do not necessarily imply the infliction of death. He maintains that the passage attributes to Jesus "the perspective of having at one and the same time to inaugurate and to submit to a terrible test"— that and no more.[146] It is certainly correct that the symbols of fire and flood do not necessarily imply the experience of death. Nevertheless, in the prophetic tradition the most common use of the figure of fire in eschatological contexts is for *destructive* judgment (see, for example, Amos 5:6, Hos. 8:14, Isa. 30:27–33 and 66:15–16, and Ezek. 21:30ff. and 29:18–19). Similarly, while the waters need not necessarily drown, they do threaten with death those engulfed by them, as in Psalms 18:4 and 69:1–2, 13–14, and as the parallels of eschatological judgment with Noah's flood attest. In Luke 12:49–50 the combination of the fire of judgment and the threat of being engulfed in water indicates more than suffering a "test"; it strongly suggests the suffering of death. The prophecies of the passion and other intimations from Jesus that a violent death awaits him should not be *contrasted* with Luke 12:49–50 but viewed as *confirming* the natural meaning of the passage—namely, that Jesus sees the climax of his mission as the suffering of death under the judgment of God.[147]

Two questions arise. How does this death entail "judgment"? And what relation does it have to the end of the age? No answer to either question is given in the sayings themselves. If the representative of the kingdom of God suffers under the judgment of God, however, we can be sure that it can have the purpose only of serving the kingdom and the people for whom the kingdom is intended. Assuming that the judgment falling on Jesus comes at the climax of his work of bringing the kingdom in his ministry, we must view it as the ultimate step in his mediation of the kingdom of God to man; it serves to open the gates of the kingdom in this time (Matt. 16:19) and to enable such as enter it to inherit it at the end (Luke 22:29–30). At the same time, it is assumed that the suffering under judgment entails a negative judgment upon those who reject the word of the kingdom that Jesus brings and who thereby bring about his death. The death of the mediator of the kingdom of God can hardly be thought of as confirming the inheritance of the kingdom for those who unite in opposing that kingdom—unless, of course, they repent of the sin of rejecting the representative of the kingdom and accept his message. In any case, the judgment of fire clearly creates a separation. The symbolism could extend to the idea that the suffering of judgment by Jesus initiates an era in which on the one hand those who receive his word share with him in suffering at the hands of a hostile world, in harmony with the call to discipleship in terms of shouldering a cross with Jesus (Mark 8:34), and on the other hand those who refuse his message thereby condemn themselves to suffer the divine displeasure that will culminate in the judgment in which the Son of Man will participate (Mark 8:38). This would be in line with the oft-cited *agraphon*,

> Whoever is near to me is near to the fire,
> and whoever is far from me is far from the Kingdom.[148]

But how far an *agraphon* should be viewed as supplying a key to a *graphe* of the Lord is a moot point.

It is undeniable that Luke 12:49–50 has a riddle-like quality that defies precision of exegesis. More plainly than the predictions of the passion, it implies that Jesus will meet his death on behalf of others, but it falls short of the specificity of the sayings relating to his death that were delivered at the Last Supper. Nevertheless, this passage makes one element clearer than the logia of the passion, and also anticipates a dominant note of the Last Supper: it suggests that the death of Jesus forms part of the eschatological process whereby the kingdom of God comes, and it links that death for others with his destiny to share in the judgment and rule of the divine sovereignty.

c. The Sign of Jonah
Luke 11:29–30 // Matthew 12:39–40

Luke's introduction to the saying in 11:29 ("While the crowds were swarming around") is vague, but the reference to a request for a sign harks back to verse 16: "Others, by way of a test, demanded of him a sign from heaven." That context is significant, for it conjoins the demand for a sign with the charge that Jesus is in league with "Beelzebub, prince of devils" (Luke 11:15). The context in which the statement about the sign of Jonah appears is the same in Luke as in Q, as is indicated by the fact that Matthew also places it in this context (Matt. 12:39–40). Where Luke describes the questioners as "others," Mark and Matthew make a firmer identification. Mark indicates that the charge of demonic liaison came from scribes from Jerusalem (3:22) and that the request for a sign came from Pharisees (8:11–12); Matthew elaborates the identification in 12:39 by taking up the reference to scribes and Pharisees from the Q passage and in 16:1 by taking up the reference to Pharisees and Sadducees from the Markan passage. It is likely that the opponents of Jesus were indeed linked with the Pharisaic party. The fact that Mark identifies them as such suggests the possibility that he may have set the demand for a sign at a later point in the ministry (8:11–12) precisely in order to link it to the Beelzebub controversy.[149]

The demand for a sign from a prophet would not appear unreasonable to Jews in light of the instructions given in Deuteronomy 13:1ff. regarding the testing of a prophet. But since unorthodox teachers sometimes sought to be authenticated by signs, the rabbis determined that the sign referred to in Deuteronomy 13:1–2 must be a sign "in heaven," in accordance with Genesis 1:14 ("They [the heavenly bodies] shall serve for signs"), whereas a "wonder" may take place on earth (e.g., the miracle of Gideon's fleece).[150] In keeping with this, the Pharisees demanded that Jesus produce a sign "from heaven," an apocalyptic or cosmic wonder. They did not consider his miracles proof enough; indeed, in their view his exorcisms constituted evidence that he might well be acting in collusion with the devil. They insisted that Jesus authenticate his ministry by a demonstration that God in heaven had sent him and was with him.

Each strand of the tradition contains an intimation that Jesus viewed the request as proceeding from evil motives. Mark states that Jesus "sighed deeply in his spirit," as he is said to have done when confronted with a man in need of healing (Mark 7:34), and he replied, "How this generation seeks a sign!"[151] The expression "this generation" in the words of Jesus always conveys an implied criticism.[152] This nuance is brought out in the Q tradition: "This generation is an *evil* generation; it seeks a sign" (Luke 11:29), and even "An *evil and adulterous* generation seeks a sign" (Matt. 12:39). The "generation" is adjudged evil because it rejects the message of Jesus delivered in his proclamation of the kingdom of God and attested in his deeds, which manifested the divine sovereignty operative in him. This estimate of the opponents of Jesus is yet more comprehensible when the demand is linked with their allegation that Jesus was an instrument of Satan, a charge that in Mark is viewed as blasphemy against the Spirit of God and an "eternal" sin (see Mark 3:28–29).

Mark's record of Jesus' answer diverges from the Q record: "Amen I say to you, a sign will certainly not be given to this generation" (Mark 8:12). The language employs the strongest negative possible, reflecting a form of oath in the Hebrew language (though not employed, apparently, in Aramaic).[153] There is no reference in this saying to the sign of Jonah. Strangely, however, the form of the Q version is also a strong asseveration, more forceful than the translations generally convey: "No sign will be given to this generation, but *the sign of Jonah will definitely be given it!*"[154] How are we to explain these different statements? Should we assume that Mark conveys the real answer of Jesus and hold the reference to the sign of Jonah to be a later interpolation? Some exegetes from Bousset onward have maintained that this is the case; in recent times it has been elaborately argued by R. A. Edwards.[155] In the estimate of Edwards, the response of Jesus to the request for a sign was an unqualified negative, as Mark has stated. But he contends that in the Q community the double saying given in Luke 11:31–32 // Matthew 12:41–42 was conjoined with the original reply of Jesus in order to express the community's anti-Jewish polemic. He goes on to suggest that reflection on the meaning of the Easter event led to the belief that Jesus had after all given a sign to this generation—namely, his ascension to heaven—and this led to the formation of the saying regarding the sign of Jonah: as Jonah was a preacher of judgment who was delivered from death and thus vindicated by God, so Jesus is the herald of the kingdom of God, delivered from death to be the Judge who shall come.[156] Edwards maintains that this interpretation is supported (1) by its kinship with the theology of Q, which is determined by the imminence of the kingdom of God, and (2) by the form of Luke 11:30 (what he calls an "eschatological correlative"), which he claims is evident in other Q sayings about the Son of Man (viz., Luke 17:24, 26, 28–30; Matt. 13:40)—namely, "As it was (or is) with . . . , so the Son of Man will be." Of the two remaining sayings on the Son of Man in Q, says Edwards, one is manifestly a community addition (Luke 12:39–40), and the other is a "sentence of holy law" (Luke 12:8) and so a community product also. On the assumption that Käsemann is right in identifying the *Sitz-im-Leben* of the "sentences of holy law" as the Eucharist, Edwards suggests that the same applies to the "eschatological correlative" sayings, which of course include Luke 11:30.[157]

Edwards's assignment of the four "eschatological correlative" sayings to a special class and his contention that they originated in the churches' Eucharist is not a plausible idea, however. The comparisons of Luke 17:24, 26, 28ff. are in no sense artificial or strange on the lips of Jesus—"As it was in the days of Noah . . . in the days of Lot . . . so shall it be in the days of the Son of Man"—and the same applies to Luke 11:30: "As Jonah was a sign . . . so the Son of man will be a sign." The real objection to these passages stems from the fact that they include mention of the Son of Man. Even before Edwards adopted this view, he was convinced that all the Son of Man sayings were unauthentic; his hypothesis merely provides what he considers to be an additional reason for supporting that view regarding four of them. But the case is not strong.

As is so frequently the case with disputed dominical sayings, the authenticity of the logion in Luke 11:29 // Mark 12:39 cannot be proved, but this scarcely constitutes a reason to suppose that it contradicts Mark 8:12. Both passages indicate that Jesus rejected his opponents' demand for a "sign from heaven" such as a cosmic miracle, or at least a flash of lightning! The sign of Jonah, whatever that phrase may signify, is not of that order. The simplest way to explain the fact that the sign of Jonah is not mentioned in Mark is to suppose that it did not appear in the tradition before him. It is not plausible to argue that Mark would have suppressed it.[158]

As it stands, the majority of exegetes agree that the logion containing the reference to the sign of Jonah is authentic; their interpretations of what the phrase means differ widely, however. Many writers are impressed with the importance of Jonah's mission to proclaim judgment and also with its success, as evidenced in the repentance of the Ninevites; indeed, following the logion, Jesus almost immediately contrasts the unresponsiveness of "this generation" to his message with the responsiveness of the Ninevites to Jonah's message (see Luke 11:32 // Matt. 12:41). Many take this to be an indication that the "sign of Jonah" relates to the appearance of another preacher of judgment, calling on this generation to repent as Jonah called on the Gentiles to repent.

A special application of this interpretation identifies the preacher as John the Baptist, a comprehensible speculation in view of the record in Q of John's preaching (see Luke 3:7–9 // Matt. 3:7–10).[159] In support of this view, some scholars maintain that confusion arose in the tradition between the names *Jona(h)* and *Jona*, the latter being an abbreviation for *Jochanan*—that is, John. The name Jochanan is occasionally rendered in the LXX as Jonah, and the mistake could have come about in this passage through the influence of the saying concerning Jonah and the Ninevites in Luke 11:32 // Matthew 12:41.[160] Granting that all things are possible, this interpretation could be valid, but it is hardly compelling. Vögtle characterizes it as "a solution of embarrassment."[161]

The belief, however, that Jesus viewed himself *in his proclamation* to Israel as a counterpart to Jonah in preaching judgment to a guilty nation is widely favored. This appears to be supported not only by the mention of the preaching of Jonah in Luke 11:33 but also through the explanatory statement of verse 30 (note the *gar*, "for"), which makes the "sign of Jonah" to be Jonah himself (genitive of apposition), the counterpart to which is the person of the Son of Man. Jonah wrought no sign among the Ninevites; his sole credentials were that he brought a message from God with awful urgency. So, it is suggested, Jesus appeared with his urgent message of the impending end, bringing the kingdom of God for those who would be responsive and judgment for those who would reject his message.[162]

The prime difficulty of this interpretation is its dependence on a doubtful use of the term *semeion* ("sign"). In the context of the question put to Jesus, to which the logion supplies an answer, preaching cannot be regarded as a sign; rather, he was requested to produce a sign to demonstrate that his preaching was from God. On the basis of this interpretation, the answer of Jesus as given in Mark would be wholly right, and the version in Q tautologous. Schlatter observes that

> The "sign" does not consist in what men do, either the prophet or the king of Nineveh, but without doubt is an intervention of the divine omnipotence in the course of events. If a contemporary of Jesus was asked where in the Book of Jonah there was mention of a sign, then he would certainly have answered, *In the first part of the book, not in the second.*[163]

A solution to the problem to which an increasing number of exegetes are attracted confines itself to verse 29, reserving judgment concerning the authenticity of verse 30 if not rejecting it outright. In the words of the best-known exponent of this view, "Just as Jonah came to the Ninevites from a distant country, so will the Son of Man come to this generation from heaven; i.e. the sign asked for the preaching of Jesus is *the Son of Man himself, when he comes to judgment.*"[164] Several points can be adduced in favor of this view. It can be said to correspond with the notion of a sign from heaven, since the Son of Man comes "from heaven." It accords with Jesus' recognition of the unbelief that prompted the request for a sign and the condemnation that awaits this generation, since for those who demand the sign, the parousia will signify not satisfaction but judgment. And finally, if the explanatory comment in verse 30 is authentic, it finds a striking parallel in "the sign of the Son of Man" in heaven mentioned in Matthew 24:30, which appears to denote the Son of Man in his parousia as the sign of the end.[165]

While this may initially appear to be a plausible interpretation of the logion, there are formidable difficulties in the way of our accepting it. First, there is no obvious parallel between Jonah's journey to Nineveh and the concept of the parousia of the Son of Man from heaven to man. Bultmann's comparison of the two on the basis of the distance traveled is a curious bit of exegesis. Jonah went to Nineveh to communicate a message of impending judgment; the Son of Man is to appear as the executor of the judgment of God *and* the bearer of the salvation of the kingdom of God for the righteous, and there is a universe of difference between those two functions, as any Jew would acknowledge. If we suppose that this interpretation is valid, then we will have to grant that there is no likelihood that any of those who heard Jesus deliver the logion would have had any way of identifying the reference to the sign of Jonah with the parousia of the Son of Man. Nor is the likelihood of their having been able to make the connection much improved by the explanatory addition of verse 30, for, unlike modern exegetes, it is unclear whether the hearers of Jesus had ever heard of the transcendent Son of Man. They knew, of course, of Daniel's prophecy of the chaos monsters and the one like a son of man, but which of them would have linked the prophecy of Daniel to the book of Jonah? Moreover, the sign of the Son of Man in heaven mentioned in Matthew 24:30 belongs to a different realm of thought from that of Jonah and Nineveh. It is an allusion to the oracle following the description of the Messiah and his kingdom in Isaiah 11, where it is said,

> In that day *the root of Jesse shall stand as an ensign to the peoples*; him shall the nations seek, and his dwellings shall be glorious. . . .
>
> He will raise an ensign for the nations [LXX: *kai arei semeion eis ta ethne*] and will assemble the outcasts of Israel, and gather the dispersed of Judah from the four corners of the earth. (Vv. 10, 12)

The pertinence of this passage to the action of the Son of Man regarding the nations and the gathering of the elect from the ends of earth and heaven in Matthew 24:30 is apparent, but it has no connection with Jonah in Nineveh, nor with any correspondence between the deeds of Jonah and the Son of Man envisaged in Luke 11:29ff.

The truth is that Jews of Jesus' generation did not share the presuppositions of twentieth-century critical exegetes any more than have the vast majority of Christians throughout the ages, including our own. As among the ancient Jews, so in the church through the centuries, the book of Jonah has been linked in the minds of men with the adventure of Jonah and the great fish. If Luke 11:29 is considered in its own right, the most natural thought conveyed by the phrase "the sign of Jonah" will relate to the signal miracle of deliverance from death through the great fish appointed by the Lord for that purpose. The prayer of Jonah recorded in the book relates the belly of the whale to the belly of Sheol (2:2), to the heart of the seas (2:3), and to the pit (2:6), where the bars of the underworld closed over him "for ever" (2:6). But Jonah was able to declare, "Thou didst bring up my life from the pit, O Lord my God," and his prayer concludes with the exclamation of praise, "Deliverance belongs to the Lord!" (2:9). The adventures of Jonah and the fish are elaborated in Jewish haggada, as may be learned from the (at times amusing) collection drawn from Jewish literature by Billerbeck.[166] Significantly, the homilies include mention of the conversion of the sailors who threw Jonah into the sea, for they saw "all these great *signs and wonders* which Yahweh did on Jonah" (*Pirqe R. El.* 10). Moreover, Jonah's experience is cited along with other passages from the Old Testament that prove the Rabbinic dictum "God does not leave the righteous in distress more than three days."

In light of these considerations, it is most natural to deduce that the sign of Jonah in Luke 11:29 // Matthew 12:39 signals a similar deliverance from death through the mercy and might of the Lord. It is not said in the logion *for whom* the deliverance will be wrought; this is indicated in the comment of 30: "For as Jonah . . . so the Son of Man." One cannot fail to recall the predictions of the passion, which we have just considered, with their stress on the suffering and death of the Son of Man and his deliverance from death.

Admittedly Luke 11:30 entails a problem: it is not stated in the book of Jonah that the prophet told the Ninevites of his miraculous rescue, thereby authenticating his mission and becoming a sign of the Lord's deliverance. It is doubtful, however, that this consideration would have occurred to the early readers of the book. Jonah's proclamation to Nineveh is given in one brief sentence: "In forty days Nineveh shall be overthrown" (3:4). By contrast the prayer of Jonah occupies a chapter of the book, and the prayer is essentially a testimony to the Lord's deliverance of his prophet; it would have been natural to assume that that testimony was included in the prophet's proclamation. More importantly, the analogy is in any case sufficiently close for Jesus to adduce it as a parallel to his own mission, for his emphasis falls on the sign of the Son of Man to his own generation.

This, of course, is the interpretation that Matthew (or his source) has elaborated in Matthew 12:40 by citing Jonah 1:17: "Jonah was in the belly of the fish three days and three nights."[167] While the emphasis in Matthew's statement is on the correspondence of time between Jonah's stay in the belly of the fish and the sojourn of the Son of Man in the heart of the earth, and his resurrection is not actually mentioned, there can be no doubt that the resurrection of Jesus is in view. The form of the statement has been dictated by the citation from Jonah 1:17, and there is no reason to believe that Luke would have had any other event in view here.

Some scholars have posited an interpretation of the sign of Jonah that combines elements of the two views we have just considered. They contend that the sign will be that of the Son of Man delivered from death at his parousia. Attractive as this view may be, it remains the case that the text itself gives no indication of any reference to the parousia, whereas the element of deliverance from death is certainly present and is in harmony with the predictions of the passion and resurrection of the Son of Man. All in all, the simpler view seems to be the most satisfactory interpretation of the saying. Probably the greatest single reason that some exegetes have been hesitant to adopt it has been the belief that the only authentic sayings about the Son of Man are those relating to his parousia and that the rest are community formulations. We have seen that this view is questionable, however, and that there are solid grounds for accepting the tradition that Jesus did in fact instruct his disciples concerning his impending rejection, death, and deliverance. The reference to the sign of Jonah in this logion comports with that tradition.

d. The Last Supper
Mark 14:22–25, Matthew 26:26–29, Luke 22:15–20

An examination of the narratives of the Last Supper confronts us with an unwelcome paradox. These passages contain the most important evidence in the New Testament as to how Jesus interpreted his death, but the significance and authenticity of the words attributed to him in these narratives are among the most strongly controverted in the whole story of Jesus.

The magnitude of the issue can hardly be exaggerated. For the death of Jesus as a physical phenomenon does not necessarily possess redemptive significance. If Jesus had fallen from a donkey and broken his skull, for example, it is doubtful that any special meaning would have been attributed to the event. The crucifixion of Jesus gains its unique meaning from the context of his mission in relation to the kingdom of God and from his singular approach to his death. A. E. J. Rawlinson has made this point with considerable clarity. Speaking of the words and acts of Jesus in the Last Supper, he says,

> Interpreting in advance the significance of his coming Passion, he was in effect making it to be, for all time, what it otherwise would not have been, viz. a sacrifice for the sins of the world. *It is the Last Supper which makes Calvary sacrificial.* It was not the death upon Calvary per se, but the death upon Calvary as the Last Supper interprets it and gives the clue to its meaning which constitutes our Lord's Sacrifice.[168]

The question posed by critics today is whether, in the light of modern research, the interpretation of our Lord's death that appears in the Last Supper narratives is in fact an accurate representation of what Jesus actually said and thought. We ought not to regard this question as perverse or as an expression of the native skepticism of New Testament scholars; these narratives are, after all, unique among all of the gospel pericopae in that they owe their place in the New Testament to their constant use in the worship of the churches. The Lord's Supper has from the beginning maintained a primary place in Christian worship. The tradition of the *Last* Supper was handed down and established as a pattern for the observance of the *Lord's* Supper, as Paul clearly attests in 1 Corinthians 11:23–25. The variations in the accounts of the Supper given by the evangelists and by Paul illustrate how differences were bound to arise in the passing on of the tradition. It is not mere skepticism, then, that leads some scholars to wonder whether the celebrations of the Lord's Supper might not have influenced the narration of the Last Supper just as the descriptive statements about the Last Supper provided the pattern to be followed in the churches' observance of the Lord's Supper. The crucial question therefore is whether such an influence might have effected a decisive change in the tradition of the Last Supper. To determine this it will be necessary to examine the records of the Last Supper, to learn what they actually say, and then to test their authenticity in the light of the teaching of Jesus gained from the gospels as a whole.

Obviously we cannot set out to produce any sort of exhaustive treatment of the topic in these pages. I will proceed to survey some of the related historical problems only briefly and include references to fuller discussions of the essential issues elsewhere.

The Last Supper and the Passover Festival.

The relation of the Last Supper to the passover festival has been a matter of endless debate, with disappointing results. Jeremias's comprehensive examination of the evidence convinced him that the Last Supper took place in the context of the passover meal,[169] but Schürmann's similarly careful assessment of the evidence led him to say, "We renounce all uncertain arguments from the character of the passover meal (*which Jeremias also has hardly proven*)."[170] Admittedly Schürmann made this statement in the context of a defense of the Last Supper narratives against claims that they are unreliable, and so he was compelled to leave aside "all *uncertain* arguments," but his procedure nevertheless illustrates the current mood even of cautious scholars. It is my perception that the majority of scholars agree that the Last Supper probably *did* take place during a celebration of the passover meal; it is simply the case that there are too many contrary features in the evidence for them to express complete assurance about it.

It is a curious fact that although the synoptic evangelists unambiguously state that the disciples prepared for Jesus to celebrate the *passover* meal with them (Mark 14:12–16 par.), the varied traditions of the words and acts of Jesus within the meal make virtually no mention of the passover (there is, for example, no mention of the passover lamb). The special tradition preserved within Luke's narrative (Luke 22:15–18) of the Supper forms an exception, and we must examine its peculiar contribution. The Johannine narrative raises problems of its own. If some too readily dismiss the Johannine testimony in the interests of the synoptic witness, and others too readily discount the synoptic narratives for the sake of the Johannine, there are yet others who too readily seize on uncertain solutions for harmonization of the traditions.[171] What is significant is the presence within the Johannine narrative of elements that appear to intimate agreement of the tradition *behind* that narrative with the synoptic dating of the Last Supper.[172] Of particular importance here is the recognition that John 19:14 must represent the same date as 19:31 and the implications that may have for the determinative statement of 18:28, since 19:31 denotes the eve of the sabbath in the passover week, not the eve of the passover meal.[173] Bultmann further points out that if the "high Sabbath" of 19:31 was the day of the sheaf offering, that would make it Nisan 16, which in turn implies that Jesus was crucified on Nisan 15, as indicated in the synoptic gospels.[174]

Clearly there ought to be further patient investigation of the relationships between the traditions lying behind the synoptic and Johannine accounts of the Last Supper. Still, this much seems beyond dispute at the outset: regardless of one's interpretation of the evidence, the passover associations of the Last Supper are presupposed in *all* the traditions concerning it. This is as much the case in John as in the synoptics, for the narrative of 19:31–36 has the evident intention of showing how the testimony of John the Baptist in 1:29 found fulfillment:

Jesus is the Lamb of God who was slain as God's passover Lamb; through that event the passover feast was fulfilled, just as Jesus fulfilled the feast of Tabernacles (John 7:1–39) and the feast of the Dedication (John 10:22–36).

The Original Text of the Account in Luke.

The original text of the Lukan account of the Last Supper has figured prominently in the work of textual critics on the New Testament. In Britain the influence of Westcott and Hort sufficed to make almost axiomatic the assumption that the shorter version of the narrative in Luke 22:15–20 (i.e., the version omitting vv. 19b–20) is original. This position has been adopted by the translators of the RV, the RSV, and the NEB, as well as by most English-speaking commentators on the gospel of Luke. In recent years, however, there has been a notable reaction to this opinion, as evidenced in the discussions of Schürmann, Jeremias, and Metzger.[175] The longer text is included in the third edition of the United Bible Societies' Greek Text of the New Testament, as well as in the Jerusalem Bible, the Good News Bible, and the New American Standard Version. I myself have at length been persuaded by the weight of the arguments in favor of the longer text, and will proceed on the assumption that it is authentic. One thing should be emphasized, however: our decision concerning which version of Luke 22:19–20 is the original will not have any decisive effect on our interpretation of the significance of the Supper, regardless of which version we adopt, since almost all of the details of both versions are also contained in the accounts of Mark and Paul. Luke's contribution to the understanding of the Last Supper is more significant in the preceding passage, Luke 22:15–18.

The Original Form of the Last Supper Tradition.

Speculations as to the original form of the Last Supper tradition involve substantial complexities. We cannot avoid considering the issue, but neither can we discuss it in a definitive manner. Three accounts of the Supper have come down to us—those in Mark 14:22–25, Luke 22:15–20, and 1 Corinthians 11:23–26. (The Matthean account is manifestly dependent on Mark, and does not constitute a separate version in its own right.) Jeremias contends that John 6:51c offers an additional independent report of one element of the Supper.[176] It has been a long-standing assumption that the text of Luke 22:15–18 assumed its present form as a result of Luke's editing of the Markan text, and that Luke 22:19–20 is a mixed text, manifesting dependence on the Markan and Pauline traditions.[177] The exhaustive investigations of Schürmann, along with those of Jeremias, have nevertheless demonstrated at least the serious possibility that Luke's account is independent of the traditions of both Mark and Paul.[178] The evidence adduced for this position is too intricate and detailed for us to review it here; I should like instead briefly to describe my own position on the matter.

Pesch makes a powerful plea for the originality of the Markan account, and contends that the Lukan account is dependent upon it,[179] but it does not seem to me that his argument is strong enough to overturn Schürmann's massive accumulation of evidence supporting the contention that the Lukan account is at least independent. And I think that Jeremias's argument that we cannot claim any of the Last Supper accounts to be *the* original one (even though he himself

inclines to the Markan narrative as closest to it) has to be taken with seriousness, especially in light of his plausible contention that "Already in the
Semitic stage of tradition the number of current variations of the eucharistic
words was greater than our texts allow us to discern."[180] Accordingly, we can
assume that the primitive tradition lies *behind* the various forms that have come
down to us in our Greek texts. If that carries the corollary that we cannot
recover the *ipsissima verba* of Jesus at the Last Supper, it by no means implies
that we cannot hope to arrive at an understanding of the essential content of the
tradition to which the varied accounts of the Last Supper bear witness. For
beyond the differences of formulation, there is considerable agreement relating
to the significance of the acts of Jesus in the Supper. It is to the elucidation of
that significance within the varied formulations that we now turn our attention.

The Eschatological Anticipation
Mark 14:25, Matthew 26:26, Luke 22:15–18, 1 Corinthians 11:16

While we accept the longer text of Luke 22:15–20 as authentic, verses 15–18
are clearly separable from verses 19–20. Verses 15–18 contain the equivalent of
the statement that Mark set at the end of his narrative (Mark 14:25 // Matt.
26:26) and that also seems to be reflected in 1 Corinthians 11:16. The striking
feature of Luke's record is its *double* reference to the anticipation of the feast of
the kingdom—the first in relation to eating in the kingdom of God and the
second in relation to drinking "when the kingdom of God comes." It is generally
agreed that Mark's wording of the anticipation of drinking the "produce of the
vine" in the kingdom of God is closer to the original than the wording of Luke's
version, but the greater question is whether Luke is right in suggesting that
Jesus expressed this expectation twice in the Supper. Schürmann is confident
that Luke is correct in so doing. He views the double eschatological sayings in
verses 16 and 18 as the nucleus of an independent account of the Supper set
within the passover context, the cup mentioned in verse 17 being the third cup,
the so-called cup of blessing.[181]

Luke 22:19–20 provides a tradition of the Last Supper parallel to the
traditions in Mark 14:22–24 and 1 Corinthians 11:23–25, which were drawn
up for the guidance of churches in the celebrations of the Lord's Supper. These
emphasize the explanations of the bread and wine in relation to the death of
Jesus. In Luke 22:15–18 no interpretation of bread and wine is given; the
emphasis falls on the nature of the Last Supper as a farewell meal of Jesus with
his disciples. His death is imminent, this is his last occasion of sharing a meal
with them, and he now looks forward to the great feast in the perfected kingdom
of God. The connection is natural in view of the persistent hope in which the
Jews celebrated the passover; the remembrance of redemption in the past was
conjoined to an anticipation of a second exodus under the second Redeemer.[182]
We also know that Jesus held the image of the feast of the kingdom of God to be
very important. His table fellowship with disciples and repentant sinners anticipated that feast (Mark 2:19), and the Last Supper was a final celebration of such
anticipatory meals. On this occasion his eyes were clearly on the great day.

Jeremias follows Schürmann in viewing Luke 22:15–18 as an independent tradition parallel to Mark 14:25. He specifies that verses 15–18 constitute the Palestinian tradition of the Supper and that verses 19–20 constitute the liturgical tradition, and he maintains that the former provides the setting for the latter. He suggests that the cup referred to in verse 17 is the *first* cup at the beginning of the preliminary course of the passover meal, and the cup referred to in verse 19 is the third cup, poured after the main meal is completed.[183] Patsch develops this view further, rejecting the approach that separates verses 15–18 and 19–20 as though they reflect two different views of the Supper. While recognizing that the two sections have come from different sources (the Semitisms in verses 15–18 demand that acknowledgment), he maintains that they find their unity in the passover context. He argues that verses 15–18 form an authentic *introduction* to the account of the Supper that follows in verses 19–20. This entails the corollary that the setting of the Supper was in truth the passover meal held by Jesus with his disciples and that the cup referred to in Luke 22:17 is the first cup of the passover meal, the "kiddush" cup. The *Sitz-im-Leben* of Luke's verses 15–20, he suggests, lies not in "cult aetiology" but in instruction given in early catechesis.[184]

An obscure feature in the eschatological anticipation is Jesus' indication that he will refrain from further (eating and) drinking until the feast of the kingdom of God. Luke's statement is particularly strong in 22:15. This statement has commonly been taken to mean "I have very much desired to eat this passover with you because this is the last time I shall do so," and the narrative is understood to record the fulfillment of that desire. Jeremias, however, interprets the statement to mean "I would very much have liked to eat this passover lamb with you before my death. (But I must deny myself this wish.) For I tell you I do not intend to eat of it again until God fulfills (his promises) in the kingdom of God."[185] He views Jesus' words as an "avowal of abstention" signifying his intention to maintain a fast. It would have been highly unusual to commit oneself to a vow during the passover period, but Jeremias maintains that Jesus would have undertaken just such an unusual and fittingly symbolic act as an accompaniment of his prayer for Israel regarding its guilt in rejecting the Messiah.[186]

Attractive as Jeremias's view might be, however, there is no hint of such a motive in the accounts of the Last Supper. That the narratives imply an intention on the part of Jesus to abstain from the meal is contested by many scholars, not a few of whom cite the uncertainty of precisely those points on which Jeremias supports his contention.[187] Nevertheless, there can be no doubt that in Luke 22:17 Jesus is indicating his intention to abstain from drinking the cup that he distributes to his disciples. And although Mark placed the statement at the end of his account of the Supper, he appears to have the same understanding of its significance as Luke. Thus, it seems most likely that Luke understood 22:16 in the same way as 22:17.

The interesting point of this apparently trivial detail is that the two halves of Luke's double statement are set at the *beginning* and the *end* of the meal. Even if the enigmatic *auto* of verse 16 refers to the bread rather than the passover lamb, we can be certain that the bread was broken and distributed at the beginning of the meal, whereas the cup referred to in verse 17 is most plausibly understood to be the cup of blessing at the end of the meal.[188] This means that *the Last Supper is bracketed by Jesus' affirmations that he will neither eat nor drink until he eats and drinks in the kingdom of God.* We need not look far for the reason behind the abstention; Luke 22:16 states "For I tell you, I shall not eat it *until it is fulfilled in the kingdom of God.*" Jesus had a task to perform in order to bring about that fulfillment![189] The nature of his task is indicated in the sayings regarding the bread and wine: he is to surrender his life that men and women may share the feast of the kingdom with him. His resolution to complete the mission that God had given him in relation to the kingdom and his confidence that he would soon be participating in its joy sound the keynote of his last meal with his disciples. The Last Supper is framed in affirmations of the death of Jesus in prospect of the kingdom of God.

The Saying concerning the Bread
Mark 14:22, Matthew 26:26, Luke 22:19, 1 Corinthians 11:24

"This is my *soma*," says Jesus. Does *soma* here represent the Aramaic term *gupha* (body) or the Aramaic *bisra* (flesh)? Jeremias argues for the latter, noting that the terms "flesh" and "blood" were commonly used among Jews to refer to the two component parts of the body. Used in their most common context, in reference to sacrificial animals, the terms presuppose a slaying that has separated flesh and blood. In the setting of the passover meal, such a usage would most naturally relate the death of Jesus to that of the passover lamb. In that case, writes Jeremias, " 'I go to death as the true Passover sacrifice' is the meaning of Jesus' last parable."[190]

Schürmann has objected to Jeremias's interpretation on varied grounds: (1) he maintains that the translator of the Lord's words would have used *sarx* rather than *soma* if the Aramaic terms indicated the flesh-blood contrast; (2) he notes that outside Leviticus and Numbers *soma* is rarely used to translate *basar* (he cites four such instances, over against 122 instances of *sarx*), and where *soma* is used it is used to refer to the body itself rather than to flesh as a component of the body; (3) the *soma-haima* terminology is retained not only in 1 Corinthians 11:23–24 but also in 1 Corinthians 10:16–17, in which the sacrificial concept in the Lord's Supper is central; and (4) the parallelism of flesh and blood with the bread and cup is unlikely here, since the the bread and cup sayings are separated by the account of the meal.[191] This last point, of course, ceases to apply outside the context of the Last Supper, when the two sacramental sayings of institution are placed together; it is therefore the more remarkable that none of the eucharistic accounts changes *soma* to *sarx* in order to secure the flesh-blood contrast.

In this, Schürmann appears to have the better of the argument. Nevertheless, one or two points are worthy of note. Even if it is the case that *soma* means "body," the sacrificial concept remains important in the context of the account of the Supper. Moreover, the same first-person suffix can be used with *bisra* and with *gupha* to denote the person of the speaker.[192] It is evident, however, that the early church found it easy to recognize in the loaf the representation of the *soma* that is *the Christ in his totality*, and from there to see in the one loaf the unity of the partakers as one body in Christ (see 1 Cor. 10:17). Significantly, that concept is found in the exposition of the Lord's Supper in 1 Corinthians 10:16–17, wherein the sacrificial language and thought of the sacrament are most strongly emphasized. The *soma* concept stresses that the value of that which is exhibited in the supper stems from Jesus himself and from fellowship with him. "This is my body" means "This is I myself"; as Pesch has suggested, Jesus "interprets *himself* as the source of blessing and salvation, as mediator of salvation."[193] This is wholly in keeping with Jesus' consciousness of being the representative and mediator of the saving sovereignty of God.

The Saying concerning the Cup
Mark 14:23–24, Matthew 26:27–28, Luke 22:20, 1 Corinthians 11:25

The wording of the different traditions is closely similar in substance, despite differences in construction. Mark's "This is my blood" stands in parallelism to the earlier saying "This is my body." The existence of the parallelism has been counted as evidence both for and against its originality; in the tradition of the church it would have been tempting to make the parallelism more precise (strangely, the parallelism is supported by 1 Cor. 10:16–17, yet not reproduced in the tradition cited by Paul in 1 Cor. 11:23). On the other hand, the difficulty (not to say offensiveness) of representing the wine that is to be drunk as "my blood of the covenant" has been seen both as supporting the originality of Mark's wording and as reason for viewing it as secondary.[194]

It was formerly maintained by some scholars that the phrase *to haima mou tes diathekes* ("my blood of the covenant") was not possible in Aramaic, but this objection has now been withdrawn in the light of related texts and the recognition that Greek idiom and word order do not necessarily correspond to an Aramaic original.[195] Jeremias, who has especially been involved in this discussion, is anxious to stress the agreement in content between the Markan and the Lukan/Pauline forms of the cup saying. He maintains that the Markan form should be rendered "This is my covenant-blood," and he argues that in the Lukan/Pauline version "the cup" indicates its contents, so that "the new covenant in my blood" means "the new covenant made in virtue of the shedding of my blood."[196]

Clearly the Markan and Lukan/Pauline versions are exceedingly close. It has even been suggested that they are different renderings of a single Aramaic statement.[197] The significant difference between the two renderings is the variation in Old Testament associations that they evoke. Mark's wording recalls Exodus 24:8: "See the blood of the covenant" (*idou to haima tes diathekes*); the sacrificial death of Jesus initiates a covenant in a manner comparable to the rites of the covenant-making at Sinai. The primary passage recalled by the Lukan/Pauline language is the prophecy of the new covenant in Jeremiah 31:31: "Behold, the days come, says the Lord, that I will make a *new* covenant with the house of Israel and with the house of Judah." It is clear, of course, that the Markan saying assumes that the blood of Jesus initiates a *new* covenant; similarly, the reference of Luke and Paul to the new covenant "in my blood" presupposes that Jeremiah's new covenant is made possible through the death of the Christ, a feature not represented in Jeremiah's prophecy.

But despite the similarity of the two versions, there is a difference of emphasis between them. Mark's language, reflecting Exodus 24, reflects the terms of the *cult*, while that of Luke and Paul, reflecting Jeremiah 31, is fundamentally *eschatological*. This latter emphasis is undoubtedly central to the intention of Jesus. The "new covenant" is to bring into existence a people renewed for life in the kingdom of God.[198] In the oft-cited words of Behm, the new covenant is "a correlative of the *basileia tou theou*," and its purpose is "to put into effect the eschatological saving will of God."[199] Käsemann has similarly pointed out that the *kaine diatheke* denotes "not a temporal repetition, but the eschatological new beginning of the two aeons."[200] This is of a piece with the doubly affirmed relation of the Last Supper to the feast of the kingdom of God. It is fitting to recall the predictions of the passion and the categories of thought presupposed in them: Jesus goes to his death as the Righteous One par excellence, as the Servant of the Lord, as the rejected Prophet, as the Martyr for God's cause, as the Son of Man whom God is to vindicate in his kingdom. It would appear that the new covenant is being conceived of as having been initiated by the Lord with precisely such concepts in mind.

The Vicarious Atonement

In the accounts of both Paul and Luke, the bread is said to represent the body of Jesus that is given *huper humon*—"on behalf of *you*." It is similarly indicated that the cup relates to the covenant in the blood that is shed *huper humon*. Mark's version contains the prepositional phrase once only, in connection with the blood, which is said to be shed *huper pollon* ("for *many*"). Again questions of origin are difficult: was the explanatory statement made in connection with the bread alone as in Paul's version, or in connection with the cup alone as in Mark's version, or in connection with both as in Luke's version—or not at all, the expression being attributable to later liturgical expansion? Schürmann has strongly defended the originality of *huper humon* in connection with the bread, arguing that from the beginning the account was set in the context of a liturgical event, and the phrase is needed in the early part of the meal if the saying "This is my body" is to make sense. He contends that the phrase became transferred to the cup saying in Mark through the influence on the text of the passion story, for Mark was especially interested in the soteriological significance of the Last Supper. But he also recognizes the possibility that the Markan tradition in turn led to the introduction of the *huper* phrase into Luke's cup saying.[201] Jeremias, on the other hand, maintains that the form of the phrase *to huper humon (didomenon)* is not characteristically Semitic in the Pauline and Lukan bread saying, and he considers this to be strong evidence that it is a later insertion; he also maintains that since Mark's *to ekchunnomenon huper pollon* is Semitic in construction and terminology, it therefore ought to be considered original. He suggests that the phrase was transposed in the Lukan version (1) in order to provide an explanation relating to the bread, (2) under the influence of liturgical practice, which contributed to the tendency to parallel the sayings relating to the bread and wine, and (3) on account of the fact that poor Palestinian congregations often celebrated the Lord's Supper with bread alone because they were unable to afford wine.[202]

The discussion is inconclusive. The problem would be simplified if we could determine whether the *huper* phrase originally contained the term *humon*, as in the versions of Paul and Luke, or *pollon*, as in Mark's version. Schürmann opts for the Pauline/Lukan version ("on your behalf"), chiefly because he sees in the Markan phrase an echo of Isaiah 53:12, and it seems to him that a reference to scripture is less likely to be dropped where it exists than introduced where it does not.[203] Jeremias contends that *pollon* as such is a Semitic usage that was employed because there was no more suitable term for "all" in Hebrew and Aramaic, and he suggests that the modification to "on *your* behalf" is a natural result of liturgical usage.[204] In this Jeremias is most likely right. If the *huper* phrase was originally attached to the bread saying, as Schürmann believes, then *huper pollon* is certainly no more than an "echo" of Isaiah 53, rather than an actual citation; while the phrase does recall Isaiah 53:12 ("he bore the sin of many"), it equally recalls the theme of *the whole* last Servant Song.

The possibilities of the Last Supper narrative now become more open. Patsch has given reason for believing that Paul's brief *huper* phrase in connection with the bread could have appeared in Aramaic if it originally read *to huper pollon*.[205] Nor is there cause to dismiss as linguistically unacceptable the presumed original of the Lukan phrase—*to huper pollon didomenon*—simply on the grounds of the position of the participle *didomenon*; Jeremias holds Mark's phrase "my covenant blood" to be acceptable on the grounds that Greek idiom and word order do not necessarily correspond to the Aramaic it translates, and that same observation is pertinent here. The importance of determining which saying the *huper* expression was attached to is clearly secondary to the importance of determining whether it applies to the bread and/or wine.

We must keep in mind that Israel never conceived of the sufferings of the Righteous One or the Rejected Prophet as vicarious, although they did in some instances adopt the vicarious view regarding the Suffering Servant of the Lord and the Martyr. The Jews were confused about the sufferings of the Servant.[206] It was easier for the contemporaries of Jesus—notably the Jews of the Dispersion, but also the Jews in Palestine—to recognize the atoning value of the sufferings of the martyrs. But of course there is no need to burden Jesus with the hesitations of his contemporaries to recognize the implications of the Fourth Servant Song. Jesus, it would seem, was unique among his people in his perception of the significance of the sufferings of the Servant of the Lord for the iniquity of humanity.[207] In light of his profound conviction that he had been sent as the representative of the saving sovereignty of God, we can well imagine that he would have seen in the image of the Servant of the Lord the supreme example of the Righteous One suffering as a martyr,[208] albeit on behalf of the guilty, in order to establish a new covenant to ensure the release of the sinful from their guilt and and to secure their entrance into the kingdom of God.

In this connection it is worthwhile to recall the references in Deutero-

Isaiah to the Servant as the means to a new covenant relation (see Isa. 42:6–7, 49:6–10, and 55:3–4; see also 54:10, 56:4, 59:21, and 61:8). These passages serve to link the role of the Servant with the establishment of the eschatological covenant described in Jeremiah 31:31. Although we may not immediately associate the notion of the body and blood of Jesus given for the forgiveness of sins with Jeremiah 31:31 (despite the fact that forgiveness of sins is integral to the new covenant—see Jer. 31:34), it does clearly come close to the heart of the last Servant Song. For this reason some scholars believe that even if the *huper humon* of Luke and Paul is original, it is nonetheless inspired by reflection on Isaiah 53.[209] In any case, the closer bond between the "many" of the last Servant Song and the new covenant concept is evident and ought to be acknowledged. The Song begins and ends with the vindication of the Servant who offers himself for the "many." In Isaiah 52:13–15 the "many" refers to the nations, and in Isaiah 53:10–12 the term almost certainly includes the nations with Israel.[210]

The new covenant is correlative to the kingdom of God. Just as Jesus taught that the kingdom of God is universal and that multitudes from the world over will stream into it (Matt. 8:11–12 // Luke 13:28–29), so the teaching about the new covenant includes the nations as well as the houses of Israel and Judah (Jer. 31:31). In the hour when Jesus most starkly faced Israel's rejection of the message of the kingdom of God and its Messenger—in the hour when he faced his impending death on that account and handed the bread and the cup of the covenant to his disciples, representatives of the renewed people who would enter the kingdom of God—he could not but have had in mind the inclusive range of his sacrifice, and so he could hardly have failed to call to mind the sole precedent in the Old Testament and late Judaism for the concept of an efficacious vicarious death on behalf of mankind: the fourth Servant Song in Isaiah 52:13–53:12. The predictions of the passion that Jesus uttered included the Servant concept along with the concepts of the Righteous Sufferer, Prophet, and Martyr; surely the concept of the Suffering Servant would have been yet more vividly on his heart as he handed the bread and cup to his disciples. They, receiving the bread and cup from his hand, were the first to receive the pledge of participation in the new covenant and inheritance in the kingdom of God: when Jesus "eats" and "drinks" in the kingdom of God, they will be there, eating and drinking with him (Luke 22:30a).

The Last Supper Traditions Questioned

We have conducted our investigation to this point on the assumption that the varied traditions of the Last Supper bear witness to a content that is essentially authentic, although there has been no claim that any of the accounts actually reproduce the *ipsissima verba* of Jesus. As it stands, this position has been challenged by various scholars. Bultmann's statement of some sixty years ago continues to be representative of not a few; he holds (1) that Mark's account is "the cult legend of the Hellenistic circles about Paul"; (2) that Luke's special account (Luke 22:15–18) is earlier though not necessarily historical, and that it contains "no reference to Jesus' death, and absolutely none to his person; the saying over the cup is much rather just a pointer to the coming kingdom of God"; and (3) that the original narrative probably told how Jesus in his last meal expressed the certainty of eating the next (festival) meal in the kingdom of God.[211]

The implications of Bultmann's view of the Supper are evident in a statement that J. Roloff has made: "Our material is insufficient to lead to a convincing proof that on the occasion of his last meal Jesus interpreted his death in the sense of a service to his own, and so as the fulfilment of his work."[212] In one of Bultmann's last contributions, he expressed this interpretation in its bluntest form, in a statement that has provoked considerable attention. Concerning the death of Jesus he wrote,

> This execution can hardly be understood as the necessary consequence of his work; it happened rather through a misunderstanding of his work as political action. Historically speaking, therefore, it was a fate without significance. Whether or how Jesus found a meaning in it we cannot know. We dare not cover up the possibility that he broke up.[213]

Why Bultmann should have considered a "break-up" possible at this point is a mystery, in light of the confidence Jesus expresses in the eschatological statements of Luke 22:15–18. Vögtle is more representative in recognizing authentic eschatological expectation in those sayings, although that does not keep him from divorcing it from any notion of expiatory significance attaching to the death of Jesus.

In essence, Vögtle argues as follows: Jesus proclaimed the good news of forgiveness and life in the kingdom of God for all who repent; if it were true that a vicarious death of the Messiah was necessary for God to bestow these gracious gifts, it would certainly have been a key feature of the proclamation; had Jesus come to hold this concept at some point in his ministry, one would expect that he would have modified his message to incorporate the significant change; but there is no indication of any such modification of his teaching.[214] This argument has been refined by Vögtle's student P. Fiedler, who finds the notion unacceptable that Jesus, after having preached the willingness of God to forgive and the triumph of the love of God, would have come to the conviction when facing his death that he must renounce this message and believe instead that God willed his death as an expiatory sacrifice. It would imply that God was not so generous or sovereign in his grace as Jesus had earlier taught, says Fiedler, and that he now insisted on an atonement. If such a deduction as to the nature of God is repugnant, it is best to recognize that Jesus' proclamation of the kingdom of God and the idea of his atoning death are irreconcilable.[215]

What is to be said in face of these objections to the traditions embodied in the Last Supper narratives? We should weigh the following considerations.

1. It is generally acknowledged that the Last Supper accounts (other than Luke 22:15–18) were fashioned for use in the churches' worship. The question of whether Mark's account can justly be described as "the cult legend of the Hellenistic circles about Paul" is a wholly different matter. Jeremias's demonstration of the Semitisms within Mark's version would seem to rule out such an

assertion by indicating that the tradition behind the traditions of the Last Supper was formulated in Aramaic or Hebrew, and by demonstrating that that background shines through the present form of Mark with particular clarity.[216]

2. The authenticity of Jesus' eschatological expectation in the Last Supper accounts is very important. On the lowest level it demonstrates, as Schürmann has put it, the confidence of Jesus that "the kingdom of God comes despite his death."[217] But more than this, it indicates that *Jesus viewed his death as part and parcel of the process whereby the kingdom comes.*

We have seen that the gospels present the ministry of Jesus as a ministry of service for the kingdom of God, an essentially mediatorial ministry of deeds and words. This inheres in his teaching on the kingdom of God both in the eschatological logia and in the parables he uttered. In his own teaching, Jesus appears as the representative (Luke 17:20–21), the revealer (Mark 4:11–12; Matt. 11:25–26), the initiator (Matt. 11:12), the instrument (Matt. 12:28), the champion (Mark 3:27), the mediator (Mark 2:18–19), and the bearer (Matt. 11:5) of the kingdom of God. The unity of this ministry is evident in the range of the Son of Man sayings, which embrace his authoritative service in word and deed among the people; his sufferings as the Righteous One, the Servant of God, and so on; and his role at the end of the age in the parousia and the judgment.

Scholars have not been much inclined to acknowledge the authentic range of the Son of Man's ministry for the kingdom of God, but it is my conviction that this critical reluctance is changing and that the change will decisively affect the question that we are now considering. We have no right to isolate the public ministry of Jesus in Galilee, as though that alone was of significance to him, for he clearly expresses anticipation of the role he will play in the final revelation of the kingdom of God and the judgment. Accordingly, we must allow his instruction concerning the last day to shed its light upon the way of Jesus in Galilee (and Jerusalem). Nor can we allow the parousia sayings to be separated from the suffering Son of Man sayings. Indeed, they are intimately bound together: there is no parousia of the Son of Man apart from his suffering of death. (We must set aside consideration of the Parables of Enoch in this regard, since there is no reference to the parousia in them and they did not exist when Jesus preached in Galilee.)

The close connection between the parousia and the Son of Man is underscored in the clearest parousia saying in the gospels, Mark 14:62: it is the Son of Man who is on trial and faces the death sentence who announces his future appearance as the Judge of his judges. We must take account of the *total* service of Jesus for the sovereignty of God when we consider the meaning of Luke 22:15–18, Mark 14:25, and 1 Corinthians 11:26 in relation to the death of Jesus. As surely as Jesus considered his ministry of proclamation and action to be the instrument of the divine sovereignty, and as surely as he understood his role in the parousia and judgment to be bound up with the revelation of the divine sovereignty, so surely will he have set his approaching death in relation to the coming of the kingdom of God. In contrast to Bultmann's assertion of our ignorance about how Jesus might have viewed his "unfortunate" death, we will do well to consider the following statement of William Manson:

If Jesus throughout his work was conscious of standing in a circle of crisis, in which the powers of the world to come were seen to be breaking in all around him, he cannot, when the prospect of death cast its shadow upon the scene, have thought of that event in purely natural terms or in dissociation from the purpose and power of God which were working with him.[218]

3. The ministry of Jesus in relation to the kingdom of God went beyond a simple proclamation of the divine sovereignty after the fashion of the apocalyptists or even of the Qumran Covenanters, who saw the kingdom in some measure realized in their midst. The ministry of Jesus in word and deed was essentially *redemptive*, as is indicated by Luke's account of the ministry to Nazareth. Jesus' use of Isaiah 61:1–2 and 58:6, together with his "interpretative word"—"Today this scripture has been fulfilled in your ears"—indicate that his announcement of the arrival of the "Jubilee" of the kingdom of God included his awareness that he had the authority to initiate it and the power to effect it. His preaching of the word of the kingdom communicated the blessings of the emancipation it made known: he inaugurated the year of the Lord's favor and *let the broken victims go free* (Luke 4:18–19). The like may be seen in Matthew 11:5, and in a different manner in the logion about the exorcisms: "If it is by the finger of God that I am casting out the demons, then the kingdom of God has arrived upon you" (Luke 11:20 // Matt. 12:28). The works of Jesus are a rescue operation in the power of the Spirit, a commencement of God's emancipation of humanity fallen prey to the powers of evil, and therefore a manifestation of the presence of God's *redemptive sovereignty*. The table fellowship of Jesus with sinners should be viewed in a similar light, for in it Jesus was going beyond showing compassion and friendship to the unfortunate and outcasts; he was bringing the redeeming grace of God into the lives of sinful men and women, providing the means by which they might become different people in a new relation to God, experiencing the renewing powers of the divine sovereignty and subjecting themselves to it (note the experiences of Levi recorded in Mark 2:14, the "sinful" woman of Luke 7:37ff., and Zacchaeus in Luke 19:1–9).

And yet all these aspects of Jesus' Nazarene ministry signaled but the beginning of the operation of the saving sovereignty in the world. The one elected to be the instrument of the kingdom of God was on his way to achieve a redemption from sin and the evil powers on a universal scale, for nothing less than that was needed if the kingdom was to be for all humanity. By definition the kingdom of God is universal in its scope; hence, the redemption has to be universal also. In Jesus the kingdom of God had powerfully broken into the world—but there were powerful adversaries (Matt. 11:12). The people of the Messiah were not receptive to his message, and there were manifestly determined efforts to destroy his work (see Matt. 13:24ff.). The evil that was rampant amidst the people of God was ubiquitous among the nations. An emancipation for the whole world was needed if the Son of Man was to be the means of a sovereignty that would *deliver* from evil as well as *judge* evil. The words of Jesus at the Last Supper reveal a method by which that goal might be achieved that is wholly in harmony with the service of the kingdom of salvation to which he was appointed.[219]

4. In answer to the question of why Jesus did not refer to this element of his service in the kingdom of God earlier in his ministry—earlier, that is, than the Last Supper—we may make two observations. First, Jesus chose in general not to make his role in the coming of the kingdom of God the subject of his preaching. When he did refer to that role, he generally did so obliquely (see, for example, Mark 2:19 and 12:6ff.; and Matt. 11:5–6). It is scarcely conceivable that Jesus would have explicitly declared to the multitudes that their rejection of his message and the opposition of their rulers to his ministry would eventually lead to his death, which would then become the means of redemption for the nation and the world. Second, we may note that the gospels do indicate that as soon as Jesus' disciples recognized that he was the Messiah—that is, as soon as they were in a position to receive intimations of Jesus' understanding of the significance of his death—he did in fact proceed to give them instruction on this theme, and he did so repeatedly. He told them in no uncertain terms that the Son of Man, the representative and mediator of the kingdom of God, had to fulfill the destiny of the suffering Righteous Man, the Servant of the Lord, the rejected Prophet, and the Martyr for God's cause, and thus to accomplish his service for the kingdom of God through death and resurrection. His statement that the Son of Man would experience death and then resurrection "after three days" can be understood only in terms of God's being at work in him redemptively on behalf of the divine sovereignty. Herein lies the justification for G. Sevenster's dictum "His dying should not be understood as a lot that he undergoes, but as a deed which he accomplishes."[220] The implications of the passion predictions for the work of Jesus in the service of the divine sovereignty are enormous. The scholars who reject the testimony of Jesus' statements at the Last Supper—statements that are entirely harmonious with the passion predictions—reject this testimony also and then ask why there are no words from Jesus about it. This is the height of irony!

5. In light of the total ministry of Jesus and the fullness and variety of the kinds of instruction it comprises, Schürmann's compendious argument concerning the actions of Jesus at the Last Supper is worthy of a more positive reception than it has received in some quarters (his fellow Roman Catholics included, some of whom seem to have reacted very strongly to their own traditions). Schürmann seeks to meet with understanding the scholars who find it difficult to accept the interpretative words at the Last Supper; setting aside any attempt to argue that the Last Supper narratives contain the *ipsissima verba* of Jesus, he emphasizes that they present the *ipsissima facta*—the *acts* of Jesus in relation to the bread and the wine. In this regard, he links his own distinct treatment with the long-standing critical connection made between these acts of Jesus and the acts of prophetic symbolism described in the Old Testament.

Schürmann's first step is to establish that Jesus frequently engaged in actions related to the prophetic actions. He notes, for instance, that his sending of the disciples on mission to the towns and villages of Israel was a "sign-event," a once-for-all sending of the message of the kingdom of God to the nation before the end should come. The triumphal entry into Jerusalem was another such sign, which urgently pressed upon Israel the necessity for a decision relating to the message Jesus brought to them. The cleansing of the temple was yet another sign, more grave than that of the triumphal entry in that it portended judgment and precipitated a decision on the part of the nation's leaders regarding Jesus' mission. In the same way, says Schürmann, the acts of the Last Supper can be seen as sign actions relating to the death of Jesus. More specifically, he characterizes these actions as signs of "eschatological fulfillment." Whereas the prophets performed acts that declared and set in motion the divine purpose they portended, the sign actions of Jesus "fulfilled"—that is, brought into being the future prophesied by the prophets.

Thus, it is Schürmann's argument, in reliance on the account of the Last Supper in Luke 22:15ff. (which does not contain the interpretative words included in the other accounts), that in the giving of the bread and the wine Jesus offers the eschatological salvation in sign fashion.[221] Having made that assertion, he then proceeds with great reserve as follows:

> Perhaps then the interpretative words with their soteriological utterances only make explicit what Jesus' sign actions already imply? Jesus' Last Supper gift proclaims and gives part in the eschaton in such a manner that the death may not only offer the occasion for giving the final emphasis to the offer; the tradition should be taken more seriously that the death is seen as a *means* which makes this eschatological gift possible, so that the eschatological salvation is thoroughly understandable as the fruit of this death.

In a more emphatic manner he then goes on to say,

> In any case . . . the emphatic "gift-gestures" of the one about to die, who declares and offers the eschatological salvation, can best be interpreted as "soteriological." In these gestures of Jesus the eschatological salvation is really understandable only as proexistent salvation of the one prepared for the surrender of death. *Jesus' action at the Supper therefore may with good reason be interpreted of the pre-Easter proexistence of Jesus.*[222]

This summary of Schürmann's argument does scant justice to it; I have not found its match anywhere in critical discussions on the synoptic evidence relating to the death of Jesus, and to the Last Supper in particular. Employing caution worthy of the British, Gnilka has stated, "One must admit to Schürmann that he has succeeded, if not in proving Jesus' understanding of salvation, at least in ensuring the openness of this question." But he then proceeds to observe with regard to Schürmann's so-called *ipsissima facta* at the Last Supper that "A half dark place remains so long as these actions speak for themselves without any sayings to accompany them."[223] Vögtle agrees with Gnilka in this, apparently on the assumption that he is suggesting that Schürmann has failed.[224] On the contrary, however, a half-dark place is clearly a great improvement on the total darkness in which are sunk the writings of those who adopt Bultmann's position. And eyes can become accustomed to half-light (a preferable way of expressing "half-dark")! With the clues provided by the words and deeds of Jesus in his ministry, the half-light of the Last Supper acts suffice to enable us to see the essentials that must be discerned.

In reality, of course, we need not settle for even so little as half-light, for everything that might be said to be dimly discernible in the profoundly suggestive acts of Jesus is fully illuminated by the interpretative words of the Last Supper accounts. These logia provide a testimony that is consistent and harmonious with the acts of Jesus in the giving of the bread and wine, viewed in the context of his total ministry, and with the eschatological prospect of the messianic feast. These narratives date back further than the written gospels to the earliest days of the primitive church. The recollection of the acts and words of Jesus in the Last Supper was as important to the first-generation church as it has been to succeeding generations. The nature of the accounts they hand on indicates that the earliest believers maintained the tradition with the care that such an event warranted.

e. Thrones of Judgment
Matthew 19:28, Luke 22:28–30

This saying is generally assigned to Q. The substantial differences between the renderings in Matthew and Luke are more probably the result of the evangelists' redactions and additions than of the sayings' having come from independent traditions. Matthew 19:28a, "Jesus replied, 'Amen, I tell you . . .'" is likely Matthew's own introduction to the saying.[225] Following this, the Matthaean parallel to Luke 22:28 begins as follows:

Matthew 19:28	Luke 22:28
You who have followed me . . .	*You* are the men who have stood firmly with me in my times of trial . . .

The next clause diverges widely in the two versions:

Matthew 19:28	Luke 22:29–30
In the world that is to be, when the Son of Man is seated on his throne in heavenly splendor . . .	And now I vest in you the kingship which my Father vested in me; you shall eat and drink at my table *in my kingdom* . . .

Schürmann contends that Matthew substituted the unusual expression "in the world that is to be" (*en te palingenesia*) for the simple "in my kingdom" contained in Luke and then filled it out with the language of Matthew 25:31.[226] After this the two traditions come close together:

Matthew 19:28	Luke 22:30
You also shall sit upon twelve thrones, judging the twelve tribes of Israel.	And you shall sit upon thrones, judging the twelve tribes of Israel.

The relationship between the two forms of the saying will be greatly simplified if we recognize that Luke's verses 29 and 30a are a very remote parallel to Matthew's statement about the new world. In essence, Luke 22:29–30a should be considered a separate saying, from Luke's tradition, which he added to the statement about the apostles' thrones. The burden of the Q saying then becomes the declaration concerning authority in the *palingenesia*.[227]

The context of the Q logion is difficult to determine. Matthew has probably placed his version of the saying in accordance with his usual principle of grouping together related material. In the Markan source he found the question of Peter, "We here have left everything to become your followers; what will there be for us?" and a reply of Jesus affirming recompense "in this age" and "in the age to come" (Mark 10:29–30). Matthew considered this to be a suitable place for the insertion of the promise to the apostles of thrones at the advent of the kingdom of God. His phrase "*You* who have followed me" takes up the words of Peter in verse 27 ("*We* here have left everything to become your followers"), thus identifying the disciples of Jesus there present as the *humeis* to whom the promise of the thrones is made.[228] Luke's opening clause contains typical Lukan vocabulary; the phrase "You are the men who have stood firmly with me" employs the verb *diameno*, used elsewhere in the gospels only in Luke 1:22, and *peirasmoi* is also typical of Luke. But the basic thought of the address in both versions is similar: after the utterance of Mark 8:34 (// Matthew 16:24, Luke 9:23), "following" Jesus entails bearing a cross after him and thus enduring "times of trial" with him; the disciples who have "followed" Jesus to this point have endured with him in the testing experiences he was called to suffer throughout his ministry. It is to these disciples that Jesus covenanted to give a share in the kingdom and its joyous feast. Hence, it is easy to see why Luke should think it natural to conjoin verses 29–30a with the saying in verses 28, 30b—and it is precisely the covenanting to give the kingdom and the joy of the feast that led Luke (or his source) to set the passage in the context of the Last Supper.

Obviously we cannot be certain either of the precise wording of the logion concerning the thrones, or the occasion of its utterance. The mention of the *twelve* thrones makes it difficult to view it as having been spoken in the circumstance in which Luke has set it—namely, immediately after the defection of Judas. On the other hand, if the function of the apostles on the thrones includes (or even denotes) that of judging in a tribunal, it may be assumed to fall at a time in the ministry of Jesus when his message had been rejected by many in his nation.

Matthew 19:28; Luke 22:28, 30b

The emphatic *humeis* of the first clause and the content of the last clause of the saying in these verses make it clear that it is addressed to the Twelve and is applicable to them alone (in contrast to the saying in Luke 22:29–30a, which need not be restricted to the circle of the Twelve).

The expression *en te palingenesia* has caused no little discussion. Perhaps too much has been made of the fact, pointed out by Dalman, that there is no precise equivalent to *palingenesia* in Hebrew and Aramaic.[229] Matthew has taken a well-known term of Greek culture to represent a concept that has many facets in the Jewish tradition, just as he used the Greek term *parousia* to represent an idea expressed by Jesus in various ways.[230] It is commonly assumed that the term is intended to express the apocalyptic equivalent of the Stoic restoration of the universe after its destruction by fire.[231] Ysebaert, in a study of the term, denies this; in his view *palingenesia* renders the notion of *palin gignesthai*, from which the idea of birth is absent: "It means no more than 'restoration' or 'new beginning,' and it is not apparent that any metaphor of a new birth of the cosmos was intended."[232] Without doubt the Jews had their own way of expressing the latter notion. We find a close equivalent to Matthew's term in 1QS 4:25, in which *'asoth hadsa* = *kainopoiia*, a "making new."[233] Philo uses the term in speaking of the reconstitution of the world after the flood, and Josephus describes the reestablishment of the Jews after the exile as *anaktesin kai palingenesian tes patridos*, "the recovery and restoration of the homeland."[234]

Clearly *palingenesia* can be applied in many different ways. The meaning of the term in Matthew has to be determined by the context. The occasion for its use in Matthew 19:28 is defined by the immediately succeeding clause, "when the Son of Man sits on his glorious throne," which echoes Matthew 25:31, in which it introduces the vision of the judgment of the nations. Vögtle stresses that connection, suggesting that Matthew used *palingenesia* rather than such expressions as "in the kingdom of God," or "in the coming eon," or "in the consummation of the age," because these expressions include positive as well as negative elements, and above all the saving sovereignty of God in its abiding condition, whereas Matthew appears to have in view the *inauguration* of the kingdom of God in the judgment. He suggests that *palingenesia* here represents the *restoration* of the people of the twelve tribes.[235] If that is a less adventurous rendering than some of those proposed, it has at least the merit of suiting the context.

Of greater consequence is the significance of the main clause of Matthew 19:28 and Luke 22:30b—in particular the meaning of the declaration that the apostles will "judge" the twelve tribes of Israel. In Luke it would appear that the term *krinontes* ("judging") suggests exercise of the power of rule within the kingdom of God, since it follows the solemn promise to the disciples that they will eat and drink in the kingdom of God (v. 30a). This interpretation is accepted by a number of the leading exegetes for Matthew also, although it is of doubtful validity.[236] When the saying is separated from Luke 22:29–30a no such picture of the kingdom of God appears for its context. Dupont points out that there is no other example in the New Testament of *krino* having the meaning of "rule" and that the natural meaning of the term is "to judge," in the sense of participating in a tribunal.[237] We have already observed that Matthew's interpretation of *palingenesia* is bound up with the clause relating to the Son of Man's sitting on the throne of his glory, and this most plausibly reflects Matthew 25:31—the introduction to the scene of universal judgment. It is probable that Jesus is envisioning something along these lines in speaking of the apostles being seated on thrones "judging" Israel's twelve tribes: they are to sit as assessors in the court when Israel is judged.

This idea may sound extraordinary to the modern mind, but it has deep roots in the Bible. The source of the concept is Daniel 7:9, the vision of the coming of God to judge the impious power that defied him in the world: "Thrones were set in place and one ancient in Years took his seat." The Jews were long intrigued that the seer speaks of "thrones" in the plural, whereas the "Ancient in Years" occupies a throne of "flames of fire." Who occupy the others, they wondered. Many answers were given, among them the following:

> Our teachers said, "What does 'thrones' in Daniel 7:9 mean?" In the future God will sit, and the angels set thrones for the great men of Israel, and these sit thereon, and God sits like a presiding judge with them, and then they judge the nations of the world, as it is written: Yahweh comes to judgment with the elders of his people and his princes, Isa. 3:14.[238]

Since judgment is a function of rule, this tradition belongs to the wider teaching that the people of God will participate in God's rule in the age to come, which is the burden of the interpretation of the vision of Daniel 7 in verses 18ff. In singling out the element of judgment in this saying, Jesus reflects his consciousness of Israel's guilt in their rejection of his ministry and message. The apostles, as the emissaries of Jesus sent to make known to Israel the message of the kingdom, are destined to act as assessors in the time when the Jews are called to give account of their response to the Messiah. According to this interpretion, the "thrones" are strictly designated for the court scene, as in Daniel 7:9.[239]

Luke 22:29–30a

Schürmann makes a strong plea for acknowledging the logion in Luke 22:29–30a as belonging to the Last Supper tradition.[240] He contends that Luke 22:15–20 and 28–30 were preserved together in the pre-Lukan tradition. This suggestion is especially plausible because of (1) the unusual link between *diatheke* and *diatithemai* in verses 20 and 29; (2) the anticipation of the messianic feast in verses 16, 18, and 30; and (3) the comparable use of *en te basileia tou theou* in verse 16 and *en te basileia mou* in verse 30. The connection of thought between the eschatological covenant ratified in the giving of the body and blood of Jesus (verses 19–20) and the covenanting to give the kingdom to the disciples in verse 29 is especially striking. While the term "covenant" does not appear in verse 29, the verb *diatithemai* is closely related to it. In the LXX *diatithesthai diatheken* is regularly used to translate the Hebrew phrase *karath berith*. It occurs in the foundational passage Exodus 24:8 ("See, the blood of the covenant which the Lord has made with you . . ."), which is rendered in the LXX as *Idou to haima tes diathekes, hes dietheto kurios pros humas.* . . . Accordingly, Otto had reason to render Luke 22:29 "I appoint the kingdom unto you by covenant, as my Father appointed it to me."[241] The intention of the covenant mentioned in the distribution of the cup in verse 20 is clearly participation in the kingdom of God, pledged by the symbolic participation in the offering of Christ. Verse 29 speaks of God's covenant gift of the kingdom to him, in virtue of which Jesus pledges a like covenant gift of the kingdom to the disciples; the death of the Lord as the condition for both elements of the covenant is self-evidently presupposed.

An ambiguity exists in the saying with respect to the object of *diatithemai*;

one can interpret the object as being either *basileian* or the *hina* clause of verse 30a. On the former presupposition, one will translate the saying somewhat as in the manner of Otto: "I appoint unto you by covenant the kingdom, as my Father appointed it to me, that you may eat and drink at my table in my kingdom."[242] On the latter understanding, one will render it "I appoint by covenant unto you, as my Father appointed by covenant to me a kingdom, that you eat and drink at my table in my Kingdom."[243] There is not a great deal of difference between the two readings, since the honor of association with Jesus in the kingdom is great—the kind of privilege, indeed, that James and John sought, though without the precise seating arrangement they wanted (see Mark 10:35–40). We should not fail to note, however, that the privilege here described is not restricted to the circle of the apostles in the manner of verse 30b; verses 19–20 suggest that the group of disciples that receives the pledges of participation in (the feast of) the kingdom of God is representative of the followers of Jesus who receive his word of the kingdom and acknowledge him as the representative and mediator of the kingdom. In this sense, verses 29–30a strengthen the interpretation of verses 15–18 and 19–20. Through the death of Jesus, the covenant ensures to his followers a participation in the kingdom that was in process of coming through his whole ministry; the assurance is given of an inheritance in that kingdom and fellowship with the Lord in the joyful feast that will celebrate its advent.

Note on the Authenticity of Matthew 19:28, Luke 22:28–30

Not a few critics and exegetes have expressed doubts as to the dominical authority of the logia. Bultmann may speak for others: "It is unquestionably the risen Lord who speaks. We are dealing with a formulation deriving from the early Church, for it was there that the Twelve were first held to be the judges of Israel in the time of the end."[244] This latter feature is frequently mentioned by those who doubt the authenticity of the saying; these scholars also typically object to the reference to the *palingenesia* in Matthew 19:28 and the Lukan terminology in Luke 22:28, issues with which we have already dealt. It is the role of the Twelve in the end that is the real stumbling block, but the solution to the problem lies in their relation to Jesus.

If we are correct in interpreting the Q logion in the light of Jesus' mission to Israel, in which the Twelve played an essential role, we can recognize the affinity of the saying with the crucial Q logion concerning the confession or denial by the Son of Man in the judgment, in accordance with confession or denial of Jesus in his ministry (Luke 12:8–9 par.). Acceptance or rejection of the emissaries of Jesus entails acceptance or rejection of the Christ who sent them, which in turn involves acceptance or rejection of the God who sent him (see Matt. 10:40, Luke 10:16). From this relation springs the rationale of the role of the Twelve in the judgment of Israel. Dupont maintains that such a view belongs essentially to the pre-Easter situation rather than that which followed Easter, and says that "this archaism is a guarantee of its historical worth."[245] When we further acknowledge that the eschatological content of Luke 22:29–30a is one with that of the earliest record of the Last Supper, we may well feel that the combined logia should be accounted as belonging to the earliest traditions of the teaching of Jesus.

---

f. The Ransom of the Son of Man
Mark 10:45, Matthew 20:28, Luke 22:27

In Mark this saying forms the climax of what appears to be a catechetical collection of sayings brought together in verses 2–12, 17–27, 35–40, and 41–45 of chapter 10.[246] Among these passages, verses 41–45 form a separate paragraph, of which verse 41 makes a transition from the previous paragraph, and 42a provides an introduction to the sayings in verses 42b–44 (// Luke 22:25–26). The relationship of Mark 10:42b–44 to Mark 9:35 is instructive. Mark 9:35 is truncated; originally it must have been a double saying, like Mark 10:43–44 par. On the other hand, the same logion suggests that Mark 10:43–44 may earlier have been stated in reverse order, and that the contrast *protos-doulos* in verse 44 was originally *protos-eschatos*. In that case, we might postulate that the double saying originally read as follows:

> *hos an thele (en humin) einai protos*
> *estai panton doulos,*
> *kai hos an thele (en humin) einai megas*
> *estai humon diakonos.*

> Whoever (among you) wishes to be first
> must be slave of all,
> and whoever (among you) wishes to be great
> must be your servant.[247]

Luke's version has been rendered into more suitable Greek, and at the same time has in view the application of the saying to the community and its leaders: *neoteros* ("younger") appears in place of Mark's *eschatos*, and *hegoumenos* ("leader") appears in place of *protos*.

The pertinence of these comments to Mark 10:45 is plain: Mark 10:43–44 // Luke 22:26 appears to have been isolated and variously placed within the tradition by those who handed it on. This would in turn suggest that Mark 10:45 and Luke 22:26 were also isolated in the tradition.

The relation of these two sayings has long been discussed. They are commonly recognized as independent versions of a single saying, drawn to the previous logia by the theme of *diakonia-diakonein*. The question of priority that accordingly arises involves a number of issues.

Bultmann settled the question of origin simply and speedily, stating that Luke 22:27 is original and Mark 10:45 was formed from the redemption theories of Hellenistic Christianity.[248] That position becomes increasingly difficult to maintain. The precedents in traditional Judaism for the ransom saying have been impressively set forth by Jeremias and by Lohse.[249] They adduce considerable evidence from a wide variety of sources to demonstrate, as Jeremias puts it, that "the literature of late Judaism is filled with the concept that death possesses expiatory power"; in light of this evidence, he says, "It should be plain . . . how strongly the question of the 'ransom' due to God occupied late Judaism."[250] Jeremias follows his exposition with an attempt to demonstrate the priority of Mark's version over Luke's on linguistic grounds—chiefly on the basis of the

Palestinian character of Mark's language in contrast to the grecized setting of the Lukan form. In the two versions of the saying and its context he sees a Jewish-Christian and a Gentile-Christian form of the sayings series, and he maintains that the Palestinian form has the greater claim to trustworthiness. He reaches a similar conclusion in comparing the saying in Mark 10:45 with the version reproduced in 1 Timothy 2:6. But it should be noted that the Hellenistic Greek features in Luke 22:24–27 to which Jeremias calls attention relate to the *context* of the saying (vv. 24–26) rather than to the saying itself. Even so, he makes the following valid points: (1) the Palestinian features of Mark 10:45 are clear, (2) they are not reproduced in Luke 22:27, and (3) they are not plausibly explained as coming from a Hellenistic Jewish-Christian environment.

Schürmann develops a different approach to the two versions of the logion.[251] Because their contexts are so similar, he maintains that they go back to an identical primitive form. He further observes (1) that Luke's double question in verse 27 is characteristic of Jewish teachers, (2) that the terminology is not specifically Lukan, and (3) that the picture of table service in Luke is probably original rather than the result of Lukan redaction (he suggests that Mark's use of *diakonein* instead of *douleuein* is probably also attributable to this); it was this element, he argues, that caused Luke 22:24–27 to be inserted in the Lord's Supper narrative. If, as is likely, Mark 10:45b was an originally independent saying, it could have affected the form of verse 45a; the notion of table service was made more general through application to the service of the Servant of the Lord. Accordingly, he proposes that verse 45b was a fragment of an originally independent logion of the Palestinian form that became attached to verse 45a. It would originally have read as follows:

> ho huios tou anthropou elthen dounai ten psuchen autou lutron anti pollon.[252]

If Schürmann still adheres to this view of Mark 10:45b, he has now come to reject the authenticity of the logion: in more recent writings he has argued that the suffering Son of Man is "a paradoxical *theologoumenon* of the Markan redaction, perhaps already of the Markan tradition," and that verse 45b is dependent on the liturgy of the Lord's Supper.[253] His earlier work, however, remains of importance, since it led to further developments in the direction he took.

Roloff followed in Schürmann's path, agreeing that the traditions of Mark and Luke are independent, that Mark 10:45a is an addition reflecting a Palestinian-Aramaic background rather than "Hellenistic redemption teaching."[254] He suggests that verse 45b reflects dependence on Isaiah 53:10—not as a citation but through the tradition of the Last Supper—and he suggests that the Markan and Lukan sayings can best be explained if we assume that Luke's verse 27 belongs to the pre-Lukan account of the Last Supper, in immediate connection with verses 15–20. He then goes on to argue that in Luke the *diakonein* of Jesus refers to a concrete situation in which Jesus is the one who serves his disciples at the table, whereas in Mark the *diakonein* reflects an understanding of the Last Supper as an act of service by Jesus that summarizes in a significant way the meaning of his sending.[255] Thus, he views Mark 10:45b as an indirect equivalent of Luke 22:27 in its original narrative context: "The statement about the giving of Jesus' life 'instead of the many' appears to be a formal abbreviation of the bread and cup sayings in the account of the meal."[256]

X. Léon-Dufour agrees with Roloff's contention that Luke 22:27 should be understood as linked with the account of the Last Supper; he views the Lukan saying as an interpretation of the action of Jesus at the Supper declaring his blood to be given on behalf of others and thus as a service to the community. Although Mark reflects a dogmatic concentration and Luke a liturgical situation, says Léon-Dufour, both versions of the saying deal with service in an absolute sense. In both sayings "we are in the presence of an understanding of the sacrifice of Jesus as service."[257]

There is something of a consensus thus in recognizing the link between Mark 10:45b and the Last Supper. The question remains who forged the link—Jesus or the church at worship in the Lord's Supper. Wellhausen maintains that to pass from the service in *life* of Mark 10:45a to the service in *death* of Mark 10:45b is a *metabasis eis allo genos*, a transition to another order that can be attributed only to the church's reflection.[258] The prospect alters, however, when we take into account the nature of Jesus' ministry as the service of the saving sovereignty of God. From this perspective it becomes clear that Jesus' whole ministry was one with its climax in death, for through it all God was establishing new relations with men and women, the salvific relations of life under the sovereignty of God. "The call of Jesus had the character of the action of grace," observes Patsch, who points out that Jesus acted in God's stead in his granting of forgiveness, in his giving of table fellowship, in his calling to following. In all this, says Patsch, he gave *himself* as well as his gracious words, and in this way he established a unity between his giving of himself in life and his giving of himself in death.[259] Roloff makes the same point: "Jesus' death was the last consequence of his ministering self-giving; in this death the real dimension of Jesus' action on sinners during his ministry was revealed."[260]

In reflecting on the saying in Mark 10:45 par., we might note that there remain many things about it that are uncertain. Pointedly, its authenticity is less certain than that of most of the disputed sayings of Jesus—although this is by no means to say that there are valid grounds for dismissing it as inauthentic. Further, the relation of Mark 10:45 to Luke 22:27 is not always carefully defined. It is incorrect to state without qualification that the two passages are two versions of one saying. Luke's verse 27a has no real parallel in Mark 10:45a. That is very clear when one observes how the former is reflected in Luke 22:27b. In fact, it is only Luke 22:27c that is clearly related to Mark 10:45a:

Luke 22:27c	Mark 10:45a
ego de	kai gar ho huios tou anthropou
en meso humon	ouk elthen diakonethenai alla
hos ho diakonon	diakonesai

It is not impossible that the two sections of Luke's saying circulated alone; they are sufficiently striking to have done so. Is it possible that Mark 10:45b once took the following form?

ho de huios tou anthropou (hos) ho diakonon
kai didous ten psuchen autou
lutron anti pollon.

That would form the perfect basis for the version in 1 Timothy 2:5–6:

anthropos Christos Iesous
ho dous heauton
antilutron huper panton.

It would have been a small step from such a reading to turn the emphasis to the purpose of the ministry of Jesus by inserting *elthen* and adding a negative qualification to the positive statement in the light of Daniel 7:14. That raises the question of why the clause relating to the ransom is missing from the Lukan version. Piecemeal reproduction of the elements of the saying might account for the loss. But we should acknowledge that this phenomenon does not occur only in Luke's reproduction of Son of Man sayings in Mark. There is also the extraordinary version of Mark 14:62 that appears in Luke 22:67–69, in which the loss of the critically important last clause of Mark 14:62 has led to all kinds of improbable explanations, none of which suffices to establish the originality of the Lukan omission over against the Markan inclusion. We should probably grant that the same sort of thing applies to Mark 10:45 in relation to Luke 22:27.

Having looked at the origins of the saying, we should now turn to the question of its meaning. What is meant when it is said that the service of Jesus' life culminates in the giving of that life as "a *lutron* for many"? Etymologically *lutron* denotes "a means of release," or, more specifically, "money paid as a means of release." It was used especially of payment for the release of prisoners of war, of slaves, and of debtors. It was also applied in the cultic sphere to payment made to a deity to which an individual had incurred indebtedness, and thus it was extended to denote expiation or compensation.[261] In the Greek Old Testament *lutron* was used mainly to render *kopher* ("the price of a life," "ransom"), *pidyon* ("ransom"), and *ge'ullah* ("redemption," including the right and the price of it). The first term comes from a cultic background denoting the covering over, propitiating, or atoning for sin; it could be used in a broader sense, as in Proverbs 6:35 and 13:8, which led D. Hill to suggest that *kopher* principally connotes the means by which some particular freedom is gained.[262] The last two terms are significant, in that they come from verbs used to express the redemption or deliverance of Israel from Egypt. Hooker has urged that this Old Testament link with the redemption of God's people from the bondage of Egypt indicates where the accent should be placed in the *lutron* concept— namely, in the historical activity of Yahweh and the hope of a similar redemption in the coming of the kingdom of God.[263] While this is a thoroughly pertinent observation, it should be noted that the conjunction of *lutron* with the preposition *anti* indicates that the death of Jesus is viewed as an "atoning substitute,"[264] or "substitute gift"[265] in place of the many. The term and the phrase indicate that without that self-sacrifice the "many" would be doomed in the judgment and miss the goal of their creation in the kingdom of salvation.

It is commonly suggested that the last Servant Song of Isaiah 52:13–53:12

(particularly the final stanza, Isa. 53:10–12) forms the background for this concept. Certainly the representations of the sufferings of the Servant and their consequences are remarkably close to the content of Mark 10:45b:

Isaiah 53:10, 12	Mark 10:45b
When thou shalt make his soul an offering for sin (*'asham*) . . .	. . . to give his soul a ransom . . .
He bore the sin of many	. . . a ransom for many

Jeremias has affirmed that Mark 10:45 "relates word for word to Isaiah 53.10f, and indeed to the Hebrew text."[266] On the other hand, Barrett has objected that the terms in Mark 10:45 do not represent those in Isaiah 53; the basic concept in *'asham* is that of guilt, he contends, while *lutron* connotes equivalence. He therefore affirms that "It would be difficult . . . to claim that Mark's words point clearly to Isaiah 53 rather than to any other part of the Old Testament and Jewish literature."[267] This surely is an overstatement. *Lutron* is an equivalent rendered with a view to redemption. In Mark 10:45 it denotes redemption for debtors to God who have no hope of salvation without it. The "many" are assumed to be "sold under sin," to use the Pauline expression, and have no means of liberation from its bondage. One might suitably contend that it would be difficult to find any passage in Jewish literature *closer* in concept to Mark 10:45b than Isaiah 53:10–12.

Of course this is not to say that Mark 10:45 is not related to any other areas of Jewish thought concerning sin and redemption. Scholars have long emphasized as most important the relation between the *lutron* saying and the concept of the vicarious nature of the martyr's death. The language in Mark 10:45 relating to the giving of life (*dounai ten psuchen*) appears in a variety of contexts in the Maccabean histories—such as 4 Maccabees 6:29: *kai antipsuchon auton labe ten emen psuchen* ("Make my blood their cleansing and take my life as their life"). There is no need to oppose this type of thought to that of Isaiah 53, as though they were rival claimants for consideration as the true background of Mark 10:45. The Servant of God in Isaiah 53 can be considered the supreme example of the Righteous Man who suffers a martyr's death on behalf of others. Pesch cites G. Dautzenberg as observing that the term *antipsuchon* in 4 Maccabees 6:29 and 17:21 is "an unconventional conterpart to *'asham*" that denotes "a substitutionary and expiatory surrender of existence." Pesch adds that "The same applies to *lutron* in Mark 10:45 and *antilutron* in the grecized variant in 1 Timothy 2:6, insofar as Isaiah 53:10 is immediately in view."[268] The feature that binds Mark 10:45 more closely to Isaiah 53:10–12 is the universal range of the *lutron*. Like the *'asham* of the Servant, the *lutron* is offered "for many," which is to say "for all" (cf. 1 Tim. 2:6). This idea is unique in Jewish literature; Patsch observes that the idea of a death of a *martyr* having universal efficacy is nowhere attested within it—indeed, it is unthinkable. Accordingly, the concept in Mark 10:45 most surely reflects Isaiah 53:10–12.[269]

Of course the same thought is present in the saying relating to the cup at the Last Supper: "This is my covenant blood which is shed *for many*" (Mark

14:24). In considering the Last Supper we observed this link with the concept of the Servant's self-sacrifice for the many; it is to be pondered that this element of the teaching of Jesus concerning the ultimate service of his life finds expression in these two passages, which make so creative a use of the Fourth Servant Song.

As it turns out, this link extends beyond Mark 10:45 and 14:24. It is the Son of Man who surrenders himself in Mark 10:45, a fact that the exegetes are prone to characterize as "paradoxical" in light of the fact that in Daniel the Son of Man is said to come in order to be served (Dan. 7:14), whereas in the teaching of Jesus the Son of Man represents the kingdom of God among men precisely in terms of his coming to serve, and in Mark 8:31 that service consists in suffering death and then being vindicated by God in eschatological power. In reviewing the passion predictions, we observed the complex background of the concept, noting that the Son of Man who suffers binds together the features of the Righteous Sufferer, the Servant of the Lord, the rejected Prophet, and the Martyr. It is likely that the same is true of the Son of Man in Mark 10:45, who gives up his life as a *lutron anti pollon*, a freely offered sacrifice, in order that the kingdom of God might be opened for mankind in its totality. It is in the concept of the service of the Son of Man, the mediator of the kingdom of God, that the unity of the ministry and self-offering of Jesus is perceived. And it is because the Son of Man is the mediator of the divine sovereignty that his service spans the present and the future of the kingdom of God. The final Servant Song represents the astonished recognition of the nations in the judgment that the Servant had achieved an atonement for their sins; the Markan saying is declared in the consciousness that the deliverance achieved by the Son of Man renders possible life in the kingdom of God now and in the ultimate unveiling. And that consciousness is at one with the mind of Jesus.

4. THE SON OF MAN IN HIS PAROUSIA

a. The Son of Man and the Mission to Israel
Matthew 10:23

Before considering the meaning of this saying, we should note that some early authorities have an expanded version of the first clause. After the statement, "When they persecute you in this city, flee to the next," these read (with minor modifications), "and if they persecute you in the next, flee to the next."[270] Either the ancestor of the mass of manuscripts omitted the additional clause through homoioteleuton ("flee to the next" ends each clause), or the reverse process took place and an accidental repetition occurred. Most textual critics assume that the latter is the case. The meaning is not greatly affected whichever reading is adopted.[271]

Key to the interpretation of the saying is a decision on whether it entails one main idea or two—specifically, whether it is simply urging flight in situations of persecution or whether it is urging pursuit of the mission to Israel by means of a command to flee from places of persecution to other towns. On the former understanding, the saying conveys an assurance that "cities of refuge" for the disciples will not be lacking till the Son of Man comes. On the latter understanding, the saying emphasizes the necessity of continuing the mission to Israel despite opposition, since the task will not be completed before the coming of the Son of Man.

The difference is not automatically settled by one's view of the meaning of *telesete* here. The term can mean "come to an end" or "bring to an end," but the distinctions are not always as clear as one would wish. Matthew uses the term more than the other evangelists—a total of seven times—but five of these instances occur in his fivefold repetition of the formula "When Jesus completed these sayings" (7:28 etc.), in which context it may simply signify when he *finished* them. In the sixth instance of *telesete*, the verb means "to pay" (a tax). Bauer suggests that the seventh occurrence—the saying in Matthew 10:23—be interpreted "[you will not] finish (going through) the cities."[272] The term is most frequently used in the New Testament to mean "fulfilling" the scriptures or the requirement or purpose of God stated in them (see, for example, Luke 2:39, 18:31, and 22:37; Acts 13:29; Rom. 2:27; and James 2:8). Consonant with this, it is used in Luke 12:50 to mean "carrying through a task": "I have a baptism to be baptized with; and how I am constrained until it be *accomplished!*" If Matthew 10:23 were interpreted in keeping with this meaning of the term, it would suggest that the disciples would not *accomplish* their task in relation to the towns of Israel till the Son of Man comes, and that would denote the task of proclaiming to all Israel the good news of the kingdom and the call for repentance. Bonnard brings this out in his paraphrase: "You will not have completed evangelizing the towns of Israel"—but with some misgivings he then asks, "Can one give to *telesete* this meaning?"[273]

It is understandable that some scholars would be inclined to deny that the text is making reference to mission. It is generally accepted that the present context of the saying is attributable to the evangelist's arrangement of the material, that Matthew has enlarged the mission charge that appears in Mark (6:7–13) and Q (Luke 10:1–12) by bringing together sayings that are pertinent to the church's continuing mission. In 10:17–22 he places material that also appears in Mark 13:9–13, and to that he has added verse 23. Some scholars thus maintain that the idea that directions for mission are contained in verse 23 is due entirely to the context the evangelist has provided for it, since there is no mention of mission in the text itself.[274] Indeed, these scholars suggest that verses 17–18 provide a more immediate context, and these verses are concerned with persecution rather than the missionary task to Israel.[275]

This last observation was given a fresh turn by Schürmann, who maintains that verse 23 cannot be a Matthaean composition. He argues that the fact that the saying is reproduced with so particularistic a focus must be attributable to the evangelist's respect for the tradition in which he found it—and then, surprisingly, he suggests that the tradition in which he found it may have been Q. The bulk of Matthew 10:26–42 comes from Q, he notes, as the Lukan parallels show. And in the previous paragraph verses 19–20 are from Q (// Luke 12:11–12). Those verses have been given an introduction from Mark 13:9 (// Matt. 10:17–18) and additional material from Mark 13:12–13 (// Matt. 10:21–22); remove the introduction and the addition, says Schürmann, and verse 23 can be seen to follow verses 19–20—and this connection could have been made already in Q. The possibility is the more clearly recognizable in light of the Lukan version of verses 19–20: the link between the two passages is apparent in their phonetic consonance (*hotan de eisperosin humas . . . me merimnesete* and *hotan de diokoson humas . . . ou me telesete*) and their content: in Luke 12:11–12 the disciples are brought before authorities, and in Matthew they are persecuted. Both sayings provide comfort and encouragement (aid will be given by the Holy Spirit—the Lord will come for their help), and both sayings relate to opposition to disciples in an eschatological situation. Schürmann therefore concludes that this is the "life setting" to which Matthew 10:23 belongs: the statement is not a missionary command but an "apocalyptic persecution saying."[276]

Schürmann's argument that the saying in Matthew 10:23 was taken from Q is impressive, and it has been adopted by such differing writers as Vielhauer and Schnackenburg.[277] Nevertheless the deduction drawn from the connection of Matthew 10:23 with the Q saying verses 19–20 (// Luke 12:11–12) is not so clear. Schürmann assumed that the setting is simply the apocalyptic distress of the last days. But if we go beyond apocalyptic dogma and bear in mind that Jesus is addressing his disciples in this saying, then the wrath of synagogue leaders and rulers and authorities can most plausibly be assumed to have been caused by the disciples' proclamation of the message of Jesus. Vielhauer saw this clearly: "It is to be reckoned that the persecutions were mostly called forth through the missionary activity of the disciples and Christians."[278]

We can note the difference between the position of Jesus' followers generally and that of those who proclaimed his message by comparing the saying in Matthew 10:23 with the Q saying in Matthew 5:11–12 // Luke 6:22–23, which pronounces the blessedness of those who for the sake of the Son of Man (as Luke has it—Matthew records "for my sake") endure persecution and are rejected from the synagogue. In Luke 12:11–12 and Matthew 10:23 the situation is more severe: the disciples are brought to judgment before synagogue leaders and before the rulers and authorities, and are counseled to flee from one situation of persecution to another. This counsel is not directed to Christian residents of a town who are reviled for being followers of Jesus but rather to Christian visitors who encounter severe opposition—they should flee to the next town, on the understanding that there are many towns available to them before the Son of Man comes.

But what is meant by the "coming" of the Son of Man in this context? The question arises because the saying is addressed to the disciples, and so the prospect of the future appears to be not distant. As with Mark 9:1, attempts have been made to interpret the saying in a noneschatological fashion or to temper the eschatological prospect in an acceptable manner; indeed, the alternatives that have been proposed for interpreting this saying are virtually the same as those that have been proposed for interpreting Mark 9:1. We will be able to consider only a few of these interpretations in these pages; those interested in a fuller survey of the critical alternatives should consult the excellent study by M. Kunzi.[279]

The saying about the coming of the Son of Man has been interpreted as a reference to Jesus' return in his resurrection at Easter,[280] in the Holy Spirit at

Pentecost,[281] through the spread of the gospel and growth of the church,[282] and in judgment upon the Jews and their land, especially in the fall of Jerusalem.[283] One interpretation not applicable to Mark 9:1 is the return of Jesus to his disciples at the close of their itinerary in the Galilean towns and villages.[284] None of these suggestions appears to satisfy the plain meaning of the saying, especially when we take into account the other instances in which Matthew uses this language (e.g., in 16:28; 19:28; 23:39; 24:26–27, 29–31, 36–39, 42–44; 25:31; and 26:64). Thus, from early times scholars have acknowledged that the saying has to do with the parousia of Jesus.[285] Today the majority of scholars unhesitatingly adopt this viewpoint. The divergencies arise from attempts to relate the statement to the teaching of Jesus generally and to assess its authenticity.

It is doubtful that any interpretation of a saying of Jesus made such an impression on the church as Albert Schweitzer's exposition of Matthew 10:23. He regarded the discourse of Matthew 10 in its entirety as a mission charge of Jesus to his disciples when he sent them through Galilee. On that assumption, Schweitzer took verse 23 to mean that Jesus did not expect to see them again in the present age, for the parousia of the Son of Man would occur before the end of their itinerary. In fact, according to Schweitzer, the saying indicates that the disciples' mission would precipitate the final convulsions of this age: "Jesus' purpose is to set in motion the eschatological development of history, to let loose the final woes, the confusion and strife, from which shall issue the Parousia, and so to introduce the supra-mundane phase of the eschatological drama."[286] Then, he goes on, when the prediction was not fulfilled, Jesus had to come to terms with the fact that the parousia had not occurred. It led him to determine to go to Jerusalem and there to bring in the end by bearing the messianic woes himself. Jesus' problem in Matthew 10:23 has been the problem of the church ever since in relation to his teaching on the end, says Schweitzer:

> The whole history of "Christianity" down to the present day, that is to say, the real inner history of it, is based on the delay of the Parousia, the non-occurrence of the Parousia, the abandonment of eschatology, the progress and completion of the "de-eschatologising" of religion which has been connectd therewith. It should be noted that the nonfulfilment of Matt. x.23 is the first postponement of the Parousia. We have therefore here the first significant date in the "history of Christianity"; it gives to the work of Jesus a new direction, otherwise inexplicable.[287]

It is extraordinary that a man of Schweitzer's intellectual brilliance could not bring himself to accept the simple fact that the discourses of Matthew were constructed by the evangelist from sources available to him. It needs no more than a synopsis of the gospels to convince humbler students of that. The limits of the Markan and Q traditions relating to the mission charge appear to be reached in Matthew 10:16. The passage that follows in 10:17–22 envisages a fierceness of opposition not at all characteristic of the early ministry of Jesus. Equally out of place at this juncture is the statement of 10:38, "He who does not take up his cross and follow after me is not worthy of me." As the latter belongs to a later period of the ministry of Jesus, so Matthew 10:23 assumes a context later than that of the mission recorded in Mark 6:7–12 par. The link in Q, postulated by Schürmann (i.e. that Matt. 10:23 follows on Matt. 10:19–20 // Luke 12:11–12), harmonizes well with the saying about bearing a cross with its assumption that to follow Jesus entails sharing his suffering and dying like him on behalf of the kingdom of God. Contrary to Schweitzer's hypothesis, then, Matthew 10 reckons with the impending *death* of Jesus, not with the *parousia* of the Son of Man before the return of the disciples. Matthew's procedure in drawing up his discourse is not due to a total loss of historical sense. Writing at his distance from the ministry of Jesus, he doubtless assumed that his readers understood that in chapter 10 he was linking the charge to the Twelve on *their* mission with sayings of Jesus that have bearing on the continuing mission of *the church* (Matt. 28:18–20). By this means the address to the Twelve sent out into Galilee becomes the point of departure for an address to disciples sent out into all the world. The notion, then, that Matthew 10:23 is "the beginning of the history of Christianity" because it marks the first postponement of the parousia is based on a critical mistake of the most elementary order—a mistake, in fact, conceived in the mind of a pretheological student and never corrected by him.[288]

Though one may reject Schweitzer's view that Matthew 10:23 relates to an *immediate* parousia of the Son of Man, the saying does appear to have emanated from a context in which the parousia is anticipated in the not-distant future. It is of interest that the great conservative New Testament scholars Schlatter and Zahn did not hesitate to make this assumption in interpreting the saying. In his commentary on Matthew, Schlatter stresses the pertinence of the saying to the apostles in their mission to their people, suggesting that it is represented as a continuing battle with a hostile nation; indeed, he goes so far as to state that "the complete destruction of the Palestinian Church is anticipated," although the promise is made that the Lord will confess his followers as his own in the power of God when he comes to their rescue.[289] In his profound study *Die Geschichte des Christus*, Schlatter cites Matthew 10:23 as one of the sayings of Jesus that show that the entire picture of the future relates to his own generation; it is, he says, authentic "near expectation."[290] Zahn similarly declares that Matthew 10:23 is making reference to the ministry of the disciples in Palestine, suggesting that that is where they will live and preach from place to place till the Lord comes and brings to an end the time of their persecution. The saying presents not only the problem of the expectation of an imminent end, says Zahn, but of tension between the nations sharing in the salvation of the kingdom (Matt. 8:11), which involves the disciples' ministry to them (cf. Matt. 5:13ff. and 28:18–20) and the assumption that the disciples will remain in Palestine till the parousia (although the latter is to some extent explained through Matthew 22:1–14 and 23:38–39). Zahn holds that Matthew 10:23 constitutes evidence that the gospel was written prior to the fall of Jerusalem and suggests that the fall subsequently compelled the church to give the saying a "flexible significance."[291]

Since these two writers presented their arguments, surprisingly little has been added to the understanding of Matthew 10:23 as a saying presenting a near expectation of the parousia. Kümmel, in his various dealings with the text, has been concerned to show that it assumes neither an immediate nor a distant parousia but a parousia in the comparatively near future. He contends that the two halves of the text were originally separate and that verse 23b is a detached saying, indicating that the Son of Man will arrive before the disciples have finished proclaiming the kingdom of God in Israel; accordingly, he adds that the text assumes that the parousia will take place in the lifetime of Jesus' hearers.[292]

Resistance to such an interpretation of Matthew 10:23 is manifest in a group of exegetes who agree that the saying relates the mission of the disciples to the parousia of Christ but believe that no delimitation of the time of the parousia is thereby indicated. This viewpoint is especially associated with Schniewind. In justice to him, we should note that he acknowledges the similarity between the views presented in Matthew 10:23 and Mark 9:1 and 13:30, and he adds that "If Jesus, like the first Christians, expected the last judgment speedily, that must not be interpreted away." He attempts to ease the tension between Matthew 10:23 and 28:18–20 in two ways: first by affirming that the expectation of an imminent parousia is derived from the conviction that future judgment and eternal salvation had already begun in Jesus' word and work, and second by affirming that Matthew 10:23 accords with other sayings in that gospel that speak of Israel's unbelief and God's rejection of them (e.g., 8:11–12, 21:43, and 23:38–39; see also Mark 12:1–11 par.). Accordingly, says Schniewind, the incomplete mission to Israel presupposes that salvation was offered first to Israel and then later declared to the Gentiles also, and so "There could lie in our saying a last hope, as Paul utters it in Romans 11; only when the Son of Man comes will Israel recognize whom it has rejected and turn to him."[293] By this means a wider horizon is opened for Matthew 10:23 than is actually given in it.

Michaelis sought a mediating view of Matthew 10:23. He and Martin Werner were both professors in the university of Bern when Werner's work on the development of Christian theology appeared,[294] and Michaelis felt obliged to enter into debate with his colleague. Werner affirmed Schweitzer's interpretation of Matthew 10:23 and made the delay of the parousia the cornerstone of his reconstruction of the history of theology. Michaelis in reply urged that Matthew 10 does not really deal with the end of the age, that verse 23 is not in the first instance a declaration about the coming of the Son of Man but is rather speaking of the destiny of Israel. The issue of the delay of the parousia does pose a genuine problem in the New Testament, Michaelis admits, but this relates not to an *immediate* expectation but to a *near* expectation, which is quite different.[295] In his exposition of Matthew 10, he maintains that verse 23b is the ground for verse 23a, and that verse 23b relates to mission work, not simply to flight for safety. The negative form of the saying was intended to counteract the idea that where violent opposition is met, one should remain in order to try to win the people; Jesus counseled flight because he wanted to deter the disciples from believing that they could complete their mission to the cities of Israel in this age. According to Michaelis, the passage implies that the conversion of all Israel will be far from concluded when the Son of Man comes, although he notes that verse 23 does not state that Israel's conversion will *remain* incomplete: "Behind this saying rather the hope stands that God in his way will complete what the disciples began." From here, then, a line may be drawn to Romans

11:15, but not to further deductions about the cessation of mission to Israel in the times of the Gentiles. Of that Jesus gives no hint.[296]

We have not taken up the question of the authenticity of Matthew 10:23 in these discussions. In precritical days it simply was not questioned, and in later times it was, by virtue of being so singular a saying, commonly assumed to have emanated from Jesus (Schweitzer, as we saw, regarded it as the key to the message and ministry of Jesus). Nevertheless, this viewpoint has been opposed by some scholars, partly on historical and partly on theological grounds. On the one hand, the saying has been linked with Matthew 10:5–6 and 15:24 as expressing an attitude to the Gentiles contrary to the spirit of Jesus; some hold that it must have arisen out of the pressing situation of the Palestinian church in its mission, possibly reflecting the opposition of Jewish Christians to the Gentile mission led by Paul.[297] On the other hand, some scholars maintain that the logion embodies an eschatology characteristic of the primitive Jewish community rather than of Jesus;[298] naturally, those scholars who hold that Jesus did not refer to the Son of Man, much less to a parousia, are drawn to this interpretation.[299]

Of one thing we may be sure: this saying was *received* by Matthew, not created by him. There is little in its linguistic formation that is distinctively Matthaean. The verb *diokein* ("persecute") is an exception—Matthew employs it in various Q passages from which it is absent in Luke (see, for example, Matt. 5:11, 12, 44)[300]—but in general Matthew simply uses it to represent an idea or replace a term found in Luke (cf., for example, Luke 6:22 and Matt. 5:11). Contrary to Schürmann's contention, the term *telein* is not specifically Matthaean,[301] for apart from the fivefold formula that closes the discourses (Matt. 7:28 etc.) *telein* occurs again in Matthew only at 17:24, with a different meaning ("to pay"). Moreover, the content of the saying stands in tension with the universalist utterances of the evangelist. No doubt he had no difficulty in holding together the two traditions of mission to Israel and mission to the nations, but he is unlikely to have created so acute a tension as that between Matthew 10:23 and 28:18–20 to express a *heilsgeschichtliche* view without making that view explicit in some other saying of his creation. Matthew surely found the logion of 10:23 in one of his sources, whether it was that which Streeter calls "M" or the common sayings source, Q.

Ultimately, I believe this saying presents us with an issue to which the church has paid too little attention—namely, the Jewishness of Jesus and the way he interpreted his vocation in relation to his own people. When I commenced theological studies it was difficult to name a leading New Testament scholar in England who believed that Jesus could have uttered Matthew 10:5–6 and 23. After reading Schlatter's *Die Geschichte des Christus* I concluded that the British had forgotten that Jesus was a Jew. More precisely, they had not contemplated what it meant to Jesus that he was a Jew, sent to proclaim to his own people the dawn of the fulfillment of the promise on which they had waited through long centuries. Jeremias is surely right in maintaining (1) that Jesus limited his own ministry to Israel, (2) that he looked for the Gentiles to enter the kingdom of God and for many of his own people to be excluded through unbelief, and (3) that his redemptive work for the kingdom of God included all over whom that sovereignty was to extend—that is to say, all of mankind.[302] It is in harmony with these features that we accept the testimony of Matthew 10:5b–6 that Jesus sent his disciples on mission to Israel only. Indeed, it is likely that we are meant to understand from Matthew 10:5b–6 that the disciples were sent at this time into Galilee only, and not even into Judea. (According to the fourth evangelist, the ministry to Judea began at an earlier date—see John 3:22–30 and 4:1–3.) Matthew 10:23 belongs to a later period of time, when resistance to the message of Jesus had increased and it had become clear that the disciples in their continuing mission would face the kind of opposition that Jesus himself encountered. Why should it appear strange that Jesus should warn his disciples of this prospect and counsel them concerning it? And why should anyone complain that Matthew 10:23 contains no reference to the Samaritans or the Gentile world? The subject of the statement is the task of the disciples in relation to their own nation in their own land and the response they should expect to the end. Jesus is not yet speaking of his plan for the nations or what he willed that his disciples should do in respect to them at this point.

Here we have to recognize the limitations imposed on us by the brevity of the statement in Matthew 10:23 and the limits of its original context. It is clear that Jesus anticipated that Gentiles would participate with believing Israel in the kingdom of God (see Matt. 8:11–12, 25:34–40, etc.). Since those "sons of the kingdom" who reject the word of the kingdom given through Jesus (see Matt. 7:26ff., 11:20ff., and 12:41–42) and fail to produce the fruit of the word of God in their lives (see Matt. 7:16ff. and 25:41ff.) will be excluded from the kingdom, it is to be assumed that those Gentiles who are included will have responded to the word of the kingdom declared among them and will have lived lives well-pleasing to God. When and by whom is this proclamation made? Jeremias contends that God himself is understood as gathering the Gentiles and leading them in pilgrimage to Zion in the last days.[303] It is possible that Jesus viewed that "miracle" of the divine gathering of the nations as operative through the witness of his followers in and beyond Israel, since his exaltation in resurrection would initiate the "latter days" leading to his parousia and thus the time for the nations to be gathered to God.

This is not the place to discuss the origin of Mark 13:10 // Matthew 24:14, but we might just note that it is on the whole less than illuminating to set one isolated saying (Matt. 10:23) over against another isolated saying (Mark 13:10) when both raise problems of their own and both are closely related to Jesus' teaching on the kingdom of God and his ministry to bring Israel and the nations under the saving sovereignty. Suffice it to say that the one who viewed himself as Son of Man and mediator of the kingdom of God in his ministry, in the service of his death, in his exaltation to God's right hand, and in his parousia would inevitably have been aware of his obligation to his own people and would have acted accordingly during his life and would also have taken care to make provision for his followers to fulfill it after his death; and at the same time, he would have been aware that through his work the door of the kingdom was to be opened for the nations and that they would have to hear of it. Informed by the Easter events, Matthew would have perceived that *heilsgeschichtliche* process.[304] Reflecting on the path he had to travel for the kingdom, Jesus would have advanced to his climactic act of redemption with a sure and certain hope.

b. The Son of Man and Judgment
Mark 8:38, Matthew 16:27, Luke 9:26

We looked at the basic issues surrounding this logion when we considered the Q version (Luke 12:8–9 // Matthew 10:32–33), but there are elements in the Markan version that call for some additional investigation, particularly with respect to its conclusion.

First we must ask whether we are in fact dealing with one saying or two—that is, whether we have one statement reproduced differently in Mark than in Q or whether the two traditions offer related but separate logia. Cranfield favors the latter alternative.[305] Vincent Taylor argues that there are three statements altogether in Q and Mark—statements relating to "confessing," "denying," and "being ashamed of" Jesus—with corresponding responses of the Son of Man in the future judgment.[306] Borsch takes yet a different line, arguing that the Q saying coincides with Mark 8:38a (in a double rather than a single form) and that Mark 8:38b is a separate saying that is reproduced in a more original form in Matthew 16:27.[307] Borsch's thesis was anticipated by C. F. Burney, who maintained that Matthew's version is prior on the ground that Matthew's statement in Aramaic falls into a perfect Kina form, whereas the statement appearing in Mark and Luke shows no trace of Kina or any other form of rhythm.[308] Most exegetes, however, agree that the Markan and Q sayings should be viewed as a single saying the variants of which arose partly in the period of transmission and partly through the redaction of the evangelists. This explanation is likely correct, although it tends to gloss over the difficulties raised by the Markan additions in Mark 8:38, which are more complex than they appear at first sight. In sum, then, we should approach the whole matter with an open mind.

The fact that Mark presents only the negative couplet might reflect a concern on his part that disciples facing persecution would forsake the Christian confession—a dire possibility, since entry into the coming kingdom of God depends on the attitude toward Jesus maintained during one's life. This consideration led Tödt to observe that this saying makes "a primarily *soteriological* statement: a break in the fellowship on earth will be followed by the loss of the redemptive fellowship in God's reign."[309] While the observation is correct from the viewpoint of the intention of the saying, it remains the case that a soteriological statement of this kind has Christological implications, and these call for examination.

One simple way of disposing of the problem of Mark's additions (relative, that is, to the Q version) has been proposed by M. Horstmann; she argues that they are all secondary, mainly on the grounds that they spoil the poetic parallelism of the Q version (in v. 38b they go beyond it).[310] This argument is too simple, however. If we are to accept poetic parallelism as holding the key to the issues, then we will have to give more serious consideration to Burney's view—namely, that Mark has conjoined in abbreviated form parallel traditions of the saying in Q (Luke 12:8–9) and Matthew, and in so doing has largely destroyed their poetic forms.

Before investing too much effort in investigating any of these arguments, however, we would do well to ask whether they have not all been too quick to assume that the Q tradition has reproduced the original saying of Jesus faithfully *and in its entirety*. It is possible, after all, that the differences between the Markan and Q versions of the saying may be attributable to Mark's dependence on an earlier and fuller form of the saying. In any case, we would do well to exercise a special care in applying the criteria of poetic forms when attempting to determine the original form of a saying. Unquestionably many of Jesus' sayings manifest a clear poetic structure, but no one would suggest that Jesus undeviatingly observed poetic forms in every sentence he uttered. In Matthew 7:3–5, for example, poetic structure is clearly evident in verses 3 and 5 but not in verse 4; to my knowledge nobody has been tempted to strike out verse 4 on that account, for it is integral to the pericope and it is both striking and amusing in its right.

Mark commences his statement in 8:38 thus: "Whoever is ashamed of me *and my words in this adulterous and sinful generation. . . .*" The italicized phrases are not included in the Q version, and they obviously disturb the parallelism. The phrase "and my words" could well be a Markan addition; they find a parallel in the phrase "for the sake of the gospel" in Mark 8:35 (cf. Matt. 16:25, Luke 9:24) and Mark 10:29 (cf. Matt. 19:29). Mark gives evidence of a characteristic appreciation for double phraseology; in 8:35, for example, he expands "for the sake of *me*" with the addition "*and of the gospel*," precisely as in 10:29. Thus, it is quite possible that the phrase "of me *and of my words*" in 8:38 is a similar expansion, made in order to clarify what it means to be ashamed of Jesus: it is to repudiate Jesus as the Bearer of the word of God and so deny the truth of his proclamation from God.

This hypothesis does not explain his inclusion of the phrase "in this adulterous and sinful generation," however, for this is *not* typically Markan: the adjectives appear nowhere else in Mark. The Q version of the request for a sign (Matthew 12:39 // Luke 11:29) qualifies the term "generation," but the Markan version (8:12) does not. It is likely therefore that the reference to "this adulterous and sinful generation" in Mark 8:38 was in the tradition received by Mark, carrying the implication that the generation that rejected Jesus was thereby showing itself to be unfaithful to God much as its forebears had shown themselves to be unfaithful in the days of the prophets.[311] The phrase is not uncharacteristic of Jesus' teaching.[312]

More difficult to determine is the origin of the last clause of Mark 8:38: "when he comes in the glory of his Father and of the holy angels." Many scholars view these words as an expansion of the Q statement in light of the apocalyptic concepts that were available to Mark at the time of composition.[313] Streeter, in one of his earliest published essays, argues that this passage is a prime example of the apocalypticizing tendencies of the gospel traditions: Mark added the clause relating to the parousia to the Q version of the saying, and Matthew omitted the reference to being ashamed of the Son of Man and elaborated the remaining eschatological reference, thereby changing the character of the saying from a statement of moral purpose to a purely apocalyptic prophecy: "The series Lk. 12.9, Mk. 8.38, Mt. 16.27 gives in epitome the eschatological evolution in the Gospels."[314]

Many recent writers, while expressing themselves more cautiously than Streeter, have affirmed their basic adherence to this viewpoint. Pesch observes that through the addition of the last clause in Mark 8:38, the "where" question of the Q saying has given way to the "when" question, throwing into relief the time of the coming of the Son of Man Jesus.[315] Tödt points out that the sovereignty of the Son of Man is heightened in the Markan representation in that the glory of the Father is given to him and the angels of God become his retinue: "He is no longer confronted by the angels; they now accompany him, and are subject to him."[316] Other scholars stress that consonant with this increase in the power and glory being accorded to the Son of Man is a transformation in the representation of the role he is to play in the judgment. Says Horstmann, "He is no longer the witness, standing at the side of men before the heavenly judgment forum of the angels of God, but he is now the majestic Judge, in whose service the angels stand, indeed who are now actually 'his angels' (Mk. 13.27)."[317] Moreover, the statement that the Son of Man comes "in the glory of *his Father*" clearly indicates that the Son of *Man* is the Son of *God*—an equation that J. A. T. Robinson suggests is "unparalleled either in Jewish usage or in that of primitive Christianity."[318] Finally, many scholars argue that it is relatively easy to see how the Q version of the saying could have evolved into the version in Mark and Matthew, but it is a good deal more difficult to see how the Q version could ever have developed from the version in Mark 8:38.[319] Accordingly, the majority of scholars have come to view Mark 8:38b as a later addition to the saying preserved in Q. Despite this consensus of opinion, however, it would be best to reserve judgment on the point in light of the fact that none of the evidence adduced is sufficiently compelling to make that conclusion certain.

We would do well to take a closer look at this last argument concerning the priority of the Q version to the Markan version of the saying, since it is sometimes viewed as delivering the *coup de grace* to the discussion. The variant forms of the saying make it clear at the very least that the Q form was by no means considered sacrosanct (any more than it was in the case of any of the other sayings of Jesus). Mark, or his source, reproduced only one couplet of the original two, Matthew deleted the references to the Son of Man in both, and Luke altered the form of the second couplet, first by omitting the reference to the Son of Man and second by setting the verb in the passive in order to accommodate the saying to the context in which he placed it. In addition, it is clear that an evangelist and/or the bearers of the gospel tradition were not beyond excluding an unambiguous reference to the parousia from a dominical saying: with a few notable exceptions the majority of New Testament scholars agree both that Luke 22:67–70 is a paraphrase of the tradition preserved in Mark 14:61–62 and that the Luke passage has *eliminated* the reference to the parousia contained in the Mark passage. This would be the more significant if, as some scholars believe, Luke received the substance of 22:67–70 from an earlier tradition and was not himself responsible for the form of verse 69.[320] If this were the case, it would suggest that there was a process at work within the tradition *contrary* to that described by Streeter, a process that is in any case more drastically exemplified in the Johannine tradition. Theoretically, therefore, it should be acknowledged that the original form of the logion could have consisted of elements now preserved in both Mark and Q.

The other features mentioned appear in a different light when we note that both the Q and the Markan sayings reflect the same biblical source—namely, the judgment scene of Daniel 7:9–10, 13–14. God comes to hold a session of his court, attended by myriads of angels, for the purpose of judging the one who has disturbed the earth's peace and to initiate the kingdom of promise. One like a son of man comes with the clouds and receives the kingdom on behalf of the saints. Reflection on the passage has traditionally involved a focus on the Son of Man's coming with the clouds of heaven and his part in the judgment and advent of the kingdom of God, especially among those exegetes who see a connection with the dragon myth. The latter consideration apart, we find striking testimony to the validity of this emphasis in Jesus' declaration at his trial in Mark 14:62. We simply cannot attribute a development of this kind to the community of Jesus' followers between the formulation of Luke 12:8–9 and that of Mark 8:38.

Acknowledging then the setting of the two sayings in the Danielic scene of judgment, we must conclude that Pesch's comment about the "where" question giving way to the "when" question is hardly to the point. It is the "when" that makes the "where" conceivable: the joint theophany of God with the Son of Man becomes the theophany of God *in* the Son of Man when the latter is understood as the mediator of the divine sovereignty to man. In this situation there is bound to be a magnifying of the role of the Son of Man; as the representative of God, he is permitted to share in the divine glory and to be accompanied by angelic retinue.[321] This latter feature is not so startling as the representation in Daniel 7:13 and Mark 14:62 that the Son of Man comes with the clouds of heaven, since that image distinctively denotes appearing in the manner of God. In Mark 8:38 it is to be assumed that the Son of Man is both attended by the angels and "confronted" by such in the judgment of heaven's court.

But what is his function in that context? Is the Son of Man advocate/prosecutor, or is he judge? Recognizing the pictorial nature of the images employed, we should ask whether it is necessary to press that question, for all forms of the saying make it plain that the destiny of man is settled by the declaration of the Son of Man. Interestingly enough, there is a version, or rather development, of our saying that explicitly combines the elements of advocate and judge in relation to Jesus—namely, Revelation 3:5:

> He who is victorious shall thus be robed all in white; his name *I will never strike off the roll of the living*, for in the presence of my Father and his angels *I will acknowledge* him as mine.

Here the Christ assumes the right to declare a verdict and even act on it, yet at the same time he confesses before the court of heaven the worthiness of a faithful follower to be a citizen of the kingdom of God, as though to seek the concurrence of the court in the decision. This mode of representing the role of the Son of Man in judgment is entirely in keeping with the spirit of the saying we are considering, for it indicates that by his acknowledgment or denial of men the Son of Man determines the issue of the judgment, and therefore *participates in the judgment with God.* Accordingly, we ought not to stress a contrast between the notions of the witness of the Son of Man and the judgment by God.[322]

The fact that in Mark 8:38 the Son of Man is related to God in such manner that God may be named "his Father" calls for comment. The relationship is not asserted but assumed—it is so casually mentioned that it slips the notice of most readers. While the precise mode of statement in Mark 8:38 is not found elsewhere, the relationship between Son of Man and Son of God appears elsewhere and is fundamental in the Johannine literature.[323] The notion that the term "son of God" was unknown as a messianic expression in late Judaism is false. Once the Messiah was acknowledged to be the "Son of God," even in strictly Jewish terms, and the expression "Son of Man" came to be the preferred name for the Bearer of the kingdom of God, then it was inevitable that the Son of Man should be seen as Son of God. The fact that the phrase rarely appears in the gospel traditions of the sayings is not significant; Jesus was not inclined to use the term *Messiah* either. The expression *Son of Man* was simply better suited to his teaching and purpose. We might note, however, that since we have already seen that Jesus added his own connotations to the significance of the expression *Son of Man* in light of his understanding of his mission and destiny in relation to the kingdom of God, we should not be surprised to find in his teaching elements in the interpretation of the expression *Son of God* that are different from and supplemental to Jewish usage.

What, then, are we to conclude with regard to the origin of Mark 8:38b? Objections to the thesis that it forms part of the saying reproduced in Q and Mark appear, on closer examination, to be less significant than is frequently claimed. We saw that the original Q version must have run somewhat as follows:

> Everyone who confesses me before men
>   the Son of Man will confess before the angels (of God);
> everyone who denies me before men
>   the Son of Man will deny before the angels (of God).

The assumption that the Markan addition reflects an earlier version of the saying opens up many new possibilities. Strict parallelism would demand that the parousia would have been mentioned in both clauses in the same manner. But it could have occurred in the first clause and been understood in the latter, or it could have formed part of the second clause and been viewed as controlling the first. There could also have been a more flexible relation between Q and Mark than any of these approaches would suggest. Had Mark simply elaborated the Q version, the result would look something like this:

> Everyone who confesses me before men
>   the Son of Man will confess,
>   when he comes in the glory of his Father with the holy angels.
> Everyone who denies me before men,
>   the Son of Man will deny,
>   when he comes in the glory of his Father with the holy angels.

But this strikes me as somewhat wooden. Mark might have been moved to alter such a construction by elaborating the first sentence, as in the following reading:

> Everyone who denies me before this adulterous and sinful generation,
> the Son of Man will deny before the angels (of God).

While we are unable to determine the original form of the statement, we have good reason to suspect that there would have been some mention made of the parousia in it. We know no other instance in which Mark added a parousia reference to a saying he received without such a reference, and its presence is in keeping both with the Danielic passage on which the Q version depends and the declaration of Jesus before the Sanhedrin (Mark 14:62). If this passage was an exception to the rule, and Mark did add the parousia reference, we should view it not as a distortion but as an expansion that rightly interprets the saying, in view of its relation to Daniel 7:13. Such an introduction of a reference to the parousia could have been prompted by the same motive as Mark's reproduction of the denial clause without that of the confession—namely, to emphasize the consequences of repudiating Jesus before men. The Lord of the disciples is to come for their vindication and to bring the kingdom to its purposed conclusion; hence, the parousia should be the occasion of unparalleled joy for the Christian, and on no account be an occasion of shame (see 1 John 2:28).

c. The Son of Man Exalted and Appearing
Mark 14:62

Unlike many of the eschatological statements of Jesus, this crucial utterance is not an isolated saying but is closely bound to its context; it is represented as an answer to a question directed to Jesus on trial before the High Priest. Modern discussion of the passage has been dominated by Lietzmann's classic essay on the trial of Jesus.[324] Motivated by a desire to demonstrate that the Markan trial narrative has a sound historical basis, Lietzmann was nevertheless led to the conclusion that the account of the trial *before the Sanhedrin* is historically unsupportable. In his view the report of such a trial originated in the fact that the early Christians knew that the Jewish leaders handed Jesus over to Pilate as a messianic pretender, and they were moved by a general tendency to place the blame for Jesus' death squarely on the shoulders of the Jewish leaders. Thus, argues Lietzmann, the early Christians were motivated to construct a full trial scene (Mark 14:55–65) out of the brief meeting of the Sanhedrin recorded in Mark 15:1. Since the altercation between the High Priest and Jesus in Mark 14:61–63 forms the culminating point of the trial, those who accept Lietzmann's argument naturally assume that the saying in Mark 14:62 is a construction of the community.

Many scholars have cited and elaborated upon Lietzmann's argument, but few have acknowledged that he later restated his position more tentatively. "It must remain undecided," he wrote, "whether in this description [Mark 14:55–65] weakened reminiscences of something which really took place have been retained."[325] The grounds Lietzmann adduces for his conclusions are, in reality, surprisingly insubstantial.[326] In the light of subsequent research one point alone appears to be formidable, and it has become the subject of prolonged debate—namely, the competence of the Sanhedrin to try cases involving capital punishment and to carry out the sentence. Lietzmann accepts the judgment of J. Juster that the Sanhedrin did have this authority (contrary to the denial expressed in John 18:31),[327] and he proceeds to observe that had the Sanhedrin used its powers and condemned Jesus to death, he would have died by stoning; thus, concludes Lietzmann, the fact that Jesus died by crucifixion shows that the Romans alone were responsible for it. The vigorous debate on this issue can be followed in the excursus in the latest edition of Blinzler's work on the trial of Jesus.[328] In my judgment Blinzler, A. N. Sherwin-White, and D. R. Catchpole have put forth arguments compelling enough to make Juster's position untenable, and with it Lietzmann's view of the Sanhedrin trial.[329]

Pesch has sought a way out of the dilemma of the historical problems by calling attention to the situation of the Jewish authorities. He maintains that even if the Sanhedrin did possess authority in religious trials both to pronounce a death sentence and to carry it out, the exercise of that right in a public stoning of Jesus would have been highly inopportune in view of the possibility of an uproar among the people. Further, if the prohibition of Mishnah Sanhedrin 4.1 was in force at that time, forbidding sentence of capital punishment within a day, the wisest legal move would have been simply to pronounce a judgment and then lodge an accusation with Pilate; indeed, since the governor was staying in Jerusalem for the feast, such a procedure would have appeared unavoidable. Pesch concludes that "Insofar as the Sanhedrin was only an organ of judgment for the High Priest, who for his part was answerable to the Roman Prefect, the proceedings, as the pre-Markan passion narrative describes them, are immediately comprehensible."[330]

All this may seem a somewhat negative diversion from the path to considering the significance of the saying in Mark 14:62, but it does serve the positive function of stressing the relation of this saying to other instruction of Jesus on the vocation and destiny of the Son of Man. For the statement is no mere retort in a debate between Jesus and the Jewish leaders on the nature of the Messiah; it is rather the ultimate confession of Jesus as to his identity and the goal of his mission. In this saying he strips away the last vestige of the messianic reserve that characterized his ministry, albeit in a context of total rejection and doom. From a position of utter humiliation before his foes he claims God's vindication for himself in a coming revelation of his right to rule.[331] The saying therefore brings to completion his instruction relating to the sufferings and exaltation of the Son of Man in the predictions of the passion. In those sayings, as we have seen, there is discernible a conjunction of the destiny of the suffering righteous man, the rejected prophet, the Servant of the Lord, and the martyr for God's cause, suffering at the hands of men but raised by God to a position of glory with himself, there to be seen by his adversaries and to participate in their judgment. Significantly, in late Jewish writings there is a recurring reference to God's raising his suffering and martyred servants to his right hand. For example,

Testament of Job 33:2ff. represents Job (a former king!) as declaring to the kings who wail over his sufferings:

> My throne is in the supra-terrestrial realm,
>   and its splendor and majesty are from the right hand of the Father in the
>   heavens.

In the Apocalypse of Elijah it is written of the martyrs,

> The Lord says: "I shall place them at my right hand, they will render thanks for the others; they will conquer the Son of Iniquity, they will see the destruction of the heaven and of the earth, they will receive the thrones of glory and crowns." (37:3–4 [3:49–50 in Rosentiehl's edition])

Similarly Testament of Benjamin 10:5–6 states,

> Keep the commandments of God, until the Lord shall reveal his salvation to all Gentiles. And then shall ye see Enoch, Noah, and Shem, and Abraham, and Isaac, and Jacob, rising on the right hand in gladness.

This tradition of the suffering and martyred righteous raised to the right hand of God is so striking that it led Pesch to suggest that it would be misleading to posit a simple derivation of Mark 14:62 from Psalm 110:1 and Daniel 7:13.[332] From the viewpoint of tradition history, Pesch's point is justifiable. It should not be overlooked, however, that the conjunction of Psalm 110:1 and Daniel 7:13 is extraordinarily apt, in that the resultant thought harmonizes remarkably well with the tradition that Pesch is concerned to emphasize. Psalm 110:1 speaks of a king who is *exalted by God above his enemies and is given a place at God's right hand*.[333] So impressed is J. R. Donahue with the correspondence between Psalm 110:1 and the trial scene in Mark that he speaks of the latter as a "midrash" on the psalm.[334] In view of the broader context in Judaism of the connection between suffering and exaltation, such a suggestion is hardly necessary. There are grounds for believing that the psalm was a tributary of the stream of tradition that represented the righteous and martyrs as exalted to the right hand of God.[335]

Yet the psalm supplies only part of the imagery of Mark 14:62. He who is seated at the right hand of God is not the King-Messiah but the Son of Man, coming with the clouds of heaven, a representation taken from Daniel 7:13. In our understanding of the vision, the distinctive element in the concept of the Son of Man is his representing the element of initiative in the manifestation of the kingdom of God—he *comes* with the clouds of heaven, and as representative of the divine sovereignty he participates in the judgment that initiates the rule of God. Aspects of both judgment and rule are implied in the martyrological application of Psalm 110:1, but they are emphasized in the imagery of the appearing of the Son of Man, and in this respect the Danielic citation complements the thought of Psalm 110:1 and brings it to completion. But again, we should note that it is *the representative of the kingdom of God on trial* who declares this prophecy of vindication. As Son of Man, Jesus has served among men as representative and mediator of the divine rule, revealing it in word and action right up to the time of his arrest in Jerusalem (as witness his entry into the city, his cleansing of the temple, and his continued witness to the populace and the authorities). The hostility of the representatives of the nation to the representative of the kingdom of God reaches its apex in the Sanhedrin scene, as the rejected Son of Man confesses his identity, declares his destiny, and broadly hints at the doom of his judges. The ancient pattern of the suffering and exaltation of the righteous representative of God moves toward its supreme embodiment in the humiliation and vindication of the Son of Man.

It is in this light that we should reconsider the oft-repeated argument that Mark 14:62 is alien to the teaching of Jesus first because he did not use the Old Testament in this manner, and second because the allusion to Psalm 110:1 and Daniel 7:13 reflects the church's experience of Easter.[336] Far from being alien to the teaching of Jesus, the saying is, as we have seen, in closest harmony with it. Nor is there anything mechanical about the conjunction of motifs from Psalm 110:1 and Daniel 7:13; in this setting they are welded into an integral part of the tradition of suffering and vindication that was so important in the eschatological-apocalyptic tradition of Israel. We might note that Jesus' citation of Psalm 110:1 in Mark 12:35–37 has implications very similar to those at the heart of Mark 14:62. We should not discount this earlier pericope on the grounds that it was relevant to the teachers of the early church: it is also characteristic of the teaching of Jesus, for it is indicative of the transition from the traditional concept of the Messiah as Son of David (cf. Ps. of Sol. 17) to the concept of the Messiah as Son of Man, which is central to the teaching of Jesus and which determined the nature of his ministry. As Neugebauer has pointed out, the unanswered question raised by Jesus in Mark 12:37 receives its answer in Mark 14:62: the Messiah is David's *Lord* as well as his *son* because he is the Son of Man, destined to be revealed as the One appointed by God to judge and to rule in the kingdom of God.[337]

The idea that the linking of Psalm 110:1 and Daniel 7:13 required the church's conviction of Jesus' resurrection also fails to take into account other available evidence. In discussing this matter, Borsch expresses his conviction that the conjunction of the two texts was probably part of the Jewish tradition inherited by the church.[338] This thesis would appear to be confirmed by the Midrash on Psalm 2:7. The passage begins with the text on which comment is to be made—"I will declare the decree of the Lord. He said unto me, 'Thou art my son' "—and continues as follows:

> The children of Israel are declared to be sons in the decree of the Law, in the decree of the Prophets, and in the decree of the Writings: In the decree of the Law it is written, *Thus saith the Lord: Israel is My Son, My first-born* (Ex. 4.22). In the decree of the Prophets it is written, *Behold my servant shall prosper, he shall be exalted and lifted up, and shall be very high* (Is. 52.13), and it is also written, *Behold my servant whom I uphold; Mine elect, in whom My soul delighteth* (Is. 42.1). In the decree of the Writings it is written, *The Lord said unto my Lord: "Sit thou at My right hand, until I make thine enemies thy footstool"* (Ps. 110.1), and it is also written, *I saw in the night visions, and behold, there came with the clouds of heaven one like unto a son of man, and he came even to the Ancient of days, and he was brought near before him. And there was given him dominion. . . .* (Dan. 7.13–14)

In another comment, the verse is read *I will tell of the decree: The Lord said unto me: Thou art my son. . . . Ask of Me, and I will give the nations for thine inheritance, and the ends of the earth for thy possession* (Ps. 2.7, 8). R. Yudan said: All these goodly promises are in the decree of the King, the King of kings, who will fulfill them for the lord Messiah. And why all this? Because the Messiah occupies himself with Torah.[339]

It is extraordinary that such a collocation of Old Testament passages should relate Israel, the Servant of the Lord, the King who is the Son of God, and the Son of Man. Notably, the group includes Psalm 110:1 and Daniel 7:13 in juxtaposition. Was the tradition that linked them in this way motivated by the events of Easter? Obviously not. Was it influenced by the church? That is difficult to believe. It appears rather that there took place among the Jews an independent development of (quasi-) messianic thinking that linked these passages and that Jesus utilized the tradition in a more radical and creative manner than his contemporaries contemplated.[340]

There is however a major consensus on a point of interpretation relating to the saying that we considered earlier in our examination of Daniel 7:13 (see pp. 27–29 herein)—namely, the significance of the reference to the Son of Man's "coming with the clouds of heaven." Does it signify an *ascent* of the Son of Man to God and thus his enthronement in heaven with God, or does it denote a *descent* to the realm of man and thus a judgment and revelation of the kingdom of God to the world (and possibly even to the cosmos)? In recent years a considerable shift of opinion to the former view has been discernible as a result of the influential work of T. F. Glasson, whose views have been developed and popularized by J. A. T. Robinson. Glasson maintains that in Daniel 7:13 the coming on the clouds of heaven denotes a movement to the presence of God in his heavenly court. The vision describes the inauguration of the fifth empire, he says, and so the conjunction of Daniel 7:13 with Psalm 110:1 in Mark 14:62 indicates that this took place "from the moment of seeming defeat, when the kingdom of the saints was inaugurated."[341] In developing this interpretation, Robinson has taken care to emphasize that the direction of movement of the Son of Man is not at issue; the point, he suggests, is that the two elements of the saying, taken from Psalm 110:1 and Daniel 7:13, have the same fundamental meaning:

> The two predictions of "sitting at the right hand of God" and "coming on the clouds of heaven" are to be understood as parallel expressions, static and dynamic, for the same conviction. Jesus is not at this point speaking of a coming from God; in whatever other sayings he may refer to the coming of the Son of Man in visitation, here at any rate he is affirming his vindication.[342]

With regard to this vindication he goes on to say,

> There can be no doubt that it refers to the only moment to which all the enthronement language applied to Jesus does refer, namely to the moment of the resurrection onwards; for there is never a suggestion that Jesus enters upon his triumph only at some second coming.[343]

This interpretation becomes more plausible in light of the modifications of the saying in Matthew 26:64 and Luke 22:69. While Matthew's replacement of *ego eimi* with *su eipas* does not materially affect the import of the saying,[344] his insertion of *ap' arti* before *opsesthe* (generally rendered, "from now on you will see . . .") is more significant. Luke has a similar phrase *apo tou nun* ("from now on the Son of Man will be seated . . ."). The appearance of the two phrases in Matthew and Luke is striking, and not surprisingly it has been inferred that the two evangelists possessed a version of the saying containing such an addition, whether from a source independent of Mark, or from an earlier edition of Mark, or even from the unmodified text of the present version of Mark.[345] Luke appears to have gone further in the modification implied in *apo tou nun*, for his version eliminates all reference to the coming on the clouds: "From now on the Son of Man will be seated at the right hand of the power of God." For those who believe that Luke has reproduced an earlier version of the saying, independent of Mark and closer to the original words of Jesus,[346] two options are clearly open with regard to the Markan logion: either Mark has grasped this meaning and added the Danielic reference to emphasize that the reign of the Son of Man began in his Easter exaltation, or he has consciously modified the earlier form of the saying and added the reference to the coming on the clouds to bring it into line with the church's teaching on the parousia.[347] Matthew, who inherited the Markan form, could have indicated by his inclusion of *ap' arti* a distinction between the two moments of vindication of the Son of Man and so embraced in a single sentence the triumph of Jesus in his resurrection-exaltation and his parousia at the end.

The issues are in fact more complex than some scholars indicate. We have already considered a number of reasons for believing that Daniel 7:13 is set in the midst of a theophany description and thus that it relates, as all theophanies in the Old Testament, to an intervention of God in the affairs of men (see pp. 28–29 herein). The kingdoms of this world, in language borrowed from the book of Revelation, become the kingdom of our God and of one like a son of man. K. H. Müller has stated—rightly, I believe—that in Jewish literature clouds do not enable heavenly beings to move among each other in the transcendental sphere, but are rather used in contexts in which such beings step forth from their hiddenness into the human sphere.[349] This would have been self-evident to Jesus, and his use of the Danielic picture in Mark 14:62b would have been meant to convey that notion. Nor does the conjoining of Psalm 110:1 with the Danielic reference suggest otherwise; indeed, the exaltation motif of Daniel 7:13 would have been strengthened by such a conjunction, since it reflects the exultation of the Son of Man by God into the position of honor. But the two Old Testament motifs are not identical. As H. Traub points out,

> In Mk. 14.62 and par. *ek dexion tes dunameos* is the *terminus a quo* of the *erchesthai*. Since the right hand of God is identical with his throne, this confirms the idea that the Son of Man comes from heaven as in some sense a localizing of the initiative of the divine sovereignty.[349]

This interpretation is confirmed by contemporary Rabbinic views on Daniel 7:13. In an excursus on this subject, Vermes has affirmed that

Although Daniel 7.13 could have provided an excellent scriptural basis for the construction of the Christian belief in the resurrection of Jesus, and even more so for his ascension, there is no evidence of its direct use in any other context but that of an earthward journey at the Parousia. Here the Gospels anticipate the doctrine expressed in rabbinic literature concerning the revelation and coming of the Messiah previously concealed in heaven.[350]

In addition, we must take into account the significance of *opsesthe*: "*You will see* the Son of Man seated . . . and coming with the clouds of heaven.*" The term is reminiscent of the seer's description in Daniel 7:13: "I was watching in visions of the night, and I saw one like a son of man. . . ." This is the language of vision, as it is in Mark 14:62, but it relates to objective events—the establishment of judgment, deliverance, and the rule of God in the world. In the dominical statement, the visionary language also represents objective events corresponding to those in the Danielic vision: the High Priest and his entourage are to see the accused man, now standing before them, exalted by God as Lord of the world and "coming" to reveal the judgment and rule of God. To interpret the statement to mean that the High Priest and members of the Sanhedrin will come to perceive through historical developments such as the spread of the gospel and growth of the following of Christ in the world, that God has exalted as messianic Lord the Jesus they condemned, is to diminish unrealistically the eschatological language employed and the significance of the situation out of which it proceeded.[351]

What then is the meaning of Matthew's *ap' arti opsesthe*? Many exegetes distinguish Matthew's use of the phrase in 26:64 from its meaning in 23:39 and 26:29, holding that in 26:64 it denotes "hereafter" (as in the KJV), with the implication "very soon": "Very soon now there will be no need to put such a question, for all will see the Son of Man for themselves."[352] Hay adopts this view and suggests that the phrase was inserted by Matthew "to bring out the contrast between Jesus' present abasement and his parousia glory; the former condition is about to end."[353] Now it is true that *arti* is occasionally used in late Greek to mean "in the near future," but I have been unable to locate any instance of the phrase *ap' arti* with that meaning. Oddly enough, Luke's equivalent *apo tou nun* can be so used, and it occurs in this sense in the LXX,[354] yet it is doubtful that Luke had in view such a meaning when he chose the phrase. Perhaps Trilling is on the right track in pointing out that in the three cases in which Matthew uses *ap' arti* (23:39, 26:29, and 26:64), the term *arti* acts as a dividing wall, facing past and future: "in all three cases the forward prospect brings into view a new situation, which is always the eschatological; while in 26:29 it is described as drinking the produce of the vine in a new way in the kingdom of God, in 26:64 it is the coming of the Son of Man."[355]

We should note that each of the sayings in Matthew that contains the phrase *ap' arti* is making reference to the eschatological future in the light of the anticipated death of Jesus; 23:39 and 26:64 explicitly relate to his rejection, the former by the people, the latter by the leaders. But 26:64 stresses the point: *ap' arti* is qualified both by the confession of Jesus that he is the Messiah who will be seen as the exalted Son of Man and by his awareness that the Jewish leaders have rejected this claim; the confession and the denial will lead to his death at the hands of men and his vindication at the hands of God. Trilling therefore is right in paraphrasing Matthew 26:64 as follows: "From now, from this hour on, since you utter the judgment, you will experience the Son of Man (only) in glory and prepared for judgment (over you)."[356] It is important to notice that Matthew's *ap' arti* is not intended to weaken the reference to the parousia by stressing the resurrection exaltation of Christ; on the contrary, it sets the glorification in relation to the parousia, which till then will be concealed from his judges through their unbelief.[357] The representation of the parousia as the revelation of the exalted Christ adds to the contrast between the "now" of the trial and the "then" of the future judgment.

It is difficult to deny that Luke has a different accent in his version of the saying. The omission of the reference to the parousia and the *opsesthe* of Mark and Matthew together with the inclusion of *apo tou nun* inevitably throws weight on the exaltation of Christ, which the Christian reader knows occurred in his resurrection. It is even possible that Luke may have included in the scope of *apo tou nun* the trial scene itself: "Now, even in this state of humiliation, the exaltation begins."[358] This is not to say, however, that such an emphasis ought to be attributed to a desire on Luke's part to play down, much less to eliminate, the parousia from Jesus' teaching because of a sensitivity regarding its delay or for any other reason. Luke has preserved too many parousia sayings for such an argument to be plausible. Presumably he emphasizes the exaltation of Christ because it signifies the total reversal of his abasement at the hands of his judges. The session of the Son of Man at the right hand of God reminds us of Luke 12:8, which reflects the judgment scene in Daniel 7:13; indeed, the link with Psalm 110:1, with its reference to the subjugation of enemies beneath the King-Messiah's feet, strengthens that emphasis. The exaltation of the Son of Man signifies his authority to judge those who reject Jesus. Accordingly, the aspect of threat to those who judge Jesus is no less real in Luke than in Mark and Matthew. If we bear in mind the parousia sayings of Luke's gospel, we will have to say that the difference between Luke's version and those of the others is his emphasis on the immediate exaltation of Jesus, which presumes the subsequent parousia, whereas the emphasis in the others is on the revelation of the exaltation in the parousia. For Luke the parousia may be said to be "the revelation of that which in 22:69 applies *apo tou nun*."[359]

To sum up, then, we can draw the following conclusions about the saying in Mark 14:62:

1. It is plausible to view Mark's version of the parousia saying in the trial as the most original version available. Matthew's version is essentially the same as Mark's, and Luke's version is most likely an adaptation of the tradition reproduced by Mark that is attributable either to Luke himself or to his source.

2. Both the judgment and the rule of the Son of Man are implied in all three traditions of the saying. Luke emphasizes the exaltation of Jesus in the resurrection. The versions of the saying in Mark and Matthew assume the exaltation, but they do not suggest that the Jewish leaders will see Jesus *first* as exalted through resurrection and *then* as coming for judgment and rule; rather, they declare that the Jewish leaders will experience a revelation of Jesus as the enthroned Son of Man. As Vielhauer expresses it, "What those addressed will see is not two

actions, enthronement and coming, but an already existing circumstance—
Jesus sitting at the right hand of God—and an event—Jesus coming as Son of
Man on the clouds of heaven."[360]

3. While Mark 14:62 does make a formal distinction between Jesus and the
Son of Man ("*I am*; and you will see *the Son of Man* . . ."), there can be no doubt as
to the identity of the Son of Man in the saying. The declaration that the Son of
Man will sit at God's right hand and will come with the clouds of heaven is given
as an explication of Jesus' affirmative response to the High Priest's question of
whether he is the Messiah. It would be impossible to construe what follows as
meaning that Jesus, having confessed himself to be the messianic King of the
coming divine sovereignty, will be vindicated by the Son of Man at his appearing
to rule in the coming divine sovereignty. On the contrary, the statement clearly
substantiates the conviction running through so much of the dominical instruction that the lowly, rejected, humiliated Jesus, representative of the kingdom of
God and its mediator to man, is to be exalted by God and revealed as the
vindicated representative and mediator of the kingdom, the Son of Man coming
for judgment and rule. The saying thus defines the messianic destiny of Jesus in
terms of the Son of Man's function to judge and to rule. Its implication for other
dominical Son of Man sayings is unmistakable. Above all, it confirms our
interpretation of Luke 12:8–9, which forms the bridge between sayings relating
to the ministry and sufferings of the Son of Man and sayings that speak of his
role in the coming of the kingdom at the end.

d. He Who Comes
Matthew 23:37–39 // Luke 13:34–35

The Lament over Jerusalem is a Q passage that Matthew and Luke reproduce
with unusually close linguistic agreement despite the fact that they set it in
different contexts. It is reasonable to assume that Luke was responsible for
attaching the saying to the logion in Luke 13:31–33 since the name "Jerusalem"
forms the link between the sentences.

In Matthew the saying follows the Q prophecy of judgment upon the
contemporary generation of Jews, which in Luke is introduced by a reference to
Wisdom's sending her messengers to Israel in vain (Matt. 23:34–36 // Luke
11:49–51). The closeness of this parallel has encouraged the assumption that
the two passages stood together in Q, and that the Lament is a Wisdom saying
like that in Matthew 23:34–36, perhaps even a continuation of that utterance.
This is unlikely, however. Matthew's address in chapter 23 is as obviously a
construction as his other discourses, and it is contrary to Luke's practice to
separate Q passages in this manner. Moreover, it has been observed in another
context that Matthew 23:34–36 // Luke 11:49–51 is a prose passage, whereas
Matthew 23:37–39 // Luke 13:34–35 manifests a poetic style characteristic of
Old Testament prophecy.[361] And although both passages are rightly compared
with prophetic oracles of judgment,[362] Matthew 23:37–39 // Luke 13:34–35
conforms in a striking way to the form of the prophecy of disaster as it has been
defined by recent scholars.[363]

According to Klaus Koch, the prophecies of disaster had a common structure through the whole period of prophecy from Elijah to Jeremiah, and generally consisted of three parts: first, an *indication of the situation*, or *diatribe*; second, *a prediction of disaster*, or *threat*, the main point of which was usually contained in a brief sentence in the negative with the verb in the imperfect (in contrast to the common prophetic perfect); and third, *a concluding characterization*, either of those affected by the prophecy (e.g., as in 2 Kings 1:4) or of the sender (e.g., as in Jer. 28:4).[364] As Polag notes, Matthew 23:37–39 // Luke 13:34–35 conforms to this structure remarkably.[365] The "indication of the situation" is set forth in the first sentence, in which Jerusalem is categorized as the city that kills the prophets and stones those sent to her; the city's rejection of the prophets is continued in its resistance of Jesus' efforts to "gather" its children. The "prediction of disaster" follows: "Your house is abandoned to you." And the "concluding characterization" is expressed in a double utterance: first the phrase "You will not see me again . . . ,"[366] which implies that there will be a period during which the presence of Jesus will be withdrawn from "Jerusalem"; and second, the phrase "until you say, 'Blessed be he . . . ,' " which suggests that the period of withdrawal will be ended when Jerusalem acclaims Jesus as "the Coming One" in terms of Psalm 118:26, at which point the people will "see" him, for he will manifest himself to them. This raises two key questions: first, what is the event in which the people will "see" Jesus, and second, what significance will this event have for them?

The saying is sometimes interpreted as affirming that Jesus will not be seen by Jerusalem till the welcome to the pilgrims is sounded again in the city—namely, at the feast of the Passover,[367] but this is an implausible view. The position that Matthew assigns the saying clearly argues against such a reading, and the context in Luke similarly makes such a reading unlikely. Luke states that it was *disciples of Jesus*, not the populace of Jerusalem, who shouted to him the welcome from Psalm 118:26—"The whole multitude of the disciples began to rejoice . . . , saying, 'Blessed be the Coming One, the King' " (Luke 19:37–38)—and he underscores the fact by noting the demand of Pharisees that Jesus rebuke his disciples for such cries (Luke 19:39–40).[368] More importantly, the saying, "You shall not see me until . . ." is an integral element of the prophecy that announces the judgment of God on the people for their obduracy. The abandonment of the "house" has its closest analogy in Ezekiel's vision of the forsaking of the temple and the city by the Shekinah glory (Ezek. 10:1–22; 22–25). The absence of Jesus from Jerusalem signified by the phrase "You shall not see me until . . ." appears to coincide with the absence of God from Israel's "house" ("Your house is abandoned to you"). It is unlikely that such a connection would have been made during any period of Jesus' ministry prior to the final days, when his attempt to "gather" Jerusalem's children met with its strongest rejection. The "seeing" of Jesus by Jerusalem must be interpreted in the light of another saying of his in which he speaks of Jews seeing him in the future—namely, Mark 14:62: "You will see the Son of Man seated at the right hand of the power, and coming with the clouds of heaven." He clearly has the parousia event in mind, for it is at that point that "Jerusalem" will utter the cry "Blessed be the Coming One. . . ."

What meaning will that event have for those who utter the cry of welcome to the returned Jesus? On the face of it, there would seem to be the suggestion that Israel will repent of its sin of rejecting Jesus as the Messiah and will come to confess him as the Messiah, with the result that they will then enter into the kingdom of God, which they were in danger of forfeiting. This may indeed be correct. Some scholars, however, understand the saying to mean that the cry of recognition is uttered too late to avail in the judgment. They suggest that the "seeing" of Jesus as the exalted Son of Man by the Jewish leaders who condemned him implies that they will see him in shame as the judge who will condemn them (Matt. 26:64); the Lament over Jerusalem is burdened with judgment from God, so the acknowledgment of the Jerusalem populace that Jesus is indeed the Messiah is comparable to that expressed in Matthew 7:22–23 // Luke 13:26–27. Furthermore, they maintain that no other utterance of Jesus anticipates Israel's repentance and salvation at the end; they interpret Matthew 22:43 as implying that Israel has forfeited her right to the kingdom of God and conclude that Matthew at least could not have seen in this word an intimation of salvation for the Jews.[369]

This interpretation is self-consistent and cannot be ruled out as untrue to the intention of the saying, particularly in view of Matthew's addition of *ap' arti*, as in Matthew 26:64. Nevertheless, I think it less adequate to the total context of the teaching of Jesus than the simpler view that rejection would be followed by repentance and acceptance. The Jew did interpret the cry of Psalm 118:26 messianically, as the Mishnah on the psalm illustrates. The Mishnah views the text as antiphonally spoken by the people of Jerusalem and the people of Judaea. Significantly, it is the former who utter the cry "Blessed be the Coming One, in the name of the Lord," while the people from Judaea outside the city say "We bless you from the house of the Lord." The ascriptions of praise continue antiphonally until all join in the final utterance, "Thank Yahweh, for he is kind, for his grace endures for ever."[370] It is difficult to believe that in the saying in Matthew 23:37–39 // Luke 13:34–35 Jesus is declaring that the expression of praise in Psalm 118:26 to be given in the end time would be rejected. The warning in Matthew 7:22 // Luke 13:26–27 is not a true parallel, for it relates to a profession of faith continually falsified, whereas Matthew 23:39 par. signifies a temporary unbelief that dissolves in repentance and is replaced with faith in Jesus as the Messiah. There is no doubt about the enthusiasm with which the utterance of the psalmist was taken up by the disciples of Jesus at the entry into Jerusalem or about the fact that it was acceptable to Jesus (see Luke 19:40); the evangelists could well have assumed that the word of Jesus to Jerusalem meant that the populace of Jerusalem would one day give to the returning Lord the same welcome that his followers gave on that great day.

An indication that such could have been in the mind of Jesus is offered by the related Q saying in Matthew 8:11–12 // Luke 13:28ff., according to which multitudes from the nations are to stream into the feast of the kingdom of God, while the sons of the kingdom will be excluded from it. Taken in isolation this saying could be interpreted as meaning that apart from the patriarchs (and prophets—see Luke 13:28) all Israel will be excluded from the kingdom of God, and that only Gentiles will be admitted to it. But the saying is clearly intended as a warning to the Jews rather than as a revelation of the identity of the heirs of the kingdom of God. Moreover, the patriarchs with whom the Gentiles are to be seated are spoken of as more than mere individuals; they are representatives of the covenant people of God descended from them. It is doubtful that the Lament over Jerusalem signifies a change in Jesus' attitude toward the Jews, and particularly so radical a change as the complete exclusion of Israel, represented by Jerusalem, from the prospect of salvation. On the contrary, the purport of his teaching in general and the scope of his mediatorial service for the kingdom of God suggest that he anticipated his own people returning to God along with the multitudes from the nations.[371] The logion does not imply that Jerusalem's inhabitants will have precedence over the nations in the kingdom of God, but rather that in the triumph of the Christ the sinful city will repent of its guilty rejection of the Messiah, and in infinite mercy be accorded a place with the rest of the heirs of the divine sovereignty.

e. The Sheep and the Goats
Matthew 25:31–46

This magnificent, and always disturbing, representation of the Last Judgment is traditionally known as the Parable of the Sheep and the Goats. It is generally agreed, however, that it is neither a parable nor an allegory.[372] As Theo Preiss has observed,

> This pericope does not fall into any of the Jewish or Christian literary genres which the Formgeschichte method tries to disentangle, parable, allegory, paradigm, apophthegm, novel, legend; rather it could be classified, from the point of view of form, with apocalyptic visions which have not usually a simple and definite structure.[373]

And yet, as Preiss acknowledges, the structure of the "vision" is close-knit, with a parallelism and an almost mathematical symmetry that make it easy to remember; moreover, in contrast to apocalyptic visions generally, it has "a sobriety of feature and colour, a reserve, a bareness" that he can ascribe to no other source than Jesus.[374] Grundmann's description of the passage as "an apocalyptic revelation discourse" is too general;[375] it is better specifically to acknowledge the pericope as a visionary depiction of the judgment of the world.[376]

The origin and background of the passage are complex. It is natural to distinguish between the frame, which portrays a judgment scene initiated by the parousia of the Son of Man, and the exposition of the criterion of judgment contained in verses 35–40, 42–45. In his pioneer work relating Jewish apocalypses to the New Testament, F. C. Burkitt maintains that the vision of the judgment in 1 Enoch 62 was as clearly presupposed in the Matthaean scene as the vision of Daniel 7 in passages that speak about the Son of Man coming with the clouds of heaven. Jesus must be relating a well-known tale, he says, but with a difference: whereas in 1 Enoch the kings and the mighty are condemned by the Son of Man because they are Gentiles, in the depiction of Jesus the Gentiles are judged by the kindness they have shown to the persecuted brothers of the Son of Man.[377]

This approach has been refined through subsequent years. It has come to be widely acknowledged that the frame was supplied by the visions of Enoch, but many scholars (particularly among the British) now maintain that it was adapted not by Jesus, but by Matthew and/or his church, who used the passage to encapsulate Jesus' message about the supremacy of love in action.[378] J. A. T. Robinson made an attempt to put this view on a firm basis with a linguistic analysis of the passage. It is his contention that the apocalyptic frame is the work of Matthew, inspired in part by the Similitudes of Enoch; within that setting the evangelist incorporated a little parable of Jesus about a shepherd with his sheep and goats (vv. 32–33) as well as the dialogue of verses 35–40 and 42–45, the result being an allegory of the Last Judgment.[379]

Whereas Robinson was interested in the apocalyptic framework, others have investigated the dialogue of verses 35–40 and 42–45, and have produced some interesting parallels. For example, in chapter 125 of the Egyptian Book of the Dead there is a statement that a deceased person should make in the hall of Osiris. It begins with a long list of sins that the deceased has *not* committed and concludes with a much shorter list of good deeds that he *has* done, thus:

> I have done that which men praise
> and that whereof the gods rejoice,
> I have satisfied God through that which he loves:
> I have given bread to the hungry
> and water to the thirsty
> and clothes to the naked
> and a ferry to those without ships.[380]

More impressive are the parallels in Jewish literature, in which exhortations are given to do works of mercy such as God performs among men. In Sota 14a the question raised by Rabbi Chama ben Chanina (ca. 260)—"What does it mean, You shall walk after the Lord your God . . . and cleave unto him (Deut. 13.5)?"— is answered as follows:

> One should judge himself in accordance with the way and the manner of God. As he clothed the naked, as it says: Yahweh-Elohim made for Adam and his wife garments from skin and clothed them therewith, Gen. 3.21—so you also clothe the naked. God visited the sick, as it says: Yahweh appeared to him by the terebinth of Mamre, Gen. 18.1 (i.e. immediately after the circumcision)—so you also visit the sick. God consoled the mourners, as it says: After the death of Abraham God spoke the word of comfort for Isaac (so the Midrash on Gen. 25.11)—so you also comfort the mourners. God buried the dead, as it says: God buried (Moses) in the valley, Deut. 34.6—so you also bury the dead.[381]

The importance of such works in the judgment is illustrated by the Midrash on Psalm 118, representing what happens when one dies and the soul is judged:

> Ps. 118.19: *Open to me the gates of righteousness*: In the future world it will be said to men, "What has your work been?" If he then says, "I have fed the hungry!" it will be said to him, "That is the gate of Yahweh, Ps. 118.20; you who have fed the hungry, enter in the same!" If he says, "I have given the thirsty to drink!" it will be said to him, "That is the gate of Yahweh; you who have given the thirsty to drink, enter in

the same!" If he says, "I have clothed the naked!" it will be said to him, "That is the gate of Yahweh; you who have clothed the naked, enter in the same!" And similarly he who has brought up the orphans, and he who has given alms, and he who has practised works of love. And David said, "I have done everything, everything should be open to me!" Therefore it is said: "Open to me the gates of righteousness (compassion); I will go into them, I will praise Yah," Psalm 118.19.[382]

In light of the apocalyptic nature of the frame of Matthew 25:31–46 and this moral teaching in Jewish literature, Bultmann concludes that there is little in the passage concerning the sheep and the goats that is specifically Christian and therefore proposes to view it as a Jewish text that was taken over in the church and modified simply through substituting the Son of Man/Jesus for God as the judge.[383] Bultmann's argument is frequently cited but it is rarely endorsed, and that for a good reason: in spite of the parallels to be drawn between the vision and the literature of other religions (parallels that should indeed be welcomed rather than minimized), the relation of this passage to Jesus the Son of Man is fundamental, filling out the warp and woof of the whole.

First, it should be noted that the Matthaean redaction of the text is not essential to the structure of the vision but merely secondary. Matthew 25:31b ("then he [the Son of Man] will sit on his glorious throne") is Matthaean language; identical phraseology appears in Matthew 19:28 ("when the Son of Man sits on the throne of his glory") and is absent from the parallel in Luke 22:29, 30b. In Matthew 19:28, however, the clause serves but to explain the nature of the occasion when the associates of Jesus will "sit on twelve thrones, judging the twelve tribes of Israel"—which is to say that the clause does not *create* the situation but *explains* it. Such is its function in Matthew 25:31b as well. Whether the latter is derived from the Similitudes of Enoch is beyond our knowledge; it is possible that the work was in circulation when Matthew composed his gospel and that Matthew had had opportunity to read it. But in any case, the basic point of the clause is assumed in the authentic teaching of Jesus, above all in Mark 14:62 // Matthew 26:64.

The situation is different with Matthew 25:31a. This clause ("When the Son of Man comes in his glory and all his angels with him . . .") is very similar to that in Mark 8:38 (". . . when he [the Son of Man] comes in the glory of his Father with the holy angels"). Contrary to Robinson's view, it is reasonable to suppose that Matthew reproduced the material *in his source* to create 25:31a and that he has supplemented it with verse 31b in accordance with implications of Mark 14:62 // Matthew 26:64. The essential element in the introduction to the vision goes back to the tradition and is in harmony with teaching elsewhere attested to be that of Jesus. What applies to verse 31 also applies to Matthew's redaction of the pericope generally; it reflects the evangelist's attempt to clarify the tradition he has received. The reference to "the king" in verses 34 and 40 befits the setting: as Mark 14:62 implies, the Son of Man/Messiah is essentially king in the revelation of the final kingdom. The function of the Son of Man to participate in the judgment is assumed in Luke 12:8–9 par. and 17:24–30, 34–37; and in Mark 13:24–27 and 14:62. It has frequently been observed that in this instance, as in related representations of all four gospels, the judgment of the Son of Man is that of his Father also (v. 34), and not his own alone. Admittedly, Robinson has given reason for suspecting that the expression "of my Father" in verse 34 may be a Matthaean addition: in the first place, the phrase is characteristic of the evangelist (it appears sixteen times in Matthew, four times in Luke, and not at all in Mark), and in the second place, the parallelism with verse 41 favors its omission, and the omission would make little difference to the text. The remaining elements of the vision attributed to Matthew are not always clear, but again we can safely hold them to be at most elaborations of a text that stands essentially unaffected by them regardless of their nature.

The feature that dominates the vision is the relation of the Son of Man to those whom he calls "the least of these (my brothers)" (vv. 40, 45). Who are these "least"? Teaching elsewhere attested to be that of Jesus does not afford a precise answer. We read of his concern for "little ones," whether children and/or disciples (e.g., in Mark 9:42 par.; and Matt. 10:42 and 18:10, 14), but in content the beatitudes offer a closer parallel, particularly those on the poor, the hungry, and the sorrowful (cf. the woes on the rich, the full, and the glad in Luke 6:24–25). The universal scope of the judgment scene makes it difficult to accept suggestions that limit the range of the multitude gathered before the king or the references to the "least." The idea, for example, that those addressed are the members of the Christian communities, judged according as they have or have not shown love to Jesus in his least brothers, is an undue restriction of the text as it stands.[384] We must regard T. W. Manson's contention that the Son of Man comprises the king and his followers, and that the nations are judged according to their treatment of the representatives of the kingdom of God as they engage in mission to the world as similarly doubtful.[385] Ingenious as this interpretation is, it depends on an unacceptable view of the Son of Man. Moreover, it is likely that the scene in Matthew 25:31ff. tacitly assumes the resurrection of the dead. The concept of the judgment in apocalyptic, as distinct from prophetic thought, tends to involve a view of mankind in its totality, and it appears that such is the case here.

Contrary to the views of Jeremias and Manson, then, we can assume that the saying concerning the sheep and the goats is referring to humanity in its entirety assembled before the Son of Man for judgment—not the Gentiles alone, but all mankind, including those who confess Christ and those who know nothing of him.[386] If that is in fact the case, then all the parallels between this vision and Jewish apocalypses and the religious ethical teaching of the Jews and other nations are transcended in a unique phenomenon: *the Son of Man, revealed in the man Jesus, owns his unity with mankind in all places and at all times.* Deeds of love and compassion shown to individual members of the human race are accepted as having been shown to him, just as deeds of love withheld from individuals are viewed as having been withheld from him. To our knowledge such a concept is unknown in the literature of the Jews or of the nations surrounding them.[387]

This affects our understanding of the acceptance by the Son of Man of deeds of mercy done to the "least" of humanity. Jesus was one with his fellow

Jews in emphasizing the duty of showing love in action to one's "neighbor." His dual definition of the first commandment as embracing both God and man (Mark 12:30–31) is exemplified in many passages in his teaching—in his commands to give alms (Mark 10:21; Matt. 6:2–4), to give food and drink (Mark 9:42; Luke 14:12–14), to show pity to the sick and exploited (Luke 10:33ff.), to care for the (orphaned?) children (Mark 9:37), to lend freely to those who cannot repay (Luke 6:34), to show love to enemies (Matt. 5:32ff.), and generally to glorify God by doing "good deeds" (Matt. 5:16).[388] As Tödt has pointed out, however, we ought not to equate the deeds of love that Jesus calls for with the Jewish works of the law or to assume that the judgment is pronounced on the basis of obedience to the law; the overriding point is that from the "weightier matters of the law" (Matt. 23:23) Jesus extracted the central issue, "mercy," and it is this that he sought from men.[389] Mercy ruled the life of Jesus; he exemplified it throughout his ministry (see John 7:53–8:11), and it finally led him to the cross. The saying concerning the sheep and the goats declares that whoever shows mercy to the needy thereby shows it to the Son of Man, whose mercy would embrace all. Both those who confess Jesus and those who do not know him are tested by the extent to which they walk in the way of the Son of Man.

Is it possible to define more closely the relation between the Son of Man and mankind assumed in this vision of judgment without invoking theological categories beyond its horizon? Preiss has struggled to follow such a path.[391] In his view, the judgment scene reveals that the Son of Man "will have been mysteriously present in the wretched, in his brethren." In interpreting that, Preiss invokes the concept of the preexistence of the Son of Man as evidenced in the Similitudes of Enoch. But the crucial factor, in his estimate, is the notion of "a vast and profound juridical mysticism," the background of which is justification and eschatology. The Son of Man "freely identifies himself with each of the wretched ones by an act of substitution and identification," which is a "juridical substitution," "an effectual reality" (not simply "as if!"), "a substitution which massively includes what the Church will later call incarnation."

One sympathizes with these attempts to give expression to the presuppositions of this saying. In my judgment, however, the notion of preexistence should be set aside in this context. Further, the assumption that identification and substitution are synonymous is misleading. It would be more in keeping with the representative nature of the concept of the Son of Man to speak in terms of his *solidarity* with mankind, expressed in *self-identification* with the needy evident in a variety of ways throughout the ministry of Jesus. One may conceivably recognize it in his baptism in the Jordan and in his identification of himself with people in a variety of circumstances, perhaps above all in his table fellowship with sinners. And of course it came to climactic expression in his giving of himself in death to achieve redemption and to open the saving sovereignty for humanity. It is precisely the representative function of the Son of Man that makes possible the concept of Jesus in solidarity with mankind, achieving redemption for the race. This solidarity continues to the end and is to be revealed in the judgment of mankind.[392]

Thus the final vision of the Son of Man opens to view the ultimate meaning of his function within the divine sovereignty. By appointment of the Creator, who wills that none of his creatures should perish, the Son of Man is sent to be representative of the divine mercy and representative of the recipients of that mercy, representative of the saving sovereignty and representative of those who inherit it. Hence he was appointed to be Mediator of redemption and of judgment, and in both functions the divine mercy stands revealed in its glory.

The challenge and comfort of this vision of judgment are alike caught in an utterance of one who is reputed to have been, in a different manner, a brother of the Son of Man:

> Always speak and act as men who are to be judged under a law of freedom. In that judgment there will be no mercy for the man who has shown no mercy. Yet mercy triumphs over judgment. (James 2:12–13)

14 | Discourses of Jesus on the Parousia

1. THE Q APOCALYPSE
Luke 17:22–37

The title "Q Apocalypse" is time-honored and may be allowed to stand. It is acknowledged by all that the heart of the discourse is from Q and that a remarkably consistent viewpoint is maintained throughout. Moreover, it appears to form the conclusion of the Q tradition,[1] and therefore is fittingly concerned with the last things, with the day of the Son of Man. As to the precise limits of the Q source within the discourse, there is some uncertainty. It is generally agreed that it includes Luke 17:23–24 (Matt. 24:26–27), 26–27 (Matt. 24:37), 34–35 (Matt. 24:40–41), and 37 (Matt. 24:28). As we shall see, there is reason to suppose that it also includes Luke 17:28–29 and 31–33. That is to say that the entire discourse after the introductory verse 22 comes from Q, apart from the Lukan insertion of verse 25 (v. 36 is a late accommodation of the text to Matt. 24:40).

The discourse is clearly related to Luke 17:20–21, yet as clearly distinguished from that passage. Whereas the question answered in verses 20–21 concerns the time of the coming of the kingdom of God, verses 22–37 take up the issue of when the Messiah will come, how he may be known, and what will eventuate from his coming. The answer to the question concerning the kingdom of God assumes the presence of the kingdom in the ministry of Jesus, but the messianic issue focuses on the day of the Son of Man. Ironically, the key to the relation between the two is provided by a non-Q saying in the midst of the discourse—verse 25—although the key is also implicitly present in the Q doublet of Mark 8:35 that appears in Luke 17:33 (in light of its Q context in Matt. 10:39). The discourse is reproduced on the basis of the identification of the Son of Man in his parousia with the Son of Man/Jesus exalted after suffering in anticipation of his "Day."

a. Introduction: Yearning for the Day of the Son of Man
Luke 17:22

The opening statement of the discourse evidently comes from Luke's pen.[2] The expression "days will come" is rooted in Old Testament prophecy (see, for example, Amos 4:2, Isa. 39:6, Jer. 7:32, and Ezek. 17:12) and appears in varied forms in the New Testament (see, for example, Mark 2:20; Luke 5:35, 19:43, 21:6, and 23:39; and Heb. 8:8). An acute problem is raised by the affirmation "You will desire to see *one of the days of the Son of Man*." The expression must be set in relation to similar phrases in the discourse: verse 24, "so shall the Son of Man be in his day";[3] verse 26, "So shall it be in the days of the Son of Man"; and verse 30, "So shall it be in the day when the Son of Man is revealed." In his equivalents of verses 24, 26, and 30, Matthew replaces these varying expressions with a single phrase, which he repeats verbatim three times: "So shall the parousia of the Son of Man be" (Matt. 24:27, 37, 39). In these three passages Luke uses the plural in verse 26 only, where it corresponds with the parallel phrase "the days of Noah," but a singular in this verse would accord with the language in verses 24 and 30, and it would make Matthew's employment of the term "parousia" more comprehensible. Accordingly, it is quite possible that the expression "the day of the Son of Man" stood in the Lukan source of verses 24, 26, and 30 as well as in verse 22. The plural would then be attributable either to Luke or to his source.[4]

If we accept this explanation of verse 22, we rule out the need for a number of more problematical explanations, including the following: (1) the disciples yearn to experience again one of the days when Jesus was among them in his ministry[5] (an interpretation which is in any event not in accord with Luke's linguistic usage: he typically uses *epithumein* with an infinitive in reference to a desire directed to the future, as in Luke 10:24; cf. 22:15);[6] (2) the period in view is that between the resurrection and the parousia;[7] and (3) the "days of the Son of Man" reflect the rabbinic expression "the days of the Messiah"—which is to say, the period of the Messiah's reign.[8] While this last view is more pertinent than the others (the kingdom of the Messiah and the kingdom of God were not always clearly differentiated), it is nevertheless more probable that the language in verse 22 ought to be understood in light of verses 24, 26, and 30.

The thrust of verse 22 is its assertion that the disciples will desire to see the day of the Son of Man *in vain*—"you will not see it." What lies behind the statement? It is likely that experiences of distress are being anticipated, on account of which the disciples will yearn for the appearance of their Lord to deliver them and establish in power the longed-for kingdom. Rigaux describes verse 22 as "a prophecy of woe";[9] that is an overstatement, but it does serve to call attention to a feature of the saying commonly overlooked. Schnackenburg, it is true, thinks that the tension between this saying and the emphasis in the discourse on the suddenness of the parousia is too great, and so he is compelled to ascribe the logion to Luke's redaction.[10] This is unnecessary, for the tension between the suddenness of the parousia and the occurrence of *thlipsis* belongs to the warp and woof of apocalyptic thought.[11] The warning about the appearance of false prophets and pseudomessiahs in verse 23 is of a piece with the eschatological tradition of signs and suddenness in relation to the coming of the end.[12]

b. The Universality of the Parousia of the Son of Man
Luke 17:23–24

In considering Luke 17:20–21 we saw that the modified parallel to verse 23 in verse 21 serves to clarify the thought of verses 20b and 21b and provides a link with the discourse of verses 22–37. It is improbable that verse 23 is a Lukan composition in imitation of verse 21a,[13] for it is clearly a Q saying, the form of which is more originally preserved in Matthew (24:26).[14] Evidently the saying circulated in the gospel traditions in more than one form (cf. Mark 13:21).

It is difficult to know whether the language of Matthew's parallel to verse 23 is intended literally or whether it reflects idiomatic speech with a general meaning. "See he is in the desert . . . see he is in (one of) the secret rooms" accords perfectly with the tradition of the hidden Messiah, which some scholars believe includes the idea that he will appear in the wilderness.[15] On the other hand, "in the desert . . . in the secret rooms" (*en to eremo . . . en tois tamieiois*) can be seen as an overliteral rendering of the poetical Hebrew antithesis *miḥus umeḥodarim*, "in open country and in the inner rooms" (Deut. 32:25), more commonly expressed by *mibbayith umiḥus*, "in the house and in the (street or) country." Both phrases are used simply to denote "within and without" (in Gen. 6:14 the latter phrase is used with reference to daubing the ark inside and outside; in Exod. 25:11 it is used in reference to vessels gilded within and without). The same expression was current in Aramaic, with the substitution of *bᵉra* for *miḥus*, which would suggest that it is possible that Jesus might originally have used this idiomatic expression to denote the idea that the Messiah is appearing somewhere in the open, or in some building or other, without specifically locating him in the desert or in a secret enclave. Matthew and Luke could have had access to different translations of the Q original, Matthew's version sharpening the term "outside" or "country" to accord with the expectation of the Messiah in the wilderness, and Luke's source understanding the expression in its idiomatic sense. Whatever the interpretation of the details, it is evident that the saying embodies "an attack on the concept of the hidden Messiah."[16]

It is uncertain whether Luke 17:24a or Matthew's 24:27a is more original. Has Matthew simplified Luke, or has Luke corrected Matthew on the ground that lightning does not necessarily travel from east to west? Luke's use of *astraptousa* ("flashing") is often thought to be deliberately reminiscent of his record of the Transfiguration, in which Jesus' clothes are described as "dazzling white" (*exastrapton leukon*, literally "white, gleaming like lightning"); the suggestion that the Lord will appear like lightning at the parousia could thus be stressing his glory rather than the suddenness of the event.[17] In this context, however, the comparison of the parousia with lightning rather than, say, the onset of a storm, is made primarily to contrast the open coming of the Messiah with the secret appearances it was said that alleged messiahs would make: it implies that none need fear missing the Messiah when he comes, for the appearance of the Son of Man will be visible to all. As Schulz expresses it, "When the Son of Man appears it will be no hole-in-the-corner affair, but a powerful, yes, universal-cosmic event."[18] The key notions are visibility and universality, though in view of the comparisons that follow (in vv. 26ff.), there may be some intent to include the idea of the suddenness of the parousia's arrival as well.

c. The Necessity for the Passion of the Son of Man
Luke 17:25

There is widespread agreement that verse 25 is an originally detached saying inserted by Luke into the Q passage, verses 23–24 and 26–30. It introduces a different thought into a sequence of sayings that deal with the nature and circumstances of the parousia. The statement is remarkably close to the first passion prediction recorded in Luke 9:22 (// Mark 8:31). Luke's only departure from the wording of 9:22 in 17:25 is his use of *auton* instead of *huion tou anthropou*, and this is due to his having employed the expression in the immediately preceding sentence (v. 24). In 9:22, Luke goes on to describe those who reject Jesus (elders, chief priests, and scribes), but in 17:25 he substitutes the summary phrase "this generation." More striking is his omission of a reference to the resurrection of Jesus. Some have felt this to be significant, and view the utterance as a primitive form of the prophecy of the passion.[19] But there is a simpler explanation available. Luke summarizes the second prediction of the passion in 9:44, and since that verse follows closely on his report of the first prediction in 9:22, he is content to abbreviate the statement. In contrast to 9:44, however, 17:25 retains the term *dei* ("must"), which appears in 9:22. This would indicate that it is plausible to view 17:25 as an abbreviation of 9:22. Since its opening term *proton* is acceptably Lukan (see Luke 9:61; 10:5; 12:1; 14:28, 31; and 21:9), as is the summary phrase "this generation" (which is peculiar to Luke; see 11:29–30 and 16:8), and since there is the precedent of his having shortened the second prophecy of the passion in 9:44, there seems good reason to attribute the form of the saying in 17:25 to Luke and not to his source.[20]

If we adopt this reading of the evidence, there is no need for us to attach undue importance to the fact that this prediction of the passion set in a parousia context contains no mention of the resurrection. Among others, Bultmann has suggested that the saying provides evidence of a tradition that links the death of Jesus with the parousia (the Palestinian tradition) as opposed to a tradition that links his death with the resurrection (the Hellenistic tradition).[21] On the contrary, however, Luke knows well enough that the Son of Man who suffers and dies in the service of the kingdom of God will rise before appearing in glory.[22] The concept is primitive.

Why has Luke set the saying in this context? It must be in accordance with his parenetic purpose in redacting the Q apocalypse. We observed that verse 22 implies that the disciples will experience difficulties in the period prior to the parousia. The passage following verse 25 likens conditions in that period to those in the days of Noah and of Lot. Luke therefore reminds his readers that the Son of Man must suffer before his revelation in glory, in accordance with the law of entrance into glory via the path of suffering (Luke 24:26, 44—observe the *dei* in both sentences); it is a reminder that if Christ must suffer, his followers will have to suffer as well (cf. Acts 14:22; 2 Tim. 2:11).[23]

d. Unpreparedness for the Parousia
Luke 17:26–30

Luke 17:26–30 contains two comparisons drawn from the Old Testament and serves to "deepen the utterances of the preceding section 17:22–25 and at the same time prepare for the parenesis of the following verses 17:31–33."[24] The first comparison, relating to Noah, in verses 26–27 (// Matt. 24:37–39a), is from Q. The second, relating to Lot, in verses 28–29, is not in Matthew, although verse 30 has its counterpart in Matthew 24:39b. The question arises whether verses 28–29 also stood in Q and were omitted by Matthew,[25] or whether they constituted a detached saying that was either linked to verses 26–27 by Luke (or in the tradition on which he drew),[26] or were composed by Luke (or by the community) and inserted between the last clause of verse 27 (// Matt. 24:39a) and the parousia saying of verse 30 (// Matt. 24:39b).[27] There is no way of resolving this problem with certainty. Scholars have variously assessed the evidence. Working from the fact that the judgments upon the generation of Noah and the inhabitants of Sodom were frequently linked in Jewish writings, as they are in 2 Peter 2:5–8, for example,[28] some scholars have assumed that Jesus would naturally have cited the two events together as illustrations of judgment at the parousia,[29] while others have assumed that Luke or his source must have supplemented Jesus' single statement in order to bring it in line with contemporary Jewish tradition.[30] The latter position is not a compelling one, however. The thought in the Lot comparison accords with the Noah logion and with much else in the teaching of Jesus. There is, for instance, a double comparison in Luke 12:49–50 in which fire and water appear in an eschatological context, reflecting a consistent connection in Jewish thinking between the Flood and Sodom traditions. The content of verses 26–30 favors the authenticity of these sayings.[31]

It is undoubtedly a strong point in favor of the independence of Luke 17:27–28 that the passage would have been congenial to Matthew, but he did not reproduce it. On the other hand, the Matthaean version of the Noah saying is unusual in that it reproduces *twice* the clause *houtos estai he parousia tou huiou tou anthropou* ("so shall the coming of the Son of Man be"). That the first occurrence (Matt. 24:37) stood in Q is clear from Luke 17:26. It would be expected that the second occurrence would introduce another comparison. Did the Q passage read "As it was in the days of Lot, so (*houtos*) it will be in the day of the Son of Man"? If that is the case, Luke placed the logion after the completed comparison to bring the double saying to a stronger conclusion, and then added language of his own choosing (*kata to auta* for *houtos*, and possibly *he hemera ho huios tou anthropou apokaluptetai* for *estai he hemera tou huiou tou anthropou*). Why Matthew chose to omit the Lot saying is unclear, but Schmid's observation is worth pondering: "Matthew had to leave out Luke 17:28–29, 32 because in his context it was not the attitude of the world and the blindness of men in the last days which should be illuminated, but the surprising and unexpected coming of the Day of Judgment."[32]

As we have already noted, the original source for both verse 26 and verse 30 in all probability referred to "the day of the Son of Man." The present reading of verse 26, "in the days of the Son of Man," has clearly been modified to accommodate the phrase "as it was in the days of Noah," and accordingly refers to the period prior to and leading up to the parousia. The modification thus serves to bring out the sense that must be assumed in the simpler phrase "the day of the Son of Man." The paraphrase in verse 30 makes use of the concept of the *revelation* of the Son of Man, which again is natural in view of the likening of the parousia to the lightning in verse 24.

What is the main point in the two comparisons of the time of Noah and of Lot with that of the parousia? One is tempted to think of the notorious wickedness of the generation of the Flood and of the inhabitants of Sodom, with the implication that such is the generation of the parousia. Yet there are no obvious references to wickedness in verses 26–29. It is likely that the allusions are meant to stress two principal points of comparison: the dangers implicit in unreflective absorption in the things of everyday,[33] and the unexpectedness and therefore surprise of the end.[34]

Goppelt suggests that this attitude of worldliness as expressed in a preoccupation with eating and drinking—"Let us eat and drink, for tomorrow we die"—stands as "an elementary expression of paganism" in the teaching of Jesus.[35] Zmijewski sees similar implications in verses 27 and 28: like eating and drinking, marriage, buying and selling, planting and building can all involve us in a preoccupation with the joys of this world, can lead to an undue emphasis on earthly concerns, a dependence on false sources of security, and absorption in an earthly future that causes the hope of the kingdom of God to fade.[36] Luke 17:26–30 implies that the contemporaries of Noah and Lot were guilty of a culpable blindness and that a similar charge is to be laid against the contemporary generation, which is moving to a similar day of reckoning. Jeremias accordingly renders the appeal of this passage as follows: "You are feasting and dancing—on the volcano which may erupt at any moment!"[37] The judgment aspect of the parousia is thus being stressed; the implication is that the event will entail judgment by the Son of Man and not merely his bearing witness before the judgment throne of God (cf. Luke 12:8–9). The parousia is the *day of the Son of Man*, with a connotation similar to that of the day of the Lord.

e. Exhortations in Light of the Parousia
Luke 17:31–33

Luke 17:31–33 consists of three sayings of diverse origins, none of which was originally related to the parousia but which in this context are given an eschatological perspective.

Verse 31 is closely parallel to Mark 13:15–16. The latter preserves the right kind of setting for the saying, for it indicates the necessity for urgent flight from a situation of imminent danger. But verse 31 is more likely a Q doublet of the Markan saying than a direct citation. We have seen that in verses 21 and 23 Luke utilized a Q version of a Markan saying (Mark 13:21). The closing sentence of this paragraph (v. 33) is also a Q version of the logion in Mark 8:35. Matthew's form of the Q statement in verse 33 (Matt. 10:39) is connected with a saying about bearing one's cross, as is the version in Mark. By setting it in this context, Luke has changed its application, just as he has changed the application of verse 31 by placing it in its present setting. It is likely, then, that he constructed this paragraph from a series of originally detached Q sayings. On the other hand, since there is a link between verse 32 and verses 28–30, it is also possible that verses 31–32 were already conjoined with each other and with verses 26–30 in the Q source.[38]

In verse 31, Luke's phrase "in that day," following as it does verse 30, can refer only to the day of the Son of Man; the phrase does not appear in Matthew or Mark and must be Luke's own identification of the occasion. Since possessions will be totally irrelevant at the parousia, it is hardly of consequence to tell one not to go down from the roof into the house or turn back from the field to bring out his belongings; not even the cloak mentioned by Mark (13:16) and Matthew (24:18) will be needed on that day! The language is being applied in a figurative manner. For Luke it signifies the need for the servant of God to maintain a detached attitude to the things of this world, in contrast with the lifestyle of the people of Sodom (v. 28). Luke's failure to mention the cloak at the end of verse 31 makes the Old Testament command to Lot more plainly observable: the followers of Christ are told not to turn back, just as Lot and his family were commanded by the angels, "Do not look back or stop anywhere in the plain" (*me periblepses eis ta opiso mede stes en pase te perichoro*, Gen. 19:17). But Lot's wife did the opposite of what was commanded, and that was viewed with utmost gravity by the Jews. Yalkut Reuben 40b (on Gen. 19:26) interprets the term "back" in the sense of "away from God"—that is, despising the command of God. Lot's wife thus turned away from God in her heart toward Sodom, and her disobedience was perpetuated in a grim memorial.[39] The injunction "Remember Lot's wife" therefore both illustrates the attitude that verse 31 declares must be shunned and provides an eerie example of the maxim in verse 33. Lot's wife wanted to "save" her (old way of) life, and she lost herself. Lot was willing to lose his (old way of) life, and he saved himself. The life that men seek to "save" is that described in verses 27 and 28, the way of life among Noah's contemporaries and of the citizens of Sodom, a way of life that remains characteristic of the way of this world; whoever seeks to hold on to *that* life will lose the life that God gives—the resurrection life under his saving sovereignty. He who would know *this* life must be prepared to forfeit the way of Sodom and this age and look for the true life that will be given at the parousia.

f. Separation in the Judgment of the Parousia
Luke 17:34–35

Verses 34–35 continue the thought of verse 30. Drawn from Q, the passage most likely followed directly on verses 26–30 at one time. Its theme is the judgment that divides the closest of human relationships.

Matthew and Luke each present two comparisons.[40] Both include the image of the women grinding meal (Luke 17:35 // Matt. 24:41). Luke precedes this with the image of two sharing a bed (v. 32), and Matthew precedes it with the image of two working in a field (24:40). Do we see here an originally triple comparison, incompletely handed on in the tradition? Or is it an originally double comparison, redacted by one of the evangelists or in the source he received? T. W. Manson opts for the first alternative, convinced that the longer reading of Luke is authentic; he holds that the passage provides "a complete picture of a Palestinian household, consisting of husband and wife, two maid-servants and two menservants."[41] This is an attractive view, but the text-critical evidence argues against it.

Matthew gives us a simple picture of two conditions under which men and women work—the men in the field and the women at home in the mill. In both cases, one will be taken and one will be left. Luke's version is complicated by the initial phrase in verse 35—"on that *night*"—which is followed by the picture of two sleeping on one bed. It is somewhat surprising to encounter this phrase in the wake of verse 30 ("So shall it be in the *day* when the Son of Man is revealed" or "So shall the *day* of the Son of Man be"), especially if we are to assume that verse 34 once followed verse 30 without interruption. Could a reference to day have been followed in the source by a reference to "that night"? Some scholars say No emphatically.[42] Nevertheless, the sequence did not seem impossible to Luke. We may have to apply here the principle *difficilior lectio potior*. Rigaux points out that the structure of Luke 17:34–35 is identical: "Three little literary unities well compacted, a verb in the future indicative, two terminating in homoioteleuton in the future passive," and he concludes, "The formulation is primitive in face of Matthew 24:40–41."[43] It is by no means unique for the parousia to be represented as a night event (as in the parable of the Burglar in Luke 12:39–40 // Matt. 24:43–44). Paul's use of the parable in 1 Thessalonians 5:2ff. is noteworthy in this regard: he passes straight from the idea of the *day of the Lord* coming like a *thief in the night* to the notion that the *day* should not overtake his readers *like a thief*! Paul obviously had no consciousness of incon-cinnity here. The expression "the day of the Son of Man," like "the day of the Lord," denotes an event rather than a calendar date. Admittedly a tradition did exist among the Jews that the Messiah would come during the night of the passover, but it is unwarranted to find a reference to that notion here.[44]

The intention of the comparisons is clear. Above all they illustrate the devastating nature of the judgment that will take place at the parousia of the Son of Man, bringing about a separation among men and women bound by closest ties. In each case the separation is expressed in the language of "taking" and "leaving"; this signifies a taking to be with the Son of Man in the kingdom of his Father of those so prepared, in contrast to a "leaving" of others to the judgment of exclusion from the kingdom of God. It also entails for believers a destiny like that of the Son of Man (see Luke 9:51). "The connection of 'humiliation and exaltation' in which the disciples were integrated . . . is now finally resolved," says Zmijewski; "they participate in the glory of the exalted Son of Man."[45] It is important to observe that this takes place on the day of *the Son of Man*—which is to say through the action of the Son of Man. The passives used (*para-*

lemphthesetai . . . aphethesetai . . .) are reminiscent of the "divine" passives.[46] The mediatorial function of the Son of Man thus reaches its climax on his "day": those who have received the word of the kingdom of God are now brought by him to share with him the glory of the consummated kingdom.

g. The Parousia: An Event of Universal Judgment
Luke 17:37

Matthew's version of this saying appears to be more primitive, both in its context and language. The saying follows well on the contrast between the expectation of the hidden Messiah and that of the Son of Man appearing as the lightning (vv. 23–24; see Matt. 24:26–28); it is generally assumed that Matthew has maintained the order of these sayings in Q. Luke will have transferred the saying so as to produce a fitting conclusion to the discourse, but this entailed his having to construct a bridge between the preceding context and the saying; hence, he formed verse 37a out of the logion itself.[47] As to the language, Matthew's *ptoma* ("corpse") was viewed by the stylists as coarse; Luke's term *soma* is clearly an improvement. The verb *sunachthesontai* in Matthew, following immediately after *ekei*, preserves a more Semitic word order than Luke's; moreover, Luke's longer compound *epi-sunachthesontai* was probably chosen so as to correspond more fully with *hopou*.[48]

The difference in the setting of the saying brings about a difference in emphasis in its application. In Matthew the saying follows the comparison of the parousia with the lightning flash, and so the emphasis is likely to be on the universality of the *revelation* of the Son of Man and its suddenness. In Luke it is natural to think of the universality and swiftness of the *judgment* of the Son of Man, which is the theme of verses 34–35. The two notions are not mutually exclusive, however. The emphasis of the interpretations tends to depend on whether the exegetes pay more attention to the corpse or the vultures. Tödt stresses the former: "As inevitably as a carcass attracts the birds of prey, men will perceive the coming of the Son of Man."[49] Schlatter emphasizes the latter element: "When guilt is ripe and the distress becomes so great that it cries out for the Redeemer, then he will come with the same unexpected but absolute certainty as the vulture appears."[50] Clearly it is necessary to exercise care in examining the features of a parabolic saying. Schlatter rightly points out that it is not stated in the saying that Jesus is a vulture, nor that the Jews or mankind are a corpse; rather, *event is compared with event*.[51] Vultures appear where there is a corpse. *Visibility* therefore is a clear element in the comparison. This probably refers, as does the lightning simile, to the parousia of the Son of Man. Yet the entire discourse lays emphasis on the aspect of *judgment* in the day of the Son of Man. The coming of vultures to prey is a common picture in the Bible to denote divine judgment, as the striking saying from Hosea 8:1 exemplifies:

> Set a trumpet to your lips,
>   for a vulture is over the house of the Lord,
> because they have broken my covenant,
>   and transgressed my law.

It is likely that this feature also forms an element of the intention of our saying. The fact that Luke placed the proverb at the end of the discourse may well indicate that he was intending to emphasize these two aspects. For just as the implicit question of where the Messiah would appear is answered by the picture of the lightning visible everywhere, so the question of where the parousia judgment would take place—a question made explicit by Luke (*pou*)—is answered by the picture of the vultures which appear wherever carrion lies: it will operate where it is needed, and that is *everywhere.* "The universality of the parousia corresponds to the universality of the judgment of the world."[52]

Interpreted in its context, the saying thus brings to a focus the two leading motifs of the Lukan apocalypse: the universal revelation of the Son of Man in his day, coming swiftly and suddenly upon all men, and the unerring judgment that day will signify for all men. The simile refers immediately to all, since the "where" of the event is anywhere and everywhere. These three constituents of the discourse—the coming of the Son of Man to all, the judgment of the Son of Man on all, and the unpredictability of the event—have an unspoken corollary: "Be ready for the day!" The parenetic concern runs through the whole discourse. It becomes explicit in verses 31–33, but is presupposed in the observations about false expectations of the Messiah (vv. 22–24) and the necessity of the Son of Man's suffering (v. 25), in the comparisons regarding Noah's Flood and Sodom's destruction (vv. 26–30), and in the statements concerning the separations that will occur at the parousia (vv. 34–35). The discourse accordingly may be viewed as a commentary on Luke 17:20b, with the added dimension of a near expectation of the parousia, which will unveil the kingdom that even now is within the grasp of all.[53]

2. THE MARKAN ESCHATOLOGICAL DISCOURSE
Mark 13 (// Matthew 24, Luke 21)

The history of criticism of the discourse may be said to have established the following points:

1. The discourse is composite. The composition of the synoptic discourses generally suggests this, including Mark's collection in chapter 4. A few examples of compilation in Mark 13 will suffice: verses 9 and 11 have a parallel in the Q doublet Luke 12:11–12 // Matthew 10:19–20, where they form a single sentence; verse 10 would have been an isolated saying, set between the two halves of the sentence; verses 15–16 occur in a different context in Luke 17:31, which is probably another Q doublet; verse 21 has a Q parallel in Luke 17:23 (Matthew reproduces both versions in Matt. 24:23–24, 26–27); and so on.

2. It is likely that sources were employed, again as in other synoptic discourses, including Mark 4. The employment of parallel material in 1 and 2 Thessalonians confirms this supposition.[54]

3. The substantial disagreements among attempts to delineate a single major source in the chapter (notably speculations concerning a "little apocalypse," either of Jewish or Jewish-Christian origin) make such a proposed source doubtful.[55] The notion that the chapter was based on a *Jewish* document is particularly questionable, since no example of a Jewish description of a

parousia prior to Mark (still less to 1 Thessalonians 1:15ff.) has been found.[56] On the other hand, the descriptions of the parousia of the Son of Man in Mark and Q are rooted in authentic teaching of Jesus.

4. A more promising approach to the discourse is offered by the fact that the primitive Christian catechesis conveys traditions of the instruction of Jesus.[57] It is a feature of the catechesis that eschatological teaching occurs at the end of instruction, as may be observed in the "discourse" of Mark 8:27–9:1 and in all five Matthaean discourses. Apart from any specific tradition that Mark may have received with regard to the setting of elements in Mark 13, it is natural that his account of the ministry of Jesus should conclude with a summary of Jesus' teaching on the last things.[58]

Acknowledging that the discourse was constructed from originally disparate units, signs of rudimentary groups of sayings can be observed within the chapter. These may be classified as follows:

1. *Sayings on the tribulation of Israel*, verses 14 and 19. Bearing in mind the tradition of the doom prophecy in verse 2, it is conceivable that verses 14 and 19 should have been brought together, reflecting as they do Daniel 9:27 (and similar passages referring to the abomination of desolation) as well as Daniel 12:1. In due time verses 15–16 and 17–18 were added, and at length verse 20.

2. *Sayings on the tribulation of the church*, verses 9 and 11. Luke 12:11–12 constitutes evidence that these logia circulated together early on. Two factors would have led to verse 10 being associated with them: the witnessing activity of the disciples, which was a prime cause of their persecution, and the growing inclination to view the church's mission from an eschatological perspective. Verses 12–13a would have been conjoined for the same reasons, as would verse 13b.

3. *Sayings of pseudomessiahs and the true Messiah*, verses 21, 24–26. In these verses the contrast between the Jewish notion of the secret appearance of the Messiah and the Christian hope of the parousia of the Son of Man is set forth. The same contrast is presented in Luke 17:23–24—a remarkable parallel, since the comparison of the parousia of the Son of Man with the lightning is rooted in the same ancient tradition reproduced in Mark 13:24–25, the theophany in the storm cloud. The reference to false messiahs in verse 21 would have been reason enough to append the related sayings, verses 6 and 22. How primitive the connection between verses 26 and 27 is cannot be determined, but it was evidently prior to 1 Thessalonians 4:16–17.

4. *Sayings on the parousia and watchfulness*, verses 24–26 and 34–36. It is again noteworthy that 1 Thessalonians 4:15–5:11 reflects the thought of Mark 13:24–27 and 33–36 (–37), indicating that the theme was common to the discourse and the primitive catechesis.

These four groups of sayings form distinct items of instruction. It was natural, however, that the second and fourth groups should come together: as in the catechesis, the call to "watch" was associated with an appeal for prayer and resistance to the hostile powers in the world (see, for example, 1 Thess. 5:6–8; 1 Pet. 4:7 and 5:8–9; and Rom. 13:11–13), so in the discourse the duty of bearing suffering witness before hostile powers and endurance to the end became linked with the parousia and the call for watchfulness. It was equally natural for the traditions relating to the tribulation of Israel to be linked with that concerning pseudomessiahs and the appearing of the true Messiah (i.e., the first and third groups). This would have been encouraged, if not actually stimulated, by the Caligula episode of 39–40 A.D. It is significant that the first and third groups are reflected in 2 Thessalonians 2:1–9, whereas the second and fourth groups are echoed in 1 Thessalonians 1–3 and 4:15–5:11, since this attests the conjunction of these elements of Christian catechesis in the period of Paul's early ministry. Mark's style is evident throughout chapter 13.[59] It is likely that he brought together the varied eschatological traditions and fashioned them into a unity in the light of the contemporary situation and needs of the church.

Detailed discussions of the structure of the chapter are available in the works of Lambrecht and Pesch.[60] Despite their different methods of approaching the chapter, both scholars divide the discourse (after the introduction, vv. 1–4) along the following lines: the Tribulation (vv. 5–23), the Parousia (vv. 24–27), and the Time (vv. 28–37).

a. The Doom of the Temple
Mark 13:1–2

It is frequently thought that the utterance in verse 2 represents the negative half of Mark 14:58.[61] This is not impossible, but a closer parallel to Mark 14:58 is the Qumran view of the renewed people of God as the true temple,[62] and a more striking link with Mark 13:2 can be found in Luke 19:44: "They will bring you to the ground . . . and not leave you *one stone standing on another*." The short statement common to Luke 19:44 and Mark 13:2 is sufficiently important for it to have circulated independently in the early church, but whereas the former passage relates it to the destruction of the city, the latter relates it to the destruction of the temple. In reality, of course, the destruction of the one necessarily entails that of the other. Like Matthew 23:38, Mark 13:2 relates to the temple as the center of Israel's life and the symbol of God's relation to the nation; the broken relationship to God occasions a rejection of the place that serves as the visible embodiment of God's presence with his people, and so a judgment on the nation itself.

The setting of the prophecy in the statement in verse 1 is Markan in style.[63] It is not improbable that verses 1–2ab formed an early tradition of the context of the utterance in verse 2c, reproduced in Mark's language.[64]

b. The Disciples' Questions
Mark 13:3–4

This introductory pericope is likely to be Mark's formulation of a tradition passed on to him as the setting for at least a section of the material before him.[65] The first clause ("When will these things [*tauta*] be?") reflects a belief that the ruin of the temple could not occur as a solitary event but would have to take place in conjunction with other significant happenings. The second clause is parallel to the first, but extends it: "What will be the sign when all these things (*tauta panta*) will be accomplished?" This assumes that the ruin of the temple will occur as part of the end-time events (the language echoes Dan. 12:6–7). The conjunction of the sign with the time of the end is significant for the discourse that follows, for the whole of verses 5–23 is brought under this rubric. In this way the discourse goes beyond the disciples' question and the prophecy that occasioned it, for it proceeds on the assumption that the really important event is not the temple's ruin but the coming of the Son of Man. The repetition of *tauta* and *tauta panta* in verses 28–29 forms a "redactional clasp" for the discourse.[66]

c. Dangers from Deceivers
Mark 13:5–6, 21–22, 7–8

These sayings are linked by a single theme—namely, warnings against claims that the end of the age has begun or is immediately impending. Verses 5–6 and 21–22 are so similar that they are sometimes regarded as doublets, but this is a mistake. Verse 5 sounds out the keynote of the discourse and can hardly be viewed as parallel with verse 21, which is Mark's version of the Q saying in Matthew 24:26 // Luke 17:23. Verses 6 and 22 are closely related but distinct: verse 6 tells of claims made by messianic pretenders on behalf of themselves, verse 21 tells of claims about pseudomessiahs made by false prophets, and verse 22 tells of joint activities of false messiahs and false prophets. The suggestion that verses 5–6 and 21–22 form an *inclusio* bracketing the signs section is a sound one, however. Mark strengthened the inclusio by adding verse 23, thereby underscoring the appeal of verse 21 and the call that sounds throughout the whole of the signs section (vv. 5–23).

Verse 5.

The first word of the discourse, *Blepete* ("watch"), sets the tone for all that follows. It is a favorite term of Mark's; while Matthew and Luke use it here only in the discourse, Mark uses it to open the next paragraph (v. 9), close the signs section (v. 23), and preface the final hortatory paragraph (v. 33). The term reinforces the idea of each sentence in which it occurs. By placing the term at the beginning of the discourse, Mark makes the reader aware of the nature of the whole; it is essentially *an appeal for eschatological awareness*. The necessity to be on guard against deceivers finds an immediate application in verses 6, 21, and 22, but is also germane in verses 7–8.

Verse 6.

The meaning of the clause "Many will come in my name" is explained by what follows: "saying 'I am (he).'" That is to say, the messianic pretenders will not merely claim to act with the authority of Jesus, or to bear the name of (the returned) Jesus, or even to be invested with divinity ("I am"); rather, they will claim to be what Jesus alone is: the Messiah.[67] The claim to be the Messiah carries with it the implication that the last times have come and the final events set in motion—precisely the kind of claim against which 2 Thessalonians 2:1–12 is directed.[68] It is altogether believable that such cries would have been heard in Mark's day, when events in Palestine appeared to herald the approaching end, and indeed, such a circumstance would explain Mark's separating verses 6 and 22 by placing them at the beginning and end of the signs section of the discourse: the activity of such false prophets and messiahs is seen as the most urgent of the dangers against which Jesus warned.

Verses 21–22.

By conjoining these two sayings, Mark characterizes the persons who affirm, "Look, the Messiah is here!" and "Look, he is there!" as false prophets. The claims reflect the Jewish doctrine of the hidden Messiah, who was expected to be born and grow up in obscurity until the day of his manifestation to Israel. It is likely that verse 21 was followed in the tradition by verses 24ff., just as in Q the saying was followed by the comparison of the Son of Man in his parousia with the lightning (Matt. 24:27 // Luke 17:24), which counters the notion that the Messiah will appear in secret places by asserting that he will be manifested *openly* and seen by all.

Verses 7–8.

Wars, earthquakes, and famines (and pestilence, in Luke 21:11—the reference could have been accidentally omitted from Mark's source) are standing elements in prophetic and apocalyptic descriptions of the end and of the times leading to it. The emphasis on war, echoed in verse 7, is bound up with the fact that the Day of the Lord originally denoted a day of battle of the Lord against his enemies, just as earthquakes (and even pestilence) were the accompaniment of his coming in powerful and glorious theophany. Famines naturally were included as a result of wars. Such events were not at first associated with the end of the age, but they later came to be seen as characteristic of the day of Yahweh's intervention for the establishment of his purpose and came to be interpreted as his judgments (see, for example, Jer. 14:12 and 21:7; and Ezek. 5:12 and 14:12–23). The language of verse 7 is traditional, echoing such passages as Jeremiah 51:46 and Daniel 11:44. The language of verse 8 conflates Isaiah 19:2 and 2 Chronicles 15:6. Mark's inclusion of these items in the discourse has an evident purpose. On the one hand, the *dei genesthai* ("these things must happen") of verse 7 implies a recognition of God's sovereignty over history even in the midst of calamity. On the other hand, the tendency to identify present events as ushering in an immediately impending end is corrected: "The end is *still to come*" and "These are (but) *the beginning* of the birthpangs." As the beginning of the birthpangs, they have eschatological significance; they are signs of the judging presence of God in a history that is moving to the end he has purposed. But they are not the sign that the disciples requested (v. 4). That has yet to be described.

d. Tribulations for Disciples
Mark 13:9–13

The sayings in this section are bound together first by the use of the term *paradidonai* (to "hand over") in verses 9, 11, and 12 and second by equivalent expressions meaning "for my sake" in verses 9 (*heneken emou*) and 13 (*dia to onoma mou*). Luke does not reproduce the former in the Q equivalent, Luke

12:11–12, and in Mark's verse 11 the participial form *paradidontes* is almost redundant. Verse 13, however, appears to echo the Targum of Jonathan on Micah 7:2ff., which reads, "A man *delivers up* his brother to destruction." Since this Targum apparently influenced the conclusion of the sentence as well, it would appear to have provided the form of verses 12–13a known to Mark.[69] It is this passage that would have suggested the adoption of *paradidonai* in the earlier two sayings. *Paradidonai* has unmistakable overtones for Mark and his community; we have noted its occurrence in Mark's second passion prediction (9:31), but it also occurs ten times in the narrative of chapters 14–15, and it belongs to the confessional language about Christ's death (Rom. 4:25; cf. Rom. 8:32). Mark uses it in verses 9–13 to point to the fact that the sufferings of the disciples parallel those of Jesus in his passion. The phrase "for my sake" in verses 9 and 13 bears a related implication: the persecutions described are the result of the disciples' attachment to Jesus; they appear before courts and suffer among their own people because they confess Jesus as the Messiah. Such is the context in which the church pursues its mission. Every trial provides an opportunity for witness to the faith before men and for the advancement of the gospel in the world (v. 10, cf. Luke 21:13; Phil. 1:12–14).

Verses 9–11.

We have already noted the Q version of verses 9 and 11 in considering Luke 12:11–12 // Matthew 10:19–20. There is no need to suppose that Mark used Q;[70] it is more plausible to assume that Mark's source contained an independent version of the Q saying and that it was fuller in its opening clauses than Luke 12:11a. Matthew appears to have conflated his Q version with Mark's saying.

The disciples are warned that they will be handed over to the Jewish "sanhedrin" and beaten in synagogues—which is to say that they will be treated as apostate Jews and subject to the discipline of Jewish courts for disturbing the peace and propagating heretical beliefs.[71] The "governors and kings" signify Roman procurators and kings of Israel, which would indicate a Palestinian provenance, although the language could also be extended to areas outside Palestine, since Jewish courts existed in the Diaspora, and Christians could be dragged before Roman authorities anywhere. The reason for such trials is not in doubt: it was the public witness of disciples to their faith.

There is some uncertainty about the punctuation of verse 10. Some manuscripts follow the lead of Matthew 10:18 (*eis marturion autois kai tois ethnesin*, the disciples will stand before the authorities "for testimony to them and the nations") and continue verse 9 into verse 10 (the disciples are handed over *eis marturion autois kai eis panta ta ethne*, "for testimony to them and to all the nations"); they then place the particle *de* after *proton* to make the clause read "But first the gospel must be preached."[72] In the context, this reading does not imply a limitation of the scope of the preaching; since "first" means prior to the end, it simply amounts to a terse expression of the necessity of preaching to all before the end comes. Although it is commonly assumed that Mark was responsible for the composition of the statement, I am inclined to believe that it was precisely because verse 9 ended with the phrase *eis marturion autois* that Mark adduced the statement of verse 10. As Hahn has pointed out, there is nothing specifically Markan about the language of verse 10: *panta ta ethne* is an Old

Testament expression that frequently occurs in Old Testament citations in the New Testament (e.g., in Mark 11:17, Acts 15:17, and Rom. 15:11); *euangelion* occurs in the catechetical summary of Jesus' preaching in Mark 1:15; *kerussein* is common in early Christian mission; and *dei* appears in sayings of Jesus circulating in bilingual Palestinian churches, as we noted in connection with Mark 8:31.[73] The only term in verse 10 likely to have come from Mark is *proton*; it matches the *oupo to telos* of verse 7 and the *arche odinon* of verse 8 and emphasizes the task to be completed prior to the parousia. This is not the same as the "delay of the parousia" motif: it is not an attempt to explain why the parousia has not yet happened; rather, it stresses the disciples' present duty in light of God's purpose for the nations to participate in the saving sovereignty.

In their experiences of trial the disciples are told not to be anxious, for the Spirit will be their inspiration (v. 11). This concept is primitive. The Holy Spirit is the Spirit of prophecy, and his action in and through the disciples is strictly related to the occasions of need stated in the text.[74]

Verses 12–13.

If it is true that enmity within the family was "a commonplace in Jewish apocalyptic since Micah 7:6,"[75] the notion receives a characteristic stamp in this context: the division takes place *dia to onoma mou* (v. 13a)—that is, because one or more members of a household confess Jesus as the Messiah.[76] This motif is more strongly expressed in the Q saying, Matthew 10:34–36 // Luke 12:51–53; Jesus sees it as part of his mission to create the apocalyptic conditions described by Micah. The so-called "apocalyptic commonplace" is accordingly declared to be integral to the ministry that moves to its end in rejection and death. Those who follow Jesus must expect to experience treatment comparable to that given to him.

The last sentence in verse 13b, following the reference to Micah 7:6 in verse 13a, may echo Micah 7:7: "As for me I will look to the Lord, *I will wait for the God of my salvation*" (LXX: *hupomeno epi to theo to soteri mou*). The salvation referred to in Mark 13:13b relates to life in the kingdom of God, not simply to survival of the tribulation. We are reminded of Mark 8:35–38: the path to life is endurance in the way of Jesus.

e. Tribulations for Israel
Mark 13:14–20, 23

If the *hotan de idete* of verse 14 recalls the *hotan de akousete* of verse 7 ("When you see . . . when you hear . . ."), the statement is nevertheless more significantly related to verse 4, since verse 14 gives a direct answer to the question concerning the sign of the impending fulfillment of the prophecy of verse 2.

Verse 14.

"Abomination of desolation" is an apocalyptic expression derived from the book of Daniel (see Dan. 9:27, 11:31, 12:11). An "abomination" frequently signifies among Jews an idolatrous object. An abomination that causes "desolation" is likely to refer primarily to religious rather than physical desolation, though the former could entail the latter. In Daniel the expression appears to be a play on the name *Baal Shamaim*, "Lord of Heaven" (pronounced among some Syrians as

Baal Shamem). For *Baal* "abomination" was substituted, and for *Shamem* the term *shomem*, "desolating," was substituted; hence, "Lord of Heaven" became "an abomination that desolates." It is recorded in 1 Maccabees 1:54ff. that Antiochus Epiphanes built an "abomination of desolation" on the altar in the temple of Jerusalem and altars throughout the land. Since "abomination" is especially used of idols, it is likely that the reference indicates that an idol was set up along with the altar; there is evidence that the idol represented Zeus in the likeness of Antiochus.[77]

While the meaning of the expression in Daniel is tolerably clear, there is difference of opinion as to its application in Mark 13:14. Most commonly it has been believed to signify the Antichrist, for the participle is masculine, denoting "*one* who creates desolation," and this interpretation links up with Paul's description of the man of lawlessness in 2 Thessalonians 2:3ff.[78] Mark himself, however, would not have held this view, since he speaks of *false messiahs* and *false prophets* in addition to the abomination, even setting them after the description of the abomination (vv. 21–22).

Could the memory of the blasphemous act of Antiochus Epiphanes have led to an expectation of a similar idolatrous object being placed in the Jerusalem temple? From Jerome onward this has been maintained. In modern times it has been linked with Caligula's attempt to place a statue of himself in the Jerusalem temple in A.D. 40, and the corollary drawn that the passage (and even the discourse itself) took its rise from this event.[79] The application of the cipher to Caligula's threat will certainly have been made; the issue of whether the threat *inspired* the prophecy is less certain.

The oldest interpretation we possess is that of Luke, who translated the phrase "Jerusalem surrounded by armies"—that is, the forces of Rome (Luke 21:20). In view of the connection between verses 14, 4, and 2 and the references to flight in verses 15–20, this may be viewed as a natural interpretation. Could it be that verse 14 involves a notion that combines these ideas—namely, an anti-Christian leader of Roman armies planting in the temple a Roman standard with idolatrous images of the emperor affixed to invoke worship? According to Josephus this actually happened at the conclusion of the Jewish war, though in manifestly different circumstances from those envisaged in Mark 13:14. Perhaps we should be satisfied with a less precise answer to these questions. The memory of the sacrilegious acts of Antiochus was perpetuated annually in the feast of Dedication. The first mention of the "desolating abomination" in Daniel 9:27 is set in a context of destruction of the city and temple by the invading army of a powerful ruler. It may be that the thrust of the abomination prophecy is simply to present a horrifying picture of the "desolation" of the temple and city that is in some way reminiscent of the havoc wrought by Antiochus, but with yet more fearful consequences, and that no closer identification is intended.[80]

The parenthetic "Let the reader understand" is an editorial insertion urging the reader to note the application of the Danielic prophecy. The call to flee in the Day of the Lord is frequent in prophecy (e.g., see Amos 5:19–20), but here it may constitute a reference to the command to Lot and his family to flee to the hills (Gen. 19:17; this allusion is made clearer in Luke 17:31). If that is the case, it implies that Jerusalem is another Sodom, and its impending desolation comparable to that of Sodom.[81]

Verses 15–16.

The necessity for flight at the appearance of the abomination is emphasized. Contrary to Jewish instinct, there will be no safety in the the city or temple, for God is bringing doom on both. It has often been thought that the command to flight in this passage is the oracle to which Eusebius referred (*Ecclesiastical History*, bk. 3, chap. 5), in consequence of which the Christians in Jerusalem fled from Jerusalem to Pella beyond the Jordan. The suggestion is interesting but tenuous. The historicity of the migration to Pella is very uncertain.[82]

Verses 17–18.

The sayings in these verses continue the motif of flight in time of war. The fact that Mark has included them serves as an indication of his limited redactional activity in this section, for they are not relevant to Christian congregations outside Palestine. The lament for pregnant women and nursing mothers reflects their inability to hasten like other people. The call to pray that the flight might not take place in winter reflects the concern of a country in which streams and rivers, including the Jordan itself, become swollen with the seasonal rains, making escape difficult or impossible.

Verses 19–20.

The tribulation being referred to is still that of Jews in Palestine. Verse 14 uses a Danielic image of Israel's distress in relation to the prophecy of verse 2; verse 19 employs another Danielic text relating to the same distress (Dan. 12:1), and verse 20 stresses the gravity of that time of trouble. It is a single situation that is being referred to throughout the paragraph. The use of the Danielic language is important in that it signifies that the doom of Israel is being viewed as the Day of the Lord on the city and people. The motif of the shortening of the days has analogies within the apocalyptic literature of Judaism, but no real parallels.[83] It expresses the thought of God's mercy upon the disobedient nation, which yet contains a faithful remnant (the "elect whom he has chosen"). God will not allow his people to be exterminated; he will bring to a speedy end the agonies of those days for the sake of the faithful whom he has elected to salvation.

Verse 23.

The *humeis de blepete* of verse 23a ("As for you, watch!") balances the *blepete* of verse 5. As we have already noted, verse 23 is the final member of the *inclusio* that holds together the signs section of the discourse. The phrase "I have told you all things" harks back to the "all things" of the disciples' question in verse 4; the sign of the "abomination" has been disclosed, and the necessary word has been spoken to ensure that the disciples are not led astray by deceivers. But nothing has been said of what lies beyond the distress. Pesch compares the saying to the prophetic formulae of conclusion that we find in Isaiah, such as "The Lord, the God of Israel has spoken it" (Isa. 1:20, 40:5, 58:14, etc.).[84] The analogy is illuminating. Prophetic concluding formulae are generally followed by further oracles; so also here, the prophecy of doom is followed by an oracle of salvation that the Lord will enact in the day of the parousia.

f. The Parousia
Mark 13:24–27

It is important to remind ourselves that this paragraph, like other elements in the discourse, was at one time a separate item in the tradition. It is virtually certain therefore that the two opening phrases, "But in those days, after that tribulation," were added at some stage in the tradition to make connection with a preceding context. It is conceivable that the first phrase "in those days" was set in the text prior to Mark, since the expression was commonly used in the Old Testament in reference to the last days (see, for example, Jer. 3:16ff., 5:18, and 31:29; Joel 2:29; and Zech. 8:23). When Mark set the paragraph in its present context, the phrase gained a narrower meaning, and so he inserted the second phrase, "after that tribulation," to make it plain that the parousia is not the last element of Israel's distress but that it takes place "*after* that tribulation."[85] The modifier then fits the temporal notes observed in verses 7, 8, and 9: a near expectation that does not permit a timetable.

Verses 24–25.

This passage is a conflation of Old Testament allusions to the Day of the Lord. Note that they are *allusions*, not *citations*. Verse 24 reflects Isaiah 13:10, verse 25a echoes Isaiah 34:4, and verse 25b is reminiscent of Isaiah 34:4 and Joel 2:10 and 3:15–16 (= MT 4:15–16). This combination of biblical recollections of features of the Day of the Lord is intended to underscore the nature of the parousia as a theophany. We should not be surprised by the fact that Mark's Greek source used the language of the *Greek* Bible when referring to Old Testament sayings and concepts; the Hebrew texts behind the allusions of verses 24–25 would have conveyed exactly the intention that is desired. Mark 13:24–25 is not the only passage that represents Jesus as speaking of his parousia in theophanic terms. Luke 17:23–24 presents essentially the same thought as Mark 13:21, 24–26: the comparison of the Son of Man in his day to a lightning flash recalls the basic idea of a theophany—namely, the appearance of the Lord of the storm in the world (cf. Exod. 19:16, Hab. 3:11, Ps. 18:13–15, and Zech. 9:14–16). And, of course, the basic text for the parousia, Daniel 7:13, is itself part of a theophanic vision, of which the feature of coming in the clouds is a clear reminder, here and in Mark 14:62.

Verse 26.

Arguments that this saying is the result of a conflation of Mark 14:62 with Daniel 7:13[86] are not convincing, since the verse obviously fails to include the motif of the exaltation of Jesus, so important to Mark 14:62.[87] Pesch suggests that the term *opsontai* ("they shall see") should be interpreted in the light of 14:62 and 8:38, where to "see" the coming of the Son of Man means to see him coming *for judgment.*[88] This is by no means certain, however. Mark 14:62 is addressed to men in the act of condemning the Son of Man, whereas Mark 8:38 is an abbreviation of a double saying (on confession and denial of Jesus, the Son of Man) for the purpose of stressing the danger of denial. Mark knows that those who confess Jesus will be confessed by the Son of Man, and hence when they "see" him, it will be for them salvation, not judgment. So here, for the *elect* to see the Son of Man at his coming signifies their salvation (v. 27). In 13:26, the third person plural (*opsontai*) suggests that the coming of the Son of Man will be a universal event.

That the Son of Man comes *in* the clouds (*en*), instead of *with* the clouds (*meta*) as in the LXX of Daniel 7:13, is of no consequence. Theodotion in the same passage has *epi* (upon). The Exodus theophany speaks of God descending *en nephelais*, "in the clouds" (Exod. 34:5). It is likely that stylistic considerations led Mark to make the change; he may well have had his source before him and was about to write *meta dunameos polles kai doxes* ("with great power and glory") when he chose not to use *meta* twice.[89] It is more important to note that the Son of Man, coming as the representative of the kingdom of God in theophanic glory, comes *from* heaven to the world of man rather than going *heavenward* from man to God.[90] A theophany is always for the accomplishment of the divine purpose in the world, whether for judgment, or deliverance, or both.

Verse 27.

The climax of the parousia is the gathering of the elect for the kingdom of God. It represents the fulfillment of the hope of reunion of Israel's scattered tribes referred to in such passages as Isaiah 11:12, 27:12–13, and 60:1–2, in the light of such passages as Zechariah 2:6 (= MT 2:10) and Deuteronomy 30:3 (and perhaps also Isa. 43:6). While the Massoretic text of Zechariah 2:6 is uncertain (cf. LXX), there is no doubt about that of Deuteronomy 30:3: the Lord will gather you *ap' akrou tou ouranou heos akrou tou ouranou* ("from the end of heaven to the end of heaven"), which has been conflated with a phrase reminiscent of Deuteronomy 13:7, *ap' akrou tes ges heos akrou tes ges* ("from the end of earth to the end of earth"). We are thus presented with a pleonasm signifying the gathering of the elect from the farthest reaches of earth and heaven.[91] We ought not to assume that the scope of this statement is narrowed by the fact that the term "elect" is taken from the Old Testament texts; like Matthew 8:11–12 (cf. Zech. 2:11), this saying is likely to imply the gathering of the elect of all nations, along with Israel's faithful remnant, into a single community under the lordship of the Son of Man.

g. The Parable of the Fig Tree
Mark 13:28–29

The origin of the opening phrase of the parable in these verses is uncertain. Lohmeyer suggests that the beginning may originally have been "The kingdom of God is like a tree. . . ."[92] Or it could have commenced with a simple *hos* or *hosper*, "As . . ." (cf. Matt. 25:14). If there was such an introduction, the figure of the fig tree must have been introduced in the main sentence, since it is the blossoming of *this* tree to which the parable draws attention.

There does not appear to be sufficient reason to reject the substance of verse 28b, although the statement could hardly have been uttered alone in its present form. The focus on the fig tree's bursting into leaf as a sign of the nearness of summer most likely provided the basis for a comparison with something else, such as with the kingdom of God; such a clause is given in verse 29, and it makes explicit the comparison implicit in the first part of the sentence. In verse 29 the phrase *houtos kai humeis* could be redactional (cf. Mark 7:18); it is possible that a simple *houtos* or *houtos kai* stood in the source. *Epi thurais* is often thought to have been added by the evangelist; many take it to be an example of Mark's redundant style.[93] This is a possibility, although it should be noted that the oft-cited contention of Jeremias that the use of a spatial image for a statement of time is Hellenistic and that the plural for door (*thurai*) is classic[94] is refuted by Septuagint usages.[95]

The expression in verse 29, *hotan idete tauta ginomena* ("when you see these things happening"), relates most naturally to events that will take place in the future, as the use of *hotan* in verses 7, 11, and 14 illustrates. This orientation of the parable to the future is supported by the *engus estin* of verse 29. Luke indicates that the future event will be the arrival of the kingdom of God (21:31), while Mark is most likely referring to the parousia. The significance of the parable is stated well in Luke 21:18: "When these things are beginning to happen, straighten up and lift up your heads, because your redemption draws near."[96]

Could the parable have had a similar meaning in a different context? Theoretically it would be possible for it to have a variety of applications, since "when you see these things happening" could be given any number of settings. In the context of the gospels, however, the possibilities are limited. The great theme of the proclamation of Jesus is the coming of the kingdom of God. The future reference of the phrase "when you see these things happening" suggests that these are events that lead to the revelation of the kingdom of God at the end. This in turn implies that the coming of the kingdom of God in the future has premonitory signs of some sort.[97] Whether by his placing of the parable in this setting Mark has explicated the *tauta ginomena* rightly is a matter for discussion; that Jesus referred to certain events as heralding the end is apparently not up for discussion.

h. The Times of Fulfillment
Mark 13:30–32

The three sayings in verses 30–32 were in all probability isolated in the pre-Markan tradition. Verse 31 has a verbal link with verse 30 through the term *pareleusontai*, "will pass away" (in verse 30 *parelthe*); it makes an impressive confirmation of the truth of verse 30 and an equally impressive introduction to verse 32. Since verses 30 and 32 are unrelated and yet bound together by verse 31, it is reasonable to assume that all three statements were originally independent and that Mark was responsible for ordering them in this context.

Verse 30.

The meaning of "this generation" is now generally acknowledged. While in earlier Greek *genea* meant "birth," "progeny," and so "race," in the sense of those descended from a common ancestor, in the LXX it commonly translates the term *dor*, meaning "age," "age of man," or "generation" in the sense of contemporaries.[98] On the lips of Jesus "this generation" always signifies the contemporaries of Jesus, but at the same time always carries an implicit criticism.[99] For Mark the eschatological discourse expounds the implications of the prophecy of judgment in verse 2, and so implies the perversity of "this generation," which must suffer the doom predicted.

This generation is not to pass away until "*all these things* happen" (*tauta panta genetai*). The first term, *tauta*, appeared previously in verse 29: "When you see *these things* happening. . . ." A clearer precedent for *tauta panta*, however, appears in the question of the disciples in verse 4: "When will these things be, and what is the sign when all these things will be completed?" The response to the request for a sign has been given, above all in verses 14–15; the question concerning the "when" is answered in verse 30. In view of Mark's setting of the statement, however, it is difficult to exclude from "*all* these things" the description of the parousia in verses 24–27.

Does the significance given the saying by the context in which Mark places it reflect its original intention? We earlier saw that Pesch answered this question in the affirmative, but he did so on the basis of the conviction that the saying was constructed for the context on the basis of Mark 9:1.[100] It is more plausible to look to the Q passage in Matthew 23:36 // Luke 11:51 for illumination, however: the blood of all the prophets shed from the foundation of the world is to be required from *this generation*. Luke 11:51 reads "Yes, I tell you, it shall be required from this generation"; Matthew 23:36 reads "Amen I tell you, all these things shall come upon this generation." It is not unreasonable to suggest that *Mark 13:30 represents the form the Q saying took when it was repeated apart from its context and became an isolated saying.* This means that the saying is referring to the doom that is to fall on Israel in the near future. Originally the nature of the doom was not specified. When Mark set it in its present context, however, he related the saying to the prophecy concerning the temple, interpreted as judgment on the nation, and therefore to the oracle of verses 14–20 also.

Contrary to recent opinion, this is not a "consolatory saying"; to the contrary, it is an affirmation of inescapable judgment upon Israel.[101]

Verse 31.

The relation of the saying in Mark 13:31 to the Q utterance in Matthew 5:18 // Luke 16:17 has frequently been remarked upon, and discussed at length by Lambrecht. He concludes that the Markan and Q affirmations are mutually exclusive, that Mark either modified Luke's version (replacing the reference to the law by referring to the words of Jesus) or he constructed both Mark 13:30 and 13:31 out of Matthew 5:18 (Lambrecht actually prefers the latter alternative).[102] These proposals are questionable. Neither the Lukan nor the Markan statement is intended to convey apocalyptic lore concerning the nature or the permanence of the universe; they are simply meant to express the authority of God's law and Jesus' message. Jesus is known to have affirmed the authority of the law and prophets as well as the word sent through him to Israel (see Matt. 5:17). There was room in his teaching for both affirmations, though they would have been elicited through different circumstances.

The scope of "my words" is uncertain. Mark understood the saying to emphasize the authority of the discourse, with special reference to verse 30. Considered as an isolated saying in the tradition, it contains nothing that relates to any specific element in the teaching of Jesus. But since the great theme of Jesus' preaching is the kingdom of God, he was probably speaking as the representative of the divine sovereignty in this instance. Thus, we can view the saying as a corollary of Jesus' entire proclamation of the kingdom of God and his relation to it.[103]

Verse 32.

While some scholars have attributed the saying in verse 32 to the post-resurrection church, the majority acknowledge its essential authenticity, although some express uncertainty about the phrase "not even the Son."[104] The main thrust of the saying is assertion that the time of the end cannot be known. Set in its present context, however, it gives the impression that the events of verses 5–27 are to come upon the generation of Jesus but that the "day or hour" of the parousia is unknowable. Accordingly, I once affirmed that the saying signifies "a narrower limitation of time over against a broader period";[105] I have since come to see that such a stance reflects an insufficient appreciation of the fact that in the biblical tradition "that day" and "that hour" are used synonymously, like the *kairos* of verse 33.[106] "Day" and "hour" have the same meaning in the phrase "that day or hour." To say that none knows "that day or hour" is to affirm a universal ignorance of the time when "the day" will break or "the hour" will strike. In itself there is no indication that the logion is declaring that the kingdom will come during that generation, however. Verse 30 relates to the doom that the contemporaries of Jesus cannot escape, and verse 32 relates to the revelation of the kingdom of God. The relation of the two events is given in the assumed relation between the Day of the Lord upon the impenitent nation and the new age initiated by the parousia, but these are distinguished in the tradition. We must allow verse 32 to stand on its own feet and not insist that it be subordinated to verse 30.

To what extent does the passage suggest that Jesus is himself ignorant concerning the last day? Rigaux, followed by Vögtle, contends that it affirms an absolute rather than a relative ignorance on the part of Jesus concerning the time of the end, and both view it as a cornerstone of the eschatological instruction of Jesus.[107] Of its importance there can be no doubt. The universal ignorance of the time of the end is affirmed in contrast to the power of God alone to determine it. This does not exclude in practice a near expectation on the part of Jesus, but it does allow for a remoter expectation if the Father so wills. Hence, it is consonant with the "tremendous tension" Oepke perceives in the thought of Jesus: "that of both concentrated and extended expectation at one and the same time."[108] The implicit submission of Jesus to the Father's will in this respect is comparable to his affirmation that it is not he but the Father who will determine who will sit at his right hand and who will sit at his left in the kingdom of God (Mark 10:40). Mark 13:32 suggests likewise that the Son leaves the determination of times in the hands of the Father.

How are we to understand this attribution of "the Son" to Jesus? In an apocalyptic utterance that excludes apocalyptic reckoning one might have expected that the statement would mention the Son of Man.[109] But rather than pit one messianic expression against another, we should acknowledge that they are related. The representative nature of the expression "Son of God" in Jewish tradition is clear: in Exodus 4:22–23, Israel is said to be God's first-born son, in contrast to Pharaoh's first-born son; in 2 Samuel 7:14 it is suggested that David's progeny will be as God's son, an idea that is developed in Psalm 2:7 and Psalm 89:26–27. These passages were stamped in the consciousness of later Judaism in its thought about the messianic people and the Messiah. Jesus' conviction that he stood in relation to God as "Son," understood in the context of the service of the kingdom of God that was at the center of his life, would readily express itself in terms of the function of the "Son of God" as interpreted within the tradition of his people. Our consideration of the Son of Man passages in the gospels has shown us a figure who is also representative, serving the rule of God in all its aspects. It would be astonishing if there had been no trace in the teaching of Jesus of a coalescence of the representative figures of the Son of God and the Son of Man. As it is, there are evidences of the eschatological functions of the Son of Man strengthening the eschatological elements already attaching to the concept Son of God, and the same thing applies to the simple title "the Son."[110]

While the Christological figures of the Son, the Son of God, and the Son of Man are distinguished in the tradition, there is no little overlap in the concepts and in the functions associated with them. All are representative as well as individual figures, and the functions they fulfill relate to the service of the kingdom of God, both in the process of its establishment and in its consummation. Accordingly, they fitly denote the present and the future status and function of him who bears these names.

i. The Call for Vigilance
Mark 13:33–37

It has frequently been observed that verses 33–37 contain echoes of various parables of Jesus, specifically those of the Watching Servants (Luke 12:35–38), the Burglar (Matt. 24:42ff. // Luke 12:39–40), the Good and Bad Servants (Matt. 24:45–51 // Luke 12:42–46), and the Talents/Pounds (Matt. 25:14–30 // Luke 19:12–27). Lambrecht believes that Mark's text is a secondary combination of all four.[111] It is more likely that verses 34–36 constitute an authentic parable in their own right, complete with an introduction in verse 33 and a summary exhortation in verse 37. The parable of the Watching Servants in Luke 12:36–38 is so close to verses 34–36 that the two parables must have come down in the tradition as variants of a single parable and been edited differently by the two evangelists.[112]

Verse 33.

The characteristic *blepete* that commences the saying in this verse is doubtless attributable to Mark; it sets the tone for the whole paragraph, emphasizes the appeal made in the verse, and binds it to the discourse. It is conceivable that the material from *agrupneite* to the end of the verse stood in the pre-Markan tradition;[113] it suits the essential parable of verses 34–36 perfectly, and its emphasis on "You do not know the time" gives it an excellent link with verse 32.

Verses 34–36.

The kinship of the parable in these verses with the parable of the Watching Servants in Luke 12:36–38 is immediately evident. Luke is probably right in representing the master as going to a banquet and returning home the same night. Mark's *apodemos* indicates a considerable journey; that would be consonant with the assignment of authority to the servants but not with the instruction that the master could return at any hour of the night or with the injunction that the porter remain vigilant and not sleep. The parable in Mark's source must have begun *hos anthropos apheis ten oikian autou to thuroro eneteilato hina gregore* ("the situation is as when a man leaves his house and commands the porter to watch").[114] The continuation of the parable in verse 35 is couched in the second person and so has been accommodated to the readers: "Keep awake, then, for you do not know when the master of the house is coming." The parallel in Luke 12:37–38 suggests that this is a modification of an original continuation stated in the third person: "He will watch, for he does not know when the master of the house is coming . . . lest coming suddenly he find him sleeping."[115]

The event presented in the parable of the Porter is linked with the great theme of Jesus' proclamation—namely, the coming of the kingdom of God and the judgment that accompanies it. This representation recalls the association in Jewish thought of the judgment and the kingdom of God with the *coming* of God. In the parable, however, as in the teaching of Jesus generally, the coming of God for judgment and salvation takes place through the coming of the Son of Man. The return of the master of the house represents an event actualized in the parousia of Christ.

Verse 37.

Lambrecht has rightly perceived that on the plane of Markan redaction the *pasin lego* in this saying stands at the opposite end of the spectrum from the *kat' idian* of verse 33.[116] It makes explicit the hints scattered through the discourse that the church is being addressed through the instruction handed on to the disciples. Now the lesson of the discourse is applied to all: the end is near, but incalculable, and liable to come as a surprise; consequently, *all* must be on the alert. Essentially that means readiness for God at every moment in a life of faith and Christian service.

15 | Conclusion

We have now concluded a review of the most significant passages on the teaching of Jesus regarding the kingdom of God. It is evident that in this teaching Jesus freely used metaphorical, symbolic, and mythic images, above all in his representations of the future of the kingdom of God. Modern man finds this mode of thinking unfamiliar and strange. What significance can it have then for our outlook on life? More specifically, to what extent does the teaching of Jesus determine our expectations of our future and of mankind as a whole?

Bultmann thrust this question to the fore as part of his questioning concerning the relation of the Christian kerygma to myth. "For my part," he wrote, "the only interpretation I can give to the Pauline, and a fortiori synoptic, eschatology, is a critical one."[1] He holds that the eschatology of the gospels is fundamentally Jewish and that the Day of the Lord and coming of God are replaced by the parousia (but not materially changed thereby). He also maintains that the parousia is bound up with a mythological picture of a three-story universe, which means that "We can no longer look for the return of the Son of Man on the clouds of heaven, or hope that the faithful will meet him in the air."[2] On the other hand, he also suggests that there is in the New Testament the beginning of a demythologizing of eschatology through the emergence of realized eschatology. John took it to its radical conclusion, he says: in the coming of Jesus the expected judgment of the world took place, and that cancels out any future judgment in the traditional sense.[3] Since the end came with Christ, he suggests, the center of interest has shifted from the goal of the historic process to the salvation of the individual human being. The believer has no more concern with history, nor with traditional eschatology bound up with it.[4]

Bultmann's views are shared by not a few today. But the exegesis that I have offered in these pages entails a fundamental modification of Bultmann's understanding of the message of Jesus. The decisive shift of eschatology from the future alone to the future-in-the-present was the work of Jesus, not of Paul and John. According to Jesus, the coming of the kingdom of God is the determinative factor in his ministry of word and deed; it culminates in his death and resurrection and leads to his parousia at an undefined time. In Jesus' perspective there is no rigid distinction between the works of the Son of Man in his humble service of the divine sovereignty and his action at the end of the age: he acts for God as he mediates the saving sovereignty in his ministry and in his death and resurrection as well as in his parousia. Accordingly, it is wrong to isolate the teaching of Jesus on the parousia and assume that in that event we have a simple equivalent of Old Testament expectations of the coming of God and the Day of the Lord. The coming of God for the saving sovereignty takes place in the *total* intervention of God through the Son of Man/Jesus, and the anticipated events of the Day of the Lord are concentrated in the acts of God in the death-resurrection-parousia of that same Son of Man. The believer's experience of grace is determined by the *totality* of Jesus' action as Son of Man. Christian existence is set between an accomplished redemption and an awaited consummation, and it involves dependence on the grace of the Lord who has come, is present, and is to come. Moreover, this action of grace does not create a new existence in solitude; rather, it is intended to bring about a renewed *humanity*, wherein God's purpose for both the individual and the race reaches its fulfillment. To limit the significance of eschatology in the teaching of Jesus to the individual is to do grave injustice to it, and to threaten the historical character of the gospel.[5]

We have not yet answered the question concerning the "mythical" character of eschatological hope. Are not the concepts of the coming of God, the Day of the Lord, the kingdom of God, and the parousia all mythical symbols that have to be translated into a wholly different key for us moderns who no longer think in terms of myth? Bultmann believed so and offered a solution in existentialist categories. Norman Perrin agreed with this approach and sought to fortify it by contributing literary researches into the nature of symbolism. He draws attention to Philip Wheelwright's distinction between "steno-symbols" and "tensive" symbols. Wheelwright explains that "steno-language" is closed language, consisting of static terms with one-to-one meanings—the language of science and logic; it arises by habit and prescription. Tensive language, on the other hand, is open language, the language of poetry and liturgy, reflecting the struggle that belongs to organic life.[6] Perrin proposes that apocalyptic language be classified as steno-language on the grounds that its symbols are "hard," bearing fixed meanings. He argues that Jesus used the concept "kingdom of God" as a tensive symbol, but his followers replaced it by apocalyptic steno-symbols that misinterpreted his intention. It is therefore a mistake, in Perrin's opinion, to assume that the proclamation of the kingdom of God by Jesus refers to a single event experienced universally at one and the same time; it is instead a proclamation that claims to mediate "an experience of God as king, an experience of such an order that it brings the world to an end." The transformation of this proclamation into instruction on the cataclysmic coming of the kingdom of God at the parousia such as we find in the Q apocalypse of Luke 17 and the eschatological discourse of Mark 13 entails a transformation of the living symbolism of Jesus to an apocalyptic symbolism, says Perrin, and this is a distortion of Jesus' message.[7]

In pondering this interpretation of Jesus, one experiences the same sort of reaction that one has on reading Dodd for the first time: there is so much that is of worth here that it is a pity that the valuable points have to be accompanied by so much that is unjustifiable.

Perrin was a highly critical New Testament scholar, but his views on the eschatology of Jesus were determined by a very dubious understanding of Old Testament eschatology. He accepted without question Mowinckel's view that the notion of the kingship of God in Israel was rooted in the religious ideas of the Middle East—specifically, that God acted as king in creating the world as he overcame and slew the primeval monster, and that he maintained his kingship by annually renewing the fertility of the earth. I have presented a different account of the kingship of Yahweh. Israel's adoption of the concept of God as king had nothing to do with the creation myth; it was rooted in their existence as a nomadic people who viewed God as their Leader and Lord in the desert. The Hebrew understanding of the "kingship" of God was expanded and deepened through the people's experience of the exodus events. It was at that point in their history that they adopted notions of theophany and the Day of the Lord, which they intially understood in a noneschatological manner. The natural orientation of Israel's historical faith to the future led to an eschatological understanding of the rule of God, to a focus on the coming of God and the Day of the Lord. These elements of eschatological hope found expression in the prophetic literature in an abundance of symbolic and mythical images. Isaiah 51:9–11 provides an illustration of how the myth of the conquest of the dragon was not *formative* of Israel's eschatology, but an enriching *vehicle* for it; by no stretch of imagination can the eschatology of Deutero-Isaiah be comprehended under this myth. The vision of Daniel 7 likewise expresses the hope of the coming of God, the Day of the Lord, and the kingdom of God in terms of the combat myth; but the eschatology it communicates was forged in the prophetic tradition prior to its having been sharpened in its apocalyptic expression, and its representation of the judgment and the appearance of one like a man entails a creative use of the mythic tradition in the service of eschatological hope.

A similar lively and original use of the apocalyptic tradition is apparent in the New Testament apocalypse. Consider, as examples of imaginative use of apocalyptic myth and symbol, the representation of redemption through the Lamb in Revelation 5, the expression of the *same* reality in terms of the combat myth in Revelation 12, the portrayal of the parousia in Revelation 19, and the conglomeration of mythic symbols in the description of the City of God in Revelation 21:9–22:5. To describe these representations of the intervention of God in Christ as collections of "steno-symbols" is plainly absurd.

The symbolism employed by Jesus with respect to the kingdom of God is many-sided, drawing not only on scenes from peasant life, of which we hear much, but on the prophetic and apocalyptic traditions also. It is not without importance that there are links between the symbolism used regarding the kingdom of God and the symbolism relating to the work of the Son of Man. In the parables of the Strong Man Bound (Mark 3:27), the Sower (Mark 4:3ff.), the Seed Growing Secretly (Mark 4:26ff.), the Mustard Seed (Mark 4:30ff.), and the Tares and Wheat (Matt. 13:24ff.) we find echoes of myth and symbol employed in the prophetic and apocalyptic traditions. In Mark 2:28 we have a Son of Man saying that combines the motifs of creation and eschaton with the mission of Jesus as performed in his ministry. The utterances of Matthew 11:5 and 12:28 and Luke 10:18 set forth the ministry of Jesus in terms of strictly mythical concepts of the kingdom of God and the Day of the Lord while at the same time relating to his concrete deeds of ministry. His speech about his coming death and vindication in Luke 12:49–50 and at the Last Supper employ yet other apocalyptic images in setting forth the relation of his death to the process of the coming of the kingdom of God; and the predictions of the passion in terms of the suffering, rejection, death, and resurrection of the Son of Man (Mark 8:31, etc.) have the same sort of implications. We must not forget, with regard to the latter, that prophecy of the resurrection of Jesus strictly speaking falls under the category of myth, for resurrection connotes not a kiss of life imparted to a corpse but an apocalyptic appearance from beyond.

It is not a difficult transition from the use of myth and symbol relating to the kingdom of God in the ministry of Jesus to descriptions of the parousia and the future kingdom of God. We have already noted the living tradition of prophecy and apocalypse. An illustration of this can be seen in a passage that most scholars would view as apocalypse par excellence—Mark 13:24–27. Its description of the cosmos plunged into confusion is reminiscent of Old Testament prophecies relating to the Day of the Lord. This is no "hard" symbol, describing astronomical changes in that day. Like the similar material in Revelation 6:12–17, it reflects the tradition of the cosmos falling into fear and confusion before the Lord of creation when he steps forth in his majesty. Mark 13:24–25 employs this ancient mythical image to highlight the theophany of the Son of Man, the representative of God. If this is true of the context of the theophany, what of the theophany itself? That too is rooted in myth and symbol, employed throughout Israel's history to depict the coming of God for Israel's deliverance, and later the coming of God at the end for the greater Exodus. The parousia imagery is definitively influenced by Daniel 7:13, set in the heart of a frankly symbolic picture in which monsters from the deep rampage on earth, a "little horn" speaks great things against God, the Ancient in Years appears with his court, and one like a son of man comes on clouds to receive the rule of earth. Manifestly the Seer of Revelation understood this apocalyptic imagery and used it with great freedom. Did Jesus not understand it also?

On the supposition that he did, what did the symbol mean for him? That it had an existentialist application ("an experience of God as king of such an order that it brings the world to an end") can be dismissed. The symbol related to divine intervention that brings about judgment and redemption. That was always the purpose of a theophany, as of the Day of the Lord, and the end in view is the revelation of the kingdom of God. The coming of God for the initiation of his kingdom in the ministry of Jesus took place in historic, concrete action, which led to a deed at Golgotha and to an apocalyptic event of the third day. Jesus depicted all these acts in eschatological terms, supremely at the Last Supper, which anticipated the feast of the kingdom of God. These provide our chief clues to what the parousia means: *it is an act of God in Christ for the salvation of the world and its judgment.*

If the parousia represents the climactic intervention of God in Christ, let us acknowledge with candor that the representations of the event do not permit us to describe it. Our guide to apocalyptic, the book of Revelation, should suffice to demonstrate that. Even the best apocalyptic cryptographer could not produce an account of the birth, life, death, and resurrection of Jesus from the mythic picture of Revelation 12 alone, nor from the vision of the Lamb in Revelation 5. Why then should we suppose that anyone would be able to produce an account of the parousia from Revelation 19:11ff., in which the Word of God rides down from heaven on a white horse followed by armies of heavenly cavalry and treads the wine press of God's wrath alone, slaying men with the scimitar that issues out of his mouth? This is mythic imagery for an event that introduces the wedding of the Lamb to a bride who is depicted as a City that comes down from heaven, twelve thousand furlongs long, broad, and high. Recounting the metaphors in this fashion might make them sound nonsensical, but in the context of the vision they produce a powerful and moving depiction of the event that brings the world to its goal in God. I am persuaded that the transcendent language Jesus employed with reference to the parousia is of a similar order.

If the parousia represents the action of Christ whereby the rule of God reaches its beneficent consummation, it is a supremely *good* action—good, that is, in the sense of merciful and gracious. Why have we subordinated this element of the service of the Son of Man, seeing that it brings to a conclusion the process that began in Galilee and proceeded via Golgotha to the right hand of God, whence he shall come to reveal the saving sovereignty of heaven? The *Dies Irae*, "that dreadful day, when heaven and earth shall pass away," has all but banished from the church the association of the parousia with the happiness of the feast of God for the world, which was Jesus' favorite image for the kingdom of God. J. E. Fison wrote a book on the coming of Christ to stress the fact that the parousia is the ultimate revelation of the love of God for man. In picturesque fashion he states, "'Journey's end in lovers' meeting' puts in a sentence the secret of the eschatological transformation."[8] In a less romantic manner Karl Barth makes the same point when he characterizes the parousia as "the miracle of the divine 'Yes.'"[9] This we know by the fact that the cross precedes the parousia, and cross and parousia take place for man's participation in the kingdom of God.

Admittedly, judgment is part of the deed of the parousia. It cannot be otherwise. It is disturbing to reflect that there is no less sin in the world today since Christ's death and resurrection, but rather more. And this is serious, when we remember that in the biblical perspective sin is ultimately rebellion against God. As Karl Heim has pointed out,

> That the rebellion is limited to a tiny space is not to the point. The smallest opposing enterprise in this case has the same weight as the greatest cosmic revolution that throws whole solar systems and galaxies out of the courses allotted to them by the Creator. The condition of the case remains the same. Any event that takes place against God limits God. God is thereby dragged down to polarity. He is degraded to a terrestrial being that has a competitor with whom he has to come to terms. God is thereby robbed of his divinity.[10]

Heim concludes that if God is unable to resolve this condition that has come about in his creation, then "God is not God, but at best a demon, a limited and relative power like all other powers that measure their strength in the arena of the world."[11] These startling words underscore the point, all too easily overlooked, that there is necessarily a divine almighty *No* to man and all evil powers as well as a divine almighty *Yes*. Jesus' teaching on the kingdom of God and the parousia alike makes it clear that such a word is to be expected; for eyes and ears of faith, that message was sounded out at the cross, and it will be sounded with unmistakable clarity at the parousia.

At this point we may fittingly recall the difficulty experienced by not a few that the parousia expectation is always a *near* expectation; many hold that the fact that it has not yet occurred annuls the expectation itself. Yet near expectation is endemic to hope itself, as every page of Old Testament prophecy bears witness. Bultmann acknowledges that this is inevitable and explains it as all do: "To the prophetic consciousness the sovereignty of God, the absoluteness of his will, is so overpowering that before it the world sinks away and seems to be at its end."[12] There appears to be no other way by which the vision of the divinely determined future can be apprehended and expressed.[13] With Jesus, however, there is an added element that Bultmann did not recognize—namely, the awareness that God was fulfilling the promise of the kingdom in his ministry. The deeds of power that Jesus performed and the word of forgiveness and welcome to the fellowship of the kingdom he declared signified a real beginning of the sovereignty of God among men. His approach to the death by which the saving sovereignty would effectively come was accompanied by anticipation of resurrection for the kingdom and in God's time a parousia for its completion. Whoever acknowledges that the kingdom came with powerful efficacy in the death and resurrection of Jesus has no cause to reject the expectation of the parousia, through which the redemptive rule now powerfully present comes to its consummation. Moreover, we have seen that the near expectation of Jesus was qualified by the utterance in Mark 13:32. That saying has important implications: (1) the near expectation of Jesus should be viewed as *hope* rather than as apocalyptic *dogma*, (2) the time of the end is wholly set in the Father's disposal, and (3) whatever the time of fulfillment proves to be, *the period between Easter and the parousia is determined by the Father*, not by the accidents of history, and so it should not be a stumbling block for faith; the subjection of the Son to the Father's sovereign decision points to the attitude God desires in his lesser sons and daughters.

The old solution of the "problem" of the near expectation—namely, that a thousand years is to God as a day (2 Pet. 3:8)—remains relevant when one frankly recognizes that it merely qualifies what is inevitable. In truth, the notion of a thousand years as a day is a commonplace to scientific man, above all to the geologist and the astronomer. Heim points out that the light that began its journey from the farthest star of which we know when man *emerged* on earth will, on ordinary scientific reckoning, first reach this planet after the *disappearance* of man from the earth.[14] The history of man is only a pulse beat in the life of the universe—albeit a pulse beat that is important to God: the kingdom he causes to appear within it occupies more than a mere moment in the cosmic process. In such a context, the death and resurrection and parousia of Jesus are seen in their true significance: they are the means of *eternal* redemption.

Althaus's observation in his comment on Paul's expression of near expectation in Romans 13:11ff. is pertinent here, not as suggesting the unreality of time, but as pointing to its relation to the existence of man under the Lord of time:

> This end, whether it be temporally "near" or "far," is essentially near to everybody. For it is one with Christ, the Crucified and Risen Lord. It is there, where Christ is. The temporal end signifies only the redemption of the essential end, which is Christ, inasmuch as he is the Crucified and Risen One, and as the risen One heading for his coming, is for the world and history the Hidden One. To this extent all of us, all generations of the church, live at the same hour, in the one last hour, in a world and time that is destined to pass away—thus as in the twilight shortly before the sunrise.[15]

The ultimate meaning of the parousia is the light it casts on the significance of Jesus, appointed as Christ and Son of Man for the accomplishment of the divine will in the saving sovereignty that we call the kingdom of God. His teaching compels us to understand him as the Mediator of the saving sovereignty, alike in its initiation in his ministry, in its powerful "coming" in the cross and resurrection, and in its consummation at the parousia. The implications of this datum of Christology have to be handed over to the systematic theologians. That is a burdensome responsibility, and while they are engaged in their task the people of God must continue to work out their salvation. This they do in hope, looking to Jesus. To the question "Is he able to keep what I trust to him?" that lies in the hearts of God's people, P. T. Forsyth has given the following reply:

> I have no means of being sure about this, nor can I live as if I were, unless I know and experience Christ; unless I know him not simply as the Lover of my soul, but as Victor for it for ever, nay the very constituent of it; unless his love is the Holy One's love, love absolute. The Christian revelation is not just God is love, but *God's love is omnipotent*.[16]

It is precisely this that the cross, resurrection, and parousia of Jesus Christ our Lord proclaim and bring to actuality, for in these deeds the revelation of God reaches its perfection. And that revelation conveys the promise of eternal good.

In such faith the Evanston Assembly of the World Council of Churches concluded its message to the churches throughout the world, a message with which I concur:

> We do not know what is coming to us. But we know who is coming. It is he who meets us every day and who will meet us at the end—Jesus Christ our Lord.
> Therefore we say to you: Rejoice in hope.[17]

Notes

LIST OF ABBREVIATIONS

BEvT	*Beiträge zur Evangelischen Theologie*	NTS	*New Testament Studies*
BJRL	*Bulletin of the John Rylands University Library of Manchester*	RGG	*Die Religion in Geschichte und Gegenwart.* 3d ed. 6 vols. Tübingen, 1957.
BZ	*Biblische Zeitschrift*	RHPR	*Revue d'histoire et de philosophie religieuses*
CBQ	*Catholic Biblical Quarterly*		
DBSup	*Dictionnaire de la Supplément*	ST	*Studia Theologica*
ExpTim	*Expository Times*	TB	*Theologische Bücherei*
HST	*The History of the Synoptic Tradition,* by Rudolf Bultmann. 2d ed. Translated by John Marsh. New York, 1968.	TDNT	*Theological Dictionary of the New Testament.* 10 vols. Ed. Gerhard Kittel and Gerhard Friedrich, trans. Geoffrey W. Bromiley. Grand Rapids, 1964–76.
HTR	*Harvard Theological Review*	TLZ	*Theologische Literaturzeitung*
HUCA	*Hebrew Union College Annual*	TR	*Theologische Rundschau*
IDB	*Interpreter's Dictionary of the Bible.* 4 vols. Ed. George Arthur Buttrick et al. Nashville, 1962.	TSK	*Theologische Studien und Kritiken*
		ZA	*Zeitschrift für Assyriologie*
		ZAW	*Zeitschrift für die Alttestamentliche Wissenschaft*
JSJ	*Journal for the Study of Judaism in the Persian, Hellenistic and Roman Periods*	ZNW	*Zeitschrift für die Neutestamentliche Wissenschaft*
JSS	*Journal of Semitic Studies*		
JTS	*Journal of Tamil Studies*	ZTK	*Zeitschrift für Theologie und Kirche*

Preface

1. Lightfoot, *History and Interpretation in the Gospels* (London, 1935), p. 225. Lightfoot did not intend to express skepticism; he had in mind Job 26:14.

2. F. Young, "A Cloud of Witnesses," in *The Myth of God Incarnate,* ed. J. Hick (London, 1977), p. 18.

Chapter One

1. Pidoux, *Le dieux qui vient* (Neuchatel, 1947), p. 7.

2. Morgenstern, "Biblical Theophanies," ZAW 25 (1911): 139–93; 28 (1914): 15–60.

3. Morgenstern, "Biblical Theophanies," ZAW 25 (1911): 140.

4. Barr, "Theophany and Anthropomorphism in the Old Testament," in *Supplements to the Vetus Testamentum* (Leiden, 1960), 7: 331–32.

5. Lindblom, "Theophanies in Holy Places in Hebrew Religion," HUCA 32 (1961): 116.

6. See Westermann, *Das Loben Gottes in den Psalmen* (Göttingen, 1961), pp. 69ff.

7. Jenni, " 'Kommen' im theologischen Sprachgebrauch des Alten Testaments," in *Wort-Gebot-Glaube, Beiträge zur Theologie des Alten Testaments,* ed. Walther Eichrodt et al. (Zürich, 1970), pp. 254ff.

8. The best short introduction to the concept of Old Testament theophany I am aware of is F. Schnutenhaus, "Das Kommen und Erscheinen Gottes im Alten Testament," ZAW 76 (1964): 1–22. The definitive treatment of the subject is Jörg Jeremias's *Theophanie: Die Geschichte einer alttestamentlichen Gattung* (Neukirchen-Vluyn, 1965), to which I am deeply indebted, and on which I freely draw in this discussion.

9. Jeremias gives a detailed account of the nature and development of the structure of theophany (see *Theophanie,* pp. 7–71).

10. Schnutenhaus, "Das Kommen und Erscheinen Gottes im Alten Testament," p. 5.

11. See especially Gunkel, *Schöpfung und Chaos* (Göttingen, 1895).

12. The texts are conveniently reproduced and translated by G. R. Driver in his *Canaanite Myths and Legends* (Oxford, 1956). Regarding their significance for the Old Testament, see. F. M. Cross, *Canaanite Myth and Hebrew Epic* (Cambridge, Mass., 1973).

13. Jörg Jeremias makes a case for this assumption, pointing out that while in the Babylonian version of the myth the chaos battle precedes creation, in Ras Shamra texts it is described as having followed creation, suggesting that the psalmist probably knew the Babylonian version. But in Psalms 93:3 and 77:17 and in Habakkuk 3:8, the battle is presented as distinct from creation, which would indicate that the Ras Shamra tradition was the likely influence. It would seem that Israel knew and drew upon both versions of the myth.

14. Cited by Jeremias in *Theophanie,* p. 79.

15. *Baal,* 3.1.4–5.

16. *Keret,* 3.2.10 et passim.

17. *Keret,* 2.3.5.

18. See Jeremias, *Theophanie,* pp. 88–90, in which he presents an extensive summary of parallels between the theophany texts of the Old Testament and those of Israel's neighbors.

19. We should note that Jeremias speaks only of the fundamental notion of God's coming forth to help his people and not of the accompanying phenomena related in the Sinai tradition. Despite the undoubted importance of the theophany recounted in the Exodus narratives and its place in Israelite thought, it does not appear to have had a decisive effect on the descriptions of theophany in the Old Testament. Jeremias claims that the one text in which an epigone at a theophany description recalls the Sinai tradition is 4 Ezra 3:17–18, and even this does not indicate a dependence on the literary or traditional-historical influence of the Sinai theophany; the theophanic text of 4 Ezra 3:18 is simply used to illustrate the Sinai event (see Jeremias, *Theophanie,* p. 107; cf. Jenni, "'Kommen' im theologischen Sprachgebrauch des Alten Testaments," pp. 259–60).

20. This is explicitly expressed in Isaiah 51:9–10 and assumed in other texts, such as Job 26, 40, and 41; Isaiah 27:1; Ezekiel 29; and Daniel 7.

21. Schnutenhaus, "Das Kommen und Erscheinen Gottes im Alten Testament," p. 21.

22. Jeremias, *Theophanie,* p. 164.

Chapter Two

1. Note especially Joel 3:2, in which the prophet follows his account of "the *day* of the Lord" (2:1) with the phrase "in those *days* and at that *time*" (3:1). See also Jeremiah 7:32 and 9:25–26; and Amos 4:2, 5:13, and 8:11.

2. For a full account of the Day of the Lord and the history of its development, see L. Czerny, *The Day of the Lord and Some Relevant Problems* (Prague, 1948).

3. See Munch, *The Expression "bajjom hahu": Is It an Eschatological Terminus Technicus?* (Oslo, 1936), p. 60n.16. Buttenwieser suggests that it was often used to denote a person's end (*The Psalms* [Chicago, 1938], p. 221n.7).

4. Von Rad, "The Origin of the Concept of the Day of Yahweh," *JSS* 4 (1959): 101.

5. So argues von Rad in various discussions of this theme: in *Old Testament Theology,* 2 vols., trans. D. M. G. Stalker (New York, 1965), 2: 123ff.; in an article on *hemera* in *TDNT,* 2: 944; and in "The Origin of the Concept of the Day of Yahweh," pp. 105ff. See also Czerny, *The Day of the Lord and Some Relevant Problems,* pp. 81–82; W. E. Eichrodt, *Theology of the Old Testament,* 2 vols., trans. J. A. Baker, Old Testament Library (Philadelphia, 1961–67), 1: 460; E. Jenni, "Eschatology of the Old Testament," in *IDB,* 2: 127; and G. E. Wright, *The Old Testament and Theology* (New York, 1969), pp. 135ff. Mowinckel has developed a thesis that opposes the position of these scholars in an essay

entitled "The Day of Yahweh is the Day of His Enthronement," in *Psalmenstudien* (Oslo, 1922), 2: 230ff. For a critique of Mowinckel, see Czerny, *The Day of the Lord and Some Relevant Problems*, pp. 46–47; Eichrodt, *Theology of the Old Testament*, pp. 123–24; O. Eissfeldt, "Jahwe als König," *ZAW* 5 (1928): 81ff.; and M. Buber, *Kingship of God*, trans. Richard Scheimann (New York, 1967), pp. 126ff.

6. Th. Vriezen generalized this position when he stated that "In Israel no fundamental distinction was made between things to come (without further distinction), indicating the limit of the speaker's horizon, and the future taken absolutely" ("Prophecy and Eschatology," in *Supplements to the Vetus Testamentum* [Leiden, 1953], 1: 202).

7. See Ezekiel 13:5, 22:31, and 34:12.

8. Von Rad, "The Origin of the Concept of the Day of Yahweh," p. 107; see also *TDNT*, 2: 944.

9. Vriezen, "Prophecy and Eschatology," p. 204.

10. See, for example, Isaiah 22:4:

Then I said, Turn your eyes away from me;
Leave me to weep in misery.
Do not thrust consolation on me
for the ruin of my own people.

11. See Jenni: "Pure prophecy of calamity or pure prophecy of salvation is an abstraction" ("Eschatology of the Old Testament," p. 128).

12. See A. Jepsen, "Eschatologie im AT," *RGG*, 2: 658. For an eloquent expression of the unity of the wrath and love of God in the Old Testament view of the future, see H. H. Rowley, *The Re-Discovery of the Old Testament* (London, 1945), p. 185. See also E. Jacob, *Theology of the Old Testament*, trans. A. W. Heathcote and P. J. Allcock (London, 1958), p. 323; Eichrodt, *Theology of the Old Testament*, pp. 459ff.; Vriezen, "Prophecy and Eschatology," pp. 206–7; Von Rad, "The Origin of the Concept of the Day of Yahweh," p. 107; and *TDNT*, 2: 946.

13. See Jeremiah 31:31ff. and Ezekiel 36:26ff.

14. Von Rad, *Old Testament Theology*, 2: 119.

15. For further examples, see Isaiah 25:9ff.; 30:27ff.; 63:1ff.; and 66:5ff., 15ff.; and Zechariah 14:3ff.

16. In examining the relationships between the two kinds of portrayals, Jörg Jeremias made the determination that such elements in the Day of the Lord as the utterance of the voice of Yahweh and the shaking of heaven and earth were proper to theophanies, whereas in theophany accounts the failure of stars to give light, the desolation of the land, and the destruction of men were taken from the traditions of the Day of the Lord; the presence of dark clouds, he says, is characteristic of both theophany and the Day of the Lord traditions (see Jeremias, *Theophanie: Die Geschichte einer alttestamentlichen Gattung* [Neukirchen-Vluyn, 1965], pp. 98ff.).

17. Von Rad, *Old Testament Theology*, p. 124.

Chapter Three

1. Three terms are used to denote "kingdom" in the Old Testament: *malkūth* (in Ps. 103:19 and 145:11–13, and in Dan. 3:33 and 4:31), *melūkah* (in Obad. 21 and Ps. 22:29), and *mamlākāh* (in 1 Chron. 29:11).

2. For a list of these references, see O. Eissfeldt, "Jahwe als König," *ZAW* 5 (1928): 89.

3. Eissfeldt, "Jahwe als König," p. 89.

4. Köhler, *Old Testament Theology*, trans. A. S. Todd (Philadelphia, 1953), p. 30.

5. Buber, *Kingship of God* (London, 1967), p. 58.

6. The popularity of the later phrase *malkūth shāmayim* ("kingdom of heaven") was linked to a Jewish desire to avoid making direct comments about God. W. G. Kuhn sees in this a parallel use of the term *shekinah* in rabbinic writings: "As this is a simple

substitute for the OT saying *shākan Yhwh*: 'God dwells,' 'God is present,' so later Judaism uses *malkūth shāmayim* for 'God is king'" (*TDNT*, 1: 571). For more on *malkūth* and related terms, see Von Rad, *TDNT*, 1: 570.

7. Eissfeldt, "Jahwe als König," pp. 84ff.

8. See Buber, *Kingship of God*, pp. 2–23, 95, 99ff.

9. Preuss, *Jahweglaube und Zukunftserwartung* (Stuttgart, 1968), p. 16. For recent thought on the meaning of *Yahweh*, see *Jahweglaube und Zukunftserwartung*, pp. 15ff., and the literature Preuss cites in note 27. Frank Cross argues that the verb from which YHWH is formed is a causative-imperfect of the Canaanite-Proto-Hebrew *hwy*, "to be," and thus that it means "cause to be," "create," and *Yahweh* is a shortened form of a sentence name that means "he who creates" (*Caanite Myth and Hebrew Epic* [Cambridge, Mass., 1973], p. 50). Preuss acknowledges the viability of this interpretation, but he maintains that *hawah*, the verb at the root of *Yahweh*, should be understood as a Qal imperfect that denotes acting and working rather than being. Hence, Preuss reads Exodus 3:14 as signifying "I am he, as I will show myself to be," which is to say, "You will know in my future words and deeds what and how I am and will be and intend to be your God." If the notion of creation, which Cross finds in the name, is applied to ongoing history as well as its beginning, however, the two interpretations will not be far from each other.

10. See G. E. Mendenhall, *Law and Covenant in Israel and the Ancient Near East* (Pittsburgh, 1965). See also G. E. Wright's review of Mendenhall's position and its pertinence to the interpretation of the kingship of Yahweh in *The Old Testament and Theology* (New York, 1969), pp. 104ff. Buber had previously observed the relevance of the correspondence between the Sinaitic covenant and the Arabian *baia* covenant, a form that also has a close parallel with the covenant between the Israelites in Hebron and David (see 2 Sam. 5:3), and he had noted other examples of a like order from other Semitic peoples (see *Kingship of God*, pp. 126ff.).

11. Buber, *Kingship of God*, pp. 124ff.

12. For an extended examination of this thesis, see Preuss, *Jahweglaube und Zukunftserwartung*.

13. On this point, see V. Maag, "Malkut Jahwe," in *Supplements to the Vetus Testamentum* (Leiden, 1960), 7: 140.

14. See von Rad, *Old Testament Theology* (New York, 1965), 2: 99–107.

15. Wendland, *Geschichtsanschauung und Geschichtsbewusstsein im Neuen Testament* (Göttingen, 1938), p. 15.

16. See Gressmann, *Der Messiah* (Göttingen, 1929), p. 294.

17. Mowinckel examines and dismisses the idea in "Urmensch und 'Königsidealogie,'" *ST* 1 (1948–49), 71ff. See also chapter 3 of *He That Cometh*, trans. G. W. Anderson (New York, 1955).

18. See Mowinckel, *He That Cometh*, pp. 21, 122, 255–56, 159–60, 173.

19. In essence this is the view L. Dürr seeks to expound in *Ursprung und Ausbau der israelitisch-jüdischen Heilandserwartung* (Berlin, 1925), which depends in no small measure on Mowinckel's earlier writings; see especially pp. 56ff. This view is also propounded by Preuss (pp. 136ff.) and by H. W. Wolff in "Herrschaft Jahwes und Messiasgestalt im alten Testament," *ZAW* 13 (1936): 181ff.

20. Mowinckel, *He That Cometh*, p. 156.

21. See Wolff, "Herrschaft Jahwes und Messiasgestalt im alten Testament," p. 191.

22. Eichrodt, *Theology of the Old Testament*, 2 vols., trans. J. A. Baker, Old Testament Library (Philadelphia, 1961–67), 1: 499; italics his. I have not attempted to keep track of all Old Testament scholars who have made similar statements, but we might take note of the following: Eissfeldt argues that in Israel Yahweh's kingship had an orientation toward eschatology, that his worshipers ever considered themselves to be in Advent, ever looked to their God-King as one coming ("Jahwe als König," p. 89); E. Jenni states that "The coming of Yahweh is the central idea of OT eschatology" and that "Salvation . . .

basically consists of the coming of Yahweh" ("Eschatology in the Old Testament," *IDB*, 2: 127–28); and E. Jacob states that "The basis of Israel's hope is solely the certitude that their God Yahweh . . . would come and establish his kingship" (*Theology of the Old Testament*, trans. A. W. Heathcote and P. J. Allcock [London, 1958], p. 317). See also A. Jepsen, "Eschatologie im AT," *RGG*, 2: 661; H. D. Preuss, *Jahweglaube und Zukunfts-erwartung*, pp. 205ff.; and L. Dürr, *Ursprung und Ausbau der israelitisch-jüdischen Heilandserswartung*, p. 38.

23. See Preuss, *Jahweglaube und Zukunftserwartung*, p. 150.
24. See Mowinckel, *He That Cometh*, p. 170.
25. Wolff, "Herrschaft Jahwes und Messiasgestalt im alten Testament," p. 193.

Chapter Four

1. L. F. Hartmann and A. A. Di Lella, in their commentary on Daniel in the Anchor Bible (Garden City, N.Y., 1978), dispute this, arguing that the author of Daniel drew his pictures of the beasts of the sea and the figures of the court scene from the Bible and the common stock of folk ideas of the ancient Middle East (see pp. 212, 217, and 219). Most recent exegetes of Daniel, however, agree that in his vision in chapter 7, the Seer utilizes the mythological traditions of Israel's neighbors as well as those of Israel itself; see, for example, A. Lacocque, *Le Livre de Daniel* (Neuchatel, 1976), pp. 105–11; R. Hammer, *The Book of Daniel*, Cambridge Bible Commentary (Cambridge, 1976), pp. 74–86; and J. J. Collins, *The Apocalyptic Vision of the Book of Daniel*, Harvard Semitic Monographs no. 16 (Missoula, 1977), pp. 95–118. For discussion of the especially important Canaanite religious traditions, see J. A. Emerton, "The Origin of the Son of Man Imagery," *JTS* 9 (1958): 225–42; and F. M. Cross, *Canaanite Myth and Hebrew Epic* (Cambridge, Mass., 1973), pp. 112–44. And for related traditions in the nearer Orient generally, see A. Y. Collins, *The Combat Myth in the Book of Revelation*, Harvard Dissertations in Religion no. 9 (Missoula, 1976), chapters 2, 3, and 5, and the literature cited therein.
2. So argues K. Müller in "Der Menschensohn im Danielzyklus," in *Jesus und der Menschensohn*, ed. R. Pesch and R. Schnackenburg (Freiburg, 1975), pp. 41ff. P. Weimar calls the passage a "Son of Man psalm" as he makes a similar case in "Daniel 7, Text-analyse," in the same volume, p. 23.
3. So argue Schaeder, von Gall, and Noth; see W. Baumgartner's discussion of their argument, "Ein Vierteljahrhundert Danielforschung," *TR* 11 (1939): 214.
4. So suggests Baumgartner, after Haller, "Ein Vierteljahrhundert Daniel-forschung," p. 214.
5. So contend S. J. Coppens and L. Dequeker in *Le Fils de l'homme et les Saints du Très-Haut en Daniel VII*, 2d ed. (Bruges-Paris, 1961), p. 22. These authors point out the close interrelation of the two parts: "The man is opposed to the beast, as the light to darkness; the heavens answer to the land or the sea, the clouds of the sky to the four winds of heaven. The antithetic parallelism is striking."
6. Compare this simple pattern with the more detailed analyses of the combat myth adduced by A. Y. Collins, *The Combat Myth in the Book of Revelation*, pp. 58–61, 83, 207–10.
7. It may be observed that to postulate such an origin for the passage carries a corollary of some importance in light of contemporary studies on the Son of Man: the myth of primal man is not on the horizon of this vision.
8. In this literature, El is frequently called "the Kindly One, El Benign."
9. So contends J. A. Emerton, "The Origin of the Son of Man Imagery," p. 232.
10. Müller, "Der Menschensohn im Danielzyklus," p. 45.
11. This interpretation, though not popular, is not without support from scholars of former and present days. Dalman holds that in the vision Yahweh is represented as coming to earth (*Words of Jesus* [Edinburgh, 1909], p. 241n.2). Similar views are present-ed by H. H. Rowley (*Relevance of Apocalyptic*, 2d ed. [London, 1947], p. 30n.1), A. Bentzen (*Daniel*, Handbuch zum Alten Testament, 2d ed. [Tübingen, 1952], p. 30), and

J. A. Emerton ("The Origin of the Son of Man Imagery," p. 230). In support of this view, Müller emphasizes the parallels with Ezekiel 1:24 and Isaiah 6:2 ("Der Menschensohn im Danielzyklus," pp. 45–46). M. Black also elaborates the view that verses 9–10 reflect a form of theophanic throne vision similar to that in Isaiah 6 and Ezekiel 1 ("Die Apotheose Israels: Eine neue interpretation des danielischen Menschensohns," in *Jesus und der Menschensohn*, pp. 96–99).

12. See Noth, "Die Heiligen des Höchsten," *Norsk Theologisk Tidsskrift* 56 (1955): 146–61.

13. See especially the discussion of this by Coppens and Dequeker, *Le Fils de l'homme et les Saints du Très-Haut en Daniel VII*, pp. 35–37.

14. See Coppens and Dequeker, *Le Fils de l'homme et les Saints du Très-Haut en Daniel VII*, pp. 29–30.

15. See, for example, Müller, "Der Menschensohn im Danielzyklus," p. 59.

16. So contends J. J. Collins, *The Combat Myth in the Book of Revelation*, pp. 123–26, 146.

17. *The Scroll of the War of the Sons of Light against the Sons of Darkness*, trans. Y. Yadin (Oxford, 1962), p. 316.

18. The identification of the Son of Man with Michael was suggested by N. Schmidt as long ago as 1900 in "The 'Son of Man' in the Book of Daniel," *JBL* 19 (1900): 22–28. Ziony Zevit has argued that Gabriel was more likely: see "The Structure and Individual Elements of Daniel 7," *ZAW* 80 (1968): 385–96. The link with the angel representatives of the nations, a more recent idea, is represented by Müller, "Der Menschensohn im Danielzyklus," pp. 58–78.

19. Collins, *The Combat Myth in the Book of Revelation*, pp. 134–35.

20. See Kuhn, *Enderwartung und Gegenwärtiges Heil: Untersuchungen zu den Gemeindeliedern von Qumran* (Göttingen, 1966), p. 92. Kuhn protests that Noth overlooks the importance of the development within late Judaism of the use of the term *saints* for those who belong to the eschatological people of God (p. 92).

21. So argues A. Jeffrey, *TB* 6 (1956): 461, following J. Hempel and E. Herzfeldt.

22. So argues A. Bentzen (*Daniel*, p. 34), E. W. Heaton (*Daniel*, Torch Bible Commentary [London, 1956], p. 183), and J. A. Emerton ("The Origin of the Son of Man Imagery," pp. 230–31).

23. For evidence on which this discussion of Revelation 12 is based, see the review of interpretation of the chapter by P. Prigent, *Apocalypse 12: Histoire de l'exégèse* (Tübingen, 1959), and the following commentaries: R. H. Charles, *A Critical and Exegetical Commentary on the Revelation of St. John*, International Critical Commentary (Edinburgh, 1920), 1: 298–314; M. Kiddle, *The Revelation of St. John*, The Moffatt New Testament Commentary (London, 1940), pp. 211–18; G. B. Caird, *The Revelation of St. John the Divine*, Black's New Testament Commentary (London, 1966), pp. 147–57; A. M. Farrer, *The Revelation of St. John the Divine* (Oxford, 1964), pp. 139–47; and G. R. Beasley-Murray, *Revelation*, The New Century Bible (London, 1974), pp. 191–97.

Chapter Five

1. Collins, "Jewish Apocalyptic against Its Hellenistic Near Eastern Environment," *Bulletin of the American Schools of Oriental Research* 220 (1975): 28.

2. See Collins, "Jewish Apocalyptic," p. 29.

3. See Collins, "Jewish Apocalyptic," p. 30.

4. J. Mesnard, *Les Tendances apocalyptiques chez le Prophète Ézéchiel* (Paris, 1907), p. 23.

5. Koch, *The Rediscovery of Apocalyptic* (London, 1972), p. 33. In an extended note Koch explains what he means by "the revelation of the divine revelation." An apocalypse is intended to convey proclamation to a community: "What is laid bare is the eschatological drama, and that in such a fashion that the hearer or reader is in a position to

make 'faith' the direction of his life, thereby making possible personal salvation at the impending divine coming" (pp. 136n.38).

6. For other passages in this vein, see the Testaments of Simeon 4:5–6, Levi 2:11, Judah 22:2, Zebulun 9:8, Naphtali 8:3, and Asher 7:3.

7. For other references to the old theophanic tradition, see the Wisdom of Solomon 5:17–23, remarkable for its representing the sea to be the instrument of God instead of his enemy; Judith 16:15; Ecclesiasticus 16:18–19; Testament of Levi 3:9–10; and 2 Esdras 3:18.

8. From *The Dead Sea Scriptures in English Translation*, trans. T. H. Gaster (New York, 1956), pp. 139–40.

9. N. Messel, *Die Einheitlichkeit der jüdischen Eschatologie* (Giessen, 1915), p. 9.

Chapter Six

1. S.v. "Apocalyptic Literature," in *A Commentary on the Bible*, ed. A. S. Peake (London, 1919), p. 432.

2. Burkitt, *Jewish and Christian Apocalypses* (London, 1914), p. 2.

3. Russell, *The Method and Message of Jewish Apocalyptic* (London, 1964), p. 94.

Chapter Seven

1. Burkitt, *Jewish and Christian Apocalypses* (London, 1914), p. 7.

2. Translated by Pierre Bogaert in *Apocalypse de Baruch: Introduction, Traduction du Syriaque et Commentaire* (Paris, 1969), pp. 515–16. In contrast to some translators, Bogaert contends that this passage is referring to people rather than things. He points out that the Syriac version uses the masculine not the feminine (= neuter), and he maintains that it is more natural to read the passage as saying that the time that will "mark the end of corruption . . . is held far from the evil [persons] and it is wholly near for those who will not die" than to read it as "it is far away from evils, and near to those things which die not" (Charles's translation).

3. Among these interpreters are V. Violet (*Die Apokalypsen des Esra und des Baruch in Deutscher Gestalt* [Leipzig, 1924], p. 246) and H. H. Rowley (*The Relevance of Apocalyptic* [London, 1944], p. 99).

4. Among these commentators are R. H. Charles (*The Apocrypha and Pseudepigrapha of the Old Testament in English, with Introductions and Critical and Explanatory Notes to the Several Books,* 2 vols. [Oxford, 1913], 2: 498) and P. Bogaert (*Apocalypse de Baruch,* p. 65).

5. Müller, *Messias und Menschensohn in jüdischen Apokalypsen und in der Offenbarung des Johannes*, Studien zum Neuen Testament, nr. 6 (Gütersloh, 1972), p. 143.

6. Pryke, "Eschatology in the Dead Sea Scrolls," in *The Scrolls and Christianity*, ed. M. Black (London, 1969), p. 50.

7. Schubert, *The Dead Sea Community*, trans. J. W. Doberstein (New York, 1959), p. 108.

8. See Kuhn, *Enderwartung und Gegenwärtiges Heil: Untersuchungen zu den Gemeindeliedern von Qumran* (Göttingen, 1966).

9. Kuhn, *Enderwartung und Gegenwärtiges Heil*, p. 185.

10. See Kuhn, *Enderwartung und Gegenwärtiges Heil*, pp. 183–84.

Chapter Eight

1. Müller, *Messias und Menschensohn in jüdischen Apokalypsen und in der Offenbarung des Johannes*, Studien zum Neuen Testament, nr. 6 (Gütersloh, 1972), pp. 61–63.

2. See F. F. Bruce, *Second Thoughts on the Dead Sea Scrolls* (London, 1956), pp. 77–78.

3. W. G. Kuhn, for example, argues for this position in "The Two Messiahs of

NOTES TO PAGES 54-58

Aaron and Israel," in *The Scrolls and the New Testament*, ed. K. Stendahl (London, 1958), p. 59.

4. Among those arguing for this point of view is M. Black, in *The Scrolls and Christian Origins* (London, 1961), p. 157.

5. D. C. Duling, "The Promises to David and Their Entrance into Christianity," *NTS* 19 (1973–74): 64.

6. Endeavors to represent the Testaments of the Twelve Patriarchs as a Christian work incorporating Jewish sources (associated above all with the labors of M. de Jonge, best known for his book *Testaments of the Twelve Patriarchs*) rather than a Jewish work with Christian interpolations seem to me unconvincing. The book reflects an attitude toward the law and the piety of Judaism that a Christian would be unlikely to express, though he could approve its spirit, especially in view of its contacts with Christian messianic beliefs. K. H. Rengstorff drew attention to the fact that in the Testaments Joseph stands out even more than Levi and Judah, and that the book portrays not a duality of leadership but a triumvirate as the center and head of the whole circle of the patriarchs. Though neither priest nor king, Joseph is set forth as the ideal type of wise man, the absolutely exemplary character; it is suggested that to follow him is to be a true observer of the law and a worthy successor to Abraham, Isaac, and Jacob. This strongly points to a Jewish origin of the book. (See Rengstorff's article "Herkunft und Sinn der Patriarchen-Reden in den Testamenten der Zwölf Patriarchen," in *La Littérature juive entre Tenach et Mischna: Quelques Problèmes*, ed. W. C. van Unnik [Leiden, 1964].)

7. Charles held that the references to the Messiah from Judah indicate attempts to offset the more original statements that represent the Messiah as springing from Levi (see Charles, *Apocrypha and Pseudepigrapha,* 2: 294, as well as his comments on the passages in question throughout the commentary).

8. See F. M. Cross, *The Ancient Library of Qumran and Modern Biblical Studies* (London, 1958), p. 166; M. Burrows, *More Light on the Dead Sea Scrolls* (London, 1958), p. 306, following Yadin; and Black, *The Scrolls and Christian Origins,* pp. 154–55.

9. See the discussion in H. L. Strack–P. Billerbeck, *Kommentar zum Neuen Testament aus Talmud und Midrasch,* 6 vols. (München, 1922–28), 3: 20ff.

10. Translated by D. C. Duling in "The Promises to David and Their Entrance into Christianity," p. 66.

11. Fitzmyer, "The Contribution of Qumran Aramaic to the Study of the New Testament," *NTS* 20 (1974): 393.

12. Fitzmyer, "The Contribution of Qumran Aramaic to the Study of the New Testament," p. 393.

13. Grundmann, "Die Frage nach der Gottessohnschaft des Messiah im Lichte von Qumran," in *Bibel und Qumran* (Berlin, 1968), p. 102.

14. See, for example, M. Hengel, *Der Sohn Gottes* (Tübingen, 1974), pp. 68ff.

15. See Braun, *Qumran und das Neue Testament* (Tübingen, 1966), p. 76.

16. Lines 286ff.: "The God of heaven shall send a king, and shall judge each man with blood and flame of fire," and 652ff.: "From the sunrise God shall send a king, who shall give every land relief from the bane of war." Both passages provide a description of the kingdom of God that recalls the messianic descriptions of Psalms of Solomon 17–18.

17. Müller, *Messias und Menschensohn,* pp. 65ff.

18. Hengel, *Judaism and Hellenism: Studies in Their Encounter in Palestine during the Early Hellenistic Period,* trans. J. S. Bowden (London, 1974), 1: 188.

19. Such is the argument of M. D. Hooker (*The Son of Man in Mark* [London, 1967], p. 44) and Müller (*Messias und Menschensohn,* p. 40).

20. R. H. Charles maintained that the rule of "Mine Elect One" in 1 Enoch 45:3–4 relates to a temporary messianic rule on the earth, after which (according to 45:4ff.) the heaven and earth are to be transformed to be an eternal blessing and light (see *Apocrypha and Pseudepigrapha,* 2: 214). While the sequence of statements in chapter 45 is susceptible of that interpretation, it is doubtful that the author intended them so to be under-

352

stood; it is more likely that he looked for the transformation to take place prior to the commencement of the kingdom, and with it the resurrection of the righteous and the rule of the Son of Man.

21. Hooker, *The Son of Man in Mark,* pp. 46–47.

22. Müller, *Messias und Menschensohn,* p. 39.

23. Such is the argument of T. W. Manson ("The Son of Man in Daniel, Enoch and the Gospels," *BJRL* 32 [1950]: 171ff.), H. H. Rowley (*The Biblical Doctrine of Election,* p. 157), D. S. Russell (*Method and Message of Apocalyptic* [London, 1964], p. 352), and M. D. Hooker (*The Son of Man in Mark,* pp. 46–47).

24. Among those to have reached this conclusion are, notably, E. Sjöberg (*Der Menschensohn im Äthiopischen Henochbuch* [Lund, 1946], pp. 83ff.), S. Mowinckel (*He That Cometh,* trans. G. W. Anderson [New York, 1955], pp. 370ff.), and Müller (*Messias und Menschensohn,* pp. 47ff.).

25. C. Colpe observes that such an identification is analogous to the belief of primitive Christianity in the eschatological work of Jesus as the Son of Man (*TDNT,* 8: 427); H. R. Balz holds that 1 Enoch 71:14ff. describes an enthronement scene after the style of Psalm 21:7, but roots the Son of Man concept of the Similitudes in the visions of the glory of God in Ezekiel, combined with the Danielic vision of the man-like one (*Methodische Probleme der Neutestamentlichen Christologie,* Wissenschaftliche Monographien zum Alten und Neuen Testament, nr. 25 [Neukirchen-Vluyn, 1967], pp. 79ff.).

26. Such is the contention of M. Casey in "The Use of the term 'Son of Man' in the Similitudes of Enoch," *JSJ* 8 (1976): 25 (following on suggestions of M. D. Hooker, *The Son of Man in Mark,* pp. 42ff.).

27. Müller provides a useful synopsis of statements in 4 Ezra and 2 Baruch relating to the Messiah and his functions (see *Messias und Menschensohn,* pp. 104–5).

28. Müller, *Messias und Menschensohn,* p. 121.

29. Müller, *Messias und Menschensohn,* pp. 134ff.

30. In a discussion of the Messiah, S. Mathews states that "This is not always an explicitly described element in all the messianic conceptions. *He would of course be always implied*" (*Messianic Hope in the New Testament* [Chicago, 1905], p. 54.

31. The judgment of R. H. Charles, who had more than a passing acquaintance with apocalyptic literature, is still worth pondering: "From the middle of the first century B.C. the expectation of the Messiah becomes almost universally the central figure in the messianic kingdom" (*Eschatology: The Doctrine of the Future Life in Israel, Judaism, and Christianity* [New York, 1963], p. 359).

Excursus One

1. See Beer, *Die Apokryphen und Pseudepigraphen des Alten Testaments,* ed. E. Kautsch (Tübingen, 1900), 2: 230–32.

2. See Charles's *The Book of Enoch* (Oxford, 1893) and *The Apocrypha and Pseudepigrapha of the Old Testament in English, with Introductions and Critical and Explanatory Notes to the Several Books,* 2 vols. (Oxford, 1913), 1: 171.

3. Frey, "Apocryphes de l'Ancien Testament," in *DBSup* 1: 360–64.

4. Frey, "Apocryphes de l'Ancien Testament," 1: 364.

5. Greenfield, in the prolegomenon to the second edition of Hugo Odeberg's *3 Enoch,* The Library of Biblical Studies (New York, 1973), p. xvii.

6. See J. C. Hindley, "Towards a Date for the Similitudes of Enoch: An Historical Approach," *NTS* 4 (1968): 553.

7. See Josephus, *Jewish War,* 1.13.1–11.

8. Josephus, *Antiquities,* 17.6.5.

9. See F. T. Glasson, *The Second Advent* (London, 1945), p. 61; Glasson is following a suggestion of V. H. Stanton (see Hastings' *A Dictionary of the Bible,* 3: 356).

10. See N. Schmidt, *Encyclopaedia Biblica,* s.v. "Son of Man." N. Messel held a modification of this view, suggesting that references to the Son of Man in the Similitudes

are interpolations—except for the references in 1 Enoch 46:2–4 and 48:2, which bear the same corporate meaning of Son of Man as that which appears in Daniel 7:13ff.; Messel therefore maintained that the Jews in the time of Jesus did not view the Son of Man as a messianic term (see *Der Menschensohn in den Bilderreden des Henoch*, Beihefte zur ZAW, nr. 35 [Geissen, 1922], p. 8).

11. This view was widespread among nineteenth-century scholars. See Frey, "Apocryphes de l'Ancien Testament," 1: 359.

12. See Black, "The Fragments of the Aramaic-Enoch from Qumran," in *La Littérature juive entre Tenach et Mischna: Quelques Problèmes*, ed. W. C. van Unnik (Leiden, 1974), p. 18.

13. See Hindley, "Towards a Date for the Similitudes of Enoch," pp. 553–65.

14. See Milik, *The Books of Enoch, Aramaic Fragments of Cave 4* (Oxford, 1976), pp. 95–96.

15. Frey, "Apocryphes de l'Ancien Testament," 1: 359. See also M. D. Hooker, *The Son of Man in Mark* (London, 1967), p. 48; and M. A. Knibb, "The Date of the Parables of Enoch: A Critical Review," *NTS* 25 (1978–79): 350–52.

16. D. Flusser has suggested that the figure of the Son of Man in the Similitudes may have influenced the representation of Melchizedek in the Melchizedek fragment found in Cave XI (see "Melchizedek and the Son of Man," *Christian News from Israel* 17 [1966]: 23–29). Undoubtedly there are similarities, in that Melchizedek has become a heavenly figure and has functions of judgment in the last days. Nevertheless the traditions relating to Melchizedek have been developed by a quite different route from those of the Son of Man, being based on a different set of scriptures (notably Gen. 14:18ff. with Pss. 7, 82, and 110:4; and Isa. 52:7 and 61:1) and the mode of using those scriptures characteristic of the Qumran method. The result is a remarkable analogy to the Son of Man concept without any indication of contact between them.

17. U. B. Müller has plausibly argued this case in a lengthy discussion of the evidence, *Messias und Menschensohn in jüdischen Apokalypsen und in der Offenbarung des Johannes*, Studien zum Neuen Testament, nr. 6 (Gütersloh, 1972), pp. 104–40.

18. The inspiration of this usage appears to be Daniel 11:30, in which the reference to "ships of Kittim" is interpreted by the LXX and Vulgate as signifying ships of the Romans. The Habakkuk Commentary 6:3–5 states, "The Kittim sacrifice to their standards, and their weapons of war are the objects of their religion," a clear reference to the Roman cult of their military standards. See Y. Yadin, *The Scroll of the War of the Sons of Light against the Sons of Darkness* (London, 1962), pp. 22–25; and A. Dupont-Sommer, *The Essene Writings of Qumran* (Gloucester, Mass., 1973), pp. 341–51.

19. Yadin, *The Message of the Scrolls* (New York, 1957), p. 172.

20. Farmer, *Maccabees, Zealots and Josephus* (New York, 1956), p. 118.

22. For conditions in Palestine under the rule of Roman procurators, see M. Stern, "The Province of Judaea," in *The Jewish People in the First Century*, ed. S. Safrai and M. Stern (Philadelphia, 1974).

23. Dupont-Sommer is not impressed with the fact that the Similitudes have not been found in the Qumran Caves, partly because other works that were once believed not to have existed in the period of the Qumran sect (e.g., the Testaments of Levi and Naphtali) have subsequently been dated to that time, and partly because the relics that have thus far been recovered cannot be said to comprise the total number of manuscripts in the Essene library. See his discussion in *The Essene Writings from Qumran*, pp. 299–300.

24. See J. C. Greenfield, in the later edition of Odeberg's *3 Enoch*, p. xiii. Greenfield further follows D. Flusser in thinking that the Qumran sectarians could not have viewed the Similitudes as an orthodox work because of the manner in which tasks and roles assigned to the sun and moon are treated in chapter 41 (see p. xiv).

25. Among those scholars who concur with this assessment of the evidence are E. Sjöberg (*Der Menschensohn im Äthiopischen Henochbuch* [Lund, 1946], p. 39), F. M.

Cross (*The Ancient Library of Qumran* [London, 1958], p. 151n.7), M. D. Hooker (*The Son of Man in Mark*, pp. 47–48), and C. L. Mearns ("The Parables of Enoch—Origin and Date," *ExpTim* 89 [1978]: 118–19, and "Dating the Similitudes of Enoch," *NTS* 25 [1978–79]: 360–69). Knibb sets the Similitudes in the same period as 2 Baruch and 2 Esdras in light of the close relation of these three writings (see "The Date of the Parables of Enoch").

Chapter 9

1. L. E. Keck has persuasively set forth this view in "The Introduction to Mark's Gospel," *NTS* 12 (1966): 352ff.
2. Kelber, *The Kingdom in Mark* (Philadelphia, 1974), p. 4.
3. Pesch, *Das Markusevangelium*, 2 vols., Herders theologischer Kommentar zum Neuen Testament (Freiburg, 1976–77), 1: 100.
4. See the careful discussion in P. Stuhlmacher, *Das Paulinische Evangelium* (Göttingen, 1968), 1: 236ff., and Pesch's comments thereon in *Das Markusevangelium*, 1: 101.
5. Lohmeyer, *Das Evangelium des Markus*, Kritisch-Exegetischer Kommentar über das Neuen Testament (Göttingen, 1963), pp. 29–30.
6. "That is clearest in the second part, which contains the demands for repentance and faith," says Trilling. "The first part also is closely bound with it, insofar as it motivates this demand and concretizes the arrival of the kingdom of God as the gospel" (*Christus Verkündigung in den synoptischen Evangelien*, Biblische Handbibliothek, nr. 4 [München, 1969], p. 53).
7. Without attempting to be exhaustive in any way, I would cite the following as indicative of a consensus: Lohmeyer, *Das Evangelium des Markus*, pp. 29–30; E. Percy, *Die Botschaft Jesu* (Lund, 1953), p. 20; Grundmann, *Das Evangelium nach Markus*, Theologischer Handkommentar zum Neuen Testament (Berlin, 1959), p. 36; Moore, *The Parousia in the New Testament*, Supplements to the Novum Testamentum, vol. 13 (Leiden, 1966), p. 165; K. G. Reploh, *Markus, Lehrer der Gemeinde*, Stuttgarter Biblische Monographien (Stuttgart, 1969), p. 14; Pesch, *Das Markusevangelium*, 1: 101–2; J. Becker, *Das Heil Gottes*, Studien zur Umwelt des Neuen Testaments, vol. 3 (Göttingen, 1964), p. 200; Keck, "Introduction to Mark's Gospel," p. 359, and *A Future for the Historical Jesus* (London, 1971), p. 32; Trilling, *Christus Verkündigung in den synoptischen Evangelien*, p. 54; Schnackenburg, "'Das Evangelium' im Verständnis des ältesten Evangelisten," in *Orientierung an Jesus*, Festschrift for J. Schmid, ed. P. Hoffmann et al. (Freiburg, 1973), pp. 310–11. Older writers tended to assume without discussion the essential authenticity of Mark 1:14–15.
8. Dodd, *The Parables of the Kingdom* (London, 1935), p. 44. It is likely that Dodd was set on this path by Dalman's *Words of Jesus* (Edinburgh, 1902), pp. 106–7, though Dalman proposed *qārab* as the Aramaic verb behind *engizein* in this passage.
9. Campbell, "The Kingdom of God Has Come," *ExpTim* 48 (1936–37): 91–92.
10. Clark, "Realized Eschatology," *JBL* 59 (1940): 367–83.
11. Dodd, "The Kingdom of God Has Come," *ExpTim* 48 (1936–37): 138.
12. Dodd, "The Kingdom of God Has Come," pp. 139ff.
13. Berkey, "EGGIZEIN, PHTHANEIN, and Realised Eschatology," *JBL* 82 (1963): 181, 186–87.
14. Kelber, *The Kingdom in Mark*, p. 9.
15. Trilling, *Christus Verkündigung in den synoptischen Evangelien*, pp. 47–48.
16. Ambrozic, *The Hidden Kingdom: A Redaction-Critical Study of the References to the Kingdom of God in Mark's Gospel*, The Catholic Biblical Quarterly—Monograph Series, 2 (Washington, 1972), pp. 21–22. See also Pesch, *Das Markusevangelium*, 1: 102; Kelber, *The Kingdom in Mark*, pp. 9–10; Reploh, *Markus, Lehrer der Gemeinde*, p. 21; Via, *Kerygma and Comedy in the New Testament: A Structuralist Approach to Hermeneutic* (Philadelphia, 1975), p. 82; Becker, *Das Heil Gottes*, pp. 200–201. We should note that Lohmeyer stresses the significance of *peplerotai ho kairos*: "Now all promise and prepara-

tions have an end; now 'God's kingdom nears,' i.e. *it is here*. Mark thus sees the proclamation of Jesus not as a preliminary stage of a coming kingdom but as the fulfilment which has now entered in and which has really come to pass" (*Das Evangelium nach Markus*, p. 30).

17. Trilling, *Christus Verkündigung in den synoptischen Evangelien*, pp. 46ff.

18. Reploh, *Markus, Lehrer der Germeinde*, p. 20.

19. See Schlatter, *Die Geschichte des Christus* (Stuttgart, 1923), pp. 51, 140, 144–45.

20. Gloege, *Das Reich Gottes und Kirche im Neuen Testament* (Gütersloh, 1929), p. 111.

21. Says Pesch, "The sovereignty of God brought near, in the sense of having arrived, corresponds to Jesus' concept of the kingdom of God as a powerful, dynamic event, in which God universally sets up his rule of salvation; God's sovereignty breaks in" (*Das Markusevangelium*, 1: 102).

22. Becker, *Das Heil Gottes*, p. 206.

23. See Ambrozic, *The Hidden Kingdom*, pp. 24–25.

24. Such is maintained by Jüngel in *Paulus und Jesus: Eine Untersuchung zur Präzisierung der Frage nach der Aufsprung der Christologie* (Tübingen, 1962), p. 175n.5.

25. Jeremias, quoted by Pesch in *Das Markusevangelium*, 1: 102–3.

26. Schnackenburg, " 'Das Evangelium' im Verständnis des ältesten Evangelisten," p. 319.

27. Pesch, *Das Markusevangelium*, 1: 104.

28. Bultmann affirmed of the saying that it can "claim the highest degree of authenticity which we can make for any saying of Jesus: it is full of that feeling of eschatological power which must have characterized the activity of Jesus" (*HST*, p. 162).

29. Says Schweitzer, "Through the conquest of the demons Jesus is the man of violence who compels the approach of the kingdom" (*The Mystery of the Kingdom*, trans. Walter Lowrie [1914; rpt., London, 1950], p. 144; and "In Matthew the miracles of Jesus . . . are, according to Matthew 12:28, an indication of the nearness of the kingdom of God" (*The Quest of the Historical Jesus* [London, 1910], p. 345).

30. Werner, *Die Entstehung des christlichen Dogmas* (Bern, 1941), pp. 51–52. The statement is omitted from the English translation, *The Formation of Christian Dogma*, an abridged version of the original work.

31. See Grässer, *Das Problem der Parusieverzögerung in den synoptischen Evangelien und in der Apostelgeschichte*, Beiheifte zur ZNW, nr. 22 (Berlin, 1957), pp. 6ff.; and "Zum Verständnis der Gottesherrschaft," ZNW 65 (1957): 3–26.

32. See, for example, Conzelmann's "Gegenwart und Zukunft in der synoptischen Tradition," ZTK 54 (1957): 286–87; *An Outline of Theology of the New Testament*, trans. J. S. Bowden (London, 1969), p. 112; and *Jesus*, ed. J. Reumann, trans. J. R. Lord (Philadelphia, 1973), pp. 70, 74, 76–77.

33. See Fuller, *The Mission and Achievement of Jesus*, Studies in Biblical Theology, no. 12 (London, 1954), pp. 37–38.

34. Fuller, *The Mission and Achievement of Jesus*, p. 26. Fuller considers that the same applies to 1 Thessalonians 2:16. J. Weiss had a not unrelated view in his belief that Matthew 12:28 proceeded from a moment of "sublime prophetic enthusiasm," which from time to time Jesus had when awareness of victory came over him. Similarly, Bousset thought this to be "a saying spoken at a moment of great excitement" (*Jesus*, trans. J. P. Trevelyan, ed. W. D. Morrison [London, 1904], p. 70), presumably hinting that not too much ought to be made of it in constructing the teaching of Jesus.

35. Bultmann, *Theology of the New Testament*, trans. K. Grobel, 2 vols. (London, 1951–55), 1: 7.

36. Conzelmann, *Jesus*, pp. 70, 76–77; italics mine.

37. Perrin, quoted by Grässer in "Zum Verständnis der Gottesherrschaft," p. 23.

38. See Bultmann, "Zur eschatologischen Verkündigung Jesu," *TLZ* (1947): 271–74.

39. Bultmann, "Zur eschatologischen Verkündigung Jesu," col. 273.

40. See pp. 49–51 herein.

41. Conzelmann, "Gegenwart und Zukunft," p. 287n.1.

42. Conzelmann, *An Outline of Theology*, p. 112.

43. J. H. Moulton and G. Milligan, *The Vocabulary of the Greek New Testament* (London, 1931), p. 667.

44. F. Blass and A. Debrunner, *A Greek Grammar of the New Testament and Other Early Christian Literature* (Chicago, 1961), par. 101.

45. Fitzer, *TDNT*, 9: 92.

46. It is noteworthy that the testimony of the linguists is supported by the important translations of the New Testament, which have been produced for the most part by responsible groups of leading New Testament scholars in various countries. The RSV reads "If it is by the finger of God that I cast out demons, then the kingdom of God has come upon you." The NEB strengthens the second clause by rendering it "be sure the kingdom of God has already come upon you." The Bible de Jérusalem renders "Si c'est par le doigt de Dieu que j'expulse les démons, c'est qu'alors le Royaume de Dieu est arrivé pour vous." The English Jerusalem Bible varies the second clause: "then know that the kingdom of God has overtaken you." Earlier editions of the Luther Bible read "So ich aber durch Gottes Finger die Teufe austriebe, so kommt ja das Reich Gottes zu euch"; in recent editions the latter clause has been modified to prevent misunderstanding: "so ist ja das Reich Gottes zu euch gekommen." The Zürcherbibel gives the same wording, and F. Tillmanns is virtually the same (". . . über euch gekommen").

47. Schrenk, *biazomai*, *TDNT* 1: 610.

48. Foerster, *daimonion*, *TDNT* 2: 19.

49. Schweizer, *pneuma*, *TDNT* 6: 398. Also in *TDNT*, see K. L. Schmidt, *basileia*, 1: 584–85; A. Oepke, *iaomai*, 3: 212; Foerster, *ktizo*, 3: 1034; H. Preisker, *misthos*, 4: 718; and O. Cullmann, *petros*, 6: 106–7.

50. Percy, *Die Botschaft Jesu*, p. 179.

51. Manson, *The Sayings of Jesus* (London, 1949), p. 86. The citation from Arbesmann is from "Das Fasten bei den Griechen und Römern," *Religionsgeschichtliche Versuche und Vorarbeiten* 21 (1929): 20.

52. Schweitzer, *The Quest of the Historical Jesus*, p. 237.

53. Jüngel, *Paulus und Jesus*, p. 185.

54. Jüngel, *Paulus und Jesus*, 185. Jüngel holds that Matthew's replacement of the expression "finger of God" with "Spirit of God" emphasizes the futurist relation of the "present" first clause to the future kingdom. This is doubtful, however, since the first-century Jews would have viewed the two expressions as identical in meaning. The problem of whether the original logion read "finger" or "spirit" is more difficult than is generally recognized. Almost all scholars accept the originality of Luke on the grounds that it is unlikely that Luke would have eliminated a reference to the Spirit—and yet he effected precisely such a change in Luke 21:15 (cf. Mark 13:11 and Luke 12:11–12), substituting an allusion to the Exodus narrative (cf. Exod. 4:15) in place of a reference to the Spirit. It is just as possible that he did the same with the logion recorded in Luke 11:20, replacing "Spirit" with "finger" in allusion to Exodus 8:19.

55. Linking them with Matthew 13:16–17 // Luke 10:32–33, Bultmann writes of these sayings, "The immediacy of eschatological consciousness is given such emphatic expression . . . that it is impossible for any Jewish tradition to provide an origin" (*HST*, p. 126). A. Polag observes, "The entire wording appears to be uninfluenced by later Christological terminology" (*Die Christologie der Logienquelle* [Neukirchen-Vluyn, 1977], p. 38).

56. See, for example, Bultmann, *HST*, p. 23; Bornkamm, *Jesus of Nazareth*, trans. I.

McLuskey, F. McLuskey, and J. M. Robinson (London, 1960), pp. 49–50; P. Vielhauer, "Johannes," *RGG* 3: 805; and H. W. Kuhn, *Enderwartung und Gegenwärtiges Heil: Untersuchungen zu den Gemeindeliedern von Qumran*, Studien zur Umwelt des Neuen Testaments, vol. 4 (Göttingen, 1966), pp. 195–96.

57. The origin of the phrase "the coming one" has been sought in various Old Testament passages, notably Habakkuk 2:3, which is understood as having a masculine subject—"*he* will surely come, *he* will not delay" (on this, see Strobel, *Untersuchungen zum eschatologischen Verzögerungsproblem auf Grund der spätjüdisch-urchristlichen Geschichte von Habakkuk 2.2ff.* [Leiden, 1961], pp. 265ff.)—as well as Song of Songs 2:8 and Daniel 7:13, both of which were understood messianically in late Judaism. But Psalm 118:26, which was also interpreted as a reference to the Messiah by the Jews, is the most likely place of origin. Most Hebrew scholars recognize that it should be rendered "Blessed in the name of the Lord is he who comes" (*habbā* = "the coming one"). It is likely that the cry of greeting accorded Jesus at his entry into Jerusalem should be so rendered, as the Swedish Bible does in all four gospel accounts: *Välsignad vare han, som kommer, in Herrens namn.* The phrase is too loose to be viewed as a title, but it may be regarded as a descriptive phrase with clear connotations of the one awaited to come as judge and deliverer according to the promise of God. For a good brief discussion of the implications of the phrase, see H. Schürmann, *Das Lukasevangelium*, Herders theologischer Kommentar zum Neuen Testament (Freiburg, 1969), pp. 408–9.

58. There is no reference to the healing of lepers in the Isaianic passages. Are we to see in this, along with explicit mention of resurrection from the dead, an indication that the fulfillment in Jesus of the ancient prophecy exceeds its hopes and expectations? See Jeremias, *New Testament Theology* (London, 1971), vol. 1, *The Proclamation of Jesus*, trans. J. S. Bowden, p. 105.

59. Bultmann, *HST*, p. 23. See also Jeremias, *The Parables of Jesus*, trans. S. H. Hooke, rev. ed. (London, 1963), p. 116; and Kuhn, *Enderwartung und Gegenwärtiges Heil*, p. 196.

60. Some copyists of the New Testament text, failing to comprehend the importance of Jesus' proclamation of the kingdom, modified the text to "improve" its sequence: fam. 13 syr^c reverse the last two clauses, thereby making the list conclude with the resurrection of the dead; k syr^s Clement omit the clause relating to the preaching. Both modifications are instructive examples of the growing inability of the later church to comprehend Jesus' teaching on the kingdom of God.

61. See Fuller, *The Mission and Achievement of Jesus*, pp. 36–37.

62. See O. Kaiser, *Der Prophet Jesaja: Kapitel 13–39*, Das Alte Testament Deutsch (Göttingen, 1973), p. 286.

63. Schweizer, *The Good News according to Matthew*, trans. D. O. E. Green (Atlanta, 1975), p. 256. See also Kümmel, *Promise and Fulfilment: The Eschatological Message of Jesus*, Studies in Biblical Theology, no. 23 (London, 1961), p. 111; Barrett, *The Holy Spirit and the Gospel Tradition* (London, 1947), p. 87; Jeremias, *The Parables of Jesus*, p. 116; Grundmann, *Das Evangelium nach Lukas*, Theologischer Handkommentar zum Neuen Testament (Berlin, 1959), p. 164; Kuhn, *Enderwartung und Gegenwärtiges Heil*, p. 186; Polag, *Die Christologie der Logienquelle*, p. 196; and Schürmann, *Das Lukasevangelium*, pp. 411–12.

64. Schürmann, *Das Lukasevangelium*, p. 411.

65. On this point, see Polag, *Die Christologie der Logienquelle*, p. 37, and Schürmann, *Das Lukasevangelium*, p. 412.

66. Jüngel, *Paulus und Jesus*, p. 190.

67. The variations represent different renderings of the Aramaic particle *de*, which can signify both the relative pronoun and the conjunction *because* (see C. F. Burney, *The Poetry of Our Lord* [Oxford, 1925], p. 145n.2, and M. Black, *An Aramaic Approach to the Gospels and Acts*, 3d ed. [Oxford, 1973], p. 70). Matthew may have recognized the

ambiguity and stressed the "that" of the saying, in contrast to Luke, who emphasized the "what" (see Grundmann, *Das Evangelium nach Lukas*, p. 220).

68. See Matthew 5:45; 10:41; 13:43, 49; 23:28, 29, 35; 25:37, 46.

69. McNeile contends that there may have been a confusion in the Aramaic tradition between *yesarin*, "righteous men," and *sarin*, "princes" or "rulers" (in 3 Reg. 22:26 *basileus* renders *sar*); see McNeile, *The Gospel according to St. Matthew* (London, 1915), p. 192.

70. Manson, *The Sayings of Jesus*, p. 80.

71. Fuller, *The Mission and Achievement of Jesus*, p. 34.

72. Lohmeyer, *Das Evangelium nach Matthäus*, Kritisch-exegetischer Kommentar über das Neue Testament (Göttingen, 1963), p. 206.

73. Among those holding this view are Bultmann (*HST*, p. 32) and W. Eltester ("Israel im lukanischen Werk und die Nazareth-Perikope," in *Jesus in Nazareth* [Berlin, 1972], pp. 135ff.).

74. Among the majority of scholars who hold this view are Dibelius (*From Tradition to Gospel* [London, 1934], pp. 110ff.), Conzelmann (*The Theology of St. Luke* [London, 1960], pp. 31ff.), A. R. C. Leaney (*The Gospel according to St. Luke*, Black's New Testament Commentaries [London, 1958], pp. 50–51), Strobel (in *Jesus in Nazareth*, p. 38), Tannehill (in *Jesus in Nazareth*, p. 52), Flender (*St. Luke: Theologian of Redemptive History* [London, 1967], p. 147), and apparently Klostermann (*Das Lukasevangelium*, Handkommentar zum Neuen Testament [Tübingen, 1929], pp. 42–45).

75. See especially Schürmann's "Zur Nazareth-Pericope Luke 6:14–30," in *Orientierung an Jesus*, p. 191; and *Das Lukasevangelium*, p. 242.

76. Compare especially Luke 7:22–23 with 4:18ff. The two passages are so closely related as to suggest to some that the latter was composed in imitation of the former. The "tendency" of the entire narrative, however, is repeated in various ways throughout the Q material; cf. Luke 3:8–9 with 3:14; 7:31–35; 10:11–12, 13–15; 11:29–30, 31–32; 12:54–56; 13:28–29, 34–35; and 14:15–24.

77. The theme of warning to Israel of impending judgment if the people reject the opportunity presented by the *kairos* of Jesus' ministry is represented in Luke's special material (e.g., in Luke 13:1–5, 6–9; 19:41–44; and 21:18ff.).

78. See, for example, Streeter, *The Four Gospels: A Study of Origins* (London, 1926), pp. 209–10; V. Taylor, *Formation of the Gospel Tradition* (London, 1957), pp. 153ff., 198; and *Behind the Third Gospel* (Oxford, 1926), pp. 76, 146–48; Grundmann, *Das Evangelium nach Lukas*, p. 119; J. Schmid, *Das Evangelium nach Lukas*, Regensburger Neues Testament (Regensburg, 1960), p. 110; and K. H. Rengstorf, *Das Evangelium nach Lukas*, Das Neue Testament Deutsch (Göttingen, 1937), pp. 66–67.

79. Spitta, *Die synoptische Grundschrift und ihrer Überlieferung durch das Lukasevangelium* (Leipzig, 1912), pp. 49ff. L. Brun had a similar analysis, differing chiefly by extending the first parallel to verse 22, and separating verse 24 (see "Der Besuch Jesus in Nazareth nach Lukas," in *Serta Rudbergi*, ed. H. Holst and H. Moland [Oslo, 1931], pp. 7ff.). J. Schmid defines the units as 16–21, 22, 23, 24, 25–27, and 28–30 (*Das Evangelium nach Lukas*, pp. 110–11). F. Hahn defines them as 16–22a, 22b–24, 25–27, and 28–30 (*The Titles of Jesus in Christology*, trans. H. Knight and G. Ogg [London, 1969], p. 381). For other examples of such analysis, see Schürmann, *Das Lukasevangelium*, p. 243–164.

80. It is a matter of debate, for example, whether verses 22, 23, and 24 were produced independently of each other, whether verse 22 should be linked with verse 24, or whether verses 22b–24 were originally a unit.

81. "Opening" (*paqach*) is used primarily of opening eyes—hence the LXX translation, which was reproduced by Luke as *tuphlois anablepsin*. The term is also used to denote letting prisoners see light—hence, setting them free—which is what this text seems to intend. For an illuminating discussion of the passage, see J. A. Sanders, "From

Isaiah 61 to Luke 4," in *Christianity, Judaism and Other Greco-Roman Cults, Festschrift for M. Smith*, ed. J. Neusner (Leiden, 1975), 1: 81.

82. See Westermann, *Jesaja 40–66*, Das Alte Testament Deutsch (Göttingen, 1966), p. 292.

83. The text of the fragment and a translation into English are given by M. de Jonge and A. S. van der Woude, "11Q Melchizedek and the New Testament," *NTS* 12 (1966): 301–26, and by J. A. Fitzmyer, "Further Light on Melchizedek from Qumran Cave 11," *JBL* 86 (1967): 25–41. A brief but valuable discussion of its significance for the passage we are considering is provided by M. P. Miller in "The Function of Isaiah 61:1–2 in 11Q Melchizedek," *JBL* 88 (1969): 467–69.

84. Translated by de Jonge and van der Woude in "11Q Melchizedek and the New Testament," p. 303.

85. See the excellent exposition of these "hermeneutic axioms" of Qumran by J. A. Sanders, "From Isaiah 61 to Luke 4," pp. 94ff.

86. Schürmann contends that scribes made the omission, not Luke (see *Das Lukasevangelium*, p. 229).

87. Caird, *St. Luke*, Pelican Gospel Commentaries (Harmondsworth, 1963), p. 86.

88. The question whether any external factor led to Jesus' utilization of Isaiah 61:1ff. is frequently discussed, but disputed. Some believe that the scroll of Isaiah was handed to Jesus, and that he read Isaiah 61 because that was the appointed "haphtara" for the day (i.e., the reading from the prophets that had been chosen to follow the readings from the law). See C. H. Cave, "The Sermon at Nazareth and the Beatitudes in the Light of the Synagogue Lectionary," *Studia Evangelica*, ed. F. L. Cross, 3/2: 231–35 = *Texte und Untersuchungen* (Berlin, 1964), 88: 232ff. For contrary views, see Schürmann, *Das Lukasevangelium*, p. 229; and Eltester, *Jesus in Nazareth*, pp. 136–37. For support, see J. A. Sanders, "From Isaiah 61 to Luke 4," p. 93. It is doubtful, in the light of his teaching elsewhere, that Jesus was motivated by apocalyptic calculation of the kind suggested by Strobel in "Das Jobeljahr in der Nazarethpredigt," in *Jesus in Nazareth*, pp. 38ff.

89. This reading is based on the assumption that *emarturoun* is being used in the sense of "giving a *good* report" (see Strathmann, *TDNT* 4: 496).

90. Flender appears to see no change of tone in verse 22, though he observes that the passage indicates how Jesus can be listened to without being "heard" (see *St. Luke: Theologian of Redemptive History*, pp. 152–57).

91. The phrase "words of grace" is commonly read as the equivalent of "gracious words," but the importance of *grace* should not be wholly diminished in this manner. It is better to view the expression as containing a dynamic meaning, *grace* being related to the concept of *dunamis*, as Otto maintains emphatically (see *The Kingdom of God and the Son of Man* [London, 1938], p. 169). If the phrase means "the good news of God" (see Conzelmann, *TDNT* 9: 392n.154), then Luke is specifically emphasizing the fact that the people rejected Jesus' message.

92. See Schürmann, *Das Lukasevangelium*, p. 236.

93. As in Luke 4, *dektos* here signifies what is acceptable to God; see J. A. Sanders, "From Isaiah 61 to Luke 4," pp. 98–99.

94. Haenchen puts this construction on the passage; see *Der Weg Jesu* (Berlin, 1966), pp. 218–19.

95. See Tannehill, in *Jesus in Nazareth*, pp. 59–60. Needless to say, if the passage is understood in this way, it must be viewed as reflecting the deliberations of the primitive Church concerning the Gentile mission rather than the situation of Jesus' ministry, to which, of course, it is not applicable.

96. 1 Kings 17:1 and 18:1 speak of three years of drought and famine, but the Jews later adapted the figure to the apocalyptic tradition (see also James 5:17). See H. L. Strack–P. Billerbeck, *Kommentar in das Neuen Testament aus Talmud und Midrasch*, 6 vols. (München, 1922–28), 3: 760–61.

97. After surveying the interpretations of the logion in its contexts in Matthew and

Luke, D. Daube wrote, "It must be admitted that, both in Matthew and in Luke, the saying concerning violence to the kingdom with the area surrounding it is a *Trümmerfeld*, a heap of ruins" (*The New Testament and Rabbinic Judaism* [London, 1956], p. 300).

98. See T. W. Manson, *The Sayings of Jesus*, p. 134; W. G. Kümmel, *Promise and Fulfilment*, p. 122; Jüngel, *Paulus und Jesus*, p. 191; and Schnackenburg, *God's Rule and Kingdom* (London, 1963), p. 130.

99. In his attempts to retrovert the saying into Aramaic, Dalman supplies the phrases set in parenthesis in the main text, and they do seem to read very naturally (see Dalman, *The Words of Jesus*, pp. 141–42).

100. An excellent summary of opinions on the logion is found in Schrenk's article on *biazomai* in *TDNT*, 1: 610ff.

101. See Otto, *The Kingdom of God and the Son of Man*, p. 110.

102. See Grundmann, *Das Evangelium nach Matthäus*, ed. E. Fascher, Theologischer Handkommentar zum Neuen Testament (Berlin, 1968), pp. 309–10; and *Das Evangelium nach Lukas*, p. 232.

103. See Dalman, *The Words of Jesus*, pp. 140–43; Black, *An Aramaic Approach to the Gospels and Acts*, pp. 116, 211n.2; and Daube, *The New Testament and Rabbinic Judaism*, pp. 284–94. Daube provides a full discussion of the various options available in Hebrew and Aramaic to account for the troublesome verbs used in this passage.

104. Dalman cites Resch's *Die Logia Jesu* (1898) in *Words of Jesus*, p. 47. (Dalman rejects Resch's method and his conclusions, especially his attempt to prove that the sayings of Jesus circulated in Hebrew.)

105. For references, see F. Brown, S. R. Driver, and C. A. Briggs, *A Hebrew and English Lexicon of the Old Testament* (Oxford, 1953), p. 829.

106. See J. Levy, *Wörterbuch über die Talmudim und Midraschim* (Leipzig, 1963), vol. 4.

107. Black, *An Aramaic Approach to the Gospels and Acts*, p. 211n.2.

108. Daube, *The New Testament and Rabbinic Judaism*, p. 287.

109. Dalman, *The Words of Jesus*, p. 141. The same idea is expressed in the Aramaic of Ezra 5:16 by *min edayin wead kean* (= LXX *ap' ekeinou mechri tou nun*). Strangely enough, Jeremiah 36:2 has the full phrase, *aph' hemeron Ioseia basileos Iouda kai heos tes hemeras tautes*.

110. Among those who have adopted this position are Otto (*The Kingdom of God and the Son of Man*, p. 109) and A. N. Wilder (*Eschatology and Ethics in the Teaching of Jesus*, rev. ed. [New York, 1950], p. 149, following a written communication from C. H. Kraeling reproduced on p. 149n.5).

111. Manson, *The Sayings of Jesus*, p. 70. Similar interpretations are made by Otto (*The Kingdom of God and the Son of Man*, p. 110), W. Manson (*Jesus the Messiah* [London, 1943], p. 49), C. J. Cadoux (*The Historic Mission of Jesus* [London, 1943], p. 130), Schnackenburg (*God's Rule and Kingdom*, pp. 130ff.), and Foerster (*TDNT*, 1: 472–73).

112. Jüngel, *Paulus und Jesus*, pp. 191ff.

113. F. Dibelius cites a number of the Church Fathers as holding this view (see "Zwei Worte Jesu: II," *ZNW* 11 [1910]: 190–92); he has been followed by various modern scholars, including Cullmann (*Die Christologie des Neuen Testaments*, [Tübingen, 1957], p. 32), Grundmann (*TDNT*, 4: 535), and Michel (*TDNT*, 4: 653).

114. See Schlatter, *Der Evangelist Matthäus* (Stuttgart, 1948), p. 366; Schnackenburg, *God's Rule and Kingdom*, p. 133; Michaelis, *Der Evangelium nach Matthäus*, 2 vols. (Zürich, 1948–49), 2: 307; and Grundmann, *Das Evangelium nach Matthäus*, 2: 365–66.

115. Schweizer, *The Good News according to Matthew*, p. 263. D. Flusser provides a not dissimilar interpretation, citing Kimchi's interpretation of Micah 2:13 (viz., that the one who opens the breach is Elijah and that the king passing on before the people is the Messiah) as an illustration of the relation of John to Jesus and the kingdom (see Flusser, *Jesus* [New York, 1969], pp. 40–41).

116. See Bultmann, *HST*, pp. 25, 55; Dibelius, *From Tradition to Gospel*, p. 162; and

Taylor, *Formation of the Gospel Tradition*, p. 69. Bultmann contends that the form is secondary but the content of the saying is authentic (p. 25); see W. L. Knox's comment on Bultmann's position in *The Sources of the Synoptic Gospels*, ed. H. Chadwick, 2 vols. (Cambridge, 1953–57), 1: 107n.3.

117. R. Sneed states that "If verses 20–21 are isolated, the reader has before him a complete question and a complete answer, and regardless of the difficulty in interpreting either or both there is no impression of an unfinished narrative or saying" ("The Kingdom of God Is within You (Lk 17,21)," *CBQ* 24 [1962]: 376–77).

118. Among those holding this position are H. Schürmann (*Traditionsgeschichtliche Untersuchungen zu den synoptischen Evangelien* [Düsseldorf, 1968], p. 237) and R. Schnackenburg, who presents his argument at some length in "Der eschatologische Abschnitt, Luke 17:20–37," in *Mélanges bibliques*, Festchrift for B. Rigaux, ed. A. Descamps and R. P. Andre de Halleux (Gembloux, 1970), pp. 214ff.

119. See Bultmann, *HST*, pp. 52–53.

120. Schnackenburg examined the style of the introduction and concluded that it is an example of Luke's fondness for introducing a saying of Jesus with a question in order to enliven the narrative ("Der eschatologische Abschnitt, Luke 17:20–37," p. 217).

121. See Rustow, "ENTOS HUMON ESTIN: Zur Deutung von Lukas 17.20–21," *ZNW* 51 (1960): 218. See also Kümmel, *Promise and Fulfilment*, p. 32; and Sneed, "The Kingdom of God Is within You," pp. 376–77.

122. See the analysis of the term and its usage in Greek literature given by H. Riesenfeld, *TDNT*, 8: 148–49.

123. Both Bauer and N. Turner recognize the possibility of *meta* with the genitive having *instrumental* force (see J. H. Moulton, W. F. Howard, and N. Turner, *A Grammar of New Testament Greek*, 4 vols. [Edinburgh, 1929–76], 3: 269). It is with this in mind that R. Sneed interprets *ou meta paratereseos* as denying that the kingdom of God can be realized by the observance of the Mosaic law ("The Kingdom of God Is within You," pp. 373–74)—but it is clearly speculative to read that much meaning into this phrase alone.

124. See Percy, *Die Botschaft Jesu*, pp. 217ff.

125. From *The Gospel according to Thomas*, trans. A. Guillaumont et al. (Leiden, 1959), pp. 3, 29, 55–56.

126. See Quispel, "Some Remarks on the Gospel of Thomas," *NTS* 5 (1959): 288.

127. Also in agreement is H. W. Bartsch; see "Das Thomas-Evangelium und die synoptischen Evangelien: Zu G. Quispels Bemerkungen zum Thomas-Evangelium," *NTS* 6 (1960): 257.

128. Perrin, *Rediscovering the Teaching of Jesus*, New Testament Library (London, 1963), pp. 70–74. See also Perrin's *Jesus and the Language of the Kingdom: Symbol and Metaphor in New Testament Interpretation*, New Testament Library (London, 1976), p. 45.

129. See H. Schürmann, "Das Thomasevangelium und das lukanische Sondergut," in *Traditionsgeschichtliche Untersuchungen zu der synoptischen Evangelien*, pp. 228–47 (pp. 237ff. on Luke 17:20–21). More importantly, see W. Schrage, *Das Verhältnis des Thomas-Evangeliums zur synoptischen Tradition und zu den koptischen Evangelienübersetzungen* (Berlin, 1964), especially pp. 199–200 on Luke 17:20–21.

130. Schrage, *Das Verhältnis des Thomas-Evangeliums*, p. 200. See also H. E. W. Turner and H. Montefiore, *Thomas and the Evangelists*, Studies in Biblical Theology, no. 35 (Naperville, Ill., 1962), pp. 103ff. for similar findings on the concept of the kingdom of God in Thomas.

131. See the following articles by Strobel: "Die Passa-Erwartung als urchristliches Problem in Lc 17.20–21," *ZNW* 49 (1958): 157–96; "A. Merx über Lc 17.20–21," *ZNW* 51 (1960): 133–34; "In Dieser Nacht (Luk 17,34)," *ZTK* 58 (1961): 16ff.; and his answer to F. Mussner's criticism, "Zu Luke 17:20," *BZ* 7 (1963): 111–13.

132. See Strobel, "Die Passa-Erwartung als urchristliches Problem in Lc 17.20–21," pp. 164ff.

133. Rustow, "ENTOS HUMON ESTIN: Zur Deutung von Lukas 17.20–21," p. 201.

134. See Riesenfeld, *TDNT*, 8: 150.

135. See 4 Ezra 4:36–37 and 5:49.

136. For examples of this, see the Apocalypse of Weeks, 1 Enoch 91 and 93, and the Vision of the Cloud and the Black and White Waters in 2 Baruch 53–74.

137. Billerbeck shows this in detail in excursus no. 30, "Vorzeichen und Berechnung der Tage des Messias," in *Kommentar zum Neuen Testament aus Talmud und Midrasch*, 4/2: 977–1015.

138. This point is far from new. It was set forth in essence by J. Weiss (in *Jesus' Proclamation of the Kingdom of God*, trans. and ed. R. H. Hier and D. L. Holland [Philadelpia, 1971], pp. 89–90) and has been ably expounded by Otto (*The Kingdom of God and the Son of Man*, pp. 132ff.), Kümmel (*Promise and Fulfilment*, pp. 32ff.), J. Schmid (*Das Evangelium nach Lukas*, p. 273), A. Rustow ("ENTOS HUMON ESTIN: Zur Deutung von Lukas 17:20–21," pp. 202–3), and F. Mussner ("Wann kommt das Reich Gottes?" *BZ* 7 [1963]: 108ff.).

139. Riesenfeld, *TDNT*, 8: 150.

140. See Noack, *Das Gottesreich bei Lukas: Eine Studie zu Luk. 17.20–24*, Symbolai Biblicae Uppsalienses, 10 (Uppsala, 1948).

141. Liddell and Scott translate *entos humon* in Luke 17:21 as "in your hearts" (see Liddell and Scott, *A Greek-English Lexicon*, rev. H. S. Jones and R. Mackenzie [Oxford, 1940], p. 577).

142. The Latin translates *entos* as *intra*; the case is similar in the Peshitta (not the Old Syriac) and the Coptic.

143. "The kingdom is within you and it is without you. If you (will) know yourselves, then you will be known and you will know that you are the sons of the Living Father" (*The Gospel according to Thomas*, p. 3).

144. "The kingdom of heaven is within you and whoever knows himself will find it" (Oxyrhyncus papyrus 659).

145. Athanasius, *Contra gentes XXX*. The Greek text is given in full (in context) by Noack, *Das Gottesreich bei Lukas*, p. 10.

146. Arndt, cited by Noack in *Das Gottesreich bei Lukas*, p. 23.

147. Sneed, "The Kingdom of God Is within You," pp. 373–74.

148. See Harnack, *What Is Christianity?* 3d ed., trans. T. B. Bailey (London, 1904), pp. 57–58.

149. See Wellhausen, *Das Evangelium Lucae* (Berlin, 1904), p. 95.

150. See the comments of O. Michel and E. Käsemann on this passage in their commentaries on Romans (Michel, *Paulus und seine Bibel*, Beiträge zur Forderung christlicher Theologie, 2/18 [Gütersloh, 1972]; Käsemann, *The Epistle to the Romans*, trans. and ed. Geoffrey Bromiley [Grand Rapids, 1980]).

151. See Strobel, "In dieser Nacht," p. 28.

152. Among those who hold to this interpretation are Bultmann (*HST*, pp. 121–22), W. Michaelis (*Täufer, Jesus, Urgemeinde* [Gütersloh, 1928], p. 79), H.-D. Wendland (*Die Eschatologie des Reiches Gottes bei Jesus: Eine Studie über den Zusammenhang von Eschatologie, Ethik und Kirchenproblem* [Gütersloh, 1931], p. 47), J. Héring (*Le Royaume de Dieu et sa venue* [Paris, 1937], pp. 43–44), J. Schmid (*Das Evangelium nach Lukas*, p. 274), T. W. Manson (*The Sayings of Jesus*, p. 304), and L. Gaston (*No Stone on Another: Studies in the Significance of the Fall of Jerusalem in the Synoptic Gospels*, Supplements to Novum Testamentum, vol. 23 [Leiden, 1970], p. 349).

153. Among those who hold to this interpretation are K. L. Schmidt (*TDNT*, 1: 585–86), E. Stauffer (*TDNT* 3: 118), W. Busch (*Zum Verständnis der synoptischen Eschatologie: Markus 13 neu Untersucht* [Gütersloh, 1938], p. 141), A. Schlatter (*Das Evangelium des Lukas: Aus seinen Quellen erklärt*, 2d ed. [Stuttgart, 1960], pp. 391–32), J. M. Creed (*The Gospel according to St. Luke* [London, 1942], p. 219), C. J. Cadoux (*The*

Historic Mission of Jesus, p. 130), Kümmel (*Promise and Fulfilment*, pp. 33ff.), N. Perrin (*Rediscovering the Teaching of Jesus*, p. 74), and A. L. Moore (*The Parousia in the New Testament*, pp. 195–96).

154. Bultmann, *HST*, pp. 121–22.

155. Otto, *The Kingdom of God and the Son of Man*, p. 135.

156. Rustow, "ENTOS HUMON ESTIN: Zur Deutung von Lukas 17.20–21," p. 212.

157. Luke uses *mesos* no fewer than fourteen times in the gospel and ten times in Acts (Mark uses it five times, Matthew eight times, and Paul seven times). In Luke 22:27 and Acts 2:22 he uses the phrase *en meso humon* to convey precisely the meaning that some attribute to the phrase *entos humon* in 17:21.

158. Cyril of Alexandria, *Commentary on Luke*, sect. 368; see Noack, *Das Gottesreich bei Lukas*, pp. 11ff.

159. Roberts, "The Kingdom of Heaven (Lk. XVIII.21)," *HTR* 41 (1948): 5ff.

160. Rustow, "ENTOS HUMON ESTIN: Zur Deutung von Lukas 17.20–21," pp. 214ff.

161. For more on this point, see Schnackenburg, *God's Rule and Kingdom*, pp. 136–37. In his more recent contribution to the subject he is inclined to see Luke's hand in 17:21b, in which he rightly recognizes a close parallel to Luke 13:23–24: "The questioners are directed from their apocalyptic enquiries and exhorted to personal effort, because the kingdom of God is already discernible in the present working of Jesus (cf. Luke 11:20)" ("Der eschatologische Abschnitt, Lk. 17.20–37," p. 218).

162. Otto, *The Kingdom of God and the Son of Man*, p. 136.

163. Ambrozic points to the non-Markan elements in the vocabulary of verses 11–12 (see *The Hidden Kingdom*, p. 48). Jeremias details the elements in the passage that point to its Palestinian origin (see *The Parables of Jesus*, p. 15). See also G. Minette de Tillesse, *Le secret messianique dans l'évangile de Marc*, Lectio Divina 47 (Paris, 1968), pp. 172–73; J. Gnilka, *Die Verstockung Israels*, Studien zum Alten und Neuen Testament, nr. 3 (München, 1961), pp. 24–25; and W. Kelber, *The Kingdom in Mark*, pp. 29, 32–33.

164. Reploh is particularly clear on this; see *Markus, Lehrer der Gemeinde*, pp. 60–61.

165. See Kelber, *The Kingdom in Mark*, pp. 25–26, 30–31.

166. Gnilka contends that Mark may have been intending to convey a distinction between the new Israel around Jesus and the old Israel apart from him (see *Die Verstockung Israels*, p. 85).

167. M. Black interprets *hoi exo* as the equivalent of the Aramaic *sharkā de 'enāshā*, which in Matthew 6:7 is used in reference to the Gentiles and in Luke 18:9–11 denotes Jews not conforming to the law (see Black, *An Aramaic Approach to the Gospels and Acts*, pp. 176–77). Schnackenburg comes to a similar conclusion on the basis of the similarity between the Hebrew *ḥus* and the Aramaic *ḥusa* (see Schnackenburg, *God's Rule and Kingdom*, p. 184). See also Grundmann, *Das Evangelium nach Markus*, p. 92.

168. Matthew 13:11 and Luke 8:10 both have the reading "secrets of the kingdom" where Mark has the singular. L. Cerfaux (in "La connaissance des secrets du royaume d'après Matthew XIII:11 et par.," *NTS* 2 [1956]: 240–41), followed by Ambrozic (in *The Hidden Kingdom*, pp. 86–88), maintains that the plural reading is original and that Mark modified it to a singular. The case is hardly convincing, however. Once the statement came to be popularly interpreted as speaking of parables generally, there was a strong temptation to make the singular a plural. Most scholars agree that the version in Matthew and Luke is secondary (see, for example, Jeremias, *The Parables of Jesus*, p. 16; Schnackenburg, *God's Rule and Kingdom*, p. 184; Gnilka, *Die Verstockung Israels*, pp. 99–100; and Schürmann, *Das Evangelium nach Lukas*, p. 459).

169. The consensus is represented in scholars of all shades of thought, including Schniewind (*Das Evangelium nach Markus*, Das Neue Testament Deutsch [Göttingen,

1958], p. 75), Klostermann (*Das Markusevangelium*, Handbuch zum Neuen Testament [Tübingen, 1926], p. 41), J. Schmid (*Das Evangelium nach Markus*, Regensburger Neues Testament [Regensburg, 1954], p. 73), Cranfield (*The Gospel according to St. Mark*, 2d ed., Cambridge Greek Testament [Cambridge, 1963], pp. 153ff.), Hauck (*TDNT*, 5: 757– 78), Horst (*TDNT*, 5: 555), Grundmann (*Das Evangelium nach Markus*, p. 92), Jeremias (*The Parables of Jesus*, p. 16), Bornkamm (*Jesus of Nazareth*, p. 71, and *TDNT*, 5: 818ff.), Schnackenburg (*God's Rule and Kingdom*, pp. 189–90), Minette de Tillesse (*Le secret messianique dans l'évangile de Marc*, p. 216), Gnilka (*Die Verstockung Israels*, p. 44), Reploh (*Markus, Lehrer der Gemeinde*, pp. 65–66), Kelber (*The Kingdom in Mark*, p. 38), W. L. Lane (*The Gospel of Mark*, New International Commentary on the New Testament [Grand Rapids, 1974], p. 158), Schürmann (*Das Lukasevangelium*, p. 461), and Pesch (*Das Markusevangelium*, 2: 239).

170. On the use of *musterion* in the Wisdom Literature, see Minette de Tillesse, *Le secret messianique dans l'évangile de Marc*, p. 195.

171. Daniel 2:18, 19, 27, 28, 29, 40, and 47.

172. The Hymn Scroll, 4:13–14, 27–28, translated by Dupont-Sommer. The whole chapter is instructive for this theme.

173. Cf. The Scroll of the Rule, 3:18–25; 4:18ff.

174. 1 Enoch 46:2ff.

175. See Grundmann, *Das Evangelium nach Markus*, p. 92; Gnilka, *Die Verstockung Israels*, pp. 193–94; and Ambrozic, *The Hidden Kingdom*, p. 93.

176. Taylor, *The Gospel according to St. Mark*, Macmillan New Testament Commentaries (London, 1952), p. 256.

177. See Jeremias, *The Parables of Jesus*, p. 18.

178. "The whole thing comes to be *cryptic*," says J. W. Hunkin ("The Synoptic Parables," *JTS* 16 [1915]: 372ff.); "All becomes *riddles*," says Otto (*The Kingdom of God and the Son of Man*, p. 92); "All things are imparted in *riddles*" or "happen in *riddles*," says Jeremias (*The Parables of Jesus*, p. 16; *New Testament Theology*, 1: 120); "Everything becomes as *riddles*," says Gnilka (*Die Verstockung Israels*, pp. 26ff.); "Everything comes in *parables*," says Ambrozic (*The Hidden Kingdom*, p. 79).

179. Schniewind, *Das Evangelium nach Markus*, p. 75.

180. Von Rad, *The Message of the Prophets*, trans. D. M. G. Stalker (London, 1968), p. 126. The whole discussion of this passage (on pp. 121–26) is highly illuminating.

181. On this point, see Minette de Tillesse, *Le secret messianique dans l'évangile de Marc*, pp. 213–14; Gnilka, *Die Verstockung Israels*, pp. 47–48; and Schnackenburg, *God's Rule and Kingdom*, p. 186.

182. Jülicher maintains that the saying should be struck out as "wholly unhistorical" and that it confronts us with an either/or: "Either the evangelists or Jesus" (*Die Gleichnisreden Jesu*, 2 vols. [Tübingen, 1910], 1: 148). See also J. Weiss, *Jesus' Proclamation of the Kingdom*, p. 63; Bultmann, *Jesus and the Word*, trans. L. J. Smith and E. H. Lantero (New York, 1958), p. 71; Dodd, *Parables of the Kingdom*, pp. 14–15; A. E. J. Rawlinson, *The Gospel according to St. Mark*, 2d ed. (London, 1927), pp. 47–48; Kümmel, *Promise and Fulfilment*, p. 125n.75: E. Schweizer, *Das Evangelium nach Markus*, Das Neue Testament Deutsch (Göttingen, 1967), p. 93; and Pesch, *Das Markusevangelium*, 2: 238.

183. The idea is further approximated in Matthew 13:16–17 // Luke 10:23–24, assumed in Luke 12:32, and yet more clearly intimated in the account of Jesus weeping over Jerusalem in Luke 19:42ff.: "If only you had known, on this great day, the way that leads to peace! But no; *it is hidden from your sight*... You did not recognize God's moment when it came."

184. V. Taylor has stated that it is "an unauthentic version of a genuine saying" (*The Gospel according to St. Mark*, p. 257). M. Black (*An Aramaic Approach to the Gospels and Acts*, p. 215) and D. Nineham (*St. Mark*, Pelican Gospel Commentary [Harmonds-

worth, 1963], p. 137) have expressed similar views. Ambrozic is uncertain on the issue, maintaining that it is impossible to say whether the logion is from Jesus or not (see *The Hidden Kingdom*, pp. 47–48). Others are more forthright in their acceptance of the saying as authentic, among them being T. W. Manson (*The Teaching of Jesus*, p. 77), Otto (*The Kingdom of God and the Son of Man*, pp. 138–46), Jeremias (*The Parables of Jesus*, p. 15), Schnackenburg (*God's Rule and Kingdom*, p. 186), Minette de Tillesse (*Le secret messianique dans l'évangile de Marc*, pp. 191–92), Gnilka (*Die Verstockung Israels*, pp. 198–99), and Schürmann (*Das Lukasevangelium*, p. 461).

185. See Gnilka, *Die Verstockung Israels*, pp. 189, 204–5. Jeremias suggests that it would not have been said at any time prior to the confession of Peter (see *The Parables of Jesus*, p. 18).

186. According to Jeremias, the saying in Mark 4:11–12 describes "the perpetual twofold issue of all preaching of the gospel: the offer of mercy and the threat of impending judgment inseparable from it (Isa. 6:9f.), deliverance and offence, salvation and destruction, life and death"; nevertheless, he says that the statement of verse 11 is "nothing less than a cry of exultation" (*The Parables of Jesus*, pp. 16, 18).

Chapter 10

1. Luke's more elaborate picture is likely to be a development of Mark's. The version in the Gospel of Thomas is similar to Mark's: "It is not possible for one to enter the house of the strong (man) and take him (or: it) by force unless he bind his hands; then he will ransack his house" (*The Gospel according to Thomas*, trans. A. Guillamont et al. [Leiden, 1959], p. 23).

2. Otto, *The Kingdom of God and the Son of Man*, trans. F. V. Filson and B. L. Woolf (London, 1943), pp. 98–102. Bultmann also held that the parable has in view the conquest of Satan by God (see *HST*, p. 103).

3. Jülicher, *Die Gleichnisreden Jesu*, 2 vols. (Tübingen, 1910), 2: 226.

4. This basic viewpoint is shared by scholars of widely differing approaches, among whom are A. Schlatter (*Die Geschichte des Christus* [Stuttgart, 1923], p. 99, and *Der Evangelist Matthäus* [Stuttgart, 1948], 2: 406–8), J. Jeremias (*The Parables of Jesus*, trans. S. H. Hooke, rev. ed. [London, 1963], pp. 122–23), W. Grundmann (*TDNT*, 3: 405, and *Das Evangelium nach Markus*, Theologischer Handkommentar zum Neuen Testament [Berlin, 1959], p. 84), J. M. Robinson (*The Problem of History in Mark* [London, 1957], pp. 30–31), D. E. Nineham (*St. Mark*, Pelican Gospel Commentary [Harmondsworth, 1963], p. 121), and E. Best (*The Temptation and the Passion: The Marcan Soteriology* [Cambridge, 1965], pp. 12–13).

5. On this, see Grundmann, *TDNT*, 3: 404–5.

6. Grundmann, *TDNT*, 3: 404–5.

7. The difference in verb tenses between the two parables is significant: the historic present in verbs of the first parable is unusual for Matthew. The kingdom of heaven is likened in the first parable to the treasure and in the second parable to the merchant. In both cases, of course, it is the *event* depicted to which the kingdom is likened.

8. *The Gospel according to Thomas*, pp. 5–7.

9. See, for example, Jeremias, *The Parables of Jesus*, p. 201; M. Wilson, *Studies in the Gospel of Thomas* (London, 1960), pp. 94–95; and Crossan, *In Parables: The Challenge of the Historical Jesus* (New York, 1973), pp. 34–35.

10. See W. Schrage: "That we have to do with a modification of the well-known parable of the Dragnet, Matthew 13:47–48, and the changes in part Gnostically conditioned, seems scarcely to be doubted" (*Das Verhältnis der Thomas-Evangeliums zur synoptischen Tradition und zu den koptischen Evangelienübersetzungen* [Berlin, 1964], pp. 37–38). For similar comments, see Quispel, "Some Remarks on the Gospel of Thomas," *NTS* 5 (1959): 289.

11. H.-D. Wendland, *Die Eschatologie des Reiches Gottes bei Jesus: Eine Studie über den Zusammenhang von Eschatologie, Ethik und Kirchenproblem* (Gütersloh, 1931), p. 35.

12. Pearls were of great worth and highly sought after in the ancient world. Cleopatra is said to have owned a pearl worth a hundred million sesterces (= three million dollars); see Jeremias, *The Parables of Jesus*, p. 199.

13. Jüngel, *Paulus und Jesus: Eine Untersuchung zur Präzisierung der Frage nach dem Aufsprung der Christologie* (Tübingen, 1962), p. 143.

14. Linnemann, *Jesus of the Parables* (London, 1966), pp. 100–101.

15. Crossan, *In Parables*, pp. 34–35.

16. Otto, *The Kingdom of God and the Son of Man*, p. 128.

17. See Danker, *Jesus and the New Age according to St. Luke* (St. Louis, 1972), p. 168.

18. See especially Jeremias, *The Parables of Jesus*, pp. 132ff., and Linnemann, *Jesus of the Parables*, pp. 65–73.

19. Linnemann, *Jesus of the Parables*, p. 66.

20. Crossan, *In Parables*, p. 74.

21. Jeremias, *The Parables of Jesus*, p. 84; italics his.

22. See Schlatter, *Der Evangelist Matthäus*, p. 561.

23. Jeremias, *The Parables of Jesus*, p. 210.

24. Via, *The Parables: Their Literary and Existential Dimension* (Philadelphia, 1967), p. 141.

25. Fuchs, *Studies of the Historical Jesus*, Studies in Biblical Theology, no. 42 (London, 1964), p. 111.

26. Bonnard, *L'Évangile selon Saint Matthieu*, Commentaire du Nouveau Testament (Paris, 1963), p. 291.

27. Jeremias, *The Parables of Jesus*, p. 37.

28. Fuchs, *Studies of the Historical Jesus*, pp. 35–36.

29. Linnemann, *Jesus of the Parables*, p. 87.

30. Via, *The Parables*, p. 154.

31. This solution of the problem of the relation between the two forms of the parable is adopted by most recent exegetes; see for example Dodd, *The Parables of the Kingdom* (London, 1935), p. 122; Jeremias, *The Parables of Jesus*, p. 65; Michaelis, *Der Evangelium nach Matthäus*, 2 vols. (Zürich, 1948–49), 1: 148; Via, *The Parables*, p. 129; R. W. Funk, *Language, Hermeneutic and the Word of God: The Problem of Language in the New Testament and Contemporary Theology* (London, 1966), p. 169; and Crossan, *In Parables*, p. 70. Both Bultmann (in *HST*, p. 195) and B. T. D. Smith (in *The Parables of the Synoptic Gospels* [Cambridge, 1937], p. 206) hold that the story of the man without a wedding garment is wholly the result of Matthew's free redaction.

32. Linnemann, *Jesus of the Parables*, p. 91. See also Caird, *St. Luke*, Pelican Gospel Commentaries (Harmondsworth, 1963), p. 177; and Schweizer, *The Good News according to Matthew*, trans. D. O. E. Green (Atlanta, 1975), p. 421, for similar expositions. Dodd in his own way and from his own viewpoint had long ago emphasized this element of the parable's significance (see *The Parables of the Kingdom*, p. 121).

33. TeSelle, *Speaking in Parables: A Study in Metaphorical Theology* (Philadelphia, 1975), pp. 71–72.

34. See TeSelle, *Speaking in Parables*, p. 77.

35. So says Crossan, *In Parables*, pp. 47–49, 51.

36. So says C. W. F. Smith, *The Jesus of the Parables*, rev. ed. (Philadelphia, 1975), p. 53.

37. If the measures cited in the parable are original they signify a huge amount of flour and bread, such as no housewife would use in ordinary circumstances: three *seah* of meal would make bread to feed more than a hundred and fifty people—*enough for a feast!*

38. Dahl, "The Parables of Growth," *ST* 5 (1951): 147.

39. Polag, *Die Christologie der Logienquelle* (Neukirchen-Vluyn, 1977), p. 51.

40. See Schweizer, *The Good News according to Matthew*, pp. 306–7.

41. Lütgert, *Das Reich Gottes nach den synoptischen Evangelien: Eine Untersuchung zur neutestamentlichen Theologie* (Gütersloh, 1895), p. 99.

42. More recently Bornkamm has made the same point: "Beginning and end, however wonderful and incomprehensible the end may be, stand in a very definite relationship, one to another. The end comes from the beginning, the fruit from the seed, the harvest from the sowing, the whole leavened loaf from the leaven. Thus *our task is to understand the present in its apparent insignificance*" (*Jesus of Nazareth*, trans. I. McLuskey, F. McLuskey, and J. M. Robinson [London, 1960], p. 71).

43. Otto, *The Kingdom of God and the Son of Man*, pp. 123–24.

44. Ambrozic, *The Hidden Kingdom: A Redaction-Critical Study of the References to the Kingdom of God in Mark's Gospel*, Catholic Biblical Quarterly—Monograph Series, 2 (Washington, 1972), p. 132.

45. *The Gospel according to Thomas*, p. 17.

46. Although W. L. Lane comes close to such an emphasis in *The Gospel of Mark*, New International Commentary on the New Testament (Grand Rapids, 1974), p. 169.

47. See Stuhlmann, "Beobachtungen zu Markus IV.26–29," *NTS* 19 (1973): 153ff. He draws attention to the fact that in the only other passage in which this term occurs in the New Testament, Acts 12:10 (*pulen . . . hetis automate enoige*), the term would suitably serve as a periphrasis for a miraculous act of God, as it would in Joshua 6:5 (*peseitai automata ta teiche*).

48. Stuhlmann, "Beobachtungen zu Markus IV.26–29," p. 157.

49. See Ambrozic's excellent formulation of this argument in *The Hidden Kingdom*, p. 119.

50. Kümmel, "Noch einmal: Das Gleichnis von der selbstwachsenden Saat," in *Orientierung an Jesus*, Festschrift for J. Schmid, ed. P. Hoffmann et al. (Freiburg, 1971), p. 235.

51. There are some exceptions, however, among whom are Jeremias (*The Parables of Jesus*, pp. 151–52) and Stuhlmann ("Beobachtungen zu Markus IV.26–29," p. 159).

52. Lohmeyer, *Das Evangelium nach Markus*, Kritisch-exegetischer Kommentar über das Neue Testament (Göttingen, 1963), p. 88.

53. Linnemann, *Jesus of the Parables*, p. 117.

54. Michaelis, *Die Gleichnisse Jesu*, Die urchristliche Botschaft, 23te Abteilung (Hamburg, 1956), pp. 24–25.

55. Guardini, *The Lord*, trans. E. C. Briefs (London, 1956), p. 175.

56. Schniewind, *Das Evangelium nach Markus*, Das Neue Testament Deutsch (Göttingen, 1960), p. 74.

57. Kingsbury, *The Parables of Jesus in Matthew 13: A Study in Redaction Criticism* (Richmond, 1969), p. 135. A similar position is maintained by Schlatter (*Der Evangelist Matthäus*, pp. 434–35). Gerhardsson, whose contention that the parable exhibits the difference between hearing and not hearing the word of God as set forth in the Shema (Deut. 6:4ff.) specifically depends on the basic assumption that the parable is concerned with the seed rather than the harvest (see "The Parable of the Sower and Its Interpretation," *NTS* 14 [1968]: 165ff., 176–77, 188).

58. Crossan, *In Parables*, p. 41.

59. Dahl, "The Parables of Growth," p. 152.

60. A pointer in this direction is given by M. Black in "The Parables as Allegory," *Bulletin of the John Rylands Library* 42 (1959–60): 278.

61. So argues W. L. Lane: "The coming of the kingdom of God is presented in comprehensive terms which call attention both to its present and to its future aspects" (*The Gospel of Mark*, pp. 154–55; cf. Schnackenburg, *God's Rule and Kingdom* [London, 1963], pp. 150–51).

62. Otto has argued that the parables of the Sower and of the Seed Growing Secretly were originally parts of a single parable, the latter serving as the true conclusion of the former; he maintains that after Mark had separated out the Seed Growing Secretly

as a parable in its own right, Matthew went one stage further and produced from it the parable of the Tares (*The Kingdom of God and the Son of Man*, pp. 89–90). See also T. W. Manson, *The Sayings of Jesus* (London, 1949), pp. 192–93; C. W. F. Smith, *Jesus of the Parables*, pp. 49–50; and S. E. Johnson in *The Interpreter's Bible*, ed. G. A. Buttrick et al. (New York, 1951), 7: 414.

63. C. H. Dodd states that the possibility that the parables of the Tares was formed from the earlier parable "does not seem to me in the least probable. The Matthaean parable stands on its own feet. It depicts in characteristic fashion a perfectly perspicuous situation" (*The Parables of the Kingdom*, p. 183).

64. E. Percy is reasonably confident of the authenticity of verses 27–29 (see *Die Botschaft Jesu* [Lund, 1953], p. 211); J. D. Kingsbury accepts only verses 24b–26 (see *The Parables of Jesus in Matthew 13*, p. 65); E. Schweizer views verses 24, 26, 28b, and 29 as original (see *The Good News according to Matthew*, p. 303); and Jüngel accepts everything through verse 29 (see *Paulus und Jesus*, p. 148).

65. H. Montefiore had no doubt on this matter: "Thomas's version of the Tares and the Wheat provides a striking instance of compression to the point of absurdity, and in this respect Thomas's version is plainly inferior to Matthew" (*Thomas and the Evangelists*, by H. Montefiore and H. E. W. Turner, Studies in Biblical Theology, no. 35 [London, 1962], p. 51).

66. Jeremias suggests that Jesus alluded to an event known to his audience (*The Parables of Jesus*, p. 224) on the basis of an incident cited by H. Schmidt and P. Kahle in *Volkserzählungen aus Palästina* (Göttingen, 1918), p. 31. B. T. D. Smith relates the story of a man who found a mass of kusseb (a reed) in seed and collected the seeds: "I went to Abu Jassin's kitchen garden," said the man. "It was freshly ploughed. There I scattered the kusseb seeds. The new year had scarcely come before the garden was thick with kusseb. From that day to this—it is now some twenty years—he could not plough a single furrow in it for the mass of kusseb. The olive trees withered away" (*The Parables of the Synoptic Gospels*, p. 197). R. C. Trench has cited examples of similar acts in modern India and one occasion in Ireland, when an evicted tenant sowed wild oats in fields which he had to leave (see *Notes on the Parables of Our Lord*, 14th ed. [London, 1882], pp. 86–87).

67. In addition to Jeremias's lucid description of these details (in *The Parables of Jesus*, pp. 224–25), see the discussion of F. L. Anderson in his article on tares in *A Dictionary of Christ and the Gospels*, ed. J. Hastings, 2 vols. (Edinburgh, 1906–08), 2: 497–98.

68. See Bultmann, *HST*, p. 177.

69. Trench, *Notes on the Parables of Our Lord*, p. 92.

70. Says Lohmeyer, "As the field belongs to the farmer, so the world—not the community nor the nation—to the Son of Man; he is its sole Lord" (*Das Evangelium des Matthäus*, completed by W. Smauch, Kritisch-exegetischer Kommentar über das Neue Testament (Göttingen, 1962), p. 223.

71. Verse 49a echoes verse 40, verse 49b echoes verse 41, and verse 50 repeats verse 42 exactly. The close connection between the interpretations of the two parables indicates that they have come from the same hand—that of the Evangelist. Yet many scholars have noted the fitness of the interpretation of the parable of the Dragnet, among them being Bultmann, who said that "there is, in my view, no need to entertain doubts" of the originality of the parable (*HST*, p. 173). See also Kümmel, *Promise and Fulfilment: The Eschatological Message of Jesus*, Studies in Biblical Theology, no. 23 (London, 1961), p. 137.

72. Otto, *The Kingdom of God and the Son of Man*, pp. 127–28. To my knowledge, T. W. Manson is the only scholar to follow Otto on this point, as he does in his interpretation of the parable of the Tares and the Wheat (see *The Sayings of Jesus*, p. 197).

73. See Jeremias, *The Parables of Jesus*, p. 226, along with the references cited in note 85.

74. Jeremias, *The Parables of Jesus*, p. 225; see also p. 102.

75. Jüngel, *Paulus und Jesus*, p. 146.

76. See, for example, B. T. D. Smith, *The Parables of the Synoptic Gospels*, p. 201.

77. Lohmeyer, *Das Evangelium des Matthäus*, pp. 228–29.

78. Schlatter, *Der Evangelist Matthäus*, p. 448.

79. Says Jüngel, "Through the eschatological difference of the sovereignty of God, as it comes to expression in Jesus' parables, a man is compelled to decision (from the aspect of the separation), inasmuch as Jesus grants a man (from the aspect of the gathering) time for decision" (*Paulus und Jesus*, p. 147; for similar analyses, see Michaelis, *Die Gleichnisse Jesu*, p. 69, and Kümmel, *Promise and Fulfilment*, pp. 137–38).

80. Bultmann, *HST*, p. 19; see also pp. 39ff.

81. Among those who contend that verses 19b–20 do reflect the church's practice of fasting are the following: Jülicher (*Die Gleichnisreden Jesu*, p. 187), Klostermann (*Das Markusevangelium*, Handbuch zum Neuen Testament [Tübingen, 1927], pp. 27–28), Lohmeyer (*Das Evangelium des Markus*, p. 59), Dodd (*The Parables of the Kingdom*, p. 116n.2), B. T. D. Smith (*The Parables of the Synoptic Gospels*, p. 95), Jeremias (*TDNT*, 4: 1103), Perrin (*Rediscovering the Teaching of Jesus*, New Testament Library [London, 1963], p. 79), Kümmel (*Promise and Fulfilment*, p. 76), Schweizer (*The Good News according to Mark*, trans. D. H. Madvig [Atlanta, 1970], p. 67), Schürmann (*Das Lukasevangelium*, Herders theologischer Kommentar zum Neuen Testament [Freiburg, 1969], 1: 297), and Pesch (*Das Markusevangelium*, 2 vols., Herders theologischer Kommentar zum Neuen Testament [Freiburg, 1976–77], 1: 171).

82. E. Percy, for one, considers such an alteration highly unlikely; see *Die Botschaft Jesu*, p. 235.

83. F. G. Cremer has strongly denied that the church took either action; see *Die Fastenansage Jesu: Mk. 2.20 und Parallelen, in der Sicht der patristischen und scholastischen Exegese*, Bonner Biblische Beiträge, nr. 23 (Bonn, 1965), pp. 5–6.

84. Wellhausen, *Das Evangelium Marci* (Berlin, 1903), pp. 18–19. He argues that the whole passage was written later.

85. Taylor, *The Gospel according to St. Mark*, Macmillan New Testament Commentaries (London, 1952), p. 212.

86. The two are A. Kee, "The Questions about Fasting," *Novum Testamentum* 11 (1969): 161–73; and J. B. Muddiman, "Jesus and Fasting, Mark ii.18–22," in *Jésus aux origines de la Christologie*, ed. J. Dupont (Gembloux, 1975), pp. 271ff.

87. Kee, "The Questions about Fasting," p. 168.

88. Such is Pesch's contention (see *Das Markusevangelium*, 1: 170, 172nn.3, 6).

89. Such is the contention of Dibelius (*From Tradition to Gospel* [London, 1934], pp. 65–66) and Kümmel (*Promise and Fulfilment*, p. 76).

90. On the expression "disciples of the Pharisees" in Mark 2:18, see Rengstoff, *TDNT*, 4: 443.

91. Muddiman, "Jesus and Fasting, Mark ii.18–22," p. 276. For information on the contemporary practice of fasting among Jews and Christians, see J. Behm, *TDNT*, 4: 924–35; and W. L. Lane, *The Gospel of Mark*, pp. 108–9.

92. Such is the contention of P. Vielhauer, "Tracht und Speise Johannes' des Taufers," in *Aufsätze zum Neuen Testament* (München, 1965), p. 54. Vielhauer's point is seconded by Pesch, *Das Markusevangelium*, p. 172.

93. "The sons of the Bridechamber" can include both the closer associates of the bridegroom and the guests he has invited; see H. L. Strack–P. Billerbeck, *Kommentar zum Neuen Testament aus Talmud und Midrasch*, 6 vols. (München, 1922–28), 1: 500–501.

94. Billerbeck, *Kommentar zum Neuen Testament aus Talmud und Midrasch*, 1: 504–5.

95. Jeremias, *TDNT*, 4: 1103; see also his *Parables of Jesus*, p. 117, and *New Testament Theology*, vol. 1, *The Proclamation of Jesus*, trans. J. S. Bowden (London, 1971), p.

105. A similar interpretation is given by Klostermann in *Das Markusevangelium*, p. 28, and by Dodd in *The Parables of the Kingdom*, p. 116n.2.

96. "This world is the betrothal . . . the wedding will be in the days of the Messiah"—Exodus 15:30, cited by Jeremias, *TDNT*, 4: 1102.

97. Such is the contention of Roloff (*Das Kerygma und der irdische Jesu: Historische Motive in den Jesus-Erzählungen der Evangelien* [Göttingen, 1970], p. 227), Percy (*Die Botschaft Jesu*, pp. 234ff.), Kümmel (*Promise and Fulfilment*, p. 57n.123), Gnilka (*Die Verstockung Israels*, Studien zum Alten und Neuen Testament, nr. 3 [München, 1961], p. 72), Schürmann (*Das Lukasevangelium*, p. 295), Pesch (*Das Markusevangelium*, 1: 173), and Lane (*The Gospel of Mark*, pp. 109–10).

98. Goppelt, *TDNT*, 4: 140.

99. Says Roloff, it is "not a *Bildwort* but a *Rätselwort*"—that is, it is not so much a parable as a riddle (see *Das Kerygma und der irdische Jesu*, p. 227).

100. See F. C. Cremer, *Die Fastensage Jesu*, p. 5.

101. *The Gospel according to Thomas*, p. 53; and see Quispel, "The Gospel of Thomas and the New Testament," *VC* 11 (1957): 192. Quispel further contends that the Diatessaron and the Gospel of Thomas could both go back to a Semitic tradition of sayings of Jesus (see "L'Évangile selon Thomas et le Diatessaron," *VC* 13 [1959]: 87ff.).

102. See Muddiman, "Jesus and Fasting, Mark ii.18–22," pp. 277–78.

103. So argues H. W. Kuhn (*Enderwartung und Gegenwärtiges Heil: Untersuchungen zu den Gemeindeliedern von Qumran*, Studien zur Umwelt des Neuen Testaments, vol. 4 [Göttingen, 1966], pp. 198–99) and Roloff (*Das Kerygma und der irdische Jesu*, p. 237).

104. We might note that Matthew replaces "fast" with "mourn" in his equivalent of verse 19. For discussions of the association of fasting and mourning in this context, see Bultmann, *TDNT*, 6: 42n.16; and Lohmeyer, *Das Markusevangelium*, p. 112. Having observed that the opening words of verse 20 ("days will come") are the same as those in Luke 17:22–23, Ebeling has argued that the saying is making reference to last distress, when fasting will be fitting, but this is unlikely (see "Die Fastenfrage [Mk. 2.18–22]," *TSK* 108 [1937–38]: 387–96).

105. Kee, "The Questions about Fasting," pp. 18ff.

106. See Muddiman, "Jesus and Fasting, Mark ii.18–22," pp. 280–81.

107. For more on this point, see Grundmann, *Das Evangelium nach Markus*, Theologischer Handkommentar zum Neuen Testament (Berlin, 1959), p. 67; Jeremias, *The Parables of Jesus*, pp. 117–18 (though his cosmic interpretation of Mark 2:21 is doubtful); Pesch, *Das Markusevangelium*, 1: 176–77; and Lane, *The Gospel of Mark*, p. 113.

Excursus 2

1. Otto, *The Kingdom of God and the Son of Man*, trans. F. V. Filson and B. L. Woolf (London, 1943), pp. 102–3. The dictum has found no little assent among scholars (see especially Perrin, *A Modern Pilgrimage in New Testament Christology* [Philadelphia, 1974], p. 53).

2. Fuchs, *Studies of the Historical Jesus*, Studies in Biblical Theology, no. 42 (London, 1964), pp. 153–54.

3. See the statement of Käsemann in "The Problem of the Historical Jesus," in *Essays on New Testament Themes*, trans. W. J. Montague, Studies in Biblical Theology (London, 1964), pp. 43–44.

Chapter 11

1. On this point, see especially J. Jeremias, *The Prayers of Jesus*, trans. J. S. Bowden, C. Burchard, and J. Reumann, Studies in Biblical Theology, 2d ser., no. 6 (London, 1967), pp. 89–93, and *New Testament Theology*, vol. 1, *The Proclamation of Jesus*, trans. J. S. Bowden (London, 1971), pp. 195–96. See also W. Grundmann, *Das Evangelium*

nach Matthäus, Theologischer Handkommentar zum Neuen Testament (Berlin, 1968), p. 199; R. E. Brown, *New Testament Essays* (Milwaukee, 1965), pp. 218–21; E. Schweizer, *The Good News according to Matthew*, trans. D. O. E. Green (Atlanta, 1975), p. 149; and S. Schulz, *Q—Die Spruchquelle der Evangelisten* (Zürich, 1972), p. 86.

2. For arguments along these lines, see Brown, *New Testament Essays*, p. 220; and H. Schürmann, *Praying with Christ: The "Our Father" for Today* (New York, 1964), p. 5.

3. This is most fully discussed by K. G. Kuhn in his study *Achtzehngebet und Vaterunser und der Reim*, Wissenschaftliche Untersuchungen zum Neuen Testament, nr. 1 (Tübingen, 1950), pp. 30–40. See also C. C. Torrey, *The Translations Made from the Original Aramaic Gospels* (New York, 1912), p. 309; C. F. Burney, *The Poetry of Our Lord* (Oxford, 1925), pp. 161–62; Lohmeyer, *"Our Father": An Introduction to the Lord's Prayer* (New York, 1965), pp. 27–29; and Jeremias, *The Prayers of Jesus*, p. 94, and *New Testament Theology*, 1: 196.

4. See Jeremias, *The Sermon on the Mount*, trans. N. Perrin, Facet Books Biblical Series 2 (Philadelphia, 1963), pp. 19–23.

5. See Jeremias, *The Prayers of Jesus*, p. 88, and *New Testament Theology*, 1: 194.

6. See Billerbeck in H. Strack–P. Billerbeck, *Kommentar zum Neuen Testament aus Talmud und Midrasch*, 6 vols. (München, 1922–28), 1: 406–7.

7. See Kuhn, *Achtzehngebet und Vaterunser und der Reim*, pp. 30–33, 40–46.

8. See Jeremias, "Abba," in *The Prayers of Jesus*, pp. 11–65, especially pp. 15–29.

9. Jeremias, *The Prayers of Jesus*, p. 57.

10. See M. Dibelius, *Jesus*, trans. C. B. Hedrick and F. C. Grant (Philadelphia, 1949), p. 120; cf. *The Message of Jesus Christ*, trans. F. C. Grant (New York, 1939), p. 69. Bultmann acknowledges this as a possible explanation; see *Jesus and the Word*, trans. L. P. Smith and E. H. Lantero (1934; New York, 1958), p. 181.

11. On this, see G. Dalman, *The Words of Jesus* (Edinburgh, 1902), pp. 206–34.

12. Those who concur with this assessment include the following: Bultmann (*Jesus and the Word*, p. 181), W. Michaelis (*Der Evangelium nach Matthäus*, 2 vols. [Zürich, 1948–49], 1: 313), G. Bornkamm (*Jesus of Nazareth*, trans. I. McLuskey, F. McLuskey, and J. M. Robinson [London, 1960], p. 137), Jeremias (*The Prayers of Jesus*, p. 98 [relating to the Lukan version]), W. Grundmann (*Das Evangelium nach Matthäus*, pp. 200–201), P. Bonnard (*L'Évangile selon Saint Matthieu*, Commentaire du Nouveau Testament [Neuchatel, 1963], p. 83), E. Lohmeyer (*"Our Father,"* pp. 272–73), R. E. Brown (*New Testament Essays*, pp. 228, 238), S. Schulz (*Q—Die Spruchquelle der Evangelisten*, p. 88), and A. Polag (*Die Christologie der Logienquelle* [Neukirchen-Vluyn, 1977], p. 60).

13. Polag, *Die Christologie der Logienquelle*, p. 60.

14. The origin of this petition has been much discussed. It is commonly suggested that the prayer of Jesus in Gethsemane was inserted into the prayer for the disciples at some time prior to the time Matthew was written. But it is highly improbable that anyone would have thus radically altered its meaning by shifting it from a context of Christ's struggle to accept the terrible destiny of having to drink the cup of woe given him by the Father to the context of the glory of the theophany for the final kingdom. It is especially unlikely that such a transposition would have been made in an era when the eschatological import of the Lord's Prayer was still vivid. Schürmann points out that there is evidence of the reverse of this process in Matthew 26:46, in which the evangelist conformed the prayer in Gethsemane to the version of the disciples' prayer he had received and recorded (see *Praying with Christ*, p. 123n.192). This process of accommodation is entirely comprehensible: Jesus recalled his prayer for the kingdom in his attempt to ensure his own obedience all the way to the conclusion of his service for the kingdom of God; even so, we should note that it was simply an accommodation of the form of a tradition rather than an insertion of a petition into the tradition. It is most plausible to assume that at some point Jesus would have expressed his desire for the coming of God's kingdom, and so it found its way into the prayer he taught his disciples.

15. See Schlatter, *Der Evangelist Matthäus* (Stuttgart, 1948), p. 210.

16. Traub, *TDNT*, 5: 517–18.

17. Jeremias, *The Prayers of Jesus*, p. 102.

18. See Jeremias, *The Prayers of Jesus*, pp. 102–6.

19. Foerster, *TDNT*, 2: 591–99.

20. So argues K. G. Kuhn in *Achtzehngebet und Vaterunser und der Reim*, p. 40. His comparison of the Tefillah with the prayer of Jesus is highly illuminating, and I have freely drawn on it.

21. See Dupont, *Les Béatitudes: Le probleme littéraire*, 3 vols. (Paris, 1969–73), 1: 314–26.

22. For a broad comparison, see the blessings and curses on Ebal and Gerizim in Deuteronomy 27–28; more particularly, see the series of beatitudes and curses in 2 Enoch 52:1–14.

23. H. Schürmann contends that these three beatitudes were spoken at one time and circulated as a unit; see *Das Lukasevangelium*, Herders theologischer Kommentar zum Neuen Testament (Freiburg, 1969), 1: 328.

24. Black, *An Aramaic Approach to the Gospels and Acts*, 3d ed. (Oxford, 1973), p. 156.

25. Among those in agreement concerning the original order of the verses are A. H. McNeile (*The Gospel according to St. Matthew* [London, 1915], p. 51), A. Farrer (*St. Matthew and St. Mark* [London, 1954], pp. 162–64), M.-J. Lagrange (*L'Évangile selon Saint Matthieu*, Études Bibliques [Paris, 1923], p. 83), Grundmann (*Das Evangelium nach Matthäus*, p. 124), Black (*An Aramaic Approach to the Gospels and Acts*, p. 156), Dupont (*Les Béatitudes*, 1: 252–53), and H. T. Wrege (*Überlieferungsgeschichte der Bergpredigt*, Wissenschaftliche Untersuchungen zum Neuen Testament, nr. 9 [Tübingen, 1968], pp. 24–25).

26. On this point, see J. Wellhausen, *Das Evangelium Matthaei* (Berlin, 1904), p. 15; A. Loisy, *Les Évangiles synoptiques*, 2 vols. (Coffonds, 1907), 1: 550–51; E. Klostermann, *Das Matthäusevangelium*, Handbuch zum Neuen Testament (Tübingen, 1927), p. 38; Bultmann, *HST*, p. 110; J. Schmid, *Das Evangelium nach Matthäus*, Regensburger Neues Testament (Regensburg, 1965), p. 82; G. D. Kilpatrick, *The Origins of the Gospel according to St. Matthew* (Oxford, 1956), pp. 16–17; and Dupont, *Les Béatitudes*, 1: 224–27.

27. See the discussion of this point in Dupont, *Les Béatitudes*, 1: 274ff.

28. Dupont, *Les Béatitudes*, 1: 281.

29. See Cadbury, *The Style and Literary Method of Luke* (Cambridge, Mass., 1920), pp. 124–26.

30. Such is the contention of Loisy (*L'Évangile selon Luc* [Paris, 1924], p. 198), Lagrange (*L'Évangile selon Saint Matthieu*, p. 81), McNeile (*The Gospel according to Matthew*, p. 50), Bultmann (*HST*, p. 109), D. Daube (*The New Testament and Rabbinic Judaism* [London, 1956], p. 200), Wrege (*Überlieferungsgeschichte der Bergpredigt*, p. 8), and Schürmann (*Das Lukasevangelium*, 1: 329–30).

31. See Dupont, *Les Béatitudes*, 1: 210–12, 64.

32. See Dupont, *Les Béatitudes*, 3: 78–97.

33. See Dupont, *Les Béatitudes*, 2: 19–90.

34. See Wrege, *Überlieferungsgeschichte der Bergpredigt*, p. 23.

35. See the discussion of the addition and omission of references to the Son of Man in the gospels on pp. 224–25 herein.

36. Proponents of this view include A. H. Wilder (see *Eschatology and Ethics in the Teaching of Jesus*, rev. ed. [New York, 1950], p. 109) and C. H. Dodd (see *The Parables of the Kingdom* [London, 1935], p. 47n.1).

37. Meir, cited by Dalman in *The Words of Jesus*, p. 128.

38. Dupont points out that *estin auton* denotes belonging, not time (see *Les Béatitudes*, 2: 120).

39. Evidence concerning the texts, versions, and Patristic writers is conveniently

assembled in the United Bible Societies' Greek New Testament, pp. 11–12. For opposing views on the evidence, see B. M. Metzger, *A Textual Commentary on the Greek New Testament* (London, 1971), p. 12; and Dupont, *Les Béatitudes*, 1: 252–53.

40. Matthew 19:28 presents a different concept; see pp. 274–75 herein.

41. Schniewind, *Das Evangelium nach Matthäus*, Das Neue Testament Deutsch (Göttingen, 1964), pp. 42–43.

42. See Dupont, *Les Béatitudes*, 2: 36–37. Schürmann argues that *klaiontes* is original and that it was replaced with *penthountes* both in the woe in Luke 6:25 and in the beatitude in Matthew 5:4 in order to conform to Isaiah 61:2 (see *Das Lukasevangelium*, 1: 331n.42). Dupont, on the other hand, shows that *klaiontes* is typically Lukan, and argues that it is more likely that Luke inserted it at this point (see *Les Béatitudes*, 3: 69–75).

43. Grundmann, *Das Evangelium nach Matthäus*, p. 124.

44. See Strack–Billerbeck, *Kommentar zum Neuen Testament aus Talmud und Midrasch*, 1: 66–67.

45. Schlatter, *Der Evangelist Matthäus*, p. 135.

46. Schürmann contends that this is the case in *Das Lukasevangelium*, 1: 332.

47. The words "and thirsty" could be original even though they do not appear in Luke. The conjunction of the words "hunger" and "thirst" is common in the Bible (see Isa. 49:10, 55:1–2, and 65:13; and Rev. 7:16). Both Burney (*The Poetry of Our Lord*, p. 166) and Lohmeyer (*Das Evangelium nach Matthäus*, completed by W. Schmauch, Kritisch-exegetischer Kommentar über das Neue Testament [Göttingen, 1962], pp. 86–87) contend that the use of the entire phrase is necessary to preserve the poetic structure of the passage in Aramaic.

48. The inclusion of the words "for righteousness" is all but universally viewed as the result of Matthew's redaction in order to substantiate his ethical emphasis in the beatitudes.

49. The NEB assumes this interpretation: "How blest are those who hunger and thirst to see right prevail." For more on this point, see McNeile, *The Gospel according to Matthew*, p. 51; Schniewind, *Das Evangelium nach Matthäus*, pp. 44–45; L. Goppelt, *TDNT*, 5: 17–18; Lohmeyer, *Das Evangelium nach Matthäus*, pp. 87–88; Grundmann, *Das Evangelium nach Matthäus*, p. 127; and Wrege, *Überlieferungsgeschichte der Bergpredigt*, pp. 17–19.

50. Dupont argues for this interpretation; see his discussion in *Les Béatitudes*, 3: 355–84.

51. *Aboth* 5:19. For more on this point, see Strack–Billerbeck, *Kommentar zum Neuen Testament aus Talmud und Midrasch*, 1: 204.

52. Dupont observes that among the Rabbis works such as those enumerated in Matthew 25:35 are known as *gemilut hasadim*, "the practice of mercy" (see *Les Béatitudes*, 2: 627; see also the excursuses in Strack–Billerbeck, *Kommentar zum Neuen Testament aus Talmud und Midrasch*, 4/1: 536–610.

53. Burney, *The Poetry of Our Lord*, p. 166.

54. "That the heart of man should become pure and free," Käsemann has said, "this is the salvation of the world and the beginning of that sacrifice which is well-pleasing to God, the beginning of true worship, as the Pauline *paraenesis* in particular will expound" ("The Problem of the Historical Jesus," in *Essays on New Testament Themes*, trans. W. J. Montague, Studies in Biblical Theology, no. 41 [London, 1964], p. 39).

55. See Schniewind, *Das Evangelium nach Matthäus*, p. 47.

56. See the excellent exposition of this point in Dupont's *Béatitudes*, 3: 559–67.

57. For the rabbinic praises of peace, see Strack–Billerbeck, *Kommentar zum Neuen Testament aus Talmud und Midrasch*, 1: 215–18 (especially the hymn of R. Eleazar ben Eleazar Ha-qappar on pp. 215–16). For the saying relating to the Messiah, see 3: 587.

58. "Aaron loved peace, and pursued peace, and established peace between a man and his fellow" (*Sanh.* 6b). " 'Pursue peace.' How should one do it? One should pursue peace in Israel between individuals, as Aaron pursued peace in Israel between indi-

viduals" (*Aboth R. Nathan* 12). Both citations appear in Strack–Billerbeck, *Kommentar zum Neuen Testament aus Talmud und Midrasch*, 1: 217.

59. Foerster, *TDNT*, 2: 409.

60. See Strack–Billerbeck, *Kommentar zum Neuen Testament aus Talmud und Midrasch*, 1: 220.

61. Burney retains the addition for the sake of parallelism and assonance in the two lines (see *The Poetry of Our Lord*, p. 166).

62. See the discussion of the sufferings of the righteous man, the prophets, the Servant of the Lord, and the martyrs, on pp. 240–46 herein.

63. See Schürmann, *Das Lukasevangelium*, 1: 333n.51.

64. Such is the position of Dupont (*Les Béatitudes*, 3: 80), D. R. A. Hare (*The Theme of Jewish Persecution of Christians in the Gospel according to St. Matthew*, Society for New Testament Studies Monograph Series, no. 6 [Cambridge, 1967], p. 53), and Black (*An Aramaic Approach to the Gospels and Acts*, pp. 135–36).

65. See Black, *An Aramaic Approach to the Gospels and Acts*, p. 193.

66. Dupont aptly cites the Targum on Numbers 23:23: "Happy are you righteous! What a good recompense is prepared for you with your Father who is in the heavens in the world which is coming!"; or, in another recension, "What recompense is prepared for you before Yahweh in the world to come!" (*Les Béatitudes*, 2: 348).

67. On this, see Schürmann: "The affliction of the disciples is set in the light of the *Heilsgeschichte* and illustrated in the prophets' destiny as a 'must' of the saving history (which at the same time throws light on the significant position of a disciple of Jesus in the saving history!): as Jesus had to suffer the fate of the prophets, so is it also determined for his disciples (Lk. 11.49f)" (*Das Lukasevangelium*, 1: 335).

68. See Trilling, *Das wahre Israel: Studien zur Theologie des Matthäus-Evangeliums*, 3d ed., Studien zum Alten und Neuen Testament, nr. 10 (München, 1969), p. 88. So also G. Strecker, *Der Weg der Gerechtigkeit: Untersuchung zur Theologie des Matthäus*, Forschungen zur Religion und Literatur des Alten und Neuen Testaments, Heft 82, 2d ed. (Göttingen, 1966), p. 100n.2.

69. See Black, *An Aramaic Approach to the Gospels and Acts*, p. 82. Black is followed in this by Jeremias, in *Jesus' Promise to the Nations*, trans. S. H. Hooke, Studies in Biblical Theology, no. 24 (London, 1958), p. 55n.185.

70. See Marshall, *Luke: Historian and Theologian* (Grand Rapids, 1970), p. 567. The priority of Luke is also maintained by Lagrange (*L'Évangile selon Saint Luc*, Études Bibliques [Paris, 1941], p. 391), Schmid (*Das Evangelium nach Lukas*, Regensburger Neues Testament [Regensburg, 1960], p. 255), and R. Hummel (*Die Auseinandersetzung zwischen Kirche und Judentum im Matthäusevangelium*, Beiträge zur evangelischen Theologie, vol. 33 [München, 1963], p. 147n.25).

71. The priority of Matthew's version is maintained by a majority of exegetes, including Klostermann (*Das Matthäusevangelium*, p. 75 [hesitantly]), Hauck (*Das Evangelium des Lukas*, Theologischer Handkommentar zum Neuen Testament [Leipzig, 1934], p. 184), Perrin (*Rediscovering the Teaching of Jesus*, New Testament Library [London, 1963], pp. 161–62), Schulz (*Q—Die Spruchquelle der Evangelisten*, p. 323), F. Hahn (*Das Verständnis der Mission im Neuen Testament*, Wissenschaftliche Monographien zum Alten und Neuen Testament, 13 [Neukirchen, 1963], p. 26n.3), and Schweizer (*The Good News according to Matthew*, p. 213).

72. Such is the contention of Lohmeyer in *Das Evangelium nach Matthäus*, p. 158. Jeremias renders *polloi* as "they (shall come) in countless numbers" (see *Jesus' Promise to the Nations*, p. 55; see also pp. 55n.2 and 73n.1 for references to literature).

73. Among the many illustrations provided by Billerbeck may be mentioned "sons of the west" (= Palestinians), "sons of the east" (= Babylonians), "sons of exile" (= exiles), "sons of the world" (= all who live in the world), and "sons of the world to come" (= all who are sure of their part in the world to come); see Strack–Billerbeck, *Kommentar zum Neuen Testament aus Talmud und Midrasch*, 1: 476–78.

74. See Strack–Billerbeck, *Kommentar zum Neuen Testament aus Talmud und Midrasch*, 1: 476.

75. On this point, see the exposition of Schlatter in *Der Evangelist Matthäus*, p. 279. See also Lohmeyer, *Das Evangelium nach Matthäus*, p. 158; and Grundmann, *Das Evangelium nach Matthäus*, p. 253.

76. Jeremias, *Jesus' Promise to the Nations*, pp. 56–62.

77. See Zeller, "Das Logion Mt 8, 11f / Lk 13, 28f und das Motiv der 'Völkerwallfahrt,'" *BZ* 15 (1971): 225.

78. See especially 1 Enoch 63:5–12 and 2 Baruch 85:12–15. Among the Qumran writings, Zeller cites 1QM 12:13ff. and 4-Bt 3 IV 8ff. ("Das Logion Mt 8, 11f / Lk 13, 28f und das Motiv der 'Völkerwallfahrt,'" p. 234n.66).

79. See Polag, *Die Christologie der Logienquelle* (Neukirchen-Vluyn, 1977), p. 92; see also Hummel, *Kirche und Judentum im Matthäusevangelium*, p. 146n.19.

80. See Zeller, "Das Logion Mt 8, 11f / Lk 13, 28f und das Motiv der 'Völkerwallfahrt,'" *BZ* 16 (1972): 88–91.

81. Schulz, *Q—Die Spruchquelle der Evangelisten*, p. 328.

82. No indication is given concerning how the Gentiles will come to be present at the feast, but if Jews are to be excluded from the feast because they reject Jesus' message of the kingdom of God, it is only natural to assume that the Gentiles will be included because they have accepted the message. There is clear evidence that this was Matthew's understanding in that he linked this saying with the episode of the healing of the centurion's *pais*; the soldier who confessed a faith in the authority of the word of Jesus such as Jesus had not found in Israel is presented as the forerunner of a multitude from the nations who will share a like faith.

83. So argues Schulz, who holds that Abraham, Isaac, and Jacob are named as *pars pro toto* and cites Bultmann to the effect that "The chosen people with its heroes will form the central point in the sovereignty of God" (see *Q—Die Spruchquelle der Evangelisten*, p. 327).

84. Such is the contention of Polag, *Die Christologie der Logienquelle*, p. 92. Jeremias expresses the same thought more cautiously in *Jesus' Promise to the Nations*, p. 63.

85. "Then shall we [i.e., Israel and the Messiah] hold the Leviathan-meal and drink old wine" (Targ. HL8, 2, in Strack–Billerbeck, *Kommentar zum Neuen Testament aus Talmud und Midrasch*, 4: 1156; for rabbinic thought on the feast of the kingdom of God, see 4: 1154–61.

86. Jeremias, *Jesus' Promise to the Nations*, p. 60.

87. See H. Windisch, "Die Sprüche vom Eingehen in das Reich Gottes," *ZNW* 27 (1928): 163–92.

88. See F. Neirynck, "The Tradition of the Sayings of Jesus: Mark 9, 33–50," *Concilium* 20 (1966): 66–69; see also A. M. Ambrozic, *The Hidden Kingdom: A Redaction-Critical Study of the References to the Kingdom of God in Mark's Gospel*, Catholic Biblical Quarterly—Monograph Series, 2 (Washington, 1972), pp. 174–76.

89. On this, see Klostermann, *Das Matthäusevangelium* p. 96; Pesch, *Das Markusevangelium*, 2 vols. (Herders theologischer Kommentar zum Neuen Testament [Freiburg, 1976–77]), 2: 115; and H. W. Robinson, *The Christian Doctrine of Man*, 3d ed. (Edinburgh, 1956), pp. 20–26.

90. Observe that Matthew sets 5:27–28 immediately before these sayings.

91. Grundmann, *Das Evangelium nach Matthäus*, p. 199. Incredibly, Windisch contends that Jesus was speaking literally both here and in Matthew 19:12 (see "Die Sprüche vom Eingehen des Reich Gottes," p. 170). R. H. Charles initially held that view as well, but later retracted it (see his *Critical History of the Doctrine of a Future Life*, 3d ed. [London, 1913], pp. 474–75).

92. *Ge-Hinnom* (Aramaic *Ge-hinnam*, hence the Greek *Geenna*), "The Valley of Hinnom," lay south of Jerusalem, immediately outside its walls. The notion, still referred

to by some commentators, that the city's rubbish was burned in this valley, has no further basis than a statement by the Jewish scholar Kimchi made about A.D. 1200; it is not attested in any ancient source. The valley was the scene of human sacrifices, burned in the worship of Moloch (2 Kings 16:3 and 21:6), which accounts for the prophecy of Jeremiah that it would be called the Valley of Slaughter under judgment of God (Jer. 7:32–33). This combination of abominable fires and divine judgment led to the association of the valley with a place of perpetual judgment (see Isa. 66:24) and later with a place of judgment by fire without any special connection to Jerusalem (see, for example, 1 Enoch 27:1ff., 54:1ff., 56:3–4, and 90:26ff.). The statement of Charles on this is still valuable (see *A Critical History of the Doctrine of a Future Life*, pp. 161–63), as is the more recent article on *Geenna* by Jeremias (*TDNT*, 1: 657–58).

93. On this, see Daniel 12:2, Solomon 3:16, 2 Maccabees 7:9, and 1 Enoch 40:9 and 58:2–3.

94. Windisch was particularly interested in establishing this point in "Die Sprüche vom Eingehen in das Reich Gottes." Most exegetes agree with him on this score, including Lohmeyer (*Das Evangelium nach Markus*, p. 204), Michaelis (*Täufer, Jesus, Urgemeinde* [Gütersloh, 1928], pp. 65ff.), C. J. Cadoux (*The Historic Mission of Jesus* [London, 1943], pp. 231ff.), Kümmel (*Promise and Fulfilment: The Eschatological Message of Jesus*, Studies in Biblical Theology, no. 23 [London, 1961], pp. 52–53), Schnackenburg (*God's Rule and Kingdom* [London, 1963], pp. 161, 227), Trilling (*Das wahre Israel*, p. 107), and Ambrozic (*The Hidden Kingdom*, pp. 139–40).

95. See Dalman, *The Words of Jesus*, pp. 117–18.

96. See Kümmel, *Promise and Fulfilment*, p. 52n.106; Schmid, *Matthäus und Lukas: Eine Untersuchung des Verhältnisses ihrer Evangelien*, Biblische Studien, 23/2–4 (Freiburg, 1930), pp. 244–45; Trilling, *Das wahre Israel*, p. 189; and Grundmann, *Das Evangelium nach Matthäus*, p. 234.

97. See Lohmeyer, *Das Evangelium nach Markus*, p. 208.

98. See Strack–Billerbeck, *Kommentar zum Neuen Testament aus Talmud und Midrasch*, 1: 814–16.

99. Such is the contention of Dalman in *The Words of Jesus*, p. 206.

100. See I. Herrmann, *TDNT*, 3: 774–76.

101. See Lohmeyer, *Das Evangelium nach Markus*, pp. 214–15.

102. Some scholars have questioned whether Jesus actually contrasted "this age" with "the age to come" (e.g., Kümmel, *Promise and Fulfilment*, p. 49n.98; and Grundmann, *Das Evangelium nach Markus*, Theologischer Handkommentar zum Neuen Testament [Berlin, 1959], pp. 213–14). On this point, Pesch rightly notes that the present age is not depreciated relative to the age to come in Mark 10:30; to the contrary, Jesus indicates that the present age has a saving character in its own right in this passage, and thus the saying is quite in keeping with the rest of his proclamation. Pesch goes on to argue that secondary references to both the present age and the age to come (e.g., in Matthew 12:32; cf. Mark 3:29) should not be used as evidence to support the contention that the use of the contrasted terms is not original in Mark 10:30 (see *Das Markusevangelium*, 2: 145).

103. The link between *paidia* and the kingdom of God is sufficiently unusual to have brought the sayings together. The thought is as characteristic of Jesus as it was uncharacteristic of the Rabbis, and is without parallel in the apocalyptic writings. The following scholars assume the independence of verse 15: Bultmann (*HST*, p. 32), Schmid (*Das Evangelium nach Markus*, Regensburger Neues Testament [Regensburg, 1954], p. 188), Lohmeyer (*Das Evangelium nach Markus*, p. 202), Nineham (*St. Mark*, Pelican Gospel Commentary [Harmondsworth, 1963], p. 269), Schweizer (*The Good News according to Mark*, trans. D. H. Madvig [Atlanta, 1970], p. 206), Ambrozic (*The Hidden Kingdom*, pp. 136–38), and Pesch (*Das Markusevangelium*, 2: 133). Percy, on the other hand, believes that verse 15 was spoken by Jesus in explanation of verse 14 (see *Die Botschaft Jesu* [Lund, 1953], p. 35).

104. Among those holding this view are Windisch ("Die Sprüche vom Eingehen des Reich Gottes," p. 164n.3), Lohmeyer (*Das Evangelium nach Markus*, pp. 204–5), Kümmel (*Promise and Fulfilment*, p. 126n.77), and Schnackenburg (*God's Rule and Kingdom*, p. 142).

105. See Ambrozic, *The Hidden Kingdom*, pp. 143–48.

106. See Schnackenburg, *Das Evangelium nach Markus*, 2 vols. (Düsseldorf, 1966), 2: 134.

107. Among those in basic agreement are Klostermann (*Das Markusevangelium*, Handbuch zum Neuen Testament [Tübingen, 1926], p. 101); V. Taylor (*The Gospel according to St. Mark*, Macmillan New Testament Commentaries [London, 1952], p. 423), Schweizer (*The Good News according to Mark*, p. 207), W. L. Lane (*The Gospel according to Mark*, The New International Commentary on the New Testament [Grand Rapids, 1974], p. 361), and Pesch (*Das Markusevangelium*, 2: 133–34).

108. Among those stressing this function are Bultmann (who viewed it as a Matthaean construction for that purpose—see *HST*, p. 150), Bornkamm (in Bornkamm, et al., *Tradition and Interpretation in Matthew*, pp. 66, 73), Strecker (*Der Weg der Gerechtigkeit*, pp. 151–52), and Grundmann (*Das Evangelium nach Markus*, p. 151).

109. Schürmann, *Traditionsgeschichtliche Untersuchungen zu der synoptischen Evangelien* (Düsseldorf, 1968), p. 130.

110. This despite Oepke's contention that "*perisseuein* in Mt. 5:20 is a quantitative rather than a qualitative term" (*TDNT*, 4: 621n.88).

111. Windisch, "Die Sprüche vom Eingehen des Reich Gottes," p. 166.

112. Gutbrod, *TDNT*, 4: 1062.

113. For a discussion of the curious textual confusion that has the Jewish leaders stating that the son who said he would go into the farm and then did not do so is the one who did the father's will, see Metzger, *A Textual Commentary on the Greek New Testament* (London, 1971), pp. 55–56.

114. Among those accepting this interpretation are R. N. Flew (*Jesus and His Church* [New York, 1938], p. 25), G. Ladd (*The Presence of the Future* [Grand Rapids, 1974], p. 25), McNeile (*The Gospel according to St. Matthew* [London, 1915], p. 306), and Lohmeyer (*Das Evangelium nach Matthäus*, p. 308), who view the publicans and sinners as "on the road to life."

115. Jeremias, *The Parables of Jesus*, trans. S. H. Hooke, rev. ed. (London, 1963), p. 125.

116. Among those holding this view are McNeile (*The Gospel according to St. Matthew*, pp. 332–33), Schniewind (*Das Evangelium nach Matthäus*, p. 231), Bonnard (*L'Évangile selon Saint Matthieu*, p. 338), and Jeremias (*TDNT*, 3: 750; he affirms the same of Matt. 16:19 on p. 749).

117. Among those holding this view are Schlatter (*Der Evangelist Matthäus*, p. 673), Lohmeyer (*Das Evangelium nach Matthäus*, p. 342), Grundmann (*Das Evangelium nach Matthäus*, p. 490), Manson (*The Sayings of Jesus*, p. 103), Schulz (*Q—Die Spruchquelle der Evangelisten*, p. 111), and Strecker (*Der Weg der Gerechtigkeit*, p. 156).

118. Polag, *Die Christologie der Logienquelle*, pp. 82–83.

119. See Windisch, "Die Sprüche vom Eingehen des Reich Gottes," p. 168.

120. Trilling, *Das wahre Israel*, p. 156.

121. On the Semitic character of the text, see Jeremias, *TDNT*, 3: 749–50. On its connection with Peter's confession, see Cullmann, *Peter: Disciple—Apostle—Martyr*, trans. F. V. Filson (London, 1953), pp. 177–83; and R. N. Flew, *Jesus and His Church*, pp. 97–98.

122. Trilling, *Das wahre Israel*, p. 157.

123. On this, see Jeremias, *TDNT*, 3: 744–46, 750–51.

124. See Grundmann, *Das Evangelium nach Matthäus*, p. 391.

125. See Jeremias, *TDNT*, 3: 748n.48.

126. See the exposition of this passage by W. Bousset in *Die Offenbarung Johannis*,

Kritisch-exegetischer Kommentar über das Neuen Testament (Göttingen, 1906), pp. 226–27.

127. Schlatter, *Der Evangelist Matthäus*, p. 511.

128. Such is the contention of P. Gardner-Smith in *St. John and the Synoptic Gospels* (Cambridge, 1938), p. 83; cf. C. K. Barrett, *The Gospel according to St. John*, 2d ed. (London, 1978), p. 475; and R. E. Brown, *The Gospel according to John*, 2 vols. (Garden City, N.Y., 1966–70), 2: 1039–45.

129. See Jeremias, *TDNT*, 3: 749–50.

130. Such is the contention of Grundmann (*Das Evangelium nach Matthäus*, p. 389), Lindars (*New Testament Apologetic: The Doctrinal Significance of the Old Testament Quotations* [London, 1961], pp. 70, 181–83), Bonnard (*L'Évangile selon Saint Matthieu*, p. 245), and especially Gaston (*No Stone on Another: Studies in the Signficance of the Fall of Jerusalem in the Synoptic Gospels*, Supplements to the Novum Testamentum, vol. 23 [Leiden, 1970], pp. 163–76, 223ff.).

131. The following scholars have reached a similar conclusion: H.-D. Wendland (*Die Eschatologie des Reiches Gottes bei Jesus: Eine Studie über den Zusammenhang von Eschatologie, Ethik und Kirchenproblem* [Gütersloh, 1931], p. 175), Otto (*The Kingdom of God and the Son of Man*, trans. F. V. Filson and B. L. Woolf [London, 1943], pp. 363–64), Cullmann (*Peter*, pp. 185–93), Schnackenburg (*God's Rule and Kingdom*, pp. 226–27), Jeremias (*TDNT*, 3: 749; and *New Testament Theology*, 1: 168–69), Trilling (*Das wahre Israel*, pp. 156–61), and Gaston (*No Stone on Another*, p. 227).

132. See Windisch, "Die Sprüche vom Eingehen in das Reich Gottes," pp. 177–86.

133. See Windisch, "Die Sprüche vom Eingehen in das Reich Gottes," pp. 185–87.

134. Among those holding this position are Bultmann (*Theology of the New Testament*, trans. K. Grobel, 2 vols. [London, 1951–55], 1: 37), Jeremias (*TDNT*, 3: 749), Schnackenburg (*God's Rule and Kingdom*, p. 227), Bornkamm (*Tradition and Interpretation in Matthew*, p. 49), and Lindars (*New Testament Apologetic*, p. 183). Cullmann appears to see references to both present and future aspects of the kingdom of God in this passage while nevertheless contending that it is Peter's task to lead people into the resurrection kingdom (see *Peter*, p. 204).

135. For the significance of Luke 12:32 in Luke's redaction of the passage, see Pesch, "Zur Formgeschichte und Exegese von Lk 12.32," *Biblica* 41 (1960): 35–38. Since Luke's redaction did not affect the form of the saying and is not relevant to our purpose at this juncture, we need not explore it any further at this point. It will be apparent that in the following exposition I am deeply indebted to Pesch's article.

136. Pesch contends that the relation of Luke 12:32 to this Old Testament form, together with the fact that it comports well with the eschatological teaching of Jesus in general, suggests that Bultmann's objection to the authenticity of the saying is weak (see Bultmann, *HST*, p. 111; and *Theology of the New Testament*, 1: 47–48). Pesch holds that in general those who argue that the saying is not authentic, as the earlier expositors did, tend to be preoccupied with the way Luke uses the saying and not sufficiently appreciative of its relation to the biblical tradition and the other attested teaching of Jesus (see "Zur Formgeschichte und Exegese von Lk 12.32," p. 34). For more on the authenticity of the logion, see Jeremias, *TDNT*, 6: 501. Jeremias agrees with M. Black that the saying reflects an Aramaic original in which there was a play on words (*poimnion/eudokesan* = *mar'ita/ra'e*); see Black's *Aramaic Approach to the Gospels and Acts*, p. 168.

137. On this, see Klostermann, *Das Lukasevangelium*, Handkommentar zum Neuen Testament (Tübingen, 1929), p. 499; Flew, *Jesus and His Church*, p. 39; and T. W. Manson, in *The Mission and Message of Jesus*, by H. D. A. Major et al. (London, 1940), p. 406.

138. On this, see especially Jeremias, *New Testament Theology*, 1: 108–13.

139. Pesch, "Zur Formgeschichte und Exegese von Lk 12.32," p. 33.

140. Pesch, "Zur Formgeschichte und Exegese von Lk 12.32," p. 34.

141. The conviction that Mark 9:1 was an isolated saying placed in its present

position by Mark is shared by most exegetes of this century, including W. C. Allen (*A Critical and Exegetical Commentary on the Gospel according to St. Matthew*, 3d ed., International Critical Commentary [Edinburgh, 1912], p. 183), G. Wohlenberg, *Das Evangelium des Markus*, Kommentar zum Neuen Testament [Leipzig, 1910], p. 239), Bultmann (*HST*, p. 121), S. Johnson (*The Interpreter's Bible*, ed. G. A. Buttrick [New York, 1951], 7: 457), Lagrange (*L'Évangile selon Saint Marc*, Études Bibliques [Paris, 1941], pp. 214–15), Grundmann (*Das Evangelium nach Markus*, pp. 177–78), E. Grässer (*Das Problem der Parusieverzögerung in den synoptischen Evangelien und in der Apostelgeschichte*, Beihefte zur ZNW, nr. 22 [Berlin, 1957], p. 131), Kümmel (*Promise and Fulfilment*, p. 25), Jeremias (*New Testament Theology*, 1: 137), and Pesch (*Das Markusevangelium*, 2: 66).

142. The history of interpretation of Mark 9:1 has been traced by M. Kunzi, *Das Naherwartungslogion Markus 9.1 par*, Beiträge zur Geschichte der Biblischen Exegese, nr. 21 (Tübingen, 1977). I am indebted to Kunzi for his indefatigable labors and have not hesitated to draw on his extensive researches for literature prior to the modern period.

143. Chrysostom, *Comm. in Matt.*, homs. 56, 57, in *Patrologia Graeca*, ed. J. P. Migne, 162 vols. (Turnhout, 1857–66), 97: 937–38.

144. Basil of Seleucia, "Oratio 40: In transfigurationem Domini et Dei et Salvatoris nostri Jesu Christi," in *Patrologia Graeca*, 85: 453ff.

145. John of Damascus, *Sacra Paralleia*, 73, in *Patrologia Graeca*, 96: 497–98.

146. The most learned and eloquent attempt to justify this interpretation in recent years is that of F. J. Schierse, "Historische Kritik und theologische Exegese der synoptischen Evangelien," *Scholastik* 29 (1959): 520–36.

147. Among those resisting this interpretation are C. E. B. Cranfield (*The Gospel according to St. Mark*, 2d ed., Cambridge Greek Testament [Cambridge, 1963], pp. 287–88) and A. L. Moore (*The Parousia in the New Testament*, Supplements to the Novum Testamentum 13 [Leiden, 1966], pp. 125–31).

148. Calvin, *Commentarius in Harmoniam evangelicam*, Corpus Reformatum, 73: 483.

149. Luther, "Annotationes in aliquot capita Matt.," Weimar Ausgabe, 38: 648ff.; Melanchthon, *Ev. Matt.*, Corpus Reformatum, 14: 847–88; and Barth, *Church Dogmatics*, ed. G. W. Bromiley and T. F. Torrance, trans. H. Knight et al., 5 vols. (Edinburgh, 1955–77), 3/2: *The Doctrine of Creation*, p. 499.

150. See Dodd, *The Parables of the Kingdom*, pp. 53–54.

151. For discussion of Dodd's interpretation, see J. Y. Campbell, "The Kingdom of God Has Come," *ExpTim* 48 (1936–37): 93–94; J. M. Creed, "The Kingdom of God Has Come," *ExpTim* 48 (1936–37): 184–85; C. T. Craig, "Realized Eschatology," *JBL* 56 (1937): 20; K. W. Clark, "Realized Eschatology," *JBL* 59 (1940): 372–73; Cranfield, *The Gospel according to St. Mark*, p. 286; Taylor, *The Gospel according to St. Mark*, p. 385; and H. Anderson, *The Gospel of Mark*, The New Century Bible Commentary (London, 1976), p. 221. See also Bornkamm, "Die Verzögerung der Parusie," in *Geschichte und Glaube*, Beiträge zur evangelischen Theologie, 48 (München, 1968), pp. 46–47; and Kümmel, *Promise and Fulfilment*, pp. 26–27.

152. Gregory the Great, *Homilia*, 32, Patrologia Latina, ed. J. P. Migne, 221 vols. (Turnhout, 1844–64), 76: 1232ff.

153. See, for example, Lagrange, *L'Évangile selon Saint Marc*, pp. 214–15; and *L'Évangile selon Saint Matthieu*, p. 333; J. Huby, *L'Évangile selon Saint Marc*, 2d ed. (Paris, 1953), p. 195; M. Meinertz, *Theologie des Neuen Testaments*, 2 vols. (Bonn, 1950), 1: 62; J. Bonsirven, *Le règne de Dieu* (Paris, 1957), p. 56; and Schmid, *Das Evangelium nach Markus*, pp. 113–14.

154. Taylor, *The Gospel according to St. Mark*, p. 386.

155. Wettstein, *Novum Testamentum Graecum* (Amsterdam, 1751–52), ad loc.

156. Keil, *Evangelium des Mattäus* (Leipzig, 1877), pp. 357–58.

157. See, for example, P. Schanz, *Mattäus* (Freiburg, 1879), pp. 384–85; R. Kubel,

Handbuch zum Ev. des Mattäus (Nordlingen, 1889), pp. 322–23; J. Knabenbauer, *Commentarius in quatuor S. Evangelia* (Paris, 1893), pp. 76ff.; and A. Plummer, *The Gospel according to St. Luke*, 5th ed., International Critical Commentary (Edinburgh, 1922), p. 249.

158. Reimarus, *Fragmente des Wolfenbuttelschen Ungenannten* (Braunschweig, 1778), p. 87; Strauss, *The Life of Jesus Critically Examined*, ed. P. C. Hodgson (Philadelphia, 1972), p. 588; and Renan, *The Life of Jesus* (New York, 1859), p. 345.

159. Weiffenbach, *Der Wiederkunftsgedanke Jesu* (Leipzig, 1893), pp. 197–98.

160. Among those accepting it are Schlatter (*Der Evangelist Matthäus*, pp. 524–25), Schniewind (*Das Evangelium nach Markus*, Das Neue Testament Deutsch [Göttingen, 1944], pp. 120–21), T. W. Manson (*The Teaching of Jesus*, 2d ed. [Cambridge, 1931], pp. 278ff.), Michaelis (*Der Herr verzieht nicht die Verheissung* [Bern, 1942], pp. 34ff.), Jeremias (*New Testament Theology*, 1: 136–37), B. Rigaux ("La seconde venue de Jésus," in *La venue du Messie: Messianisme et Eschatologie*, by E. Massaux et al., Recherches Bibliques, vol. 6 [Louvain, 1962], pp. 173ff.), Kümmel (in many publications, especially *Promise and Fulfilment*, pp. 25ff.), and Ambrozic (*The Hidden Kingdom*, pp. 209–10).

161. This point has been expressed by many writers of differing views. See, for example, W. Baldensperger, *Das Selbstbewusstsein Jesu im Lichte der messianischen Hoffnungen seiner Zeit*, 2d ed. (Strassburg, 1892), p. 203; J. Weiss, *Das älteste Evangelium* (Göttingen, 1903), pp. 230–31; Schlatter, *Die Geschichte des Christus* (Stuttgart, 1923), pp. 480–81; T. W. Manson, *The Teaching of Jesus*, pp. 278ff.; Schniewind, *Das Evangelium nach Markus*, pp. 120–21; G. Gloege, *Aller Tage Tag* (Stuttgart, 1960), pp. 141–42; Rigaux, "La seconde venue de Jésus," pp. 173–74; Schnackenburg, *God's Rule and Kingdom*, pp. 199–201, and "Naherwartung," in *Lexikon für Theologie und Kirche*, 2d ed., ed. J. Hofer and K. Rahner (Freiburg, 1957–64), 8: 777–78; and Cullmann, *Salvation in History*, trans. S. G. Sowers (London, 1967), pp. 218–19.

162. Linnemann, *Jesus of the Parables* (London, 1966), p. 132n.26.

163. See Pfleiderer, *Primitive Christianity*, trans. W. Montgomery, ed. W. D. Morrison, 4 vols. (Clifton, N.J., 1965), 2: 13; Bultmann, *HST*, p.121; Bornkamm, *Geschichte und Glaube*, pp. 46–47; Grässer, *Das Problem der Parusieverzögerung in den synoptischen Evangelien und in der Apostelgeschichte*, pp. 131–33; H. Braun, *Spätjüdisch-häretischer und frühchristlicher Radikalismus*, 2 vols. (Tübingen, 1957), 2: 50; Percy, *Die Botschaft Jesu*, p. 172; H. Conzelmann, *The Theology of St. Luke* (London, 1960), p. 104; Schweizer, *The Good News according to Mark*, pp. 178–79; H. Anderson, *The Gospel of Mark*, p. 222; Pesch, *Naherwartungen: Tradition und Redaktion in Mk 13*, Kommentare und Beiträge zum Alten und Neuen Testament (Düsseldorf, 1968), p. 183 (although in *Das Markusevangelium* [2: 66] he affirms the authenticity of the saying).

164. Bornkamm, *Geschichte und Glaube*, pp. 46–48.

165. Kümmel, *Promise and Fulfilment*, pp. 27–29.

166. Michaelis, *Der Herr verzieht nicht*, p. 43.

167. Vögtle, "Exegetische Erwägungen über das Wissen und Selbstbewusstsein Jesu," in *Gott in Welt*, Festschrift K. Rahner (Freiburg, 1964), 1: 608–67.

168. Vögtle, "Exegetische Erwägungen über das Wissen und Selbstbewusstsein Jesu," p. 644.

169. Schürmann, *Das Lukasevangelium*, 1: 551n.189.

170. Others holding this view include Grässer (*Das Problem der Parusieverzögerung in den synoptischen Evangelien und in der Apostelgeschichte*, pp. 131–37), Perrin (*Rediscovering the Teaching of Jesus*, pp. 200–201), Braun (*Spätjüdisch-häretischer und frühchristlicher Radikalismus*, 2: 50), and Schürmann (*Das Lukasevangelium*, 1: 551–52).

171. See Horstmann, *Studien zur markinischen Christologie: Mark 8.27–9.13 als Zugang zum Christusbild des zweiten Evangeliums*, Neutestamentliche Abhandlungen, nr. 6 (Münster, 1969), p. 64n.146; and Pesch, *Naherwartungen*, pp. 186ff. Regrettably,

Vögtle has been persuaded by the arguments of Pesch, his own pupil. In a mere sentence (in *Das Neue Testament und die Zukunft des Kosmos*, Kommentare und Beiträge zum Alten und Neuen Testament [Düsseldorf, 1970], p. 100n.52) he states his acceptance of Pesch's view of the dependence of Mark 13:30 on 9:1. For reasons here indicated, I find Pesch's views on this issue implausible, and express the hope that the revered Professor Emeritus will revert to his own more convincing reasoning!

172. Pesch, *Das Markusevangelium*, 2: 308.

173. Lambrecht, *Die Redaktion der Markus-Apokalypse: Literarische Analyse und Strukturuntersuchung*, Analecta Biblica 28 (Rome, 1967), p. 208. At a later point in his exposition of Mark 13:30, Lambrecht gives a different account of its origin (see pp. 334–35 herein).

174. See the discussion of this issue by J. Zmijewski, *Die Eschatologiereden des Lukas-Evangeliums: Ein traditions- und redaktionsgeschichtliche Untersuchung zu Lk. 21.5–36 und Lk. 17.20–37*, Bonner Biblische Beiträge, nr. 40 (Bonn, 1972), pp. 276–77; Zmijewski considers Pesch's arguments on the priority of Mark 9:1 and finds them unacceptable.

Chapter 12

1. The size of the fully grown mustard plant is frequently commented on. In the area of Gennesaret it may reach a height of from two and a half to three metres (eight to ten and a half feet); see Hunzinger, *TDNT*, 7: 288. In *The Land and the Book* ([Grand Rapids, 1954], p. 183), W. M. Thomson tells of his uprooting "a veritable mustard tree which was more than twelve feet high."

2. Cf. Bultmann: "Both beginning and completion of God's Reign are miraculous, and miraculous is the happening which brings its fulfilment" (*Theology of the New Testament*, trans. K. Grobel, 2 vols. [London, 1951–55], 1: 8).

3. In Dahl's view, "The lesson of the parable is not so much the great results of the work of Jesus as it is the 'organic unity' between his ministry in Israel and the future kingdom of God" ("The Parables of Growth," *ST* 5 [1951]: 148).

4. See the exposition of Jüngel in *Paulus und Jesus: Eine Untersuchung zur Präzisierung der Frage nach dem Aufsprung der Christologie* (Tübingen, 1962), pp. 153–54. He contends that the intent of the parable is to gather men for the kingdom rather than to turn aside doubts of Jesus' opponents or to defend "the present oppressive experience" (Schnackenburg's expression). But could it not be serving both intentions? See the expositions of C. E. Carlston in *Parables of the Triple Tradition* (Philadelphia, 1975), pp. 160–62; and Crossan in *In Parables: The Challenge of the Historical Jesus* (New York, 1973), p. 51.

5. Jeremias classifies the parables of the Mustard Seed, the Leaven, the Seed Growing Secretly, and the Sower as "the four contrasting parables" (*The Parables of Jesus*, trans. S. H. Hooke, rev. ed. [London, 1963], p. 89).

6. Jones, "The Seed Parables of Mark," *Review and Expositor* 85 (1978): 522.

7. Among those holding this view are Bultmann (*Theology of the New Testament*, 1: 8), Schlatter (*Markus*, p. 104), Lohmeyer (*Das Evangelium nach Markus*, Kritisch-exegetischer Kommentar über das Neue Testament [Göttingen, 1963], p. 88), Jeremias (*The Parables of Jesus*, p. 91), Bornkamm (*Jesus of Nazareth*, trans. I. McLuskey, F. McLuskey, and J. M. Robinson [London, 1960], p. 73), C. W. F. Smith (*The Jesus of the Parables*, rev. ed. [Philadelphia, 1975], p. 85), Grundmann (*Das Evangelium nach Markus*, Theologischer Handkommentar zum Neuen Testament [Berlin, 1959], p. 99), Kümmel (*Promise and Fulfilment: The Eschatological Message of Jesus*, Studies in Biblical Theology, no. 23 [London, 1961], p. 128, and "Noch Einmal: Das Gleichnis von der selbstwachsenden Saat," in *Orientierung an Jesus*, ed. P. Hoffmann et al. [Freiburg, 1971], p. 232), Ambrozic (*The Hidden Kingdom: A Redaction-Critical Study of the References to the Kingdom of God in Mark's Gospel*, Catholic Biblical Quarterly—Monograph Series, 2 [Washington, 1972], p. 116), and P. R. Jones ("The Seed Parables of Mark," p. 525).

8. See the report on the teaching of Judas the Gaulonite by Josephus, *Antiquities*, 18.1.1.

9. Montefiore gathered a number of utterances of rabbis expressing this notion in varied ways (see his *Rabbinic Literature and Gospel Teachings* [London, 1930], p. 408).

10. Dahl, "The Parables of Growth," p. 150.

11. For more on this, see Schnackenburg, *God's Rule and Kingdom* (London, 1963), pp. 153ff.; Ambrozic, *The Hidden Kingdom*, pp. 118–19; and Carlston, *Parables of the Triple Tradition*, p. 210.

12. See, for example, the expositions of W. Michaelis in *Die Gleichnisse Jesu*, Die urchristliche Botschaft, 23te Abteilung (Hamburg, 1956), p. 25; E. E. Ellis in *The Gospel of Luke*, rev. ed., New Century Bible (London, 1974), pp. 126–27; R. H. Fuller in *The Mission and Achievement of Jesus*, Studies in Biblical Theology, no. 12 (London, 1954), p. 44; and J. Schniewind in *Das Evangelium nach Markus*, Das Neue Testament Deutsch (Göttingen, 1944), p. 74.

13. On this, see the comments of Dahl, "The Parables of Growth," p. 153; Schnackenburg, *God's Rule and Kingdom*, p. 150; and Crossan, *In Parables*, p. 41.

14. Such is the contention of the following: C. W. F. Smith (*Jesus of the Parables*, pp. 42–43), Dahl ("The Parables of Growth," p. 154), Jeremias (*The Parables of Jesus*, p. 92), Grundmann (*Das Evangelium nach Markus*, p. 89), Jüngel (*Paulus und Jesus*, p. 151), Schnackenburg (*God's Rule and Kingdom*, p. 150), W. L. Lane (*The Gospel of Mark*, New International Commentary on the New Testament [Grand Rapids, 1974], p. 154), Schweizer (*The Good News according to Mark*, trans. D. H. Madvig [Atlanta, 1970], p. 91), and Ambrozic (*The Hidden Kingdom*, p. 100).

15. See Kümmel, *Promise and Fulfilment*, p. 135.

16. Dahl, "The Parables of Growth," p. 151.

17. Schnackenberg, *God's Rule and Kingdom*, p. 158.

18. See, for example, Jeremias, *The Parables of Jesus*, pp. 155–57.

19. See, for example, Kümmel, *Promise and Fulfilment*, p. 137.

20. Cf. Grundmann: "Gathering and separation denote eschatological present and future, which are set in juxtaposition" (*Das Evangelium nach Matthäus*, Theologischer Handkommentar zum Neuen Testament [Berlin, 1968], p. 356).

21. "We can almost see here notes for three separate sermons on the parables as text," says Dodd, commenting on Luke 16:8b–12 (*The Parables of the Kingdom* [London, 1935], p. 30).

22. For this reason some critics view verse 8a as a secondary addition. But should not the principle of *difficilior lectio probabilior* apply here?

23. Schlatter, for one, contends that this is the case (*Das Evangelium des Lukas aus seinen Quellen erklärt*, 2d ed. (Stuttgart, 1960), p. 365.

24. Derrett, "Fresh Light on St Luke xvi: I. The Parable of the Unjust Steward," *NTS* 7 (1961): 203ff.

25. Via, *The Parables: Their Literary and Existential Dimension* (Philadelphia, 1967), p. 161.

26. For an analysis of the language of verse 1 calculated to establish the Lukan style of the sentence, see W. Ott, *Gebet und Heil: Die Bedeutung der Gebetsparänese in der lukanischen Theologie*, Studien zum Alten und Neuen Testament, nr. 12 (München, 1965), p. 19. This study contains the most exhaustive treatment of the parable to be found, providing a wealth of information concerning critical opinions on the issues raised in the parable.

27. Jülicher, *Die Gleichnisreden Jesu*, 2 vols. (Tübingen, 1910), 2: 283.

28. Jülicher, *Die Gleichnisreden Jesu*, 2: 285ff.

29. The discussion on these matters is conveniently summarized by Ott in *Gebet und Heil*, pp. 24–42.

30. See Delling, "Das Gleichnis vom gottlosen Richter," in *Studien zum Neuen Testament und zum hellenistischen Judentum* (Göttingen, 1970), pp. 204–5.

31. Regarding the figure of the widow, see Exodus 22:21ff., Isaiah 1:17, Jeremiah 7:6 and 22:3, Lamentations 1:1, and James 1:27. Regarding the figure of the judge, see especially Psalm 82:2–7. God is frequently represented as the ideal judge who rejects bribes and secures justice for widows and orphans (see, for example, Deut. 10:18 and Ps. 68:5).

32. The expression is Derrett's ("Law in the New Testament: The Parable of the Unjust Judge," NTS 18 [1972]: 86–87). The ekdikesis (literally, "vengeance"), he says, is "the technical term of administrative justice throughout the Hellenistic age," and ekdikeson me means "Take up my case." See also G. Schrenk, TDNT, 2: 442–46.

33. On this, see Ellis, The Gospel of Luke, p. 213.

34. See Derrett, "Law in the New Testament," pp. 180–91.

35. See Ott, Gebet und Heil, p. 50.

36. See Riesenfeld, "Zu Makrothumein (Lk. 18.7)," in Neutestamentliche Aufsätze, Festschrift for Josef Schmid (Regensburg, 1963), pp. 257–58.

37. H. Ljungvik independently makes the same point in criticism of Riesenfeld's view in "Zur Erklärung einer Lukas-stelle (Luk. xviii.7)," NTS 10 (1964): 290–91.

38. The Apocrypha and Pseudepigrapha of the Old Testament in English, with Introductions and Critical and Explanatory Notes to the Several Books, ed. R. H. Charles, 2 vols. (Oxford, 1913), 1: 439.

39. The knowledge possessed by Jesus of the ideas current in popular extracanonical literature requires more careful consideration than is commonly given to it. If the echo of Ecclesiasticus 35:18 is in fact attributable to a redactor, this would chiefly affect the wording of verse 7; the relation of the original parable to the Qumran outlook would then be less sharply defined but not necessarily excluded.

40. On this point, see L. Gaston, No Stone on Another: Studies in the Significance of the Fall of Jerusalem in the Synoptic Gospels, Supplements to Novum Testamentum, vol. 23 (Leiden, 1970), pp. 353–54; and Delling, "Das Gleichnis vom gottlosen Richter," pp. 232ff. W. L. Knox thinks that Luke 18:8 reflects a half-ironic expression of regret that the hope that the Pharisees would accept the kingdom of heaven had proved illusory (The Sources of the Synoptic Gospels, ed. H. Chadwick, 2 vols. [Cambridge, 1953–57], 2: 114).

41. Delling, "Das Gleichnis vom gottlosen Richter," p. 222.

42. The unusual ekeino in Matthew has been replaced in Luke with touto, Matthew's phulake has been replaced with hora in anticipation of the next sentence, and the word order in Matthew 24:44—he ou dokeite hora—has been smoothed by Luke. But in Matthew 24:43, the clause egregoresen an kai, which does not appear in Luke, is an insertion by Matthew in anticipation of verse 44 (see Schulz, Q—Die Spruchquelle der Evangelisten [Zürich, 1972], p. 268).

43. Strobel speaks of Matthew 24:42 as the "superscription" of the following cycle of parables (Untersuchungen zum eschatologischen Verzögerungsproblem auf Grund der spätjüdisch-urchristlichen Geschichte von Habakkuk 2.2ff. [Leiden, 1961], p. 210).

44. Dodd, The Parables of the Kingdom, pp. 169–70.

45. Jeremias, The Parables of Jesus, pp. 48ff.

46. See also 1 Corinthians 5:5; 2 Corinthians 1:14; and Phillippians 1:6, 10; and 2:16.

47. Lövestam, Spiritual Wakefulness in the New Testament, Lunds Universitets Årsskrift, Band 55, nr. 3 (Lund, 1963), pp. 98–99.

48. See, for example, Bultmann, Theology of the New Testament; Kümmel, Promise and Fulfilment, pp. 55–59; Strecker, Der Weg der Gerechtigkeit: Untersuchung zur Theologie des Matthäus, Forschungen zur Religion und Literatur des Alten und Neuen Testaments, Heft 82, 2d ed. (Göttingen, 1966), pp. 241–42; Strobel, Untersuchungen zum eschatologischen Verzögerungsproblem, pp. 212–13; Luhrmann, Die Redaktion der Logienquelle, Wissenschaftliche Monographien zum Alten und Neuen Testament (Neukirchen-Vluyn, 1969), pp. 69–70; Schulz, Q—Die Spruchquelle der Evangelisten, pp. 269–70; Polag, Die Christologie der Logienquelle (Neukirchen-Vluyn, 1977), p. 133; and Marshall, Luke: Historian and Theologian (Exeter, 1970), p. 538.

49. Schrage, *Das Verhältnis der Thomas-Evangeliums zur synoptischen Tradition und zu den koptischen Evangelienübersetzungen* (Berlin, 1964), p. 68.

50. Schulz, *Q—Die Spruchquelle der Evangelisten*, p. 270.

51. Strobel, *Untersuchungen zum eschatologischen Verzögerungsproblem*, p. 213.

52. See Bultmann, *HST*, p. 126 (where he states that Matt. 24:43 is among passages likely to be of Jewish origin), p. 152 (where he indicates that Matt. 24:43–44 is among sayings that could come from Jesus), and p. 128 (where he suggests that no firm conclusion about the saying is possible). On the other hand, he attributes the parable to Jesus in *Theology of the New Testament*, 1: 29.

53. Among those holding this view are E. Grässer (*Das Problem der Parusieverzögerung in den synoptischen Evangelien und in der Apostelgeschichte*, Beihefte zur ZNW, nr. 22 [Berlin, 1957], pp. 84ff.), Vielhauer (*Aufsätze zum Neuen Testament* [München, 1965], p. 73), Strecker (*Der Weg der Gerechtigkeit*, p. 241n.3), Luhrmann (*Die Redaktion der Logienquelle*, pp. 69–70), and Schulz (*Q—Die Spruchquelle der Evangelisten*, p. 259).

54. Strobel, *Untersuchungen zum eschatologischen Verzögerungsproblem*, p. 211.

55. Patsch, *Abendmahl und historischer Jesus*, Calwer Theologischer Monographien (Stuttgart, 1972), p. 115.

56. Jeremias, *The Parables of Jesus*, p. 50.

57. In Dodd's view, the appearance of the figure of the thief in both Q and 1 Thessalonians indicates that its use can be dated back to as early a stage in the history of the church as it is possible to reach (see *The Parables of the Kingdom*, p. 168; see also Lövestam, *Spiritual Wakefulness in the New Testament*, p. 96; and Marshall, *Luke: Historian and Theologian*, p. 538).

58. The bridegroom could go in procession to the home of his bride to take her to his parents' home, or he could go directly to his parents' home and there meet his bride, who had been taken there earlier (see Jeremias, *The Parables of Jesus*, p. 173, for illustrations of both customs).

59. The variant in the Greek text, "to meet the bridegroom *and the bride*," is generally believed to be an interpolation by copyists who were disturbed that no mention is made of the bride of Christ in the parable (see B. M. Metzger, *A Textual Commentary on the Greek New Testament* [London, 1971], pp. 62–63).

60. See the description of a wedding procession by Raschi, cited by Oepke, *TDNT*, 4: 17n.2.

61. According to Billerbeck, the formula was used by Rabbis as a proscription, forbidding access to a teacher for a limited period, whether for one, or seven, or thirty days (see H. L. Strack–P. Billerbeck, *Kommentar zum Neuen Testament aus Talmud und Midrasch*, 6 vols. [München, 1922–28], 1: 469; 4: 293).

62. See Dodd, *The Parables of the Kingdom*, p. 172; and Jeremias, *The Parables of Jesus*, pp. 51–53. See also F. T. Glasson, *Second Advent: The Origin of the New Testament Doctrines*, 3d ed. (London, 1963), p. 93; and J. A. T. Robinson, *Jesus and His Coming* (London, 1957), p. 69.

63. Kümmel, *Promise and Fulfilment*, pp. 58–59.

64. Bultmann, *HST*, p. 119. The statement is echoed and expanded by Grässer in *Das Problem der Parusieverzögerung*, pp. 120–21.

65. Bornkamm, *Die Verzögerung der Parusie: In memoriam E. Lohmeyer* (Stuttgart, 1951), pp. 121–25. This position is strongly supported by Strobel, who however stresses the importance of the belief in the coming of the Messiah in the passover night for the details in the parable: "All the features of the parable, including those which earlier were always felt to be questionable, can be derived from a common basis in the passover liturgy" (*Untersuchungen zum eschatologischen Verzögerungsproblem*, p. 250; and see pp. 236–50).

66. See Jeremias, *The Parables of Jesus*, pp. 52–53.

67. Linnemann, *Jesus of the Parables*, p. 127.

68. Jeremias contends that the representation of the Messiah as bridegroom is foreign to the Old Testament and literature of late Judaism (see *TDNT*, 4: 1100–1103; and *The Parables of Jesus*, p. 52), but this now appears doubtful. The Targum on the wedding psalm (45:3) reads: "Your beauty, O King Messiah, is more excellent than that of the rest of the children of men." Jeremias himself draws attention to *Pesiq.* 149:1, "The garment in which God will one day clothe the Messiah will shine ever more brightly from one end of the world to the other, cf. Isaiah 61:10: 'Like a bridegroom who puts on the priestly mitre.'" Jeremias thought this an isolated example, but the same scripture is cited in 1QIsa with the unusual reading "as a priest" (k^ekohen) for "with a garland" (y^ekahen), and Brownlee views the bridegroom and priest as having messianic reference ("Messianic Motifs of Qumran and the New Testament," *NTS* 3 [1957]: 205–6). Jeremias also fails to give enough weight to the significance of Mark 2:19 (see pp. 140–41 herein). For more on this issue, see Meinertz, "Die Tragweite des Gleichnisses von den zehn Jungfrauen," in *Synoptischen Studien*, Festschrift for A. Wikenhauser (München, 1953), pp. 101ff.; and Lövestam, *Spiritual Wakefulness in the New Testament*, p. 111.

69. Jeremias, *The Parables of Jesus*, pp. 52–53.

70. See Schnackenburg, *God's Rule and Kingdom*, p. 245.

71. See Bornkamm, *Die Verzögerung der Parusie*, p. 120. Grässer expresses the same view more succinctly: "The *chronizein* belongs to the substance of the parable, from which every individual item is explained" (*Das Problem der Parusieverzögerung*, p. 120).

72. Bauer, cited by Lövestam in *Spiritual Wakefulness in the New Testament*, p. 110n.4. Jeremias cites a comparable description from his father of a Jerusalem wedding that took place in 1906 (see *The Parables of Jesus*, pp. 173–74).

73. The bargaining is all part of the game. "To neglect this often lively bargaining might be taken to imply an insufficient regard for the relatives of the bride," says Jeremias; "on the other hand, it must be interpreted as a compliment to the bridegroom if his future relations show in this way that they give away the bride only with the greatest reluctance" (*The Parables of Jesus*, p. 174).

74. The following scholars agree on this point: Kümmel (*Promise and Fulfilment*, p. 56), Bonnard (*L'Évangile selon Saint Matthieu*, Commentaire du Nouveau Testament [Neuchatel, 1963], pp. 358–59), Meinertz ("Die Tragweite des Gleichnisses von den zehn Jungfrauen," p. 105), Michaelis ("Kennen die Synoptiker eine Verzögerung der Parusie?" in *Synoptischen Studien*, p. 119), and Strobel (*Untersuchungen zum eschatologischen Verzögerungsproblem*, p. 233).

75. See McNeile, *The Gospel according to St. Matthew* (London, 1915), p. 363; Kilpatrick, *The Origins of the Gospel according to St. Matthew* (Oxford, 1946), pp. 32–33; Bultmann, *HST*, p. 176; Jeremias, *The Parables of Jesus*, p. 52; Kümmel, *Promise and Fulfilment*, pp. 56–57; Grässer, *Das Problem der Parusieverzögerung*, p. 86; and Strecker, *Der Weg der Gerechtigkeit*, pp. 44–45.

76. Bauer, *A Greek-English Lexicon of the New Testament and Other Early Christian Literature*, rev. by F. W. Gingrich and F. W. Danker, 2d ed. (Chicago, 1958), p. 167; Oepke, *TDNT*, 2: 338.

77. Such is the contention of Bonnard (*L'Évangile selon Saint Matthieu*, p. 360), Grundmann (*Das Evangelium nach Matthäus*, p. 579), Linnemann (*Jesus of the Parables*, p. 128), and Schweizer (*The Good News according to Matthew*, trans. D. O. E. Green [Atlanta, 1975], p. 468).

78. Lövestam, *Spiritual Wakefulness in the New Testament*, p. 122.

79. Robinson, *Jesus and His Coming*, p. 67. The recognition of a distinct parable combined with that of the pounds has been common since Strauss; see, for example, Wellhausen, *Das Evangelium Lucae* (Berlin, 1904), p. 106; T. W. Manson, *The Teaching of Jesus*, 2d ed. (Cambridge, 1931), pp. 313ff.; C. W. F. Smith, *Jesus of the Parables*, p. 201; Jeremias, *The Parables of Jesus*, p. 59; Ellis, *The Gospel of Luke*, p. 222; and Caird, *St. Luke*, Pelican Gospel Commentaries (Harmondsworth, 1963), p. 210. Others prefer to see in it an elaboration of the original parable, whether in the tradition or by Luke; see, for

NOTES TO PAGES 216-220

example, B. T. D. Smith, *The Parables of the Synoptic Gospels* (Cambridge, 1937), p. 162; Michaelis, *Die Gleichnisse Jesu*, p. 254n.66; Bultmann, *HST*, pp. 195–96; Luhrmann, *Die Redaktion der Logienquelle*, pp. 70–71; and Schulz, *Q—Die Spruchquelle der Evangelisten*, p. 288.

The motif of a nobleman traveling to a distant land to receive a kingdom was common in the time of Jesus. For the missions of Herod the Great and his successor Archelaus to Rome to gain support for their rule and their revenge on their enemies see Josephus, *Antiquities*, 14.14.1–2, 17.9.3–4, and 17.11.1ff.

80. See Derrett's illuminating comments on the background of the parable in "The Parable of the Talents and Two Logia," in *Law in the New Testament* (London, 1970), pp. 18–23.

81. Crossan, *In Parables*, p. 101.

82. Samuel, BM 42a, cited in Strack–Billerbeck, *Kommentar zum Neuen Testament aus Talmud und Midrasch*, 1: 971–72.

83. Michaelis, *Die Gleichnisse Jesu*, p. 105.

84. Cf. Matthew 8:12, 13:42, 22:13, and 24:51 (but here parallel with Luke 13:28).

85. This is more plausible than the idea that the parable closed with Matthew 25:27 // Luke 19:23 (see B. T. D. Smith, *The Parables of the Synoptic Gospels*, p. 167; and Schweizer, *The Good News according to Matthew*, p. 472).

86. Dibelius, *From Tradition to Gospel*, p. 255. Joining him with similar views are Glasson (*The Second Advent*, p. 92) and C. W. F. Smith (*The Jesus of the Parables*, pp. 203–7).

87. Dodd, *The Parables of the Kingdom*, p. 151.

88. Such is the contention of B. T. D. Smith (*The Parables of the Synoptic Gospels*, pp. 168–69), Jeremias (*The Parables of Jesus*, pp. 61–62), and Grässer (*Das Problem der Parusieverzögerung*, p. 114).

89. This interpretation is supported by Michaelis (*Die Gleichnisse Jesu*, p. 112), Bonnard (*L'Évangile selon Saint Matthieu*, p. 361), and A. Weiser (*Die Knechtsgleichnisse der synoptischen Evangelien* [München, 1971], pp. 263–66).

90. Such is the interpretation of Dalman (*The Words of Jesus*, pp. 117–18), Strack–Billerbeck (*Kommentar zum Neuen Testament aus Talmud und Midrasch*, 1: 972), and B. T. D. Smith (*The Parables of the Synoptic Gospels*, p. 166). Michaelis resists equating the "joyous meal" with the feast of the kingdom (see *Die Gleichnisse Jesu*, p. 109).

91. Cf. D. O. Via: "The very fact that there is an event expected in the future—the master's return—and that it is to be an accounting marks off a real present and gives the latter its character: the present is a time for risky action" (*The Parables*, p. 121).

92. Polag, *Die Christologie der Logienquelle*, p. 165.

93. See Polag, *Die Christologie der Logienquelle*, p. 165n.523. Grässer (in *Das Problem der Parusieverzögerung*, p. 114) and Schulz (in *Q—Die Spruchquelle der Evangelisten*, p. 293) are in essential agreement with Polag on this point.

94. See, for example, Schulz, *Q—Die Spruchquelle der Evangelisten*, p. 298.

Chapter 13

1. See the discussion of T. W. Manson in *The Sayings of Jesus* (London, 1949), pp. 109–10; and of Jeremias in *New Testament Theology*, vol. 1, *The Proclamation of Jesus*, trans. J. S. Bowden (London, 1971), p. 261.

2. See Bultmann, *Theology of the New Testament*, trans. K. Grobel, 2 vols. (London, 1951–55), 1: 30.

3. Higgins, *Jesus and the Son of Man* (London, 1964); Tödt, *The Son of Man in the Synoptic Tradition* (London, 1965).

4. See Schweizer, "Der Menschensohn (Zur eschatologischen Erwartung Jesu)," *ZNW* 50 (1959): 185–209; and "The Son of Man," *JBL* 79 (1960): 119–29.

5. See Vermes's essay "The Use of *bar nash / bar nasha* in Jewish Aramaic," in M.

Black's *An Aramaic Approach to the Gospels and Acts*, 3d ed. (Oxford, 1967), pp. 310–28, and his own work *Jesus the Jew* (New York, 1973), pp. 163–68.

6. See, for example, Käsemann's *New Testament Questions of Today* (Philadelphia, 1969), pp. 77 and 101; and Vielhauer's essay "Gottesreich und Menschensohn in der Verkündigung Jesu," in *Aufsätze zum Neuen Testament* (München, 1965), pp. 55–91.

7. Vielhauer, "Gottesreich und Menschensohn in der Verkündigung Jesu," p. 80. H. Conzelmann is in essential agreement with Vielhauer's thinking; see his *Outline of the Theology of the New Testament*, trans. J. S. Bowden (London, 1969), pp. 131–37. N. Perrin reflects parallel ideas along a route of his own but in explicit accord with Vielhauer in chapters 3–5 of *A Modern Pilgrimage in New Testament Christology* (Philadelphia, 1974).

8. See pp. 63–68 herein.

9. See Meyer, *Jesu Muttersprache* (Freiburg, 1896); Lietzmann, *Der Menschensohn* (Freiburg, 1896); and Vermes, "The Use of *bar nash / bar nasha* in Jewish Aramaic," pp. 310ff.

10. See Vermes, "The Use of *bar nash / bar nasha* in Jewish Aramaic," pp. 310ff.; and *Jesus the Jew*, pp. 162ff.

11. Vermes, "The Use of *bar nash / bar nasha* in Jewish Aramaic," pp. 325–26.

12. See Jeremias, *New Testament Theology*, 1: 261n.1.

13. See Vermes, *Jesus the Jew*, pp. 188–91.

14. Bowker, "The Son of Man," *JTS* 28 (1977): 32.

15. Paul's references in 2 Corinthians 12:1–7 to the visions and revelations of the Lord given to "a man in Christ" afford a close parallel to both these elements—modesty and ambiguity. The latter is sufficiently real to have caused many expositors to insist that Paul must have been referring to another person, although the context of the argument and the fact that it issues in the description of the "thorn for the flesh" that kept Paul humble in face of the exalted visions clearly indicate that the "man in Christ" was Paul himself.

16. See Bowker, "The Son of Man," pp. 35ff.

17. Haufe, quoted by Kümmel, in "Das Verhalten Jesus gegenüber und das Verhalten des Menschensohns, Markus 8:38 par und Lukas 12.3f par Matthäus 10.32f," in *Jesus und der Menschensohn*, ed. R. Pesch and R. Schnackenburg (Freiburg, 1975), p. 210. F. Hahn also suggests that Luke 12:8–9 is a point of departure for the Son of Man sayings, in *The Titles of Jesus in Christology*, trans. H. Knight and G. Ogg (London, 1969), p. 322. See also R. Fuller, *The Foundations of New Testament Christology* (London, 1965), p. 122.

18. Michel, *TDNT*, 5: 208n.27. On *emprosthen*, see also G. Schrenk, *TDNT*, 2: 745ff.

19. Such is Käsemann's contention in his essay "Sentences of Holy Law in the New Testament," in *New Testament Questions of Today*, p. 77. Many have concurred, including Vielhauer ("Gottesreich und Menschensohn in der Verkündigung Jesu," p. 77), Jüngel (*Paulus und Jesus: Eine Untersuchung zur Präzisierung der Frage nach der Aufsprung der Christologie* [Tübingen, 1962], p. 259), and Pesch (*Das Markusevangelium*, 2 vols., Herders theologischer Kommentar zum Neuen Testament [Freiburg, 1976–77], 2: 64). Kümmel disagrees, pointing out that the term *epaischunesthai* occurs here only in the gospels, and that it is not Markan but that it is in the LXX and profane Greek; he contends that it was replaced by *arneisthai* (see *Jesus und der Menschensohn*, pp. 217–18). Jeremias believes that we are confronted here with variants of the Aramaic tradition behind the two terms: "deny" = *k^{e}par*, "be ashamed of" = *h^{a}par* (see *New Testament Theology*, 1: 7n.2).

20. See Jeremias, *New Testament Theology*, 1: 262–63, for a brief version of the argument; he works the position out more fully in his article "Die älteste Schicht der Menschensohn-Logien," *ZNW* 58 (1967): 159–72.

21. See Perrin, *Rediscovering the Teaching of Jesus*, New Testament Library (Lon-

don, 1963), p. 189. Originally "the angels" could have stood as a periphrasis for God (see Dalman's *The Words of Jesus* [Edinburgh, 1902], p. 197).

22. See Borsch, *The Christian and Gnostic Son of Man*, Studies in Biblical Theology, 2d ser., no. 14 (London, 1970), p. 27.

23. See especially S. Schulz on verse 9: *"Luke wanted to avoid a collision with the following logion about the forgivable blasphemy of the Son of Man"* (*Q—Die Spruchquelle der Evangelisten* [Zürich, 1970], p. 69). In similar vein, see I. H. Marshall, "The Synoptic Son of Man Sayings in Recent Discussion," *NTS* 12 (1966): 69; Kümmel, in *Jesus und der Menschensohn*, p. 214; and H. Schürmann, "Beobachtungen zum Menschensohntitel in der Redequelle," in *Jesus und der Menschensohn*, p. 135.

24. Higgins, " 'Menschensohn' oder 'ich' in Q: Lk. 12.8–9 // Mt. 10.32–33," in *Jesus und der Menschensohn*, p. 123. In a similar vein, see G. Bornkamm in his early essay "Das Wort Jesu vom Bekennen," in *Geschichte und Glaube,* Beiträge zur evangelischen Theologie, 48 (München, 1968), 26n., and his later *Jesus of Nazareth*, trans. I. McLuskey, F. McLuskey, and J. Robinson (London, 1960), p. 176; Bultmann, *HST*, p. 151, and *Theology of the New Testament*, p. 30; Jüngel, *Paulus und Jesus*, pp. 242–43, 260; Borsch, *The Son of Man in Myth and History*, New Testament Library (London, 1967), p. 358n.1; H. Braun, "Der Sinn der neutestamentlichen Christologie," *ZTK* 54 (1957): 345; W. Pannenberg, *Jesus: God and Man*, trans. L. L. Wilkins and D. A. Priebe (London, 1970), pp. 59–60; Kümmel, *Promise and Fulfilment: The Eschatological Message of Jesus*, Studies in Biblical Theology, no. 23 (London, 1961), pp. 44–45, and in *Jesus und der Menschensohn*, pp. 213–14; and R. G. Hamerton-Kelly, *Pre-Existence, Wisdom, and the Son of Man*, Society for New Testament Studies Monograph Series, no. 21 (Cambridge, 1973), pp. 94–95.

25. Higgins, *Jesus and the Son of Man*, pp. 215–16.

26. Tödt, *The Son of Man in the Synoptic Tradition*, p. 43.

27. Tödt, *The Son of Man in the Synoptic Tradition*, p. 57.

28. It is important to recognize that in the two other passages in which Jesus and the Son of Man are formally differentiated, a similar interpretation applies. Matthew 19:28, when compared with its parallel Luke 22:28ff., is most plausibly understood in this fashion, and Mark 14:62 cannot be interpreted in any other way. For a comparable estimate of the significance of confessing Jesus and the verdict of the Son of Man, see E. Percy, *Die Botschaft Jesu* (Lund, 1953), p. 249; T. W. Manson, *The Teaching of Jesus*, 2d ed. (Cambridge, 1931), p. 263; Bornkamm, *Jesus of Nazareth*, p. 176; Higgins, *Jesus and the Son of Man*, pp. 207–8; Jüngel, *Paulus und Jesus*, p. 261; Kümmel, in *Jesus und der Menschensohn*, pp. 222–23; Marshall, "The Synoptic Son of Man Sayings," p. 101; J. Becker, *Johannes der Täufer und Jesus von Nazareth* (Neukirchen-Vluyn, 1972), p. 101; and Hamerton-Kelly, *Pre-Existence, Wisdom, and the Son of Man*, pp. 26, 94–95.

29. See Bultmann, *Jesus and the Word*, trans. L. P. Smith and E. Huntress (New York, 1958), pp. 216–17.

30. Käsemann, *Essays on New Testament Themes*, trans. W. J. Montague, Studies in Biblical Theology, no. 41 (London, 1964), p. 44.

31. See Käsemann, *New Testament Questions for Today*, p. 77.

32. Käsemann's thesis that the "Sentences of Holy Law in the New Testament" originated from Christian prophets in the primitive church has been subjected to searching examination by K. Berger (see "Zu den sogenannten Sätzen heiligen Rechts," *NTS* 17 [1970]: 21–40), and by D. Hill ("On the Evidence for the Creative Role of Christian Prophets," *NTS* 20 [1974]: 262–74). Berger demonstrates that the idea of correspondence between actions and rewards was rooted in the Wisdom literature and that it found an eschatological application in apocalyptic thought; he argues that its presuppositions were too widely held to limit its *Sitz-im-Leben* in the church to the activity of a special group of prophets. Hill agrees and affirms not just that a connection between prophecy and the "sentences" has not been critically demonstrated but also that no proof has been

forthcoming of a custom in the primitive church of attributing Spirit-inspired utterances to the historical Jesus; indeed, the Pauline letters and the book of Revelation suggest that no such confusion arose.

33. See Kümmel, in *Jesus und der Menschensohn*, p. 222.

34. See Marshall, "The Synoptic Son of Man Sayings," pp. 350–51.

35. F. J. Foakes-Jackson and K. Lake, *The Beginnings of Christianity*, 5 vols. (London, 1920–33), 1: 379.

36. V. Taylor, *The Gospel according to St. Mark*, Macmillan New Testament Commentaries (London, 1952), p. 199.

37. Wellhausen, *Das Evangelium Marci* (Berlin, 1903), p. 16; Klostermann, *Das Markusevangelium*, Handbuch zum Neuen Testament (Tübingen, 1926), p. 23; and Colpe, *TDNT*, 8: 430.

38. Colpe, *TDNT*, 8: 431.

39. Schürmann, *Das Lukasevangelium*, Herders theologischer Kommentar zum Neuen Testament (Freiburg, 1969), p. 284.

40. Other scholars holding this view include Taylor (*The Gospel according to St. Mark*, p. 198), C. K. Barrett (*The Holy Spirit in the Gospel Tradition* [London, 1947], p. 82), Kümmel (*Promise and Fulfilment*, p. 46n.93), W. Grundmann (*Das Evangelium nach Markus*, Theologischer Handkommentar zum Neuen Testament [Berlin, 1959], p. 58), Borsch (*The Son of Man in Myth and History*, pp. 321–22, and *The Christian and Gnostic Son of Man*, pp. 7–8), H. Anderson (*The Gospel of Mark*, New Century Bible Commentary [London, 1976], p. 102), Tödt (*The Son of Man in the Synoptic Tradition*, pp. 126–27), A. Higgins (*Jesus and the Son of Man*, pp. 26ff.), and Percy (*Die Botschaft Jesu*, pp. 27n and 242–43). Tödt, Higgins, and Percy agree as to the interpretation of the text but concur with Bultmann in viewing Mark 2:5–10a as an interpolation, whether by Mark or his source, into the original narrative of the healing of the Paralytic (see Bultmann, *HST*, pp. 15–16).

41. Tödt, *The Son of Man in the Synoptic Tradition*, p. 129.

42. H.-D. Wendland saw this clearly: "Jesus in Mark 2:10 affirms that his authority is grounded in the fact that he is the Son of Man. Here again the representation of the coming sovereignty of God issues into the question of the relation of the Messiah to the kingdom, of the proclaimer to his proclamation. The kingdom of God is forgiveness; but this circumstance gains its reality in that it is not taught as a new doctrine of God, but in that the kingdom here and now meets man as forgiveness through the action of Jesus. . . . The kingdom of God is real through him who forgives sin" (*Die Eschatologie des Reiches Gottes bei Jesus: Eine Studie über den Zusammenhang von Eschatologie, Ethik und Kirchenproblem* [Gütersloh, 1931], pp. 65–66).

43. Note the *kai elegen autois* of verse 27, which is constantly used by Mark to introduce additional material (e.g., in 4:11, 21, 24; 7:9; 9:1).

44. Indeed, among those holding this view are the following: Wellhausen (*Das Evangelium Marci*, p. 20), Bultmann (*HST*, p. 16), Klostermann (*Das Markusevangelium*, p. 31), T. W. Manson (*The Teaching of Jesus*, p. 214), C. J. Cadoux (*The Historic Mission of Jesus* [London, 1943], p. 75), Jeremias ("Die älteste Schicht der Menschensohn-Logien," p. 165, and *New Testament Theology*, 1: 261), and R. Pesch (*Das Markusevangelium*, 1: 184ff.).

45. Manson, "Mark 2.27f," in *Coniectanea Neotestamentica* 11 (Lund, 1947), pp. 145–46. F. W. Beare has adopted the idea of the Son of Man as subject of the two statements, but not Manson's interpretation, and views the passage as a later church formation (see *The Earliest Records of Jesus* [Oxford, 1962], pp. 91–92, and "The Sabbath Was Made for Man?" *JBL* 79 [1960]: 130–36).

46. Among those holding such a view are Lohmeyer (*Das Evangelium des Markus*, Kritisch-exegetischer Kommentar über das Neue Testament [Göttingen, 1963], p. 66), W. Manson (*Jesus the Messiah* [London, 1943], p. 116), Taylor (*The Gospel according to St. Mark*, p. 118), Fuller (*The Foundations of New Testament Christology*, p. 149), E. Lohse

(*TDNT*, 7: 22), Colpe (*TDNT*, 8: 452), Tödt (*The Son of Man in the Synoptic Tradition*, pp. 130–32), Higgins (*Jesus and the Son of Man*, pp. 29–30), Hahn (*The Titles of Jesus in Christology*, p. 35), and Anderson (*The Gospel of Mark*, p. 111).

47. See Cranfield, *The Gospel according to St. Mark*, 2d ed., Cambridge Greek Testament (Cambridge, 1963), p. 118; and Lane, *The Gospel of Mark*, New International Commentary on the New Testament (Grand Rapids, 1974), p. 120.

48. See Braun, *Jesus of Nazareth*, trans. E. R. Kalin (Philadelphia, 1979), pp. 82–83.

49. Käsemann, *Essays on New Testament Themes*, p. 102.

50. Abrahams, *Studies on Pharisaism and the Gospels*, 2 vols. (Philadelphia, 1917–24), 1: 129.

51. "This principle does not have general validity, but says only that the Sabbath may be deconsecrated solely for the saving of a human life" (Simeon, in H. L. Strack–P. Billerbeck, *Kommentar zum Neuen Testament aus Talmud und Midrasch*, 6 vols. (München, 1922–28), 2: 5.

52. Braun, *Jesus of Nazareth*, p. 81.

53. On this, see J. Schmid, who draws attention to the loose use of *dia touto* in Matthew 12:31, 13:52, and 21:43, and Mark's similar use of *gar* in Mark 8:35, 36, 37, 38, and 9:41 (*Das Evangelium nach Markus*, Regensburger Neues Testament [Regensburg, 1958], p. 56). Schürmann agrees (see *Das Lukasevangelium*, p. 304n.21), as does Lane (see *The Gospel of Mark*, p. 118n.93).

54. See Pesch, *Das Markusevangelium*, 1: 184ff.

55. On this, see Borsch's perceptive statement: "It should not be surprising that the Son of Man would speak and act as sovereign of the sabbath, the day which is a memorial of the creation, especially created for the blessing of mankind, among whom Adam is first. And it is this day of rest which is associated with the coming of the new age, with the ceremonial activity of the ruler, and through its observance, with the coming of the Messiah. In this sense, both in terms of its first purpose and its final purpose, it could be seen as the day of the Man" (*The Son of Man in Myth and History*, p. 322). M. D. Hooker's exposition of Mark 2:28 is essentially the same as Borsch's (see *The Son of Man in Myth and History*, New Testament Library [London, 1967], pp. 98–102), as is that of J. Roloff (*Das Kerygma und der irdische Jesu: Historische Motive in den Jesus-Erzählungen der Evangelien* [Göttingen, 1970], p. 62).

56. On this, see Kümmel, *Promise and Fulfilment*, p. 46n.93.

57. Jeremias, *New Testament Theology*, 1: 121.

58. Among those holding this view are Bultmann (*Theology of the New Testament*, p. 30), Jeremias ("Die älteste Schicht der Menschensohn-Logien," p. 165), Colpe (*TDNT*, 8: 432), and Bonnard (*L'Évangile selon Saint Matthieu*, Commentaire du Nouveau Testament [Neuchatel, 1963], p. 437).

59. Among those holding this view are T. W. Manson (*The Sayings of Jesus*, p. 70) and Vermes (*Jesus the Jew*, pp. 182, 260n.77).

60. Among those holding this view are Tödt (*The Son of Man in the Synoptic Tradition*, p. 116), Higgins (*Jesus and the Son of Man*, p. 123), Fuller (*The Foundations of New Testament Christology*, p. 125), and Bornkamm (*Jesus of Nazareth*, pp. 229–30).

61. Jeremias, *New Testament Theology*, 1: 262.

62. Borsch, *The Son of Man in Myth and History*, p. 326n.1.

63. On this, see Percy, *Die Botschaft Jesu*, pp. 252–53; Grundmann, *Das Evangelium nach Matthäus*, Theologischer Handkommentar zum Neuen Testament (Berlin, 1968), p. 312; Schürmann, *Das Lukasevangelium*, p. 426n.134; and Hamerton-Kelly, *Pre-Existence, Wisdom, and the Son of Man*, p. 130.

64. The LXX renders the italicized phrase *sumbolokopon oinophlugei*, "given to feasting and drinking wine." Delitsch, in his translation of the New Testament into Hebrew, must have seen the connection, for in Matthew 11:19 he translates the expression *phagos kai oinopotes* with precisely the words that appear in Deuteronomy

21:20, *zolel wesobe* (see *Eine neue hebräische Übersetzung des Neuen Testaments* [Leipzig, 1864]).

65. On this, see R. Hummel, who points out that Matthew does not in fact oppose scribalism as such, but only in its Pharisaic form (*Die Auseinandersetzung zwischen Kirche und Judentum im Matthäusevangelium*, Beiträge zur evangelischen Theologie, vol. 33 [München, 1963], pp. 17, 27).

66. See Bultmann, *HST*, pp. 27, 102; and *Jesus and the Word*, p. 49.

67. See T. W. Manson, *The Sayings of Jesus*, p. 72; Percy, *Die Botschaft Jesu*, p. 251; and Schweizer, "Der Menschensohn: Zur eschatologischen Erwartung Jesu," p. 199.

68. See Colpe, *TDNT*, 8: 433; and Jeremias, *New Testament Theology*, p. 262.

69. See Otto, *The Kingdom of God and the Son of Man*, trans. F. V. Filson and B. L. Woolf (London, 1943), p. 234. For a similar interpretation, see Fuller, *The Foundations of New Testament Christology*, p. 125.

70. Tödt, *The Son of Man in the Synoptic Tradition*, p. 123.

71. See Tödt, *The Son of Man in the Synoptic Tradition*, p. 122.

72. Bonnard, *L'Évangile selon Saint Matthieu*, p. 118; Colpe, *TDNT*, 8: 433. See also Fuller, *The Foundations of New Testament Christology*, p. 148; Schniewind, *Das Evangelium nach Matthäus*, Das Neue Testament Deutsch (Göttingen, 1956), pp. 113–14; and Schweizer, *The Good News According to Matthew*, trans. D. O. E. Green (Atlanta, 1975), p. 220.

73. Luke's editorial work in the concluding sentences of the Zacchaeus story has been variously estimated. Bultmann holds that the original narrative consisted of verses 1–7 and 9 and that Luke added verses 8 and 10 (*HST*, pp. 33–34). E. Bammel thought that the original was verses 1–7 and 9b and that Luke added verses 8–9a and 10 (*TDNT*, 6: 907n.197). Higgins contends that verses 1–9a are pre-Lukan and that verses 9b–10 are Lukan additions (*Jesus and the Son of Man*, pp. 76–77). The reasoning behind these conjectures is not always compelling; Bultmann's belief that verse 8 is mere Lukan moralizing should be compared with Michel's statements concerning Jewish requirements regarding the restitution of expropriated property (*TDNT*, 8: 105).

74. Schmid, *Das Evangelium nach Lukas*, 4th ed., Regensburger Neues Testament (Regensburg, 1960), p. 287.

75. See Colpe, *TDNT*, 8: 453. Tödt makes the same point in *The Son of Man in the Synoptic Tradition*, p. 133.

76. See Jeremias, "Die älteste Schicht der Menschensohn-Logien"; *TDNT*, 6: 492; and *New Testament Theology*, 1: 262n.6.

77. See Michel, *TDNT*, 8: 104.

78. See Lagrange, *L'Évangile selon Saint Luc*, Études Bibliques (Paris, 1921), p. 491.

79. Otto, *The Kingdom of God and the Son of Man*, p. 251.

80. See F. Field, *Notes on the Translation of the New Testament* (Cambridge, 1899), pp. 11–13; for a recent discussion, see K. Lehmann, *Auferweckt am Dritten Tag nach der Schrift, Früheste Christologie, Bekenntnisbildung und Schriftauslegung im Lichte von 1 Kor. 15.3–5*, 2d ed., Quaestiones Disputatae 38 (Freiburg, 1969), pp. 165–66.

81. See the excursus of Pesch on the pre-Markan passion story in *Das Markusevangelium*, 2: 1–25, especially pp. 3 and 24.

82. Jeremias suggests that the threefold repetition came about because "among the complexes of tradition that Mark took up there were by chance three that contained the prediction of the passion: 8.27–9.1 (confession and the cost of discipleship), 9.30–50 (the great collection built on link-words), and 10.32–45 (suffering and discipleship)" (*New Testament Theology*, 1: 281n.1).

83. See especially Strecker, "Die Leidens- und Auferstehungsvoraussagen im Markusevangelium (Mk 8,31; 9,31; 10,32–34)," *ZTK* 64 (1967): 31.

84. The originality of 8:31 is favored by the following scholars: Lohmeyer (*Das Evangelium des Markus*, pp. 164–65), H. Horstmann (*Studien zur markinischen Christologie: Mark 8.27–9.13 als Zugang zum Christusbild des zweiten Evangeliums*, Neu-

testamentliche Abhandlungen, nr. 6 [Münster, 1969], pp. 171ff.), Strecker ("Die Leidens- und Auferstehungsvoraussagen im Markusevangelium," pp. 24ff.), L. Goppelt ("Zum Problem des Menschensohns: Das Verhältnis von Leidens- und Parusieankündigung," in *Christologie und Ethik* [Göttingen, 1968], pp. 69–70), and P. Hoffmann ("Mk. 8.31: Zur Herkunft und markinischen Rezeption einer alten Überlieferung," in *Orientierung an Jesus*, Festschrift for J. Schmid, ed. P. Hoffmann [Freiburg, 1973], pp. 171ff.).

The originality of 9:31 is favored by Grundmann (*Das Evangelium nach Markus*, p. 192), Hahn (*The Titles of Jesus in Christology*, pp. 41–42), Jeremias (*New Testament Theology*, 1: 281–82), W. Popkes (*Christus Traditus: Untersuchung zum Begriff der Dahingabe im Neuen Testament*, Abhandlungen zur Theologie des Alten und Neuen Testaments, Band 49 [Zürich, 1967], p. 161), Schweizer (*The Good News according to Mark*, trans. D. H. Madvig [Atlanta, 1970], p. 190), and Pesch (*Jesus und der Menschensohn*, p. 176).

85. Such is the contention of Taylor (in *The Gospel according to St. Mark*, p. 377) and Hooker (in *The Son of Man in Mark*, p. 134). See also Popkes, *Christus Traditus*, p. 160, and H. Patsch, *Abendmahl und historischer Jesus*, Calwer Theologische Monographien, Band 1 (Stuttgart, 1972), p. 187.

86. Hahn, *The Titles of Jesus in Christology*, pp. 40 and 53n.163; Hahn is drawing on Michaelis, *TDNT*, 5: 904ff.

87. See Ruppert, *Jesus als der leidende Gerechte?* Stuttgarter Bibelstudien 59 (Stuttgart, 1972), pp. 65–66.

88. Pesch contends that the term is also linked with the motif of the rejection of the prophets in the Deuteronomic tradition (see *Jesus und der Menschensohn*, p. 170).

89. Daniel 2:28 states, "He has made known to the king what shall be [*mah di leh*wa'*] in the end of the days." The LXX renders the Aramaic phrase as *ha dei genesthai*.

90. On this, see E. Fascher, "Theologische Beobachtungen zu *dei*," in *Neutestamentliche Studien für R. Bultmann*, 2d ed. (Berlin, 1957), pp. 229ff.; and Lohmeyer, *Das Evangelium des Markus*, pp. 164–65.

91. See Grundmann, *TDNT*, 2: 22–23; and *Das Evangelium nach Markus*, p. 169.

92. Patsch suggests that those who conveyed the tradition would have had all three meanings in mind (see *Abendmahl und historischer Jesus*, pp. 190ff.).

93. See Jeremias, *New Testament Theology*, 1: 281.

94. See the discussion on this in Patsch, *Abendmahl und historischer Jesus*, pp. 193–94.

95. It should be pointed out that this tendency is not confined to those who translate from Aramaic into Greek; it belongs to the tradition of translating Holy Scripture in all instances, as is evidenced in the frequency with which the strong negative *ou me* occurs in the LXX and in the New Testament. Of the sixty-four occurrences of *ou me* in the gospels, fifty-seven are in sayings of Jesus; apart from citations of Old Testament scriptures and words of Jesus, *ou me* is as rare in the New Testament as it is in secular literature. Moulton concludes, "Since these are just the two elements which made up 'scripture' in the first age of Christianity, one is tempted to put it down to the same cause in both—a feeling that *inspired language was fitly rendered in words of a peculiarly decisive tone*" (in Moulton et al., *A Grammar of New Testament Greek*, 4 vols. [Edinburgh, 1929–76], 1: 192). The same phenomenon is apparent in the use of "shall" and "will" in the AV: "will" is uniformly used in translating utterances of inspired men in the first person, and "shall" is uniformly used in translating such utterances in the third person, both being emphatic (see, for example, Isa. 51:3ff., "The Lord *shall* comfort Zion"; "I *will* make my judgment to rest for a light of the people").

96. See Pesch, "Die Passion des Menschensohnes," in *Jesus und der Menschensohn*, p. 193.

97. See Jeremias, *New Testament Theology*, 1: 281–82. Strecker's objection that the play on words is as evident in Greek as in Aramaic and hence that there is no need to appeal to an Aramaic original (see "Die Leidens- und Auferstehungsvoraussagen im

Markusevangelium," p. 30) is not valid; in the postulated Aramaic original not only is the play on words more precise, but it includes an interplay of ideas—*the Man*, and *men*. Patsch further points out that one would not think of a play on words in the Greek text unless one knew what lay behind it (see *Abendmahl und historischer Jesus*, p. 195).

98. Such is the contention of Hoffmann, in *Orientierung an Jesus*, p. 176. Strecker thinks that its formation reflects the influence of the passion narrative (see "Die Leidens- und Auferstehungsvoraussagen im Markusevangelium," p. 30).

99. Such is the contention of Jeremias (see *New Testament Theology*, 1: 281n.2); the "soon" is added because the participle in Aramaic relates to the near future.

100. Such is the contention of Popkes, *Christus Traditus*, p. 181.

101. See Hoffmann, in *Orientierung an Jesus*, p. 195.

102. See Jeremias, *New Testament Theology*, 1: 278–80; and Schürmann, *Jesu Ureigener Tod: Exegetische Besinnungen und Ausblick* (Freiburg, 1975). The chief points that this view focuses on are (1) the dangers to Jesus associated with his *teaching*, which was in opposition to that of both the Pharisees and the Sadducees; (2) the dangers associated with his *conduct*, which highlighted the radical nature of his teaching, especially in relation to his solidarity with sinners and his breaking of the ceremonial laws and the sabbath laws as they were understood at the time; (3) his reflection on the fate of John the Baptist (see Matt. 11:12 and Mark 9:12); (4) his evident danger in the hands of Herod, who did not suffer prophets gladly (see Luke 13:31–32), and from the Romans, who did not suffer messianic pretenders gladly; and (5) the peril in which his cleansing of the temple, following on the entry into Jerusalem, placed him, indicative as it was of his popularity and therefore danger to the Jewish establishment.

103. While many writers have drawn attention to the importance of the concept of the Righteous Sufferer in the teaching of Jesus, none has been more indefatigable in this than Schweizer, who elaborated it in his book *Erniedrigung und Erhöhung bei Jesus und seinen Nachfolgern* (ET, *Lordship and Discipleship*, Studies in Biblical Theology, no. 28 [London, 1960]) and also in various articles on the Son of Man as well as in his commentaries on Matthew and Mark. His writings stimulated Ruppert to produce his significant *Jesus als der leidende Gerechte?* in which Schweizer's thesis is tested and evaluated, and its valid insights set on a firmer foundation. To this book I am deeply indebted, and in the discussion which follows I freely refer to Ruppert's findings.

104. See Ruppert, *Jesus als der leidende Gerechte?* pp. 19–20.

105. See Ruppert, *Jesus als der leidende Gerechte?* pp. 23–24.

106. See Suggs, "Wisdom of Solomon 2.10–5: A Homily Based on the Fourth Servant Song," *JBL* 76 (1957): 26–33.

107. See Gnilka, "Die Verhandlungen vor dem Synhedrion und vor Pilatus nach Markus 14:3–15:5," in *Evangelisch-katholischer Kommentar zum Neuen Testament*, Vorarbeiten Heft 2 (Zürich, 1970), pp. 11–12.

108. Pesch includes the passion predictions within the complex of the pre-Markan passion story. He reckons the latter to consist of 8:27–33; 9:2–13, 30–35; 10:1, 32–34, 46–52; 11:1–23, 27–33; 12:1–17, 34c–37, 41–44; 13:1–12; and 14:1–16:8. He has estimated that no less than two-thirds of this material is stamped with allusions to or citations of the motifs of the righteous sufferer. To substantiate the claim, he provides a detailed listing of the Psalms that employ this pattern and the passages in the Markan narrative that allude to them or cite them (see the excursus "Die vormarkinische Passionsgeschichte," in *Das Markusevangelium*, 2: 1–27, especially pp. 12–14).

109. See G. von Rad, *Old Testament Theology*, 2 vols., trans. D. M. G. Stalker (New York, 1962–65), 1: 340.

110. See Jeremias, *New Testament Theology*, 1: 280n.2.

111. Jeremias, *TDNT*, 5: 714.

112. See Jeremias, *New Testament Theology*, 1: 280.

113. See pp. 297–99 herein on the destiny of the martyrs.

114. C. R. North contends that there is in fact a reference to the resurrection of the Servant in Isaiah 53:10 but that it is masked by vague language resulting in part from a lack of analogy to the exaltation of the Servant and in part to the fact that the Song was composed before the doctrine of a resurrection from the dead became general (see *The Second Isaiah* [Oxford, 1964], p. 242).

115. On this, see W. Zimmerli, in Zimmerli and Jeremias, *The Servant of God*, Studies in Biblical Theology, no. 20 (London, 1957), p. 26; C. Westermann, *Jesaja 40–66*, Das Alte Testament Deutsch (Göttingen, 1966), pp. 20–21; and Ruppert, *Jesus als der leidende Gerechte?* pp. 19–20.

116. See Jeremias, in *The Servant of God*, p. 96n.438; and *New Testament Theology*, 1: 296n.4.

117. Jeremias, *New Testament Theology*, 1: 299.

118. See Pesch, *Jesus und der Menschensohn*, p. 177.

119. W. Bousset, *Die Religion des Judentums*, 3d ed., rev. H. Gressmann (Berlin, 1926), p. 374.

120. The book of Daniel in its entirety illustrates this, with Daniel 12:2 making plain the doctrine of resurrection.

121. The strong emphasis on the resurrection faith in 2 Maccabees (see 12:43ff., as well as 7:9, 11; 14:36; and 14:46) gives some indication of this. C. C. Torrey writes of 4 Maccabees that "The religion which the book preaches is Judaism through and through, somewhat enriched from Greek thought, but nonetheless loyal to the faith of the fathers" (*The Apocryphal Literature* [New Haven, 1945], p. 104).

122. See the references in Jeremias's *New Testament Theology*, 1: 288nn. 4–8.

123. For references, see Pesch, *Jesus und der Menschensohn*, p. 185; and *Das Markusevangelium*, 2: 438.

124. *Midrash Rabbah*, trans. and ed. H. Freedman and M. Simon, 10 vols. (London, 1939), 1: 491.

125. See Lehmann, *Auferweckt am Dritten Tag*, p. 269.

126. Lehmann, *Auferweckt am Dritten Tag*, p. 181.

127. Such is the contention of Schürmann in *Traditionsgeschichtliche Untersuchungen zu der synoptischen Evangelien* (Düsseldorf, 1968), pp. 213n.24 and 234.

128. See Jeremias, *The Parables of Jesus*, trans. S. H. Hooke, rev. ed. (London, 1963), p. 163n.46.

129. See Black's discussion of this idiom in *An Aramaic Approach to the Gospels and Acts*, pp. 121–23.

130. See Delling, *Studien zum Neuen Testament und zum hellenistischen Judentum* (Göttingen, 1970), pp. 240–43. The construction occurs frequently in the LXX—250 times altogether (p. 242n.37).

131. On this, see H. Köster, *TDNT*, 7: 884–85; and S. Légasse, "Approche de l'Épisode préévangelique des Fils de Zébédée (Marc x.35–40 par.)," *NTS* 20 (1974): 165.

132. See Wellhausen, *Das Evangelium Lucae* (Berlin, 1904), p. 69; Koster, *TDNT*, 7: 885n.77; Légasse, "Approche de l'Épisode préévangelique des Fils de Zébédée," p. 165; and Delling, *Studien zum Neuen Testament und zum hellenistischen Judentum*, p. 246.

133. See Légasse, "Approche de l'Épisode préévangelique des Fils de Zébédée," p. 165.

134. See Zahn, *Das Evangelium des Lucas* (Leipzig, 1913), p. 515.

135. See Plummer, *The Gospel according to St. Luke*, 5th ed., International Critical Commentary (Edinburgh, 1922), p. 334.

136. Among those holding this point of view are J. M. Creed (*The Gospel according to St. Luke* [London, 1930], p. 178), B. S. Easton (*The Gospel according to St. Luke* [Edinburgh, 1923], p. 209), Lang (*TDNT*, 6: 942), and Schmid (*Das Evangelium nach Lukas*, p. 225).

137. Among those holding this point of view are N. Geldenhuys (*Commentary on

the Gospel of Luke, New London Commentary [London, 1950], pp. 366–67), Grundmann (Das Evangelium nach Lukas, Theologischer Handkommentar zum Neuen Testament [Berlin, 1959]), and Bultmann—although he links this interpretation with the Gnostic redeemer myth (see HST, pp. 153–54).

138. Ellis, The Gospel of Luke, rev. ed., New Century Bible Commentary (London, 1974), p. 182.

139. Among the Qumran writings, see for example 1QpHab 10:13 and 1QH 3:24–31, 7:3–4. Among the apocalyptic writings, see for example 1 Enoch 102:1; Psalms of Solomon 15:4–5; and 2 Baruch 28:39. On the references to the fire of Gehenna and the abyss of fire, which are, of course, numerous in this literature, see Charles, A Critical History of the Doctrine of the Future Life (London, 1889), pp. 244, 292ff., 358ff.

140. For non-Septuagintal renderings of Psalm 7:16, Job 9:31, and Jeremiah 38:22, see Delling, Studien zum Neuen Testament und zum hellenistischen Judentum, p. 243.

141. This is evident in 2 Peter 3:6–7. It finds explicit expression in the Books of Adam and Eve 49:3: to Adam it is said, "On account of your transgression our Lord will bring upon your race the anger of his judgment, first by water, the second time by fire; by these two will the Lord judge the whole human race."

142. See the discussion in Légasse, "Approche de l'Épisode préévangelique des Fils de Zébédée," pp. 167–68. Illustrations can be found in J. P. Lewis's Study of the Interpretation of Noah and the Flood in Jewish and Christian Literature (Leiden, 1968), pp. 34–35, 169–70.

143. See, for example, Sibylline Oracles 3:689–90: "God shall judge all with war and sword, and with fire and cataclysms of rain." See also Lewis, Study of the Interpretation of Noah and the Flood in Jewish and Christian Literature, pp. 115–16, 169–73.

144. See, for example, 1QH 3:29–30, in which it is stated that in the day of the Lord

The torrents of Belial overflowed all the high banks
like a fire consuming all their shores,
destroying from their channels every tree green and dry
and whipping with whirlwinds of flame
until the vanishing of all that drinks there. . . .

145. See Vögtle, "Todesankündigungen und Todesverständnis Jesu," in Der Tod Jesu: Deutungen im Neuen Testament, ed. K. Kertelge, Quaestiones Disputatae 74 (Freiburg, 1976), pp. 83–85.

146. See Légasse, "Approche de l'Épisode préévangelique des Fils de Zébédée," p. 169.

147. For evidence indicating that Jesus expected a violent death, see Jeremias, New Testament Theology, 1: 277–86.

148. The Gospel according to Thomas, trans. A. Guillaumont et al. (Leiden, 1959), p. 45 (log. 82); cf. Origen, In Jerem. hom. lat., 3:3.

149. See Lane, The Gospel of Mark, p. 176.

150. Sifre 92a on Deuteronomy 13:2; see Strack–Billerbeck, Kommentar zum Neuen Testament aus Talmud und Midrasch, 1: 726–27.

151. See Black, An Aramaic Approach to the Gospels and Acts, p. 89.

152. See Behm, TDNT, 1: 663.

153. See Lagrange, L'Évangile selon Saint Marc, Études Bibliques (Paris, 1910), p. lxxxvii.

154. Colpe gives this rendering in TDNT, 8: 449, citing Kuschke, "Das Idiom des relativen Negation im NT," ZNW 43 (1950–51): 263.

155. See Edwards, The Sign of Jonah in the Theology of the Evangelists and Q, Studies in Biblical Theology, 2d ser., no. 18 (London, 1971). Among those to have championed the view before him are Bousset (Kyrios Christos, 2d ed. [Göttingen, 1921], p. 7), H. B. Sharman (Son of Man and Kingdom of God [London, 1943], p. 15), H. B. Branscomb (The

Gospel of Mark, Moffatt New Testament Commentary [London, 1937], pp. 138–39), and Lohmeyer (*Das Evangelium des Markus*, p. 156n.4).

156. See Edwards, *The Sign of Jonah in the Theology of the Evangelists and Q*, pp. 83–87.

157. See Edwards, *The Sign of Jonah in the Theology of the Evangelists and Q*, pp. 48–57.

158. Bultmann thought otherwise: "Mark could easily have omitted the (to him) incomprehensible saying about the sign of Jonah" (*HST*, p. 118n.1). But in what is perhaps the most significant contribution on the sign of Jonah in modern critical discussions, Vögtle rejects Bultmann's conclusion (see "Der Spruch vom Jonaszeichen," in *Synoptischen Studien*, Festschrift for A. Wikenhauser, ed. J. Schmid and A. Vögtle [München, 1953], p. 240).

159. See T. K. Cheyne and J. S. Black, *Encyclopaedia Biblica*, 4 vols. (London, 1899–1903), 2: 2502; W. Brandt, *Die jüdische Baptismen* (Giessen, 1910), pp. 82ff.; and B. W. Bacon, *The Sermon on the Mount* (London, 1902), p. 232.

160. See C. Moxon, "To semeion Iona," *ExpTim* 22 (1911): 566–67; J. H. Michael, "The Sign of Jonah," *JTS* 21 (1920): 146ff.; Creed, *The Gospel according to St. Luke*, p. 163; and Kraeling, *John the Baptist* (New York, 1951), pp. 136–37.

161. Vögtle, "Der Spruch vom Jonaszeichen," pp. 246–47.

162. Among those holding this view are the following: A. E. J. Rawlinson (*The Gospel according to St. Mark*, 2d ed. [London, 1927], p. 227), Branscomb (*The Gospel of Mark*, pp. 138–39), T. W. Manson (*The Sayings of Jesus*, p. 90), Taylor (*The Gospel according to St. Mark*, p. 363), Kümmel (*Promise and Fulfilment*, pp. 68–69), Borsch (*The Son of Man in Myth and History*, p. 327n.3), Perrin (*Rediscovering the Teaching of Jesus*, pp. 194–95), Schulz (*Q—Die Spruchquelle der Evangelisten*, pp. 255–56), A. R. C. Leaney (*The Gospel according to St. Luke*, Black's New Testament Commentaries [London, 1958], p. 192), and G. B. Caird (*St. Luke*, Pelican Gospel Commentaries [Harmondsworth, 1963], p. 156).

163. Schlatter, *Der Evangelist Matthäus* (Stuttgart, 1948), p. 416.

164. Bultmann, *HST*, p. 118. The interpretation of the sign of Jonah as denoting the parousia is maintained by Klostermann (*Das Matthäusevangelium*, Handbuch zum Neuen Testament [Tübingen, 1927], p. 112), Hahn (*The Titles of Jesus in Christology*, p. 32), Ellis (*The Gospel of Luke*, p. 167), Schmid (*Das Evangelium nach Lukas*, p. 207), Tödt (*The Son of Man in the Synoptic Tradition*, p. 138), Jüngel (*Paulus und Jesus*, p. 257), Strecker (*Der Weg der Gerechtigkeit: Untersuchung zur Theologie des Matthäus*, Forsuchung zur Religion und Literatur des Alten und Neuen Testaments, Heft 82, 2d ed. [Göttingen, 1966], p. 104), and Schweizer (*The Good News according to Matthew*, pp. 292–93).

165. Such is the contention of Jeremias, *TDNT*, 3: 410; and O. Glumbitza, "Das Zeichen des Jonah (zum Verständnis von Matth. xii.38–42)," *NTS* 8 (1962): 363.

166. See Strack–Billerbeck, *Kommentar zum Neuen Testament aus Talmud und Midrasch*, 1: 642–49.

167. Matthew clearly was not troubled by the difference between "three days and three nights" and the "third day" of the kerygma (see Matt. 16:21, etc.); the expressions denote the same length of time (see Strack–Billerbeck, *Kommentar zum Neuen Testament aus Talmud und Midrasch*, 1: 649).

168. Rawlinson, "Corpus Christi," in *Mysterium Christi*, ed. G. K. A. Bell and A. Deissmann (London, 1930), p. 241.

169. See Jeremias, *The Eucharistic Words of Jesus* (London, 1966), pp. 15–88.

170. Schürmann, *Jesu Ureigener Tod*, p. 85.

171. Mme. Jaubert's argument that Jesus celebrated the passover on the Tuesday evening of passover week in accordance with a solar calendar that was also followed by the Essenes, and that John is reporting the observance of the passover by the Jewish authorities on Friday in accordance with the official lunar calendar (see *The Date of the*

Last Supper [New York, 1965]) should be viewed with caution in view of the uncertainty of the evidence. Having reviewed the thesis, Jeremias commented, "I can only regard this as unfounded" (see *The Eucharistic Words of Jesus*, pp. 24–25).

172. See Jeremias, *The Eucharistic Words of Jesus*, pp. 80–82.

173. See J. B. Segal, *The Hebrew Passover* (London, 1963), pp. 36–37; and C. C. Torrey, "The Date of the Crucifixion according to the Fourth Gospel," *JBL* 50 (1931): 227.

174. See Bultmann, *The Gospel of John*, trans. G. R. Beasley-Murray, R. W. N. Hoare, and J. K. Riches (Oxford, 1971), p. 524n.5.

175. See Schürmann, *Traditionsgeschichtliche Untersuchungen der synoptischen Evangelien*, pp. 159–92; Jeremias, *The Eucharistic Words of Jesus*, pp. 139–59; and Metzger, *A Textual Commentary on the Greek New Testament* (London, 1971), pp. 173–77.

176. See Jeremias, *The Eucharistic Words of Jesus*, pp. 100, 190.

177. Among those making this assumption are H. Lietzmann (*Mass and Lord's Supper* [Leiden, 1979], pp. 175ff.), Klostermann (*Das Lukasevangelium*, 2d ed., Handkommentar zum Neuen Testament [Tübingen, 1929], p. 208), Dibelius (*From Tradition to Gospel* [London, 1934], p. 210), Kümmel (*Promise and Fulfilment*, p. 31), and Pesch (*Das Markusevangelium*, 2: 368–69).

178. See Schürmann, *Der Paschamahlbericht Lk. 22, (7–14) 15–18* (Münster, 1953), pp. 1–74; and *Der Einsetzungsbericht Lk. 22, 19–20* (Münster, 1955), pp. 17–132; and see Jeremias, *The Eucharistic Words of Jesus*, pp. 97–100, 161–91.

179. See Pesch, "Das Abendmahl und Jesu Todesverständnis," in *Der Tod Jesu*, especially pp. 145–71.

180. See Jeremias, *The Eucharistic Words of Jesus*, p. 190.

181. See Schürmann, *Der Einsetzungsbericht Lk. 22, 19–20*, pp. 133–50.

182. See Jeremias, *The Eucharistic Words of Jesus*, pp. 206–7.

183. See Jeremias, *The Eucharistic Words of Jesus*, pp. 99–100. See also Goppelt, *TDNT*, 6: 153–54.

184. See Patsch, *Abendmahl und historischer Jesus*, pp. 90–100.

185. Jeremias, *The Eucharistic Words of Jesus*, pp. 207–9. The following scholars hold views essentially similar to that of Jeremias on the abstention of Jesus from the meal: C. H. Dodd (*The Parables of the Kingdom* [London, 1935], p. 56), K. H. Rengstorf (*Das Evangelium nach Lukas*, Das Neue Testament Deutsch [Göttingen, 1937], p. 235), Kümmel, *Promise and Fulfilment*, p. 31), Grundmann (*Das Evangelium nach Lukas*, p. 393), Patsch (*Abendmahl und historischer Jesus*, pp. 136–39), and D. Palmer ("Defining a Vow of Abstinence," *Colloquium* 5 [1973]: 38–41).

186. See Jeremias, *The Eucharistic Words of Jesus*, pp. 216–18.

187. Among those scholars who question whether Jesus expresses an intent to abstain from the meal are Wellhausen (*Das Evangelium Lucae*, p. 121), Plummer (*The Gospel according to St. Luke*, pp. 495–96), Creed (*The Gospel according to St. Luke*, p. 265), Schmid (*Das Evangelium nach Lukas*, pp. 321–22), W. Manson (*The Gospel of Luke*, Moffatt New Testament Commentary [London, 1930], p. 239), Taylor (*The Gospel according to St. Mark*, p. 547), J. A. Ziesler ("The Vow of Abstinence: A Note on Mark 14:25 and Parallels," *Colloquium* 5 [1972–73]: 12–14; and "The Vow of Abstinence Again," *Colloquium* 6 [1973–74]: 49–50), Schürmann (*Der Paschamahlbericht Lk. 22, [7–14] 15–18*, p. 11), Pesch (*Das Markusevangelium*, 2: 360), I. H. Marshall (*Luke: Historian and Theologian* [Exeter, 1970], p. 796), and Gnilka ("Wie urteilte Jesus über seinen Tod?" in *Der Tod Jesu*, p. 34).

188. On this, see Schürmann, *Der Paschamahlbericht Lk. 22, (7–14) 15–18*, pp. 48–50. See also D. Daube, *The New Testament and Rabbinic Judaism* (London, 1956), pp. 330–31.

189. See Patsch, *Abendmahl und historischer Jesus*, p. 139.

190. Jeremias, *The Eucharistic Words of Jesus*, p. 224; and see pp. 198–201.

191. See Schürmann, *Der Einsetzungsbericht Lk. 22, 19–20*, pp. 18–19; 107–10. For a similar opinion, see Dalman, *Jesus-Jeshua*, trans. P. L. Levertoff (London, 1929), pp. 141–43; Taylor, *The Gospel according to St. Mark*, p. 544; Behm, *TDNT*, 3: 736; Cranfield, *The Gospel according to Mark*, p. 426; Kümmel, *Promise and Fulfilment*, pp. 119–20; Schweizer, *TDNT*, 7: 1059; and Patsch, *Abendmahl und historischer Jesus*, pp. 73, 83.

192. See Pesch, *Das Markusevangelium*, 2: 357, and the references to other literature on p. 357n.6 therein. I might add that while *bisra* and *gupha* can both convey the meaning of "person," *soma* conveys it more fitly than *sarx*.

193. Pesch, *Das Markusevangelium*, 2: 357.

194. Jeremias affirms the originality of the Markan wording (see *The Eucharistic Words of Jesus*, pp. 169–71); Schürmann opposes it and supports the originality of the Lukan/Pauline tradition (see *Der Einsetzungsbericht Lk. 22, 19–20*, pp. 94–112).

195. See especially J. A. Emerton, "The Aramaic Underlying *to haima tēs diathēkēs* in Mark xiv.24," *JTS* 6 (1955): 238–40; see also "*to haima tēs diathēkēs*: The Evidence of the Syriac Versions," *JTS* 13 (1962): 111–17, and "Mark XIV.24 and the Targum to the Psalter," *JTS* 15 (1964): 58–59. Jeremias withdraws his earlier objections to the legitimacy of the language in *The Eucharistic Words of Jesus*, pp. 193–95.

196. See Jeremias, *The Eucharistic Words of Jesus*, pp. 169–71, 195.

197. See Patsch, *Abendmahl und historischer Jesus*, p. 83. Patsch cites Gottlieb ("TO HAIMA MOU TES DIATHEKES," *ST* 14 [1960]: 117), who holds that *berit* or *qim'* is understood as a genitive of apposition and has been reproduced through *he diatheke en*.

198. See Schürmann's discussion of this point in *Der Einsetzungsbericht Lk. 22, 19–20*, p. 97.

199. Behm, *TDNT*, 2: 134.

200. Käsemann, "Das Abendmahl im NT," in "Abendmahlsgemeinschaft?" *BEvT* 3 (1937): 69.

201. See Schürmann, *Der Einsetzungsbericht Lk. 22, 19–20*, pp. 75–79. For similar analyses, see Marxsen, *Die Einsetzungsbericht zum Abendmahl* (Kiel, 1948), pp. 63–64; and Patsch, *Abendmahl und historischer Jesus*, p. 78. Patsch also points out that the remarkably close parallel in John 6:51 favors the originality of the *huper* phrase in connection with the bread (p. 73).

202. See Jeremias, *The Eucharistic Words of Jesus*, pp. 166–68. Pesch is in agreement with Jeremias on this point (see "Das Abendmahl und Jesu Todesverständnis," in *Der Tod Jesu*, pp. 154, 162; and *Das Markusevangelium*, 2: 373–74).

203. See Schürmann, *Der Einsetzungsbericht Lk. 22, 19–20*, pp. 75–77.

204. See Jeremias, *The Eucharistic Words of Jesus*, pp. 167–68, 179.

205. See Patsch, *Abendmahl und historischer Jesus*, p. 77.

206. See Jeremias, *The Eucharistic Words of Jesus*, pp. 227–30; and Patsch, *Abendmahl und historischer Jesus*, pp. 153–55.

207. See Jeremias, *The Eucharistic Words of Jesus*, pp. 229–31.

208. In this Jesus was anticipated by the author of the diptych in Wisdom 2 and 5; see Suggs, "Wisdom of Solomon 2.10–5: A Homily Based on the Fourth Servant Song."

209. See Grundmann, *Das Evangelium nach Lukas*, 397; and Schnackenburg, *God's Rule and Kingdom* (London, 1963), p. 251.

210. Such is the contention of Jeremias in *TDNT*, 4: 537–38, and in *The Eucharistic Words of Jesus*, pp. 227–29. See also O. Procksch, *Theologie des Alten Testaments* (Gütersloh, 1949), p. 706; von Rad, *Old Testament Theology*, 2: 257; Zimmerli, *Old Testament Theology in Outline*, trans. D. O. E. Green (Atlanta, 1978), pp. 223–24; and North, *The Suffering Servant in Deutero-Isaiah* (London, 1948), p. 151.

211. See Bultmann, *HST*, pp. 265–66.

212. Roloff, "Anfänge der soteriologischen Deutung des Todes Jesu (Mk. x.45 und Lk. xxii.27)," *NTS* 19 (1972): 62.

213. Bultmann, *Das Verhältnis der urchristlichen Christusbotschaft zum historischen Jesus*, Sitzungsberichte der Heidelberger Akadamie der Wissenschaften, Phil.-hist. Klasse, 1960, 3. Abhandlung, 3. Aufl. (Heidelberg, 1962), p. 12.

214. See Vögtle, "Todesankündigungen und Todesverständnis Jesu," in *Der Tod Jesu*, pp. 101, 110–12.

215. See Fiedler, "Sünde und Vergebung im Christentum," *Concilium* 10 (1974): 568–71.

216. See Jeremias, *The Eucharistic Words of Jesus*, pp. 173–86.

217. Schürmann, *Jesu Ureigener Tod*, pp. 36–37.

218. Manson, *Jesus the Messiah*, pp. 125–26.

219. Cf. H.-D. Wendland: "In opposition to all theological definitions which would isolate one aspect or another of his work, we must emphasize the totality of this mission of his, by which God's kingdom is brought into the world. In other words, we speak here neither only of the incarnation, nor only of the cross, nor only of the redeemer's Spirit-filled words and deeds, but the acts of his mission are to be seen where they belong: in his mission as a whole" ("Church, Community and State," in H. G. Wood, C. H. Dodd, Edwyn Bevan, et al., *The Kingdom of God and History* [Chicago, 1938], p. 147. See also Schürmann, *Jesu Ureigener Tod*, pp. 44–58; and Patsch, *Abendmahl und historischer Jesus*, pp. 142–49.

220. Sevenster, *De Christologie van het Nieuwe Testament* (Amsterdam, 1946), p. 111.

221. See Schürmann, *Jesu Ureigener Tod*, pp. 90–95, 38–40.

222. Schürmann, *Jesu Ureigener Tod*, pp. 58, 59.

223. Gnilka, "Wie urteilte Jesus über seinen Tod?" in *Der Tod Jesu*, pp. 40–41.

224. See Vögtle, "Todesankündigen und Todesverständnis Jesu," in *Der Tod Jesu*, p. 92.

225. See Dupont, "Le logion des douze trônes (Mt 19, 28; Lc 22, 28–30)," *Biblica* 45 (1964): 356–57.

226. See Schürmann, *Jesu Abschiedsrede, Lk 22.21–38* (Münster, 1957), pp. 48–51.

227. Such is the contention of the following scholars: Creed (*The Gospel according to St. Luke*, p. 268), Schmid (*Das Evangelium nach Lukas*, p. 330), Dupont ("Le logion des douze trônes," pp. 358–61), and Marshall (*Luke: Historian and Theologian*, p. 817).

228. On this, see Schürmann, *Jesu Abschiedsrede, Lk 22.21–38*, p. 37; and Dupont, "Le logion des douze trônes," pp. 361–62.

229. See Dalman, *The Words of Jesus*, pp. 177–78.

230. On this, see Black, *An Aramaic Approach to the Gospels and Acts*, p. 236.

231. Among those holding this view are Bousset (*Die Religion des Judentums*, pp. 280–81), W. C. Allen (*A Critical and Exegetical Commentary on the Gospel according to St. Matthew*, 3d ed., International Critical Commentary [Edinburgh, 1912], p. 281), Schlatter (*Der Evangelist Matthäus*, p. 582), Vielhauer ("Gottesreich und Menschensohn," p. 68), and Schulz (*Q—Die Spruchquelle der Evangelisten*, pp. 332–33).

232. Ysebaert, *Greek Baptismal Terminology: Its Origins and Early Development* (Nijmegen, 1962), pp. 92–93.

233. See Dupont, "Le logion des douze trônes," p. 365.

234. See Philo, *De vita Mosis*, 2, 65; and Josephus, *Antiquities*, 11, 66.

235. See Vögtle, *Das Neue Testament und die Zukunft des Kosmos*, Kommentare und Beiträge zum Alten und Neuen Testament (Düsseldorf, 1970), pp. 163–65. I. Broer agrees with Vögtle (see "Das Ringen der Gemeinde um Israel: Exegetischer Versuch über Mt. 19, 28," in *Jesus und der Menschensohn*, pp. 152–53).

236. Among those holding the view are Bultmann (*HST*, p. 171), Buchsel (*TDNT*, 3: 923), Colpe (*TDNT*, 8: 447), and Bornkamm (*Jesus of Nazareth*, p. 209n.13).

237. See Dupont, "Le logion des douze trônes," p. 372.

238. Tanuch B1 (36a), cited by Strack–Billerbeck, *Kommentar zum Neuen Testament aus Talmud und Midrasch*, 4: 1210.

239. Such is the contention of Dupont (see "Le logion des douze trônes," pp. 388–91). In essential agreement on this point are Strack–Billerbeck (*Kommentar zum Neuen Testament aus Talmud und Midrasch*, 1: 828; cf. 4: 1029ff.), Rengstorf (*TDNT*, 2: 327), Lohmeyer (*Das Evangelium des Matthäus*, completed by W. Smauch, Kritisch-exegetischer Kommentar über das Neue Testament [Göttingen, 1956], p. 289), Kümmel (*Promise and Fulfilment*, p. 47), Strecker (*Weg der Gerechtigkeit*, p. 109), and Polag (*Die Christologie der Logienquelle* [Neukirchen-Vluyn, 1977], p. 97n.302). Those who hold that *krinontes* means "rule" in this passage frequently equate the Twelve Tribes with the new Israel here; among those who do so are Lagrange (*L'Évangile selon Saint Luc*, p. 552), Dodd (*According to the Scriptures* [London, 1952], p. 68), Ellis (*The Gospel of Luke*, p. 255), Bonnard (*L'Évangile selon Saint Matthieu*, p. 289), and Jeremias (*New Testament Theology*, 1: 274).

240. See Schürmann, *Jesu Abschiedsrede, Lk 22.21–38*, pp. 37–62.

241. See Otto, *The Kingdom of God and the Son of Man*, p. 292. See also Schlatter, *Das Evangelium des Lukas: Aus seinen Quellen erklärt*, 2d ed. (Stuttgart, 1960), p. 424.

242. Among those scholars agreeing with Otto in this interpretation are Dalman (*The Words of Jesus*, p. 134), Wellhausen (*Das Evangelium Lucae*, p. 122), Klostermann (*Das Lukasevangelium*, p. 212), Schürmann (*Jesu Abschiedsrede, Lk 22.21–38*, pp. 44–45), and Marshall (*The Gospel of Luke*, p. 816). The NEB is among those translations adopting the reading.

243. Among those who hold to this reading are Lagrange (*L'Évangile selon Saint Luc*, p. 551), Creed (*The Gospel according to Saint Luke*, p. 269), Behm (*TDNT*, 2: 105), and Caird (*St. Luke*, p. 239). Westcott and Hort and the RSV have also adopted this reading.

244. Bultmann, *HST*, pp. 158–59.

245. Dupont, "Le logion des douze trônes," p. 388.

246. See the excursus "Die vormarkinische katechetische Sammlung (10.2–12, 17–27, 35–45)," in Pesch, *Das Markusevangelium*, 2: 128–30; Pesch follows a similar study by H. W. Kuhn (*Ältere Sammlungen im Markusevangelium* [Göttingen, 1971], pp. 146–91).

247. Cf. Bultmann, *HST*, pp. 143–44.

248. See Bultmann, *HST*, p. 144; Bultmann is following Bousset (*Kyrios Christos*, pp. 7–8).

249. See Jeremias, "Das Lösegeld für Viele (Mk. 10.45)," *Judaica* 3 (1947–48): 249–64; and Lohse, *Märtyrer und Gottesknecht* (Göttingen, 1955), p. 118.

250. Jeremias, "Das Lösegeld für Viele (Mk. 10.45)," pp. 216–17, 223.

251. See Schürmann, *Jesu Abschiedsrede, Lk 22.21–38*, pp. 80–92.

252. Schürmann, *Jesu Abschiedsrede, Lk 22.21–38*, p. 91.

253. See Schürmann, "Beobachtungen zum Menschensohn-Titel in der Rede-quelle," p. 125n.5.

254. See Roloff, "Anfänge der soteriologischen Deutung des Todes Jesu," p. 51.

255. See Roloff, "Anfänge der soteriologischen Deutung des Todes Jesu," pp. 54–58.

256. Roloff, "Anfänge der soteriologischen Deutung des Todes Jesu," p. 59.

257. Léon-Dufour, "Jésus devant sa mort a la lumière des textes de l'Institution eucharistique et des discours d'adieu," in *Jésus aux origines de la christologie*, ed. J. Dupont (Leuven/Gembloux, 1975), p. 165.

258. See Wellhausen, *Das Evangelium Marci*, pp. 84–85.

259. See Patsch, *Abendmahl und historischer Jesus*, pp. 214–19.

260. See Roloff, "Anfänge der soteriologischen Deutung des Todes Jesu," p. 63.
261. See Büchsel, *TDNT*, 4: 340.
262. See Hill, *Greek Words and Hebrew Meanings* (Cambridge, 1967), p. 61.
263. See Hooker, *The Son of Man in Mark* (London, 1967), p. 144, and *Jesus and the Servant* (London, 1959), p. 76. Hill has expressed a similar point of view (see *Greek Words and Hebrew Meanings*, p. 81).
264. So says Hill, *Greek Words and Hebrew Meanings*, p. 81.
265. So says Pesch, *Das Markusevangelium*, 2: 164.
266. Jeremias, *New Testament Theology*, 1: 291.
267. Barrett, "The Background of Mk. 10.45," in *New Testament Essays*, Festschrift for T. W. Manson, ed. A. J. B. Higgins (Manchester, 1959), p. 7.
268. See Pesch, *Das Markusevangelium*, 2: 163–64.
269. See Patsch, *Abendmahl und historischer Jesus*, p. 178.
270. Such is the reading of Codex D (Bezae). Another variant—"and if they persecute you out of this city, flee to the next"—is found in Codex θ (Koridethi) and other representatives of the Caesarean text and in Origen.
271. See Metzger, *A Textual Commentary on the Greek New Testament*, p. 28.
272. Bauer, *A Greek-English Lexicon of the New Testament and Other Early Christian Literature*, rev. by F. W. Gingrich and F. W. Danker, 2d ed. (Chicago, 1958), p. 810.
273. Bonnard, *L'Évangile selon Saint Matthieu*, p. 149.
274. See, for example, Polag: "The wording of the saying offers no point of contact for maintaining that the saying has been taken by Matthew from a mission context" (*Die Christologie der Logienquelle*, p. 98n.305).
275. See, for example, A. H. McNeile, *The Gospel according to St. Matthew* (London, 1915), p. 142; cf. Strecker, *Der Weg der Gerechtigkeit*, p. 42n.2.
276. See Schürmann, "Zur Traditions- und Redaktionsgeschichte von Mt 10, 23," *BZ* 3 (1959): 82–88.
277. Schürmann cites a letter he received from Vielhauer in which Vielhauer stated that "The origin of Matthew 10:23 from Q you have made very probable. . . . I am now convinced by it" (*Traditionsgeschichtliche Untersuchungen zu der synoptischen Evangelien*, p. 150); Schnackenburg states his position in *God's Rule and Kingdom*, p. 204.
278. Vielhauer, "Gottesreich und Menschensohn," p. 59.
279. Kunzi, *Das Naherwartungslogion Matthäus 10.23: Geschichte seiner Auslegung*, Beiträge zur Geschichte der Biblischen Exegese, nr. 9 (Tübingen, 1970).
280. Among those holding this view are Ephraem Syrus (*Commentary on Tatian's Diatessaron*, ad loc.), Thomas Aquinas (*Matt. Evang. expositio*), and Barth (*Church Dogmatics*, 5 vols., ed. G. W. Bromiley and T. F. Torrance, trans. H. Knight et al. [Edinburgh, 1955–77], 3/2: *The Doctrine of Creation*, pp. 499–500).
281. Among those holding this view are Calvin (*Commentary on the Harmony of the Gospels*, ad loc.) and Grotius (*Annotationes in quatuor Evangelia et Acta Apostolorum* [Basileae, 1732], pp. 111–12).
282. This view has appealed especially to British writers, including the following: A. B. Bruce (in *The Expositor's Greek Testament*, 5 vols., ed. W. R. Nicoll [London, 1901], 1: 164), A. H. Curtis (*The Vision and Mission of Jesus* [Edinburgh, 1954], p. 171), and R. V. G. Tasker (*The Gospel according to St. Matthew* [London, 1961], p. 109).
283. Among those holding this view are Bucer (*In sacra quatuor Evangelia enarr. perpetuae* [Basileae, 1536], p. 270), Lagrange (*L'Évangile selon Saint Matthieu*, Études Bibliques [Paris, 1923], pp. 204–5), J. A. T. Robinson (*Jesus and His Coming* [London, 1957], pp. 76, 80, 91), and A. Feuillet ("Le sens du mot Parousie dans l'Évangile de Matthieu," in *The Background of the New Testament and Its Eschatology*, Festschrift for C. H. Dodd, ed. W. D. Davies and D. Daube [Cambridge, 1956], pp. 262–72).
284. For this view, see Chrysostom (*Comm. in Matt. evang.*, homs. 34–35), Eras-

mus, *Novum Testamentum Annotationes* [Basileae, 1527], p. 45), Bengel (*Gnomon*, 1: 238, 245), and A. T. Cadoux (*The Theology of Jesus* [London, 1940], pp. 192–93).

285. See, for example, Hilary, *Evang. Matt. comm.* 10, 14; Augustine, *Contra Gaudentium Donatistarum episcopum*, 1, 18; and Luther, *Annotationes in aliquot capita Matthaei*.

286. Schweitzer, *The Quest of the Historical Jesus* (London, 1910), p. 369. For comment on Matthew 10, see pp. 357–58, 361.

287. Schweitzer, *The Quest of the Historical Jesus*, p. 358.

288. It is well known that Schweitzer hit upon his understanding of Matthew 10:23 during a year of military service prior to commencing theological studies. Holtzmann's contention that Matthew 10 is a composition of the evangelist's seemed to Schweizer too easy an explanation of an embarrassing text and so he rejected it.

289. Schlatter, *Der Evangelist Matthäus*, p. 342.

290. Schlatter, *Die Geschichte des Christus* (Stuttgart, 1923), p. 481.

291. See Zahn, *Das Evangelium des Matthäus* (Leipzig, 1913), pp. 405ff.

292. See Kümmel, *Promise and Fulfilment*, pp. 61–64; see also his essay "Eschatological Expectation in the Proclamation of Jesus," in *The Future of Our Religious Past: Essays in Honour of R. Bultmann*, ed. J. M. Robinson (London, 1971), p. 46.

293. Schniewind, *Das Evangelium nach Matthäus*, p. 131. Among those scholars putting forth interpretations similar to that of Schniewind are F. Fluckiger (*Der Ursprung des christlichen Dogmas: Eine Auseinandersetzung mit Albert Schweitzer und Martin Werner* [Zürich, 1955], pp. 25–26), A. L. Moore (*The Parousia in the New Testament*, Supplements to the Novum Testamentum 13 [Leiden, 1966], p. 145), F. Busch (*Zum Verständnis der synoptischen Eschatologie: Markus 13 neu Untersucht* [Gütersloh, 1938], p. 135), D. Bosch (*Die Heidenmission in der Zukunftsschau Jesu*, Abhandlungen zur Theologie des Alten und Neuen Testaments, nr. 36 [Zürich, 1959], pp. 156–57), and Bonnard (*L'Évangile selon Saint Matthieu*, p. 149).

294. The work in question is Werner's *Die Entstehung des christlichen Dogmas* (Bern, 1942; 2d ed. 1954). The English translation, *The Formation of Christian Dogma* (London, 1957), abbreviates the work and omits Werner's discussion of Matthew 10.

295. See Michaelis's essay in *Die grosse Enttäuschung* (Kirchenfreund, 1942), 226ff., republished separately under the title *Irrefuhrung der Gemeinden?* (1942).

296. *Das Evangelium nach Matthäus*, 2 vols. (Zürich, 1948–49), 2: 93–96.

297. Among those holding this view are B. H. Streeter ("Synoptic Criticism and the Eschatological Problem," in *Oxford Studies in the Synoptic Problem*, ed. W. Sanday [Oxford, 1911], p. 429n.1); and *The Four Gospels: A Study of Origins* [London, 1926], p. 255), Bultmann (*HST*, p. 122), Klostermann (*Das Matthäusevangelium*, p. 86), T. W. Manson (*The Teaching of Jesus*, pp. 221–22), E. Grässer, *Das Problem der Parusieverzögerung in den synoptischen Evangelien und in der Apostelgeschichte*, Beihefte zur ZNW, nr. 22 [Berlin, 1957], pp. 137–38), Tödt (*The Son of Man in the Synoptic Tradition*, p. 61), Higgins (*Jesus and the Son of Man*, pp. 100–104), and Hahn (*Mission in the New Testament* [London, 1965], pp. 55–56).

298. Among those holding this view are T. Colani (*Jésus Christ et les croyances messianiques de son temps* [Stuttgart, 1864], p. 186), T. F. Glasson (*The Second Advent: The Origin of the New Testament Doctrine*, 3d ed. [London, 1963], pp. 103–4), Jüngel (*Paulus und Jesus*, pp. 237–38), Vögtle ("Exegetische Erwägungen über das Wissen und Selbstbewusstsein Jesu," in *Gott in Welt*, Festschrift for K. Rahner [Freiburg, 1964], 1: 650), E. Linnemann (*Die Gleichnisse Jesu* [Göttingen, 1962], pp. 138–39), and Hahn (*Mission in the New Testament*, pp. 56–57).

299. See, for example, Käsemann, *New Testament Questions of Today*, pp. 105–6; and Vielhauer, "Gottesreich und Menschensohn in der Verkündigung Jesu," p. 66; see also A. N. Wilder, *Eschatology and Ethics in the Teaching of Jesus*, rev. ed. (New York, 1950), p. 39.

300. See G. D. Kilpatrick, *The Origins of the Gospel according to St. Matthew* (Oxford, 1946), p. 16.

301. See Schürmann, *Traditionsgeschichtliche Untersuchungen zu der synoptischen Evangelien*, p. 150n.2.

302. See Jeremias, *Jesus' Promise to the Nations*, trans. S. H. Hooke, Studies in Biblical Theology, no. 24 (London, 1958), especially pp. 25ff., 46ff., and 51ff. The whole book is an invaluable discussion of the subject.

303. See Jeremias, *Jesus' Promise to the Nations*, pp. 56–62.

304. On this, see Goppelt, *Christentum und Judentum im ersten und zweiten Jahrhundert* (Gütersloh, 1954), pp. 180ff.

305. See Cranfield, *The Gospel according to St. Mark*, p. 283.

306. See Taylor, *The Gospel according to St. Mark*, p. 384.

307. See Borsch, *The Son of Man in Myth and History*, pp. 358n.1, 380; and *The Christian and Gnostic Son of Man*, p. 19.

308. See Burney, *The Poetry of Our Lord* (Oxford, 1925), p. 142. Burney observes that the Kina rhythm in the Matthew passage requires the term "holy" (angels), which he says must have been adopted from Mark.

309. See Tödt, *The Son of Man in the Synoptic Tradition*, pp. 41–42.

310. See Horstmann, *Studien zur markinischen Christologie: Mark 8.27–9.13 als Zugang zum Christusbild des zweiten Evangeliums*, Neutestamentliche Abhandlungen, nr. 6 (Münster, 1969), pp. 41ff. For analyses in a similar vein, see Tödt, *The Son of Man in the Synoptic Tradition*, pp. 44ff.; Jüngel, *Paulus and Jesus*, p. 259; Higgins, *Jesus and the Son of Man*, p. 59; Schürmann, *Das Lukasevangelium*, pp. 549–50; and Pesch, *Das Markusevangelium*, 2: 64–65.

311. Among those holding this view are Hauck (*TDNT*, 4: 734) and Grundmann (*Das Evangelium nach Markus*, p. 177).

312. See Kümmel, *Jesus und der Menschensohn*, pp. 213, 216.

313. The list of those who do so includes the following: C. H. Dodd (*The Parables of the Kingdom*, pp. 93ff.), Glasson (*The Second Advent*, p. 750), Taylor (*The Gospel according to St. Mark*, pp. 383–84), J. A. T. Robinson (*Jesus and His Coming*, pp. 53ff.), Colpe (*TDNT*, 8: 456), Perrin (*Rediscovering the Teaching of Jesus*, pp. 185ff.), Tödt (*The Son of Man in the Synoptic Tradition*, p. 44), Horstmann (*Studien zur Markinischen Christologie*, p. 50), and Schürmann (*Das Lukasevangelium*, pp. 549–50).

314. See Streeter, "Synoptic Criticism and the Eschatological Problem," p. 429.

315. See Pesch, *Das Markusevangelium*, 2: 65.

316. Tödt, *The Son of Man in the Synoptic Tradition*, p. 45.

317. Horstmann, *Studien zur Markinischen Christologie*, p. 47; J. A. T. Robinson holds a similar point of view (see *Jesus and His Coming*, pp. 55–56).

318. Robinson, *Jesus and His Coming*, pp. 54–55. Cf. Pesch, *Das Markusevangelium*, 2: 65. Kümmel also contends that the representation of the Son of Man as the Son of God must be a Christian addition, but he maintains that it came about through the intrusion of a reference to "my Father" in an otherwise authentic saying of Jesus (see *Jesus und der Menschensohn*, p. 219).

319. See, for example, Glasson, *The Second Advent*, p. 75; and J. A. T. Robinson, *Jesus and His Coming*, p. 54.

320. Among those holding that this is the case are H. B. Sharman (*The Teaching of Jesus about the Future according to the Synoptic Gospels* [Chicago, 1909], pp. 83–85), Colpe (*TDNT*, 8: 435–36), Bammel (*Erwägungen zur Eschatologie Jesu*, Texte und Untersuchungen nr. 88 [Berlin, 1964], p. 24), Jeremias (*New Testament Theology*, 1: 273–74), O. Michel (in *Theologisches Begriffslexikon zum Neuen Testament*, ed. L. Coenen, E. Beyreuther, and H. Bietenhard, 3 vols. [Wuppertal, 1967–71], 3: 1162), and, with some hesitation, I. H. Marshall (*Luke: Historian and Theologian*, p. 850).

321. Traditional concepts of theophany may well have contributed, along with Daniel 7:9ff., to the formation of this element in parousia concepts; see Deuteronomy

33:2 and Zechariah 14:5, and observe the application of 1 Enoch 1:9 (the coming of God with ten thousands of his holy ones) to the Lord Christ in Jude 14–15.

322. This applies to Luke 12:8–9 as well as to Mark 8:38. Bornkamm states that in the Lukan saying, denial serves the same function as the "shame" of Mark 8:38: it is a periphrasis for judicial condemnation by the Son of Man (see *Geschichte und Glaube*, Beiträge zur evangelischen Theologie, 48 [München, 1968], pp. 34–35). Operating on the assumption that Luke's passive "shall be denied" is authentic, A. J. B. Higgins (*Jesus und der Menschensohn*, pp. 119–20) and F. Hahn (*Titles of Jesus*, pp. 30–31) maintain that the verb must denote the action of God *and* the action of the Son of Man. Says Higgins, "The Son of Man is participant in the judge's role as one who sits at the side or in the presence of God the highest Judge, who alone has the right to utter judgment over those who have denied Jesus in his work on earth. It is not necessary to distinguish too strictly between the Son of Man as witness and judge." Such is also the contention of Colpe (*TDNT*, 8: 447), Kümmel (*Jesus und der Menschensohn*, p. 220), and Polag (*Die Christologie der Logienquelle*, p. 99).

323. Note especially John 5:21–29, and 1 Thessalonians 1:10, an early kerygmatic fragment that similarly equates the Son of God with the Son of Man. See also Schweizer, *TDNT*, 8: 370, and pp. 335–36 herein.

324. Lietzmann, "Der Prozess Jesu," in *Sitzungsberichte der Preussischen Akadamie der Wissenschaft* (Berlin, 1934), pp. 313–22.

325. Lietzmann, *Geschichte der Alten Kirche*, 4 vols. (Berlin, 1937), 1: 50.

326. Lietzmann's first four points are (1) that there is no source of information concerning the Sanhedrin trial that makes it credible; (2) that the threat against the temple in Mark 14:58 cannot be reconciled with Jesus' cleansing of the temple; (3) that the High Priest's question in Mark 14:62 is not characteristically Jewish—"Son of God" was not a messianic title; and (4) that the Jews would not have held a confession to be the Messiah (as in Mark 14:62) to be a blasphemy. In response, I would suggest (1) that if the Jews had condemned Jesus and handed him over to the Romans, the news would have gone round Jerusalem "like wildfire" (see W. Weiffenbach, *Der Wiederkunftsgedanke Jesu* [Leipzig, 1893], p. 206; and Jeremias, *New Testament Theology*, 1: 267n.7); (2) that the citation of Jeremiah 7:11 in Mark 11:17 indicates that the cleansing of the temple was an act of prophetic symbolism embodying warning and threat, in harmony with Mark 14:58 and other sayings of Jesus on the temple (e.g., Mark 13:2); (3) that there is a good deal of evidence that the expression *Son of God* was indeed understood to be a messianic title among the Jews (H. Braun states that the title was "simply Jewish" in *Qumran und das Neue Testament*, 2 vols. [Tübingen, 1966], 1: 76; see also M. Hengel, *The Son of God: The Origin of Christology and the History of Jewish-Hellenistic Religion* [Philadelphia, 1976], pp. 41–56); and (4) that it is correct that the claim to be Messiah was not technically blasphemous, but this is not to the point; it was the further definition of Jesus' reply to the High Priest that proved offensive to the Jewish leaders. In saying "I am," Jesus was saying that he would be *seated at the right hand of God, coming in the clouds of theophany*, and by implication he was saying that he would be coming as *judge of the High Priest and his court*. For more on this, see Dalman, *The Words of Jesus*, pp. 313–14, and *Der Gottesname Adonaj und seine Geschichte* (Berlin, 1889), pp. 44–45; Strack–Billerbeck, *Kommentar zum Neuen Testament aus Talmud und Midrasch*, 1: 1017; J. Blinzler, *Der Prozess Jesu*, 3d ed. (Regensburg, 1960), p. 155; K. Berger, "Die königlichen Messiastraditionen des Neuen Testaments," *NTS* 20 (1973): 19; and Pesch, *Das Markusevangelium*, 2: 440.

327. See Juster, *Les juifs dans l'empire romaine* (Paris, 1914), pp. 132–42.

328. See Blinzler, *Der Prozess Jesu*, 4th ed. (Regensburg, 1969), pp. 229–44.

329. In addition to Blinzler's *Der Prozess Jesu*, see Sherwin-White's *Roman Society and Roman Law in the New Testament* (Oxford, 1963) and *The Trial of Christ: Historicity and Chronology in the New Testament*, SPCK Theological Collections no. 6 (London, 1965); and see Catchpole's *The Trial of Jesus* (Leiden, 1972).

330. Pesch, *Das Markusevangelium*, 2: 418.

331. Says Berger, "From the form-critical point of view the scene in Mk. 14.61–3 concurs with the confession scenes in the martyrdoms" ("Die königlichen Messiastraditionen des Neuen Testaments," p. 19).

332. See Pesch, "Die Passion des Menschensohnes," in *Jesus und der Menschensohn*, p. 185.

333. Such is the contention of H. Gunkel: "The oracle, shorn of its fantastic imagery, proclaims that to the king comes the highest honour next to Yahweh himself, and that he will overcome and humble the many enemies which now press on him" (*Die Psalmen*, 5th ed. [Göttingen, 1962], p. 482). For a similar point of view, see W. O. E. Oesterley, *The Psalms*, 2 vols. (London, 1939–54), 2: 462–63.

334. Donahue, *Are You the Christ? The Trial Narrative in the Gospel of Mark*, Society of Biblical Literature Dissertation Series, no. 10 (Cambridge, Mass., 1973), pp. 173–74.

335. The speculation concerning the destiny of the martyrs in a passage such as Testament of Job 33:2ff., for example, may well have been influenced by Psalm 110:1. For the use made of Psalm 110:1 throughout Jewish literature, see D. M. Hay, *Glory at the Right Hand: Psalm 110 in Early Christianity*, Society of Biblical Literature Monograph Series, no. 18 (New York, 1973), pp. 22–33, 52–56.

336. N. Perrin is a key proponent of this view; see "Mark XIV.62: The End Product of a Christian Pesher Tradition?" *NTS* 12 (1965–66): 150–55; *Rediscovering the Teaching of Jesus*, 173–85; and *A Modern Pilgrimage in New Testament Christology*, pp. 10–23.

337. See Neugebauer, "Die Davidssohnfrage (Mark xii.35–7 parr.) und der Menschensohn," *NTS* 21 (1974): 81–108. Hay also provides an excellent review of the treatment of Psalm 110:1 in contemporary Jewish thought, in the teaching of Jesus, and in the primitive church (see *Glory at the Right Hand*).

338. See Borsch, "Mark xiv.62 and I Enoch lxii.5," *NTS* 14 (1968): 556–57.

339. *Midrash on Psalms*, trans. W. G. Braude, 2 vols., Yale Judaica Series, no. 13 (New Haven, 1959), 1: 40.

340. On the significance of the Midrash for Mark 14:62, see J. D. M. Derrett, *Law in the New Testament* (London, 1970), pp. 223, 424; and Lane, *The Gospel of Mark*, p. 536.

341. Glasson, "The Reply to Caiaphas (Mark xiv.62)," *NTS* 7 (1960): 91; see also *The Second Advent*, pp. 64–65; and *His Appearing and His Kingdom* (London, 1953), p. 3.

342. Robinson, *Jesus and His Coming*, p. 45.

343. Robinson, *Jesus and His Coming*, p. 51.

344. Too much has been read into this Semitic idiom. Catchpole is surely right in stating that "*su eipas* means 'Yes,' modified only by the implication that more is needed for a complete understanding of Jesus, which indeed the kingly Son of Man saying immediately provides" ("The Answer of Jesus to Caiaphas (Matt. XXVI:64)," *NTS* 17 [1971]: 221). In view of the discussions on this point, Bultmann's comment is noteworthy: "The Rabbinic example given by [Schlatter] and [Strack-Billerbeck] I 990 on Mt. 26.25, and the comparison of Mt. 26.64 with Mk. 14.62, show that the *su* does not need to be stressed, as if the sense were: "*You* say that," and the responsibility for the assertion were pushed on to the questioner (contrary to [Blass-Debrunner] §441 3). Apart from [John 18:36], where the question is indeed factually affirmed, the continuation shows that in Jn. 18.37 *su legeis* = 'Yes,' for the continuation becomes senseless if one attempts to understand it otherwise" (*The Gospel of John*, p. 654n.6). A number of scholars suggest that Mark's text originally read *su eipas*—among them Lohmeyer (*Das Evangelium des Markus*, 328n.2), Taylor (*The Gospel according to St. Mark*, p. 568), Hooker (*The Son of Man in Mark*, p. 164n.5), and D. E. Nineham (*St. Mark*, Pelican Gospel Commentary [London, 1963], p. 408)—but this is implausible; its presence in the Caesarean text (*su eipas hoti ego eimi*) is surely a clear instance of assimilation to Matthew (see Blinzler, *Der Prozess Jesu*, p. 112n.51; Catchpole, "The Answer of Jesus to Caiaphas [Matt. XXVI:64]," p. 220; and Anderson, *The Gospel of Mark*, p. 331).

345. Glasson supports the contention that Matthew and Luke worked from an unmodified version of Mark as we now know it, noting that the Sinaitic Syriac in Mark has the same phrase for *ap' arti* = *apo tou nun* as it has in Matthew and Luke (see *The Second Advent*, p. 66). Glasson acknowledges his debt to B. H. Streeter for this insight (*The Four Gospels*, p. 321), and Streeter in turn acknowledges his debt to Sir John Hawkins for the observation. The suggestion has not commended itself to expositors generally.

346. Among those who do hold to this view are Colpe (*TDNT*, 8: 435) and Jeremias (*New Testament Theology*, 1: 273).

347. See Jeremias, *New Testament Theology*, p. 274.

348. See Müller, in *Jesus und der Menschensohn*, p. 45.

349. Traub, *TDNT*, 5: 522.

350. Vermes, *Jesus the Jew*, p. 187. See also pp. 171–72, 185.

351. Among those who hold this point of view are Kümmel (*Promise and Fulfilment*, p. 65), J. E. Fison (*The Christian Hope: The Presence and the Parousia* [London, 1954], p. 192), Cadoux (*The Historic Mission of Jesus*, p. 293), Moore (*The Parousia in the New Testament*, pp. 105–6), and Borsch ("Mark xiv.62 and 1 Enoch lxii.5," p. 565).

352. B. T. D. Smith, *The Gospel According to St. Matthew* (Cambridge, 1927), p. 203. Among those holding similar points of view are W. C. Allen (*A Critical and Exegetical Commentary on the Gospel according to St. Matthew*, p. 284), J. C. Fenton (*Saint Matthew*, Pelican Gospel Commentaries [London, 1963], p. 428), Grässer (*Das Problem der Parusieverzögerung*, p. 176), Tödt (*The Son of Man in the Synoptic Tradition*, p. 84), and Schweizer (*The Good News according to Matthew*, p. 499).

353. Hay, *Glory at the Right Hand*, p. 68.

354. See Genesis 46:30: "kai eipen Israel pros Ioseph, Apothanoumai apo tou nun, epeide heoraka to prosopon sou. . . ." And Tobit 11:9, in which Hannah says to Tobit, "Eidon se, paidion, apo tou nun apothanoumai."

355. Trilling, *Das Wahre Israel: Studien zur Theologie des Matthäus-Evangeliums*, 3d ed., Studien zum Alten und Neuen Testament, nr. 10 (München, 1969), pp. 86–87.

356. Trilling, *Das Wahre Israel*, p. 86. Presumably Wellhausen had some such understanding in mind when he rendered the meaning of the saying as "From now on you will see me only as manifest Messiah" (*Das Evangelium Matthaei*, pp. 141–42). J. Weiss's paraphrase is clearer: "From now on you have nothing more to expect than . . ." (*Die Schriften des Neuen Testaments* [Göttingen, 1917], 1: 393). In essential agreement with Trilling are H. Frankemölle (*Jahwebund und Kirche Christi*, Neutestamentliche Abhandlungen, Band 10 [Münster, 1973], p. 356) and R. Walker (*Die Heilsgeschichte im ersten Evangelium*, Forschungen zur Religion und Literatur des Alten und Neuen Testaments, nr. 91 [Göttingen, 1967], p. 70).

357. Such is the contention of Hay, *Glory at the Right Hand*, p. 69.

358. Such is the reading of Stählin, *TDNT*, 4: 1113. It is important to observe that in making this interpretation, Stählin saw the *apo tou nun* as a paradoxical anticipation of Jesus' glorification and coming again, as his entire statement makes plain.

359. J. Zmijewski, *Die Eschatologiereden des Lukas-Evangeliums: Ein traditions- und redaktionsgeschichtliche Untersuchung zu Lk. 21.5–36 und Lk. 17.20–37*, Bonner Biblische Beiträge, nr. 40 (Bonn, 1972), pp. 248–49. See also H. Flender, *St. Luke: Theologian of Redemptive History* (London, 1967), pp. 99ff.; and Marshall, *Luke: Historian and Theologian*, p. 850.

360. Vielhauer, "Erwägungen zur Christologie des Markusevangeliums," in *Zeit und Geschichte*, Festschrift for R. Bultmann, ed. E. Dinkler (Tübingen, 1964), pp. 160–61. Lambrecht is in agreement with Vielhauer on this point (see *Die Redaktion der Markus-Apokalypse: Literarische Analyse und Strukturuntersuchung*, Analecta Biblica 28 [Rome, 1967], p. 181n.1). See also Hay, *Glory at the Right Hand*, pp. 65–66.

361. See M. Plath, "Der neutestamentliche Weheruf über Jerusalem," *TSK* 78

(1905): 457. Burney holds that Matthew's version reflects a *kina* rhythm (see *The Poetry of Our Lord*, p. 146), a view with which Jeremias agrees (see *The Eucharistic Words of Jesus*, p. 259).

362. See Steck, *Israel und das gewaltsame Geschick der Propheten*, Wissenschaftliche Monographien zum Alten und Neuen Testament, nr. 39 (Neukirchen-Vluyn, 1967), pp. 47, 51ff.

363. See Plath, "Der neutestamentliche Weheruf über Jerusalem," pp. 458ff.

364. See Koch, *The Growth of the Biblical Tradition: The Form Critical Method* (New York, 1969), pp. 211–13.

365. See Polag, *Die Christologie der Logienquelle*, p. 93.

366. The phrase *ap' arti* ("from now on") is clearly attributable to Matthew's redactional activity, which serves to underscore the futurity of the event (see Matt. 26:29, 64).

367. Among those holding this view are Otto (*The Kingdom of God and the Son of Man*, p. 172) and Glasson (*The Second Advent*, p. 100). W. L. Knox assigns the saying to an early date in the ministry of Jesus, when Jesus wanted to go to Jerusalem but believed that he would not find a hearing; accordingly, he holds that the saying means "I will not visit you until you are prepared to receive me as coming in the name of the Lord" (*The Sources of the Synoptic Gospels*, 2 vols. [Cambridge, 1953–57], 2: 82).

368. See H. van der Kwaak, "Die Klage über Jerusalem (Matth. XXIII.37–39)," *Novum Testamentum* 8 (1966): 158–59.

369. Among those who endorse this negative interpretation of the saying are T. W. Manson (*The Sayings of Jesus*, p. 128), Gaston (*No Stone on Another: Studies of the Significance of the Fall of Jerusalem on the Synoptic Gospels*, Supplements to the Novum Testamentum, vol. 23 [Leiden, 1970], p. 455), Strecker (*Der Weg der Gerechtigkeit*, pp. 114–15), Trilling (*Das wahre Israel*, pp. 87–88), Hummel (*Die Auseinandersetzung zwischen Kirche und Judentum im Matthäusevangelium*, p. 142), Schulz (*Q—Die Spruchquelle der Evangelisten*, p. 358), and Polag (*Die Christologie der Logienquelle*, p. 94).

370. See Strack–Billerbeck, *Kommentar zum Neuen Testament aus Talmud und Midrasch*, 1: 850.

371. Says Jeremias, "Jesus is certain that the promise of God will be fulfilled and that even in the blind and obdurate city God will arouse a remnant which will greet the coming one, the returning one in the name of God" (*The Eucharistic Words of Jesus*, pp. 259–60). Those holding a similar view include Schlatter (*Der Evangelist Matthäus*, p. 691), Schniewind (*Das Evangelium nach Matthäus*, p. 237), Bonnard—hesitantly (*L'Évangile selon Saint Matthieu*, pp. 343–44), Kümmel (*Promise and Fulfilment*, p. 81), Grundmann—in the case of Luke but not Matthew (*Das Evangelium nach Lukas*, p. 290), and Marshall, who states that "The possibility . . . is a live one" (*Luke: Historian and Theologian*, p. 577).

372. Dodd points out that the only parabolic element in the pericope is the simile of the shepherd separating the sheep and the goats, and this is only a passing allusion; the sheep and the goats play no part in the main scene (*The Parables of the Kingdom*, p. 85n.1). For this reason Dodd does not treat the passage in his book, nor do most writers on the parables (e.g., B. T. D. Smith, Michaelis, C. W. F. Smith, Linneman, Crossan).

373. Preiss, *Life in Christ*, trans. H. Knight (Chicago, 1954), p. 46.

374. Preiss, *Life in Christ*, p. 46.

375. See Grundmann, *Das Evangelium nach Matthäus*, p. 46.

376. McNeile characterizes it as "a prophetic picture of the judgment" (*The Gospel according to St. Matthew*, p. 368), and Klostermann calls it "a homiletic delineation of the judgment of the world" (*Das Matthäusevangelium*, p. 204).

377. See Burkitt, *Jewish and Christian Apocalypses* (Oxford, 1914), pp. 22–25.

378. Among those holding this view are Dodd (*The Parables of the Kingdom*, p. 85n.1), T. W. Manson (*The Sayings of Jesus*, p. 249), Glasson (*The Second Advent*, pp.

129–30), Higgins (*Jesus and the Son of Man*, pp. 115–18), and Hill (*The Gospel of Matthew*, New Century Bible Commentary [Grand Rapids, 1972], p. 330).

379. See Robinson, "The 'Parable' of the Sheep and the Goats," *NTS* 2 (1956): 225–37. Robinson maintains that verse 31 is Matthaean and that Matthew's redaction can also be detected in verse 34 (especially with regard to the introduction of "the king" and "my Father"), and in verses 32, 34, 37, 40, 41, 46—the last saying in its entirety being added by the evangelist.

380. See H. Gressmann, *Altorientalische Texte und Bilder zum Alten Testament* (Berlin, 1926), 1: 186–89. For references to Parsee parallels, see Bultmann, *HST*, p. 124; and Klostermann, *Das Matthäusevangelium*, p. 206.

381. Cited in Strack–Billerbeck, *Kommentar zum Neuen Testament aus Talmud und Midrasch*, 4/1: 561.

382. Cited in Strack–Billerbeck, *Kommentar zum Neuen Testament aus Talmud und Midrasch*, 4/1: 1212.

384. See Bultmann, *HST*, pp. 123–24.

384. Among those holding to this restricted view are Wellhausen (*Das Evangelium Matthei*, 134–35), Bonnard (*L'Évangile selon Saint Matthieu*, p. 367), and Hill (*The Gospel of Matthew*, p. 330).

385. See T. W. Manson, *The Sayings of Jesus*, pp. 249–51. Those who accept Manson's interpretation include G. E. Ladd (*A Theology of the New Testament* [Grand Rapids, 1974], pp. 118–19), J. R. Michaels ("Apostolic Hardship and Righteous Gentiles: A Study of Matthew 25:31–46," *JBL* 84 [1965]: 27–37), and W. D. Davies (*The Setting of the Sermon on the Mount* [Cambridge, 1964], p. 98). The position was anticipated by Sharman: "The whole paragraph seems to be a form of appeal for the favorable reception and the benevolent treatment of the itinerant propagandists of the faith in the early age of the Church" (*The Teaching of Jesus about the Future*, p. 242).

386. See Jeremias, *The Parables of Jesus*, p. 209.

387. So says Braun, *Spätjüdisch-häretischer und frühchristlicher Radikalismus*, 2 vols. (Tübingen, 1957), 1: 94n.2.

388. On this see Jeremias, "Die Salbungsgeschichte," in *Abba* (Göttingen, 1966), pp. 110–14.

389. See Tödt, *The Son of Man in the Synoptic Tradition*, pp. 74–77.

390. Cf. Schlatter: "Neither the one group nor the other has acted with eyes on Jesus (a parallel to *eis onoma mathetou*, 10.42, is lacking here). . . . That which love does is here deliberately freed from all particular presuppositions. Only acts are mentioned which lie in the range of each one, for which no theological instruction is needed" (*Der Evangelist Matthäus*, p. 726).

391. See Preiss, *Life in Christ*, pp. 50–58.

392. The implications of verses 34–36 for soteriology are considerable. As Schlatter has written, "By the fact that Jesus speaks with men not of their sins but only of their good works, he reveals himself as the one who has procured forgiveness for all. On this the saying is founded which leads those also, who did not know him, into his Kingdom" (*Der Evangelist Matthäus*, p. 726). This, I believe, is the inspiration for Jeremias's comment that "for them justification is available on the ground of love, since *for them also the ransom has been paid*" (*The Parables of Jesus*, p. 210).

Chapter 14

1. The origin and composition of Luke 22:28–30 // Matthew 19:28 is a disputed matter; I believe there is reason to assign the *common* element of the passages to an earlier period than the Last Supper.

2. On this, see B. Rigaux, "La petite apocalypse de Luc (XVII, 22–37)," in *Ecclesia a Spiritu Sancto edocta Lumen Gentium*, Mélanges théologiques à G. Philips 53 (Gembloux, 1970), pp. 408–9; and J. Zmijewski, *Die Eschatologiereden des Lukas-Evangeliums: Ein*

traditions- und redaktionsgeschichtliche Untersuchung zu Lk. 21.5–36 und Lk. 17.20–37, Bonner Biblische Beiträge, nr. 40 (Bonn, 1972), p. 398.

3. The phrase "in his day" is omitted by P75 B D it sah, but included by the majority of critics; the idea is not affected by the omission.

4. Such is the contention of Higgins (*Jesus and the Son of Man* [London, 1964], pp. 88–90), Tödt (*The Son of Man in the Synoptic Tradition* [London, 1965], pp. 51–52), and Rigaux ("La petite apocalypse de Luc [XVII, 22–37]," p. 436).

5. Such is the contention of C. H. Dodd (*The Parables of the Kingdom* [London, 1935], p. 81n.31) and Colpe (*TDNT*, 5: 458n.396).

6. See Rigaux, "La petite apocalypse de Luc (XVII, 22–37)," p. 409.

7. Such is the contention of Flender (*St. Luke: Theologian of Redemptive History* [London, 1967], pp. 94ff.), who is followed by Zmijewski (*Die Eschatologiereden des Lukas-Evangeliums*, pp. 400–403).

8. See Strack–Billerbeck, *Kommentar zum Neuen Testament aus Talmud und Midrasch*, 6 vols. (München, 1922–28), 2: 237, 4/2: 826ff.; and Jeremias, *New Testament Theology*, vol. 1, *The Proclamation of Jesus*, trans. J. S. Bowden (London, 1971), p. 261.

9. See Rigaux, "La petite apocalypse de Luc (XVII, 22–37)," p. 412.

10. See Schnackenburg, "Der eschatologische Abschnitt Lk 17.20–37," in *Mélanges bibliques: Festschrift for B. Rigaux*, ed. A. Descamps and R. P. Andre de Halleux (Gembloux, 1970), p. 222.

11. This is clearly observable in 1 Thessalonians 5:1ff. (cf. Rev. 16:15). It is evident that Matthew was not conscious of an undue tension in his setting the Q apocalypse within the context of the Markan eschatological discourse (see Matt. 24:26ff., 37ff.).

12. In contrast to Schnackenburg, Rigaux sets to Luke's redaction the *reduction* of premonitory signs to a simple mention of the distress of the times (v. 22) and to a mere allusion to the activity of false prophets by a repetition in verse 23a of verse 20b ("La petite apocalypse de Luc [XVII, 22–37]," p. 433).

13. See Schulz, *Q—Die Spruchquelle der Evangelisten* (Zürich, 1972), p. 278.

14. Such is the contention of J. Lambrecht (*Die Redaktion des Markus-Apokalypse: Literarische Analyse und Strukturuntersuchung*, Analecta Biblica 28 [Rome, 1967], p. 101), Schulz (*Q—Die Spruchquelle der Evangelisten*, p. 278), Zmijewski (*Die Eschatologiereden des Lukas-Evangeliums*, pp. 410–11), and Marshall (*Luke: Historian and Theologian* [Exeter, 1970], p. 659). Dissenting from this consensus are Schnackenburg ("Der eschatologische Abschnitt Lk 17.20–37," p. 220) and Rigaux ("La petite apocalypse de Luc [XVII, 22–37]," p. 416).

15. In Midrash Ruth 2:14 (132b) it is stated: "As the first redeemer (i.e. Moses) acted, so will the last redeemer act. As the first redeemer manifested himself and then hid again from them . . . so the last redeemer will manifest himself to them and again hide himself from them. . . . Whither will he lead them? Out of the land to the wilderness of Judah, Hos. 2.16, 'See, I will allure them and will lead them into the wilderness'" (Strack–Billerbeck, *Kommentar zum Neuen Testament aus Talmud and Midrasch*, 1:86–87).

16. See Klostermann, *Das Matthäusevangelium*, Handbuch zum Neuen Testament (Tübingen, 1927), p. 194. Klostermann is followed by Tödt (*The Son of Man in the Synoptic Tradition*, p. 49) and Schulz (*Q—Die Spruchquelle der Evangelisten*, pp. 283–84).

17. See Zmijewski, *Die Eschatologiereden des Lukas-Evangeliums*, pp. 404ff. Cf. Jeremias, *The Parables of Jesus*, trans. S. H. Hooke, rev. ed. (London, 1963), p. 221.

18. Schulz, *Q—Die Spruchquelle der Evangelisten*, p. 284. See also Colpe, who adds: "This thought, which plainly sets aside the idea of a political Messiah in favor of a heavenly bringer of salvation, constitutes a decisive argument for the authenticity of the saying" (*TDNT*, 8: 433); for similar statements, see Bultmann, *HST*, p. 163; Tödt, *The Son of Man in the Synoptic Tradition*, p. 206; and Lührmann, *Die Redaktion der Logienquelle*, Wissenschaftliche Monographien zum Alten und Neuen Testament, Band 33 (Neukirchen-Vluyn, 1969), p. 73.

19. Among those holding this view is Kümmel (*Promise and Fulfilment: The Eschatological Message of Jesus*, Studies in Biblical Theology, no. 23 [London, 1961], pp. 70–71).

20. Among those holding this view are Higgins (*Jesus and the Son of Man*, pp. 78–79), Schmid (*Das Evangelium nach Lukas*, Regensburger Neuen Testament [Regensburg, 1960], p. 276), Leaney (*The Gospel according to St. Luke*, Black's New Testament Commentaries [London, 1958], p. 231), Schnackenburg ("Der eschatologische Abschnitt Lk 17.20–37," p. 222), and Rigaux ("La petite apocalypse de Luc [XVII, 22–37]," p. 417). Zmijewski prefers to view the saying as a mixture of texts, specifically Mark 8:31 and 9:12 and Luke 24:26, and hence as a purely Lukan redaction (see *Die Eschatologiereden des Lukas-Evangeliums*, p. 419).

21. See Bultmann, *Theology of the New Testament*, trans. K. Grobel, 2 vols. (London, 1951–55), 1: 30.

22. See Rigaux, "La petite apocalypse de Luc (XVII, 22–37)," p. 419.

23. See Schnackenburg, "Der eschatologische Abschnitt Lk 17.20–37," p. 222; and Zmijewski, *Die Eschatologiereden des Lukas-Evangeliums*, pp. 419–20.

24. Zmijewski, *Die Eschatologiereden des Lukas-Evangeliums*, p. 430.

25. Such is the contention of T. W. Manson (*The Sayings of Jesus* [London, 1949], p. 143), Schnackenburg ("Der eschatologische Abschnitt Lk 17.20–37," p. 223), Rigaux ("La petite apocalypse de Luc (XVII, 22–37)," p. 420), and Marshall (*Luke: Historian and Theologian*, p. 662). Bultmann suggests that the passage may have stood in a later redaction of Q that was unknown to Matthew (see *HST*, p. 117); Tödt agrees with Bultmann on this point (see *The Son of Man in the Synoptic Tradition*, p. 49).

26. Such is the contention of Colpe, *TDNT*, 8: 434n.257.

27. Such is the contention of Lührmann (*Die Redaktion der Logienquelle*, pp. 73–74, 82–83) and Schulz (*Q—Die Spruchquelle der Evangelisten*, pp. 279–80). See also Higgins, *Jesus and Son of Man*, p. 85; and Zmijewski, *Die Eschatologiereden des Lukas-Evangeliums*, pp. 449–56.

28. Lührmann provides an excursus on this theme in *Die Redaktion der Logienquelle*, pp. 78–83.

29. Among those making this assumption are Klostermann (*Das Lukasevangelium*, Handkommentar zum Neuen Testament [Tübingen, 1929], p. 539), Schlatter (*Das Evangelium des Lukas: Aus seinen Quellen erklärt*, 2d ed. [Stuttgart, 1960], p. 395), and Schmid (*Das Evangelium nach Lukas*, p. 276).

30. Among those making this assumption are Lührmann (*Die Redaktion der Logienquelle*, pp. 82–83) and Zmijewski (*Die Eschatologiereden des Lukas-Evangeliums*, p. 452).

31. Such is the contention of Colpe (*TDNT*, 8: 434n.257), Tödt (*The Son of Man in the Synoptic Tradition*, pp. 50, 224), Jeremias (*New Testament Theology*, 1: 263), Rigaux ("La petite apocalypse de Luc (XVII, 22–37)," pp. 421–22), and Marshall (*Luke: Historian and Theologian*, p. 663).

32. Schmid, *Das Evangelium nach Matthäus*, Regensburger Neues Testament (Regensburg, 1965), pp. 340–41.

33. See Tödt, *The Son of Man in the Synoptic Tradition*, pp. 50–51.

34. See Colpe, *TDNT*, 8: 434.

35. See Goppelt, *TDNT*, 6: 139–40.

36. Zmijewski, *Die Eschatologiereden des Lukas-Evangeliums*, pp. 433–34, 438–39.

37. Jeremias, *The Parables of Jesus*, p. 163.

38. See T. W. Manson, *The Sayings of Jesus*, pp. 144–45; Polag, *Die Christologie der Logienquelle* (Neukirchen-Vluyn, 1977), p. 100n.313; Marshall, *Luke: Historian and Theologian*, pp. 664–65; and Lambrecht, *Die Redaktion des Markus-Apokalypse*, p. 157.

39. Wisdom 10:7 tells of the five Cities "whose wickedness is still attested by a smoking waste, by plants whose fruit can never ripen, and a pillar of salt standing there as a memorial of an unbelieving soul."

40. It is generally agreed that Luke 17:36, which is contained in manuscripts of the Western Text (D, It, OS, and Diatessaron), assimilates the passage in Matthew 24:40 (see B. M. Metzger, *A Textual Commentary on the Greek New Testament* [London, 1971], p. 168).

41. Manson, *The Sayings of Jesus*, p. 146.

42. Among those who object to such a possibility is Klostermann (*Das Lukasevangelium*, p. 540); he is followed in this by Zmijewski (*Die Eschatologiereden des Lukas-Evangeliums*, pp. 491–92, 497–98).

43. Rigaux, "La petite apocalypse de Luc (XVII, 22–37)," p. 427.

44. See A. Strobel's exposition of this theme, "In dieser Nacht (Luk 17, 34)," *ZTK* 58 (1961): 16–29. In relation to this passage, Rigaux wrote, "It is temerarious to report on the New Testament, every time that the night is mentioned in an eschatological context, the traditions on the Passover and the night of the Passover" ("La petite apocalypse de Luc (XVII, 22–37)," p. 427).

45. Zmijewski, *Die Eschatologiereden des Lukas-Evangeliums*, p. 505.

46. See Schulz: "The covert passive manifestly stands here for the divine action of the Kurios Judge of the world" (*Q—Die Spruchquelle der Evangelisten*, p. 285).

47. Such is the contention of Schnackenburg ("Der eschatologische Abschnitt Lk 17.20–37," p. 225), Schulz (*Q—Die Spruchquelle der Evangelisten*, p. 280), Zmijewski (*Die Eschatologiereden des Lukas-Evangeliums*, p. 507), and Marshall (*Luke: Historian and Theologian*, p. 669).

48. See Rigaux, "La petite apocalypse de Luc (XVII, 22–37)," p. 430.

49. Tödt, *The Son of Man in the Synoptic Tradition*, p. 50.

50. Schlatter, *Der Evangelist Matthäus* (Stuttgart, 1948), p. 709.

51. See Schlatter, *Der Evangelist Matthäus*, p. 709.

52. Zmijewski, *Die Eschatologiereden des Lukas-Evangeliums*, pp. 515–16.

53. The notion that the discourse is determined by a consciousness of delay of the parousia that is maintained by such scholars as Conzelmann (*The Theology of St. Luke* [London, 1960], pp. 122–23) and Grässer (*Das Problem der Parusieverzögerung in den synoptischen Evangelien und in der Apostelgeschichte*, Beihefte zur ZNW, nr. 22 [Berlin, 1957], pp. 171–72) is unacceptable. There is no hint in the discourse of a far expectation. On the contrary, the spirit of the discourse is that of a "continuous orientation to the end." On this see Rigaux, "La petite apocalypse de Luc (XVII, 22–37)," pp. 432–35; and Zmijewski, *Die Eschatologiereden des Lukas-Evangeliums*, pp. 524, 539.

54. The reflections of the eschatological discourse in Paul's writings have been underestimated in recent years. A fresh examination of the evidence makes it appear highly probable to me that the following passages are linked:

Mark 13:5	2 Thess. 2:3a
Mark 13:6	2 Thess. 2:2, 9
Mark 13:7	2 Thess. 2:2
Mark 13:14	2 Thess. 2:3–4
Mark 13:22	2 Thess. 2:9
Mark 13:24–27	1 Thess. 4:15–17
Luke 21:34–36	1 Thess. 5:3, 6 and 2 Thess. 1:5

The following echoes are less certain but also noteworthy:

Mark 13:10	Rom. 11:25 and Col. 1:23
Mark 13:13	1 Thess. 5:9 and 2 Thess. 2:13
Mark 13:17	1 Cor. 7:28
Mark 13:19	1 Thess. 2:16 (cf. Luke 21:23b)
Mark 13:32	1 Thess. 5:1ff.
Mark 13:33ff.	1 Thess. 5:4ff.

In addition, Colossians 1:23–29, 2 Corinthians 4:5, and 2 Timothy 2:12–13 and 4:1–5 show viewpoints similar to those in Mark 13:9ff. without apparent citation.

55. I have observed that in endeavors to define this "little apocalypse," every verse within the chapter has been proposed for inclusion in it by one scholar or another, and every verse omitted from it; see *A Commentary on Mark Thirteen* (London, 1957), p. 10.

56. In addition to the fact that it is most unlikely that the Similitudes of Enoch were composed before the Christian era, it must be noted that they contain no reference to the parousia of the Son of Man like those in Daniel 7:13 and the gospels; he is simply described as seated on the throne of glory.

57. On this, see especially C. H. Dodd, "The 'Primitive Catechism' and the Sayings of Jesus," in *New Testament Essays: Studies in Memory of T. W. Manson* (Manchester, 1959) (revised in *More New Testament Studies* [Manchester, 1968], pp. 12ff.). See also P. Carrington, *The Primitive Christian Catechism* (Cambridge, 1940) and G. Bornkamm, "End Expectation and Church in Matthew," in *Tradition and Interpretation in Matthew*, by G. Bornkamm, G. Barth, and H. J. Held, trans. P. Scott, New Testament Library (London, 1963), pp. 15–51.

58. See D. A. Koch, "Zum Verhältnis von Christologie und Eschatologie im Markus-evangelium," in *Jesus Christus in Historie und Theologie*, Festschrift for H. Conzelmann, ed. G. Strecker (Tübingen, 1975), pp. 396ff., 408.

59. I believe this has been sufficiently demonstrated by Lambrecht in *Die Redaktion des Markus-Apokalypse*.

60. Lambrecht, *Die Redaktion des Markus-Apokalypse*, pp. 261–94; Pesch, *Naherwartungen: Tradition und Redaktion in Mk 13*, Kommentare und Beiträge zum Alten und Neuen Testament (Düsseldorf, 1968), pp. 74–82.

61. Among those holding this view are Colani (*Jésus Christ et les croyances messianiques* [Stuttgart, 1864], p. 180) and many later exegetes.

62. See Gaston, *No Stone on Another: Studies of the Significance of the Fall of Jerusalem in the Synoptic Gospels*, Supplements to the Novum Testamentum, vol. 23 (Leiden, 1970), pp. 126–28, 168–76.

63. Such is the contention of Lambrecht (*Die Redaktion des Markus-Apokalypse*, pp. 68–72) and Pesch (in *Naherwartungen*, pp. 84–86, although he qualified his position in *Das Markusevangelium*, 2 vols., Herders theologischer Kommentar zum Neuen Testament [Freiburg, 1976–77], 2: 269).

64. Such is the contention of Pesch in *Das Markusevangelium*, 2: 270. Note the earlier observation of K. L. Schmidt: "Here the announcement of place is firmly anchored in the saying itself" (*Der Rahmen der Geschichte Jesu* [Berlin, 1919], p. 290).

65. See Pesch, *Das Markusevangelium*, 2: 273–74.

66. See Ambrozic, *The Hidden Kingdom: A Redaction-Critical Study of the References to the Kingdom of God in Mark's Gospel*, Catholic Biblical Quarterly—Monograph Series, 2 (Washington, 1972), p. 225. See also Busch, *Zum Verständnis der synoptischen Eschatologie: Mark 13 neu Untersucht* (Gütersloh, 1938), p. 44; Marxsen, *Der Evangelist Markus: Studien zur Redaktionsgeschichte des Evangeliums* (Göttingen, 1959), p. 166; Lambrecht, *Die Redaktion des Markus-Apokalypse*, p. 227; and Pesch, *Naherwartungen*, pp. 79, 176.

67. Such is the understanding of most exegetes, including Schniewind (*Das Evangelium nach Markus*, Das Neue Testament Deutsch [Göttingen, 1944], p. 167), Cranfield (*The Gospel according to St. Mark*, 2d ed., Cambridge Greek Testament [Cambridge, 1963], p. 395), Schmid (*Das Evangelium nach Markus*, Regensburger Neues Testament [Regensburg, 1954], p. 188), Taylor (*The Gospel according to St. Mark*, Macmillan New Testament Commentaries [London, 1952], pp. 503–4), and Pesch (*Naherwartungen*, p. 111).

68. See W. Manson, *Christ's View of the Kingdom of God* (London, 1918), pp. 176–78; and Pesch, *Naherwartungen*, pp. 110–11.

69. See the discussion by Hartman in *Prophecy Interpreted: The Formation of Some Jewish Apocalyptic Texts and of the Eschatological Discourse Mark 13 Par.*, Coniectanea Biblica, New Testament Series 1 (Lund, 1966), pp. 168–69.

70. This is contrary to Lambrecht's contention (see *Die Redaktion des Markus-Apokalypse*, pp. 119–20).

71. On the nature of these courts, see D. R. A. Hare, *The Theme of Jewish Persecution of Christians in the Gospel according to St. Matthew*, Society for New Testament Studies Monograph Series, no. 6 (Cambridge, 1967), pp. 101–9.

72. The evidence of the textual tradition is examined by F. C. Burkitt, who favors the alternative reading (see *Christian Beginnings* [London, 1924], pp. 145–47). For G. D. Kilpatrick's construction based on this reading, see "The Gentile Mission in Mark and Mark 13:9–11," in *Studies in the Gospels*, ed. D. E. Nineham (Oxford, 1955), pp. 145–48. For a critique of his interpretation, see Cranfield, *The Gospel according to St. Mark*, p. 398; Pesch, *Naherwartungen*, p. 126; and Lambrecht, *Die Redaktion des Markus-Apokalypse*, pp. 133–35.

73. See Hahn, *Das Verständnis der Mission im Neuen Testament*, Wissenschaftlich Monographien zum Alten und Neuen Testament (Neukirchen-Vluyn, 1963), pp. 60–62.

74. Among those scholars who stress this point are Lohmeyer (*Das Evangelium des Markus*, Kritisch-exegetischer Kommentar über das Neue Testament [Göttingen, 1963], p. 273), Taylor (*The Gospel according to St. Mark*, p. 509), Schweizer (*TDNT*, 6: 4), and C. K. Barrett (*The Holy Spirit and the Gospel Tradition* [New York, 1947], p. 139).

75. Wellhausen, *Das Evangelium Marci* (Berlin, 1903), p. 102.

76. The connection between verses 12 and 13a is seen through a comparison with Targum Jonathan on Micah 7:6: after the statement "A man delivers up his brother to destruction" as in Mark 13:12a, it renders the clause in Micah 7:6 "a man's enemies are his own household" as "those who hate a man are the men of his own house," as in Mark 13:13a (strangely, LXX reads "a man's enemies are *all* the men in his house"). See Hartman, *Prophecy Interpreted*, pp. 168–69.

77. See Strack–Billerbeck, *Kommentar zum Neuen Testament aus Talmud und Midrasch*, 1: 951, 945; Rigaux, "Bdelygma tēs erēmōseōs (Mc 13, 14; Mt 24, 15)," *Biblica* 40 (1959): 675–66, with literature there cited; and my *Commentary on Mark 13*, pp. 54–55.

78. This interpretation has been especially popular in Germany; among those advocating it are J. Weiss (*Das älteste Evangelium* [Göttingen, 1903], pp. 77–78), Klostermann (*Das Markusevangelium*, Handbuch zum Neuen Testament [Tübingen, 1926], p. 135), Lohmeyer (*Das Evangelium des Markus*, pp. 275–76), and Marxsen (*Der Evangelist Markus*, p. 181).

79. Such is the contention of Pfleiderer (*Das Urchristenthum, seine Schriften und Lehren, in geschictlichen Zusammenhang beschrieben* [Berlin, 1887], p. 104), Weiss (*Das älteste Evangelium*, p. 78), and A. Piganiol ("Observations sur la date de l'apocalypse synoptique," *RHPR* 4 [1924]: 247–49).

80. On this, see Schlatter, *Der Evangelist Matthäus*, p. 703.

81. Such is the contention of Hartman (*Prophecy Interpreted*, pp. 151–52) and Pesch (*Das Markusevangelium*, 2: 293).

82. In a paper delivered to the Colloquium Biblicum Lovaniensis XXX in 1979, F. Neirynck examined the evidence for the Eusebian report and concluded that it is too precarious to use as a basis for interpreting the Markan discourse.

83. See *A Commentary on Mark 13*, pp. 80–82, and Lambrecht, *Die Redaktion des Markus-Apokalypse*, p. 164.

84. See Pesch, *Naherwartungen*, p. 155n.591.

85. See G. Neville, *The Advent Hope: A Study of the Context of Mark 13* (London, 1961), p. 64; Pesch, *Naherwartungen*, p. 157; and Marxsen, *Der Evangelist Markus*, p. 167.

86. See Gaston, *No Stone on Another*, pp. 33, 388–89; and Lambrecht, *Die Redaktion des Markus-Apokalypse*, p. 190.

87. See Zmijewski, *Die Eschatologiereden des Lukas-Evangeliums*, p. 238.

88. See Pesch, *Naherwartungen*, p. 170.

89. Such is the contention of Lambrecht in *Die Redaktion des Markus-Apokalypse*, pp. 182–83; he disagrees with Dalman, *The Words of Jesus* (Edinburgh, 1902), p. 241.

90. Jeremias disagrees with this; see *New Testament Theology*, 1: 274. See also the related discussion of Mark 14:62, pp. 300–2 herein.

91. See Lambrecht, *Die Redaktion des Markus-Apokalypse*, p. 189.

92. See Lohmeyer *Das Evangelium des Markus*, p. 280.

93. Among those who argue that this is the case are Jeremias (*The Parables of Jesus*, pp. 119–20) and Rigaux (*Témoignage de l'évangile de Marc* [Louvain, 1965], p. 90).

94. See Jeremias, *TDNT*, 3: 173–74.

95. See Isaiah 46:12–13. For an example of the interchangeability of *thura* and *thurai* in the LXX, see Exodus 40:5–6 and Leviticus 1:3, 5; 4:4, 7; 17:4, 5, 7, 9; and so on.

96. Contrary to Jeremias's argument (see *The Parables of Jesus*, pp. 119–20), this shows that the blossoming of the fig tree can relate to trials that point to the outcome in a joyful redemption.

97. Cf. Kümmel: "It can safely be concluded from the clear parallelism of the parable and its application that *tauta* must signify some kind of premonitory signs of the end, whilst as the subject of *engus estin*, the end, the parousia, the entry of the kingdom of God must be presumed" (*Promise and Fulfilment*, p. 21).

98. So says Büchsel, *TDNT*, 1: 662–63.

99. See Büchsel, *TDNT*, 1: 663.

100. See Pesch, *Naherwartungen*, pp. 181–90. In *Das Markusevangelium*, 2: 308–9, Pesch adds Matthew 10:23 and Matthew 23:36 and suggests that Mark 13:31 supplies additional aid in the formulation of the saying.

101. This contrary to the contention of Grässer (see *Das Problem der Parusieverzögerung in den synoptischen Evangelien und in der Apostelgeschichte*, pp. 128–31).

102. See Lambrecht, *Die Redaktion des Markus-Apokalypse*, pp. 221–26.

103. Such is the contention especially of Lohmeyer (*Das Evangelium des Markus*, p. 282).

104. Among those who hold this view are Dalman (*The Words of Jesus*, p. 194), Kümmel (*Promise and Fulfilment*, p. 42), Oepke (*TDNT*, 5: 867), Schrenk (*TDNT*, 5: 989), Bornkamm (*Jesus of Nazareth*, trans. I. McLuskey, F. McLuskey, and J. Robinson [London, 1960], p. 226), and Jeremias (*New Testament Theology*, 1: 131).

105. See my *Commentary on Mark 13*, p. 107.

106. The phrase "in that day" is rendered sometimes by *en te hemera ekeine* (e.g., in Josh. 6:26 and Zech. 1:12) and with equal frequency by *en to kairo ekeino* (e.g., Gen. 38:1 and Jer. 3:17); in Esther 8:1 it is rendered in LXX ms. S by *en taute te hora* and in mss. A and B by *en taute te hemera*. Similarly, in Daniel 11:40 "the time of the end" (*eth qeṣ*) is rendered by *hora tes sunteleias*, and in 12:4 it is rendered by *kairos sunteleias*. In 12:1 the time of tribulation appears in LXX as *hemera thlipseos* and in Symmachus as *kairos thlipseos*.

107. See Rigaux, "La seconde venue de Jésus," in *La venue de Messie: Messianisme et eschatologie*, by E. Massaux et al., Recherches Bibliques, vol. 6 (Louvain, 1962), p. 191n.1; and Vögtle, "Exegetische Erwägungen über das Wissen und Selbstbewusstsein Jesu," in *Gott in Welt*, Festschrift for K. Rahner (Freiburg, 1964), 1: 610.

108. Oepke, *TDNT*, 5: 867.

109. So notes Fuller in *The Mission and Achievement of Jesus*, Studies in Biblical Theology, no. 12 (London, 1954), p. 83; and in *The Foundations of New Testament Christology* (London, 1965), p. 114.

110. This is now being affirmed of Matthew 11:27 as well, the background of which is apocalyptic rather than Hellenistic; see also 1 Thessalonians 1:10 (an early kerygmatic fragment), 1 Corinthians 15:24–28, and John 5:19ff.

111. See Lambrecht, *Die Redaktion des Markus-Apokalypse*, pp. 249ff.

112. Such is the contention of Dodd (*The Parables of the Kingdom*, p. 161), Jeremias (*The Parables of Jesus*, pp. 53–54), Dupont ("La parabole du mâitre qui rentre dans la nuit," in *Mélanges Bibliques*, pp. 90–91), and A. Weiser (*Die Knechtsgleichnisse der synoptischen Evangelien* [München, 1971], p. 139).

113. Such is the contention of Pesch in *Das Markusevangelium*, pp. 314, 316.

114. Such is the contention of Weiser in *Die Knechtsgleichnisse der synoptischen Evangelien*, p. 137.

115. See Weiser, *Die Knechtsgleichnisse der synoptischen Evangelien*, p. 142.

116. See Lambrecht, *Die Redaktion des Markus-Apokalypse*, p. 248.

Chapter 15

1. Bultmann, in *Kerygma and Myth: A Theological Debate*, ed. H. W. Bartsch, trans. R. H. Fuller (London, 1953), p. 116.

2. Bultmann, *Kerygma and Myth*, p. 4, and his contribution to *Die Christliche Hoffnung und das Problem der Entmythologisierung*, by G. Bornkamm, R. Bultmann, and F. K. Schumann (Stuttgart, 1953), p. 22.

3. See Bultmann, *Die christliche Hoffnung und das Problem der Entmythologisierung*, pp. 30–31.

4. See Bultmann, "History and Eschatology in the New Testament," *NTS* 1 (1954–55): 13ff.

5. Cf. A. N. Wilder: "The 'mythology' of the two testaments sees God's action always as having a social and corporate reference. The future in the gospel announcement is a future of the people of God, and the future of the individual is inseparable from it. It is at this point that the 'plan of salvation' is to be maintained. It is here that Bultmann's reinterpretation verges toward Gnosticism and psychologism" (*Eschatology and Ethics in the Teaching of Jesus*, rev. ed. (New York, 1950), p. 65.

6. See Wheelwright, *Metaphor and Reality* (London, 1962), pp. 37, 45ff.

7. See Perrin, *Jesus and the Language of the Kingdom: Symbol and Metaphor in New Testament Interpretation*, New Testament Library (London, 1976), p. 54. See also "Eschatology and Hermeneutics: Reflections on Method in the Interpretation of the New Testament," *JBL* 93 (1974): 13.

8. Fison, *The Christian Hope: The Presence and the Parousia* (London, 1954), p. 50.

9. Barth, *The Epistle to the Romans*, trans. E. C. Hoskyns (London, 1933), p. 417.

10. Heim, *Jesus der Weltvollender* (Hamburg, 1952), pp. 146–47.

11. Heim, *Jesus der Weltvollender*, p. 145.

12. Bultmann, *Theology of the New Testament*, trans. K. Grobel, 2 vols. (London, 1951–55), 1: 22.

13. Cf. Althaus, who suggests that near expectation is "the transitory and broken form in which the essential eschatological estimate of the world at all times expresses itself to faith, as also its knowledge concerning the actual possibility of the last day which exists at any time" (*Die letzten Dinge*, 4. Aufl. [Gütersloh, 1933], p. 273).

14. See Heim, *Weltschöpfung und Weltende* (Hamburg, 1958), p. 15.

15. Althaus, *Der Brief an die Römer*, Das Neue Testament Deutsch (Göttingen, 1966), ad loc.

16. Forsyth, *This Life and the Next: The Effect of This Life of Faith on the Next* (New York, 1918), p. 71.

17. "A Message from the Second Assembly of the World Council of Churches, Evanston," *Ecumenical Review*, 7 (1954–55): 65.

Bibliography

NOTE: *Titles of journals are for the most part abbreviated in this list. For a list of abbreviations, see page 345.*

Abrahams, I. *Studies on Pharisaism and the Gospels.* 2 vols. Philadelphia, 1917–24.

Allen, W. C. *A Critical and Exegetical Commentary on the Gospel according to St. Matthew.* 3d ed. International Critical Commentary. Edinburgh, 1912.

Althaus, P. *Der Brief an die Römer.* Das Neue Testament Deutsch. Göttingen, 1966.

_____. *Die letzten Dinge.* 4. Aufl. Gütersloh, 1933.

Ambrozic, A. M. *The Hidden Kingdom: A Redaction-Critical Study of the References to the Kingdom of God in Mark's Gospel.* Catholic Biblical Quarterly—Monograph Series, 2. Washington, 1972.

Anderson, H. *The Gospel of Mark.* New Century Bible Commentary. London, 1976.

Bacon, B. W. *The Sermon on the Mount.* London, 1902.

Baldensperger, W. *Das Selbstbewusstsein Jesu im Lichte der messianischen Hoffnungen seiner Zeit.* 2d ed. Strassburg, 1892.

Balz, H. R. *Methodische Probleme der neutestamentlichen Christologie.* Wissenschaftliche Monographien zum Alten und Neuen Testament, nr. 25. Neukirchen-Vluyn, 1967.

Bammel, E. *Erwägungen zur Eschatologie Jesu.* Texte und Untersuchungen, nr. 88. Berlin, 1964.

Barr, James. "Theophany and Anthropomorphism in the Old Testament." In *Supplements to the Vetus Testamentum.* Leiden, 1960. 7: 331–32.

Barrett, C. K. "The Background of Mark 10:45." In *New Testament Essays.* Festschrift for T. W. Manson. Ed. A. J. B. Higgins. Manchester, 1959. Pp. 1–18.

_____. *The Gospel according to St. John.* London, 1955. 2d ed. London, 1978.

_____. *The Holy Spirit and the Gospel Tradition.* London, 1947.

Barth, K. *Church Dogmatics.* Ed. G. W. Bromiley and T. F. Torrance, trans. H. Knight et al. 5 vols. Edinburgh, 1955–77.

_____. *The Epistle to the Romans.* Trans. E. C. Hoskyns. London, 1933.

Bartsch, H. W. "Das Thomas-Evangelium und die synoptischen Evangelien: Zu G. Quispels Bemerkungen zum Thomas-Evangelium." *NTS* 6 (1960): 249–61.

Bauer, W. *A Greek-English Lexicon of the New Testament and Other Early Christian Literature.* Rev. by F. W. Gingrich and F. W. Danker. 2d ed. Chicago, 1958.

Baumgartner, W. "Ein Vierteljahrhundert Danielforschung." *TR* 11 (1939): 59–83, 125–44, 201–28.

Beare, F. W. *The Earliest Records of Jesus.* Oxford, 1962.

_____. "'The Sabbath Was Made for Man?'" *JBL* 79 (1960): 130–36.

Beasley-Murray, G. R. *A Commentary on Mark Thirteen.* London, 1957.

_____. *Revelation.* The New Century Bible. London, 1974.

Becker, J. *Das Heil Gottes.* Studien zur Umwelt des Neuen Testaments, vol. 3. Göttingen, 1964.

_____. *Johannes der Täufer und Jesus von Nazareth.* Neukirchen-Vluyn, 1972.

Beer, G. *Die Apokryphen und Pseudepigraphen des Alten Testaments.* Ed. E. Kautsch. Tübingen, 1900.

Bell, G. K. A., and A. Deissmann, eds. *Mysterium Christi.* London, 1930.

Bentzen, A. *Daniel,* Handbuch zum Alten Testament. 2d ed. Tübingen, 1952.

Berger, K. "Die königlichen Messiastraditionen des Neuen Testaments." *NTS* 20 (1973): 1–44.

_____. "Zu den sogenannten Sätzen heiliger Rechts." *NTS* 17 (1970): 10–40.

Berkey, R. F. "EGGIZEIN, PHTHANEIN, and Realised Eschatology." *JBL* 82 (1963): 177–87.

Best, E. *The Temptation and the Passion: The Marcan Soteriology.* Cambridge, 1965.

Black, M. *An Aramaic Approach to the Gospels and Acts.* 3d ed. Oxford, 1973.

_____. "The Fragments of the Aramaic-Enoch from Qumran." In *La Littérature juive entre Tenach et Mischna: Quelques Problèmes,* ed. W. C. van Unnik. Leiden, 1974. Pp. 15–28.

_____. "The Parables as Allegory." *Bulletin of the John Rylands Library* 42 (1960): 273–87.

_____. *The Scrolls and Christian Origins: Studies in the Jewish Background of the New Testament.* London, 1961.

Black, M., ed. *The Scrolls and Christianity: Historical and Theological Significance.* London, 1969.

Blass, F., and A. Debrunner. *A Greek Grammar of the New Testament and Other Early Christian Literature.* Chicago, 1961.

Blinzler, J. *Der Prozess Jesu.* 3d ed. Regensburg, 1960.

Bogaert, Pierre. *Apocalypse de Baruch: Introduction, Traduction du Syriaque et Commentaire.* Paris, 1969.

Bonnard, P. *L'Évangile selon Saint Matthieu.* Commentaire du Nouveau Testament. Neuchatel, 1963.

Bonsirven, J. *Le règne de Dieu.* Paris, 1957.

Bornkamm, G. *Geschichte und Glaube.* Beiträge zur evangelischen Theologie, 48. München, 1968.

_____. *Jesus of Nazareth.* Trans. I. McLuskey, F. McLuskey, and J. M. Robinson. London, 1960.

_____. *Die Verzögerung der Parusie: In memoriam E. Lohmeyer.* Stuttgart, 1951.

Bornkamm, G., G. Barth, and H. J. Held. *Tradition and Interpretation in Matthew.* Trans. P. Scott. New Testament Library. London, 1963.

Bornkamm, G., R. Bultmann, and F. K. Schumann. *Die Christliche Hoffnung und das Problem der Entmythologisierung.* Stuttgart, 1953.

Borsch, F. H. *The Christian and Gnostic Son of Man.* Studies in Biblical Theology, 2d ser., no. 14. London, 1970.

_____. *The Son of Man in Myth and History.* New Testament Library. London, 1967.

_____. "Mark xiv.62 and I Enoch lxii.5." *NTS* 14 (1968): 565–67.

Bosch, D. *Die Heidenmission in der Zukunftsschau Jesu.* Abhandlungen zur Theologie des Alten und Neuen Testaments, nr. 36. Zürich, 1959.

Bousset, W. *Jesus.* Trans. J. P. Trevelyan, ed. W. D. Morrison. London, 1904.

_____. *Kyrios Christos.* 2d ed. Göttingen, 1921.

_____. *Die Offenbarung Johannis.* Kritisch-exegetischer Kommentar über das Neuen Testament. Göttingen, 1906.

_____. *Die Religion des Judentums.* 3d ed. Rev. H. Gressmann. Berlin, 1926.

Bowker, J. A. "The Son of Man." *JTS* 28 (1977): 19–48.

Brandt, W. *Die jüdische Baptismen.* Giessen, 1910.

Branscomb, H. B. *The Gospel of Mark.* Moffatt New Testament Commentary. London, 1937.

Braude, W. G., trans. *Midrash on Psalms.* 2 vols. Yale Judaica Series, no. 13. New Haven, 1959.

Braun, H. *Jesus of Nazareth.* Trans. E. R. Kalin. Philadelphia, 1979.

_____. *Qumran und das Neue Testament.* 2 vols. Tübingen, 1966.

_____. *Spätjüdisch-häretischer und frühchristlicher Radikalismus.* 2 vols. Tübingen, 1957.

_____. "Der Sinn der neutestamentlichen Christology." *ZTK* 54 (1957): 341–77.

Brown, F., S. R. Driver, and C. A. Briggs. *A Hebrew and English Lexicon of the Old Testament.* Oxford, 1953.

Brown, R. E. *New Testament Essays.* Milwaukee, 1965.

_____. *The Gospel according to John.* 2 vols. Garden City, N.Y., 1966–70.

Brownlee, W. H. "Messianic Motifs of Qumran and the New Testament." *NTS* 3 (1957): 195–210.

Bruce, F. F. *Second Thoughts on the Dead Sea Scrolls.* London, 1956.

Brun, L. "Der Besuch Jesus in Nazareth nach Lukas." In *Serta Rudbergi.* Ed. H. Holst and H. Moland. Oslo, 1931. Pp. 7–17.

Buber, Martin. *Kingship of God.* Trans. Richard Scheimann. New York, 1967.

Bultmann, R. *Jesus and the Word.* Trans. L. P. Smith and E. H. Lantero. New York, 1958.

_____. *Kerygma and Myth: A Theological Debate.* Ed. H. W. Bartsch, trans. R. H. Fuller. London, 1953.

_____. *The Gospel of John.* Trans. G. R. Beasley-Murray, R. W. N. Hoare, and J. K. Riches. Oxford, 1971.

_____. "History and Eschatology in the New Testament." *NTS* 1 (1954–55): 5–16.

_____. *The History of the Synoptic Tradition.* 2d ed. Trans. J. Marsh. New York, 1968.

_____. *Theology of the New Testament.* Trans. K. Grobel. 2 vols. London, 1951–55.

_____. *Das Verhältnis der urchristlichen Christusbotschaft zum historischen Jesus.* Sitzungsberichte der Heidelberger Akadamie der Wissenschaften, Phil.-hist. Klasse, 1960, 3. Abhandlung, 3. Aufl. Heidelberg, 1962.

_____. "Zur eschatologischen Verkündigung Jesu." *TLZ* (1947): 271–74.

Burkitt, F. C. *Christian Beginnings*. London, 1924.

————. *Jewish and Christian Apocalypses*. Oxford, 1914.

Burney, C. F. *The Poetry of Our Lord*. Oxford, 1925.

Burrows, M. *More Light on the Dead Sea Scrolls*. London, 1958.

Busch, F. *Zum Verständnis der synoptischen Eschatologie: Markus 13 neu Untersucht*. Gütersloh, 1938.

Buttenweiser, M. *The Psalms*. Chicago, 1938.

Cadbury, H. J. *The Style and Literary Method of Luke*. Cambridge, Mass., 1920.

Cadoux, A. T. *The Theology of Jesus*. London, 1940.

Cadoux, C. J. *The Historic Mission of Jesus*. London, 1943.

Caird, G. B. *St. Luke*. Pelican Gospel Commentaries. Harmondsworth, 1963.

————. *The Revelation of St. John the Divine*. Black's New Testament Commentary. London, 1966.

Campbell, J. Y. "The Kingdom of God Has Come." *ExpTim* 48 (1936–37): 91–94.

Carlston, C. E. *Parables of the Triple Tradition*. Philadelphia, 1975.

Carrington, P. *The Primitive Christian Catechism*. Cambridge, 1940.

Casey, M. "The Use of the term 'Son of Man' in the Similitudes of Enoch." *JSJ* 8 (1976): 11–29.

————. *The Son of Man: The Interpretation and Influence of Daniel 7*. London, 1979.

Catchpole, D. R. *The Trial of Jesus*. Leiden, 1972.

————. "The Answer of Jesus to Caiaphas (Matt. XXVI:64)." *NTS* 17 (1971): 213–26.

Cave, C. H. "The Sermon at Nazareth and the Beatitudes in the Light of the Synagogue Lectionary." In *Studia Evangelica*. Ed. F. L. Cross 3/2:231–35 = *Texte und Untersuchungen*. Berlin, 1964. 88: 231–35.

Cerfaux, L. "La connaissance des secrets du royaume d'après Matt. XIII.11 et par." *NTS* 2 (1956): 238–49.

Charles, R. H. *The Apocrypha and Pseudepigrapha of the Old Testament in English, with Introductions and Critical and Explanatory Notes to the Several Books*. 2 vols. Oxford, 1913.

————. *The Book of Enoch*. Oxford, 1893.

————. *A Critical and Exegetical Commentary on the Revelation of St. John*. International Critical Commentary. Edinburgh, 1920.

————. *A Critical History of the Doctrine of a Future Life*. London, 1889.

————. *Eschatology: The Doctrine of the Future Life in Israel, Judaism, and Christianity*. New York, 1963.

Cheyne, T. K., and J. S. Black. *Encyclopaedia Biblica*. 4 vols. London, 1899–1903.

Clark, K. W. "Realized Eschatology." *JBL* 59 (1940): 367–83.

Coenen, L., E. Beyreuther, and H. Bietenhard, eds. *Theologisches Begriffslexikon zum Neuen Testament*. 3 vols. Wuppertal, 1967–71.

Colani, T. *Jésus Christ et les croyances messianiques de son temps*. Stuttgart, 1864.

Collins, A. Y. *The Combat Myth in the Book of Revelation*. Harvard Dissertations in Religion no. 9. Missoula, 1976.

Collins, J. J. *The Apocalyptic Vision of the Book of Daniel*. Harvard Semitic Monographs no. 16. Missoula, 1977.

————. "Jewish Apocalyptic against Its Hellenistic Near Eastern Environment." *Bulletin of the American Schools of Oriental Research* 220 (1975): 27–36.

Conzelmann, H. "Gegenwart und Zukunft in der synoptischen Tradition." *ZTK* 54 (1957): 277–96.

————. *Jesus*. Ed. J. Reumann, trans. J. R. Lord. Philadelphia, 1973.

————. *An Outline of the Theology of the New Testament*. Trans. J. S. Bowden. London, 1969.

————. *The Theology of St. Luke*. London, 1960.

Coppens, S. J., and L. Dequeker. *Le Fils de l'homme et les Saints du Très-Haut en Daniel VII*. 2d ed. Bruges-Paris, 1961.

Craig, C. T. "Realized Eschatology." *JBL* 56 (1937): 17–26.

Cranfield, C. E. B. *The Gospel according to St. Mark*. 2d ed. Cambridge Greek Testament. Cambridge, 1963.

Creed, J. M. *The Gospel according to St. Luke*. London, 1930.

————. "The Kingdom of God Has Come." *ExpTim* 48 (1936–37): 184–85.

Cremer, F. G. *Die Fastenansage Jesu: Mk. 2.20 und Parallelen, in der Sicht der patristischen und scholastischen Exegese*. Bonner Biblische Beiträge, nr. 23. Bonn, 1965.

Cross, F. M. *Canaanite Myth and Hebrew Epic*. Cambridge, Mass., 1973.

_____. *The Ancient Library of Qumran and Modern Biblical Studies.* London, 1958.

Crossan, J. D. *In Parables: The Challenge of the Historical Jesus.* New York, 1973.

Cullmann, O. *Die Christologie des Neuen Testaments.* Tübingen, 1957.

_____. *Peter: Disciple—Apostle—Martyr.* Trans. F. V. Filson. London, 1953.

_____. *Salvation in History.* Trans. S. G. Sowers. London, 1967.

Curtis, A. H. *The Vision and Mission of Jesus.* Edinburgh, 1954.

Czerny, L. *The Day of the Lord and Some Relevant Problems.* Prague, 1948.

Dahl, N. A. "The Parables of Growth." *ST* 5 (1951): 132–66.

Dalman, G. *Der Gottesname Adonaj und seine Geschichte.* Berlin, 1889.

_____. *Jesus-Jeshua.* Trans. P. L. Levertoff. London, 1929.

_____. *The Words of Jesus.* Edinburgh, 1902.

Danker, F. W. *Jesus and the New Age according to St. Luke.* St. Louis, 1972.

Daube, D. *The New Testament and Rabbinic Judaism.* London, 1956.

Davies, W. D. *The Setting of the Sermon on the Mount.* Cambridge, 1964.

Davies, W. D., and D. Daube, eds. *The Background of the New Testament and its Eschatology.* Festschrift for C. H. Dodd. Cambridge, 1956.

Delitsch, F. *Eine neue hebräische Übersetzung des Neuen Testaments.* Leipzig, 1864.

Delling, G. *Studien zum Neuen Testament und zum hellenistischen Judentum.* Göttingen, 1970.

Derrett, J. D. M. "Fresh Light on St Luke xvi: I. The Parable of the Unjust Steward." *NTS* 7 (1961): 198–219.

_____. *Law in the New Testament.* London, 1970.

_____. "Law in the New Testament: The Parable of the Unjust Judge." *NTS* 18 (1972): 78–91.

Descamps, A., and R. P. Andre de Halleux, eds. *Mélanges bibliques.* Festschrift for B. Rigaux. Gembloux, 1970.

Dibelius, F. "Zwei Worte Jesu: II." *ZNW* 11 (1910): 190–92.

Dibelius, M. *From Tradition to Gospel.* London, 1934.

_____. *Jesus.* Trans. C. B. Hedrick and F. C. Grant. Philadelphia, 1949.

_____. *The Message of Jesus Christ.* Trans. F. C. Grant. New York, 1939.

Dinkler, E., ed. *Zeit und Geschichte.* Festschrift for R. Bultmann. Tübingen, 1964.

Dodd, C. H. *According to the Scriptures.* London, 1952.

_____. "The Kingdom of God Has Come." *ExpTim* 48 (1936–37): 138–42.

_____. *The Parables of the Kingdom.* London, 1935.

_____. "The 'Primitive Catechism' and the Sayings of Jesus." In *New Testament Essays: Studies in Memory of T. W. Manson.* Manchester, 1959. And in *More New Testament Studies.* Manchester, 1968. Pp. 11–29.

Donahue, J. R. *Are You the Christ? The Trial Narrative in the Gospel of Mark.* Society of Biblical Literature Dissertation Series, no. 10. Cambridge, Mass., 1973.

Driver, G. R. *Canaanite Myths and Legends.* Oxford, 1956.

Duling, D. C. "The Promises to David and Their Entrance into Christianity—Nailing down a Likely Hypothesis." *NTS* 19 (1973): 55–77.

Dupont, J. *Les Béatitudes: Le probleme littéraire.* 3 vols. Paris, 1969–73.

_____. "Le logion des douze trônes (Mt 19,28; Lc 22,28–30)." *Biblica* 45 (1964): 355–92.

_____. "La parabole du mâitre qui rentre dans la nuit." In *Mélanges Bibliques.* Festschrift for B. Rigaux. Gembloux, 1970.

Dupont, J., ed. *Jesus aux origines de la Christologie.* Gembloux, 1975.

Dupont-Sommer, A. *The Essene Writings of Qumran.* Gloucester, Mass., 1973.

Dürr, L. *Ursprung und Ausbau der israelitisch-jüdischen Heilandserwartung.* Berlin, 1925.

Easton, B. S. *The Gospel according to St. Luke.* Edinburgh, 1923.

Ebeling, H. J. "Die Fastenfrage (Mk. 2.18–22)." *TSK* 108 (1937–38): 387–96.

Edwards, R. A. *The Sign of Jonah in the Theology of the Evangelists and Q.* Studies in Biblical Theology, 2d ser., no. 18. London, 1971.

Eichrodt, W. E. *Theology of the Old Testament.* 2 vols. Trans. J. A. Baker. Old Testament Library. Philadelphia, 1961–67.

Eissfeldt, O. "Jahwe als König." *ZAW* 5 (1928): 81–105.

Ellis, E. E. *The Gospel of Luke.* Rev. ed. New Century Bible Commentary. London, 1974.

Eltester, W. "Israel im lukanischen Werk und die Nazareth-Perikope." In *Jesus in Nazareth.* Ed. W. Eltester. Berlin, 1972. Pp. 76–147.

Emerton, J. A. "The Aramaic Underlying *to haima tēs diathēkēs* in Mark xiv.24." *JTS* 6 (1955): 238–40.

———. "Mark XIV.24 and the Targum to the Psalter." *JTS* 15 (1964): 58–59.

———. "The Origin of the Son of Man Imagery." *JTS* 9 (1958): 225–42.

———. "to haima tēs diathēkēs: The Evidence of the Syriac Versions." *JTS* 13 (1962): 111–17.

Farmer, W. R. *Maccabees, Zealots and Josephus.* New York, 1956.

Farrer, A. M. *The Revelation of St. John the Divine.* Oxford, 1964.

———. *St. Matthew and St. Mark.* London, 1954.

Fascher, E. "Theologische Beobachtungen zu *dei.*" In *Neutestamentliche Studien für R. Bultmann.* 2d ed. Berlin, 1957. Pp. 228–54.

Fenton, J. C. *Saint Matthew.* Pelican Gospel Commentaries. London, 1963.

Feuillet, A. "Le sens du mot Parousie dans l'Évangile de Matthieu." In *The Background of the New Testament and Its Eschatology.* Festschrift for C. H. Dodd. Ed. W. D. Davies and D. Daube. Cambridge, 1956. Pp. 261–80.

Fiedler, P. "Sünde und Vergebung im Christentum." *Concilium* 10 (1974): 568–71.

Field, F. *Notes on the Translation of the New Testament.* Cambridge, 1899.

Fison, J. E. *The Christian Hope: The Presence and the Parousia.* London, 1954.

Fitzmyer, J. A. "The Contribution of Qumran Aramaic to the Study of the New Testament." *NTS* 20 (1974): 382–407.

———. "Further Light on Melchizedek from Qumran Cave 11." *JBL* 86 (1967): 25–41.

Flender, H. *St. Luke: Theologian of Redemptive History.* London: 1967.

Flew, R. N. *Jesus and His Church.* New York, 1938.

Fluckiger, F. *Der Ursprung des christlichen Dogmas: Eine Auseinandersetzung mit Albert Schweitzer und Martin Werner.* Zürich, 1955.

Flusser, D. *Jesus.* New York, 1969.

———. "Melchizedek and the Son of Man." *Christian News from Israel* 17 (1966): 23–29.

Foakes-Jackson, F. J., and K. Lake. *The Beginnings of Christianity.* 5 vols. London, 1920–33.

Forsyth, P. T. *This Life and the Next: The Effect of This Life of Faith on the Next.* New York, 1918.

Frankemölle, H. *Jahwebund und Kirche Christi.* Neutestamentliche Abhandlungen, Band 10. Münster, 1973.

Freedman, H., and M. Simon, eds. *Midrash Rabbah.* 10 vols. London, 1939.

Frey, J. B. "Apocryphes de l'Ancien Testament." *DBSup* 1: 360–64.

Fuchs, E. *Studies of the Historical Jesus.* Studies in Biblical Theology, no. 42. London, 1964.

Fuller, R. H. *The Foundations of New Testament Christology.* London, 1965.

———. *The Mission and Achievement of Jesus.* Studies in Biblical Theology, no. 12. London, 1954.

Funk, R. W. *Language, Hermeneutic and the Word of God: The Problem of Language in the New Testament and Contemporary Theology.* London, 1966.

Gardner-Smith, P. *St. John and the Synoptic Gospels.* Cambridge, 1938.

Gaster, T. H., trans. *The Dead Sea Scriptures in English Translation.* New York, 1956.

Gaston, L. *No Stone on Another: Studies in the Significance of the Fall of Jerusalem in the Synoptic Gospels.* Supplements to the Novum Testamentum, vol. 23. Leiden, 1970.

Geldenhuys, N. *Commentary on the Gospel of Luke.* New London Commentary. London, 1950.

Gerhardsson, B. "The Parable of the Sower and Its Interpretation." *NTS* 14 (1968): 165–93.

Glasson, T. F. *His Appearing and His Kingdom.* London, 1953.

———. "The Reply to Caiaphas (Mark xiv.62)." *NTS* 7 (1960): 88–93.

———. *The Second Advent: The Origin of the New Testament Doctrine.* 3d ed. London, 1963.

Gloege, G. *Aller Tage Tag.* Stuttgart, 1960.

———. *Das Reich Gottes und Kirche im Neuen Testament.* Gütersloh, 1929.

Glombitza, O. "Das Zeichen des Jona (zum Verständnis von Matth. xii.38–42)." *NTS* 8 (1962): 359–66.

Gnilka, J. "Die Verhandlungen vor dem Synhedrion und vor Pilatus nach Markus 14:3–15:5." In *Evangelisch-katholischer Kommentar zum Neuen Testament.* Vorarbeiten Heft 2. Zürich, 1970.

———. *Die Verstockung Israels.* Studien zum Alten und Neuen Testament, nr. 3. München, 1961.

Goppelt, L. *Christentum und Judentum im ersten und zweiten Jahrhundert.* Gütersloh, 1954.

———. "Zum Problem des Menschensohns: Das Verhältnis von Leidens- und Parusieankündigung." In *Christologie und Ethik.* Göttingen, 1968. Pp. 66–78.

Gottlieb, H. "TO HAIMA MOU TES DIATHEKES." *ST* 14 (1960): 115–18.

Grässer, E. *Das Problem der Parusieverzögerung in den synoptischen Evangelien und in der Apostelgeschichte.* Beihefte zur ZNW, nr. 22. Berlin, 1957.
————. "Zum Verständnis der Gottesherrschaft." *ZNW* 65 (1974): 3–26.
Gressmann, H. *Altorientalische Texte und Bilder zum Alten Testament.* Berlin, 1926.
————. *Der Messiah.* Göttingen, 1929.
Grundmann, W. *Das Evangelium nach Lukas.* Theologischer Handkommentar zum Neuen Testament. Berlin, 1959.
————. *Das Evangelium nach Markus.* Theologischer Handkommentar zum Neuen Testament. Berlin, 1959.
————. *Das Evangelium nach Matthäus.* Theologischer Handkommentar zum Neuen Testament. Berlin, 1968.
————. "Die Frage nach der Gottessohnschaft des Messias im Lichte von Qumran." In *Bibel und Qumran.* Berlin, 1968. Pp. 86–111.
Guardini, R. *The Lord.* Trans. E. C. Briefs. London, 1956.
Guillamont, A., et al., trans. *The Gospel according to Thomas.* Leiden, 1959.
Gunkel, H. *Die Psalmen.* 5th ed. Göttingen, 1962.
————. *Schöpfung und Chaos in Urzeit und Endzeit.* Göttingen, 1895.
Haenchen, E. *Der Weg Jesu.* Berlin, 1966.
Hahn, F. *Das Verständnis der Mission im Neuen Testament.* Wissenschaftlich Monographien zum Alten und Neuen Testament, 13. Neukirchen-Vluyn, 1963.
————. *Mission in the New Testament.* London, 1965.
————. *The Titles of Jesus in Christology.* Trans. H. Knight and G. Ogg. London, 1969.
Hamerton-Kelly, R. G. *Pre-Existence, Wisdom, and the Son of Man.* Society for New Testament Studies Monograph Series, no. 21. Cambridge, 1973.
Hammer, R. *The Book of Daniel.* Cambridge Bible Commentary. Cambridge, 1976.
Hare, D. R. A. *The Theme of Jewish Persecution of Christians in the Gospel according to St. Matthew.* Society for New Testament Studies Monograph Series, no. 6. Cambridge, 1967.
Harnack, A. *What Is Christianity?* 3d ed. Trans. T. B. Bailey. London, 1904.
Hartman, L. *Prophecy Interpreted: The Formation of Some Jewish Apocalyptic Texts and of the Eschatological Discourse Mark 13 Par.* Coniectanea Biblica, New Testament Series 1. Lund, 1966.
Hastings, J., ed. *A Dictionary of Christ and the Gospels.* 2 vols. Edinburgh, 1906–08.
Hauck, F. *Das Evangelium des Lukas.* Theologischer Handkommentar zum Neuen Testament. Leipzig, 1934.
Hay, D. M. *Glory at the Right Hand: Psalm 110 in Early Christianity.* Society of Biblical Literature Monograph Series, no. 18. New York, 1973.
Heaton, E. W. *Daniel.* Torch Bible Commentary. London, 1956.
Heim, K. *Jesus der Weltvollender.* Hamburg, 1952.
————. *Weltschöpfung und Weltende.* Hamburg, 1958.
Hengel, M. *Judaism and Hellenism: Studies in Their Encounter in Palestine during the Early Hellenistic Period.* Trans. J. S. Bowden. London, 1974.
————. *The Son of God: The Origin of Christology and the History of Jewish-Hellenistic Religion.* Philadelphia, 1976.
Héring, J. *Le Royaume de Dieu et sa venue.* Paris, 1937.
Higgins, A. J. B. *Jesus and the Son of Man.* London, 1964.
Higgins, A. J. B., ed. *New Testament Essays for T. W. Manson.* Manchester, 1959.
Hill, D. *The Gospel of Matthew,* New Century Bible Commentary. Grand Rapids, 1972.
————. *Greek Words and Hebrew Meanings.* Cambridge, 1967.
————. "On the Evidence for the Creative Role of Christian Prophets." *NTS* 20 (1974): 262–74.
Hindley, J. C. "Towards a Date for the Similitudes of Enoch: An Historical Approach." *NTS* 4 (1968): 551–65.
Hofer, J., and K. Rahner, eds. *Lexikon für Theologie und Kirche.* 2d ed. 10 vols. Freiburg, 1957–64.
Hoffmann, P., et al., eds. *Orientierung an Jesus.* Festschrift for J. Schmid. Freiburg, 1971.
Hooker, M. D. *Jesus and the Servant.* London, 1959.
————. *The Son of Man in Mark.* London, 1967.
Horstmann, M. *Studien zur markinischen Christologie: Mark 8.27–9.13 als Zugang zum Christusbild des zweiten Evangeliums.* Neutestamentliche Abhandlungen, nr. 6. Münster, 1969.

Huby, J. L'Évangile selon Saint Marc. 2d ed. Paris, 1953.

Hummel, R. Die Auseinandersetzung zwischen Kirche und Judentum im Matthäusevangelium. Beiträge zur evangelischen Theologie, Band 33. München, 1963.

Hunkin, J. W. "The Synoptic Parables." JTS 16 (1915): 372ff.

Jacob, E. Theology of the Old Testament. Trans. A. W. Heathcote and P. J. Allcock. London, 1958.

Jaubert, A. The Date of the Last Supper. New York, 1965.

Jenni, E. "'Kommen' im theologischen Sprachgebrauch des Alten Testaments." In Wort-Gebot-Glaube: Beiträge zur Theologie des Alten Testaments. Ed. Walther Eichrodt et al. (Zürich, 1970), pp. 251–61.

Jepsen, A. "Eschatologie im AT," RGG, 2: 661.

Jeremias, J. Abba. Göttingen, 1966.

————. "Die älteste Schicht der Menschensohn-Logien." ZNW 58 (1967): 159–72.

————. The Eucharistic Words of Jesus. London, 1966.

————. Jesus' Promise to the Nations. Trans. S. H. Hooke. Studies in Biblical Theology, no. 24. London, 1958.

————. "Das Lösegeld für Viele (Mk. 10.45)." Judaica 3 (1947–48): 249–64.

————. New Testament Theology. Vol. 1, The Proclamation of Jesus. Trans. J. S. Bowden. London, 1971.

————. The Parables of Jesus. Trans. S. H. Hooke. Rev. ed. London, 1963.

————. The Prayers of Jesus. Trans. J. S. Bowden, C. Burchard, and J. Reumann. Studies in Biblical Theology, 2d ser., no. 6. London, 1967.

————. The Sermon on the Mount. Trans. N. Perrin. Facet Books Biblical Series 2. Philadelphia, 1963.

Jeremias, Jörg. Theophanie: Die Geschichte einer alttestamentlichen Gattung. Neukirchen-Vluyn, 1965.

Jones, P. R. "The Seed Parables of Mark." Review and Expositor 75 (1978): 519–38.

Jonge, M. de, and A. S. van der Woude. "11Q Melchizedek and the New Testament." NTS 12 (1966): 301–26.

Jülicher, A. Die Gleichnisreden Jesu. 2 vols. Tübingen, 1910.

Jüngel, E. Paulus und Jesus: Eine Untersuchung zur Präzisierung der Frage nach der Aufsprung der Christologie. Tübingen, 1962.

Juster, J. Les juifs dans l'empire romaine. Paris, 1914.

Kaiser, O. Der Prophet Jesaja: Kapitel 13–39. Das Alte Testament Deutsch. Göttingen, 1973.

Käsemann, E. "Das Abendmahl im NT," in "Abendmahlsgemeinschaft?" BEvT 3 (1937): 60–93.

————. The Epistle to the Romans. Trans. and ed. Geoffrey Bromiley. Grand Rapids, 1980.

————. Essays on New Testament Themes. Trans. W. J. Montague. Studies in Biblical Theology, no. 41. London, 1964.

————. New Testament Questions of Today. Philadelphia, 1969.

Keck, L. E. A Future for the Historical Jesus. London, 1971.

————. "The Introduction to Mark's Gospel." NTS 12 (1966): 352–70.

Kee, A. "The Question about Fasting." Novum Testamentum 11 (1969): 161–73.

Kelber, W. The Kingdom in Mark. Philadelphia, 1974.

Kertelge, K., ed. Der Tod Jesu: Deutungen im Neuen Testament. Quaestiones Disputatae 74. Freiburg, 1976.

Kiddle, M. The Revelation of St. John. The Moffatt New Testament Commentary. London, 1940.

Kilpatrick, G. D. The Origins of the Gospel according to St. Matthew. Oxford, 1946.

————. "The Gentile Mission in Mark and Mark 13:9–11." In Studies in the Gospels. Ed. D. E. Nineham. Oxford, 1955. Pp. 145–58.

Kingsbury, J. D. The Parables of Jesus in Matthew 13: A Study in Redaction Criticism. Richmond, 1969.

Klostermann, E. Das Lukasevangelium. Handkommentar zum Neuen Testament. Tübingen, 1929.

————. Das Markusevangelium. Handbuch zum Neuen Testament. Tübingen, 1926.

————. Das Matthäusevangelium. Handbuch zum Neuen Testament. Tübingen, 1927.

Knabenbauer, J. Commentarius in quatuor S. Evangelia. Paris, 1893.

Knibb, M. A. "The Date of the Parables of Enoch: A Critical Review." NTS 25 (1978–79): 345–59.

Knox, W. L. The Sources of the Synoptic Gospels. Ed. H. Chadwick. 2 vols. Cambridge, 1953–57.

Koch, D. A. "Zum Verhältnis von Christologie und Eschatologie im Markus-evangelium." In Jesus

Christus in Historie und Theologie. Festschrift for H. Conzelmann. Ed. G. Strecker. Tübingen, 1975.

Koch, K. *The Growth of the Biblical Tradition: The Form Critical Method.* New York, 1969.

————. *The Rediscovery of Apocalyptic.* London, 1972.

Köhler, L. *Old Testament Theology.* Trans. A. S. Todd. Philadelphia, 1953.

Kraeling, C. H. *John the Baptist.* New York, 1951.

Kubel, R. *Handbuch zum Evangelium des Mattäus.* Nordlingen, 1889.

Kuhn, H. W. *Ältere Sammlungen im Markusevangelium.* Göttingen, 1971.

————. *Enderwartung und Gegenwärtiges Heil: Untersuchungen zu den Gemeindeliedern von Qumran.* Studien zur Umwelt des Neuen Testaments, vol. 4. Göttingen, 1966.

Kuhn, K. G. *Achtzehngebet und Vaterunser und der Reim.* Wissenschaftliche Untersuchungen zum Neuen Testament, nr. 1. Tübingen, 1950.

————. "The Two Messiahs of Aaron and Israel." In *The Scrolls and the New Testament.* Ed. K. Stendahl. London, 1958.

Kümmel, W. G. "Eschatological Expectation in the Proclamation of Jesus." In *The Future of Our Religious Past: Essays in Honour of R. Bultmann.* Ed. J. M. Robinson. London, 1971. Pp. 29–48.

————. *Promise and Fulfilment: The Eschatological Message of Jesus.* Studies in Biblical Theology, no. 23. London, 1961.

Kunzi, M. *Das Naherwartungslogion Markus 9.1 par.* Beiträge zur Geschichte der biblischen Exegese, nr. 21. Tübingen, 1977.

————. *Das Naherwartungslogion Matthäus 10.23: Geschichte seiner Auslegung.* Beiträge zur Geschichte der Biblischen Exegese, nr. 9. Tübingen, 1970.

Kwaak, H. van der. "Die Klage über Jerusalem (Matth. XXIII.37–39)." *Novum Testamentum* 8 (1966): 158–59.

Lacocque, A. *Le Livre de Daniel.* Neuchatel, 1976.

Ladd, G. E. *The Presence of the Future.* Grand Rapids, 1974.

————. *A Theology of the New Testament.* Grand Rapids, 1974.

Lagrange, M.-J. *L'Évangile selon Saint Luc.* Études Bibliques. Paris, 1921.

————. *L'Évangile selon Saint Marc.* Études Bibliques. Paris, 1910.

————. *L'Évangile selon Saint Matthieu.* Études Bibliques. Paris, 1923.

Lambrecht, J. *Die Redaktion des Markus-Apokalypse: Literarische Analyse und Strukturuntersuchung.* Analecta Biblica 28. Rome, 1967.

Lane, W. L. *The Gospel of Mark.* New International Commentary on the New Testament. Grand Rapids, 1974.

Leaney, A. R. C. *The Gospel according to St. Luke.* Black's New Testament Commentaries. London, 1958.

Légasse, S. "Approche de l'Épisode préévangelique des Fils de Zébédée (Marc x.35–40 par.)." *NTS* 20 (1974): 161–77.

Lehmann, K. *Auferweckt am Dritten Tag nach der Schrift, Früheste Christologie, Bekenntnisbildung und Schriftauslegung im Lichte von 1 Kor. 15.3–5.* 2d ed. Questiones Disputatae, vol. 38. Freiburg, 1969.

Léon-Dufour, X. "Jésus devant sa mort a la lumière des textes de l'Institution eucharistique et des discours d'adieu." In *Jésus aux origines de la christologie.* Ed. J. Dupont. Leuven/Gembloux, 1975. Pp. 141–68.

Levy, J. *Wörterbuch über die Talmudim und Midraschim.* Leipzig, 1963.

Lewis, J. P. *Study of the Interpretation of Noah and the Flood in Jewish and Christian Literature.* Leiden, 1968.

Liddell, H. G., and R. Scott. *A Greek-English Lexicon.* Rev. H. S. Jones and R. Mackenzie. Oxford, 1940.

Lietzmann, H. *Geschichte der Alten Kirche.* 4 vols. 2d ed. Berlin, 1937.

————. *Mass and Lord's Supper.* Leiden, 1979.

————. *Der Menschensohn.* Freiburg, 1896.

————. "Der Prozess Jesu." In *Kleine Schriften,* vol. 2. Ed. K. Aland. Texte und Untersuchungen zur Geschichte der altchristlichen Literatur, vol. 68. Berlin, 1958. Pp. 251–63.

Lightfoot, R. H. *History and Interpretation in the Gospels.* London, 1935.

Lindars, B. *New Testament Apologetic: The Doctrinal Significance of the Old Testament Quotations.* London, 1961.

Lindblom, J. "Theophanies in Holy Places in Hebrew Religion." *HUCA* 32 (1961): 91–106.

Linnemann, E. *Die Gleichnisse Jesu.* Göttingen, 1962.

————. *Jesus of the Parables.* London, 1966.

Ljungvik, H. "Zur Erklärung einer Lukas-stelle (Luk. xviii.7)." *NTS* 10 (1964): 289–94.

Lohmeyer, E. *"Our Father": An Introduction to the Lord's Prayer.* New York, 1965.

————. *Das Evangelium des Markus.* Kritisch-exegetischer Kommentar über das Neue Testament. Göttingen, 1963.

————. *Das Evangelium des Matthäus.* Completed by W. Schmauch. Kritisch-exegetischer Kommentar über das Neue Testament. Göttingen, 1962.

Lohse, E. *Märtyrer und Gottesknecht.* Göttingen, 1955.

Loisy, A. *L'Évangile selon Luc.* Paris, 1924.

————. *Les Évangiles synoptiques.* 2 vols. Coffonds, 1907.

Lövestam, E. *Spiritual Wakefulness in the New Testament.* Lunds Universitets Årsskrift, Band 55, nr. 3. Lund, 1963.

Lührmann, D. *Die Redaktion der Logienquelle.* Wissenschaftliche Monographien zum Alten und Neuen Testament, Band 33. Neukirchen-Vluyn, 1969.

Lütgert, W. *Das Reich Gottes nach den synoptischen Evangelien: Eine Untersuchung zur neutestamentlichen Theologie.* Gütersloh, 1895.

Maag, V. "Malkut Jahwe." In *Supplements to the Vetus Testamentum.* Leiden, 1960, 7: 140.

McNeile, A. H. *The Gospel according to St. Matthew.* London, 1915.

Major, H. D. A., et al. *The Mission and Message of Jesus.* London, 1940.

Manson, T. W. "Mark 2.27f." In *Coniectanea Neotestamentica* 11. Lund, 1947.

————. *The Sayings of Jesus.* London, 1949.

————. "The Son of Man in Daniel, Enoch and the Gospels." *BJRL* 32 (1950): 171–93.

————. *The Teaching of Jesus.* 2d ed. Cambridge, 1931.

Manson, W. *Christ's View of the Kingdom of God.* London, 1918.

————. *The Gospel of Luke.* Moffatt New Testament Commentary. London, 1930.

————. *Jesus the Messiah.* London, 1943.

Marshall, I. H. *Luke: Historian and Theologian.* Exeter, 1970.

————. "The Synoptic Son of Man Sayings in Recent Discussion." *NTS* 12 (1966): 327–51.

Marxsen, W. *Die Einsetzungsbericht zum Abendmahl.* Kiel, 1948.

————. *Der Evangelist Markus: Studien zur Redaktionsgeschichte des Evangeliums.* Göttingen, 1959.

Massaux, E., et al. *La venue de Messie: Messianisme et eschatologie.* Recherches Bibliques, vol. 6. Louvain, 1962.

Mathews, S. *Messianic Hope in the New Testament.* Chicago, 1905.

Mearns, C. L. "Dating the Similitudes of Enoch." *NTS* 25 (1978–79): 360–69.

————. "The Parables of Enoch—Origin and Date." *ExpTim* 89 (1978): 118–19.

Meinertz, M. *Theologie des Neuen Testaments,* 2 vols. Bonn, 1950.

————. "Die Tragweite des Gleichnisses von den zehn Jungfrauen." In *Synoptischen Studien.* Festschrift for A. Wikenhauser. München, 1953.

Mendenhall, G. E. *Law and Covenant in Israel and the Ancient Near East.* Pittsburgh, 1965.

Mesnard, J. *Les Tendences apocalyptiques chez le Prophète Ézéchiel.* Paris, 1907.

Messel, N. *Die Einheitlichkeit der jüdischen Eschatologie.* Giessen, 1915.

————. *Der Menschensohn in den Bilderreden des Henoch.* Beihefte zur ZAW, nr. 35. Giessen, 1922.

Metzger, B. M. *A Textual Commentary on the Greek New Testament.* London, 1971.

Meyer, A. *Jesu Muttersprache.* Freiburg, 1896.

Michael, J. H. "The Sign of Jonah." *JTS* 21 (1920): pp. 146ff.

Michaelis, W. *Das Evangelium nach Matthäus.* 2 vols. Zürich, 1948–49.

————. *Die Gleichnisse Jesu.* Die urchristliche Botschaft, 23te Abteilung. Hamburg, 1956.

————. *Die grosse Enttäuschung.* Kirchenfreund, 1942.

————. *Der Herr verzieht nicht die Verheissung.* Bern, 1942.

————. *Täufer, Jesus, Urgemeinde.* Gütersloh, 1928.

Michaels, J. R. "Apostolic Hardship and Righteous Gentiles: A Study of Matthew 25:31–46." *JBL* 84 (1965): 27–37.

Michel, O. *Paulus und seine Bibel*. Beiträge zur Forderung christlicher Theologie, 2/18. Gütersloh, 1972.

Milik, J. T. *The Books of Enoch, Aramaic Fragments of Cave 4*. Oxford, 1976.

Miller, M. P. "The Function of Isa 61:1–2 in 11Q Melchizedek." *JBL* 88 (1969): 467–69.

Minette de Tillesse, G. *Le secret messianique dans l'évangile de Marc*. Lectio Divina 47. Paris, 1968.

Montefiore, C. J. G. *Rabbinic Literature and Gospel Teachings*. London, 1930.

Montefiore, H., and H. E. W. Turner, *Thomas and the Evangelists*. Studies in Biblical Theology, no. 35. London, 1962.

Moore, A. L. *The Parousia in the New Testament*. Supplements to the Novum Testamentum 13. Leiden, 1966.

Morgenstern, J. "Biblical Theophanies." *ZAW* 25 (1911): 139–93; and 28 (1914): 15–60.

Moulton, J. H., and G. Milligan, *The Vocabulary of the Greek New Testament*. London, 1931.

Moulton, J. H., W. F. Howard, and N. Turner. *A Grammar of New Testament Greek*. 4 vols. Edinburgh, 1929–76.

Mowinckel, S. *He That Cometh*. Trans. G. W. Anderson. New York, 1955.

————. "Der Tag Jahwäs ist der Thronbesteigung." In *Psalmenstudien II*. Oslo, 1922. Pp. 230–44.

————. "Urmensch und 'Konigsidealogie.'" *ST* 1 (1948–49): 71ff.

Moxon, C. "To semeion Iona." *ExpTim* 22 (1911): 566–67.

Muddiman, J. B. "Jesus and Fasting, Mark ii.18–22." In *Jésus aux origines de la Christologie*. Ed. J. Dupont. Gembloux, 1975. Pp. 271–81.

Müller, U. B. *Messias und Menschensohn in jüdischen Apokalypsen und in der Offenbarung des Johannes*. Studien zum Neuen Testament, nr. 6. Gütersloh, 1972.

Munch, P. A. *The Expression "bajjom hahu": Is It an Eschatological Terminus Technicus?* Oslo, 1936.

Mussner, F. "Wann kommt das Reich Gottes?" *BZ* 7 (1963): 108ff.

Neirynck, F. "The Tradition of the Sayings of Jesus: Mark 9, 33–50." *Concilium* 20 (1966): 66–69.

Neugebauer, F. "Die Davidssohnfrage (Mark xii.35–7 parr.) und der Menschensohn." *NTS* 21 (1974): 81–108.

Neville, G. *The Advent Hope: A Study of the Context of Mark 13*. London, 1961.

Nicoll, W. R., ed. *The Expositor's Greek Testament*. 5 vols. London, 1901.

Nineham, D. E. *St. Mark*. Pelican Gospel Commentary. Harmondsworth, 1963.

Nineham, D. E., ed. *Studies in the Gospels*. Oxford, 1955.

Noack, B. *Das Gottesreich bei Lukas: Eine Studie zu Luk. 17.20–24*. Symbolae Biblicae Uppsalienses, 10. Uppsala, 1948.

North, C. R. *The Second Isaiah*. Oxford, 1964.

————. *The Suffering Servant in Deutero-Isaiah*. London, 1948.

Noth, M. "Die Heiligen des Höchsten." *Norsk Theologisk Tidsskrift* 56 (1955): 146–61.

Odeberg, Hugo. *3 Enoch*. The Library of Biblical Studies. New York, 1973.

Oesterley, W. O. E. *The Psalms*. 2 vols. London, 1939–54.

Ott, W. *Gebet und Heil: Die Bedeutung der Gebetsparänese in der lukanischen Theologie*. Studien zum Alten und Neuen Testament, nr. 12. München, 1965.

Otto, R. *The Kingdom of God and the Son of Man*. Trans. F. V. Filson and B. L. Woolf. London, 1943.

Palmer, D. "Defining a Vow of Abstinence." *Colloquium* 5 (1973): 38–41.

Pannenberg, W. *Jesus: God and Man*. Trans. L. L. Wilkins and D. A. Priebe. London, 1970.

Patsch, H. *Abendmahl und historischer Jesus*. Calwer Theologische Monographien, Band 1. Stuttgart, 1972.

Peake, A. S. *A Commentary on the Bible*. London, 1919.

Percy, E. *Die Botschaft Jesu*. Lund, 1953.

Perrin, N. "Eschatology and Hermeneutics: Reflections on Method in the Interpretation of the New Testament." *JBL* 93 (1974): 3–14.

————. *Jesus and the Language of the Kingdom: Symbol and Metaphor in New Testament Interpretation*. New Testament Library. London, 1976.

————. "Mark XIV.62: The End Product of a Christian Pesher Tradition?" *NTS* 12 (1965–66): 150–55.

————. *A Modern Pilgrimage in New Testament Christology*. Philadelphia, 1974.

————. *Rediscovering the Teaching of Jesus*. New Testament Library. London, 1963.

Pesch, R. *Das Markusevangelium*. 2 vols. Herders theologischer Kommentar zum Neuen Testament. Freiburg, 1976–77.

BIBLIOGRAPHY

————. *Naherwartungen: Tradition und Redaktion in Mk 13*. Kommentare und Beiträge zum Alten und Neuen Testament. Düsseldorf, 1968.

————. "Zur Formgeschichte und Exegese von Lk 12.32." *Biblica* 41 (1960): 35–38.

Pesch, R., and R. Schnackenburg, eds. *Jesus und der Menschensohn*. Freiburg, 1975.

Pfleiderer, O. *Primitive Christianity*. Trans. W. Montgomery, ed. W. D. Morrison. 4 vols. Clifton, N.J., 1965.

————. *Das Urchristenthum, seine Schriften und Lehren, in geschichtlichen Zusammenhang beschrieben*. Berlin, 1887.

Pidoux, Georges. *Le dieu qui vient*. Neuchatel, 1947.

Piganiol, A. "Observations sur la date de l'apocalypse synoptique." *RHPR* 4 (1924): 245–49.

Plath, M. "Der neutestamentliche Weheruf über Jerusalem." *TSK* 78 (1905): 455–60.

Plummer, A. *The Gospel according to St. Luke*. 5th ed. International Critical Commentary. Edinburgh, 1922.

Polag, A. *Die Christologie der Logienquelle*. Neukirchen-Vluyn, 1977.

Popkes, W. *Christus Traditus: Untersuchung zum Begriff der Dahingabe im Neuen Testament*. Abhandlungen zur Theologie des Alten und Neuen Testaments, Band 49. Zürich, 1967.

Preiss, T. *Life in Christ*. Trans. H. Knight. Chicago, 1954.

Preuss, H. D. *Jahweglaube und Zukunftserwartung*. Stuttgart, 1968.

Prigent, P. *Apocalypse 12: Histoire de l'exégèse*. Tübingen, 1959.

Procksch, O. *Theologie des Alten Testaments*. Gütersloh, 1949.

Pryke, J. "Eschatology in the Dead Sea Scrolls." In *The Scrolls and Christianity*. Ed. M. Black. London, 1969. Pp. 45–57.

Quispel, M. "L'Évangile selon Thomas et le Diatessaron." *VC* 13 (1959): 87–117.

————. "The Gospel of Thomas and the New Testament." *VC* 11 (1957): 189–207.

————. "Some Remarks on the Gospel of Thomas." *NTS* 5 (1959): 276–90.

Rad, G. von. *The Message of the Prophets*. Trans. D. M. G. Stalker. London, 1968.

————. *Old Testament Theology*. 2 vols. Trans. D. M. G. Stalker. New York, 1962–65.

————. "The Origin of the Concept of the Day of Yahweh." *JSS* 4 (1959): 97–108.

Rawlinson, A. E. J. "Corpus Christi." In *Mysterium Christi*. Ed. G. K. A. Bell and A. Deissmann. London, 1930. Pp. 225–44.

————. *The Gospel according to St. Mark*. 2d ed. London, 1927.

Reimarus, H. S. *Fragmente des Wolfenbüttelschen Ungenannten*. Braunschweig, 1778.

Renan, E. *The Life of Jesus*. New York, 1859.

Rengstorff, K. H. *Das Evangelium nach Lukas*. Das Neue Testament Deutsch. Göttingen, 1937.

————. "Herkunft und Sinn der Patriarchen-Reden in den Testamenten der Zwölf Patriarchen." In *La Littérature juive entre Tenach et Mischna: Quelques Problèmes*. Ed. W. C. van Unnik. Leiden, 1964. Pp. 29–47.

Reploh, K. G. *Markus, Lehrer der Gemeinde*. Stuttgarter Biblische Monographien. Stuttgart, 1969.

Riesenfeld, H. "Zu *Makrothumein* (Lk. 18.7)." *Neutestamentliche Aufsätze*. Festschrift for Josef Schmid. Regensburg, 1963.

Rigaux, B. "Bdelygma tēs erēmōseōs (Mc 13,14; Mt 24,15)." *Biblica* 40 (1959): 675–83.

————. "La petite apocalypse de Luc (XVII, 22–37)." In *Ecclesia a Spiritu Sancto edocta Lumen Gentium*. Mélanges théologiques à G. Philips 53. Gembloux, 1970. Pp. 407–38.

————. "La seconde venue de Jésus." In *La venue de Messie: Messianisme et eschatologie*, by E. Massaux et al. Recherches Bibliques, vol. 6. Louvain, 1962. Pp. 173–216.

————. *Témoignage de l'évangile de Marc*. Louvain, 1965.

————. *La venue du Messie: Messianisme et Eschatologie*. Recherches Bibliques, vol. 6. Paris, 1962.

Roberts, C. H. "The Kingdom of Heaven (Lk. XVIII.21)." *HTR* 41 (1948): 1–8.

Robinson, H. W. *The Christian Doctrine of Man*. 3d ed. Edinburgh, 1956.

Robinson, J. A. T. *Jesus and His Coming*. London, 1957.

————. "The 'Parable' of the Sheep and the Goats." *NTS* 2 (1956): 225–37.

Robinson, J. M. *The Problem of History in Mark*. London, 1957.

Robinson, J. M., ed. *The Future of our Religious Past: Essays in Honour of R. Bultmann*. London, 1971.

Roloff, J. "Anfänge der soteriologischen Deutung des Todes Jesu (Mk. x.45 und Lk. xxii.27)." *NTS* 19 (1972): 38–64.

————. *Das Kerygma und der irdische Jesus: Historische Motive in den Jesus-Erzählungen der Evangelien*. Göttingen, 1970.

Rowley, H. H. *The Re-Discovery of the Old Testament*. London, 1945.

_____. *The Relevance of Apocalyptic*. London, 1944.

Ruppert, L. *Jesus als der leidende Gerechte?* Stuttgarter Bibelstudien 59. Stuttgart, 1972.

Russell, D. S. *The Method and Message of Jewish Apocalyptic*. London, 1964.

Rustow, A. "ENTOS HUMON ESTIN: Zur Deutung von Lukas 17.20–21." *ZNW* 51 (1960): 197–224.

Safrai, S., and M. Stern. *The Jewish People in the First Century*. Philadelphia, 1974.

Sanday, W., ed. *Oxford Studies in the Synoptic Problem*. Oxford, 1911.

Sanders, J. A. "From Isaiah 61 to Luke 4." In *Christianity, Judaism and Other Greco-Roman Cults*. Festschrift for M. Smith. Ed. J. Neusner. Leiden, 1975.

Schanz, P. *Mattäus*. Freiburg, 1879.

Schierse, F. J. "Historische Kritik und theologische Exegese der synoptischen Evangelien." *Scholastik* 29 (1959): 520–36.

Schlatter, A. *Das Evangelium des Lukas: Aus seinen Quellen erklärt*. 2d ed. Stuttgart, 1960.

_____. *Der Evangelist Matthäus*. Stuttgart, 1948.

_____. *Die Geschichte des Christus*. Stuttgart, 1923.

Schmid, J. *Das Evangelium nach Lukas*. Regensburger Neues Testament. Regensburg, 1960.

_____. *Das Evangelium nach Markus*. Regensburger Neues Testament. Regensburg, 1954.

_____. *Das Evangelium nach Matthäus*. Regensburger Neues Testament. Regensburg, 1965.

_____. *Matthäus und Lukas: Eine Untersuchung des Verhältnisses ihrer Evangelien*. Biblische Studien, 23/2–4. Freiburg, 1930.

Schmidt, H., and P. Kahle. *Volkserzählungen aus Palästina*. Göttingen, 1918.

Schmidt, K. L. *Der Rahmen der Geschichte Jesu*. Berlin, 1919.

Schmidt, N. "The 'Son of Man' in the Book of Daniel." *JBL* 19 (1900): 22–28.

Schnackenburg, R. "Der eschatologische Abschnitt Lk. 17.20–37." In *Mélanges bibliques*. Festschrift for B. Rigaux. Ed. A. Descamps and R. P. Andre de Halleux. Gembloux, 1970. Pp. 213–34.

_____. "'Das Evangelium' im Verständnis des ältesten Evangelisten." In *Orientierung an Jesus*. Festschrift for J. Schmid. Ed. P. Hoffmann et al. Freiburg, 1973. Pp. 309–24.

_____. *Das Evangelium nach Markus*. 2 vols. Düsseldorf, 1966.

_____. *God's Rule and Kingdom*. London, 1963.

Schniewind, J. *Das Evangelium nach Markus*. Das Neue Testament Deutsch. Göttingen, 1944.

_____. *Das Evangelium nach Matthäus*. Das Neue Testament Deutsch. Göttingen, 1956.

Schnutenhaus, F. "Das Kommen und Erscheinen Gottes im Alten Testament." *ZAW* 76 (1964): 1–22.

Schrage, W. *Das Verhältnis der Thomas-Evangeliums zur synoptischen Tradition und zu den koptischen Evangelienübersetzungen*. Berlin, 1964.

Schubert, K. *The Dead Sea Community*. Trans. J. W. Doberstein. New York, 1959.

Schulz, S. *Q—Die Spruchquelle der Evangelisten*. Zürich, 1972.

Schürmann, H. *Der Einsetzungsbericht Lk. 22,19–20*. Münster, 1955.

_____. *Jesu Abschiedsrede, Lk 22.21–38*. Münster, 1957.

_____. *Jesu Ureigener Tod: Exegetische Besinnungen und Ausblick*. Freiburg, 1975.

_____. *Das Lukasevangelium*. Herders theologischer Kommentar zum Neuen Testament. Freiburg, 1969.

_____. *Der Paschamahlbericht Lk. 22, (7–14) 15–18*. Münster, 1953.

_____. *Praying with Christ: The "Our Father" for Today*. New York, 1964.

_____. *Traditionsgeschichtliche Untersuchungen zu der synoptischen Evangelien*. Düsseldorf, 1968.

_____. "Zur Traditions- und Redaktionsgeschichte von Mt 10,23." *BZ* 3 (1959): 82–88.

Schweitzer, A. *The Mystery of the Kingdom of God*. Trans. Walter Lowrie. 1914; rpt., London, 1950.

_____. *The Quest of the Historical Jesus*. London, 1910.

Schweizer, E. *Lordship and Discipleship*. Studies in Biblical Theology, no. 28. London, 1960.

_____. *The Good News according to Mark*. Trans. D. H. Madvig. Atlanta, 1970.

_____. *The Good News according to Matthew*. Trans. D. O. E. Green. Atlanta, 1975.

_____. "Der Menschensohn (Zur eschatologischen Erwartung Jesu)." *ZNW* 50 (1959): 185–209.

_____. "The Son of Man." *JBL* 79 (1960): 119–29.

Segal, J. B. *The Hebrew Passover*. London, 1963.

Sevenster, G. *De Christologie van het Nieuwe Testament*. Amsterdam, 1946.

Sharman, H. B. *Son of Man and Kingdom of God*. London, 1943.

———. *The Teaching of Jesus about the Future according to the Synoptic Gospels*. Chicago, 1909.

Sherwin-White, A. N. *Roman Society and Roman Law in the New Testament*. Oxford, 1963.

———. *The Trial of Christ: Historicity and Chronology in the New Testament*. SPCK Theological Collections, no. 6. London, 1965.

Sjöberg, E. *Der Menschensohn im Äthiopischen Henochbuch*. Lund, 1946.

Smith, B. T. D. *The Gospel According to St. Matthew*. Cambridge, 1927.

———. *The Parables of the Synoptic Gospels*. Cambridge, 1937.

Smith, C. W. F. *The Jesus of the Parables*. Rev. ed. Philadelphia, 1975.

Sneed, R. "The Kingdom of God Is within You (Lk 17,21)." *CBQ* 24 (1962): 363–82.

Spitta, F. *Die synoptische Grundschrift und ihrer Überlieferung durch das Lukasevangelium*. Leipzig, 1912.

Steck, O. H. *Israel und das gewaltsame Geschick der Propheten*. Wissenschaftliche Monographien zum Alten und Neuen Testament, nr. 39. Neukirchen-Vluyn, 1967.

Stern, M. "The Province of Judaea." In vol. 1 of *The Jewish People in the First Century*. Ed. S. Safrai and M. Stern. Philadelphia, 1974. Pp. 308–76.

Strack, H. L. and P. Billerbeck. *Kommentar zum Neuen Testament aus Talmud und Midrasch*. 6 vols. München, 1922–28.

Strauss, D. *The Life of Jesus Critically Examined*. Ed. P. C. Hodgson. Philadelphia, 1972.

Strecker, G. "Die Leidens- und Auferstehungsvoraussagen im Markusevangelium (Mk 8,31; 9,31; 10,32–34)." *ZTK* 64 (1967): 16–39.

———. *Der Weg der Gerechtigkeit: Untersuchung zur Theologie des Matthäus*. Forschungen zur Religion und Literatur des Alten und Neuen Testaments, Heft 82. 2d ed. Göttingen, 1966.

Strecker, G., ed. *Jesus Christus in Historie und Theologie*. Festschrift for H. Conzelmann. Tübingen, 1975.

Streeter, B. H. *The Four Gospels: A Study of Origins*. London, 1926.

———. "Synoptic Criticism and the Eschatological Problem." In *Oxford Studies in the Synoptic Problem*. Ed. W. Sanday. Oxford, 1911. Pp. 425–36.

Strobel, A. "In dieser Nacht (Luk 17,34)." *ZTK* 58 (1961): 16–29.

———. "A. Merx über Lc 17.20f." *ZNW* 51 (1960): 133–34.

———. "Die Passa-Erwartung als urchristliches Problem in Lc 17.20f." *ZNW* 49 (1958): 157–96.

———. *Untersuchungen zum eschatologischen Verzögerungsproblem auf Grund der spätjüdisch-urchristlichen Geschichte von Habakkuk 2.2ff*. Leiden, 1961.

———. "Zu Luke 17:20." *BZ* 7 (1963): 111–13.

Stuhlmacher, P. *Das Paulinische Evangelium*. Göttingen, 1968.

Stuhlmann, P. "Beobachtungen zu Markus IV.26–29." *NTS* 19 (1973): 153–62.

Suggs, M. J. "Wisdom of Solomon 2.10–5: A Homily Based on the Fourth Servant Song." *JBL* 76 (1957): 26–33.

Tasker, R. V. G. *The Gospel according to St. Matthew*. London, 1961.

Taylor, V. *Behind the Third Gospel*. Oxford, 1926.

———. *Formation of the Gospel Tradition*. London, 1957.

———. *The Gospel according to St. Mark*. Macmillan New Testament Commentaries. London, 1952.

TeSelle, S. *Speaking in Parables: A Study in Metaphorical Theology*. Philadelphia, 1975.

Thomson, W. M. *The Land and the Book*. Grand Rapids, 1954.

Tödt, H. E. *The Son of Man in the Synoptic Tradition*. London, 1965.

Torrey, C. C. *The Apocryphal Literature*. New Haven, 1945.

———. "The Date of the Crucifixion according to the Fourth Gospel." *JBL* 50 (1931): 227–41.

———. *The Translations Made from the Original Aramaic Gospels*. New York, 1912.

Trench, R. H. *Notes on the Parables of Our Lord*. 14th ed. London, 1882.

Trilling, W. *Christus Verkündigung in den synoptischen Evangelien*. Biblische Handbibliothek, nr. 4. München, 1969.

———. *Das wahre Israel: Studien zur Theologie des Matthäus-Evangeliums*. 3d ed. Studien zum Alten und Neuen Testament, nr. 10. München, 1969.

Turner, H. E. W., and H. Montefiore, *Thomas and the Evangelists*. Studies in Biblical Theology, no. 35. Naperville, Ill., 1962.

Unnik, W. C. von, ed. *La Littérature juive entre Tenach et Mischna: Quelques Problèmes*. Leiden, 1974.

Vermes, G. *Jesus the Jew*. New York, 1973.

————. "The Use of *bar nash* / *bar nasha* in Jewish Aramaic." In M. Black, *An Aramaic Approach to the Gospels and Acts*. 3d ed. Oxford, 1967. Pp. 310–30.

Via, D. O. *Kerygma and Comedy in the New Testament: A Structuralist Approach to Hermeneutic*. Philadelphia, 1975.

————. *The Parables: Their Literary and Existential Dimension*. Philadelphia, 1967.

Vielhauer, P. *Aufsätze zum Neuen Testament*. München, 1965.

————. "Erwägungen zur Christologie des Markusevangeliums." In *Zeit und Geschichte*. Festschrift for R. Bultmann. Ed. E. Dinkler. Tübingen, 1964. Pp. 155–70.

————. "Johannes." *RGG* 3: 805.

Violet, V. *Die Apokalypsen des Esra und des Baruch in Deutscher Gestalt*. Leipzig, 1924.

Vögtle, A. "Exegetische Erwägungen über das Wissen und Selbstbewusstsein Jesu." In *Gott in Welt*. Festschrift for K. Rahner. Freiburg, 1964.

————. *Das Neue Testament und die Zukunft des Kosmos*. Kommentare und Beiträge zum Alten und Neuen Testament. Düsseldorf, 1970.

————. "Der Spruch vom Jonaszeichen." In *Synoptischen Studien*. Festschrift for A. Wikenhauser. Ed. J. Schmid and A. Vögtle. München, 1953. Pp. 230–77.

————. "Todesankündigungen und Todesverständnis Jesu." In *Der Tod Jesu: Deutungen im Neuen Testament*. Ed. K. Kertelge. Quaestiones Disputatae 74. Freiburg, 1976. Pp. 51–113.

Vriezen, Th. "Prophecy and Eschatology." In *Supplements to the Vetus Testamentum*. Leiden, 1953. 1: 202.

Walker, R. *Die Heilsgeschichte im ersten Evangelium*. Forschungen zur Religion und Literatur des Alten und Neuen Testaments, nr. 91. Göttingen, 1967.

Weiffenbach, W. *Der Wiederkunftsgedanke Jesu*. Leipzig, 1893.

Weiser, A. *Die Knechtsgleichnisse der synoptischen Evangelien*. München, 1971.

Weiss, J. *Das älteste Evangelium*. Göttingen, 1903.

————. *Jesus' Proclamation of the Kingdom of God*. Trans. and ed. R. H. Hier and D. L. Holland. Philadelpia, 1971.

————. *Die Schriften des Neuen Testaments*. Göttingen, 1917.

Wellhausen, J. *Das Evangelium Lucae*. Berlin, 1904.

————. *Das Evangelium Marci*. Berlin, 1903.

————. *Das Evangelium Matthaei*. Berlin, 1904.

Wendland, H.-D. "Church, Community and State." In *The Kingdom of God and History*, by H. G. Wood, C. H. Dodd, Edwyn Bevan, et al. Chicago, 1938.

————. *Die Eschatologie des Reiches Gottes bei Jesus: Eine Studie über den Zusammenhang von Eschatologie, Ethik und Kirchenproblem*. Gütersloh, 1931.

————. *Geschichtsanschauung und Geschichtsbewusstsein im Neuen Testament*. Göttingen, 1938.

Werner, M. *Die Entstehung des christlichen Dogmas*. Bern, 1941.

Westermann, C. *Jesaja 40–66*. Das Alte Testament Deutsch. Göttingen, 1966.

————. *Das Loben Gottes in den Psalmen*. Göttingen, 1961.

Wheelwright, P. *Metaphor and Reality*. London, 1962.

Wilder, A. N. *Eschatology and Ethics in the Teaching of Jesus*. Rev. ed. New York, 1950.

Wilson, M. *Studies in the Gospel of Thomas*. London, 1960.

Windisch, H. "Die Sprüche vom Eingehen in das Reich Gottes." *ZNW* 27 (1928): 163–92.

Wohlenberg, G. *Das Evangelium des Markus*. Kommentar zum Neuen Testament. Leipzig, 1910.

Wolff, H. W. "Herrschaft Jahwes und Messiasgestalt im alten Testament." *ZAW* 13 (1936): 181ff.

Wrege, H. T. *Uberlieferungsgeschichte der Bergpredigt*. Wissenschaftliche Untersuchungen zum Neuen Testament, nr. 9. Tübingen, 1968.

Wright, G. E. *The Old Testament and Theology*. New York, 1969.

Yadin, Y. *The Message of the Scrolls*. New York, 1957.

Yadin, Y., trans. *The Scroll of the War of the Sons of Light against the Sons of Darkness*. Oxford, 1962.

Young, F. "A Cloud of Witnesses." In *The Myth of God Incarnate*. Ed. J. Hick. London, 1977. Pp. 87–121.

Ysebaert, J. *Greek Baptismal Terminology: Its Origins and Early Development*. Nijmegen, 1962.

Zahn, T. *Das Evangelium des Lucas*. Leipzig, 1913.

Zeller, D. "Das Logion Mt 8, 11f / Lk 13, 28f und das Motiv der 'Völkerwallfahrt.'" *BZ* 15 (1971): 222–37 and 16 (1972): 84–93.

Zevit, Z. "The Structure and Individual Elements of Daniel 7." *ZAW* 80 (1968): 385–96.

Ziesler, J. A. "The Vow of Abstinence: A Note on Mark 14:25 and Parallels." *Colloquium* 5 (1972): 12–14.

_____. "The Vow of Abstinence Again." *Colloquium* 6 (1973): 49–50.

Zimmerli, W. *Old Testament Theology in Outline*. Trans. D. O. E. Green. Atlanta, 1978.

Zimmerli, W., and J. Jeremias. *The Servant of God*. Studies in Biblical Theology, no. 20. London, 1957.

Zmijewski, G. *Die Eschatologiereden des Lukas-Evangeliums: Ein traditions- und redaktionsgeschichtliche Untersuchung zu Lk. 21.5–36 und Lk. 17.20–37*. Bonner Biblische Beiträge, nr. 40. Bonn, 1972.

Index of Authors

Index of Scripture References

New Testament

Apocryphal and Pseudepigraphal Literature

Qumran Writings

Gnostic Writings

Rabbinic Writings